Collected Poems and Songs
of
George Campbell Hay
(Deòrsa Mac Iain Dheòrsa)

George Campbell Hay, c. 1975.
Reproduced by kind permission of Gordon Wright.

Collected Poems and Songs
of
George Campbell Hay
(Deòrsa Mac Iain Dheòrsa)

Edited by
Michel Byrne

EDINBURGH UNIVERSITY PRESS

Edinburgh University Press
22 George Square, Edinburgh

Poems and Songs © the estate of George Campbell Hay, 2000, 2003

Editorial Principles, Review and
editor's translations © Michel Byrne, 2000, 2003

First published in hardback in two volumes
by Edinburgh University Press in 2000.
First published in paperback
by Edinburgh University Press 2003.

Designed and typeset in New Caledonia
by Jack Osborne,
and printed and bound in Great Britain by
Cambridge University Press, Cambridge

A CIP record for this book is available
from the British Library

ISBN 0 7486 1621 7

The right of George Campbell Hay and Michel Byrne
to be identified as authors of this work
has been asserted in accordance with
the Copyright, Design and Patents Act 1988.

The Publisher acknowledges subsidy from

THE SCOTTISH **ARTS** COUNCIL

towards publication of this volume

Publication of the paperback edition
has also been made possible by a subsidy kindly provided
by the W. L. Lorimer Memorial Trust Fund.

mar chuimhneachan air

Deòrsa Mac Iain Dheòrsa
(1915–1984)

agus

Robin L. C. Lorimer
(1918–1996)

and to O. D.

L'arte non è malattia perché è sanità, … è ragione di vita e di maggiore umanità. Piccoli cuori, piccoli cervelli, piccoli anime, che siano stati grandi poeti, non sono noti nella storia …

Benedetto Croce

Art is not sickness, for it is health … it brings life and greater humanity. Small hearts, small brains, small minds that have been great poets are unknown in history …

George Campbell Hay, 1983, Tarbert Loch Fyne.
Reproduced by kind permission of Angus Martin.

CONTENTS

POEMS 1938–1940

CONTENTS

POEMS 1942–1944

CONTENTS

x

CONTENTS

CONTENTS

CONTENTS

POEMS 1964–1973

xiii

CONTENTS

CONTENTS

POEMS 1978–1979

GEORGE CAMPBELL HAY: A REVIEW

COMMENTARY TO THE POEMS

CONTENTS

APPENDICES

INDEXES

Summary of Editorial Coding

In poems:

    * by poem number and title: denotes previously published poem.

    [ ]: emendation by editor or specified agent.

In translations:

    [ ]: editorial interference (e.g. supplying missing text).

    italics: translation by editor or as indicated.

PREFACE

The publication of George Campbell Hay's collected poetry has been long awaited. His position as a Scottish Renaissance figure and associate of Douglas Young, C. M. Grieve, Sorley MacLean and Francis George Scott is perfectly well known, his poetic facility in both Gaelic and Scots giving him a special niche in that illustrious circle. The publication of *Fuaran Slèibh* and *Wind on Loch Fyne* (both 1948) and *O na Ceithir Àirdean* (1952) amply established his claim to be ranked with the best of the post-war writers. His appearance beside Sorley MacLean, Willie Neill and Stewart MacGregor in *Four Points of a Saltire* (1971), and beside Sorley MacLean, Iain Crichton Smith, Derick Thomson and Donald MacAulay in *Nua-bhàrdachd Ghàidhlig/ Modern Gaelic Poems* (1976), brought his qualities to the attention of the younger, wider literary audience of the 1970s.

These publications earned for Hay's poetry a considerable measure of critical respect, and he was urged on several occasions to gather at least a substantial portion of his work, including unpublished material and poems that had appeared in out-of-the-way journals, with a view to publishing a "collected works" or at least a "selected works". Alternating bouts of ill-health and fresh creativity prevented him from gathering and editing to his satisfaction the large (and increasing) corpus of material which would inevitably have been involved, though he made a start on the work more than once. The present publication aims to remedy that omission by presenting to the public as complete and authoritative a "collected poems" as may be, thereby bringing this remarkably neglected, undeniably major Scottish voice to the attention which he deserves.

Given the particular circumstances of Hay's creative life, work methods and difficult later years, the task of bringing his work to the stage now reached has been a challenging one, and would have been impossible but for the intercession of certain heroes and guardian angels along the way. A small band of loyal friends, including members of the Heretics group of writers, helped him in various ways to retain confidence in the value of his work. Dolina Maclennan, John MacInnes and Willie Neill spring to mind, but there were others too. In particular, Gordon Wright, who had published him in *Four Points of a Saltire*, visited him regularly during his last years, and encouraged him to order and edit his poems with a view to publication. Professor Derick Thomson published individual poems of Hay's in *Gairm* over many years, commissioned translation work from him for the Gaelic

Books Council, and published what could be garnered of Hay's incomplete magnum opus, "Mochtàr is Dùghall" (1982). Angus Martin offered support and understanding when Hay contemplated and then made his heroic attempt to return to Tarbert near the end of his days. A debt of a different sort is owed to Donald MacCormick, who correctly recognised Hay's papers for what they were when he came across them in an old suitcase at Edinburgh's Lane Sales, rescued them from the alternative threat of destruction and export, and saw to it that at least this part of the Hay family's literary effects came safely to the National Library of Scotland.

Robin Lorimer had known Hay since they were contemporaries at Oxford in the late 1930s, and became a champion of his work over many years. Hay was one of the poets whom he wished to publish when he was setting up Southside, as an independent publisher of the best of contemporary Scottish literature, in the late 1960s. (The times were not propitious, and *Nuabhàrdachd Ghàidhlig* (1976), together with *Reothairt is Conntraigh/Springtide and Neap-tide* (1977), containing selected poems of Sorley MacLean, were eventually published in association with Canongate.) Later on, the huge success of W. L. Lorimer's *New Testament in Scots* (1983) gave Robin (who had prepared his father's work for the press) the means to support "uneconomic" publishing proposals of outstanding literary merit and importance to Scotland. The recovery of Hay's papers after his death in 1984 greatly increased the volume and range of his poetic *œuvre*, and brought a renewed urgency to the case for making it available in print. Accordingly, the collected work of George Campbell Hay became accepted as the next project to be undertaken by the Lorimer Trust Fund. Our debt to them is immense.

Robin Lorimer recognised, better than most, the extraordinary challenge which Hay presented to a prospective editor, on account of his frequent rewriting and redrafting of poems and ideas for poems, his linguistic experimentation involving transpositions from one language to another, and his creative translations and imitations of the works of others. It was my privilege to be associated with the plan which emerged as a response to this challenge: we sought a young scholar with the necessary linguistic equipment and critical gifts to tackle the intellectual spadework as a Ph.D. thesis to be undertaken within the Celtic Department at Edinburgh University. There was an especially appropriate aspect of this association, inasmuch as Professor James Carmichael Watson had encouraged Hay to pursue Gaelic lexicographical work within the Celtic Department when he returned to Scotland after finishing (somewhat ingloriously) at Oxford in 1938. It was my pleasure, together with Dr (now Professor) Donald Meek, to supervise Michel Byrne's dissertation, which rose splendidly to the challenge of establishing the canon, the chronology and the textual principles to be applied. Thanks are also due to Professor D. Ellis Evans and his fellow Trustees for awarding Michel the Sir John Rhys Junior Fellowship at Jesus College,

Oxford, for 1990–1, to enable him to complete his thesis, which was accepted in 1992.

The task of making "the book of the thesis" fell naturally to Dr Byrne, with the added benefit of Robin Lorimer's commitment, wisdom and enormous experience as an editor of scholarship and literature. The philosophy and practices adopted in the present work (as described below under "Editorial Principles") have been designed to bring the work of an author of the first rank from a sometimes primitive, sometimes chaotic state to a near-definitive one. It has taken very considerable time, skill and devotion, and by far the greatest debt we owe is to the editor, who has shown himself equal to the many problems he faced. I also feel particular pleasure that Edinburgh University Press has become associated with the project and has provided the book with the degree of material and visual excellence which the Lorimer Trustees have stipulated. The result is, beyond doubt, a *tour de force* of scholarship and a publishing *coup*. It is a cause of sadness that Robin died before the work was published, but a consolation that he lived to see the end within sight, and an occasion for rejoicing that his vision has been fulfilled so worthily.

George Hay would, I am sure, have taken pride in this publication. Among his papers there have survived the draft contents lists and the beginnings of textual revisions which show how he himself had sought to tread that road, though he was not able to complete the journey. The scholar and philologist in him would have appreciated the painstaking elaboration of principles and their meticulous application once established. While his characteristic modesty would have prevented feelings of personal aggrandisement at the effort thus lavished on his work, he would have felt proud on behalf of his family and for Scotland's sake.

William Gillies
Edinburgh, 1 May 1998

ACKNOWLEDGEMENTS

Ged as fad a-mach Barraigh ruigear e, says the proverb – "though Barra is a long way out, it can be reached". It is over twelve years now since the Trustees of the W. L. Lorimer Memorial Trust Fund first undertook to publish a definitive edition of George Campbell Hay's poems and songs, and almost as long since I embarked on the task of preparing the edition. So long, indeed, that some may have thought our boat lost at sea. Had it been a solitary venture, I would no doubt have gone under, but thankfully, many have helped, some at the steering, some at the oars and others again blowing invigorating winds into the sails. I am indebted to them all, and apologise to any whom I have omitted from the following account.

Professors William Gillies and Donald E. Meek, my original academic supervisors, were inspiring in their enthusiasm and constant in their encouragement. In spite of unending demands on them from so many other quarters, their advice was readily offered and always deeply considered, and has kept me on track from start to finish.

Angus Martin, poet and social historian, shared his vast knowledge of Kintyre and his memories of Hay with generosity and warmth, and he and the late Professor Robert Rankin both patiently responded in painstaking detail to my persistent questioning on biographical points. Their published testimonies (see Martin 1984, chapter 3, and Rankin 1984) remain the finest of tributes.

For additional biographical information and reminiscences of Hay from the 1930s and 1940s, I am indebted to Frank Cameron-Yeaman, the late John Lorne Campbell, Ronald Daffern (who also kindly offered a photograph from Oxford days), Ian Haig, Dr D. Jenkins (Moray House College, Edinburgh), the late Arnold H. Jennings, Maurice Lindsay, the late Robin L. C. Lorimer, Professor Angus MacIntosh, Flora MacLean, the late Sorley MacLean, Elizabeth MacPherson, Mrs Christopher MacRae, the late Naomi Mitchison, Duncan Murray, George N. Scott, D. Ainslie Thin, Sir Keith Thomas (Corpus Christi College, Oxford), J. O. Urmson, and Mrs L. Yeamans of the Ministry of Defence. My approach to the Ministry was facilitated by Ivor R. Guild, Hay's executor.

For sharing information about Hay from the 1960s onwards, I am grateful to Alastair Cherry, Alexandra M. Jones, Pauline Scott and Hamish Seaton (all presently or formerly of the National Library of Scotland), Jeremy Bruce-Watt, John Burns, Hamish Henderson, Elizabeth Kirk, Eddie Linden,

Professor Donald MacAulay, Donald MacCormick, Iain MacDonald (Gaelic Books Council), Kenneth MacDonald (formerly of the Historical Dictionary of Scottish Gaelic), Dr John MacInnes, the late Rayne Mackinnon, Professor John MacQueen, Gerald Mangan, Willie Neill, Paul H. Scott, Professor Derick Thomson and Gordon Wright. For information and advice on aspects of Hay's mental health, I am most grateful to Dr Andrew K. Zealley of the Royal Edinburgh Hospital, and also to John Boa, Bill Cook and Mairi Wilmott. Additional thanks are due to Gerald Mangan, Angus Martin and Gordon Wright for permission to reprint their fine portraits of Hay.

The following people provided, or helped track down, sources for the poems: Jeremy Bruce-Watt, John Burns, Catriona Campbell, Rachel Craig, Lillias Forbes and George N. Scott, Giuseppe Greco, Tom Hubbard, Elizabeth Kirk, Martin McGregor, Professor Angus MacIntosh, Flora McLean, Dodo and Willie Neill, the late Tom Scott, and Ronald Stevenson. I am particularly indebted to Christopher Whyte for alerting me to the existence of Hay material in Aberdeen University Library's Historic Collections (MS 2864/2).

The erudition of Ronald Black, the late Donald Archie MacDonald and John MacInnes helped elucidate some problems of translation, although I am fully responsible for any remaining inaccuracies or infelicities. Yassin Dutton kindly translated some Arabic drafts by Hay and threw valuable light on aspects of Arabic culture and literature; advice in this was also given by A. H. Beeston (St John's College, Oxford), Bruce Ingham (University of London School of Oriental and African Studies) and the Reverend James Ritchie. Dr Arne Kruse translated and commented on Hay's Norwegian writings, as did Peter Anderson (National Archives of Scotland). Iain Fraser of the Place-name Survey (School of Scottish Studies) was helpful beyond the call of duty.

Fiona Carmichael and her colleagues at the University of Edinburgh Language and Humanities Centre masterfully kept technical gremlins at bay during the first phase of the project, and the staff of the National Library of Scotland and of the Scottish Poetry Library were ever courteous and helpful. A generous studentship from Professor D. Ellis Evans (Jesus College, Oxford) and the Trustees of the Sir John Rhys Memorial Fund helped ensure the successful completion of that phase.

I am hugely indebted to my parents, family and friends for their support and forbearance, and hope they will forgive my frequent neglect of them for "The Book". Allison Alexander, Meg Bateman, Thomas Clancy, Julian Goodare, Paul Matheson, Gillian Munro and Christopher Whyte were particularly helpful in their advice and criticisms at various stages of writing. I have much appreciated the support of my colleagues in the Department of Celtic at Glasgow University, in particular that of Professor Cathair Ó Dochartaigh. And for his patience and good humour throughout, special thanks to Odrán Doherty.

I had great pleasure working with the late Jack Osborne, who undertook the book's design and page-layout – including the gruelling labour of type-setting – with remarkable enthusiasm and good cheer. His sudden death in May 1999 was a sad blow. Thanks to Jackie Jones, Ian Davidson and the team at EUP, and especially to Ivor Normand for his awesomely rigorous copy-editing. The generosity of the Governors of Catherine MacCaig's Trust (that same body which underwrote the publication of Hay's work some fifty years ago) and funds gifted by the Celtic Departments of the Universities of Edinburgh and Glasgow secured the services of Dr Richard Cox for proof-reading the Gaelic material, which he undertook with expert thoroughness. Further thanks are due to the Celtic Department in Glasgow for allowing us to publish "Mochtàr is Dùghall" (previously published by the Department in 1982).

The Trustees of the Lorimer Trust generously provided technical and financial support at various stages and have been constant in their dedica-tion to the project. The indefatigable Priscilla Lorimer, Secretary to the Trustees, provided the warmest hospitality at Balcorrachy, while Robin Hodge's energetic assistance was particularly crucial in the last three years.

The Trustees gratefully acknowledge receipt of a donation towards the cost of publishing these volumes from the Richard Traill Charitable Trust.

My debt to the late Robin Lorimer, publisher to the Trustees, is incalcu-lable. Having initiated the project, one which had been close to his heart for many years, he tactfully bided his time until the initial postgraduate study was completed, firm in his belief that haste would not serve the cause of Hay's literary rehabilitation, but never sparing in supportive advice when called on. As the time came to plan the design and typography of the col-lected edition, he threw himself into the daunting task with characteristic single-mindedness, tackling complex problems at a time when his own health was beginning to cause concern. Although this was his first involvement with computer-based publishing, the speed with which – at 76 – he mastered the intricacies of his new technological tools was astonishing, though it should not have surprised those who knew him. I greatly valued his advice and was honoured by his friendship, and the sadness of his death was only mitigated by the knowledge that he had steered our boat so assuredly close to harbour that it was inconceivable we would not come to safe berth. It is fitting that this edition should stand as testimonial to a great scholar-publisher as well as to a great scholar-poet.

Michel Byrne

EDITORIAL PRINCIPLES

This edition aims to present Hay's *œuvre* as a chronological record of his poetic activity. The text of each poem (barring "Mochtàr is Dùghall") derives from one copy-text, chosen after all the available sources (as listed in the Commentary) had been collated. Variants, that is, forms departing from the copy-text, have generally not been given as they are fully documented in Byrne 1992, but the more substantial are mentioned in the Commentary.

Sources

All manuscript and typescript copies by Hay himself were taken as sources, even if identical, since each represented a potential recension by the poet. Texts produced by Hay through other agents (for example, published works, typescripts by his mother or by Douglas Young) were also accepted, unless they derived exclusively from a surviving prototype by Hay.

Thus, for example:

- Republications from Hay's three collections, in anthologies such as Oliver and Smith's *A Scots Anthology* (Edinburgh and London, 1949), and in various periodicals from the late 1940s, were not accepted as sources. However, MacQueen and Scott's Oxford anthology, *Four Points of a Saltire* and *Nua-Bhàrdachd Ghàidhlig*, for which Hay prepared at least some fresh texts, were included (Sources G, H and J). Similarly, Francis George Scott's collections of lyrics, Maurice Lindsay's important anthology of the Scottish renaissance and Douglas Young's 1952 anthology all preserve versions of Hay's poems predating his printed collections, and they have therefore served as sources for the edition (Sources D, E and F).
- Young's transcripts for which no certain prototype survives have served as important sources (Sources 37 and 39), but his typescripts of extant prototypes (for example, of the French poems sent to him by Hay in 1943) were not included.
- In the case of published texts, when the prototype sent by Hay for publication has survived (as in the case of "Mochtàr is Dùghall"[109]), the manuscript has superseded the printed text as a source, but the printed incidence is detailed in the Commentary.

Choosing the Copy-text

Axiomatic in the editorial treatment of sources has been the principle that printed sources can lay claim to a finality, and thus an authority, which cannot be presumed of manuscript sources. The concept of text finality here refers to the irrevocable actualisation of a version in the public domain, with the author's consent, through publication. A printed version, presuming it has enjoyed the full cooperation and consent of the author, is one which we know the poet at a specific time judged fit for public appreciation; a manuscript text, however, presents a version which may or may not be "final". Bibliographical analysis may help distinguish between an initial draft, a rough copy or a publication-ready script, but further revision by the poet prior to publication can never be ruled out.

This distinction of finality between published and unpublished texts has obviously informed the choice of copy-texts for the edition, so that, as a rule, the printed text of a poem (or its prototype) has taken precedence over manuscript versions. The status of *Fuaran Slèibh*, *Wind on Loch Fyne* and *O na Ceithir Àirdean* is primordial, since these are collections carefully planned and prepared by Hay (in collaboration with other agents) and ratified by him at every stage. This of course did not prevent instances of textual corruption, and I have corrected indisputable typographical errors without comment, but any other departures from the copy-text of a poem, or intrusions in the text by another hand, have been indicated by square brackets and glossed in the Commentary.

The present edition has operated an inclusive chronological policy, foregoing any segregation of published and unpublished poems. In order, therefore, that the status of copy-text sources should be clearly recognisable, all published poems have been signalled by an asterisk before their title, and in the Commentary printed sources have been codified by letter (in the case of periodicals, P plus numeral) and manuscript sources by numeral alone.

Hay's Revisions: The Dilemma

The issue of finality becomes more problematic when we take into account Hay's numerous revisions post-dating publication, some of which were effected twenty-five to thirty-five years after the original composition. This extreme time lapse accentuates the basic methodological dilemma: does an "original" version of a text retain primordial status over later variants, or should ultimate authority go instead to the last version approved by the poet?

Of course, one could posit that all versions are inherently equal, and that editors should simply choose whichever version they prefer, letting readers agree or disagree with the editorial judgement. To do full justice to the demands of a historically oriented critical edition, however, it seemed more satisfactory to base editorial choice on a methodological principle. If writers do indeed retain artistic authority over their work ad infinitum, then it would follow that revised readings should be given precedence over early texts. Such a policy in this edition would have yielded a small number of texts which were arguably (in one instance undoubtedly) inferior to their originals.

Some textual critics, on the other hand, have suggested that authorial right expires at some point after the initial creative process. This idea has a certain plausibility in the case of a poet like Hay, whose creative peak, it could be said, was followed by debilitating illness and uneven poetic activity. As a guiding principle, however, it offers little help, since the question remains: when do we deem the creative impulse to have cooled off sufficiently for the poet to lose automatic authority over a particular text? The editor, it seems, is left to judge each revision.

Hay's Revisions: The Editorial Practice

To resolve this dilemma, I have based the choice of copy-text for revised poems not on the perceived quality of specific revisions but on the status of the sources involved. The sources for Hay's revisions are of various kinds:

- the republished texts in *Nua-Bhàrdachd Ghàidhlig*;
- a typescript of collected Gaelic poems (Source 21);
- poems from periodicals subsequently revised and even republished;
- unpublished poems surviving in more than one form;
- annotations by Hay in his own copies of the printed collections (Sources 29, 30, 32, 33 and 57);
- a list of revisions to *Wind on Loch Fyne* (Source 11: 63–4).

As a general principle, revisions have been taken as carrying a "final" authority only if the status of their source is equal to (or supersedes) that of the original source. Thus, revised versions published in periodicals have not been given precedence over original versions from Hay's three collections. To give specific examples:

- *Nua-Bhàrdachd Ghàidhlig* has provided the copy-text for its eleven poems, superseding *Fuaran Slèibh* and *O na Ceithir Àirdean*.
- The copy-text of "Òran Nàiseantach"[192], a song published in three periodicals, is that of its final periodical appearance. The song thus figures chronologically among poems of 1961, but in a recension of twenty years later.
- That song's Scots counterpart, "Nationalist Sang"[206], was published twice in periodicals, later sent for publication but not published, then again redrafted. I have taken the manuscript text sent for publication as

the copy-text, as it represents the author's last intended printed version. Again, however, the song is given its original chronological placing.

- Hay's annotated revisions holding no "final" authority, Sources 29, 30, 32, 33 and 57 have in no instance provided copy-texts, although their revisions may be noted in the Commentary. Thus, for example, two additional lines intended for "Seeker, Reaper"[158] are noted but have not been incorporated into the poem.

It follows that even Hay's substantial manuscript expansions of such poems as "Homer"[2] (expanded from two to four verses, fifty years after composition) or "The Smoky Smirr o Rain"[151] (from three verses to five, then eight, thirty-five years later) should not supersede the published originals as copy-texts. However, since the edition defers to a historical orientation, prioritising both Hay's intentions and the chronological accuracy of the historical record, it seemed appropriate to present each poem twice, first in its original published form then in its expanded manuscript version[367, 368], the later text being seen as the product of a second creative fire, rather than a tentative tampering.

For poems existing only in manuscript form, I have adopted the more finalised draft, or, faced with equally finalised drafts, the later version. Thus:

- Source 21, by virtue of its importance as a major, sustained recension by Hay of most of his Gaelic work up to 1973, has taken precedence over all other manuscript sources.
- "Spring Here Northaway"[159] was composed in 1947 in Tarbert dialect, but altered to a broader Scots register some thirty years later. The two versions are not sufficiently distinct to warrant the treatment given to "Homer" and "The Smoky Smirr o Rain"; however, a typescript copy of the first version was sent by Hay to F. G. Scott, giving it marginally more "final" authority than the later text found only in notebooks. The copy-text is thus that of the Tarbert version.

Transgressions

The above should make reasonably clear the limits to the editorial judgements applied in this edition. Once the initial choices had been made regarding the status of each source (taking into account the totality of bibliographical and historical information, and based on an assessment of Hay's intentions), no further literary criticism was brought to bear on editorial decisions. It follows that versions have not been amalgamated in order to produce "improved" texts.

In several specific cases, however, editorial practice has transgressed the policies outlined above:

- First, two lines in "Còmhradh an Alltain"[112], omitted in Source C but previously published and present in all translations, have been reinserted into the copy-text, on the basis that the omission was accidental. This interpretation, however, is open to dispute.
- Second, some of Hay's poems in French and Norwegian are problematic, in that they contain linguistic errors which any editor sufficiently acquainted with those languages would have had him correct, but which went unnoticed (or at any rate uncorrected) into publication. The correction of obvious errors is a basic editorial task, yet it would be wrong to falsify the historical record and give a mistaken impression of Hay's mastery of these languages. I have therefore effected the minimal revisions required in "Le Montagnard"[249], "Enhver Seiler"[262], "Skottland til Ola Nordmann"[257] and "Steinen på Fjellet"[259] (all indicated in the Commentary), but have left untouched more debilitating linguistic confusions such as the penultimate verse of "Épreuve de Doute"[99].
- Finally, it was clear from the fragmentary state of "Mochtàr is Dùghall"[109] that factors beyond authorial control or intention – namely the loss of sources and Hay's inability to restore his text within the necessary time limits – reduced the primacy of the published text (or more accurately its prototype, Source 47) over all other sources, and that this poem would require a more flexible, eclectic approach. An excessive historicism in adherence to one copy-text source would only have obscured Hay's intentions, perpetuating the misapprehension that he composed two different endings to the poem. The unified ending undeniably intended and written by Hay has therefore been restored by the piecing together of disparate texts, although I have resisted (with perhaps excessive caution) an editorial interpolation suggested by Hay's translation (see the gloss on line 1,220).

Exclusions from the Edition

I have excluded from the edition:

- Hay's juvenilia, bar the three poems which he himself absorbed into his adult corpus;
- most of the drafts from Source 9 (c. 1949?) – a fascinating run of multilingual outpourings based on traditional songs and previous writings;
- some very fragmentary drafts in Sources 25 and 27.

All of these are accessible either in Byrne 1992 or in the National Library of Scotland collection.

Gaelic Orthography

Given the varied nature and provenance of the copy-texts, an orthographically non-standardised edition would present readers with a bewildering variety of spelling practices, many of these reflecting editors' policies rather than Hay's own preference. At a time when the modernisation of spelling in Gaelic is universally accepted in principle though still a matter for debate in its details, Hay's own changing practice over the years, and the conventions followed by his editors, are undoubtedly of interest and can be consulted in Byrne 1992. For this edition, however, it was decided to standardise Gaelic spelling along the lines recommended by the SCE Examination Board, but also taking into account the more recent proposals from the Board of Celtic Studies Scotland (see SEB 1981 and McLeod 1998).

Hay's own attitude to orthographical simplification was approving: "the more dots and dashes we eliminate from the Gaelic orthography the better", he wrote when planning *Fuaran Slèibh* (Source 36, 12 March 1944), although he warned against simplifications which would create confusion. He eliminated some apostrophes and hyphens in his collections, and continued to modernise his spelling in later years, shedding such usages as *gu'n* and *ag cumail*, and expressing no apparent disapproval of the evolving conventions applied by *Gairm* to his new poems and to "Mochtàr is Dùghall". (Some of his own usages – for example, *maith, s, gu'n, cha n-eil* – can be seen in the quotes from his letters in Volume 2, which have not been standardised.)

Care has been taken in the edition, however, not to allow standardisation to affect the phonetic integrity of the verse. Thus, for example:

- Instances of dialect (always clearly indicated by Hay) have been retained.
- I have added some length marks dictated by rhyme (such as *oìdhche*), following Hay's own example.
- There has been no attempt to standardise Hay's treatment of the *do* and *de* prepositional pronouns after an *n*. Although he uniformly used the unlenited forms (*domh, duinn* and so on) in the 1930s and 1940s, in later years Hay tended to follow the more standard usage (only intermittently in *Nua-Bhàrdachd Ghàidhlig*, but more consistently in Source 21).
- Hay's consistent use of *roimh* and *troimh* has been retained to respect any possible phonetic particularity. I have, however, standardised *allt/ alld* (plus declined forms) and pre-nominal *sean/seann*, where Hay's highly inconsistent usage, even within the same poem, suggests that the orthographic difference carried no phonetic significance.

Scots Orthography

Given the acceptance of greater variation in Scots orthography, I have refrained from regularising the spelling of Scots in this edition, except within each poem. The conventions shown are usually, but not always, Hay's own (with some input from Douglas Young in the earlier texts). Some spelling revisions for *Wind on Loch Fyne* were noted by Hay in Source 30 (such as the differentiation between present participle and verbal noun), but these were neither sustained nor consistent enough to warrant adoption.

The instability of Scots spelling, clearly discernible in the sources, could in itself provide a valuable field of study. Douglas Young played an important role in the development of a standardised Scots orthography and in the drawing-up of the Makars' Club style sheet in 1947 (printed in *Lines Review* 9, August 1955, and again in *Scotia*, March 1970), and his typescripts of Hay's poems offer valuable evidence of the experimentation that preceded this attempt at stabilising the writing of Scots.

Punctuation

The punctuation shown, as a rule, is that of the copy-text, only modified when necessary for the sake of clarity. Modifications have generally been made in the light of other sources.

Translations

Hay's prose translations of his poems were collated on the same principles as the original poems. Texts have only been altered when they reflect a version other than that of the copy-text (for example in "Ùrnaigh Oisein as Ùr"[27] or "Truaighe na h-Eòrpa"[136]), or when occasionally they do not adequately reflect the lexical richness of the original. All such changes by the editor are shown in square brackets. On the rare occasion that the required substitution has been supplied by another of Hay's own versions, the change has not been indicated.

Where no translations by Hay were available, I have supplied translations to the Gaelic and French poems, and Dr Arne Kruse has kindly translated the Norwegian poem "Skottland til Nordsjøfarerne"[88]. All translations not by Hay are given in italics. The difficulties inherent in translation have often been rehearsed, perhaps never more succinctly than by Benedetto Croce, who in the early twentieth century spoke of the

> impossibility of translations … insofar as they claim to present one expression in the guise of another, as the same body of liquid may be given a different form by being decanted into a vessel of a different shape … "Ugly but faithful, or beautiful but faithless": this proverbial

saying neatly captures the dilemma with which every translator is faced.
(Croce 1992: 76)

My primary concern in translating has been to convey the meaning of the
original – faithfulness at the expense of beauty, the rich accented music of
Gaelic being impossible to sustain in English in any case. When translating
poems composed in traditional song metres, however, I have sometimes
attempted to convey rhythms and occasionally hint at rhyme patterns.

Titles

No poem has been left untitled, and, for the sake of clarity, no title has been
duplicated. All titles for which the editor is responsible are in square brack-
ets. Titles in a language other than that of the poem have been translated in
a subtitle, following the practice in *Four Points of a Saltire*.

Dating

The decision to present Hay's work chronologically has entailed meticulous
efforts at a precise dating of sources. This is not meant to simplify the
process of poetic creation to a neat linear process, with a clear genesis and a
clear end; the dates should only be taken as relative indicators of com-
position. That said, however, and accepting that we cannot measure the
unwritten gestation period of a poetic idea, there is evidence that the written
creative process for Hay could be very rapid, and that poems, particularly in
the later years, often came to him in a spate.

With a small number of poems, all efforts at precise dating were un-
successful, and editorial ignorance or doubt has been indicated. When no
specific reference for the date is quoted in the Commentary, dating has been
arrived at by inference from the texts (position in source, calligraphy, bio-
graphical circumstance and so on).

Some dates noted by Hay indicate mere transcription rather than composi-
tion, and whenever there is reason to believe that a cited date is a transcription
date substantially removed from actual composition, this has been stated.

Poems and Songs

POEMS 1932–1938

*1 *The Hind of Morning*

She snorts and stamps upon the eastern hill,
the Hind of Morning, longing for the day,
the Hind of Morning, mad to leap away,
and flings her head up, scorning to be still.   4

On high her hooves strike up a streaming fire,
that wavers, slanting past the haloed peaks;
her quick feet spurn the summits, and she seeks
to trample night and burn it up entire.   8

The Hind of Morning leaps and will not stay,
she stretches West and West with flinging stride,
the Hind of Morning pacing in her pride,
the Hind of Morning is away, away.   12

*2 *Homer*

They say that you were blind, yet from the shore
    you saw the long waves cresting out at sea;
before the climbing dawn from heaven's floor
    you saw the dark night flee.   4

The torrents whirling in the springtime thaw,
    the shady slopes of Ida many-pined,
the curving flash of falling swords you saw –
    they lie; you were not blind.   8

*3 *Cumha Ruaraidh Mhòir*
Lament for Ruaraidh Mòr MacLeod

Ruari dead – now Skye lament and wail your spoiling,
and the [dread] tale that I tell; and all slowly toiling
   on your shoulders raise him – then never more.   3
He was your shield; across the stormy seas he led you
to the far fields of the foreign men; on spoil he fed you,
   and your arms grew strong from the sword and the oar.   6

Quiet at their chains his long-boats lie, for past their sailing;
and their gear rots in the rain, and the cold wind goes wailing
   through their straining shrouds as evening falls.   9
Now let them laugh that hated him and feared his coming,
and their wine flow, and in feeble cheer their tuneless strumming
   make the echo wake on their castle walls.   12

Here will no harper stir his strings to music's measure,
nor the song ring in our halls; nor ever joy or pleasure
   will Patrick bring to us ever more.   15
For what can we see or hear again with Ruari sleeping,
but the grey rain on the dreary hills weeping, weeping,
   and the sea's mouth mourning along the shore?   18

4 For the Corrie

After her, days are sad and cheerless;
that was a ship that was first and peerless,
ran through the midst of fear all fearless.   3

Tide-rips snatched, and blind reefs fenced us
stark [heads] hurled their squalls against us,
storm winds wearied and sleep unsensed us.   6

Three reefs down and the long seas pouring
over her bows, with the North-West roaring
down from Kintyre, and the stays loud roaring.   9

Tramping along with the lee-rail dripping,
soft through the dark to an anchorage slipping,
anchor up and the dawn wind nipping.   12

Long days sailing, and long nights singing,
setting the shores of the anchorage ringing,
there we lay out our anchor swinging.   15

Staunch in squalls and sweet in steering,
smashing the waves on her way careering,
ready to answer the sly winds veering.   18

*5 Aisling

Gàir nan tonn an-raoir am chluasan,
   leamsa 's truagh mo dhùsgadh maidne,
mi nam shuain air taobh Loch Fìne,
   na mo dhùisg an tìr na machrach.   4

Bha mi 'n-raoir, a Dhia, am bhruadar
   air a' chruaich os cionn Glac Calltainn,
air a' chruaich os cionn na tràghad,
   cnocan fàsail, fasgach, crannach.   8

Chunna mi 'n-sin an là 'glasadh,
   grian a' lasadh air Loch Fìne;
chuala mi – 's bu bhinn am fonn e –
   nuall nan tonn ri taobh na tìre.   12

Nuall nan tonn ri tràigh 'nan leumnaich,
   'tighinn 'nan treud o Chaolas Bhreanain,
's ghabh i seachad, seud nam bàta –
   b'e sin thug bàrr air gach aisling.   16

[B'e sin

---

5 [A Vision]

The thunder of waves last night in my ears, | *sad for me is my morning waken-*
ing; | *on Lochfyneside in my sleep,* | *but waking up in Lowland country.*   4

Last night, oh Lord, in my dreams | *I was on the hill above Hazel Hollow,* | *on the*
hill above the shoreline, | *a desolate hillock, sheltered and wooded.*   8

There I saw the day dawning, | *the sun setting fire to Loch Fyne;* | *and I could*
hear – how sweet the music!– | *the raging of the waves along the coast.*   12

The raging of the waves bounding on the shore, | *coming in herds from Kilbrannan*
Sound – | *and past she glided, the jewel of boats,* | *a sight surpassing every vision.*   16

B'e sin thug bàrr air gach aisling,
    an darach cridhe 'tighinn 'na cabhaig;
sloistreadh stuadh fo cheann mo ghaoil-sa,
    fuaim nan seòl sa ghaoith ri crathadh.   20

Fuaim nan seòl sa ghaoith ri crathadh,
    bid a h-aisnean, 's i fo shiùbhal;
crònan sunndach aig mo ghràdh-sa
    bhàrr gach bàirlinn 'geàrradh shùrdag.   24

Crònan sunndach aig mo ghràdh-sa
    bhàrr gach bàirlinn 'geàrradh shùrdag;
òran sùgraidh aig mo leannan,
    's i 'na deann a' dèanamh ùspairn.   28

'Dèanamh ùspairn ris na tonntan,
    'bualadh trom le guala làidir,
socrach, eutrom anns na gleanntan,
    air gach beann gu beòthail dàna.   32

Air gach beann gu beòthail dàna,
    's gaoth le ràn 'cur luaths 'na casan –
och, chan ionnan sin 's an saoghal
    th'aig na daoine seo sa mhachair.   36

Dhè, chan ionnan sin 's an saoghal
    th'aig na daoine seo sa mhachair:
gàir nan tonn an-raoir am chluasan,
    leamsa 's truagh mo dhùsgadh maidne.   40

A sight surpassing every vision: | the darling oak swiftly approaching; | dashing of billows at the prow of my love, | the noise of the sails as they crack in the wind.   20

The noise of the sails as they crack in the wind, | the creaking of her ribs as forward she goes, | a cheerful droning from my dear one | as she cuts a leap over every breaker.   24

A cheerful droning from my dear one | as she cuts a leap over every breaker, | a playful song from my beloved | as on she rushes into battle.   28

Into battle against the waves, | striking hard with a strong shoulder, | calm and light in the valleys, | on each mountain spirited, fearless.   32

On each mountain spirited, fearless, | as the wind with a shriek puts speed in her step. | Och, there's no comparing that and the life | of the people here in the Lowlands.   36

God, there's no comparing that and the life | of the people here in the Lowlands. | The thunder of waves last night in my ears, | sad for me is my morning wakening.   40

6 *Na Geamairean*

[incomplete text]

Mi sgìth a' siubhal garbhlaich
   's na frasan na mo shùilean,
earb no boc chan fhaca mi,
   ge fada mi am shiùbhal;   4
nach olc an obair sealgaireachd,
   air leacainn lom le gunna,
air allaban on mhadainn seo
   gun srad a thoirt le m'fhùdar.   8

Ghabh mi sìos don Lagan sin,
   's tric tathaich nam fear ruadh ann,
b'e sin an ceum an-asgaidh dhomh,
   oir earba fhèin cha d'fhuair mi;   12
chuartaich mi gach bealach
   is gach glac, le sùil thar gualainn,
mun tigeadh orm na geamairean
   sa cheathaich – sin bu chruaidh leam.   16

O hì o hò na geamairean,
   mo sheanmhair, gum b'fheàrr i,
ri siubhal slèibh is leacainnean,
   ri faire air an fhàsaich;   20
air leam gur sibhs' na cailleachan,
   chan ainmig rinn mi làmhach,
a-mach gu moch sa chamhanaich,
   is sibhs' nur cadal sàmhach.   24

[Bidh cromag

6 [The Gamekeepers]

Tired with wandering the rough moorlands | and the rainshowers blinding me, | no sign I've seen of roe or buck | though far and wide I've wandered; | what miserable work is hunting, | on a bare slope with a gun, | roaming since the morning | and not one spark from the powder.   4   8

I headed for that Lagan, | a usual haunt of the red fellows; | no gift of a trip that was for me, | for not even a doe did I catch; | I walked round every pass | and every dip, looking over my shoulder | lest the gamekeepers should come upon me| in the mist – a fate to be dreaded!   12   16

O hee o ho the gamekeepers, | my grannie herself was better | at travelling the moors and rockfaces, | keeping a look-out on the wildernesses. | Methinks it's you are the old wifies – | not seldom have I gone shooting, | away till the early dawn,| while you were all sleeping soundly.   20   24

Bidh cromag ac' is gunnaichean,
  is cù mòr busach grannda,
bidh prosbaig aig gach bùrraidh ac',
  's gun sùilean ac' 'nan ceann-sa,   28
cho pròiseil iad ri Prionnsaichean
  's iad siùbhal air a' chabhsair,
ach feuch a-nis 'ad measg nan stùc,
  gur crùbach iad 's gur mall iad.   32

*7   Siubhal a' Choire

Thog sinn a-mach air a' mhachair uaine;
chuir sinn a' Gharbhaird ghailbheach, ghruamach,
leum on iardheas sìontan cruaidh oirnn.   3
  Thog i 'ceann ri ceann nam fuarthonn,
  an tè dhubh chaol nì gaoir 'na gluasad;
  thog i 'seinn is rinn i ruathar.   6

Shìn i a sgòd le cruas na cruadhach,
shìn i 'taobh ri taobh nan stuadhan,
shìn i 'ceum a cheumadh chuantan.   9
  Bhuail i beum le 'beul 's i 'tuairgneadh,
  thug i sad le sgar a guailne,
  gheàrr i leòn le 'sròin 's i 'luasgan.   12

A crook they take with them and guns, | and a huge, ugly, big-mawed hound; | every one of the boors with binoculars, | as they lack good eyes in their head; | 28 *they are arrogant as princes | when walking down the causey, | but watch them now among the crags, | how slow they are and squatting.* 32

7   The Voyaging of the Corrie

We lifted out on to the green plain, | we weathered Garvel the tempestuous and scowling, | hard rain-squalls leaped upon us out of the south-west. | She raised 3 her head against the heads of the cold waves, | the black narrow one who makes a clamour as she goes, | she raised her singing and made an onrush. 6

She stretched her sheet as hard as steel, | she stretched her side to the sides of the [breakers], | she stretched her stride to pace the oceans. | She struck a 9 blow with her gunnel as she buffeted, | she struck a dunt with the seam of her shoulder, | she clove a wound with her beak as she lurched. 12

Eilean Aoidh – bu aoibh a nuallan;
Àird MhicLaomainn – a gaoir gum b'uaibhreach;
os cionn na h-Innse sheinn i duanag. 15
    Cha robh nar sùilean ach smùid a stràcan,
    cathadh is sìoban o chìr nam bàirlinn,
    cha robh nar cluais ach fuaim a stàirneil. 18

*8   *An Gleannan*

Pàrrthas sìth' an gleann suaimhneach –
dìon a chrann 's a luachair lòin –
gleann as sèimhe sruth fo bhruachaibh,
an gleann feurach, lusach, uaine; 4
uain' a bharrach 's a riasg ròmach,
    cluain nam fiadh – còrr am fàrdach;
glasanach ciar binn an crònan,
    bruidhinn am beòil 's a' ghrian air fàire. 8

Trì fuinn as gnàth sa ghleannan –
gàir aig na tuinn 'teachd fann a-nìos,
toirm an uillt le slios nam beannaibh,
gaoth bheag shoirbh a' seinn sna crannaibh. 12
Cromar cinn nan craobh le chèile
    a dh'èisteachd nam port faondrain aice.
Allt na leacainn, buan a labhairt
    a-nuas sa ghlaic fo Chreag an Fhasgaidh. 16

Eilean Aoidh – joyous was her roaring; | Ardlamont – haughty was her shouting; | up off Inchmarnock she sang a ditty. | In our eyes there was nothing but the smoke of her strokes, | spindrift and driven spray from the crests of the billows; | in our ears there was nothing but the sound of her snorting. 15 18

8   *The Glennan*

A paradise of peace the tranquil glen – | the shelter of its trees and meadow rushes – | glen whose stream goes quietest under its banks, | the grassy, flowering, green glen; | green are its birch tops and shaggy moor-grass, | meadow of the deer – no common one their dwelling place; | in the grey dawning light sweet is their [bellowing], | the speech of their mouths when the sun is on the skyline. 4 8

Three melodies that are habitual in the little glen – | the thunder of the waves coming faintly from below, | the roar of the burn down the slopes of the mountains, | a small easy wind singing in the trees. | The trees stoop their heads all together | to listen to its vagrant tunes. | The stream of the slope, everlasting is its talking | downwards in the hollow below the Shelter Craig. 12 16

*9 Òran don Oighre

'S ioma gleann a tha fod làimh-sa,
    beanntan, 's àilein rèidh 'nam bonn,
's ioma calamh seasgar, sìtheil,
    's acarsaid gu dìdean long;   4
srathan ìosal, slèibhtean, 's coilltean,
    's coireachan an fhèidh san àird,
le cinnt 's le ceartas fhuair thu t'fhearann
    od shinnsir fhèin, 's gum meal thu à.   8

Gum meal thu fhèin t'oighreachd fharsainn,
    far nach faic thu fear a' tàmh,
gach tobhta falamh, 's fàrdach fhuaraidh,
    's goirtean luachrach gun fhàs;   12
seall a-mach, a thriath, ad uinneag,
    air na bailtean cruinn sa ghleann,
far nach cluinnear guth no gàire,
    na làraichean gun mhuinntear annt'.   16

Gum meal thu fhèin do chàs 's do chor-sa,
    fearann falamh, sporan gann,
mheud a chosgas tu ga chumail,
    's gun tuath chumas nì riut ann;   20
peacadh 'n athar air a chlann-sa,
    's teann an lagh, 's cha bhacar à;
's àrsaidh t'oighreachd sin, 's cha ghann i,
    's ioma gleann a tha fod làimh.   24

9 [Song to the Heir]

Many's the glen that's under your hand, | mountains with level meadows at their foot, | many the secluded peaceful haven, | and anchorage for ships to shelter; | 4 low-lying straths, hills and woodlands, | and the deer corries up on the heights; | with certitude and justice you have acquired your land | from your own fore-bears, and may you enjoy it.   8

May you enjoy your vast estate, | where you'll not see a single inhabitant, | each empty ruin, each cold hearth, | each uncultivated plot overrun with rushes; | look 12 out from your window, great chief, | onto the huddled townships in the glen, | where no talk or laughter can be heard, | the ruined remains bereft of people.   16

May you enjoy your fate and predicament, | your vacant land, your empty purse, | all you will have to spend to maintain it, | and no tenantry providing you with anything; | the sin of the father upon his children, | harsh is the law and ineluct- 20 able; | ancient is that estate of yours and not meagre, | many's the glen that's under your hand.   24

10 [*What Song Is Ours*]

[incomplete draft]

In roussedness of fire,　　in flames roaring
passed in the night　　Priam's people;
wild through Troy　　the red sword wandered.
Their end is a song　　that men will mind of,
folk far off　　will sorrow for them.　　　　　　　5

What song is ours　　but a change-house chorus
cursing the sheep
They that browse　　through broken townships,
sleep in the rain　　on ruined thresholds,
bracken their bed　　on hearths that are harried.　　10

These have the glens　　and we must wander
strange and unsought　　in a changed country,
walk like ghosts　　where once they were welcome
and now their friends　　are gash before them.

Dearer than hearths　　herds on the hillside,　　15
stag and hind　　in the high corries;
dearer than men　　is money among them.

*11 [*An t-Sàbaid*]

"Mur cùm thu Sàbaid Dhè, a mhic,
　　chan èirich leat gu bràth."
Mo thruaighe, bhris Clann Dòmhnaill i
　　aig Inbhir Lòchaidh là.　　　　　　　4

11 [*The Sabbath*]

"If you fail to keep God's Sabbath, son, | no good will ever befall you." | Alas, the
MacDonalds broke it | that day at Inverlochy.　　　　　　　4

12 [Dùrachdan Nollaige, 1936]

Bhon tha Nollaig nar cois
   bi gu sodalach èibhinn,
gabh do dheoch, seinn do phort,   3
   gun sprochd is gun èislean,
's nuair a thig a' Bhliadhn' Ùr
   gum bi sùlas gach ceum dhuit.   6

*13 Tìr Thàirngire
The Land of Promise

I've heard o a land that lies westward. Weel it's set
in the lee o aa the wunds that are but the saft Sooth.
There isna hurtin in't or the sting o a sherp mooth,
there isna woundin or greetin, they canna grieve or fret.   4

Shinin evar in sun the slopes, bricht the sand;
singin evar an' laughter. They ken nae keen
the people thonder. The Lord's hand lies atween
that fowk an' daith, that fowk an' Adam's clan.   8

Thon was the land whar Brendan came; but his coorach's track
has fadeit for aye on the sea's face. Folla ye may,
but ye'll folla no more than yere awn wish an' the wund's way;
an' the wish o man is wake lik a rash. Ye'll but sleep in the wrack. 12

Summar an' Wunter, a weary while, ye'll run on yere rodd,
wi many's the dreich wundward bate, an' yere eyes aheid
seekin thon shore. On the sea's groond ye wull herbar deid,
for Brendan's land is hidden from men by the hand o God. 16

Ye wull sail yere boat by flann an' gale while her sides last,
an' yere eyes onstarein ayont the bows grow ridd an' fey.
But nevar thon coast wull leap lik a flame thro haar or spray;
an' then end o't, a scraich. The big sea wull grup ye fast. 20

12 [Christmas Greetings, 1936]

*Since Christmas is upon us | be expansive and merry, | have your dram, play your
tune, | banish misery and sadness, | and come the New Year |* *may there be joy in* 3
each step for you.   6

Ye wull druft wi the tides as they shuft an' swing by the side o the land
an' quate the fush wull glim at ye oot o cauld eyes,
an' there ye wull rock in the tangle an' turn, till the deid rise,
an' the hunners that socht a shore that seeker nivar fand.   24

*14 The Three Brothers

Thon night the three put the sails tie her,
cheerily, heidin home from Ayrshir.
A gale o southerly wund came on them
by the Cumbrae light, but they werena carein.   4

Oot thonder by Garroch Heids she trevellt,
runnin lik smok, an her daicks streamin.
When the rip was risein roond her shoothers,
seas that wad swalla, she didna heed them.   8

West she trampt, an' the white ridges
lik bauchkans oot o the night came breengein
against her quarter. Slack they werena
thon night, but the night had a sore endin.   12

It wasna the wave that the wund wakent,
a steep-faced sea brekkin aboard her,
or a white lump shaken over her shoothers,
that fillt her so that she sank below them.   16

Ootside o Laggan Heid it struck her.
Doon from the home hills came boondin
a livin squaal that whupt the watter.
It raxt her sail, an' over it threw her.   20

To their folk's hoose came the hand o somethin,
through the derk tie the door, an' clasht upon it
three times. At thon uncanny knockin
they couldna speak for the thoughts that were in them.   24

Their eyes stood in their heid, starein,
an' they wisht they couldna hear the howlin
that the wund made, or the soond o the brekkers
doon on the shore. But it aye was louder.   28

They gazet in the fire wi gash faces,
an' nevar talkt, for they couldna speak it.
They werena for lyin doon or sleepin,
an' they daurna say for why they werena.   32

[Afore

Afore the brekk o day in the moarnin,
when it wasna derk an it wasna dawnin,
from the rocks on the *rubh'* they heard a cryin,
a *cèinteach*'s keenin. They kent their story.　　　36

They kent what thon sore cry was sayin,
an' whose lair was laid in the wrack an' seaweed,
an' they sat there wi the day brekkin,
grey face on the men an' the wummen greetin.　　　40

*15　*Luinneag*

Hug ò hoireann ò,
gura fada, cian fada,
hug ò hoireann ò.

B'e gairbhe na gaoithe
chùm an-raoir mi nam chaithris.　　　5

Gaoth à deas air Loch Fìne,
'teachd gu fìochar le tartar.

Na tuinn chaoirgheal mun Gharbhail,
neart na fairge 's a faram.

Is ann an-raoir a bha 'n nuallan　　　10
na mo chluasan 's mi 'n Sasainn.

Gun tig fuaim an Uillt Bheithe
eadar mise 's mo chadal.

15　[Chorus Song]

Hug ò hoireann ò, | it is far, endlessly far, | hug ò hoireann ò.
It was the hardness of the wind | that kept me awake last night.　　　5
A wind from the south on Loch Fyne, | coming fiercely with uproar.
Waves blazing with foam round Garvel, | the might of the sea and its clangour.
Last night its roaring | was in my ears, and I was in England.　　　10
The sound of the Birch Burn comes | between me and my sleep.

Abhainn nan Gillean 's a gaoir aic'
bho Loch a' Chaorainn 'na cabhaig.   15

Lagan Ròaig 's Tràigh na Lùibe
eadar mo shùilean 's mo leabhar.

Agus Rudha Clach an Tràghaidh
a' snàmh air a' bhalla.

*16 *Fada–Geàrr*

*Bidh fear thall 's a-bhos a' cumail a-mach nach eil feum dhuinn ann a
bhith 'cur chomharraidhean air faidead agus air giorrad (no* accents
*mar a ghoirear dhiubh sa Bheurla) os cionn nam facal. Ach ma ghabhas
sinn an comhairle bithidh mòran troimhe-chèile agus dìth chinnte againn,
nach bi? Feuch a-nis:*

B'fheàrr leam gàd na gad, is clach ra dùsgadh,
cuir àit an àite ait, 's is tearc gheibh tùr ann;
ma tha thu gàgach gagach, mabach ciùrrta,
mo chràdh do chàs, do chas 's do chab bhith brùite.   4
Mas càraid caraid, 's dithist fear sa chunntas,
mas gàradh garadh, 's lios gach creag san dùthaich,
mas còir an coireach, 's carach am fear fiùghail,
's mas bòchdan bochdan, 's tannasg fear gun iunntas.   8

[No mur tig

The River of the Youths with its outcry, | hastening from the Rowan Loch.   15
Lagan Ròaig and the strand of the Bight | between my eyes and my book.
And Ebbing Stone Point | swimming on the wall.

16 [Long–Short]

*The odd person here and there maintains that we've no need to write length marks (or
accents, as they're called in English) above words. But if we go along with that advice, it
will give rise to much confusion and uncertainty, won't it? Have a try:*

I'd pick a crowbar *before a* withe *were a stone to be shifted, | put a* place *in place
of* pleased *and you'll rarely make sense; | if you're* chap-footed *and* stuttering*,
stammering and disabled, | your* fate *pains me, your* feet *and mouth both in-
jured. | If a* friend *is a* couple*, one man counts for two, | if a* den *is a* garden*, every   4
rock in the land is an orchard; | if the* guilty *are* good*, the righteous man is crooked,
| and if a* beggar's *a* bogle*, a man without wealth is a phantom.*   8

No mur tig thu às do bharail le sin, cluinn seo:

> Mo thruaigh do cheann, 's neo-Chrìostail thu 'charaid
>> mas ionnan leat sabaid is Sàbaid;
> 's mo thruaigh an Rìgh, nì e suidhe neo-thaitneach
>> mur toir sibh dha cathair ach càthair;   12
> air mo shon dheth, nam b'fheudar dhomh triall thar mara,
>> b'e 'bhochdainn leam bata airson bàta,
> 's an àm togail nan seòl, 's a bhith 'fàgail a' chala,
>> 's e bu ghoireas dhuinn rac, 's cha bu ràc e.   16

17 A' Chas air Tìr

Feet Ashore

To sit at ease by day and through the night
to sleep unlet; careless though secretly
the cheating wind should veer, and morning's light
break upon shores foam-girdled by the sea,
where shelter was; to go one's way in spite   5
of storm or thwarting calm, unharmed and free;
we thought on this in wind-torn haggard dawns
when daylight came across the racing heads
of driven seas. And now this ease that awns
o'erhead from windy skies is tried, and sheds   10
its sweetness. Now we'd hear her wake's hoarse cry,
and nurse her heeled and straining, anxiously
groping among the curtained squalls, or see
the long swell marching ridged against the sky.

Or if that doesn't make you change your mind, listen to this:

Alas for your head, you're no Christian my friend, | if you equate the Sabbath with fighting; | and alas for the king, he'll be sat none too comfortably, | if the throne that you give him's a peatbog; | for myself, if I had to cross over the ocean, | a stick   12 for a boat would mean trouble, | and when the sails were hoisted for leaving the port, | it's not a rake that we'd need but a parrel.   16

*18 Mi 'Fàgail na Tìre
Leaving the Land

The way I went some spite had planned,
  to know the homes of other men,
the time I turned to leave the land,
  it was not well with me then.   4

That these old headlands falling back
  could draw such dim eyes to their hold,
that hills beyond a steamer's track
  could hurt so sore, I was not told.   8

There Sleea swung away from me,
  hidden by hills I never crossed.
I had not heard that rock and scree
  and rain-scarred slope were precious lost.   12

My eyes on Laggan, and the sound
  of homely waters loud astern:
that day the ancient grief I found
  of songs sung lightly, in my turn.   16

19 Soraidh Slàn le Cinntìre

Soraidh slàn le Cinntìre
  's le Loch Fìne mo ghràidh;
ceud soraidh leis na cuantan,   3
  mo cheòl cluais' iad gach là;
slàn om chridhe leis an Tairbeirt
  is le garbh thìr an àigh.   6

[Leam

19 A Long Farewell to Kintyre

A long farewell to Kintyre | and to Loch Fyne that I love; | a hundred farewells to
the oceans – | music for my ear every day were they; | goodbye from my heart to   3
Tarbert | and the glorious, rough land.   6

17

Leam bu ro-luath am bàta
   àrd a-mach air an loch,
nuair a ghabh i gu astar   9
   anns a' mhadainn glè mhoch.
Chaill mi sealladh air Garbhail.
   Thuit mo mheanmna gu sprochd.   12

Sin am fearann nach fuath leam
   mo thìr chuanar bheag fhèin;
shìn i 'taobh ris na cuantan;   15
   shìn i 'cruachan gus an speur.
Gluaisidh stuadhan mun cuairt oirr'
   as nuallanach geum.   18

Dè do sgeul, fhir a chunnaic
   is a shiubhail an tìr
o shruth gàireach na Maoile   21
   gu Slia' Gaoil an t-slios mhìn?
Bidh do bhruadar gach oidhche
   air an loinn a bha innt'.   24

Bha mi uair is cha ghèillinn
   gum feumadh mi fhèin
beannachd fhàgail aig mo dhùthaich, 27
   ach cha tig mùthadh air feum –
soraidh slàn le Cinntìre
   's le Loch Fìne nam dhèidh.   30

Too swift to me was the boat | high out on the loch, | when she gathered speed | in 9 the morning very early. | I lost sight of Garvel. | My mood fell to melancholy. 12

That is the land that is not hateful to me, | my own snug, little country; | it has stretched its side to the oceans, | it has stretched its hillcrests to the sky. | Waves 15 move about it | of sonorous lowing. 18

What is your tale, you that have seen | and travelled the land | from the roaring tide of the Moyle | to Slia' Gaoil of the smooth flank? | Every night your dream 21 will be | of the fineness that was there. 24

There was a time that I would not give in | that I myself would have | to bid farewell to my [native land], | but necessity knows no changing. | A long farewell 27 to Kintyre | and to Loch Fyne after me. 30

*20 *To a Loch Fyne Fisherman*

Calum thonder, long's the night to your thinking,
night long till dawn and the sun set at the tiller,
age and the cares of four and a boat to keep you
high in the stern, alone for the winds to weary.   4

A pillar set in the shifting moss, a beacon
fixed on the wandering seas and changing waters,
bright on the midnight waves and the hidden terrors;
the ancient yew of the glen, not heeding the ages.   8

Set among men that waver like leaves in the branches,
still among minds that flicker like light on the water.
Those are the shadows of clouds, the speckled and fleeting;
you are the hill that stands through shadow and sunlight.   12

Little you heed or care to change with changes,
to go like a broken branch in the grip of a torrent;
you are your judge and master, your sentence unshaken,
a man with a boat of his own and a mind to guide her.   16

*21 *'S Leam Fhèin an Gleann*

An gleann sam biodh na smeòraichean
   gun sòradh 'cur ri rainn,
an gleann sam faighte fialachd
   is biatachd chnò bhàrr chrann,   4
chaidh bacadh air bhith 'tadhal ann
   le maoidheadh mar ri sgraing,
tha faire ann aig forsairean –
   tha 'n coigreach sa ghleann.   8

[Bha òl

21 [Mine is the Glen]

*The glen where the thrushes | would break into song unstintingly, | the glen which
offered bounteous provision | of nuts from its trees, | obstruction has been placed*   4
*on frequenting it | by threats as well as scowls, | and foresters now keep watch – |
the foreigner's in the glen.*   8

Bha òl à sruth gu farsaing ann
    gun lacha bhith ga ghairm,
bha 'n t-eun 's an t-allt gun euradh ann,
    's na smeuran crotach garbh;   12
gheibheadh fir an domhain ann
    gach sochair bha 'na shealbh,
ach obaidh an troich gortach seo
    cead coise ann gu falbh.   16

Obadh, euradh, sòradh e,
    cha mhòr a' bhuannachd dhà,
oir cò bheir feart air abartachd
    gach balaich thig don àit?   20
Air m'fhallaing fhèin, ge miosa e
    na 'dhriseag tha 'na phàirc,
tha 'n gleann aig' aoidheil sùlasach
    's cha diùlt sinn gibht bho 'làimh.   24

*22 *Do Bheithe Bòidheach*

Neul a' snàmh air an speur,
    duilleach eadar è 's mo shùil;
ùr bàrr-uaine gruag a' bheithe,
    leug nan leitir cas mun Lùib.   4

There was plenty drink from its running waters | with no accounts to settle, | bird and burn denying none, | and plump coarse brambles; | there any man in the 12 *world could enjoy | every comfort it possessed, | but this miserly midget now forbids | all right of way to the walker.* 16

Let him forbid, refuse, begrudge, | little good will it do him, | for who'll pay heed to the impudence | of every lad that comes to the place? | By my own cloak, 20 *although he's more prickly | than the briarbush in his park, | his glen is hospitable and comforting, | and we'll refuse no gift from its hand.* 24

22 *To a Bonny Birch Tree*

A cloud drifting in the sky, | leafage between it and my eye; | fresh and green-crested are the tresses of the birch, | jewel of the steep descents about the Bight. 4

Oiteag 'tighinn bhàrr an tuim,
   a' toirt fuinn às do dhos;
cruit na gaoithe do bhàrr teudach,
   cuisleannan nan geug ri port.   8

Àilleagan nan glac seo shìos,
   sìthbhrugh do na h-eòin do dhlùths,
thu gan tàladh às gach àirde,
   iad a' teàrnadh ort le sunnd.   12

Ceileireadh 's e binn binn,
   seirm is seinn air a' chnoc,
nuair a chromas na h-eòin Shamhraidh
   air do mheanglain 's mil 'nan gob.   16

Is fheàrr na 'n ceòl t'fhaicinn fhèin
   air bhogadan rèidh fon chnap,
seang bàrr-snìomhain amlach ùrar,
   is dealt 'na chùirnein air gach slait.   20

*23 *Cuimhne Nach Tèid Às*

A Memory that will not Fade

For though it were in Paradise
   or the far islands of the blest,
the sound of water down a glen
   would come between me and my rest.   4

[If only

A gentle breeze from the knowe | wins music from your crest; | harp of the wind is your stringed top | as the tendrils of the boughs make melody.   8

Gem of the hollows down [here], | a fairy-mound for the birds is your close-set fastness; | you charming them out of every airt, | and they stooping down on you with cheer.   12

Sweet, sweet the chorusing, | carolling and singing on the hillock, | when the birds of summer alight | on your sprays with honey in their beaks.   16

Better than their music is to see yourself, | gently nodding below the scaur, | slim and fresh, with crest enlaced and plaited, | and beads of dew on every branch.   20

If only over sleeping seas
    one breath of wind should wander there,
straying from off the hills I knew,
    I'd think upon a land more fair.   8

There is no Lethe that would drown
    the longing or the memory,
whose kindly stream would bear away
    my tears, if that wind blew on me.   12

For if I thought on sea and wind
    and Sleea under rainy skies,
and minded of another land,
    little to me were Paradise.   16

*24 *The Fisherman Speaks*

Along the shore the solans strike,
    and rise, and strike again in spray,
and I myself, and all my like,
    can curse our fate and look away.   4

On sheltered rocks the black scarts bask
    full fed, and rise to meet again;
we bend our shoulders to the task
    they threw to us like beggar men.   8

The skiff I had for thirty years
    has gone to pay her debts and mine.
My son a stranger's cutter steers.
    I delve the roadway by Loch Fyne.   12

From Kenmore south to Saddell Bay
    the blind shoals wander in the sea.
I ply my spade and watch them play –
    God, what is it but mockery?   16

*25 Looking out from Kintyre

Rest on the hill and look beyond the sea.
  Eastward the smoke hangs over Clyde and Ayr.
Yonder is all that Britain is, will be;
  the blossoming of years is garnered there.   4

Look from this widowed land, wed to the deer,
  and see uprise the incense offering,
the smoky mist that chokes the stars, and hear
  the thunder of toom barrels rattling.   8

Here is regret, and memory and song;
  the long hills lie indifferent and smile.
Yonder the heirs of all their eras throng
  their hives, with their inheritance of bile.   12

Had all our past and all our future, both,
  to go like spindrift when the great wind blows;
had our green shoot to shrivel for the growth
  of this gaunt sprawling weed that is their rose?   16

They sing no song. They see nor sun nor earth.
  All are gone crazed with babbling. All shape ill.
Where is there mark for reverence, where is worth?
  Where is the word that hand should yield to still?   20

There is no robe we should give back before,
  no honour that should walk the causey's crown.
Had this to be – that we should come once more
  to iron counsels, long thought cassen down?   24

This is the end of precedent and gown,
  of court, debate, procession, learning prim –
each will be quick to strike his striker down,
  and he that bars the way, be hard with him.   28

*26 *Cinntìre*

Sìth o Dhia air màthair m'altraim,
    le spreigeadh gràidh chan fhaigh mi clos;
sòlas duit Chinntìr' is sonas –
    cuim nach molainn crìoch gun lochd?   4

Gnàthach sunnd is aobhachd inntinn
    san dùthaich ghaoil a dh'àraich mi;
gràin no gruaim cha tig 'na còir-se,
    gàire 's ceòl as dual di.   8

Ghràdhaich mi do mhuir 's do mhonadh,
    lom do chnoc fo ghuirm' an speur,
drilseach grèin' air an slios taobhgheal,
    lios aost' as milse gasta gnè.   12

Binn guth gaoithe air do chruachan,
    ag èigheach air an guaillean àrd;
gur rìomhach do ghealchrios umad,
    a' mhuir a' teannadh gu tràigh.   16

Seann tìr ud air oir an aigeinn,
    monmhar mara buan mu 'Maoil,
còrr a slèibhtean os cionn sàile,
    rèidh a tràigh, tonnbhàn a taobh.   20

26 *Kintyre*

Peace from God on my fostering mother, | with the incitement of love I get no rest. | Joy and happiness be to you, Kintyre – | why should I not praise a land that is faultless ?   4

Cheer and gladness are customary | in the beloved land that reared me. | Hate or gloom come not near her. | Laughter and music are her heritage.   8

I have loved your sea and moorland, | the bareness of your hills under the blue of the sky; | the shimmer of sun on their fair-sided flanks, | old pleasance of sweetest and finest nature.   12

Sweet is the voice of the wind on your summits, | crying on their high shoulders; | lovely your white girdle about you, | the sea closing in on the shore.   16

That ancient land on the edge of the deep, | the murmur of the sea ever about her Moyle, | steep her hills above the salt sea, | smooth her strand, wave-white her side.   20

Tìr nan Òg nam fonn gun truimead,
   iomadh tonn ga sgaradh ruinn;
Tìr fo Thuinn gun sgur air gàire –
   thugadh tìr as àillidh dhuinn.   24

Is daor a cheannaich mi mo bheòshlaint'
   mas e mo stòras fanachd uait,
crom gach là os cionn mo leabhair
   gun amharc ort, mo ghoirtein uain'!   28

A bhith 'fuaradh Àird MhicLaomainn,
   long 's a lorg 'na gaoir fo 'druim,
slèibhtean Ròaig romham a' sìneadh –
   togail cinn is cridhe siud.   32

Air ruigsinn domh à tìr aineoil
   gu crìoch m'aithne o shiubhal thuinn,
cur mo chois' air fòd na dùthcha –
   saoil nach pògainn ùir an fhuinn?   36

Breugadh sùla do na chì e,
   sgeul an tì a chunnaic e –
slios fad' àillidh an fhuinn shona,
   oighreachd àrsaidh sliochd nan treun.   40

Cinneadh Iain Mhòir, an curaidh,
   Ìle 's Uladh ac' am bann,
cleas nan neul gun deach iad thairis –
   och, gun ach an sgeul orr' ann !   44

[Is domhain

Tìr nan Òg, of the melodies without melancholy, | many a wave parts us from it; | Tìr fo Thuinn with laughter unceasing – | to us has been given a land more lovely. 24

Dearly have I bought my livelihood | if my wealth is to stay away from you; | bent every day over my book | without looking upon you, my little green garth. 28

To be weathering Ardlamont, | a ship with her wake droning under her keel, | the hills of Ròaig stretching before me – | that would be a lifting of head and heart. 32

When I reach the country I know | from a strange land, after traversing waves; | when I put my foot on the soil of my native land – | why would I not kiss the earth of my native place ? 36

A charm to the eye of all who see it, | the tale of the one who has seen it – | such is the long, beautiful sweep of the happy land, | the ancient heritage of the race of heroes. 40

The clan of Iain Mòr, the warrior, | who had Islay and Ulster in bond, | like the clouds they have passed by – | alas, the tale of them alone remains! 44

Is domhain a chaidh freumh do sheanchais,
  luingeas Lochlainn, airm is trod,
Clanna Lìr air Sruth na Maoile,
  Calum Cille caomh nad phort.   48

Talla rìoghail cruadhlach t'aonach,
  cluasag shìoda fraoch do chòs;
is mìls' an deoch e, deur od shruthain
  na fìon tìr eile an cupan òir.   52

Leannan mo shùgraidh is mo shuirghe,
  fearann mo rùin, crò nan sliabh,
leug is àilleagan gach tìre,
  seunadh ort is sìth o Dhia.   56

*27 *Ùrnaigh Oisein as Ùr*

Oisein

  Innis dhuinn, a Phàdraig,
    air onair do lèighinn –
  a bheil nèamh gu h-àraid
    aig Fionn is Fianna Èireann?   4

Deep has gone the root of your tradition: | ships of Norway, arms and strife, | the Children of Lìr on the Moyle Race, | gentle Columba in your port.   48

A royal hall your stony hills, | a silken pillow the heather of your hollows; | sweeter the drink a drop from your streamlets | than the wine of another land in a golden cup.   52

Sweetheart of my love-talk and my wooing, | land of my desire, fold in which the hills are gathered together, | gem of all lands and loveliest of them, | a blessing on you and peace from God.   56

27 *Ossian's Prayer Revised*

Ossian: Tell me, Patrick, | for the honour of your learning, | have Fionn and the Fiann of Erin | attained to heaven truly?   4

26

*Thug Pàdraig na speuclairean bhàrr a shròine, phaisg e
Mìosachan na h-Eaglaise, is thubhairt e:*

A Oisein, mhic an fhlatha,
  seo mar rinneadh an t-òrdan –
cha bhi nèamh aig na peacaich
  a bhios ri feadail Di-Dòmhnaich.   8

Oisein

B'fheàrr feadail nan sealgair
  air an leargaidh Di-Dòmhnaich,
na a bhith 'g èisteachd do shearmon
  agus seirm do shailm còmhla.   12

Pàdraig

Ach ma nì thu fìor aidmheil,
  a' gabhail aithreachais ìosail,
sa cheann thall bidh do dhùil-sa
  ri Hallelùia nach crìochnaich.   16

Oisein

Nach mi a bhiodh falamh,
  an dèidh na ghabh mi 'dhàin rìomhach,
a bhith a' seinn "Thalla laoghaibh"
  air an aon teud gu sìorraidh,   20
is thuirt thu fhèin rium an duan ud
  a bhith buan, gun sgur aca.
Chìthear fòs iad, ge àrd iad,
  is an càrsan gan tachdadh.   24

[*Pàdraig*

Patrick took the spectacles from off his nose, [folded the Church Monthly] and said:

Ossian, son of the prince, | this is how it [has been] laid down in the regulations – | heaven is not for the sinners | that whistle on Sunday.   8

Ossian: Better the whistling of the hunters | on the hillside of a Sunday | than [to be listening to your sermons | and your psalm-singing] together.   12

Patrick: [But] if you become a professing churchgoer | and [make humble repentance, | you may look forward eventually | to] a Halleluia without cease.   16

Ossian: [Wouldn't I be] the blockhead, | [after all the splendid verses I've recited in my time, | to be singing "Get moving, calves" | on an endless monotone – | for you yourself have just told me that the ballad | goes on endlessly. | We'll see them yet, high as they are, | choked by their own hoarseness.]   24

Pàdraig

Cha tig glochar air sgòrnan
   an taigh glòrmhor mo Rìgh-sa,
is uisge beò ann 'na ghalain
   a chaisgeadh an ìota.   28
Chaoidh chan fhaicear ann pathadh,
   ged nach fhaighear an Stuth ann,
oir tha tì ann is cofaidh,
   a bhios 'na dheoch aig na Turcaich.   32

Oisein

Mas e teaghlach tì-tòtail
   a th'ann taigh glòrmhor do Rìgh-sa,
b'fheàrr leam bàs san taigh òsta,
   measg nan stòp 's mi làn fiona.   36
B'fheàrr aon sgailc às an fhuaran
   ud shuas air Beinn Èadair,
na tì cairtidh na ciste
   is do bhriosgaidean dèilidh.   40

Pàdraig

Cuist, a thrusdair na misge,
   bus gun ghliocas, gun Sgrìobtair,
agus t'athair 's a shinnsreachd
   cruinn ud shìos anns a' ghrìosaich.   44

Oisein

Is beag tha dh'eòlas nad spuaic-sa.
   Is e uaimh fhuar reòta
a th'ann Ifrinn an dùbhraidh –
   is chan eil Fionn ann a chòmhnaidh.   48

Patrick: Never wheezing will come on throat | in the glorious house of my King, | with living water there by the gallon | to put a stop to their thirst. | [Never will 28 thirst be felt there, | though the hard stuff isn't on offer, | for there's tea to be had and coffee, | the staple drink of the Turks.]   32

Ossian: If it's a teatotal household, | the glorious dwelling of your King, | dearer to me were death in the pub, | among the stoups, and me brimful of wine. | 36 [Dearer one good swallow from yon stream | up on the Hill of Howth | than tinted tea from the chest | and your jam biscuits.]   40

Patrick: Wheesht, scullion of the drunkenness, | gab without sense, without Scripture, | and your father and his ancestry | [down there together on the cinders]. 44

Ossian: Little knowledge there is in your scruffy pate. | Dark Hell | is a cold frozen [cave] – | and Fionn hasn't his quarters there anyway. | 48

Toll làn snagardaich fhiaclan,
   chan fhaic m'Fhiann-sa no Fionn e,
is e làn casadaich 's lòinidh
   is mìle sròn ann gan srùbadh.   52

Pàdraig
Nach do leugh thu Chriosostom?
   Bi 'd thost, a Anachriost dhearbhta,
oir tha an t-àit 'na loch lasrach,
   mar bhios mi 'canainn san t-searmoin.   56
Sin sloc teinteach nan coire,
   nach fhaic solas na grèine,
is tha Fionn 's Tarbh Bhàsain
   agus Bàl ann le chèile.   60

Oisein
B'fheàrr mo gharadh an Ifrinn
   na blasad dibhe do Rìgh-sa,
mas E fhèin a chuir m'athair
   gu baile na grìosaich.   64
Cuir nam làimh claidhe sgaiteach,
   biodag mhath no sgian luthaidh,
is do Rìgh 's a luchd cùirte,
   chuirinn smùid asta uile.   68

Pàdraig (ris fhèin)
Cluinnibh sin! Claidhe sgaiteach,
   is e 'n ath-leanabas 'aoise –
Fionn 's a mhusgaid 's a chlogaid,
   agus Osgar 's a straoillean.   72

                                              [(*ri Oisein*)

[The abyss where there is gnashing of teeth, | my Fianna or Fionn won't set eyes on it, | and it full of coughing and rheumatism | and a thousand noses sniffing.]   52

Patrick: Have you not read Chrysostom? | [Be silent, you] proven Antichrist, | for the place is a loch of [flame, | as I shall be expounding in my sermon.] | That   56 is the fiery pit of the stewpans, | that sees not the light of the sun, | and Fionn and the Bull of Bashan, | and Baal are there together.   60

Ossian: [I'd rather warm up in Hell | than take one sip of your King's drink], | if it's himself who sent my father | to the township of the cinders. | [Hand me] a   64 cleaving sword, | a good dirk or [a clasp-knife, | and your King and his courtiers | I'd send them all packing.]   68

Patrick [(to himself)]: Listen to that now! A cleaving sword, | and him in the infancy of his old age – | Fionn with his musket and his helm, | and Oscar with his thumps.   72

(ri Oisein)

Ma thig Fionn an rùn catha
    don chaisteal tha shuas ud,
bheir mo Rìgh staigh am fàradh
    's e 'dòrtadh teàrra mu 'chluasan.   76

Oisein (a' beucaich agus 'anail 'na uchd is e a'
smeurachadh mun chagailt)

Bheireadh Osgar cruinnleum às
    a chur greim air a' bharran.
Bheireadh e maoim às na h-ainglean,
    is e a-staigh ac' gun taing dhaibh.   80
A dh'aindeoin Sheraphim 's aingeal
    bhiodh do cheannard san daorsa –
is a Phàdraig dhuibh stiallaich,
    b'fheàirrd thu sgian na do chaolan.   84

Pàdraig (le meud mòr is tarcais)

Sin thu fhèin ann, a Oisein.
    Leig dhìot an clobha 's cuir saod ort,
is tu làn aineolais pheacaich –
    is b'fheàirrd thu ealtainn ri t'aodann.   88

Oisein

A Phàdraig naoimh, cha bu mhist' thu –
    fhad 's a dh'fhiosraich mi t'aogasg,
's mur deach mi ceàrr leis an doille –
    corra ghaoisid nad mhaol-chnap.   92

[(to Ossian): If Fionn comes with fighting in mind | to the castle up yonder, | my King will draw in the ladder | and pour tar about his lugs.]   76

Ossian [(rasping and out of breath, and fumbling around the fireplace)]:

[Oscar would take a whirling leap | and gain a foothold on the ramparts. | He would spread terror among the angels | and force his way in, despite them all.] | In spite of Seraphim and angels, | your chief would be in chains – | and, dirty streaky Patrick, | you'd be the better of a knife in your guts.   80
      84

Patrick [(with great superiority and contempt)]:   There you go again, Ossian. | Put down the tongs and behave yourself, | and you so full of wicked ignorance – | and you would be none the worse of a [razor to] your face.   88

Ossian: Well, [Blessed] Patrick – | as far as I can make out your appearance | and if my blindness doesn't lead me astray – | you'd be the better of a little fur on your bald [pate].   92

Pàdraig (is an rudhadh 'na ghruaidh)

Ma leanas tu, mo ghaisgich,
    gu stailceach sa cheum sin,
cha toir mi branndaidh no rùm dhuit,
    no tì làn siùcair no dèilidh.   96

Oisein (ri miolaran)

Na bi gu dona nis, abstoil,
    don t-seana dhallan 's e rùiste.
Bidh mi rèidh riut, Mhic Ailpein,
    's gur ann agad an siùcar.   100

*28 Òran

Gràdh nan gruagach, on dh'fhàs i fuar rium,
    chan eil dol suas domh no suain 'na dèidh,
on chuir i suarach a' bhruidhinn chluaineis
    's gach coinneamh uaigneach dh'fhàg luath mo cheum.   4
Èiridh 'n latha is a' ghrian le 'gathannaibh,
    èiridh 'n ceathach rith' on achadh rèidh,
èiridh 'n driùchda bhàrr fhlùr is gheugan –
    och, cùin' a dh'èireas mo chridhe fhèin?   8

[Shiubhail

Patrick [(getting red in the face)]: If you carry on so stubbornly | in that way, my hero, | I won't give you any brandy or rum, | [or sugary tea or jam].   96

Ossian [(fawningly)]: Oh, apostle, don't be bad now | to the poor blind old man. | I give in to you, son of Alpin, | since it's you that have the sugar.   100

28 [Song]

Since the bonniest of lassies has grown cold towards me, | no cheer I'll find after her nor sleep, | since she despises all the whispered promises | and each secret meeting that lightened my step. | The day will rise and the sun will spread its   4 rays | and lift the mist from the level plain, | the dew will lift from flowers and branches – | oh when will my own heart lift?   8

Shiubhail mi anmoch fonn dall is garbhlach,
    sìos leis a' Gharbh Allt 's mi 'falbh gu sgìth,
gus an d'ràinig mi 'n cnocan càrnach
    os cionn na fàrdaich a b'àras dì;   12
an ciar a' mhochthrath 's an speur a' gormadh
    chaidh an t-eun gu gairm ann a baile shìos,
chunnaic mi 'n smùid 'teachd o thaigh mo rùin-sa,
    shil mo shùilean is thionndaidh mi.   16

Tha tasgaidh luachmhor am falt mo ghruagaich,
    mar bheairteas uaislean 'na chruachan ann,
òr nan cuailean os cionn a gruaidh-se,
    am pailteas ruadh-òir 'na chuachan trom;   20
fìon dearg a beul is e ruiteach leusach,
    's a muineal glègheal mar èiteag thonn,
mar aiteal grèine air chathadh bheucthonn,
    no sneachd ga shèideadh air slèibhtean lom.   24

Nuair thig a' ghaoth bhàrr an àilein bhraonaich
    bidh fàile mhaothlus 's e caoin 'na beul,
is cridheil faoilidh thig oiteag chaoilghlinn,
    roid an aonaich 's am fraoch 'na sgèith;   28
mas gaoth à deas i a thig gar tatadh
    o shliosan cadaltach blàth ri grèin,
thig smuain mo ghràidh leath' is smuairean cràidhte,
    a' ghaoth a thàinig o h-àite fhèin.   32

Late I walked dark forbidding country, | heading down Garvalt, my progress slow, | till I came to the rocky hilltop | overlooking the dwelling that was her home; | in 12 *the dawn's half-light as the sky was paling, | the cock crowed in her township down below, | I saw smoke rise from the house of my darling, | tears filled my eyes and I turned to go.* 16

There is priceless treasure in my lass's tresses, | like the wealth of nobles in piles high, | the golden ringlets about her temples | the red-gold profusion of heavy curls; | her mouth is red wine, with deep glow gleaming, | her throat pure white as 20 *a sea-smoothed stone, | as a sun-gleam in the spray of roaring breakers, | or as drifting snow across bare hills blown.* 24

When the wind comes over from the drizzly meadow, | it breathes a sweet scent of fragrant herbs, | and a mild kindly breeze comes from narrow defiles, | mountain myrtle and heather in its wing; | if it's a south wind which comes to lull us | from 28 *sleepy hillslopes warmed by the sun, | it brings thoughts of my love and a searing sadness, | this wind which from her own place is come.* 32

*29 *Lomsgrios na Tìre*
The Destruction of the Land

In flames o fire, in a reid furnace, in bluidreid licht
    passt away Priam's fowk; an' the lowe lept
up in the luft lik a bricht stab in the breist o the nicht.
    Daith wandert, an' wudd in the streets the sword swept.   4

Priam's people passt in the flames. Fowk that war fey,
    led on a heidlong rodd by a lass wi a bricht face.
Man there isna that hasna heard o their gait astray;
    come there wilna that wilna greet for thon brokkin place.   8

Here brokk as deep a wave o ruin an' scowred the shore;
    truly, for here the land is harrowt bare o men.
Lowe tae licht the sky there wasna. Wull sorrow gar
    sangs be made tae lift oor names tae the licht again?   12

Fowk that deed lik a fire on the hull, smowldert oot?
    Left in a lee by the man that made it, an' gaed his way;
deein black in the driftin rain at a rock's foot,
    ashes steerd by the hand o the wund, cauld an' grey.   16

Nae sign tae see that heat an' the quick flame war there;
    an' no' a sign in the herriet straths, that we should ken
hoo life, a balefire, bleezed on the ridges, reid an' fair,
    hoo sword an' the sang there lept in the hand an' the mooth o men. 20

An' us the lave – tae gang lik ghaists in a strange land?
    Stumblin steps an' unsiccar gait in oor awn glens;
shuffle lik coos in ways that are waa'd on either hand;
    keep tae the causey, no' a fowk, but a flock o men.   24

"Keppoch is wasteit" – weel we may sing it. The ebb tide
    has bared oor beach lik a besom. This is oor tune o tunes,
the daft bleating o grey sheep in tumblet toons,
    an' the shepherd caain his dogs heich on the hullside.   28

30 [*Rann Aoire air Bàta*]

I gun ùrlar a b'fhiù iomradh,
   creag 'n àm iomraim, uaigh 'n àm seòlaidh;
i cho stailceach 's gun i socrach,
   b'e 'n "soraidh slàn" air cois air bòrd dhith.   4

31 Do na Daoine Muladach nach Gabh Òran ach Òran Gaoil, 's e Fìor Bhrònach

Tha mìle Màiri Bhàn san dùthaich
   is thrèig gach sgliùrach dhiubh a rùn;
tha mìle rìbhinn donn a bhàrr orr',
   's chan iad as fheàrr mas fìor bhur tùrs,   4
tha mìle nighean dubh làn chuireid,
   's tha corra nighean bhuidh' sa chùis;
ach bàn no buidh' iad, breac no stiallach,
   bidh creach is cianalas 'nan lùib.   8

30 [*Satirical Verse about a Boat*]

*Without a deck worthy of the name, | she was a rock to row, a tomb to sail in; | she
so thrawn and none too stable, | it was "forever farewell" to step aboard her.*   4

31 [*For the Melancholy Folk who only ever sing
Highly Plaintive Lovesongs*]

*A thousand Fair Marys there are in the land, | and each one of the hussies has
ditched her beau; | there are a thousand brown-haired maidens, moreover, | who
aren't much better if your sorrow speaks true; | and a thousand black-haired girls*   4
*full of wiles, | and the odd golden-haired girl to mention too; | but fair or golden,
speckled or streaked, | ruin and regret they'll bring in tow.*   8

Och och, nach searbh e, cor fear Albann,
   's gach tì ri gairm 's ri gul 's ri èigh,
a' caoidh mar dh'fhàg e fhèin a dhachaigh,
   's mar dh'fhàg a chaileag mhìn e fhèin.   12
Nach eil Cùil Fhodair fhèin gu leòir leibh?
   Thoir beagan sgòid dhith 's mùth bhur gleus.
Nach b'fheàrr leibh "Fair a-nall am botal"
   na oiteag mhnà gun bhonn gun stèidh?   16

*32 *An Sealgair agus an Aois*

Cuing mo dhroma an aois a-nis,
   rib' mo choise, robach, liath;
fear thig eadar soills' is sùilean,
   fear thig eadar rùn is gnìomh.   4

Fàgaidh e am faillean crotach,
   fo gach dos 's e chuireas sgian;
is och, b'e 'm bàrr air gach miosgainn
   'thighinn eadar mi 's an sliabh.   8

[Thug e

Och, bitter the plight of the men of Scotland, | *every one of them cries out, and weeps and wails,* | *lamenting how he left his home,* | *and how his gentle lass has now left him.* | *Is Culloden itself not enough for you?* | *Tighten the sails some and* 12 *change your tune.* | *Would you not prefer "Pass over the bottle"* | *to a baseless, whimsical feminine waft?* 16

32 *The Hunter and Age*

A yoke on my back Age is now, | *a snare for my foot, shaggy and grey:* | *a man who comes between the light and my eyes,* | *one who comes between intention and deed.* 4

He leaves the sapling crooked, | *under every thicket he wields the knife,* | *and och, to top his every malice,* | *he comes between me and the hill.* 8

Thug e dhìom a' Chruach Chaorainn,
  's an gunna caol san ealchainn shuas;
bhuin e dhìom mo neart, am meàirleach;
  dh'fhàg e mi gun làmh, gun luaths.   12

Nan robh aige corp a ghlacainn,
  's nan tachrainn ris leis fhèin sa bheinn,
bhiodh saltairt ann is fraoch ga reubadh,
  is fuil air feur mun sgaradh sinn.   16

*33   *Age and the Hunter*

Yoke of my neck, this Age comes o'er me,
  snare of my feet, the gray, the still.
Between my eyes and the light he is standing;
  he stands between the deed and the will.   4

There is the hand that warps the sapling,
  that sets the knife to the apple's root;
and, oh, 'twas the crown of all his malice
  to snatch the hill from beneath my foot.   8

He has taken from me the paths of the Cruach;
  he has rusted my gun like an autumn leaf;
he has taken away from me strength and laughter,
  and hand and foot, like a heartless thief.   12

If Age were a man that hands could grapple,
  and I could come on him secretly
up on the hill where no man passes,
  grass would be reddened or he went free.   16

He has taken from me the Rowan Summit | and the slender gun, up on its hook: | he has plucked my strength from me, the bandit, | and left me without speed or agility of hand.   12

Had he a body that I could seize, | and were I to chance on him in the hills alone, | there would be much trampling, much wrenching of heather, | and blood on the grass before we'd part.   16

*34 Song

Day will rise and the sun from eastward,
    the mist in his rays from marsh and plain;
the dew will rise from the bending branches –
    och, when will my own heart rise again?   4
For a treasure shines on the head that haunts me,
    like old kings' vaults or the spoils of Spain,
gold hair falling about her shoulders,
    the red gold pouring like burning rain.   8

Her mouth is the sun through red wine shining;
    lips that are tender and fine with pride.
White is the neck where the ringlets cluster,
    like a white stone under the running tide;   12
like a burst of sun on broken water,
    when the mad wind scatters the spindrift wide,
or the drifting snow that the wind is blowing,
    whispering, cold on the bare hillside.   16

By night I travelled rough lonely places,
    and down by Garvalt I took my way,
till I reached at dawning the rocky summit
    above the town where my darling lay;   20
the stars were fading, the sky was paling,
    the cock told loud in her home of day;
I saw the smoke from her hearthstone rising;
    I wept and sighing I turned away.   24

From showery meadows the wind comes softly
    with a scent of blossoms and tender grass.
Heartsome the breezes from narrow valleys;
    myrtle and heather they breathe, and pass.   28
But the south wind singing, that comes to lull us
    from sleepy hillsides and seas of glass,
brings to me thoughts of care and sorrow
    out of the airt where dwells my lass.   32

*35 *Kintyre*

Leaving those men, whose hearts
   are hearths that have no fire,
my greetings, westward go
    to lovely long Kintyre.   4

Her uplands draw my thoughts,
   till over lands and seas
my dreamings go, like birds
    that seek the leafy trees.   8

Of names sweet to the mouth,
   of names like the sounding sea,
for my delight alone
    I'll write this litany.   12

Ròaig and Àirigh Fhuar,
   words from some fairy tale,
the Grianan and Davaar,
    Carradale, Sunadale.   16

These on my mouth, I walk
   among grey walls and chill;
these are a flame to warm,
    a sain against all ill.   20

*36 *Tiomnadh*

Ach cò a bheir gu beachdaidh dhuinn,
  gun teagamh bhith san sgeul,
nuair thig dalladh air na sùilean,   3
  dùnadh air a' bheul,
fios air an tìr aineoil ud,
  's air rathad rùin ar ceum?   6

Cò dh'innseas e mas cadal duinn
  's e maireannach gun là,
smàladh dhuinn gun ùrachadh   9
  is mùchadh gu bràth,
no an tadhail sinn tìr-èigin
  sìor èibhinn thar gach àit?   12

Mas Tìr nan Òg no Abhalon
  am fonn as lainnreach lìth;
mas Pàrrthas naomh na glaine e,   15
  gun anuair ann ach sìth,
's e cliarach, seirmeil, seunta –
  O fèathail e, gun sìon!   18

An Tìr nan Òg bios ealtan
  a' seinn air frasan ciùil,
glòir nan dùl nco-lochdach   21
  is slànadh lot 'na sunnd;
bios Tìr fo Thuinn, mar chualas e,
  gun ghluasad ànraidh dhùir.   24

[Is gann

36 [Testament]

Who then will give us, with certainty | and not a shadow of doubt in the tale, |
when blindness falls on the eyes | and the mouth is silenced, | information on that   3
unknown land | and on the mysterious road we are to travel?   6

Who will tell if sleep awaits us, | eternal with no dawn of day, | if we are to be
extinguished and never revived, | snuffed out for ever, | or if we shall haunt some   9
land | perpetually happy beyond all other places?   12

If the land of brightest hue | is the Land of the Young or Avalon, | or if it is blessed
Paradise of the pure, | with no tempestuousness but only calm, | full of poesy,   15
melody, enchantment – | how peaceful it must be, untouched by the elements!   18

In the Land of the Young flocks of birds | sing on showers of music, | the voice of
untarnished creation | with a balm in its cheer to heal all wounds; | the Land   21
Under Waves, it is said, | is undisturbed by any grim storm.   24

Is gann a mhosglas cuiseag ann
   no duilleag air a' ghèig;
is gann a lùbas luachair ann   27
   air bruaich nan caochan slèibh;
bidh drillsein cois an t-sàile ann
   de thràighean ris a' ghrèin.   30

Ciod e mur ruig an aois orra
   a-chaoidh san t-samhradh bhuan?
Oir chluinninn coill' an Lagain ann   33
   ri latha sèididh chruaidh.
Sgeir Leathann 's i ri beucaich,
   bhreug i mo chridhe uam.   36

Dh'iarrainn gaoth is sgairt aice
   a' cur sgapadh fo na neòil,
a' teachd à tuath bhàrr Chruachain   39
   's an fhuachd an teum a beòil;
marcan sìne a' màrsaladh
   air clàr a' chuain le pròis.   42

Cur froise mar bhrat falaich
   's e 'faicheachd thar nan stuadh;
an sìoban searbh, sgathach   45
   mar ghathan neimh' air gruaidh;
iomagain an stiùramaich,
   b'e sin m'ionndrainn uam.   48

Rarely will a blade of grass stir there | or leaf on a branch; | rarely will the rushes stoop | on the banks of its mountain streams; | along its sea the strands | will glitter in the sun. 27 30

What of it, if age should never touch them, | in that eternal summer? | For I would still hear the woodland of Lagan | on a day of hard winds. | The roar of Sgeir Leathann | has stolen my heart. 33 36

I would want a howling wind | putting the clouds to flight, | coming down from the north over the ridge of Ben Cruachan | with cold clutched in its jaws, | and the storm-steeds marching | proudly on the ocean's plain. 39 42

A downpour like a heavy curtain | advancing over the billows; | the sharp stinging sea-spray | like poison-darts on the cheek; | the anxiety of the steersman – | those would be my longing. 45 48

Uainlios mhìn na meala,
　　bheil fois aig Breannan innt'?
A dheòraidh lèith a' churaich,　　51
　　nach miann leat lunn ri 'shlinn,
's nach b'fheàrr leat faire fhairge
　　na sailm an cùirt do Rìgh?　　54

Thigeadh an eallach dhroma orm
　　is cromadh a' chinn lèith,
ma gheibh mi dhomh, mun druid sin orm,　　57
　　mo chuid de ghaoith 's de speur,
's mo laighe far am b'eòlach mi –
　　cha mhòr mo ghuidh', a Dhè.　　60

Air Rudha Lagan Ròaig
　　biodh tòrramh 's tional fhear,
is àras chlach ga chàrnadh　　63
　　fo sgàirneach dubh nam preas;
is fàgaibh ann air m'uilinn mi
　　is uinneag ris an ear.　　66

Chì mi na luing chaola
　　is caoirein diubh 'nan steud,
's mo chluas ri dùrd na gaoithe　　69
　　is ri glaodh mo dhaoine fhèin.
Laighidh mi san ionad
　　far an tric a bhiodh mo cheum.　　72

The calm honeyed verdant garden, | *has Brendan found peace there?* | *Silver-haired pilgrim of the coracle,* | *do you not yearn for the surge against its wicker,* | 51
and would you not prefer the watch of the deep | *to psalms in the court of your King?* 54

Let the back-burden come upon me | *and the stooping of a greying head,* | *if I can have, before those ensnare me,* | *my share of wind and sky,* | *and can be laid to rest* 57
in the territory of my people – | *my request, O God, is not excessive!* 60

On Lagan Ròaig Point | *let there be a funeral assembly and a gathering of men,* | *and let a stone dwelling be amassed* | *below the thicketed black scree,* | *and there* 63
leave me on my side | *with a window to the east.* 66

I will see the slender ships | *like steeds in blazing foam,* | *and my ear will catch the hum of the wind* | *and the shouts of my own folk.* | *I will lie in the place* | *where* 69
often my feet have trod. 72

*37 Brìodal Màthar

Mo luran thu,
mo dhuinein thu,
èh, m'ultachan is m'eallach clèibh;   3
's tu luchd sàibhir
nan long Spàinteach,
sìod' an-àird riu 's lìon fo ghrèis.   6

M'Osgar mòr thu,
m'usgar òir thu,
mo mhogal chnò a chromas geug;   9
lìonadh cupain,
riarach' guidhe,
crìoch mo shiubhail, freagairt m'fheum.   12

Leabaidh èirigh
do mo ghrèin thu,
iùl mo cheum thu thar gach reul;   15
cuilean suairc thu,
faillean uain' thu,
fearan cruaidh thig gu bhith treun.   18

37 Mother's Fondling Talk

My bonnie thing art thou, | my mannie art thou, | eh, my arm load and breast burden; | thou art the rich lading | of the Spanish ships, | silk aloft on them and 3 linen embroidered. 6

My great Oscar art thou, | my golden jewel, | my cluster of nuts that curves the bough; | my cup-filling, | my prayer-fulfilment, | end of my journeying, answer to 9 my need. 12

The bed from which my sun | rises art thou, | the guidance of my steps more than every star; | a pleasant puppy art thou, | a green shoot, | a hardy wee man who will 15 come to be strong. 18

POEMS 1938–1940

38–54: The Scottish Scene
[A Satirical Sequence]

38 *Gather, Gather, Gather*

I got his hat in lend from Chames,
    and asked Rob Cam to mind the coo,
and went to the Druim Neònach games
    to see our Highland Who Iss Who.   4

Never a scenery so fair
    was heard of yet on Scotland's shores;
my Cot, the Duke of Brill wass there
    in Hunting Cameron plus fours.   8

The leddies from the U.S.A.
    sat row on row like chugs on shelves;
their tartan bonnets, surely they
    would melt the fery stones themselves.   12

Pipe Major Tamson won the day,
    och, his wass the MacCrimmon's fist!
the cabar prize wass born away
    by Al the Olive Pugilist.   16

Our fathers' ways are with us yet,
    our ancient backbone is unbent,
the only Highlandmen I met
    I found in the Refreshments Tent.   20

*39 *Renaissance*

Mac Ruaraidh 'ic Hiram Mhòir
   for exiled centuries atones,
regains his long-lost native shore,
   and studies Gaelic Without Groans.   4

A kilted brave – a piper too –
   advanced my way, his head on high.
I asked him, "Ciamar tha thu 'n-diugh?"
   He swore at me. I wonder why.   8

Miss Annabella (Deirdre) Sharp
   of Rumbleriggs' artistic group,
assumes a bun and buys a harp,
   and wears a Hebridean droop.   12

Sir Percy can say "Slàinte mhòr",
   and sports his learning through the town;
Lord Bangem-buts of Gleann nan Deòir
   has bought a tartan dressing-gown.   16

Burn burn, ye bonfires; pipers play
   (our grandeur springs from scenes like these)
while Tennessee and Kent display
   their atavistic tendencies.   20

40 *International Repercussions*

Ye grouse, bid fame your last adieus,
   ye hinds (fourfooted) deign a tear,
you are no longer in the news;
   Wall Street is looking pretty queer.   4

The tartan maker's head is bowed,
   the Highland Ball, its glory dim,
stags in the corries groan aloud;
   Wall Street is looking pretty grim.   8

Good Highland folk who lately quailed,
   let joy enlustre all your looks,
no longer will ye be assailed
   through Gaelic conversation books.   12

But what of all our tartan dolls?
   And what of all these bonnets bright?
What is the use of Falloch Falls?
   In Wall Street all is not quite right.   16

Ye stalkers all, unlace your boots,
   and firewards stretch the stockinged toe;
rest well, ye ghillies. No one shoots,
   for Wall Street's down the drain, you know.   20

No more to hook the sportsmen's trout,
   no more to shoot their deer for them;
no more will kilts be seen about;
   for Wall Street's gone to – well – ahem!   24

41 The Soccer Scene

The English team was pretty fair,
   MacQuilken's dribbling stirred the crowd,
Ross had considerable flair,
   so had Mackenzie and MacLeod.   4

But Scotia triumphed through the work
   of Con O'Flaherty at half;
O'Brien, Connel, and McGurke
   made our attack, and so did Taaffe.   8

This migratory age has more
   than many mysteries to show.
The greatest? To what southern shore
   do Anglo-Saxon players go?   12

42 The Proper Procedure

A fellow can, as someone said,
   (why not indeed?) dream noble dreams;
ideas will assail one's head;
   one entertains all sorts of schemes.   4

Life offers oh! so many larks:
   fill up the Tay and trick the tide,
make candles from Kilbrennan sharks,
   remove the Mound to Morningside.   8

[Should you

Should you have some such scheme in hand,
 (perhaps you want to dam the Clyde?)
just tell it to your Member, and
 the English Members will decide.   12

43 *The Scottish Chelsea*
or "Ged as fad a-mach Barraigh ruigear e"

("Though Barra is far out it can be reached", a Gaelic proverb)

It spoils the sleep of poor and rich,
 this crowding of our tenements,
but there are farflung outposts which
 are just as bad to all intents.   4

An isle there is, where to and fro
 phoneticists do roam unchecked,
and Danish savants row on row,
 all jotting down the dialect.   8

This island has been scrutinised,
 examined, viewed, turned inside out,
oh, criticised and analysed,
 described, depicted, talked about.   12

The crowding passes all belief;
 dense swarms of poets block the view,
and novelists, and a Highland Chief!
 What will the wretched natives do?   16

44 Life's Little Compensations

The Scottish scene looks rather glum,
 but there are compensations too.
Our Secretary's sure to come
 and rhapsodise about the view.   4

Farming and grazing are – you know,
 "where are the snows of yesteryear?"
Good chap, good chap, to ease the blow
 he'll shed a ministerial tear.   8

Our men encased in khaki slacks
    fly South like flocks of homing rooks.
Northward good Colville will make tracks,
    and give us sympathetic looks.   12

The Highlands are devoured by deer,
    the Herring Industry is dead.
Faint not, my soul. He will appear
    and pat the bairnies on the head.   16

45 Our Culture Still Counts

No, we are not forgotten quite,
    though we have known neglect and wrongs;
Paul Robeson, to my delight,
    has started singing Gaelic songs.   4

The interest spreads in every way;
    another case occurs to me;
an English judge the other day
    said "Harry Lauder, who is he?"   8

Yet one more case I will subjoin,
    ungrudging fellow that I am!
Madame Tabouis intends to join
    the Piping Girls of Dagenham.   12

They can't forget us. Why? Oh well,
    our haggis, Piping Girls, Braemar,
and tartan spats, and Harry L.,
    will never let them get so far.   16

46 Tìr nan Òg

The Land of the Young

"This *Tìr nan Òg*! – well, dash and drat,
    it's placed so flaming far away."
My friend, it's not so bad as that;
    you can get there within a day.   4

David MacBrayne will take you out,
    for a con-sider-ati-on,
where no one's ever put about
    though Time itself should all be gone.   8
                                    [Should Kent

Should Kent be blown up to the skies,
    they'd say "Well well, indeed", and draw
their bonnets down across their eyes,
    and sleep within the lion's maw.   12

There's no one minds or cares a dime,
    and no one does, and no one knows,
and if you ask them "What's the time?"
    they say "Och, Monday, I suppose."   16

To gaze upon a scene so fair
    not everyone is fully fit.
A Yankee business man went there,
    and died of nightmares after it.   20

47   *How to Deal with "Revelations"*

The fat's in the fire, and we're all in the soup,
the reporters are out on the scent of a scoop,
the bag that we made has emitted the cat,   3
why, even the public is smelling a rat!
    So gather, gather, gather Griogaraich.
    Gather? Rather – gather Griogaraich.   6

Set up a committee to ponder awhile,
and a new sub-committee to docket and file,
and a sub-sub-committee to get in the way,   9
and your deed is a deed that is nameless for aye.
    Oh, gather, gather, gather Griogaraich.
    Gather? Rather – gather Griogaraich.   12

48   *Nature Notes*

Should I be asked to choose the beast
which, speaking roughly, differs least
from old Sir Blank, I should of course   3
select his closest friend the horse;
its teeth are large, its voice is gruff,
it is so tactless and so tough.   6

A soul-mate must be found at once
for one of these Commissions
that roost. I'd pair it at a stab   9
with Partan or the Common Crab;

48

its little eyes that hardly see,
its gait with its obliquity.   12

In this free land I'd rather not
talk frankly of the Empire Scot,
or of his pals; but in my eyes   15
they're very like a swarm of flies:
they're irksome, but their aims are safe;
a little sugar's all they crave.   18

To higher things. Where would you park
the Secret'ry in Noah's ark?
He'd have to swim, so much does he   21
resemble that great mystery
the herring – whence he comes, where goes,
and why and wherefore no one knows.   24

*49   Buffalo Bill in Gaiters

Our ministers are apt to stick
in principles, and haven't tact;
the English prelate is more slick,
he is a two-gun man in fact.   4

Upon his left side, lo, there swings
a holster stuffed with Luke and John;
Psalms, Judges and the Book of Kings
his good right side he bears upon.   8

While quiet reigns and Europe snores
he keeps to merely Christian lines,
but should a crisis sprout, he roars
of "smiting" and the Philistines.   12

He is adaptable, he boasts;
and it intrigues a man to see
him excavate the Lord of Hosts
in moments of emergency.   16

The Foreign Office like it; so
if he can please them why can't we?
Our ministers are learning, though:
wait till the crisis and you'll see.   20

50 'S Leam Fhèin an Gleann
The Glen is Mine

The Glen Is Mine (and at a cost
   of thousands it is pretty sweet).
I've put a notice on a post
   to say so, and the thing's complete.   4

I've bought some crofters too, and though
   it is their country, yet it's clear –
The Empire Needs Them. They must go.
   (Besides they might disturb the deer.)   8

There is a drove-road running through,
   I'm told an ancient right of way.
Barbed wire, a notice-board or two,
   and it is Holy Ground for aye.   12

How jollah, what! For miles and miles
   in peace I stroll as I incline,
and no one sees, as wreathed in smiles
   I skip, and shout "The Glen is mine."   16

51 An Informative Volume Bound Tastefully in Blue

"From Solway Firth to John o' Groats
look at our herring and our oats."
"Neglected? Nothing of the sort.
You cad, you've had a new report."   4

Westminster is in fact a dear,
and gives us almost every year,
a volume bound in blue. (Quite right;
the colour is most apposite.)   8

It tells us just how doomed are we,
and drips "alarm" and "sympathy".
We should be honoured. What a fuss!
Pages and pages all for us!   12

Go ask the anecdotard hoar:
for half a century and more
Blue Books have fall'n like gentle rain;
and yet some people will complain.   16

52 *Am Fiann air an Uilinn*
The Fiann on Their Elbows

According to a yarn, which you need not believe, a man once found his way into a cave, the existence of which he had never suspected before. Leaning up against the end of the inner wall were a number of great boulders, and on the floor before him lay a horn. He picked it up and blew it, out of curiosity, and the rocks seemed to him to take on the appearance of men. However, he blew a second blast, and sure enough the huge men raised themselves up on their elbows and fixed their saucer-like eyes on him. "Sèid a-rithist, a dhuine bhig" ("Blow again, little man") rumbled one of them. The little man dropped the horn and made for the mouth of the cave as fast as he could, and a bitter shout followed him: "Is miosa dh'fhàg thu na mar fhuair" ("Worse you left us than you found us"). These great men were the Fiann, and it is said that the third blast will be blown yet and they will rise again.

The bus arrives. They tumble out
   and hurry screeching to the cave;
they babble, jostle, grope about,
   and feel adventurous and brave.   4

Out by their hidden dwelling's gate
   the tourists fumble, whisper, stare,
and far within the Fiann wait
   leaning on their elbows there.   8

What if some Cockney brave at last
   should find the horn where still it lies,
and blow upon it that third blast,
   and Fionn and all the Fiann rise?   12

"Most undesirable. Would they
   be Empah Spirited, and bar
the ceds who jeer at Empah Day?
   No, let them stay the stones they are."   16

True, true. Their blood could never be
   Red, White and Blue. But don't forget
the horn's still there. (It seems to me
   someone will blow the damned thing yet.)   20

53 *Is Coma Leam Cogadh no Sìth*
War or Peace, I Care Not

The war will come in Spring, they say;
and if it comes I bet, my friend,
they'll find some "Belgium" to defend.
(Invest In Steel, while yet you may.)   4

The Fiery Cross from London flies,
and caterans (encased in spats)
all mount their tanks, and cock their gats,
and gallop off with shining eyes.   8

And thus we fight for gutters fit
for Scottish heroes, where they may
(complete with begging licence) play
trombones – they "having done their bit".   12

Weeping through Scotland, shore to shore,
and pipers puffing, red and wudd,
and Donald choking in his blood –
the "little Belgiums" matter more.   16

54 *Our National Building*

That whatnot on the Calton Hill
(no, not the jail) is said to fill
a long-felt want. You know the way
our daring journals talk today.   4

No more will Scotland, it transpires,
be governed through some dozen wires,
as in the bad days tha' are goane,
but through a single telephone.   8

The Cabinet will be ringing through,
and sending wires and letters too,
so, when you come to think of it,
the G.P.O. will benefit.   12

God help me! What munificence!
How free they are with Scotland's pence!
What will they give us next? The moon?
The salts! I feel inclined to swoon.   16

*

*55 [Banaltram nam Bàrd]

(trì rainn is amhran)

Banaltram nam bàrd mo rùn-sa,
   's a cuid stiùiridh domhain gu leòir.
Dh'ionnsaich mi le meud mo ghràidh dhi
   c'as a thàinig *Och och-òin*.   4

Their mi gur feàrr na gach naomh i
   gu saoghaltachd a chur fo chois.
On dh'iarr mi gràdh 's a dhiùlt i gràdh dhomh,
   thigeadh am bàs – is beag mo thoirt.   8

Chrath i 'ceann, is fhuair mi eòlas
   air màthair-uisg' a' bhròin 's nan deur.
Thug i cùl rium, 's dh'fhàg i glic mi,
   's cha b'e 'n gliocas eutrom e.   12

Ceangal

A bhean lurach neo-chaomh, gad chaoineadh dh'ionnsaicheadh mì.
'S tu thug dhomh bhith naomh 's an gaol air uirigh sa chill.
Sheall thu dhomh aobhar gach glaoidh a bhuidhneadh o chrì,
is nach cuir thu mi saoghalta, saobh, beò, sunndach a-rìst?   16

55 *The Nurturer of Poets*
(three verses and envoi)

The nurturer of poets is my love, | and her guidance is profound. | I have learned through the greatness of my love, | whence came *Och ochone*.   4

I maintain she is better than any saint | for teaching contempt for the love of this world. | Since I asked her for love and she refused it, | let death come – I care little.   8

She shook her head, and I attained knowledge | of the fountainhead of sorrow and tears. | She turned her back on me and left me wise – | and it was no light, easy wisdom.   12

Envoi

Lovely, unkind woman, I have had my schooling in weeping for you. | It is you who have taught me saintliness and longing for a bed in the churchyard. | You have revealed to me the cause of every cry that was ever wrung from a heart; | will you not make me worldly, foolish, alive and cheerful again?   16

*56 An Gaol a Bh'ann

Leigear an gaol an dìochuimhne,
   is dìobrar leis na leannain e.
Nìthear cainnt is coinneamh leo
   cleas choigrich fuar' is aineolaich.   4

Is e 'n dìochuimhne as suaineadh dhaibh,
   is e 'n suarachas as fasgadh dhaibh,
's a' ghrìosach fhuar gun chridhealas
   sa chridh' a-staigh ga saltairt leo.   8

57 Love Is Forgotten

Love is forgotten, lovers stray,
   and one another they deny;
they meet and talk upon their way
   like strangers or like passers-by.   4

They meet and play the casual part,
   with gaiety they bolt their door,
while still they stifle in their heart
   embers of fire that warm no more.   8

58 [Rann Comhairle]

Is olc do dhuine bhith 'na thost,
   b'fheàrr an trod na bhith ad thàmh,
oir gheobh càch an cuid den chlos
   nuair thuiteas iad 'nan tost gu bràth.   4

---

56 Love That Was

Love is forgotten | and is banished by the lovers. | They meet and talk | like cold strangers or people unacquainted.   4

Forgetfulness is the mantle that haps them, | indifference is their shelter, | while they stamp out the feeble, cheerless ember in their inward hearts.   8

58 [Cautionary Verse]

One should not remain so silent, | better a quarrel than your calm, | for folk will get their fill of quiet | when eternal silence falls on them.   4

*59 *An Dèidh Tràghaidh Thig Lìonadh*
After Ebb Comes Flood

I thought this tide would rise and lip the grass,
    so that the waves would break among the trees,
spring flood of spirit soften our clenched mass   3
    of dry root tendrils; burst in blooms a frieze.
Scotland's gapped forest, great boles tumbled, meet
the running tide that roared about its feet.   6

Who will take pains to say what none will see?
    This tide is set to ebbing, leaving dry
the staring boulders. Greed sets murder free.   9
    (When rogues fall out, then good men go to die).
We saw too dimly. Flood for evermore
slips down our beach to climb some other shore.   12

The spirit ebbs, and all our visions pass.
    Now lifts another tide and thickly runs,
brochan of blood. When it draws down across   15
    bare stones, then, barren Scotland, where are your sons?
Will none be here to do as we were fain,
and think that after ebb comes flood again?   18

*60 *A Ballad in Answer to Servius Sulpicius Rufus*

Rufus leans owre the gunnel o his ship,
    skelpin afore the snappin wund frae Thrace,
the shores he conned at schule, astern they slip,
    strawn wi the shards o toons, a stony place;   4
the thochts he droned at schule fa' intae place –
    "We girn at deein? *Nos homunculi*,
wi Athens doon!" Yet, Servius, by yere grace,
    she lived her day, syne deed, an' sae maun I.   8

Noo Nineveh is nocht, Argos a name;
    the quays o Carthage, nae man moors thereat,
the lang groond-swell has drawn thaim til its wame;
    sand is the hauld whar the queen Dido grat;   12

[Troy toon

Troy toon an' Tyre hard fates hae trampit flat,
    by tyrant time owrecassen, lo, they lie –
yet, *air a shon sin uile*, for aa that,
    they lived their day, syne deed, an' sae maun I.   16

Teamhair 'na féar – Tara is grass, they say;
    Durlus o Guaire, o the open door,
nane but the wund gangs guestin there the day;
    Sycharth o Owen the saft rain ootwore.   20
Emain an' Tailtiu, heard ye these afore?
    MacEwen's Kerry keep, that wance was high,
sin time is thrawn ye may speir lang therefor.
    They lived their day, syne deed, an' sae maun I.   24

Whar are thy choirs noo, Jedburgh, whar, Scone?
    Iona, whar thy monks? Dunadd, thy kains?
The Lia Fàil lies penned in London toon;
    Canmore, auld hoolets bicker owre his banes.   28
Duntuilm an' Carnaborg o the MacLeans,
    an' Mingarry, ill-kent, aft-sung they lie;
the Stewarts mak a rant for dandlin weans –
    they lived their day, syne deed, an' sae maun I.   32

Envoi

Dia (Loard Goad), Prince o the Coal-Black Beard,
    tho Aiberdeen an' Glesca toon should lie
twa smowlderin cowps, my sang wad be (I'm feard):
    they lived their day, syne deed, an' sae maun I.   36

61   *1918–1939*

They deed, thae men ablow the mools,
    for fules that played at history.
Aye, boys. Oor turn tae thrapple daith
    for fules grown auld wha winna dee.   4

*62 *Alba*

Scotland

The blaffering wind blows from the South-west;
    it strikes, and our boat louts low on her side;
ridge runs upon ridge boarding her, storm-pressed,
    but lightly she lifts and scatters the seas wide.   4

Here we must bide, work her to win home,
    though the decks welter and swim, and the grinding gale
storms white on the crests, trailing their cold foam,
    for nothing is here but the sea when her seams fail.   8

Death girns from the grey glens that her stem rives,
    and rows her in sharp seareek as she goes.
Oh, blinding the spray, bitter the rain drives,
    and dim in the drift only the scudd of the land shows.   12

*63 *An Gaol Cha d'Fhiosraich Mi*

(trì rainn is amhran)

An gaol cha d'fhiosraich mi uair –
    dè, cha chualas e bhith ann –
ach nise chuartaich e mì
    eadar chas, mo dhìth, is cheann.   4

Bean ghuanach a thàlaidh mì;
    a sheallas bìth 's a ceann crom.
Tha 'cridhe corrach fada uam
    mar ghaoth chruaidh a' falbh nan tonn.   8

[Chan eil

63 *Love I Never Knew*
(three verses and envoi)

Love I never knew of, | I had not heard that there was such a thing, | but
now it has encircled me | between foot and head, my loss.   4

[It is a fickle woman that has] lured me, | that looks quietly, her head bent. | Her
wavering heart [is far] from me | like a hard wind travelling the waves.   8

Chan eil truas aice rium,
   cha do chuir i suim nam chor,
ise 'càradh a cùil bhàin,
   mise 'dol bàs air a son.   12

Ceangal

A nighean an sgàthain, is clàr do bhathais mar chèir,
a sheallas nam ghnùis is rùn do chridh' agad fhèin,
ge tais orm do shùil, cha dlùth do smuaintean 'na dèidh –
cùm agad an t-amharc is aisig mo chridhe làn chreuchd.   16

*64 Is Duilich an t-Slighe

'S tiamhaidh dùsgadh a' mhochthrath,
's càch 'nan crùban gu socrach;
làn an dùirn seo a mhosgail ron ghrèin.   3

Dhaoine cridhe, aig ar gainne
chan eil ann duinn sa ghleac seo
ach gach fear a bhith fearail dha fhèin.   6

Chan eil buidheann nar deaghaidh
bhiodh gar stuigeadh air adhart
le moladh 's le gleadhar 's le eubh.   9

She has no pity for me, | she has given no heed to my plight, | she arranging her fair hair, | and I dying for the sake of her!   12
Envoi
Lass with the mirror, your forehead white as wax, | that gazes in my face keeping the counsel of your heart to yourself; | though softly your eye rests on me, your thoughts do not follow closely after your glance – | keep to yourself the gaze and give me my [sorely wounded] heart again.   16

64 [Difficult Is the Road]

Sad the daybreak awakening, | as others curl up quietly; | only a handful have stirred before dawn.   3
We are so few, my friends, | our one recourse in this struggle | is for each to be manful alone.   6
There is no team behind us | to urge and to prod us | with encouragement and cheering and praise.   9

Chan eil fodhainn de bhunait
ach dà chois aig gach duine,
b'fheàrr am forcadh is fulang gach beum.   12

Beum teanga ar dùthcha,
beum slat an fhir sgiùrsaidh,
bàs fuar anns na cùiltean gun sgeul.   15

Ghabh sinn toiseach an àtha,
nì na sheachain e gàir' oirnn,
seal san t-sruth 's bidh a ghàirich nar dèidh.   18

Och on dhiùlt mi an gàbhadh,
's a rinn mi stad aig beul àtha,
tha mo chridhe ga chnàmh gu ro-gheur.   21

Ach a chuideachd na seasmhachd,
moladh beò cha do mheath sibh,
ged a choisinn mi masladh dhomh fhèin.   24

Nuair a ghlaodhas mi 'n ath-uair
le mòralachd fhacal,
bidh mo ghnìomhan, mo ghealladh, dan rèir.   27

Mo chompanaich ghaolach,
thuit iad bhuam air gach taobh dhiom,
is dh'fhàgadh ris mi sa chaonnaig leam fhèin.   30

---

*We have below us for prop | only each man's two legs – | plant them firmly and
suffer each blow.*   12

*The tongue-lash of our country, | the whiplash of the flogger, | cold death in the
backstreets unnoticed.*   15

*We entered the ford, | those who dodged it will mock us, | a while in the torrent
and behind us its roar.*   18

*Oh since I stepped back from danger | and stopped at the mouth of the ford, | a
canker gnaws at my heart too sorely.*   21

*But you, steadfast comrades, | no praise ever softened you, | though I earned
disgrace for myself.*   24

*The next time I trumpet | with grand rhetoric, | I swear my actions will match my
words.*   27

*My beloved companions | fell away all around me, | and left me exposed and alone
in the fray.*   30

*65 *Ceithir Gaothan na h-Albann*

M'oiteag cheòlmhor chaoin 'teachd deiseil nam bheitheach Samhraidh i,
mo stoirm chuain le dìle 'cur still 's gach alltan domh,
a' ghaoth tuath le cathadh sneachda nì dreachmhor beanntan domh,
a' ghaoth tha 'g iomain m'fhalaisg Earraich ri leathad ghleanntaichean.

Duilleach an t-Samhraidh, tuil an Dàmhair, na cuithean 's an àrdghaoth
Earraich i; 5
dùrd na coille, bùirich eas, ùire 'n t-sneachda 's an fhalaisg i;
tlàths is binneas, àrdan, misneach, fàs is sileadh nam frasan i;
anail mo chuirp, àrach mo thuigse, mo làmhan, m'uilt is m'anam i.
Fad na bliadhna, rè gach ràithe, gach là 's gach ciaradh feasgair dhomh,
is i Alba nan Gall 's nan Gàidheal is gàire, is blàths, is beatha dhomh. 10

66 *The Waukrife Corp*

Frae the cannle licht whar he ligged his lane
in the nocht the deid man cem tie the door,
an' fain was he tie win there ben,
but bolt an' bar stood stench afore. 4

"O the morn tie ma lair they wull cairry me,
an' hap me close in the yird, ma dear,
my langsome spale in the mools tie dree;
come, leave me farweel or I gang frae here." 8

My melodious, gentle breeze blowing from southward in my Summer birchwood
is she; | my ocean storm, with downpour sending in headlong spate each burn for
me; | the north wind with driving snow that makes beautiful the hills for me; | the
wind that drives my Springtime muirburn up the slopes of glens is she.

The leaves of Summer, the spate of Autumn, the snowdrifts and the high Spring
wind is she; | the sough of the woodland, the roaring of waterfalls, the freshness 5
of the snow and the heather ablaze is she; | mild pleasantness and melody, angry
pride and courage, growth and the pouring of the showers is she; | breath of my
body, nurture of my understanding, my hands, my joints and my soul is she. | All
year long, each season through, each day and each fall of dusk for me, | it is
Scotland, Highland and Lowland, that is laughter and warmth and life for me. 10

"When the cock has crawed an' the day comes up,
    then I'll rise ma last farweel tie gie,
for the nicht is derk an' the shaddas strange;
    but, och, ma dear, is it weel wi' ye?"   12

The deid man grat. "The lanesome deid,
    that their kin should speir 'Is it weel wi' ye?'
when they coor at thaim in the nicht wi' dreid,
    an' steek the door that they come tie."   16

*67   *Na Baidealan*

Neòil iongantach gan càrnadh suas
    le ruaim ghàbhaidh 's tòcadh borb;
turaidean treuna, tùir làn pròis,
    brataichean bagraidh, ceò is colg.   4

Snàgaidh rompa duibhre 's oillt,
    's na dealain bhoillsgeach ast' a-nuas;
slaodar leò an t-uisge glas
    'na chùirtein dallaidh trast' an cuan.   8

Siud tuinn is tìr air call an dath,
    gan dubhadh às le steall nan speur,
is Arainn bheàrnach uainn fo chleòc –
    glòir uamharr e de ghlòiribh Dhè.   12

67   *The Battlements*

Wondrous clouds are heaped aloft, | with a dark flush and a fierce swelling; | strong turrets, towers full of pride, | threatening banners, mist and rage.   4

Fearful darkness creeps before them, | and down out of them dart the lightning flashes; | they trail after them the grey rain | like a blinding curtain across the sea.   8

Yonder are waves and land, their colour lost, | blotted out by the torrent from the skies, | and gapped Arran gone from us under a cloak – | it is a terrible glory of the glories of God.   12

*68 Grunnd na Mara

"Tha iad ann an grunnd na mara,
is cha b'e siud an rogha cala" –
rug siud orm o dh'fhalbh mo mhacan,
an cuilean a bhithinn ga thatadh,
a dhèanadh gàire na mo ghlacaibh.   5
Thàinig an seann sgeul air a chasan.
Tha an speur a' ciaradh mu fheasgar,
goir aig na h-eòin air na sgeirean,
geumnaich a' chruidh a' teachd dhachaigh,
èigheach nan giullan anns a' bhaile,   10
's mi 'm thurraman leam fhèin mun chagailt,
a' smuaineachadh air na bh'agam.
Chì mi do chòta air an tarran,
is, och! an taigh gun fhuaim, gun fhacal,
an stairsneach nach bi fuaim chas oirr',   15
an seòmar fàs 's an leabaidh fhalamh.
Mas e an osna thèid fada,
cluinnear m'osnaich far an laigh thu
nad chadal luasganach san fheamainn,
's na fuathan a' sìor dhol seachad,   20
cruthanna aognaidh na mara!

Am marbh a' bruidhinn:

"Èist, a bhean, is na bi rium,
   is truimide mo dhìol do bhròn;

---

68   *[The Bottom of the Sea]*

"They are down at the bottom of the sea – | *that was not their chosen haven" –* | *that has overtaken me since my lad departed,* | *the young pup I used to fondle* | *and who would make merry in my arms.* | *The old tale has come to pass.* | *The*   5 *evening sky is growing dark,* | *as the birds cry out on the skerries,* | *the cattle bellow their way home,* | *and the boys' shouts echo in the village,* | *while I rock by*   10 *the fire, alone,* | *my thoughts on that which once was mine.* | *I see your coat hanging on its nail,* | *and oh! not a sound, not a voice in the house,* | *the threshold on which no footstep will sound,* | *the vacant room and the empty bed.* | *If it's the*   15 *sigh that goes far,* | *my sighing will be heard where you lie,* | *tossed in your sleep among the tangle,* | *the water demons going ever past you,* | *terrible spectres of the*   20 *sea!*

The dead man speaking:
"Hold your wheesht, woman, do not disturb me, | *my burden is made heavier by*

sgàin is leagh an long for buinn –
    thriall an cuimhn' an cois an deò.   25
Lunnainn a mharbh mi,
    a mhill an t-sùil nach fhaca i.
Theagamh gum b'aithne dhomh thu,
    sgùr an sàl mo chuimhne nis.
Tha mi air sabhd sa chuan mhòr;   30
    bu Dòmhnall mise an-dè.
Laigh do ghul orm 'na lòd,
    ge b'e cò thu, a bhean, èist."

Mo losgadh, mhuinntir nan Eilean,
is daor a phàigh sibh mòrachd Bhreatainn!   35

69 *Soothwards owre the Sea*

The Englishmen hae taen tie dunts, an' sterted on a splore,
I hope they may get dunts an' clours, for every ane a score;
they spoilt oor land an' thirlet oor men, an' cleaned us fore an' aft
an' garred auld Scotlan' drift an' drive, a herriet hirplin' craft.   4

Tie Flanders for tie fecht for thaim they fain wad hae me gang,
wi' pokes ahint an' guns afore, an' baynets thin an' lang,
wi' claes the colour o' the sharn, a basin on ma bree,
but I'll awa' an' tak a rant tie Soothward owre the sea.   8

They thocht tie herd us lik' a wheen o shochlin' hairy yowes,
I think they'll find us thrawn eneuch, an' ragged fowk tie rowse;
their cratur King an' me, ma boys, we little do agree,
I'll no come rinnin' lik' a tyke though he should whustle me.   12

[Then farweel

your grief; | the ship burst and dissolved beneath us – | memory fled with the
breath of life. | London it is that murdered me, | that destroyed the eye it had 25
never seen. | It may be that once I knew you, | but the salt-sea has scoured my
memory now. | I go adrift in the ocean deep; | Donald I was, in a former day. | 30
Your weeping has weighed on me like a load, | whoever you are, woman, hold
your wheesht."

It sears me, people of the Islands, | how dearly you have paid for the greatness of
Britain! 35

Then farweel Scotlan' for a wee, farweel the lang Kintyre,
ye'll see us yet, we'll raise a lowe an' set yere hills on fire;
we'll bide a bit, an' watch a bit, an' counsel patiently,
then ready we'll come rinnin' wi' a Sooth wund owre the sea.   16

When Scotlan's Lion loups again, an' breenges up fu' reuch,
then we will baste the gangerils, an' gie thaim clours aneuch,
an' a' the herm they did tie us, we'll richt it speedily,
when North awa' for Scotlan' we come skelpin' owre the sea.   20

*70 *The Old Fisherman*

Greet the bights that gave me shelter,
they will hide me no more with the horns of their forelands.
I peer in a haze, my back is stooping;
    my dancing days for fishing are over.   4

The shoot that was straight in the wood withers,
the bracken shrinks red in the rain and shrivels,
the eyes that would gaze in the sun waver;
    my dancing days for fishing are over.   8

The old boat must seek the shingle,
her wasting side hollow the gravel,
the hand that shakes must leave the tiller;
    my dancing days for fishing are over.   12

The sea was good night and morning,
the winds were friends, the calm was kindly –
the snow seeks the burn, the brown fronds scatter;
    my dancing days for fishing are over.   16

*71 The Kerry Shore

Blow, good wind from westward, blow against the dawn,
blow across this livid loch with shadows strawn.
Sweetly blew the breeze from westward, o'er she lay,
coming down the Kerry Shore at break of day.   4

Up from hills of dreaming Cowal came the sun,
clear he stood and struck with fire the waters dun,
waves green-sided, bright, white-crested glittered gay,
coming down the Kerry Shore at break of day.   8

Branches rocking, waves of shadow, all the trees
becked and swung in Glennan to the singing breeze,
Caisteal Aoil, the Bròg, the Buck to leeward lay,
coming down the Kerry Shore at break of day.   12

Head on Tarbert, through the seas she raised a cry,
jewels of foam around her shoulders tossed on high,
green waves rose about her bows and broke away,
coming down the Kerry Shore at break of day.   16

*72 Fuar Fuar
Cold Cold

Heich o,
braes that the green things brockit are clootit wi snaw,
mavis an merle wi the spent sun hae socht awa.
Sooth aye, for the birk is nae bield wi the drift ablow.   4

Cauld, alas,
the Nor' wind hunts the kairrie frae cairn tae cairn,
the scowry cratur drants owre soopit flats o airn,
whar the green rash dandlet its hacklet heid, an' the laverock was. 8

Sair, sair –
whar the gowd nuts bendit the boos the straucht rods stan!
What ails the grizzlet airts that they tak sic a pick tae this lan?
Laggan was leafy; the snaw blins the sma birds there.   12

73 *Am Maraiche Gàidhealach sa Chogadh*

Is iomadh oidhch' air bheag socair,
   eadar Lochlann is Sealtainn,
a thug mi 'marcachd nan sùghan,
   a' ruith nan spùinneadair falaich;   4
cha b'e fuaim nan tonn copach,
   's i ri postadh 's gan sadadh,
a bha nam chluasan san àm sin,
   ach dùrd an alltain sa Ghleannan.   8

Eadar Narvik 's am Bùta,
   a' falbh nan sùmainn 'nan sreathaibh,
is sinn a' cliathadh an liathchnaip,
   ag iarraidh na creiche;   12
gaoth tuath ann, sneachd dùmhail,
   muir a' brùchdadh a-steach oirr' –
chìthinn na sùghan geal deàrrsach
   mun Gharbhaird a' spreadadh.   16

Ged a leanainn an streup seo
   gu cùl na grèine thar mara,
le gach stuadh a' sgoltadh
   a th'eadar Lochlann 's an Aifric,   20
bhiodh bàghannan m'eòlais,
   is mi 'seòladh air m'aineol,
a' cur aighear fo m'inntinn,
   's gam chumail dìreach ri anuair.   24

73 [*The Gaelic Sailor at War*]

Many a restless night | between Norway and Shetland | I've spent riding the billows, | tracking the hidden marauders; | it wasn't the noise of the frothing waves, | as trampling she dashed them, | that filled my ears at that time, | but the hum of the wee burn in Glennan. 4 8

Between Narvik and the Butt of Lewis, | travelling the ranked breakers, | as we harrowed the grey hill | in search of the foray; | a north wind, the snow thick | and the sea rushing aboard her – | I would see the glittering white billows | crashing about Garvel. 12 16

Though I should continue this warring | to seas behind the sun, | cleaving every wave | between Norway and Africa, | my own familiar bays | as I sailed unknown waters | would lift my spirits to gladness | and keep me upright in the storm. 20 24

74 [Brang air na Sasannaich]

Cuiridh sinn brang air na Sasannaich,
sparraidh sinn glas air am beulaibh,
cuiridh sinn brang air na Sasannaich,
brang air na Sasannaich, glas air am beulaibh. 4

'Illean, on chaill sinn deagh chleachdainn ar n-athair,
    chaidh a h-uile rud tarsainn nar dùthaich bhig fhèin oirnn;
thigeadh na spadairean, chuireadh iad dhachaigh iad,
    thurraich air tharraich a' gabhail ratreuta. 8

Dh'fhàg iad ar dùthaich 'na caile sna cùiltean,
    tromcheannach tùrsach 's a h-àlach ga trèigsinn,
mheall iad le cùinneadh i, rinn iad a spùilleadh,
    ghàir iad is thionndaidh iad uaipe gu h-eutrom. 12

Ged bhiodh iad ri feadail cha ruith sinn mar mheasain,
    ealamh gu claisteachd nuair chuireadh iad feum air;
is coma leinn spaglainn nam fear a chuir falamh i,
    seasaidh sinn daingeann ged chrathadh na speuran. 16

74 [A Muzzle on the English]

A muzzle we'll put on the English, | a gag we'll force on their mouths, | a
muzzle we'll put on the English, | muzzle on the English, gag on their mouths. 4

Lads, since we lost the good ways of our fathers, | all has slipped from us in our
own little land; | the braggarts would come, they would send them packing home, |
falling over each other in panicked retreat. 8

They left our land like a girl in the backstreets, | lethargic, grief-stricken, as her
children abandoned her. | They seduced her with wealth, they stripped her of
all, | they laughed and light-heartedly turned away from her. 12

Whistle as they may, we won't come running like lapdogs, | alert of hearing when
it suits their need; | we care not for the bluster of the men who despoiled her, |
firm we will stand though the skies should cave in. 16

*75 *Alba Ghaoil Ò*

Ged tha thu nis bochd ìseal,
    Alba ghaoil ò,
bidh sùil is seirc gach tìr' ort,
    a mhùirneach chaomh ò.   4
Ged tha t'aodach dìblidh,
càirear gùn den t-sìod' ort.
Thèid thu a-mach fo uidheam rìoghail,
    a Alba ghaoil ò.   8

Chaidh t'ainm 's do chliù a dhìtheadh,
    Alba ghaoil ò;
is suarach t'àit is t'ìre,
    a mhùirneach chaomh ò;   12
ach togar leinn a-nìos thu,
òlar fhathast fìon ort,
is gheibh luchd t'fhuath' an dìol dinn,
    a Alba ghaoil ò.   16

Is fheàirrde tàir a dìoladh,
    Alba ghaoil ò;
b'e 'n troich a ghabhadh dìmeas,
    a mhùirneach chaomh ò.   20
Cha b'àbhaist dhuit bhith cìosnaicht',
is mithich dhuit bhith 'dìreadh,
mosgail do sheann innsginn,
    a Alba ghaoil ò.   24

75 *Dear Scotland O*

Though you are now poor and lowly, | dear Scotland o, | the love and gaze of every land will be on you, | dear and kindly o; | though your clothing is mean, | a   4 gown of silk will be set about you, | you will go forth garbed royally, | dear Scotland o.   8

Your name and your renown are blotted out, | dear Scotland o, | wretched is your place and your rank, | dear and kindly o; | but you will be raised up by us, | wine   12 will be drunk to you yet, | and those who hate you will get their fill of us, | dear Scotland o.   16

Despising is the better for being repaid, | dear Scotland o, | he'd be a dwarf that would accept contempt, | dear and kindly o; | it was not your custom to be   20 subdued, | and it is time for you to be ascending. | Rouse your old spirit, | dear Scotland o.   24

76 [*Alba Àrsaidh*]
[fragment]

Alba àrsaidh ghleannach ghorm,
  choillteach, tholmach, mhachaireach,
Alba iongantach, mo stòr,
   's tu thug beò 's a dh'altraim mi;   4
b'òg a sheas mi air do shon,
   's mo chridhe goirt mar thachair dhuit,
bhon thagh mi thu tha 'm fraoch fom cheann,
   's a ghaoil, nach seall thu fasgadh dhomh?   8

77 [*Sgairt Mo Dhaoine*]
[incomplete draft]

Sgairt mo dhaoine 's am mòrachd,
am fialachd 's an tròcair,
thug na bliadhnachan leò siud 's b'e 'm beud.   3

Cha do sheall sibh [   ]
is sibh a shealladh gu h-ìosal,
brù is sporan a' sìor ghabhail rèim.   6

Cearcan sgròbain rinn cumasg
ach cò bu mhò dhèanadh trusadh –
thèid bhur stòras 'na dhuslach nur beul.   9

[Leig sibh

76 [*Ancient Scotland*]

Ancient Scotland, blue and valleyed, | of woods and knowes and plains, | wondrous Scotland, my treasure, | 'twas you who brought me to life and nourished me; | young I stood on your behalf, | and my heart sore for what had befallen you,   4
| since I have chosen you the heather is under my head, | and my love, will you not show me shelter?   8

77 [*The Fiery Spirit of My People*]

The fire and dignity of my people, | their liberality and compassion, | all have gone with the years – great the loss!   3

You did not look [ ], | Your gaze you kept lowered, | purse and belly holding sway more and more.   6

Like scratching hens you caused mayhem | to see whose hoard would be greatest – | your wealth will turn to dust in your mouths.   9

Leig sibh srian le luchd fòirneirt,
cha do chaisg sibh an dòrn ac' –
bidh e dùinte for sròin gu bhur n-èis.   12

Bhon a ruaig sibh na b'fhiach dhibh
a-mach gu iomall na h-iarmailt
tha sibh airceach bochd crìon air bheag spèis.   15

Na h-òga do-chìosnaicht'
a phut an t-àr às an tìr seo,
is ann tha dubh phrasgan dìolain 'nan dèidh.   18

Na coimhich a b'fhiù leibh
air na mhill sibh bhur dùthaich,
fastaidh iadsan mar chù sibh air èill.   21

*78 *Còmhradh nan Rubha*
The Talk of the Headlands

Says Ebbing Point to Laggan Head:
"Where do they watch their nets to spread
on the black lifting of the sea,
that laid their homeward course on me?   4

"When the sun stoops and leaves the sky
the loch lies dead, with not a cry
or torch to mark from far or near.
It leaves me lonely, watching here."   8

You gave free rein to oppressors, | you did not stay their hand – | it will clench under your noses in your need.   12
Having driven your best | to the ends of the earth | you are poor, needy, paltry, of no worth.   15
The indomitable youths | whom war drove from this land | left a vile pack of mongrels behind.   18
The strangers you looked up to, | for whom you spoiled your country, | will secure you like dogs on the leash.   21

Says Laggan Head across the bight:
"What sounds the men must rienge to-night,
not Holy Isle or Ailsa know,
who flashed farewell and saw them go.   12

"They search dark seas they never kent,
seeking out death, ill-rested, spent;
yet sweet it drones aye in their ear,
the swell that breaks upon us here."   16

79 Òran a Rinneadh ann an Ainm Fir Eile

A hill òro och is ochan,
thrèig an comann a bha treis ann,
a hill òro och is ochan.

Chaidh an gaol gu snìomh 's gu fuachd oirnn;
a chridh', bu luath a thrèig an t-seirc ud.   5

Chùm mi mach gun robh mi coma,
's mi gam bhrodadh le rinn sgeine.

Thuirt gum bu choingeis leam siud,
's dubhan teann am chliabh air greimeadh.

'S ann tha stobadh fo m'aisnibh;   10
cha dèan cainnt no bòst a leigheas.

[Thug thu

79 *A Song Composed in Another Man's Name*
A hill òro och is ochan, | gone the accord that once we had, | a hill òro och is ochan.

Love has turned painful and cold on us; | my heart, how soon that affection was lost!   5

I maintained that I was unconcerned, | pricked all the while by the point of a knife.

It left me quite indifferent, I said, | while in my breast a hook lodged tight.

A stabbing pain grips my ribs, | which talk or bravado cannot heal.   10

Thug thu guin dhomh fhèin ri ghiùlan
gach àit an tionndaidh mi fo m'eire.

A chinn duibh is 'aghaidh ghaolach,
cò shaoileadh mis' is tu bhith 'deasbad? 15

Cò chunnaic àmhghar riamh air domhan
mar sheann chomann 'dol air deireadh?

Mo shùil ri gàire 's ri suairceas,
thug thu sùil shuarach rathad eile.

*80 Cuimhneachan do Ealasaid agus Anna NicMhaoilein

Is ann 'nan laighe an Cill Aindreis
 tha dithist bhan a dh'altraim mì,
mnài chuir maise air a' bheatha-s',
 ged bu sean iad, len cuid gnìomh; 4
Ealasaid maraon is Anna,
 bha iad farsaing, caomh, neo-chrìon:
thug iad saoghal mòr ri fialachd,
 is thug aon bhliadhna iad don chill. 8

You have given me a stinging wound to endure, | everywhere I turn with my burden.
You of the dark head and lovely face, | who would have thought we two would argue? 15
Who ever saw a more grievous thing in the world | than an old accord coming to an end?
When I had an eye to laughter and pleasantness, | your disdainful eye looked the other way.

80   In Memoriam *for Elizabeth and Anne Macmillan*

There lying in Tarbert graveyard | are two women who nurtured me; | women who made this life beautiful, | although they were old, with their deeds. | 4 Elizabeth together with Anne, | they had breadth of spirit and kindliness and liberality; | they spent a long life in generosity | and one year took them to the grave. 8

Uaisle ghiùlain, cainnt bu chiùine,
    suairceas, sunnd is cridhe mòr,
cò a shaoileadh mnathan aosta
    a bhith 'nan aobhar ioghnaidh leò?   12
Mar sin bha Ealasaid is Anna,
    le sgairt a fhreagradh don aois òig;
bha seann fharsaingeachd nan Gàidheal
    a-rìst 'nan gnàths a' tighinn beò.   16

An seann saoghal còir bha 'nochdadh
    riamh tromhaibh anns gach ceum
feumaidh sinn a ràdh, mo thruaighe,
    gum "b'aisling uaireigin è".   20
Is math a bhiodh sinn dheth, a dhithist,
    nam fàgadh sibh mar ghibht nur dèidh,
's nam faigheadh daoin' an t-saoghail ghoirt seo,
    leth nan sochair bh'annaibh fhèin.   24

Cha do chrom thu ceann no inntinn,
    Ealasaid, gu rud crìon nach b'fhiù;
is Anna phàirteach ghaoil an t-sonais
    làmh no doras cha do dhùin.   28
Chì mi thu fo fhiamh a' ghàire
    a' roinn air càch air ceann do bhùird,
's ma tha thu fhathast mun t-seann àite
    is spiorad fàilteach, coibhneil thù.   32

Nobility of bearing, great gentleness of speech, | pleasantness, cheer and a great heart, | who would think that aged women | would be a cause for wonder with such? | Thus were Elizabeth and Anne, | with a smeddum that would befit young years; | the old breadth of spirit of the Gael | came alive again in their habitual ways.

The decent old world that always | showed through you at every step, | we may well say, alas, | that "it was a vision once upon a time". | Well would we be off, the two of you, | if you had left behind you as a gift, | and if the people of this sore world could get, | the half of the good qualities that were in yourselves.

You never lowered your head or mind, | Eliza, to any paltry worthless thing; | and sharing, dear, happy Anne | closed nor hand nor door. | I see you with your smile | sharing to the rest at the head of your table; | and, if you are still about the old place, | you are a kindly, welcoming spirit.

*81 Aonarain na Cille

Ochan, aonarain na cille,
   gach aon 'na ionad fhèin fa leth,
'na thighearna air taigh gun tathaich
   far nach dèanar farraid air.   4

Chan èirich grian ann no reul,
   cha tig neul no fras no gaoth,
gormadh an là no 'n dùthrath,
   sìth no ùspairt, gràin no gaol.   8

82 Teisteas Mhic Iain Deòrsa

Nach seall sibh a' chraobh ud
   's i ag aomadh gu tuiteam?
Dheòl a freumhan ar brìgh oirnn,
   ach nis chrìonaich a duilleach;   4
chaill i 'greim anns an talamh –
   fuich, b'e 'n dallan gun tuigsinn
dhèanadh suidhe fo 'sgàile
   is a' bhàrrgheug air udal.   8

81 The Lonely Ones of the Churchyard

Alas, the lonely ones of the churchyard, | each one in his own place apart, | master
of a house unvisited, | where no one comes to ask after him.   4

Neither sun nor star rises there; | no cloud comes, or rain, or wind; | no day's
dawning or dusk of evening; | peace or tumult, hate or love.   8

82 [Mac Iain Deòrsa Testifies]

Take a look at that tree | tipping over, near falling. | Its roots sucked all our sap, |
but now its foliage has withered; | it has lost its hold in the soil – | why, only the   4
blind would be fooled | into sitting in its shade | while the topbranch is rocking.   8

An cuileann cruaidh, craobh nam mollachd
   nach fàs fochann 'na sgàile,
a sgaoil thar iomall an domhain,
   is seacadh fodha 's gach àirde,   12
is teann a spàrr e na freumhan
   a thraogh fèithean gach àlaich,
ach thig fàs air fonn goirticht'–
   tha e bogadh, a chàirdean!   16

Gu dè as cleachdadh do Shasainn?
   Siuthad, farraid an Èirinn;
no thig freagairt an fhuathais
   à iomadh uaigh an tìr chèin ort;   20
greas is feòraich sna h-Innsean
   feuch an innis iad sgeul duit:
och, is farsaing an eachdraidh,
   's truagh mar chreach iad an Èiphit.   24

Rachadh an talamh air udal
   nan robh guth aig na cnàmhan,
is iad ag èigheach 's a' tagairt
   na rinn Sasainn de chràdh orr':   28
guth Uallais chaidh shracadh,
   guth Ghilleasbaig, guth Màiri,
gàir nan leòint' air Cùil Fhodair,
   glòir na gort' ann an Dàrien.   32

[Cha do chaochail

The coarse holly, tree of curses | that not a shoot can grow under, | that has spread to the world's rim | and withered every continent, | ruthlessly it pushed the roots | 12 *that drained the channels of each people, | but growth will come to parched soil – | it is softening, friends!*   16

What are the customary ways of England? | Go enquire in Ireland; | or spectres can answer you | from many a grave overseas; | hurry and ask in India, | see what   20 *story they tell you: | oh, their history spreads far, | how shamefully they stripped Egypt!*   24

The ground would start rocking | if bones had a voice, | were they to shout and claim redress | for all the torments England brought on them; | the voice of Wallace   28 *torn limb by limb, | the voice of Archibald, the voice of Mary, | the wails of the wounded on Culloden, | the moan of famine in Darien.*   32

Cha do chaochail iad nàdar
 is iad gur tàladh le bruidhinn
gus am faicear bhur sreathan
 fon chlò lachdann 's fon ghunna.   36
Siud an trù chaidh a chealgadh
 'dol 'na armaibh gu duineil,
feuch a shùil air an fhàire
 is a nàmhaid aig 'uilinn.   40

Och bhuainn e dhaoine!
 Nach do thaom sibh ur cuislean
anns gach dùthaich fon iarmailt,
 ri breun riasladh 's ri murtadh?   44
Is na Sasannaich stràiceil
 a' marcachd àrd air bhur muineal,
's ann an deireadh gach tuasaid
 is beag a fhuaireadh ga chionn leibh.   48

Cha deic na bh'againn de ghòraich,
 b'fheàirrde crònan a' chait sinn –
's ann da fhèin, mar a theireir,
 bhios a cheilear ga ghabhail.   52
Is ma thogas sinn gunna
 's ma bhios buillean gan tarraing,
's ann duinn fhèin is do dh'Albainn
 a dheargar ar n-acfhainn.   56

*Their nature has not changed, | as they seduce you with fine talk | till ranks of you appear | in the khaki, gun in hand. | That doomed wretch who's been duped | see   36
him go bravely in arms | with his eye on the skyline | and his enemy at his elbow.*

*Oh let's be rid of it, men! | Haven't you drained your blood-vessels | in every land under the sun, | in foul carnage and murder? | While the arrogant English | rode   44
high on your backs, | and after every stramash, | precious little it won you.*   48

*Our gullability did not help us, | the purring cat should be a lesson – | for itself alone, says the proverb, | does it murmur its music. | And if we take up the gun | 52
and if blows are to be struck, | it's for ourselves and for Scotland | that our arms will be bloodied.*   56

An e 'chrùbadh san làthaich
    am sglàbhaiche aca?
Ghin m'athair-sa saor mi
    is cha d'fhoghlaim mi gealtachd.   60
Ged bu toigh leo mo shracadh
    is a' ghreallach thoirt asam,
's iomadh beinn a tha 'm dhùthaich –
    's am bithinn ùmhal don phaca?   64

Bidh sinn sealan gar ruagadh
    feadh nan uaimh is nan dùslainn,
ach thig là a bheir teisteas
    gun robh ceartas nar cùrsa;   68
is ma thèidear gu buillean
    's mi bhuidhneas sa chùnnradh –
chan fhaigh iad ach mise
    's gheobh mi dithist no triùir dhiubh.   72

B'fhada ìosal sinn, fhearaibh,
    tha 'n t-àm againn bhith dìreadh;
's och, na leigibh an dearmad
    ar n-Albainn bhochd dhìleas,   76
ach forcaibh ur casan
    's cumaibh carraid ri mìltean,
is seasaibh gu daingeann,
    is daibhsan na strìochdaibh.   80

·

Am I to crouch in the mud | as if I were their slave? | My father begot me free | and
I have not learnt to be a coward. | Though they'd like to rip me open | and tear the 60
guts out of me, | there are hills in my country, | and would I grovel to the pack? 64

They will pursue us a while | through the dens and the thickets, | but a day will
come to bear witness | that our course was a just one; | and if it comes to blows, | 68
I'll win in the deal: | they will get only me, | but it's two or three that I'll hit. 72

We've lain low a long while, men, | it's now time to ascend; | do not permit the
neglect | of our poor loyal Scotland; | but plant your legs firmly | hold the fight 76
against thousands, | stand firm and determined, | and to them do not yield. 80

POEMS 1942–1944

*83 *Casan Sìoda*

Air tilleadh dhachaigh feasgar dhomh 's an teine a' cur ruaim dheth,
chunnaic mi an creachadair 'na laighe socair suaimhneach;
chan fhaicinn ach an druim dheth, fionnadh dubh is bàrr a chluasan –
fhuair mi Casan Sìoda 'na shìneadh anns an luaithre.   4

"Siud thusa na do chuachaig gun smuain air làimh do bhiathaidh,
nad stidean leisg, mì-thaingeil, làn aingidheachd is mialaich.
B'olc gu leòir nad phiseig thu, droch stic nam prat mì-rianail,
ach nis is làn-chat feusaig thu, a rèir na chaill mi dh'iasg leat.   8

"Sealgair nan trannsa is fear rannsachaidh nan cùiltean;
Òrd nan Luch gan tòireachd le do chròcan, 's cha b'e 'n sùgradh;
Freiceadan Dubh gach tollaig, is tu roimpe na do chrùban;
ceatharnach sa chidsin nì na measraichean a sgrùdadh.   12

83 *Silk Feet*

Coming home in the evening, when the fire was throwing out a ruddy glow, | I
saw the plunderer lying peacefully at his ease; | I could only see his back, black
fur and the tips of his ears – | I found Silk Feet reposing on the ashes.   4

"There you are coiled up without a thought for the hand that feeds you, | a bad,
ungrateful pussy full of ungodliness and meowing. | You were bad enough when
a kitten, a bad stick full of disorderly pranks, | but now you are a full-grown whisk-
ered cat, judging by the amount of fish I have lost through you.   8

"Huntsman of the lobbies and investigator of the nooks and crannies; | Hammer
of the Mice, pursuing them with your grappling-hooks, and it's no joking
matter; | Black Watch of every chink, crouching before it; | cateran in the kitchen,
who will scrutinise the dishes.   12

"'S e Spògan Sròil a b'athair dhuit, fear caithreamach na h-oìdhche,
a fhuair ri Coiseachd Chlùimh thu, bean chiùin a b'fhaide ìghnean.
Fhuair thu do thogail leis a' ghoid, 's cha b'ann gu dìomhain –
's nach olc an sgoil a thug iad dhuit, a mhurtair nan eun bìdeach?   16

"Chan eil gealbhonn no smeòrach o Ghleann Cró gu ruig Loch Fìne,
lon-dubh no gobhlan gaoithe o Àrd Laoigh gu Gleann Sìora,
chan eil eireag bheag no luchag, no eun guir am preas san rìoghachd,
nach eil air 'fhaicill roimh do spògan – och-òin, a Chasan Sìoda!   20

"Seachain an cù aosta le a chraos 's a shùilean gruamach;
thugad bean na còcaireachd 's a' phòit 'na làimh gu bualadh;
seachain an cat buidhe ud, laoch guineach air leth-chluais e,
no bheir e Inbhir Lòchaidh dhuit, mo Spògan Sìoda uallach!   24

"Seo rabhadh dhuit, a mhic ud, is na leigear e an dìochuimhn'.
Nuair thig mi dhachaigh anmoch leth-mharbh 's air mo mhìobhadh,
ma gheibh mi na mo chathair thu, o seallaidh mi le cinnt dhuit
nach *persona grata* thu, a ghràidh, a Chasan Sìoda."   28

"Satin Paws was your father, the loud musician of the night; | he had you by Downy Tread, a gentle lady with claws of the longest. | You were brought up to thieving, and not idly – | and wasn't it a bad education they gave you, murderer of the tiny birds?   16

"There's not a sparrow or a thrush from Glen Croe to Loch Fyne, | a blackbird or a swallow from Ardlui to Glen Shira, | there's not a little chicken or a mouse or a broodie bird in any bush in the kingdom, | but it's on its guard against your paws. Alas, Silk Feet!   20

"Avoid the aged dog with his maw and his glum eyes; | look out for the cook with the pot in her hand to hit you; | avoid yon yellow cat – he's a ferocious warrior with one ear | or he'll give you an Inverlochy, my jaunty Silk Paws!   24

"Here's a warning for you, you son of the devil, and don't let it be forgotten. | When I come home late, half dead and battered by the weather, | if I find you in my chair, oh, I will show you quite decidedly | that you are not *persona grata*, my darling Silk Feet."   28

*84 Rabhadh

Na bi null 's a-nall, a bhean;
　　thoir fa-near nach measan mì,
's tu ga theumadh 's ga chur suarach,
　　ga smèideadh 's ga ruagadh a-rìst.　　　　　4

Aotrom, dubhach, loisgeach, fionnar,
　　inntinn eadar fuireach 's folbh;
bioradh beag on chogais chursta,
　　seal eile t'fhuil 'na lasair bheò.　　　　　8

Cha leanabh mi is tu ga bhreugadh;
　　cha dèideag mi no peata bog;
tha geat' iarainn air mo chridhe,
　　a chrannas mi a chlisgeadh ort.　　　　　12

Mas cluich leat a bhith coimheach fuar rium,
　　a bhith cruaidh bu shùgradh leinn;
thig thu a dh'òl às an fhuaran,
　　's gheibh thu 'na uachdar an deigh.　　　　　16

84 Warning

Do not waver this way and that, woman. | Take heed and know that I am no lapdog | for you to entice, then despise, | to call to you, then chase away.　　4

Light-hearted then gloomy, burning then cool; | your mind half set on going, half set on staying; | now a little prick from the cursed conscience, | and, at another moment, your blood aflame with living fire.　　8

I am not a child for your beguiling. | I am not some toy or a soft pet. | There is a gate of iron to my heart, | which I can bar against you in an instant.　　12

If you think it a game to be distantly strange and cold with me, | I would think it sport to be hard. | You will come to drink from the spring, | and will find on its surface ice.　　16

*85 *Sguabag 1942*

Chan àm caoinidh seo no osnaich,
àm gu brosnachadh 's gu sùrd,
àm gu deachdadh, cainnt is òrain,
àm gu dòchas is gu dùil;   4
    àm gu bòrcadh, snodhach, sùgh,
    àm gu gràbhaladh 's luchd ciùil,
    àm gu smaointean, sunnd is gàire,
    àm gu beatha 's fàs as ùr.   8

Chan e seo ach stoirm an Earraich,
a sguabas sneachd a' Gheamhraidh uainn,
bean ghlùin neo-thruasail a' Chèitein,
Sguabag gheur le 'meuraibh cruaidh.   12
    Is i as dèine dh'èigheas fuachd,
    sneachd 'na dèidh 'na rèis gu cuan –
    's a h-uile crann gun smuais 'na shlataibh,
    nì ligh' an Earraich a ghrad bhuain.   16

Seann mhaide mosganach an t-saoghail,
crìonach aost' a' grod san ùir,
slatan nach cùm taic ri daoine,
is iad a' faoisgneadh às an rùisg;   20
    thèid an sgaoileadh mar le sùist
    air glas aodann nan sruth dùr;
    bheirear rùm don ùr fhàs aobhach
    a nì caoin an Samhradh ciùin.   24

85 [*Spring Sweeper 1942*]

This is no time for lamenting or sighing, | it is a time for incitement and activity; | it is a time for inditing, speech and songs, | a time for hope and expectation; | a   4 time for burgeoning, sap and juice, | a time for sculpting and musicians; | a time for thoughts, cheer and laughter; | a time for life and renewal of growth.   8

This is only the Springtime storm | that sweeps away from us the snow of Winter, | Maytime's pitiless midwife, | keen Sguabag with her hard fingers. | It is   12 she who shouts most vehemently, proclaiming cold. | After she has passed snow goes racing to the sea, | and every tree that has no pith in its branches | will be swiftly plucked away by the [Springtime] thaw.   16

All the old, dry-rotted wood of the world, | the aged, withered timber [decaying] in the earth, | rods that give no support to men, | their bark peeling off them – | 20 they will be scattered as by a flail | on the grey face of the grim streams; | room will be made for the joyous new growth, | which will make pleasant the tranquil summer.   24

*86 Fàire M'Òige

Siud e m'fhàire san Earrach is crìochan mo fhradhairc sa Chèitein,
tràth thilleadh gealghrian a' mhochthrath 's a h-uilinn sna cnocain ag èirigh,
cnoc air muin cnuic anns a' Cheathramh, mullaichean 's leacainnean èibhinn,
guala 's guala bhòidheach, na tomain an Còmhal 's na slèibhtean,
uchdach air uchdaich a' dòmhlachadh, aonach is mòinteach nam fèithean. 5
Seall, Sliabh Gaoil a' sìneadh san ògsholas fhìondhearg ghrèine,
rogha is taghadh nan sliabh, beinn sheilge Dhiarmaid 's na Fèinne,
druim fada mìn air dheagh shnaidheadh mar bhalla a chasgadh na sèisde,
a' sruthadh 'na shliosan 's ag aonadh 'na ruigheachan faon ris an rèidhlean.
An rìgh am meadhan a shluaigh, deagh bhuachaill am meadhan a threudan –
còir gach rìgh sin 's a urram 'na àite suidhe is èirigh;
seasadh a mhuinntir deas air is clì air ag amharc 's ag èisteachd –
an cridhe na h-àirde tuath siud Cruachan Beann fo bhrèid ghil,
stuadh a' chìrein àrdghil 'sìor bhriseadh air fàire 's leus deth.
B'e sin clach-tharraing mo shùla, an casthonn trìcheannach glègheal. 15

86 My Youth's Horizon

Yon was my horizon in the Spring and the bounds of my sight in the Maytime, | when the white sun of morning would return with its elbow on the knowes arising: | hill upon hill in Kerry, the summits and the joyous hillsides, | shoulder upon bonny shoulder, the hillocks in Cowal and the high hills; | ascent crowding upon ascent, upland and moorland of the bog-runnels. | See Sliabh Gaoil stretched out 5 in the young wine-red light of the sun, | pick and choice of all hills, hunting-mountain of Diarmad and the Fiann; | a long smooth ridge, finely carved, like a wall to check the siege, | streaming down in flanks and joining in long gentle slopes with the flatland. | The king in the midst of his people, a good shepherd in the midst of his flocks – | that is the right and honour accorded to every king in his 10 place of sitting down and rising up. | Let his people stand to right of him and to left of him, looking and listening – | in the heart of the northern airt Cruachan under a white snood, | the wave of the high white crest ever breaking and gleaming on the horizon. | That was the lodestone of my eye, the steep bright wave, triple-crested. 15

*87 [Duilleach an Fhoghair]

(trì rainn is amhran)

Duilleach an fhoghair a chaidh às,
  fochainn an earraich seo 'teachd trìd;
na sgap a' bhliadhna is i 'meath,
  a' bheatha ùr a dh'fhàs 'na cill.   4

Thug thusa cùl ri t'òige fhèin
  nad Chèitein blàth le claonadh glic.
Nuair thuiteas do dhuilleach donn
  feuch nach trom a' chuimhne sin.   8

Fuar do ghliocas, aghaidh dhonn,
  thoirt car-mu-thom dod bhith le moit.
Breithnich ciaradh gach là,
  's an dàimh a thagras an ùir ort.   12

Ceangal

Saobh ghliocas sheann ùghdar a thùraich faoineas an-dè,
a chuir thusa an-diugh o t'iùl an ceannairc riut fhèin.
Dhiùlt thu an sùgradh, is dhiùlt thu baileach mo bheul.
Biodh agad, a rùin – ach is dlùth an talamh don chrè.   16

87 [This Autumn Foliage]
(three verses and envoi)

The foliage of this dead autumn that is gone, | the shoots of this spring's grass coming through it; | what the year scattered as she decayed, | the new life that has grown in her graveyard.   4

You have turned your back on your own youth, | in your warm Maytime with perverse "wisdom". | When your yellow leafage falls, | take heed that the memory of that be not heavy.   8

Cold is your wisdom, brown face, | to play hide and seek with your being in petulant pride. | Judge (the meaning of) the darkening of each day, | and the kinship that the earth will claim on you.   12

Envoi

The false wisdom of old authors who devised foolishness yesterday | has put you today off your path in rebellion against yourself. | Fondling you have refused, and you have refused completely my mouth. | So be it, my dear – but the earth is close to the clay.   16

*88 Skottland til Nordsjøfarerne

Vestover hele natten uten ende
som røyken jager hun, uredd, alene;
hun luter under bygene, vil skjene –
østen er tatt, vestover må de vende.   4
   Hvitt død på svarte gangere, med makt
   tordner de drevne bølger som hun stamper;
   fram under bleke faner, hør, de tramper,
   sjøens nordøstkavaleri på jakt.   8

Slik før de lange skip, da harde hender
holdt Skottlands øyer under røveråket
(ennu gjentar vår munn Norrøna språket).
Da var vi fiender, nu er vi frender.   12
   Nei, Norges kjøler fører ikke nu
   den gamle terror gjennom storm og bølger.
   Krigsbrødre, følgende det håp vi følger,
   velkommen til vårt land fra havets gru.   16

88 [*Scotland to the North Sea Farers*]

Westwards the whole night without end, | quick as smoke she hunts, fearless, alone; | she stoops and swerves under the squalls – | the east is taken, westwards they must turn. | White death on black steeds, | with might the driven waves thunder as she stamps; | forward under pale banners, listen, they tramp, | the sea's north-east cavalry on the hunt.

Thus in times past the longship, when hard hands | held Scotland's isles firm under the plunderer's yoke | (still our mouths repeat the Norse language). | Then we were enemies, now we are friends. | No, Norway's keels no longer carry | the old terror through storm and waves. | Brothers of war, you who are following the hope we follow, | welcome to our country from the ocean's terror.

[A. Kruse]

*89 Deux Vers

Hélas, les morts muets, solitaires!
   Chacun dans son endroit dort immuré,
maître d'une maison noire, amère,
   où personne ne vient le saluer.   4

Ni soleil s'y lève, ni étoile.
   On n'y sent pas le vent ni voit nuée.
Jamais n'y flambe l'aube, pays pâle,
   sans peur, sans amour, sans paix, sans épée.   8

89 *[Two Verses]*

*Alas, the mute, solitary dead! | Each one sleeps in his place, walled in, | master of
a black, bitter house, | where no one comes to greet him.*   4

*Neither sun nor star rises there. | There no wind is felt, nor mist-cloud seen. |
Never does the dawn blaze there, pallid country, | without fear, without love,
without peace, without sword.*   8

*90 *Le Revenant du Marin Parle*
à sa Mère

Femme, lâchez-moi. Ne pleurez plus.
  Sur moi la douleur pèse, où je suis.
Sous nos pieds le bateau s'est fendu.
  La mémoire aveugla cette nuit.   4

Percé par vos larmes, de l'oubli
  pourquoi m'attirez-vous, inconnue?
Pourquoi m'éveillez-vous, endormi?
  Est-ce que jadis je vous ai vue?   8

Une fois j'étais Donald, je crois.
  Les courants m'emportent et les flots.
Femme, que fait frissoner ma voix,
  je vous laisse. Cessez vos sanglots.   12

90 [*The Sailor's Ghost Speaks to his Mother*]

Woman, release me. Weep no more. | *Pain weighs heavily on me, where I am.* | *Under our feet the ship split asunder.* | *Memory blinded that night.*   4

Piercing me with your tears, from oblivion | *why do you draw me, stranger?* | *Why do you wake me, when I sleep?* | *In bygone times have I ever seen you?*   8

Once I was Donald, I think. | *The currents and the waters carry me away.* | *Woman, who shudders at the sound of my voice,* | *I will leave you now. Cease your sobbing.*   12

*91   Trois Vers et Envoi

Tu vois? La vie ne reste pas.
   Ces feuilles mortes font des fleurs.
Au tombeau où l'été sombra,
   elle renaît de l'an qui meurt.　　　　　　4

Ta jeunesse, tu la renies
   dans ton avril ensoleillé.
Quand la feuille tombe jaunie,
   comment vas-tu t'en rappeler?　　　　　8

Les morts sévères t'ont gelée.
   Leurs mots t'exilent du corps doux.
Pense au soir, port de tout soleil,
   aux droits qu'a la terre sur nous.　　　12

Envoi

La fausse sagesse des moines encloîtrés
t'a rendue rebelle à ton être et ta beauté.
Ma bouche tu fuis, mes bras tu as repoussés.
Ainsi soit, chérie – mais la terre est toujours près.　　16

91　[*Three Verses and Envoi*]

You see? Life does not stay. | These dead leaves beget flowers. | At the tomb where summer sank into darkness, | life is reborn out of the dying year.　　4

You renounce your youth, | in your sunny April years. | When the faded leaf falls, | how will you remember it?　　8

The grim dead have frozen you. | Their words banish you from the body's sweetness. | Think of the evening, the port to every sun, | of the rights which the earth holds over us.　　12

Envoi
The false wisdom of the cloistered clerics | has made you rebel against your being and your beauty. | My mouth you avoid, my arms you have pushed away. | So be it, love – but the earth is ever close.　　16

*92 Le Gaël Réfléchit

Le goéland qui là-haut balance
    derrière mon bateau,
les soirs, plongeant, quitte les horizons,
    s'envolant à son îlot.   4

Fidèle à sa niche de falaise,
    il a son lit connu;
mais les miens s'étendent et s'éveillent,
    toujours nouveaux venus.   8

Le soleil les voit toutes les heures
    entre les deux minuits;
avec l'épée, la charrue, la nostalgie
    ils errent sans répit.   12

Tous les promontoires de la terre
    leur cachent les baies d'ici;
tous les monts du monde rejettent l'écho
    de leur musique hardie.   16

Ils ont pris les remparts des continents;
    les océans ils ont rougi;
leur sang abreuve les royaumes lointains,
    vêtus en cramoisi.   20

92 [The Gael Reflects]

The seagull that hovers up there | behind my boat, | in the evenings dives off beyond the horizons, | flying to his searock.   4

Faithful to his nook in the cliff | he has his familiar bed; | but my folk lie down and wake up, | always newly come.   8

The sun sees them every hour | between the two midnights; | with sword, plough and nostalgia | they wander without respite.   12

All the promontories of the earth | hide from them the bays of this place; | all the mountains of the world return the echo | of their hardy music.   16

They have taken the ramparts of the continents; | they have reddened the oceans; | their blood quenches faraway kingdoms, | dressed in scarlet.   20

*93 *L'Écosse M'Accompagne*

J'oublie
mes sombres monts, fauves, nus,
esclave las du beau soleil?
Or, lis
ces vers à toi tendus   5
du cœur splendide de l'été,
et dis
si tu me vois changé.
Sous les vagues de l'Algérie
la mémoire s'est-elle donc noyée?   10

Je vois
ses sommets solitaires.
Leurs maîtres sont en ma patrie.
L'effroi
des falaises sévères,   15
des rochers ascètes, surgit.
Les rois
de la Haute Kabylie
menacent impérieux, et moi,
je tiens ces fronts superbes en mépris.   20

Les champs
y donnent et redonnent,
dans ce pays bien-aimé du soleil;

[et dons

93   [*Scotland Goes With Me*]

I forget | my untamed, stark, dark mountains, | a weary slave to the fine sun? |
Yet, read | these lines proffered to you | from the resplendent heart of summer, | 5
and say | if you see me changed. | Under the waves of Algeria, | then, has memory
drowned?   10

I see | these lonely summits. | Their masters are in my homeland. | The terror | of
the grim cliffs, | of the ascetic rocks, suddenly looms. | The kings | of High Kabylia | 15
imperiously threaten, and as for me | I hold these superb brows in disdain.   20

Fields | here yield and yield again, | in this country beloved of the sun; |

et dons
y courbent et couronnent   25
les branches des arbres rangés;
fruits dont
un peuple vit bercé.
Vaincues de mains durcies, elles ont
plus de gloire, nos pentes labourées.   30

Ce Dieu
seul et impitoyable,
et son prophète guerrier –
affreux
ses saints naissent du sable,   35
conquistadors, prêchant l'épée.
Tous creux,
ses dogmes entonnés.
Les saints des îles parlent mieux,
Colum et sa royale humilité.   40

Blême
sous la bourrasque d'hiver,
fouetté par la grêle du nord;
même,
mon pays là-bas, m'est-il cher   45
sous l'averse aveugle qui mord.
Gemme
quand le dur temps s'endort,
et le vent du large sème,
mourant, pleurnichant, la paix sur ses bords.   50

and gifts | here bend and crown | the branches of the well-ordered trees; | fruits | 25
on which a people sweetly lives. | Conquered with hardened hands, they hold |
more glory, our ploughed slopes. 30

That God, | solitary and ruthless | and his warrior prophet – | frightful, | his saints
rise to life from the sands, | conquistadors, preaching the sword. | All hollow, | his 35
intoned dogmas. | The saints of the isles speak better, | Colum and his kingly
humility. 40

Ghostly pale | under the winter squall, | whipped by the hailstones from the north;
| even, | my country yonder, is it dear to me | under the blind, biting shower. | 45
Gem | when the harsh weather goes to sleep, | and the wind from off the sea, | with
a dying whimper, sows peace on its banks. 50

94–98: Stances de Simple Soldat

*94 *Hypocrite*

Il veut passer pour exemplaire,
    et sermonise, Dieu le sait;
mais il y a bien des pas à faire
    de comme il faut à comme il fait.   4

*95 *L'Essentiel*

L'enfant que vous châtiez,
    pourquoi faut-il l'éduquer,
vu que tout le monde naît
    maître du système D?   4

*96 *Crime et Punition*

"Le sergent dit que l'accusé
    a eu l'audace de penser."
"Quoi! Penser?" (ébahi, il tousse)
"Toi! Quinze jours de calabouse."   4

94–98: [Verses from a Mere Private]

94   [*Hypocrite*]

*He'd like to pass for a paragon, | and, God knows, he pontificates; | but there's a
long way separates | what one should do and how this one acts.*   4

95   [*The Essential Thing*]

*The child you were chastising, | why should it need educating, | when everyone is
born | a master of the art of coping?*   4

96   [*Crime and Punishment*]

*"The sergeant says that the accused | had the audacity to think." | "What! Think?"
(he coughs, amazed) | "You! Two weeks in the clink."*   4

*97 *Le Capitaine*

"Il m'en veut de partis pris.
　Sait-il ce que 'troupe' vaut?"
"Vieille noix, pour lui – tant pis –
　'troupe' veut dire 'troupeau'."　　　　4

*98 *"Ne t'en fais pas, c'est pas la peine ..."*
(chanson populaire)

Ces goujats m'insultent sans le savoir guère.
　Je me tais après tout.
Eux, ils sont chiens; je suis fils de mon père.
　Je m'en fais? Je m'en fous.　　　　4

*

97　[*The Captain*]
*"He holds some grudge against me. | Does he realise what 'troop' is worth?" |
"Old chap, for him – too bad – | 'troop' means only 'herd'."*　　　　4

98　[*"Don't worry, it's not worth it ..." (popular song)*]
*These boors insult me unwittingly. | I keep my silence after all. | Them, they are
dogs; I am my father's son. | Worry? I don't give a damn.*　　　　4

*

*99   Épreuve de Doute

Inaperçu dans ce feu
   la Mort si je passerai,
marchant sous la main de Dieu,
   enfin je la reverrai –   4

La belle face fière
   que tu montres à l'océan;
la mine joyeuse altière
   dont tu vois ses flots criants.   8

Je verrai croître – magie –
   renaître à mes yeux avides
ton front hautain, ma patrie,
   qui dit: "J'ignore leurs brides".   12

Regard qui dit: "Voyez
   si j'ai l'air assujetti!
Qui a vu mes pics courbés?
   Devant qui ai-je fléchi?"   16

Mais, mon pays, j'ai peur pour toi.
   Les monts durent: meurt la flamme.
L'autel survit à la foi.
   Auras-tu gardé ton âme?   20

[Le pouvoir

99   [Trial of Doubt]

Unnoticed in this fire | if I should slip past Death, | walking under God's protection, | I will see it again at last –   4

The noble, bonnie face | that you turn to the ocean; | the proud, joyful expression | with which you see its roaring waves.   8

I will see grow as if by magic, | rise again for my avid eyes, | your lofty brow, my homeland, | that says: "I know not their bridles".   12

A look which says: "See | if I appear subjugated! | Who has seen my peaks bowed? | Before whom have I stooped?"   16

But, my country, I fear for you. | The mountains endure: the flame dies. | The altar outlives the faith. | Will you have kept your soul?   20

Le pouvoir noir de la guerre
     m'ayant rendu inquiet,
peut-être, élève de l'ère,
     bas je me demanderai: 24

"C'est mon Arran crénelé,
     qu'en partant j'ai vu bleui;
mais est-il le parapet
     d'un château dedans trahi?   28

"Ce faste de faîtes longs,
     marge de la mer rieuse
et du ciel clair, est-il donc
     une façade trompeuse?   32

"Entourés de telles cîmes,
     autels de la liberté,
se peut-il, cœur, que s'abîme
     un peuple qui s'est troqué?   36

"Sont-ils, ces monts, une frise,
     décor d'une tragédie
où une nation qui vise
     chacun son but, perd sa vie?"   40

Mais, je le sais, quand je vois
     les hauts remparts de ma terre,
devant leur fierté fuira
     ce cauchemar qui me serre.   44

The black power of war, | having driven me to anxiety | perhaps, a pupil of the age, | I will silently ask myself: 24

"It is my serrated Arran, | that on leaving I saw tinted blue; | but is it the parapet | of a castle betrayed within?   28

"This pageant of long crests, | fringe of the laughing sea | and of the bright sky, is it then | a deceptive façade?   32

"Surrounded by such peaks, | altars of liberty, | could it be, heart, that a people | which has bartered itself is rotting?   36

"Are they a frieze, these mountains, | the set for some tragedy | in which a nation which aims | each for his own goal (sic) loses its very soul?"   40

But I know it when I see | the high ramparts of my land, | before their pride will flee | this nightmare that grips me.   44

*₁₀₀ *Fhearaibh 's a Mhnài na h-Albann*

Fhearaibh 's a mhnài na h-Albann,
  stoc gailbheach mo ghràidh,
sluagh nach gabh saltairt
  is nach saltair air muin chàich;
a chridheachan nach marbha,   5
  guma fairge sibh nach tràigh
am bailtean 's glinn na h-Albann,
  air a garbh chnuic 's a blàir.
    Fearann mo shinnsre Alba,
      clann Albann mo dhàimh,   10
      m'fheòil is sùgh mo chridhe sibh,
        mo mhisneach 's mo dheas làmh.

Seann dùthaich ghorm nam bidein,
  is i thug bith dhuinn 's a thug brìgh;
is garbh, is geanail, coibhneil i,   15
  's i toinnte 's gach aon dhìnn;
air a' mhachair, air na monaidhean
  dheoghail sinn a cìoch;
mas Goill, a ghaoil, mas Gàidheil sinn,
  dh'àraich ise sìnn.   20
    Fearann mo shinnsre Alba,
      clann Albann nach strìochd,
      mo bhiadh, mo dheoch is m'anail sibh –
        chan fhaic mi sibhse sìos.

---

100 *Men and Women of Scotland*

Men and women of Scotland, | tempestuous race that I love, | people who are not
to be trampled on, | and who will not trample on the necks of others; | oh, hearts
that are not dull and dead, | may you be a sea that will never ebb | in the towns   5
and glens of Scotland, | on her rough knowes and her plains.

Land of my forebears, Scotland, | children of Scotland, my kin, | you are my flesh   10
and the sap of my heart, | my courage and my right hand.

The old blue land of the mountain pinnacles, | it is she that has given us being and
pith; | she is rough, she is cheerful and kindly, | she is interwoven in every one of   15
us; | on plain and on upland | we have suckled at her breast; | be we Lowland, my
dear, or Gaels, | it was she that nurtured us.   20

Land of my forebears, Scotland, | children of Scotland that will not yield, | my
food, my drink and my breath are you – | I will not see you brought low.

*101 [Rann fo Chraoibh Orainse]

An dèidh coiseachd beanntan Tùnais,
  is sìoda chùbhraidh bhur cnuic gharbh.
An dèidh cluinntinn "Allah! Allah!"
  is guth meala leam bhur sailm.   4

*102 Athair nan Cluas

O Sfax gu Casablanca
  chan eil rathad garbh no rèidh
air nach fhaicear thu gad chosnadh
  le cnàimh do dhroma chur gu feum.   4

Fo chuail cheithir tunna,
  's tu a' tuisleachadh fon luchd,
is do bhiorain spàg gan lùbadh
  aig an dùn a th'air do dhruim.   8

101 [Verse under an Orange Tree]

After walking the hills of Tunis, | like perfumed silk are your wild braes. | After the sound of "Allah! Allah!" | a honeyed voice to me your psalms.   4

102 The Father of the Ears

From Sfax to Casablanca | there is not a road, rough or smooth, | where you are not to be seen earning your living | by putting your backbone to good use.   4

Under a four-ton burden, | stumbling beneath the load, | and your twigs of legs buckling | under the heap that is on your back.   8

Bù Udnìn, nach eil na cluasan
   as suaicheantas dod threubh,
cho fada ris an fhaighidinn
   a thug Allah dhuit mar sgèimh?   12

Is iomadh Arabach mòr, sultmhor,
   is do dhà uiread ann gu lèir,
a dh'èigheas "Gaodam!" (Bi air t'aghaidh!)
   ga do shlacadh gus an fhèill;   16

Air a shuaineadh 'na bhurnus,
   is a chuifein gaoil 'na bheul,
is 'uile bhathar air a thorradh
   roimhe is 'na dhèidh.   20

Air bhith tric a' gabhail beachd ort
   is e mo bhreith – 's is math breith mhall –
gur cochur thu nan eileamaid
   a leanas san ath rann: 24

Paidhir chluas is ceithir chasan,
   faighidinn is peall,
fichead punnd den ùmhlachd
   is unnsa den stailc.   28

Bû Udnîn, are not the ears, | which are the badge of your tribe, | as long as the patience | which Allah gave you for beauty?   12

Many a big, fleshy Arab, | with fully twice your bulk in him, | yells "Qeddam!" (Get a move on!), | as he belts you to the fair;   16

Swathed in his burnous, | with his beloved cigarette in his mouth, | and all his wares piled up | in front of him and behind him.   20

After having often taken notice of you, | it is my judgement – and a leisurely judgement is a good one – | that you are a synthesis of the elements | that follow in the next verse: 24

A pair of ears and four feet, | patience and a shaggy pelt, | twenty pounds of obedience | and an ounce of stubbornness.   28

*103 *Brosnachadh*

Alba ghràidh, thoir crathadh ort
  le braise, 's tuig na th'ann;
tha cas gach glaoic air t'amhaich-sa,
  's do bheatha geal an geall: 4
's nach searbh an sgeul air t'iomchar e,
  's e iomraiteach 's gach ball,
gun d'aithnich càch mar chaochladh ort,
  do dhaoine bhith cho fann?   8

Och Alba, mas e 'm bàs a th'ann,
  's mas cnàmhadh dhuit ad shuain,
mas crìonadh le caoin shuarachas,
  gur fuar a' chrìoch dod shluagh.   12
Am fàg thu do na ghràdhaich thu
  's le 'm b'àill thu a bhith suas,
ach gul ri àm do ghiùlain-sa
  is t'ionndrainn uap' san uaigh?   16

Ach gu ma h-e nach fhaicear sin:
  bidh lasair mar ri leus,
's tu fhèin ad shlèibhtean falaisge,
  is glanadh roimp' 's 'na dèidh;   20
on Pharbh gu muir na Maoil' annad
  bidh 'chaoir ud suas ri speur,
's is iomadh tighearn 's coigreach
  their "Oit" air chorraig chreucht'.   24

103 [*Incitement to Battle*]

*Beloved Scotland, give yourself a brisk shake | and understand the situation: |
every fool has a foot on your neck | and your precious life is at stake. | Is it not a*   4
*bitter comment on your bearing, | so renowned in every part, | that others have
recognised the change in you | from the feebleness of your people?*   8

*O Scotland, if death is your fate, | and mouldering in your sleep, | if it is to be a
withering away through apathy, | then a cold end awaits your people. | Will you*   12
*leave for those who loved you | and wished to see you flourish, | nothing but
weeping at the time of your funeral procession | and regret when you lie in the
tomb?*   16

*But may that not be seen; | there will be a flame and a blaze, | and you will be like
hills alight with heather-burning, | everything cleansed before it and after; | from*   20
*Cape Wrath to the waters of the Mull of Kintyre | that conflagration will stretch
to the heavens, | and many a lord and foreigner | will cry "Ouch" as his fingers
smart.*   24

*104 An Cnocan Fraoich

Och, a chuideachd ghràidh sa bheil fuil nan sàr,
    feuch a' chuing air a càramh le làmhan nan daoi,
is ar sealbhachd àrsaidh a' searg mu làr,
    is tost nam bailtean fàis air ar Cnocan Fraoich.   4
Dà cheud bliadhna 's an còrr – mar a dh'iarradh daonnan leò –
    fhuair iad iall mu n-ar còirichean, teann is caol.
Chaidh ar creic air òr anns a' Bhargan Mhòr,
    is leag iad an dubh chròg air ar Cnocan Fraoich.   8

Am Bliadhn' a' Phrionnsa 'nan rangaibh dlùth
    theann na lasgairean le dùrachd an tìr a chur saor;
a h-uile math is mith gus na h-èill a bhriseadh,
    gillean san robh misneach is cridh' an laoich.   12
Là Chùil Fhodair a' dol sìos chaidh an dochann air an t-sliabh;
    fhuair na Sasannaich am miann orra 's oirnn maraon.
Sgaoil iad teine 's crochadh, coin luirg is mort,
    geur-leanmhainn is gort feadh a' Chnocain Fhraoich.   16

Och, mar thrèigeadh gun truas e fo fhèidh is luachair,
    's an clàdan 's an cluaran 'nam bàrr air gach raon;
gun ach mèilich uan anns an Earrach fhuar
    far an cluinnte duan air a h-uile gaoith.   20

[E gun daoine

104 [The Heather Knowe]

Alas, dear companions of the line of the great men, | see the yoke imposed by the hands of the rogues, | our ancient dominion withering to the ground, | and the silence of emptied townships on our Heather Knowe. | Two hundred years and   4
more – as was ever their desire – | they got a leash round our rights, fast and tight; | we were sold for gold in the Great Bargaining, | and they set loose their black paw on our Heather Knowe.   8

In the Year of the Prince, in tight ranks marching, | the valiant sought earnestly to set their land free; | noble and commoner, all sought to break the thongs, | lads who had the courage and the heart of heroes. | As Culloden day passed, they were   12
felled on the moor; | the English got their way with them and likewise with us. | They spread fire and hanging, set loose lurchers and murder, | persecution and famine throughout the Heather Knowe.   16

Oh, how ruthlessly it was abandoned to the deer and the rushes, | with the burr and the thistle each field's only crop, | and in the cold Spring air only the bleating of lambs, | where a song was once carried on every wind. | 20

E gun daoine, gun chòmhnaidh, gun ghealbhan, gun cheòl,
    is na h-allmharaich ri spòrs air le gàire faoin;
's e cho aonranach, brònach, aognaidh, dòite
    ri aon chnoc san Eòrpa, ar Cnocan Fraoich.   24

Tha e 'n dàn don linn seo na h-èill a chur dhinn,
    às na banntaibh dìomhair gar cur fo sgaoil.
Is na biomaid dìomhain, ach siuthad ri gnìomh
    le duinealas is dìlseachd dar dìleab aost'.   28
Bidh a' bhratach ghorm is gheal a' stoirmrich ri gath,
    mar a bha i ann o shean, Crois ar n-Ainndreis Naoimh.
Far an robh cromadh cinn cluinnear coireal binn,
    is a' phìob ga seinn air ar Cnocan Fraoich.   32

Bidh bàigh an speur ris is fàbhar Dhè,
    is togar dheth 'na dhèidh sin dreach lom an aoig,
le bruthainn ghrèine is bog dhealt Chèit,
    chuireas snodhach anns gach gèig air ar Cnocan Fraoich.   36
Gum bi fàs agus beatha 'na bhlàth lagain fhasgaidh,
    snàmhaidh smùid a theallach mu bhàrr nan craobh;
is bidh 'òigridh cheutach tràth-nòin ag èisteachd
    ri ceòlan eunlaith ar Cnocain Fraoich.   40

Stripped of people and habitation, of hearthfire and music, | while foreigners made sport there in fatuous mirth, | it is as solitary and sad, as wasted and scorched | as any hill in Europe, our Heather Knowe.   24

It is this generation's mission to cast off the fetters, | that we be set free from our invisible thongs. | So let us not be idle, but forward into action | with manfulness and with loyalty to our ancient legacy. | The blue and white flag will fly high on its pole, | as it did of old, our Holy Andrew's cross; | sweet chorusing will be heard where heads once were cowed, | as the pipes are sounded on our Heather Knowe.   28   32

The heavens will be kind to it, it will be in God's favour, | and from it in the end the deadly bleakness will lift, | with the sun's sultry heat and the fresh Maytime dew | sending sap up each branch of our Heather Knowe. | There will be growth and life in its warm sheltering hollows, | about the treetops will drift the smoke from its hearths, | and in the afternoon hours its fine youths will be listening | to the warbling of the birds on our Heather Knowe.   36   40

105 [Bail' Ìomhair]

(trì rainn is amhran)

Is uasal leibh bhur saobhadh mhèirleach,
  màthair ghuir nan ceudan àr;
ma tha e sluaghmhor, ainmeil, rìoghail,
  tha Bail' Ìomhair an tost a' bhàis. 4

Thog sibh bhur lùchairtean àlainn
  le clachaibh ar làrach fuar.
Am fuil phrìseil bhlàith ar daoine
  bhàth sibh saorsa nan sluagh. 8

Is e bhur buannachd ar calldachd,
  is e bhur n-alladh cleith ar n-ainm,
is e bhur n-uabhar ar cinn chroma,
  is e bhur tromalaigh' ar fearg. 12

Amhran

Le sprùidhlich nam balla a b'fhasgadh dor sluagh o thùs,
thog sibh bhur n-aitreabh, a chlachairean shom nan lùb.
B'ann air cuirp ar fear dàna, a chàrnadh leibh glùn air ghlùn,
a rinn sibh am màrsal gu stàtail gu cumhachd is cùirt. 16

105 [Baliver]

(three verses and envoi)

Your lair of thieves is a cause of pride to you, | queen bee of the countless wars. | It may be populated, famous, royal, | but Baliver meanwhile lies in the silence of death. 4

You built your splendid castles | with the stones of our cold empty townships. | In the warm, precious blood of our people | you drowned the freedom of nations. 8

Your gain means our loss, | your fame means the suppression of our name, | your pride is in our stooped heads, | your nightmare is our anger. 12

Envoi

With the rubble of the walls that sheltered our people from earliest times, | you built your mansions, you sleekit stonemasons of guile. | It was over the corpses of our brave, for generations piled up high, | that you made your stately advance to honour and might. 16

*106 *Dleasnas nan Àirdean*

A' bheinn dhorcha fon dìlinn,
   ris na sìontan 'na h-innein,
tha sìor shèideadh ma creachann,
   tha sìor cheathach ma sliosaibh;   4
is doirbh fo na casan
   a h-aisridhean snidheach;
is seasgar ma bonnaibh
   taighean, gortan is liosan.   8

Dheònaich beagan an sàrach
   tric los càch a bhith 'blasad
air an t-sonas chaidh bhuinnig
   ri uchd Chumhachdan 's gaillinn.   12
Sgal na gaoith' air a' mhullach,
   deò cha chluinnear sna srathaibh.
Is e tuairgneadh nan àirdean
   a bheir sàmhchar don ghleannan.   16

A òigridh mo dhùthcha,
   an e ciùine nan rèidhlean,
fois is clos nan gleann ìosal,
   air an dìon on gharbh shèideadh?   20
Biodh bhur ceum air a' mhullach,
   is bhur n-uchd ris na speuran.
Dhuibh sracghaoth nam bidean,
   mun tig sgrios 'na bheum slèibh' oirnn.   24

106 *The Duty of the Heights*

The dark mountain under the downpour, | exposed as an anvil to the tempest, | the wind ever blows about its summit, | the mist ever drifts about its sides; | difficult under the feet | are its dripping paths through the rocks; | [snug 4
and safe] about its base | are houses, corn-plots and gardens. 8

Often a few have assented to trials | so that others should taste | the happiness that was won | in the face of Powers and tempest. | The scream of the wind on the 12
crest; | not a breath is heard on the straths. | It is the buffeting of the heights | that gives tranquillity to the little glen. 16

Youth of my country, | is it to be the [mildness] of the plains, then? | The peace and slumber of the low valleys, | sheltered from the rough blast? | Let your step 20
be on the summit, | and your breast exposed to the sky. | For you the tearing wind of the pinnacles, | lest destruction come on us as a landslide. 24

107   *[Rinn Sibh Cuan …]*

Rinn sibh cuan de dheòir 's de fhuil,
   's a stuadhan tiugha 'ruith 's a' bòcadh.
Feuch a-nis, a làmhan lapach,
   an tèid agaibh air a sheòladh.   4

Bhur beul sìoda 's bhur làmhan mìne
   (is ruadh for n-ìghnean sal na feòlachd)
tha sibh air lobhadh, air lobhadh,
   ge dàicheil othail bhur n-òraid.   8

Thig Saorsa 's Ceartas gu slìogach ungta
   'nan srùileadh crèis' or slugan ròiceil.
Tha iad 'dol fodha sna ceithir àirdean
   an srùileadh àir a' ghaorr a dhòirt sibh.   12

Thèid bhur long spùinnidh o stiùradh.
   Tha 'n taoim air feadh a h-ùrlair lòdte.
I trom le pròis is le plunndrainn,
   's na tuinn a dhùisg sibh ma bòrdaibh.   16

I 'ruith o chuan nan sluagh a reub i,
   gu sgeirean geur nan Stàitean mòra.
Feuch a-nis, a làmhan lapach,
   an tèid agaibh air a steòrnadh.   20

107   *[You Made an Ocean …]*

You made an ocean of tears and blood, | and its viscous waves are rushing and swelling. | See now, hands of failing strength, | just how well you are able to sail it.   4

With your silken mouth and fine delicate hands | (the stain of butchery rusty under your nails), | you are putrefied, putrefied, | however plausible the clamour of your rhetoric.   8

Freedom and Justice come out, sleek and oily, | like some greasy spillage from your gluttonous gullet. | But in the four airts they are floundering | in the slaughter-spill of gore you have caused to flow.   12

Your pirate ship will veer out of control. | Bilge-water runs over her water-logged deck. | Laden down with pride and plunder she wilts, | as the waves you have wakened assault her planks.   16

She flees from the sea of the peoples she ravaged, | onto the sharp skerries of the mighty Powers. | See now, hands of failing strength, | just how well you are able to steer her.   20

*108 An Ceangal

Seadh, chaith mi mo thìom 's mo dhìcheall ri dàin, fhir chòir,
gan snaidheadh 's gan lìomhadh sa bhinn chainnt is àrsaidh glòir,
an Dùn Àd a thug binn, is an Ì a rinn cràbhadh fòil,
a labhair mo shinnsre 's na rìghrean an Sgàin o thòs.   4

Thèid sibh, a dhàin, thèid gu dàna, gun fhiaradh ròid,
ag èigheach 's gach àird rim luchd clàistneachd fìor chiall mo cheòil:
"Troimh cheusadh is sàrach nan Gàidheal tha 'n dian fhuil beò,
is cha trèig iad an làrach gus an smàlar a' ghrian fa-dheòidh."   8

108 Envoi

Yes, I have spent my time [and my greatest energies on poems, dear man], | chipping them and polishing them in the sweet speech of ancient utterance, | that delivered judgement in Dunadd, and that practised quiet piety in Iona, | the speech my forefathers spoke, and the kings in Scone from the beginning.   4

You will go, poems, you will go boldly, not looking aside on your road, | crying to my listeners in all the airts the true meaning of my music: | "Through the crucifixion and trials of the Gaels their fervid blood lives on, | and they will not forsake the field of battle till the sun is blotted out in the end."   8

POEMS 1944–1946

(i)

*109 *Mochtàr is Dùghall*
(Sgeula-dhàn fada neo-chrìochnaichte)

109.1 [FOSGLADH]

Mhochtàir is Dhùghaill, choinnich sibh
an comann buan gun chòmhradh.

B'iad fraighean an taigh chèilidh dhuibh
an cactas ceuste, leònte.

B'i 'n aoigheachd an dèidh furain dhuibh   5
làn beòil den duslach ròsta.

B'i fàilte an ùr chomainn sin
guth obann, cruaidh a' mhòrtair.

Am fear a sgrìobh an dùnadh
le bloighean, bùirich 's ceò dhuibh,   10

Am fear a sgaoil an urchair,
cha bu shuilbhear e no deònach.

[A bhrù

109 *Mokhtâr and Dougall*
[A long unfinished narrative poem]

109.1 [PROLOGUE]

Mokhtâr and Dougall, you have met | in an everlasting fellowship without conversation.

The walls of your gossiping house | were the tortured, wounded cactus.

The hospitality that followed welcome for you | was the fill of your mouth of hot dust.   5

The greeting of your new companionship | was the sudden, hard voice of the mortar.

The man who wrote the closing words of your song | with splinters, roaring and smoke,

The man who fired the shot, | he was no cheerful, eager warrior.   10

A bhrù gu 'chur gu tuireadh
le droch uisge plodach lòintean.

A shùilean dearg is sreamach   15
le cion cadail 's an schnapps a dh'òl e.

Is e a' speuradh is a' mallachadh
an stùir, an teas 's a' chòirneil.

                              *

A bheil fhios ciod e 'n dubh chumhachd
a chuir cruinn sibh air an sgòrr seo?   20

A stiùir thar bheann 's thar chuan sibh,
gur cruadhachadh le dòrainn?

Nur triùir – sibh fhèin rinn bràithreachas
's an làmh a naisg bhur n-eòlas,

A' sèapail is a' màgaran,   25
a' snàgail mar bhèistean feòlachd.

An *Gefreit* a thug am bàs dhuibh,
's a thàrr às gur fàgail còmhla,

Dh'fhalbh e crom is gearanach
fo 'eagal 's luchd a' mhòrtair.   30

Ghlacadh, 's an sgreuch 'na mhuineal,
'na fhear cuthaich air Ceap Bòn e.

His belly driving him to weep | with the bad, tepid water of the flats.
His eyes red and watering | with want of sleep and the schnapps he had drunk.   15
He blaspheming, and cursing | the dust, the heat and the colonel.
                              *
Who knows what black power | brought you together on this pinnacle,   20
Guided you over mountains and oceans, | hardening you with misery?
The three of you – you two who formed your brotherhood, | and the hand that
bound you together in acquaintance,
Sneaking, crawling on all fours, | snaking like beasts of prey.   25
The Gefreiter who gave you your death, | and pulled out, leaving you together,
[He went off, stooping and whimpering | under his fear and the weight of the
mortar.]
He was captured with the scream in his throat, | a madman on Cape Bon.   30

"Der Krieg ist Scheiss! Der Führer, Scheiss!" –
b'e sin an *Sieg Heil* fa-dheòidh aig'.

Ach dh'fhuirich sibh san làrach   35
measg diumàir an debeil chròin seo.

An seo tha 'n "trustar Arabach"
's an "Rùimi rapach" còmhla.

Am b'e sin a' chainnt a bh'agaibh
nuair a thachradh sibh sna ròidean?   40

No 'n do nochd sibh daonnachd chaidreabhach
san aiteal am bu bheò sibh?

Daoine nach gabhadh fionnaireachd
le burnus no dath còta?

Nach coma! Air an leathad seo   45
rinn sibh mu dheireadh còrdadh,

Is chan eil foirfeach no marbat
a thearbas sibh le 'eòlas;

Tàileab, iomàm no ministear
chuireas ioghnadh, crith no bròn oirbh.   50

                              *

Fear-rèite treun is tìoranach
deagh shìbhealtachd na h-Eòrpa!

"Der Krieg ist Scheiss! Der Führer, Scheiss!" – | that was his Sieg Heil in the end.
But you stayed on the battlefield | amongst the jumar of this swarthy jebel.   35
Here are the "lousy Arab" | and the "dirty Roumi" together.
Was that the speech you used | when you used to meet on the highways?   40
Or were you humane and affable | in the glimpse of time you were alive?
Men who would not turn coldly hostile | on account of a burnous or the colour of
a coat?
What does it matter? On this hillside | you agree at last,   45
[And] there is no elder or marabout | who can estrange you with his knowledge;
Taleb, imam, or minister | to fill you with wonder, or trembling or sorrow.   50
                              *
A powerful, tyrannous reconciler | is the goodly civilisation of Europe!

109.2 MOCHTÀR

109.2.1 *Bean Mhochtàir is Mnathan an Dùair*

A h-uile nì an làmh Allah!
Mharbhadh Mochtàr. Cha tig e dhachaigh.

Cluinnibh, a mhnathan uile an dùair!   55
Chruinnich armailtean nan Rùimi
am falachd uachdaran is dùthcha;
thug iad bruidhinn air an fhùdar
sna beanntan sear am fearann Tùnais,
is bha m'fhear fhèin 'na Thiorailliùr ann.   60
Mar a chomharraich Dia 's a rùnaich,
ràinig e 'm bad bu cheann do 'chùrsa,
fòd air an amais tràill is prionnsa.
Athair mo chloinne, dh'fheac e 'ghlùinean,
's chan fhios domh cò a dhùin a shùilean,   65
no cà'n do chàraich iad san ùir e.

Mo bhràithreachan is bràithreachan m'athar,
leughaibh an lorg is siribh adhar
an fhir nach fhac' e is a spad e!
Fallas bhur làmhan air a chraiceann;   70
geiltchrith a ghuaillean for basan!

109.2 MOKHTÂR

109.2.1 *Mokhtâr's Wife and the Women of the Douar*

Everything is in the hand of Allah! | Mokhtâr has been killed. He will not come home.

Hear, all ye women of the douar! | The armies of the Roumis gathered | in 55 the feud of rulers and country; | they made the powder speak out, | among the mountains eastward in the land of Tunis, | and my own man was there, a Tirailleur. | 60 As God had marked it out and planned it, | he reached the spot which was the end of his course, | the turf on which both slave and prince must tread. | The father of my children, he bent his knees, | and I do not know who has closed his eyes, | or 65 where they have laid him in the earth.

My brothers, and the brothers of my father, | read the trail and seek the wind | of the man who never saw him, and yet who killed him. | The sweat of your hands be on his skin; | the terrified trembling of his shoulders be under your palms! | 70

Mo chuimhne! – chan e sin a thachras.
Rinneadh crodh dhinn ri linn m'athar.

Beannachd Allah is A shìth air!
Cha b'e sin an Càifir dìtidh   75
a dhèanadh smugaid air an Fhìrinn,
a dhèanadh mùin air uaigh nan Dìleas.
B'e sin an làmh bha deas gu sìneadh,
's nach druideadh air ocar nan dìblidh,
's nach dèanadh cù òtraich a shlìogadh.   80
Beannachd an Tròcairich 's A shìth air!
Beul nach do bhlais air salchar fìona;
a ghabhadh na h-ùrnaighean gun dìochuimhn',
còig uairean san là gu h-ìosal
ga shleuchdadh, air 'ionnlaid sa mhodh dhìreach.   85
Anam nach fhairich teintean Ìblis,
nach seachnadh dleasnas Creidmhich dhìlis
leis fhèin ri teas nan raointean sgìthe.
Ge b'fhad' o shumanadh 's o innse,
's o ghuth caol binn a' Mhuaidìn e,   90
bheanadh a bhathais gu h-ùmhail strìochdte
do dhuslach pronn nan iomair ìotmhor.
Shloinneadh e gach ainm rìomhach
a bh'aig an Fhàidh, 's gach fàidh san sgrìobhadh,
Maois, Ìbrahìm 's ar Tighearn Ìosa;   95
gidheadh, am fianais aoin a shìolaich

[o Àdhamh

I forget – these things do not happen. I In my father's time we were turned into cattle.

The blessing of Allah and His peace be on him! I Yon was no condemned Kaffir I 75
who would spit upon the Truth, I and piss on the graves of the Faithful. I That was
the hand that was ready to reach out in help, I and that would not close over usury
wrung from the weak, I that would not caress the dunghill dog. I The blessing of the 80
Merciful and His peace be on him! I Mouth that never tasted the filth of wine; I
that would repeat the prayers without forgetfulness, I five times a day in lowly
guise I prostrating himself, purified in the lawful manner. I Soul that will not feel 85
the fires of Iblis; I that would not shun the duty of a faithful Believer, I even alone
by himself in the heat of the weary fields. I Though he was far from summons and
the report of men, I and from the shrill, sweet voice of the Muezzin, I humbly and 90
submissively his forehead would touch I the crumbled dust of the thirsty furrows. I
He would repeat every gorgeous name I that the Prophet ever had, and every
prophet in the holy writing, I Moses, Ibrahim and Our Lord Jesus; I yet, in the 95
presence of any being who sprang I

o Àdhamh, ge sgàrlaid, àrd a chìrein,
chan fhaicte a' cromadh a chinn e,
marsanta, tàileab, càid no sìch e.
A ghruaim no 'ghràin, a thlachd no 'mhìothlachd,   100
shealladh e steach an sùilean rìghrean.

Rinneadh 'ionnlaid, 's cha d'rinn e ùrnaigh:
tharrainn e is cha do thionndaidh.

Tha fùirneis mo chlèibh a' gabhail
airson mo chèile, stèidh mo thaighe,   105
mo chrodh, mo threudan is m'fhear agairt.
Cha sìn a sgàile air an rathad,
a' ghrian a' cromadh 's e 'dol dhachaigh.
'Na thaigh dìochuimhnichear e fhathast
gun tigeadh e tràth-nòin gu baile.   110

A mhnathan an dùair, leughaibh ar faoineas!
Na biodh bhur n-earbsa às an t-saoghal,
's gur cealgach, an-iochdmhor, claon e.
Cha taigh seilbh' e ach taigh aoigheachd.
Seallaibh mun cuairt! Cà bheil bhur daoine?   115

Èighibh is buailibh bhur basan!
Mharbhadh Mochtàr an cèin air 'aineol.
An nì a sgrìobhadh dhà, 's e thachair.

from Adam, however high and scarlet his comb might be, | he was never seen
bending his head, | be it merchant, taleb, caid or sheikh. | Scowls or laughter,   100
pleasure or displeasure, | he would look into the eyes of kings.

His ablutions were performed, yet he performed no prayer. | He set out and did
not turn back.

The furnace of my heart is kindling | for the sake of my husband, stay of my
house, | my flocks, my herds and my pleader. | No more will his shadow lengthen   105
on the road, | as he goes homeward with the declining sun. | In his house it will be
forgotten yet | that he ever came home at evening.   110

Women of the douar, consider the vanity of us! | Put not your trust in the world, |
for it is treacherous, merciless and perverse. | It is no house that we own, but a
guesting house. | Look about ye! Where are your people now?   115

Cry and strike your hands together! | Mokhtâr has been killed far away in a strange
country. | What was written for him has befallen him.

109.2.2 *Ahmad*

Bha bean an taighe den t-seann fhasan,
ach bha do spiorad fhèin na b'fharsaing,
ged bha do làmhan cruaidh, lachdann,
air dhath na h-ùrach, air bheag maise.

Dh'innseadh do sheanair mar thriall 'athair
am feachdan naomhaicht' Abd al-Cadar
(maitheanas Dhè air!). A ghunna fada
tarsainn air diallaid a chapaill;
crios leathann sìod' air lìth na fala
mu 'bhurnus geal ga chumail teannaicht';
dag air an robh an t-òr 'na bhannaibh
a' nochdadh fodha, deas gu tarraing;
a lann Innseanach, 's ainm Allah
gràbhailt' air an sgrìobhadh casdhlùth,
an truaill mhìn den leathar mhaiseach,
is càrnaid Thafilalet mar dhath oirr'.
Air a cheann bha seun nan cailleach,
gu dìon a chuim an tiugh nan cathan
o làmhach luath 's o shàthadh chlaidheamh.
Rola 'na bhroilleach am falach,
air an do sgrìobh an tàileab faclan
an Leabhair Naoimh, is trompa sgap e
àireamhan dìomhar an deagh mhanaidh.

[Maitheanas

109.2.2 *Ahmed*

The woman of the house was of the old style, | but your own spirit was less narrow, | although your hands were hard and dark brown, | the hue of the soil, | and without any beauty.

Your grandfather used to tell how his father rode away | in the sanctified hosts of Abd el-Qader | (God's mercy on him!). His long gun | across the saddle of his mare; | a broad silken girdle the colour of blood | about his white burnous drawing it tight; | a pistol bound with strips of gold | showing from under it, ready to draw; | his Indian blade, with the name of Allah | engraved on it in close twining lettering, | in a fine scabbard of lovely leather, | with the carnation dye of Tafilalet to give it colour. | On his head was the saining of the old women, | to shield his body in the thick of the battle | from swift volleying and the thrust of swords. | Hidden in the breast of his clothing he bore a scroll, | on which the taleb had written words | from the Holy Book, and through them had scattered | mystical numbers of good omen.

Maitheanas Dhè air Abd al-Cadair!
Nuair a bhriseadh cath is cath air,
's a rùnaich an t-Aon làn mhasladh
nan Creidmheach, 's a' Bhratach Uaine allail   145
ga leagadh, ga saltairt is ga sracadh,
's a shìobadh mar dhuslach uaith a smala,
thug Aimìr nan Dìleas thairis,
is thill do shinnseanair slàn dhachaigh,
gun chreuchd, ach reubte 'na anam.   150
Chuir e a ghunna am falach
a-muigh, is thaisg e a chlaidheamh
an cist' a sheòmair fhèin. Mun aisith
riamh ri dùil cha tubhairt e facal.

Lean e fuar, tostach, dùinte,   155
is, air cho mion 's a dhèante sgrùdadh
's a leughte reothadh marbh a ghnùise,
a cheusadh cridhe theth cha rùisgte.
Bhuidhinn e rèim air gus an ùine
san d'fhàisg an tìom an smachd 's an tùr às.   160
Chunnacas e 's a shaibhlean siùbhlach,
a threudan, 's e gun fhois, mar ùigean,
feadh àite teàrnaidh na dùthcha,
air an àrd mhachair nach cunglaich
an radharc, 's a thàirneas toil is sùilean   165
air aghaidh o innis gu innis ùdlaidh

The mercy of God on Abd el-Qader! | When battle upon battle had gone against him, | and the One God willed the complete humiliation | of the Believers, and willed that the renowned Green Banner | should be cast down, trampled under   145
foot and torn; | when his smala was swept away from him like dust, | the Emir of the Faithful gave over, | and your grandfather's father returned home unhurt, | without a wound, but wounded in his soul. | He hid his gun away | outside the   150
house, and laid by his sword | in the kist in his own room. About the warfare | he never spoke a word to any soul.

He went on cold and silent and withdrawn, | and however minutely he was   155
scrutinised, | however closely the dead frost of his face was read, | the crucifixion of his hot heart was not to be laid bare. | He warred it down and mastered it until the season | when Time wrung the mastery and sense out of him. | He was to be   160
seen with his moving granaries, | his flocks, travelling restless, like some gloomy solitary, | wandering through all the camping-grounds of the country, | on the high plateau that does not confine | the sight, but draws both eye and desire | 165
onward from dark remote pasture to pasture |

eadar Batna is Mansùra.
Cha chreidte, is 'fhaicinn bhith measg ùspairt
nan aoghaire, 's an treud ga chunntadh,
gun do reub e riamh bian nan Rùimi.   170

Ach millidh tìom is sìneadh uidhe
am fulangas as buaine, suidhicht',
air 'fhaghart am mìle bròn is tubaist.
Mharcaich an aois e, shrian i 'thuigse,
rinn i 'mhac-meanmna a chuipeadh   175
ga chur air bhall-chrith, is e a' cluinntinn,
ar leis, na mairbh a b'eòl da 'bruidhinn.
Ghearaineadh e a cheann 's a thruimead,
a tholladh 's a chreimeadh le gob cnuimhe.
Dà bhliadhna 'na phàilliun thug e,   180
uair an neul is uair air chuthach,
sa chùil bu duirche dheth 'na shuidhe.
Cha ghluaiseadh e làmh san Iuchar
gu ruagadh uaith nan sgaothan chuileag
bhiodh fad an là a' srannraich uime.   185
Chìte corr uair 'na ghruaidh rudhadh,
is chlisgeadh e le brodadh cuimhne.
Dh'èigheadh e: "Daingneach àrd ar curaidh –
tâh as-sûr! – tha 'm mùr air tuiteam,
mùr Thakideimt!" Is thigeadh gul air,   190
no loireadh e e fhèin san duslach

                                            [a' guidhe

between Batna and Mansoura. | None would have believed, as they saw him so quiet among the bustle | of the shepherds as the flocks were counted, | that he had ever rent the skins of the Roumis.   170

But time and the long onward reaching of the way will wreck | the most everlastingly settled endurance, | tempered in a thousand griefs and misfortunes. | Age rode him as a horseman, bridled his understanding | and gave the whip to his fancies, | setting him trembling as he heard | (it seemed to him) the dead he once 175 knew speaking. | He would complain of his head and its heaviness, | and how the beak of a worm was boring and gnawing at it. | Two years he passed in his tent, | 180 at times in a stupor, at times in a frenzy, | sitting away in the darkest corner of it. | In the Dogdays he would not move a hand | to chase away the swarms of flies | that buzzed about him all day long. | At times a flush would be seen on his cheek, | 185 and he would start as memory stabbed him. | He would cry: "The high stronghold of our warrior – | tâh es-sûr! – the rampart has fallen, | the rampart of Takidemt!" And a fit of weeping would come over him, | or he would roll himself in the dust, | 190

a' guidhe damnadh Còirneil Iussuf,
an Rùimi bhrath a Chreud dà thuras.

Ach nuair a bha e tràighte, breòite,
thaisbein an Tròcaireach A thròcair.   195

Oir, madainn labharghaothach chitheach,
is càch a' dèanamh deas gu imeachd,
a' seinn 's a' teannachadh nan girteag,
air dha bhith cho fad' air iomall
a ghaolaich uile, 'na chùis frionais   200
don chuid gun mhothachadh, gun mhionach,
dh'èalaidh e 'na thost, gun lideadh,
à comann Chloinn' Àdhaimh driopail.
Is e leag Ahmad, 'àirde spioraid.
Nuair as glaine criostal a' chridhe,   205
mar tha e furasta a bhriseadh!

Rinneadh 'ionnlaid, rinneadh èideadh
ann an gile mhìn a lèine,
air an do fhrois iad uisge seunta
tobar Zemzem, on tìr chèin ud   210
a dh'fhògair am Fàidh is a ghèill dha.
Chaidh a ghiùlan air na dèilean
gu mall, mùirneach gus an rèilig
bu cheann-uidhe do luchd a threuda.
Thog an luchd caoinidh an t-èigheach   215

praying for the damnation of Colonel Yussuf, | the [Roumi] who betrayed his creed twice over.

But when he was drained and feeble | the Merciful revealed His mercy.   195

For on a loud, windy, showery morning | when the others were making ready to raise camp, | singing and tightening the girths, | having been so long out on the margin | of his loved ones, a cause of impatience | to those that were insensible 200 and had no bowels of compassion, | he crept away in silence, without a word, | from the bustling fellowship of Adam's Clan. | It was the loftiness of his spirit that brought Ahmed down. | When the crystal of the heart is at its purest, | how easy it 205 is to shatter it!

He was washed, he was arrayed | in the smooth whiteness of his shroud; | and on it they sprinkled blessed water | from the well of Zemzem in that far-off land | 210 which drove out the Prophet, then yielded to him. | He was borne upon the boards | slowly, affectionately, to that graveyard | which was the journey's end for the people of his tribe. | The keeners raised their crying |
                                                                        215

am farsaingeachd na machrach cèire,
is mhùch a' ghailleann, a bu bheus da,
fo chùirtein siùbhlach nan neul e.
Trì chuairt thuit an ùir troimh mheuraibh
an fhir den t-sluagh bu ghile feusag.   220
Thogadh mar chomharra 'na dhèidh sin
an dà chloich fhianais measg an fheuraich;
is dh'fhàgadh 'na laighe leis fhèin e
air a thaobh deas, 's a bhathais chèirgheal
ri àird an ear. Fhuaradh a Lèigh dha.   225

109.2.3 *Òmar*

Sin na chuala thu aig Òmar,
am bithbhriathrach, deasbhriathrach, eòlach
a chuireadh snas is lìth air còmhradh,
a ghlèidheadh fo gheasaibh a ròsgeul
air Deaha 's air Harùn na Còrach   230
an taistealach, ged b'fhaisg a' ghlòmainn.
Ghuidh thu air, is thug e 'n còrr dhuit.

Oir stuigeadh e le teas a nàdair
gu fulang mòr sgìos an fhàsaich;
an òige 's miann an òir ga thàladh   235

[gu sireadh

in the vastness of the dark steppe, | and the storm that roared bass to it drowned | it under the shifting curtain of the clouds. | Three times the earth fell through the fingers | of the man whose beard was whitest among the people. | Afterwards they 220 raised as a sign | his two witness-stones among the grass, | and he was left lying there alone | on his right side, his wax-white forehead | towards the east. His Healer had been found for him.   250

109.2.3 *Omar*

That was what you heard from Omar, | the garrulous, fluent, knowing one, | who could give finish and colour to speech, | and who would keep fast under the spell of his far-fetched yarns | about Djeha and Haroun the Just | the traveller, even 230 though the gloaming was near. | You begged him, and you got the rest from him.

For he was egged on by the heat of his nature | to endure the great weariness of the desert, | youth and the lust of gold wiling him | 235

gu sireadh ioghnaidhean troimh ghàbhadh,
is eòlas air a shlighean cràidhte.

Chreic e a chaoraich air na fèilltean,
is chuir e a bhathar ri chèile –
pasgain shìoda fo obair ghrèise,   240
cotan, bratan ùrlair, lèintean,
soithichean umha, copain, seunan,
sgeanan nan cas snaidhte leugach;
burnuisean Shùsa 's iad cho eutrom
ri lìon an damhain-allaidh ghleusda;   245
fàinneachan adhbrainn 'nan ceudan,
's am pailteas de gach cungaidh sgèimhe,
an heana, an còhl, luibhean is freumhan;
coifidh is mìlseanan gun euradh,
innealan ciùil is cìrean feusaig   250
agus Coràin an dathaibh èibhinn,
le caignidhean is cuairteagan rèidhe
a chuireadh le tlachd air mhisg an lèirsinn.

Le a shreath chàmhal fon luchd ud
thog e 'n àird air mochthrath fionnar,   255
mun do nochd a' ghrian cùl nan tulach
a gharadh nam pàilliuna dubha.
Thuirt e: "An ainm a' Chruithir!"
is rinn e an cùrsa a chumail
air Biosgra, 's e air mhearan subhach   260

to seek out wonders through peril, | and acquaint himself with its tortured pathways.

He sold his sheep at the markets | and put his wares together – | rolls of silk worked with embroidery, | cotton, rugs, shirts, | vessels of brass, cups, amulets; | 240 knives with carved jewel-set hilts; | burnouses from Souse, as light | as the web of the cunning spider; | ankle-rings in their hundreds, | and an abundance of every 245 beautifying preparation, | henna, kohl, herbs and roots; | coffee and sweetmeats without stint; | instruments of music and combs for the beard, | and Corans in 250 joyous colours, | with interlocking letters and smooth whorls | which would inebriate the sight with pleasure.

With his string of camels under that burden | he took the road on a cool early morning, | before the sun showed from behind the knowes | to warm the black 255 tents. | He said "In the name of the Creator!" | and held his course | on Biskra, and he in a delirium of pleasure, | 260

a' tilgeadh os a chionn a mhusgaid
's ga ceapadh, a' gabhail na luinneig:
   Bhith 'dol nad leum air muin cùrsain,
   cù bhàrr èille 'falbh 'na dheann,
   bhith 'g èisteachd gliongartaich nan usgar,   265
   bheir sin a' chnuimh às a' cheann.

B'e fhèin an luinneagach, gòrach,
sgeulachdach, gàireachdach, pògach
air bhoile le fion na h-òige.
Bu cheusadh leis mall imeachd stòlda   270
a' charabhain sin, ach, is dòcha,
nuair a dhìrich e sa ghlòmainn
cas bhealach Sfa, is dhearc e cròn mhuir
na Sahara, 's i aibhiseach dòite
ghrad dh'fhuirich e gun cheòl, gun chòmhradh.   275

Fhuair e fir iùil ann am Biosgra,
eòlach, cinnteach, fir gun ghiorag.

Stiùir an luchd iùil iad gun bhruidhinn
seachad air cnàmhan luchd thurais
's air fuarain mharbha, thachdte, dhruidte   280
air an sèideadh 's air an slugadh.
Choisich iad gun sgeul, gun luinneag
troimhn fhàsach bhalbh far nach cluinnte
ach cagarsaich na gainmhich uidhre
's an siomùm ga cur gu sruthadh –   285

                 [uachdar

throwing his musket into the air | and catching it, while he sang the song: | "To race bounding on a charger, | a hound off the leash streaking away, | to listen to 265 the tinkling of jewels, | these things drive the worm from the head."

'Tis he that was the songful, daft one, | the man for tales and laughter and kisses, | mad with the wine of youth. | He thought the placidly dignified slow pace | of the 270 caravan a torture, but yet, it is likely | when he topped in the gloaming | the steep pass of Sfa, and gazed on the saffron sea | of the Sahara, vast and grimly glooming, | that he quickly fell silent of music and conversation.   275

He got guides in Biskra, | knowing, certain, not men to panic.

Their guides led them with never a word spoken | past the bones of travellers, | and past dead springs, choked, closed up, | drifted over, swallowed. | They walked with 280 neither song nor story | through the dumb wilderness, where was heard only | the whispering of the dun sand | as the simoom set it streaming – | 285

uachdar an fhuinn air snàmh mar uisge.
Lios Allah, gun a seis air luimead,
far an trèig an deargan am fear siubhail!
Neo-chaochlaidheachd na fàire buidhe,
air chrith 's a' dannsadh, do-ruigheachd.   290

Mar nàmhaid nach robh dol às air,
fear dìoghailt nach cuirte bhàrr 'fhalachd,
dh'èirich a' ghrian a h-uile latha.
Nuair sheas i dìreach anns an adhar
aig a h-àirde, fo phreas no carraig   295
cha robh sgàile. Bhrùth a gathan
gach beò bha gluasad air an talamh.
Is nuair a bhiodh an oidhche aca,
an oidhche, 's iad a' buidhinn astair
ri 'fionnarachd, an corp air chrathadh   300
fon aodach bàite le fallas,
bu deoch à fuaran àrd don anam
bhith 'leughadh balbh chuairt nam plainead,
air buidhnean nan reul a bhith 'cur aithne,
mion duslach òrdha air a shadadh   305
trast an speur, is troimhe 'nan lasair
prìomh lòchrain steòrnaidh gach aon rathaid,
ri eadarsholas na tundra failte,
san fhàsach sheasg, air druim na mara –
Veuga, Altàir is an Crann Airein,   310
Orìon a' stailceadh a chasan,

the surface of the land drifting like water. | The Garden of Allah, without its match for bareness, | where the very flea forsakes the traveller! | The unchangingness of the yellow horizon, | quivering and dancing, unattainable.   290

Like an enemy from whom there was no escaping, | an avenger not to be turned aside from his feud, | the sun rose up every day. | When it stood overhead in the air | at its zenith, under bush or rock | there was no shadow. Its rays crushed | 295 every living thing that was moving on the earth. | But when the night was with them, | the night, and they were winning distance | during its coolness, their bodies shaking | under their clothes drowned in sweat, | it was as a drink from a 300 high hill spring to their souls | to be reading the silent wheeling of the planets, | to be making acquaintance with the companies of the stars, | a fine golden dust dashed | across the sky, and through it blazing | the prime guiding lanterns of 305 every road, | be it in the twilight of the barren tundra, | in the [arid] desert, on the ridge of the sea – | Vega, Altair and the Plough, | Orion planting fast his feet, | 310

an Grioglachan a thagh an gabhail
do stiùireadairean luingeas Tharsis,
's o Abhlais do luchd iùil nan gaisgeach.
Bu bhallan ìocshlaint tuil na gealaich 315
a' dòrtadh sìos 'na stuadhan taise;
bu tròcair, bu draoidheachd, bu tatadh,
bu làmh an leighis an dèidh a' chath' i.
Dh'èireadh fonn à tost an tlachda,
is shiùbhladh e an sreath is at leis, 320
cleas buidealaich a' fàs à sradaig;
laoidhean do Rianadair na maidne,
no duain achrannach, dhlùth-chaste
a dh'oibricheadh an cùirt Dhamascais,
dàin an fhìona 's nam ban maiseach: 325
   Nì sinn a phòit 'na neart gun mheasgan,
   's a òl an ceann glan-uisge shneachda;
   is nì sinn ceòl is rainn a phleatadh
   an àras mòrail màrmair dhreachmhoir.
Leis na seann turbain bu sgreat iad, 330
ach leis na giullain blàithean ealaidh.

Chan eil leigheas an àm gorta
ach diasan troma, 's air a' bhochdainn
ach an Sudàn, an tìr san coisinn
burnus dà thràill, mas mìn bog e. 335
B'e sin an ràdh a bh'aig na bodaich

[feadh

the Pleiades that chose their tack | for the steersmen of the ships of [Tarshish], | and for the pilots of the heroes out of Aulis. | A magic vessel of healing was the flooding of the moon, | pouring down in soft waves; | it was mercy, it was enchant- 315 ment, it was a dandling; | it was the hand of healing after battle. | A melody would rise up out of the silence of their contentment, | and travel down the line of the caravan swelling as it went, | like a blaze growing from a spark; | holy hymns to the 320 One who rules the morning, | and intricate, closely-twined poems | that were fashioned at the court of Damascus, | songs of wine and beautiful women: | 325 "We will drain it in its pure strength with no admixture, | and we will drink it mingled with pure snow water; | and we will plait music and verses together | in a lordly dwelling of lovely marble." | To the old turbans they were loathsome, | but to the lads flowers of art. 330

There is no healing in time of hunger | but the heavy ears of corn, and no cure for poverty | but the Sudan, the land where a burnous | will earn two slaves, if it is soft and fine. | That was the saying which the old men had | 335

feadh nan caifidh, 's b'fhìor an gogail.
Fhuair iad maoin an-sin is onair,
is iad ri cunnradh air an socair
aig na daoine dubha, a' tomhas   340
coifidh chùbhraidh, sìoda 's cotain
air mnathan seanga 's gillean toirteil.
An dèidh bheagan làithean fosaidh
ghreas iad treud làn deur is osnaich
troimh cheart làr an fhàsaich dhomhain.   345
An inntinn leagta air na choisneadh,
tràillean is ìobhraidh is mill throma
den òr, air ceistean bìdh is fodair,
air an t-snàth fhada thana thobar
a bu bheatha 's bu dìdean phort dhaibh;   350
bu neòni leò na gearain ghoirte
a dh'èireadh suas ospag air ospaig
o rangaibh brùite a' mhì-fhortain.
Gun truas bheireadh iad gu tost iad
le stràcan slaite is le fochaid,   355
is iad gan iomain air an socair
o mhuin chàmhal gun losgadh coise.
Theich an t-iochd roimh shannt na toice,
is fhreagair iad le cruas is corraich
atach an co-dhaoine bochda;   360
oir bha an cridhe claon air 'fhosgladh
do stuigeadh anspiorad na toile,

through the cafes, and there was truth in their clucking. | They found riches there and honour, | bargaining at their ease | with the black men, measuring out | fragrant 340 coffee, silk and cotton | for slender women and stout lads. | After a few days of quiet and rest, | they urged a flock full of tears and sighing | through the very heart of the deep wilderness. | Their minds taken up with what they had gained, | slaves and 345 ivory and heavy lumps | of gold, with questions of food and fodder, | with the long thin thread of wells | that meant life and haven-sheltering for them, | they made 350 naught of the wounded complaints | that rose up, gust upon gust, | from the crushed ranks of misfortune. | Pitilessly they would bring them to silence | with strokes of the rod and mocking, | driving them on at their ease | from the backs of their camels, 355 without any scorching of foot. | Mercy fled before greed for wealth, | and they answered with hardness and anger | the beseeching of their poor fellow men; | for 360 their hearts, perverted, were opened | to the inciting of the evil spirit of the will, |

is chrann iad air daonnachd an doras.
Ach car mar a rinn iad rinneadh orra.

"Le rùn Allah", orsa Òmar   365
a' cìreadh 'fheusaige le 'mheòirean,
"air cho eagach, creagach, dòite,
sgorrach, clachach 's a bhios còrrbheinn
no sgreagan seasg air machair chòmhnaird,
gheibhear daonnan anail bheò ann,   370
bèistean neimhe ann a chòmhnaidh,
nathraichean, sgoirpeanan 's an còrr dhiubh.
Is ann mar sin don dìthreabh òirtheth.
Tha sùilean ann gu sireadh feòlachd;
tha bilean ann a bhruidhneas fòirneart;   375
tha casan ann gu cur na tòireachd ...

"Latha 's a' ghrian aig a h-àirde,
's an saoghal gu lèir le 'teas gu sgàineadh,
a losgadh air toirt air na tràillean,
mu dheireadh, leigeil dhiubh an tàsain,   380
is sinn gu stad chur air a' mhàrsal,
chunnaic sinn coltas fir air fàire,
dìreach deas oirnn air muin càmhail.
Cha do charaich ceann no làmh dheth,
ach e mar chraobh no carraig àrsaidh   385
anns a' ghainimh air a sàthadh.

                                                            [Stad

and they had barred the door on humanity. | But very much as they had done, others did to them.

"By the purposes of Allah" said Omar, | combing his beard with his fingers, | 365 "however notched, rocky, scorched, | pinnacled and stony a precipitous mountain may be, | or the barren hard ground on a level plain, | living breath is always to be found in it, | venomous beasts dwelling there, | serpents, scorpions and the 370 rest of them. | So it is with the golden-hot desert. | There are eyes in it to seek out slaughter, | there are lips in it to speak of violence, | there are feet in it to come 375 pursuing after ...

"One day when the sun was at its height, | and the whole world ready to split with its heat, | its burning having at last | made the slaves give up their whining, | just 380 when we were on the point of halting the march, | we saw the appearance of a man on the horizon | directly south of us, on a camel. | Neither head nor hand of him moved, | but still he was, like a tree or an ancient rock | thrust in the sand. | 385

Stad sinn shuas air eagal nàimhdean
a theachd a sgapadh oirnn a' ghràisg ud,
is chròth sinn iad an lagan 's geàrd orr'.
Thuirt m'fhear iùil is e a' teàrnadh   390
bhàrr a bheathaich: 'Bhuainn an gàbhadh!'
is à guth ìosal: 'Latha m'àmhghair!
Chìthear fòs, a Thriath, mo chnàmhan
a' gealachadh san dìthreabh ghràineil.
Seall, beachdair Tuargach thall air fàire.'   395
Chuir sinn ar luaidh 's ar fùdar làmh ruinn,
is dh'ullaich sinn ar n-airm gu làmhach,
is ged nach do dh'ith sinn rè an là ud
mu fheasgar bha sinn cheana sàthach.
(Gum mallaich Dia an fheusag bhàn seo,   400
mur b'ann mar sin 's gach car a thàrla.)
A-nis bha ciaradh nan tràth ann,
àm na doille is nan sgàile.

"San oidhche shuidhich sinn an fhaire
ceithir thimcheall an lagain,   405
is cha robh gin nach robh a' caithris,
gun bhiadh, gun deoch, gun fhois, gun chadal,
gun sùil ri grian no madainn fhaicinn,
is gul nan tràill gar cur an laigead,
a' tolladh 's a' treachailt for n-anam.   410

We pulled up for fear of enemies | coming to scatter our slave rabble on us, | and we penned them into a hollow with a guard over them. | Said my guide, as he dismounted | from his beast: 'Far from us be danger!' | and then, in a low voice: 390 'Day of my affliction! | My bones will yet be seen, oh Lord, | whitening in the hateful wilderness. | See yonder a Touareg scout on the horizon.' | We laid our 395 powder and our lead beside us, | and made ready our arms for firing; | and although we did not eat all that day, | at evening we were already replete. | (May God curse this white beard | if it was not thus that it happened in every point.) | 400 And now it was the darkening tide, | time of blindness and of shadow.

"In the night we set the watch | round all four sides of the hollow, | and there was 405 not one that was not waking, | without food or drink or rest or sleep, | without hope of ever seeing sun or morning, | and the weeping of the slaves weakening us, | burrowing and undermining our souls. 410

"Seall domh fear tha beò air thalamh,
is musg 'na dhòrn, no sgiath, no claidheamh,
bhithinn gun smuain, 's mi òg, 'na bhadaibh.
Ach dol a ghleac san dìthreabh aineoil
ri Tuargach, b'e bhith cur a' chatha   415
ri uilebhèist chuain san fhuar aigeann.
Gun spìon Dia an teanga asam
ma tha mi breugach. Cia b'às daibh?
Cò dh'innseas sin duit ach am Maighstir,
no nathair adharcach nan clachan?   420
Thigeadh iad 'nan sgaoth mar phlathadh
às an aon àird is ionad fhalaich
ris na locaist, 's an dà chuid aca
'nam plàigh 's 'nan sgiùrs 's gach àit an laigh iad.
Shèap iad, na mortairean luatha bradach,   425
à saobhadh air choreigin nach fhacas
le sùilean Creidmhich chneasta, m'anam.
Chluinnte feasgar 's an teine 'lasadh
an luchd iùil a' teachd an cagar,
beul ri cluais, air Tamanrassat,   430
Tenesruft, dìthreabhan na Haggar
is Iomuisear. Sàr bhrùchdadh fhacal
a b'euchd leò uile a bhith aca,
ged nach aithnicheadh iad 'nan clabhas

[sruth

"Show me any man living on earth, | with a musket in his fist, or a knife or a sword |
and without a thought I would have been at his throat when I was young. | But to
go and fight in the unkent desert | with a Touareg, that was to give battle | to a 415
monster of the ocean in the cold sea depths. | May God tear out my tongue | if I
lie! Whence did they come? | Who can tell that but the Master, | or the horned
viper of the stones? | They would come in a swarm suddenly | from the same airt 420
and hidden place | as the locusts, and both of them | are a plague and a scourge in
every place they alight. | They sneaked, the swift thieving murderers, | out of some 425
lair or other that has never been seen | by the eye of a decent Believer, my soul.
| At evening when the fire was blazing | the guides used to be heard talking in a
whisper, | mouth close to ear, of Tamanrasset, | Tenezruft, the wastes of the Haggar 430
| and Imusharh. A fine belching of words | which they thought it a remarkable
feat to know, | although in their chatter they could not tell the difference |

sruth seach cinneadh, beinn seach baile.   435
A-nis bha a' chuideachd dhìomhair againn.

"Bu sheachd feàrr leam, a ghrian mo bheatha,
ceud Turcach a dhòmhlachadh a-steach orm
le tartar is raspars mar chleachd iad,
ag èigheach cuid oidhche is dibhearsain   440
dhaibh fhèin, don gillean is don eachaibh;
ged bhiodh e 'teannadh gu feasgar,
na fraighean cho lom ris na leacaibh,
's iad fhèin ri cnàmhan is ri deasbad,
gun bhlas na h-oidhche – fir no beathaich –   445
às an craosaibh gionach, leathann.
B'fheàrr leam sin na aiteal fhaicinn
uam air fàire den luchd chreich' ud.

"Cha robh guth air clos no cadal
fad na h-oidhch' ud gus an latha;   450
chan fhacas oidhche riamh a b'fhaide.

"Oidhche bhiothbhuan san rath dhorcha,
bu dùinte dall a mall uairean gorma.
Bu bhagairt leinn gach cagar 's monmhar
a bh'aig an osaig feadh nan tolman;   455
bu ghuth nàmhaid gach gluasad soirbheis,
's gach ospag ionnsaigh mhèirlich borba.

between stream and tribe, mountain and town. | And now the mysterious band 435
was upon us.

"I would rather seven times, sun of my life, | that a hundred Turks should crowd
in on me | with uproar and overbearing swagger as was their wont, | shouting for
food and lodging and diversion | for themselves, their lads and their horses; | even 440
though it should be drawing on to evening, | the shelves as bare as the flagstones, |
and they snarling and disputing, | not yet [– man or beast –] having put the taste
of the night | out of their gluttonous, wide maws. | I would rather that than see, | 445
even far off on the horizon, a glimpse of those plunderers.

"There was no mention of repose or sleep | all that night till daylight, | and never 450
was seen a night that was longer.

"An eternal night in the moon's last quarter, | shut in and blind were its dragging
blue hours. | A threat we thought every whisper and murmur | that the breeze
made through the dunes; | the voice of an enemy was each stirring of the wind, | 455
and every gust an onset of wild robbers.

"Is beag a b'fheàirrde sinn ar n-èisteachd
is cur ar cluasan gus an deuchainn.
Nuair a b'airgead òr nan reultan,   460
's a ghlas an là am bun nan speuran
'na sholas tiamhaidh, fann, air èiginn
a' taisbeanadh dlùth theachd na grèine,
thug sinn sùil mun cuairt le chèile –
siud againn sealladh truagh ar lèiridh!   465
Air gach làimh dhinn 'nan luchd sèistidh,
feuch, na Tuargaich mar fhad èigh dhuinn,
mar armachd thaibhse no aisling èitigh,
a' gabhail beachd oirnn 's iad 'nan ceudan.

"Gu h-obann, a Dhia, le tuiltean òmair   470
thar an fhàsaich ghlais gan dòrtadh,
leum a' ghrian san speur is dreòs dith;
gach preas is tolman ri 'h-ògleus
a' seasamh a-mach air a leth-òradh
air ghrunnd a sgàile gu riochdail, beòdha.   475
Sheall i dhuinn fìor chruth nam bòcan;
gach aon le 'aodann air a chòmhdach,
brèid uaine gu bàrr a shròine,
cleas ar maighdeann 's ar ban pòsta.
Bu chosmhail iad 'nan uidheam còmhraig   480
ri feachdan àrsaidh Shidi Òcba
nuair mharcaich e 's an Creideamh còmhla,
iuchair gach daingnich 'na thruaill òrdha,

[fear iùil

"We were little the better of our listening | and the putting of our eyes to the test. | When the gold of the stars was silver, | and the day showed pale at the foot 460 of the sky, | a melancholy, feeble light scarce | revealing the close approach of the sun, | we all threw a glance around together – | and yonder was the wretched sight of our misfortune! | On every side of us, as besiegers, | behold the Touaregs within 465 shouting distance of us, | like an army of spectres or a ghastly vision, | watching us in their hundreds.

"Suddenly, oh God, with floods of amber | pouring over the grey wilderness, | the 470 sun leaped into the sky, shedding forth a blaze; | every fold and dune stood out | in its young light, half-gilded, | defined and vivid on the background of its own shadow. | It revealed to us the real appearance of those terrors, | each one with 475 his face covered over, | a green veil to the top of his nose | in the manner of our maidens and married women. | They were similar in their war-gear | to the 480 antique hosts of Sidi Oqba, | when he and the Faith rode together, | the key of every stronghold in his gilded sheath, |

125

fear iùil gach bealaich a lann shròiceach,
o Chairuàn gu ruig am mòrchuan.   485
Bha sleaghan aca bu tana còrrdhias,
sgiathan cruinne, claidhnean mòra,
is bogha aig gach fear den chòmhlan
air fiaradh cùl slinnein mar ri dòrlach.
Chan fhaca sinn aon mhusg 'nan dòidibh,   490
's bha gunnachan is luaidh gun sòradh
againn fhèin; ach thug mi òrdugh
gun teannadh ri làmhach no ri trògbhail.
Bha am fàsach farsaing mun cuairt òirnne,
sinn air ar n-aineol, iad air an eòlas.   495

"Treis duinn ann gun ghuth, gun ghluasad,
crùibte, làn iomagain is uabhais,
mar chrodh casgraidh ann am buaile,
is iadsan 'nan grunnaibh fuaimneach
a' marcachd thall 's a bhos gu luaineach,   500
a' cur an comhairle rin uaislean.

"An-sin a chlisgeadh sguir a' bhruidhinn,
stad an gluasad is sheas iad uile
mar a bh'aca. Sheall mi 's chunnaic
dithist a' teachd à broilleach grunnain,   505
laoch leathann àrd mar ri duinein,
a' dèanamh oirnn gu stàtail, ruighinn.

his rending sword the guide of every pass | from Kairouan to the great ocean. | 485
They had spears with fine tapering points, | round shields and great swords, | and
each man of the company had a bow | aslant behind his shoulder, along with a
quiver. | We did not see one musket in their hands, | and we ourselves had guns 490
and lead without stint, | but I gave the order | not to take to firing or fighting. |
The wide desert was around us, | we in a region we did not know, they in a place
where they were well acquainted.   495

"A while we passed there without speech or movement, | crouching, full of
apprehension and terror, | like cattle for the slaughter in a fold, | while they rode
to and fro in noisy groups, | and strayed hither and thither | taking counsel with 500
their nobles.

"Then, in a clap, their talking ceased, | the movement stopped, and they all stood
fixed | where they were. I looked and saw | two men coming from the breast of a
group, | a tall, broad warrior and a wee mannie, | making towards us at a stately 505
unhurried pace. |

Stad iad suas is iad air ruigsinn
mar dheich troigh dhuinn. Thog an curaidh
a làmh dheas mar chomharra furain,   510
is bheannaich mi fhèin don deamhan fhuilteach.
Shìn e an-sin ri cainnt is glugail
nach dèanadh Creidmheach beò a tuigsinn;
's bu rogha dibhearsain e ri 'chluinntinn,
mur b'e am Bàs a bhith rir n-uilinn   515
a' feitheamh ri brosnachadh on bhus ud.
Lean e a' cluich a làimhe 's uchd air,
's a' phlabartaich 'na sruth 's 'na sriut às;
bu mhanntach, briste, tùchte, tiugh i
mar chàrsan duine, 's a chìoch shlugain   520
air at 's ga thachdadh. Dh'èist mi gu h-umhail,
's cha b'fhada gàire 's cha b'fhada gul uam.
Fad an t-siubhail bha mi 'guidhe:
'A Chruthadair a rinn a chumadh,
's a chuir na th'aige chainnt 'na shlugan,   525
deònaich dhuinne meadhan tuigsinn,
air neo cha slàn a bhios mo mhuineal!'
An-sin mhothaich mi don duinein,
's bha fiamh a' ghàire air an trustar.

"Is roghnaiche beul sìoda na tachdadh,   530
is cumaidh teanga mheala 's masgall
an sgian is gèire o na h-aisnibh.
Fhreagair mi ma-tà ceann a' phaca

[le modh

They stopped short when they had reached | ten paces from us; the warrior raised | his right hand as a sign of greeting, | and I myself greeted the bloody devil. | 510 Then he set to in a gurgling speech | that no Believer living could understand, | and it would have been a choice diversion to listen to it | had not Death been at our elbow | waiting to be urged on by that maw of his. | He went on gesturing with 515 his hand and swelling out his chest, | while his blabbering streamed and poured from him; | it was stammering, broken, stifled and thick | like the hoarseness of a man whose uvula | is swollen and is choking him. | I listened humbly, | and 520 neither laughter nor weeping was very far away from me. | All the time I was praying: | 'Oh Creator, who fashioned him | and who put such speech as he has in his gullet, | grant to us means of understanding, | or else my throat will not be 525 whole and sound!' | Then I noticed the wee mannie, | and there was a smile on the scoundrel's face.

"It is better to have a mouth of silk than to be strangled, | and a tongue of honey 530 and flattery will keep | the sharpest knife away from the ribs. | I answered, then, the leader of the pack |

le modh 's le cuir bhinn shlìogach shnasmhor,
gun fhios am b'fhiach an cur 'nan altaibh.   535
Chuir mi mìlsead is deagh bhlas orr'
le dòchas gun tuigeadh am madadh
a' chiall, gun tuigsinn nam facal.

" 'Fhir uasail a thàinig o chèin oirnn,
is binne do chòmhradh na 'n liùt theudach,   540
mìneachadh mùinte ollamh na h-Èiphit
is duain Andalùis le chèile.
Chan fhios domh, air mo cheann 's air m'fheusaig,
an samhlaich mi do chruth 's do bheusan,
do ghliocas dìomhar domhain is t'euchdan   545
ri Sultan Stambùil nan steud-each,
no ri rìgh Ghranàda rèimeil
air an innsear a liuthad sgeulachd.
Thug do thadhail beannachd Dhè oirnn,
's – cha cheil mi – an dèidh t'fhaicinn 's t'èisteachd,   550
a-chaoidh chan iarr mi feadh nam fèilltean
ach sgeul do bheatha bhith fada èibhinn.
Bu bheairteas leam a bhith nam dhèircein
gad amharc am-feast, a ghnùis na grèine.
Ach seall le truas air t'òglach feumach,   555
is innis a-nis do thoil mhath fhèin da.'
Chuir an sgiùrsair braoisg is drèin air,
an duinein 's e fhèin a' gnùst ri chèile.

with courtesy and musical, sleekit, well-turned phrases, | not knowing whether it
was worth my while to joint them together. | I put sweetness and a savoury taste 535
on them, | hoping that the hound would understand | the sense without under-
standing the words.

" 'Oh noble man that has come from afar to us, | your converse is more melodious
than the stringed lute, | the learned expositions of the sages of Egypt | and the 540
songs of Andalusia all together. | By my head and by my beard, I do not know | if
I am to liken your form and your virtues, | your deep secret wisdom and your
prowess | to the Sultan of Stamboul of the steeds, | or to the King of Granada who 545
reigned so wide, | and of whom are told so many tales. | Your visit has brought the
blessing of God upon us, | and – I will not conceal it – after seeing you and listen-
ing to you, | never more will I seek aught throughout the markets | but news that 550
your life is long and joyous. | And it would be riches to me to be a beggar | and
gaze upon you for ever, oh countenance of the sun. | But look with pity upon your
needy servant, | and tell him now your own good will.' | The gallows-bird put a 555
twisted grimace on him, | while he and the mannie grunted to one another.

"Thionndaidh an duineachan a ghnùis oirnn,
ghreas e a chàmhal na bu dlùithe, 560
bhean e do 'bhathais, rinn e ùmhlachd
is thòisich e – O anabarr ioghnaidh! –
an Arabais cho taghte cùirteil
's a chluinnear am Bàrdo rìoghail Thùnais:
'Cha ruig thu leas a bhith cùinneadh 565
nam briathar òir mar ghibht don bhrùid seo.
Cha dèan cainnt a chraos a dhùnadh,
ach a lìonadh leis na spùinn e,
's gur mèirleach air rathaidean na dùthch' e,
a nì an deòraidh fhèin a rùsgadh. 570
Air sgàth aghaidh Allah, na dùisg e.
Bi iriseal, 's na tairg dha dùlan,
is gheibh sibh bhur beatha leis on ùraisg,
ged sgobadh e uaibh cosnadh bhur cunnraidh.
Fichead bliadhn' air ais, mo shùilean, 575
rinn e mo charabhan a spùinneadh,
is, leis gun robh mi dreachmhor lùthmhor,
rinn e ciomach is tràill gun diù dhiom.

"'Cnàmhan mo chompanaich, a thùirse,
thog gaoth nan dìthreabh 's i sìor smùidrich 580
gainmhe mìne tòrr is dùn orr'.
Leugh mi mo ghliocas, theann mi 's dh'ionnsaich
an donnalaich cainnt a th'aig na brùidean;
is tha mi 'n-diugh mar chomhairleach cùirte

['s mar

"The mannikin turned his face to us, | nudged his camel closer, | touched his 560 forehead, made obeisance | and began – oh wonder of wonders! – | in Arabic as choice and courtly | as is to be heard in the royal Bardo of Tunis: | 'It does not profit you to coin | words of gold as a gift for this brute. | Speech will not close his 565 maw, | but only its fill of what he has plundered, | for he is a robber of the highways of this region | who will strip even the pilgrim bare. | For the sake of Allah's 570 countenance, do not rouse him. | Be humble and offer him no defiance, | and you will escape with your life from the monster, | although he should snatch from you the winnings of your trading. | Twenty years ago, my eyes, | he plundered my 575 caravan, | and, as I was handsome and strong, | he made me a captive and a slave of no account.

"'My companions' bones, oh grief! – | the wind of the wastes endlessly smoking | 580 with fine sand has raised a heap and a mound upon them. | I studied my wisest course, set to and learned | the yowling speech of the brutes, | and this day I am court counsellor |

's mar chompanach creiche aig a' chù sin. 585
Their e rium: "Is tu a thùras
gach car glioc 's gach annas ùr dhuinn.
Is tu mo chasan leis an siùbhlainn,
is tu mo làmhan 's mo sgiathan cliùiteach
gam thoirt air ite às mo chrùban." 590
Fhuair mi le sin droch inbh' a' chùirteir,
's bu phrìosanaich riamh anns gach cùirt iad.
An e dol às gun chead bu rùn domh?
Chan fhad' a shìninn riamh an cùrs' ud,
oir bhiodh am fàsach marbh ga stiùradh, 595
a' brath mo shlighe 's ga thoirt gam ionnsaigh.
Ghoireadh a' ghaoth ris: "Tionndaidh! Tionndaidh!
Ghabh e mar sin", 's gach bruan ùrach
's gach clach a dh'fhairicheadh trom mo chùrsain:
"Tha e 'n-seo, an-seo, a dhiùlnaich!" 600
Ya Rabbi, Rabbi! Fèilltean Tùnais,
an caladh, na sràidean sgàile, an lùchairt,
's an t-iomlan fionnar, sneachdgheal, ùrgheal –
gu bràth chan fhosgail mo dhà shùil air.
Ach seall a-nis. Tha ceathach mùgach 605
a' ciaradh aogas grànd' an ùmaidh.
Is leòir dhuinn na thuirt mi, a rùnaich;
ach fhuair mi 'n t-òrdan mar ri bùitich
innse dhuit gu bheil an cù sin
air mhiann ruamhair is rùraich 610

and reiving companion of that dog. | He says to me: "It is you that devise | each 585
wise plan and fresh novelty for us. | You are my feet for me to travel, | you are my
hands and my famed wings | bearing me up in flight out of my crouching." | And 590
so I have the wretched rank of a courtier, | and they have ever been prisoners in
every court. | And should my intent be to escape without his leave, | I would
never stretch that course very far, | for the inanimate desert would be guiding
him, | betraying my path and bringing him towards me. | The wind would cry to 595
him: "Turn! Turn! | He went yon way"; and each particle of earth | and every stone
that felt the weight of my charger would shout: | "He is here, here, warrior!" | Ya Rabbi 600
Rabbi! The markets of Tunis, | the harbour, the shadowy streets, the palace, |
and all of it cool, snow-white, fresh-white – | never will my two eyes open on it
again. | But see now, a surly mist | is darkening the ugly face of the boor. | What I 605
have said suffices us, dear man; | but I have had the command, along with threats,
| to tell you that the dog | desires to delve and rummage | 610

am measg do bhathair. Sìon as fiù leis
bidh aige mar chomharra do dheagh dhùrachd.'

"Ged bha an cridh' annam is smùid às
thuirt mi – 's mi dèanamh mìn mo ghnùise –
'Air mo cheann is air mo shùilean'.   615
Thill an duinein le coltas sunndach
a ràdh gum b'onair leam mo spùinneadh.
Thionndaidh mac Ìblis a chùl ruinn,
thog e 'làmh dheas, 's a Dhia an ùpraid!

"Ri bhith 'bruidhinn an-diugh fhèin air,   620
thig brat fala air mo lèirsinn.
Gum buidhich Allah gnùis an treubh ud!
Cha robh faolchu tana, feumach,
dam bu ghreim 's bu deoch an eucoir,
nach robh 'na fhicheadan 's 'na cheudan   625
an sàs nar seilbh, is iad a' speuradh,
a' tarraing, ag utadh 's a' malairt spèicean.
Gach pasgan againne, chaidh 'fheuchainn
's a shracadh sìos às a chèile.
Rinn iad na tràillean fhèin a dheuchainn,   630
gam brodadh 's gan stobadh len dubh mheuraibh.
Fad an latha lean na bèistean,
is mi gan amharc à geimhlibh m'èiginn,
fiamh a' ghàire air mo dheudach.

[A mholadh

amongst your wares. Everything he thinks of worth | will be his, as a sign of your
good will.'

"Although the heart within me was smoking, | I said, making my countenance
smooth: | 'On my head and on my eyes'. | The mannie returned cheerfully | to say   615
that I held it an honour to be plundered. | The son of Iblis turned his back on us, |
and raised his right hand – oh God, the uproar!

"When I speak of it this very day | a mantle of blood comes over my sight. | May   620
God turn yellow the faces of that tribe! | There was not a thin, needy wolf | to
whom wrongdoing was food and drink, | that was not in his scores and hundreds | 625
among our possessions, blaspheming, | tugging, jostling and exchanging blows. |
Every bundle we had was tried, | rent and torn asunder. | Even the slaves them-
selves were tested | and they prodded them and jabbed them with their black   630
fingers. | All day long the monsters continued, | and I watched them out of the
fetters of my necessity, | baring my teeth in a smile.

"A mholadh sin do Thriath nan Saoghal,   635
an Tròcaireach, Truacantach, an t-Aon Dia,
Maighstir na Camhanaich, a shaor sinn
is a chuir nam cheann an smaoin ud.

"Anns gach conaltradh mun ghealbhan,
fhuair na Tuargaich an t-ainm sin,   640
bhith beò gun sògh air nòs nan ainmhidh,
beatha chaol air fodar garbh ac'
air meas buidhe nan craobh pailme,
is air bainne an gobhar anfhann
a dh'ionailtreadh measg chlach is gainmhe.   645
Dheasaich mi, ma-tà, is thairg mi
tì meannta milis don mhèirleach gharg ud,
dh'fheuch an tigeadh e o 'aintheas
le tlachd, 's an callachadh a bhalg e.
Bhlais e air, a Chruithir m'anma,   650
sgob e às e an aon bhalgam,
is shìn e air a ghlugail bhalbhain.

"'Thuirt e,' ors' an duinein sgeigeil,
'"Is math an gobhar a shil a leithid,
ge b'e càite no cò leis e"   655
's da-rìribh sin na tha e 'creidsinn.'
'A ghrian an fhàsaich,' rinn mi freagairt
'cha ghobhar dubh no bàn ga leigeil
a rinn an deoch, ach luibhean seacte

"Praise be for it to the Lord of all the Worlds, | the Merciful, the Compassionate, 635
the One God; | the Master of the Dawn, who saved us, | and who put in my head
the thought.

"In every conversation around the fire | the Touaregs had got the name | of living 640
without any luxury, after the manner of animals, | having a lean life on rough
fodder, | on the yellow fruit of the palm trees, | and the milk of their weakly
goats | that browsed through stones and sand. | I made ready, therefore, and 645
offered | sweet mint tea to the wild robber, | to see if pleasure would make him
give up his fury, | and if his belly would tame him. | He tasted it, oh Creator of my
soul, | and drained it in one mouthful; | then started his dumbie's mouthings.   650

"'He said', said the mocking mannie, | '"Good is the goat that gave such milk, |
wherever it might be and whoever might own it" – | and in truth that is what he 655
believes.' | 'Sun of the desert', I answered, | 'it was no goat, black or white, | that
made the drink on being milked, but dried herbs |

an ceann uisge, is fodha teine.   660
Mas toigh led chridhe leòmhain, bheir mi
am pailteas duit den luibh, is fleasgach
a thàirneas gu mion-eòlach ceart i,
air mhodh gum bi i daonnan deas duit
nuair as trom an là 's a theas ort.'   665

"An dèidh ròlais nach do thuig sinn:
'Their grian an fhàsaich', ors' an duinein
'gur fiach le 'chridhe àrd na chuir thu
'na thairgse a ghabhail; is, tuilleadh,
an èirig do dhùrachd is an urraim   670
an còrr ded ghibhtean thèid a liubhairt
dhuit mar thà e, is t'òr-sa cuideachd.
(Dh'fhàilnicheadh ar beathaichean fo 'chudthrom.)
An fheadh 's a tha e a' casg a chuideachd
's gan toirt gu 'shàil, gun amharc umad   675
bi 'falbh gud bhathar is cuir cruinn e,
beannaich Dia is lean air t'uidhe.
Ma chìthear an-seo a-rìst do bhuidheann,
gheibh i an aon rùsgadh dunach.
Soraidh leat! Is ann duit as buidhe,   680
thusa tha 'falbh nuair tha mi 'fuireach.'
Rug mi fhèin air làimh an duinein,
sheachain mi 'shùilean 's iad a' sruthadh.
Thionndaidh e is lean e 'n curaidh,

[a bha

in water with a fire underneath. | If it pleases your lion heart I will give | you abun- 660
dance of the herb, and a youth | who will mask it cunningly and rightly, | so that it
will always be ready for you | when the day and its heat are heavy upon you.'   665

"After some vapouring we did not understand – | 'The sun of the desert says', said
the mannie, | 'that his lofty heart deigns | to accept what you have offered, and,
furthermore, | to recompense your good will and the honour, | what remains of 670
your gifts will be restored | to you as it stands, and your gold also. | (Our beasts
would fail under its weight.) | While he is restraining his company | and bringing
them to heel, without looking about you, | go to your wares and gather them 675
together, | bless God and continue your journey. | If your company is seen here
again | it will get the same disastrous stripping. | Farewell, fortunate that you are, | 680
you who are going, while I am biding.' | I took the mannie by the hand, | but avoided
his eyes, for they were wet with tears. | He turned away and followed the warrior, |

a bha 'saodach pac a chuilean   685
le crann a shleagha 's roinn a ghutha.

"Dh'ullaicheadh an-sin ar triall leinn.
Chuir sinn cruinn na bh'ann de iarmad,
tràillean is bathar. Dh'fhan mun trian deth.

"Làn èibhneis – ar ceann a' snàmh leis   690
's ar cridhe a' falbh air sgiathan àrda –
thug sinn ar cùl ris a' ghràisg ud.
Bu teàrnadh gach dìreadh leinn gam fàgail."

                              *

Is tric a lean thu snàth a ròsgeul,
snàth fada mìn ga chur fod chòir leis;   695
snàth sìoda a shnìomhadh e le 'chòmhradh,
dearg na fala is buidhe an òir ann,
is tu nad shuidhe ri uilinn Òmair
fo sgàil' an dorais, a' mealtainn còmhla
na h-oiteig ag osnaich trast an còmhnard.   700
Ach air na ghabh sibh asta 'shòlas,
le t'athair caomh, le aon mhac Òmair,
b'fhaoineas peacach iad 's bu ròlais.

who was herding his pack of whelps | with the shaft of his spear and the edge of 685
his voice.

"Then we prepared our departure, | and gathered what remnants were left | of
slaves and goods. About a third remained.

"Full of joy – our heads swimming with it, | and our hearts away on lofty wings 690
– | we turned our back on yon rabble. | Every ascent was a descent to us as we left
them."
                              *

Often you followed the thread of his romances. | A long, fine thread that he
unwound before you, | a silken thread of speech that he twined | with the yellow 695
of gold and the red of blood in it, | while you sat by Omar's elbow | under the
shadow of the door, and you enjoyed together | the breeze sighing over the plain. | 700
But for all the pleasure that you had from them, | in the eyes of your dear father,
Omar's only son, | they were sinful vanity and vapouring.

109.2.4 *Obàïd*

An nead na h-iolaire ga àrach,
air a' bhearradh ghuanach, ghàbhaidh,   705
chan fhaighear dreathan-donn nan àilean.
Chan altraim eilid luath an fhàsaich
mac a thionndaidhear le gàradh,
sliochd a ghlèidhear ann am bàthaich.
Cha ghin measan a' chomhairt dhàna   710
gadhar dan rèidhlean sgòrr is sgàirneach,
abhag bheir aghaidh don ghille Mhàirtinn.
Feuch an dèan sibh druid den steàrnal;
feuch an claon sibh dualchas nàdair.
Chan ann mar sin a bhios Clann Àdhaimh.   715
Cha luaidh iad san aon seann chàmas;
cha dealbhar iad air chumadh gnàthach.
Is tric a ghin fìor ùmhlachd àrdan,
's a rugadh suarachan am pàileas;
's cha d'fhuaras riamh air meud an àireimh,   720
draoidhean, fiosaichean is fàidhean,
o àm rìoghachdan Iuphràtais,
beul a rachadh dhiubh an ràthan
air leanaban, mun tigeadh fàs da,
gun fheitheamh glic ri binn a làithean.   725
Cha b'ionnan Òmar is am pàisde
ris an d'rinn e uiread fàilte,
ga phògadh 's e air uchd a mhàthar.

["Ciod e

109.2.4 *Obayd*

In the nest of the eagle, | aloft on the dizzy, perilous precipice, | you do not find ₇₀₅
the meadow wren being reared. | The swift hind of the wilderness will not mother |
a son who would be turned by a dyke, | offspring who could be kept in a byre. |
The messan of the bold barking will beget | no hound to which rock pinnacles and ₇₁₀
tumbled boulders are level ground, | no terrier which will defy the fox. | See if
you can make a starling of the tern; | see if you can divert the hereditary character
given by Nature. | But not so with Adam's Children. | They are no lead in the one, ₇₁₅
same old mould; | they are not formed after a customary pattern. | Often has true
humility begotten pride, | and often has a worthless being been born in a palace. |
And never yet, for all their numbers, | druids, soothsayers and prophets, | never ₇₂₀
from the time of the kingdoms of the Euphrates, | has one been found who would
go surety | [on a little child before it grew, | without wisely waiting for the judge-
ment of its days. | Very dissimilar were Omar and the child | whom he welcomed ₇₂₅
with so much fuss, | kissing it as it clung to its mother's breast.]

"Ciod e an duine?" orsa Pìondar.
"Ciod e nach gabh e bhith 'na thìoman?"   730
Cò leis an dàna roimh-innse
cur a shruthan, at a shìontan,
tlàths is grian a fhèathan tìorail?
Cà bheil mairnealaich a shìde?

Cha sàsaichear an cridhe 's 'ionndrain,   735
tagairt na h-inntinn 's a geur sgrùdadh
le fios, le fianas radharc a dhùsgaidh,
's gach fàire 'na cloich tharraing ùir dha.

Tha marcach ann a chuireas spuir ris,
neo-fhaicsinneach ann fhèin ga chuipeadh;   740
tha sealgair ann fhèin ga stuigeadh,
's e fhèin a mhìolchu fhèin. Is uime
an iall a shnaidhmeadh dha le 'Chruithear.
Fiadh an spioraid ga shìor ruith leis;
corr aiteal clis, cha mhò a chuid dheth,   745
a dh'aindeoin ruaig na h-ionndrain tuislich.

Mhochtàir, am bothan bochd do chinnidh
chuala neach o ghuth a spioraid
ràdh a theireadh ris a' chridhe
    eunan luaineach 'na chiomach,   750
    air a chunglachadh an ciste;

"What is man?" said Pindar. | "What can he not be in his times?" | Who is bold 730
enough to foretell | the set of his tides, the swelling of his gales, | the pleasant
sunshine of his kindly calms? | Where is the weather prophet of his weather?

The heart and its longing will not be satisfied | nor the case-pleading of the 735
intellect and its keen scrutiny, | by the knowledge and the witness borne by his
waking sight. | Every horizon is a new lodestone to draw him.

There is a rider in him who sets spurs to him, | invisible within him, whipping him
on; | there is a hunter within him who eggs him onward, | and he himself is his 740
own hound. About him | is the leash which his Creator knotted for him. | The
deer of the spirit is for ever coursed by him; | a glimpse that goes in a flash, seen
from time to time, he is fated to have no more than that of it, | in spite of the 745
pursuit made by stumbling desire.

Mokhtâr, in some poor hut of your race, | a man heard from the voice of his spirit |
a saying that spoke this way of the heart: | "a wandering bird made captive | and 750
penned in a kist; |

gu àird an ear thèid e 'sireadh,
gu àird an iar bheir e sitheadh,
's a-chaoidh chan fhaigh e mach air ite.
Bha 'n t-eunan sin an cliabh na dithist   755
a dh'altraim thu le seirc 's le gliocas.

Bu draoidh do Òmar oir an fhàsaich,
'na stuadhan òir air ghrunnd na fàire,
gaoth gun neòil mar anail àmhainn,
an dipeardan ri dannsa bàinidh;   760
gach tìr nach b'eòl da, treubh is cànain,
na margaidhean, na tùir, na sràidean,
sgreagan nam bealach, bùrn nan oàsais,
's am bàs 's an cunnart orra 'nan geàrdaibh.

T'athair Obàïd, 'athair-san Òmar,   765
's gach fear aca 'na chuan eòlais
le gnè an t-sireadair 'na dreòs ann;
b'ionnan an stuigeadh a bha fòpa,
ach cha b'ionnan fiadh an tòireachd.
Mharcaich Òmar cnoc is còmhnard;   770
b'fhalbhanach 'inbhe agus 'òige.
Dh'fhan Obàïd 'na shuidhe stòlda
– ceann crom 'na thost – ag èisteachd còisir
a smaointean fhèin, an seinn 's an còmhradh.

[Geasan

eastward it goes seeking, | westwards it goes darting, | but it will never win out on the wing." | That bird was in the breast of the two | who brought you up with 755 affection and wisdom.

Omar's enchanter was the rim of the desert, | running in waves of gold on the background of the horizon, | a cloudless wind like the breath from a furnace, | the mad dancing of the heat tremors; | all the lands that he did not know, the tribes 760 and their tongues, | the markets, the towers, the streets; | the rocky, stony ground of the passes, the water of the oases, | and death and danger as guards standing over them.

[Your father Obayd, his father Omar, | each one of them an ocean of knowledge | 765 set ablaze by the seeker's temperament; | the same spur prodded them both, | but quite different was the deer each man pursued.] | Omar rode hill and plain; | ever 770 on the way were his youth and his manhood. | Obayd stayed sitting quietly | – a head bent in silence – listening to the chorus | of his own thoughts, their singing and their talk.

Geasan saoghalta cha do thàlaidh 775
'inntinn no 'shùilean riamh len àilleachd,
ach fàire a b'fhaide uaith 's a b'àirde
's a b'fhìrinniche na gach fàire;
fàire gun mhuir-làn gun tràghadh,
gun neul, gun ghrian, gun fhèath, gun ànradh, 780
gun sìor chuairt oidhcheannan is làithean,
taobh thall de chrìochan rìoghachd Nàdair.
Doimhne na Cruitheachd is a h-Àirdead;
am Prìomh Adhbhar a thùr 's a ghràbhail
gach dùl ann eadar bhuan is bhàsmhor; 785
a chuir air ghluasad le 'làimh ghràdhmhor
na plaineidean 's na reultan àrda,
's a dh'fhadaidh leus na beatha blàithe;
Tobar a' Bhith, Àithne nan àithntean,
an Fhìrinn far am foirfe làn i, 790
b'e sin fiadh a sheilge dàna.
B'e sin a shealg, 's a dhùil ri teàrnadh
seallaidh, mar aiteal a' Bhàird Shlàbhaich
    nuair a bheanas Muire Màthair,
    sa chamhanaich ghil òig, le fàitheam 795
    a màntail ris an ùr fheur bhàite
a' foillseachadh car priobaidh Pàrras.

The world's enchantments did not lure | his mind or his eyes with their beauty, | 775 but a horizon that was farther from him, and higher | and truer than all the horizons that are; | a horizon where there is neither full tide nor ebb, | cloud nor sun, calm nor tempest, | a horizon that does not know the eternal cycle of nights 780 and days, | beyond the bounds of Nature's kingdom. | The depths of Creation and its heights, | the Prime Cause that conceived and formed | every created thing that is, be it everlasting or mortal; | that set in motion with its loving hand | the 785 planets and the lofty stars, | and that kindled the flame of warm life; | the Well from which flows all Being, the Commandment from which arose all commandments, | Truth where it is perfect and whole, | such was the deer of his bold 790 hunting. | Such was his hunting, and his hope was ever for the descent | of some vision like the moment's glimpse of the Slav poet: | "when Mother Mary, | in the white young morning, brushes | the fresh, drenched grass with the hem of her 795 mantle", | revealing Paradise for an instant.

B'i earail Òmair dhuit, 's tu 'd bhalach:
"Guidheam ortsa, air cheann t'athar,
meal an saoghal 's na toill masladh.   800
Biodh làmh is cridhe fosgailt' agad;
biodh misneach agus cruadal annad;
thoir uait an nàimhdeas is an caidreabh.
Brath an aoigh is brath an t-salainn –
is miosa fear mosach agus sgraing air,   805
's gur fial Cruthadair nan anam,
's le fialachd shèid e 'anail annainn."

Shèideadh Obàïd ort à àird eile,
gad chur air ghabhail ùir le 'earail.

"Gabh ealla ris an t-saoghal mhosach.   810
Chan eil 'na bhòidhchead is 'na shodal
ach gile oillteil duine lobhair.
A bheairteas uile, ciod e ach closach?
A luchd sanntachaidh, is coin iad.

"Ma tha do thìth gu fìor air gràsaibh,   815
ionnsaich irisleachd, trèig t'àrdan.
Chan uisgich uillt na raointean àrda.

         ["Na sàsaicheadh

This was Omar's advice to you when you were a boy: | "I pray you, by your father's head, | enjoy the world and earn no disgrace. | Let your heart and hand   800 be open; | let there be spirit and hardiness in you; | give freely in enmity and fellowship. | Betrayal of a guest, betrayal of the salt – | still worse is a mean man with an ill-tempered look, | for the Creator of souls is generous, | and in   805 generosity he breathed his breath into us."

Obayd would blow upon you out of another airt, | setting you on a fresh course with his counsel.

"Watch apart, and take nothing to do with the vile world. | Its beauty and flattery | 810 are but the horrible whiteness of a leprous man. | All its wealth, what is it but carrion? | Those who are greedy for it are dogs.

"If you truly desire grace, | learn humility, forsake your pride. | Streams do not   815 water lofty fields.

"Na sàsaicheadh deagh ìota t'anma
geàrr thomhas eòlach nan nithean talmhaidh,
is dealan truagh gach nì a dh'fhalbhas.   820

"Chan eil àite do thlachd
    eadar nèamh is talamh dhuinne.
Ciamar a thèid gràinein às
    eadar dhà chloich bhreith gun bhruthadh?

"Dèan rud coibhneil 's na iarr ìocadh,   825
comain, 's caith uait i san Tìgris;
aisigidh Dia dhuit i san dìthreabh.

"Is gaoth an spiorad. Is sruth sìobain
an saoghal, is toiseach is crìoch ann
a' marcachd a chèile gu dìlinn;   830
cnàmhadh às is teachd gu ìre;
fàs, gucag, blàithean, meas is mìlsead
's an duilleag dhonn air làr a' crìonadh.
Gidheadh, tha nì ann a tha cinnteach,
a sheasas fìor ann fhèin gu sìorraidh.   835
Sir an t-eun seunta sin led lìontaibh."

B'e sin a chomhairle dhuit, a b'àirde
is a bu dorra na tuigse pàiste,
is nach do thuig thu gus am bu bhàs da.

"Let not the good thirst of your soul be quenched | by the brief, accustomed measure of earthly things, | or by the piteous lightning-flash of that which passes away."   820

"There is no place for pleasure | between heaven and earth for us. | How will grains issue | from two grinding-stones that do not crush?

"Act with kindness and demand no reward; | any indebtedness you incur, cast 825 from you into the Tigris; | God will restore it to you in the waste lands.

"A wind is the spirit. A torrent of spindrift | the world, in which beginning and end | forever ride on each other; | corrosion to nothing and coming to fruition; | 830 growth, bud, blossoms, fruit and sweetness, | and the brown leaf withering on the ground. | But there is one thing which is constant, | and stands in its own truth for ever. | Seek that enchanted bird with your nets."   835

Such was his advice to you, too lofty | and difficult for a child's understanding, | and which you did not understand till he had died.

Bu toigh le Òmar spòrs is aighear,   840
is toirm nan ceàrrach anns a' Chaifidh
'nan suidh' air bratan ùrlair alfa
a' cluich air dìsnean 's air na cairtean;
a' giorrachadh nan oidhche fada
is eallach teth nan latha lasrach   845
le toimhseachain is sgeulachd Antair.
Bhiodh an tambùr 's a' ghàita aca,
cofaidh na h-Iemen, seinn is aiteas.

Sin far an robh an dòmhlan aobhach,
nach leigeadh durc 'nan còir no daormann –   850
clàr feòirne, còmhradh, feadain chaola,
uain air biorain is feòil gu saor ann,
an deòiridh 's an dèircein a' glaodhach:
"Rudeigin air ghaol Dè, a dhaoine!"
's an sgeulaiche a b'fheàrr 's a b'aosta   855
'na thost, nuair thogadh Òmar gaolach
a ghuth an tiugh a' chòmhlain aotroim.
Ach bhiodh a mhac ri làithean maotha
a òige fhèin a' tighinn daonnan
air fàidhean is air nithean naomha,   860
a' dèanamh tarcais air an t-saoghal,
air foill na beatha is a faoineas.

["An òtrach

Omar enjoyed fun and high spirits, | and the din of the gamblers in the café | as 840
they sat on their alfalfa rugs | playing chess and cards; | shortening the long nights |
and easing the hot burden of scorching days | with riddles and the tale of Antar. | 845
As the tambur and gaïta played, | they would drink coffee from Yemen, | they
would sing and be merry.

There one would find the cheerful throng, | that admitted no oafs or churls into
their midst – | chess-board, banter, slender chanters, | lambs on spits and meat 850
free for the having, | the beggar and the vagrant calling out: | "Something for the
love of God, good people!", | and the best and most venerable storyteller | falling 855
silent when dear Omar would raise | his voice in the thick of the light-hearted
group. | His son, however, in the tender days | of his own youth would always
bring the talk round | to prophets and matters spiritual, | expressing contempt for 860
the world, | for life's deceitfulness and its vanity.

"An òtrach gu lèir an domhan?"
orsa Òmar. "Is reòthadh t'fhoghlam.
Smaointean buidhe mar dhuilleach foghair,   865
nach eil san t-saoghal no sa cholainn
ach prìosan bruid' is cuibhreach trom dhuinn.

"Ged ràinig mi air radharc ceòthar
is anail gheàrr na h-aoise breòite,
air tuisleachadh 's air teàrnadh glòmainn;   870
ged thàinig orm an aimsir leòinte
bheir lùth gu sèapail [den] mhòrchuid
a dhìth fuath, gràidh, eagail, dòchais,
tha cridhe sgàrlaid blàth na h-òige
nam chom, nam smaointean is nam chòmhradh.   875

"Cluinnibh, fhearaibh, m'ògmhac naomha!
Èistibh a bhreith 's a bheachdan aosta.
Chan eil a bheatha measg nan daoine,
chan eil a shealladh air an t-saoghal;
is fad' o àit a shuidhe 'smaointean,   880
cha cheann uidhe sliabh no raon daibh."

"Ge òg mi an làthair bhur n-aoise,"
ors' Obàïd gu ciùin, "chan aom mi
le fanaid, no le buaireadh aoibhneis
na tha a-bhos 'na shruth a' caochladh   885

"Is the world nothing but a dungheap?" | asked Omar. "Your teaching is a chilling frost. | Yellow as autumn foliage, these thoughts | that the world and the 865 body | are but a prison of captivity and a heavy chain holding us down.

"Though I have now reached frail old age | with its clouded vision and shortness of breath, | though my step falters and I am in the gloaming of my days; | although 870 that wounded time has come upon me | that deprives most people of their vigour, | empty of hate, love, fear, or desire, | the warm scarlet heart of youth | is in my breast yet, in my thoughts and in my talk. 875

"Hear, men, my saintly young son! | Listen to his judgement and his elderly opinions. | His life is not among the people, | his sight is not set on the world; | far are his thoughts from where he sits, | and their journey's end is neither hill nor 880 plain."

"Though I may be young before your seniority," | said Obayd gently, "I will not give in | to derision, or to the lure of gladness | offered by this world like a passing stream, | 885

gu meallta diombuan, a' tighinn le faoilte
's a' falbh gar n-antoil 'na chùis chaoinidh.
Tha nì nach ceannsaich an t-Aog e:
an t-anam buan, is cleiteag aotrom
den t-sneachd a dh'iomaineas a' ghaoth e,   890
ach bheir a chùrsain leuman saora
gu iomall thall nan grian 's nan saoghal.
Ciod e a their mi ris, a dhaoine?
Blàth de na blàithean as maoithe,
aig nach eil freumh no fàs as t-saoghal   895
ach gu h-àrd an gàradh naomha."

"Mo mhicein!" orsa Òmar 's uaill às,
"Tha do ghuth nas tiamhaidh suairce
na mac-talla an gleann uaigneach,
nuair cluinnear mèilich fhann nan uan ann,   900
feasgar 's an cìobair sgìth gan cuallach."

"Is e mo Mhaighstir an t-Aon Dia coibhre,
bheir fàs don fhìonan is don droigheann;
Rianadair beul an là 's na h-oidhche,
bheir òrdugh don ghrèin 's their 'Soillsich!'   905
thàirneas na neòil à dubhar na doimhne,
's a their, gan tilleadh chum a broinne,
'Dòirtibh an-siud is fàgaibh loinneil
sgrìodan nan sgòrr 's am fàsach oillteil.

[Ùraichibh

deceptive and transient, welcomed with delight when it appears | but leaving us in tears when it moves on regardless. | There is something which Death cannot conquer: | the lasting soul, it is a light flake | of snow driven by the wind, | but its 890 *coursings take wild leaps | to the far rim of suns and worlds. | What name shall I give it, good people? | The blossom of most delicate blossoms, | which has neither roots nor growth in this world | but on high in the holy garden."* 895

"My darling son!" said Omar with pride, | "Your voice is more melancholy and soothing | than the echo in a desolate glen, | when the faint bleating of lambs is heard | in the evening as the weary shepherd gathers them in." 900

"My Master is the One God of salvation, | who brings growth to the vine and the bramblebush; | the Governor of dawn and dusk, | who commands the sun, saying 'Shine forth!', | who draws the clouds from the darkness of the deep | and says, 905 *returning them to its womb: | 'Pour yonder, and leave brightly gleaming | the gullies on the pinnacles and the terrible desert. |*

Ùraichibh ler sgàile sgìos fuinn loisgich.   910
Tromaichibh diasan buidhe mo chloinne.'
Is fial E, 's is iochdmhor, coibhneil,
is chan e bròn no deòir a thoilleadh
Pàrras uaith, no fuachd do 'shoillse."

"Mas e naomhachd cùl ri aighear,   915
ceusadh na colla, 's a bhith air sgaradh
ris an t-saoghal a rinn ar n-Athair,
carson a chuir e A chuid mhac ann,
's a thug E dhuinn fìon ar fala,
lòchran ar radhairc is, car tamaill,   920
a' cholainn uallach òg gu aiteas?"

"Chuir E ann sinn gu ar tearbadh",
orsa Obàïd, "le mìlsead 's seirbhead
gu ar deuchainn 's ar gnè a dhearbhadh.
An stàilinn neo-fhoirfe chearbach,   925
nì an saoghal buairt' a meirgeadh.

"Nì e an droch chruaidh a lùbadh
no mhaolachadh, is smal is smùrach
a chruinneachadh air a faobhar dùsail;
ach an deagh stàilinn fhaghairt gu sùrdail   930
le feum 's le deuchainnibh dlùtha,
ga cur an gèiread 's gach aon ionnsaigh.

Relieve in your shadow the weariness of a scorching soil. | Fill out for my children the 910
golden ears of corn.' | He is generous, He is compassionate and kind, | and it is not grief
or tears that would earn | Paradise from Him, nor cold indifference to His radiance."

"If saintliness is the shunning of gaiety, | the mortification of the body, and 915
rejection | of the world which our Father created, | why has He placed His sons in
its midst, | and given us the wine of our blood, | the lantern of our sight, and, for
a short spell, | a vigorous young body quick to merriment?" 920

"He has placed us there to separate us out", | said Obayd, "to test us | with
life's sweet and bitter and let us prove our nature. | Steel which is imperfect and
blemished, | the chaotic world will cause to rust. 925

"It will make the bad metal bend | or go blunt, and cause stains and blots | to
collect on the dulled blade; | but it will eagerly temper the good steel | through 930
necessity and rigorous trials, | sharpening it with every encounter.

"Thèid steud-each na colla uaibhrich
o rian a dh'easbhaidh smachd is bualaidh,
's am marcaich a leig srian fhuasgailt   935
le 'roidean dalla is le 'ruathar
a' ruith air cunnart is sìor thruaighe
is sitrich nam miann 'na chluasan.

"A bhith cuidhte is a cìocras!
Is crom mall mi, dall is dìblidh   940
anns na geimhlibh dualach sìorraidh
as cuid den bheatha a thug an Rìgh dhuinn.
Tha freumhach ann a cheanglas sìos mi
air leathad gaothach 's rèidhlean ìosal,
gam chumail ann ri uisg' is sìontan   945
's fo bhruthainn thruim na grèine fiochmhoir,
measg cealgaireachd is ceò na tìme,
ion is nach ruig mi air an Fhìrinn
san t-Sìorraidheachd far an riochdail fìor i.

"Is fad-fhulangach ar n-Athair rùnach;   950
is iochdmhor E; ach dèanaibh tionndadh
or n-amaideas, or n-uaill, or sùgradh,
no thig latha A throm sgiùrsa oirbh,
is nìthear nithean na bhur dùthaich
bheir oirbh, ge neo-sgàthach lùthmhor,   955
cur bhur làmhan roimh bhur sùilean,

                                                    [is mil

"The steed of the arrogant body | will lurch out of control for lack of discipline and beating, | and the rider who gave free rein | to its blind dashes and bolting | will find himself running a course of danger and constant misery, | deafened by the neighings of desire.

"Oh to be done with the body's rapacious appetites! | I am slow and stooped, blind and abject | in the eternal ineluctable bonds | which are the share of life the King has accorded us. | There is a root holding me down | on windswept slope and low-lying plain, | which keeps me there through rain and tempest | and in the crushing sultriness of the merciless sun, | amidst the hypocrisy and blind fog of time, | and which prevents me from attaining the Truth | in the Eternity where it is manifest and real.

"Long-suffering is our loving Father, | and forgiving; but turn ye all | from your foolish ways, your overweening pride and your sporting, | or the day of His terrible scourge will come upon you, | and there will be done deeds in your land | which, for all your fearlessness and valour, will cause you | to cover your eyes with your hands, |

is mil a ràdh, seadh mil is siùcar,
ris a' Bhàs is sibh ga ionndrainn."

B'i sin an fhàistneachd a rinn t'athair,
's a thàinig air a cois rid latha. 960

*

"Ràinig aoigh sinn is rinn sinn aiteas,
rinn sinn boch ris, rinn sinn aighear;
ràinig o thìr gun ùir, gun chlachan,
's cha b'ann a chois, air each, air asail.
  Dh'ìobair sinn caora 965
  le fèist is faoilte,
  le buidheachas is gàire
  air a thàillibh.
Thàinig e taobh ruinn, is rinn e suidhe an sìth;
shocraich e e fhèin againn, is rinn e fuireach fo dhìon." 970

Air t'athair is ort fhèin cha deachaidh
ach deich bliadhna 'nam plathadh seachad
on là a ghabhadh do dhuan breith leis
gus an do laigh a ghrian feasgair,
's a thuirt iad riut, 's tu maoth is meachair: 975
"Guma beò do cheann! Mu dheireadh
o 'nàmhaid an domhan theich e."

and speak of Death as of honey, aye, honey and sugar, | and long for it to come."
Such was the prophecy uttered by your father, | and which came to pass in your
day. 960

*

"A guest came to us and we rejoiced, | we celebrated and made merry; | he came
from a land without soil or stones, | he did not come on foot, on horseback or
donkey. | We sacrificed a sheep | amidst feasting and cheer, | thankfulness and 965
laughter | on his account. | He came to our side, and sat down in peace; | he made
himself at home with us, and settled in security." 970

Ten years only, quick as a glimpse, | passed by your father and you | from the day
he recited your birth-song | till the setting of his evening-sun | when they said to
you, still a delicate boy of tender age: | "Long life to you! He has finally | escaped 975
from his enemy the world."

B'iriseal e, is cha robh sgàth ann.
Thuirt do sheanair ri fear de 'nàimhdean:
"Ged thilleadh tu am broinn do mhàthar,   980
spadaidh mi thu, spadaidh, a ghàrlaich!"
Ach thuirt t'athair ri fear rinn tàir air:
"Seo mo lethcheann. Buail, a bhràthair."

Deich bliadhn' air fhichead dha air thalamh.
Bu ghobha 'anma fhèin e, ag amharc   985
sgàthan a chridhe fhèin, gun fhaileas
on t-saoghal a-muigh, ach gann, ri fhaicinn
an gile chiùin gun smal a ghlaine.
Bu bheag a shuim do thaigh no achadh,
do sprèidh no treudan, no òr an tasgaidh –   990
bha maoin neo-fhaicsinneach aige.

A' chuid nach robh ach feòil is fuil annt',
thuirt iad ris "a' choinneal spultach",
ach bha leus ann air nach ruigeadh
sùil air a dorchnachadh le duslach.   995
Bha solas caomh dheth nach do thuig iad,
ged a dh'fhoillsicheadh dhuit e.

He was humble, and there was no shadow in him. | *Your grandfather told one of his enemies:* | *"Though you should crawl back into your mother's belly,* | *I will* 980 *squash you, squash you, you piece of dirt!"* | *But your father told a man who was causing him grievance:* | *"Here is my cheek. Strike, brother."*

Thirty years was his span on earth. | *He was the smith of his own soul, looking into* | *the mirror of his own heart, where hardly a shadow* | *from the outside world* 985 *could be detected* | *in its bright, gentle, unblemished purity.* | *Little did he care for house or field,* | *for herds or flocks, or golden treasure –* | *his was an invisible* 990 *wealth.*

Those who were but flesh and blood | *called him "the dripping candle",* | *but there was a flame in him which* | *the dust-blinded eye could not perceive.* | *There was a* 995 *gentle light from him which they did not understand,* | *although to you it was revealed.*

147

109.2.5 *Deòir Ìblis*

Fhuair taisdealach san dìthreabh –
 an teas is ìota ga cheusadh –
caochan a' ruith à beul uamhach,   1,000
 sgàile is fuaran le chèile.

Chrom e is rinn e a bhlasad,
 ga thoirt às am bois a làimhe.
Thrèig a dhùil e an taom feirge;
 bha e searbh air bhlas an t-sàile.   1,005

Dh'èalaidh e a-steach on bhruthainn,
 a shireadh fionnarachd na h-uamhach.
Fhuair e sa chùil bu mhotha dubhar
 fear mòr crom 'na shuidhe 'n uaigneas.

Fear mòr crom a' gul 's ag osnaich,   1,010
 coltas àrdain air is uaisle.
B'iad a dheòir gan sileadh daonnan
 a rinn caochan searbh na h-uamhach.

B'e sin Ìblis a bha 'na aingeal,
 a rinn ceannairc, a chaidh fhògradh,   1,015
is e a' gul an dèidh na chaill e,
 aghaidh Allah, amharc A Mhòrachd.

109.2.5   [*The Tears of Satan*]

A wanderer in the desert – | *wracked by heat and thirst –* | *found a runnel*
flowing from the mouth of a cave, | *shade and spring in one.*   1,000

He crouched and had a taste of it, | *drinking it out of his cupped hand.* | *His*
expectation fled in a surge of anger; | *it was bitter with the taste of sea-water.*   1,005

He crept inside away from the sweltering heat, | *seeking the coolness of the*
cave. | *He found in the darkest recess* | *a large stooped man sitting in solitude.*

A large stooped man weeping and sighing, | *of lofty and noble countenance.* | 1,010
His tears it was, shed unceasingly, | *that formed the bitter streamlet of the cave.*

That man was Satan, once an angel, | *who had rebelled and been banished,* | 1,015
crying now for that which he had forfeited, | *the face of Allah, the sight of His*
Greatness.

Lean am fear turais air a rathad
  gun smuain air tart, no air a' bhruthainn,
ga fhaighneachd fhèin, 's e 'g imeachd, cùine   1,020
  dh'aonaichte dùilean agus Cruithear.

Cùin a dh'èighte sìth is caidreabh
  eadar na rinneadh is Na thùr e,
is rèite eadar na th'ann
  agus Na chuir ann air thùs e.   1,025

109.2.6 [Turas Mhochtàir]

Bu ghiorra an duan, a Mhochtàir, dhuit.
Cha do ghin do fhreumhach blàithean;
cha do bhàrc meas do shnodhaich air bàrrgheug;
do bhith, is gann gun do bhlàthaich
bean no clann, luchd gaoil no càirdean   1,030
aig lughad is aig luaths do làithean.

Treiseag dhuit ri uilinn Òmair,
treiseag sna raointean 's mu na cròithean,
treiseag an caidreabh do mhnà pòsta,
is dh'fhalbh thu, 's cha b'ann gu deònach,   1,035
air thuras gu craos a' mhòrtair.

*

The traveller went on his way, | with no thought now of thirst or swelter, | asking himself, as he walked, when | creation and Creator would ever be one.   1,020

When would peace and fellowship be proclaimed | between what has been made and That which fashioned it, | and harmony declared between that which exists | and That which first put it in place?   1,025

109.2.6 [Mokhtâr's Journey]

Shorter was your song, Mokhtâr. | Your roots yielded no blossom; | the fruit of your sap never burst forth on a topmost branch; | hardly did your being give warmth | to wife or children, loved ones or friends, | for the brevity and haste of 1,030 *your days.*

A short while you had at Omar's elbow, | a short while in the fields and at the folds, | a short while in the intimate company of your spouse, | and you left, not willingly, | on a journey that led you to the gaping maw of the mortar.   1,035

*

149

Clach aoil a' sgagadh fon teas,
   sgreuthadh nan creag 'na ghathan duslaich;
an ùir bhruante suas 'na smùid
   fo chrùidhean aindeonach nam muileid.   1,040

An nathair adharcach 's gach gleann;
   an dipeardan is srannraich chuileag;
druim mar sgian gun neul, gun deò
   's na sgiathalain a' crònan uime.

Am Bàs grad am measg nam preas,   1,045
   ri feallfhalach air slios gach tulaich,
a' faire o sgàil' an alltain chèir,
   air Saghuàn fo ghrèin gun dubhar.

Limestone splintering in the heat, | the shrivelling of rocks in its dust-speckled rays; | pounded soil up in puffs | under the recalcitrant hooves of the mules.   1,040

The horned viper in every defile; | the shimmering heat and buzzing of flies; | a knife-sharp ridge without cloud or breath of air, | circled by the droning planes.

Nimble Death among the thickets, | ready to ambush on the flank of every hill, | 1,045 *keeping watch from the shade of the gloomy wee burn, | on shadeless sunbaked Saghouan.*

109.3 DÙGHALL

109.3.1 [Sa Mhadainn eadar Cadal 's Dùisg]

Mi ag èirigh mochthrath blàidhealtrach
   sa Bhàghan shìos,   1,050
bha an speur is uinneag sgàrlaid air,
   bu chràidhearg grìs;
dhùisg fonn na h-oiteig tràthaile,
ri osnaich 's cagar gàirdeachais,
sna dosan far am b'àbhaisteach   1,055
   sàmhchar, sìth.

A' mhuir ri monmhar ataireachd
   ri cladach dùr;
deò bheag ri seirm chadaltaich,
   gaoth mhara chiùin.   1,060
Fann torghan uisge chaisreagaich
an clais an uillt, fo shlatagaibh
a' challtainn 's a' bheithe bhachlagaich
   's fon bharrach ùr.

Ceòl nan eun ri turraraich,   1,065
   's e sriutach, saor.
An smeòrach cheutach, ghuibeineach
   air stuibein caol.

[Cantail

109.3 DOUGALL
109.3.1 [In the Morning between Sleep and Wakening]

As I rose early on a warm, dewy morning | in the wee bay down below, | there 1,050 was a scarlet window in the sky, | flushing flaming red. | The melody of the early breeze awakened, | sighing and whispering joyfully | in the clumps of trees where quiet and peace | had their accustomed place. 1,055

The sea sent its swell murmuring | against a frowning shore; | a little breeze sang sleepy music, | a gentle wind of the sea. | Faint sounded the purling of 1,060 eddying water | in the channel of the burn, beneath the branches | of the hazel and the tressed birch, | under the fresh green tops of the trees.

Out sounded the music of birds warbling | in free, unchecked torrents. | The 1,065 bonny thrush with his melodious beak, | perched on a slender branch. |

Cantail, sòlas, fionnarachd
'n àm tràghadh dreòs nan rionnagan,   1,070
's an là ga dhòrtadh ruiteagach
    thar chnuic an fhraoich.

An dùsgadh no an cadal dhomh?
    An sealladh fìor
a chunnaic mi san aiteal sin,   1,075
    no an aisling sgìos?
Dhùisg geur iolach àrdghuthach
aig iomainiche nan càmhal mi
à fionnarachd ghlas Phàrrasail
    a' Bhàghain shìos.   1,080

109.3.2 [*Folachd is Àrach*]

Ciod e a th'annainn, a chlann mo dhùthcha?
Ciod e a th'annainn is a bha 'n Dùghall?
Ciod e tha an dualchas is an dùthchas?
Cainnt is eachdraidh, snàth nan glùinean,
na ginealaich druim air dhruim a' cùrsachd,   1,085
a' casruith a chèile cleas nan sùghan.

Chanting, cheer and coolness | at the time when the flaming of the stars was
drained to paleness, | and the new day pouring ruddy in floods of fire | over the   1,070
heathery hills.

Am I awake or sleeping? | Was it real, | what I saw in that glimpse, | or was it a   1,075
vision of weariness? | The high-pitched, shrill shouting | of the camel-driver
awoke me | out of the grey, Paradise coolness | of the wee bay down below.   1,080

109.3.2   [*Lineage and Rearing*]

What are we, children of my country? | What makes us and what made Dougall? |
What is in us by heredity and what by tradition? | Speech and history, the
thread of generations, | the generations coursing back on back, | racing head-   1,085
long over each other like rolling waves. |

Breith is bàs mar fhàs na h-ùrach,
àrach, is àbhaistean nach do mhùthadh
ler sluagh on rinn e Alb' air thùs deth.
Am b'oighre air guth 's air cumadh gnùis' e   1,090
air faireachdainnean, inntinn, sealladh sùla
aig daoine a dh'fhàiltich sìos gan ionnsaigh
luchd am faraire is an giùlain,
riamh mun d'iarr iad a' bhean ghlùin da?
Bu Ghàidheal e, 's bu bhlàth a dhùrachd   1,095
don chànain àrsaidh a rinn a dhùsgadh
o 'chadal creathlach; san d'rinn e sùgradh
ri leannan anns a' choille chùbhraidh.
B'Albannach e, a fhuair mar dhùthaich
an tìr bheag ghailbheach, ghrianach, chliùiteach   1,100
nach dèan saltairt is nach gabh lùbadh.
B'ann de Chloinn Àdhaimh rinn Dia dùileach
Fodha Fhèin 's os cionn nam brùid e.

Eachdraidh nan Gàidheal! Sgeul nan lotan,
buill' air bhuille, nach d'ràinig plosgadh   1,105
a' chridhe, 's a liuthad cuisl' air fosgladh.
Bu chuspair iad do shaighdean goirte,
is b'amaiseach urchraichean a' Mhì-fhortain,
bu chuimseach an sàthadh is bu domhain.
B'i siud a' choille a rinn sona,   1,110
a rinn lurach, 's a lìon le 'h-osnaich

                                                    [gleann

Birth and death like the growth of the soil, | rearing, and customs unaltered | by our people since they first settled in Scotland. | Was he heir to the voice and physical appearance, | the feelings, the turn of mind and the outlook | of people 1,090 *who welcomed among them | their wakeholders and their pallbearers, | long before they fetched the midwife for him? | He was a Gael, and warm was his regard | for the ancient tongue which woke him | from his cradle sleep; and in* 1,095 *which he courted | his love in the fragrant woods. | He was a Scot, given for country | the small tempestuous sunny land of renown | that will trample on* 1,100 *none and that none can bend. | Of Adam's Clan the Creator made him, | under Himself and above the beasts.*

The history of the Gaels! The tale of the wounds, | inflicted blow by blow, which failed to reach the palpitating | heart despite so many open veins. | They have 1,105 *been the target of painful arrows, | well-aimed have been the gunshots of Misfortune, | unerring the knife-lunges and deep. | Yon was the forest which made happy, | made beautiful and filled with its sighs |* 1,110

gleann is eilean, còs is cnocan.
B'ùrar a bàrr is bu dosrach;
bu bhinn a h-eòin earraich is, as t-fhoghar,
bu chrom a geugan fon cuid toradh.   1,115
B'i siud a' choille a fhuair sgrìob doininn,
fhuair a leagadh, fhuair a lomadh,
fhuair beàrn air bheàrn le sèideadh ospag,
is an tuagh ga geurachadh mu 'coinneimh.
Ach fhad 's a dh'fhanas freumh a dheoghal   1,120
brìgh na h-ùrach, 's a chur snodhaich
suas fon rùisg, le driùchd is soineann,
thig failleanan ùra o na stocaibh
gu 'cur 'na tuiltean uaine molach
air ais far am b'uaine i roimhe.   1,125
A dh'aindeoin fògraidh, fhiadh is bochdainn,
's na thàinig uile à Là Chùil Fhodair,
cha leagadh buan a fhuair ar doire.

A Dhùghaill, chunnaic t'athair 's do sheanair
an daoine a' falbh ri luaths le leathad,   1,130
agus san là bu chruaidhe greim ac'
air an dìleab thar luach a theasairg
an tuath on tìom is o a ceathach.
B'ann sa chlais ghàbhaidh a bha 'n eathar
ga fuadan leis fo làn a sreathan;   1,135
ach bhris rid latha latha eile,
a gheall soirbheas rathail leatha.

glen and island, crevice and hillock. | Fresh and luxuriant were its topmost branches; | melodious were its birds of springtime, and in the autumn | heavy were its boughs under their load of fruit. | That forest was torn open by tem- 1,115 pests, | it was felled and maimed, | and saw gap after gap blown by gusts, | and the axe being whetted in its very presence. | But as long as one root survives to suck | the juice of the earth and to send sap | rising under the bark, in dew and 1,120 sunshine, | fresh saplings will sprout from the stumps | and in time restore floods of green bush | where there was greenness before. | In spite of expulsions, deer 1,125 and poverty, | and all that befell in the wake of Culloden, | it is no permanent felling our grove has suffered.

Dougall, your father and your grandfather saw | their people fleeing fast down a brae, | and even in days of cruellest hardship still holding firm | to that price- 1,130 less inheritance which the common people | protected from time and its mist. | In a perilous track was their boat, | blown to leeward with all sails reefed; | but 1,135 in your day there broke a new day, | promising fair winds and good fortune.

Bha thu fhèin cho mear ri minnein,
nad bhalachan air tràigh is fireach,
cho aotrom ri eun os cionn a nidein,   1,140
t'ùidh am bàtaichean 's an iomain,
ràmh is caman, slat mu linne.
Ruith na maighich, snàmh a' bhricein;
stiùir is seòl is dorgh, a shireadh
tacar èisg ri grèin is sileadh.   1,145
Feadan beag agad gu binneas
a' cneatraich fo do bhuillean cliste.
Thu gun teagamh, gun eagal, gun tioma,
gun smuain fhalaich annad idir,
do ghnùis 'na sgàthan glan dod chridhe.   1,150
Thug thu treis ri cluich is mire;
deireadh foghair, sac cùl slinnein,
a' buain chnò is smeuran drise;
oidhche Shamhna – bàrr san iodhlainn –
le aodann fuadain a' falbh fo ghighis   1,155
a' faoighe ùbhlan 's rudan milis,
air do chur buileach às do riochd-sa
le seann aodach màs na ciste.
An grian do shaoghail chaidh thu 'n sinead,
gus an robh thu 'd spealp de ghille,   1,160
is chaidh thu 'n eòlas ceàird do chinnidh –
ceàird an amhsain a-nuas a' tighinn,
eun na faire 's an tuitim shithich –
is air an gàradh meas 's an lios-san,
a' mhuir chobhrach, gharbh, gheal-bhriste.   1,165

You yourself were as merry as a little kid, | a boy on beach and hilltop, | as light as a bird above its nest, | your mind taken up with boats and shinty; | an oar, a 1,140 caman, a rod about a pool. | A hare for running, a trout for swimming; | tiller and sail and handline to go seeking | provision of fish in sun and rain. | A little chanter 1,145 you had for sweet music, | warbling under the nimble beats of your fingers. | You knew neither doubt, nor fear, nor grief; | there was not one single hidden thought in you, | your face a clean bright mirror to your heart. | A while you 1,150 spent in merry playing; | at the end of autumn with a sack over your shoulder, | gathering nuts and brambles from the bush; | Hallowe'en – with the harvest in the yard – | away [you would go,] masked with a false face, | thigging apples and 1,155 sweet things, | disguised beyond all recognition | with the old clothes from the bottom of the kist. | Living in the sunshine of your world you grew older, | until you were a strapping lad | and grew acquaint with the trade of your folk – | the 1,160 trade of the solan coming down, | the bird of the long [watch and of the attacking dive] – | with their fruit-garden and their plot, | the foaming, rough, white-broken sea. 1,165

109.3.3 *Bean an Iasgair*

Cha d'fhuair mi 'n cadal fad na h-oidhche,
  o dhubh gu soillse 's mi faisg air gul:
a' ghaoth cho sgalail is mi ga h-èisteachd,
  is m'fhear fhèin is an sgoth a-muigh.

Bha mi a' guidhe dìon is fasgadh   1,170
  on ghaillinn dhorcha don sgoth dhuinn
eadar Arainn is bàghan Chòmhail.
  Is mairg dom beòshlaint lìon is muir.

Buidseach na foille 's an aodainn phreasaich,
  àilleag nan geas 's nan ceudan cruth,   1,175
brù às an d'èirich rèidhlean 's garbhlach –
  dubh fhairge nan stuadh 's nan sruth.

109.3.4 *A' Mhuir*

A' mhuir dhìomhar, mheallta, mhùthach,
le 'cunnartan àillidh a thàirneas sùilean
is rùn na h-òige, 'toirt beò a h-ionndrainn   1,180
le draoidheachd 'fhàire is chòrsaichean ùra.
An geasadair, an cleasaiche làn rùintean,
sìor ùr, thar fiosrachaidh, làn ioghnaidh.

109.3.3 *The Fisherman's Wife*

I got no sleep all the night, I from dark to daylight, and I near crying: I the wind
so shrill, and I listening to it, I and my own man and the skiff out at sea.

I was praying for shielding and shelter I from the dark gale for the brown skiff I   1,170
between Arran and the bays of Cowal. I Unlucky is he whose livelihood is a net
and the sea.

Treacherous witch of the wrinkled face, I bonny enchantress of the hundreds of
shifting shapes, I womb out of which arose plains and rough mountain land – I   1,175
wretched sea of the waves and the tides.

109.3.4 *The Sea*

The secret, deceitful, changing sea, I with its lovely perils that draw the eyes I
and the desire of youth, bringing his longing to life I with the wizardry of hori-   1,180
zons and new coastlines. I Weaver of spells, the trickster, full of secrets; I ever
knew, beyond knowing, full of wonder.

Faoilte na fairge is greann a dùsgaidh;
a' ghaoth obann o àirdean dùra,   1,185
a h-ospagan cleas ùird a' tùirling,
a h-oiteagan, a fèath, a ciùineas;
gob nan sgeir 's nan creagan crùbte
ri feallfhalach air saidh is sùidhean.

Mòrshluagh bras fo chathadh sìobain,   1,190
ròshluagh, marcshluagh, cathshluagh sìne,
eachraidh ghrad 'na sreathaibh fìochmhor,
muing-gheal, ceanngheal, steud-eich strìthe.

Mòrfhairge mhòr 's a' ghaoth ga ruagadh,
ròshluagh, mòrshluagh, marcshluagh uaibhreach;   1,195
am Bàs geal o thaobh an fhuaraidh
shuas 'na dhìollaid 's e ri nuallan;
steudan glasa na srannraich uabhais,
cìrein nan stuadh a' teachd le ruathar.

Is ann tha rubha cùl gach rubha,   1,200
bàghan nach eòl duinn 's bailtean puirt ann.
Tha bàta fodhainn gu 'cur a shiubhal,
a' ghaoth ri sàiltean 's an t-seann mhuir umainn,
's chan eil, a ghràidh, air thalamh uile
làn shàsachadh no fìor cheann uidhe   1,205
do mhiann an fhalbhain anns an duine.

The welcoming smile of the sea, and the surly bristling of its awakening; | the
sudden wind out of grim airts; | its squalls coming down like a hammer. | Its 1,185
light breezes, its calm, its peacefulness; | the long points of the skerries and the
crouching rocks | waiting in ambush for stem and seams.

A mighty headlong host mantled in driving spindrift, | a great host, a host of 1,190
horsemen, a tempest host of battle, | quick cavalry in fierce raging ranks, | white-
maned, white-headed, steeds of strife.

A mighty sea, a great sea with the wind driving it on; | a mighty host, a great
host, a haughty host of cavalry; | white death from windward | in his saddle 1,195
roaring; | grey steeds snorting terribly, | the crests of the waves coming onwards
with a rush.

There is a headland beyond every headland; | bays that we do not know and 1,200
ports there are. | There is a boat under our feet to set sailing, | the wind at her
heels and the old sea round us. | And there is not, dear, on all the earth, | full
satisfying or a true journey's end | for the love of wandering in man.   1,205

109.3.5 *A' Bhean a' Bruidhinn*

Na falbh m'ulaidh, ach dèan fuireach air cladach t'eòlais,
cois làn a' phuirt far an dèan sruth nan caisreag ceòl duit,
is e a' seinn gu fairge troimh ghile ghainmhe, 's an t-suain
                             'na chrònan,
– calltainn 's beithe gu dubhar leth ris – o chnuic is còsan.   1,210

Bi gum mhiann. Na gèill don fhiabhras chuain, 's gur leòir dhuit
ar puirt, ar n-eileanan 's ar sgeirean, is mol an òbain
far an deachaidh do cheud eathar air sàil fod steòrnadh.
Dèan thusa fanachd. Na lean braise dhall na h-òige.

Teas gun fhois nan caladh coimheach, 's an dòmhlachd shluaigh annt', 1,215
na taighean solais nach fhac' thu roimhe, 's an leus a' sguabadh
nan eirthir aineoil; 's cùl bheann nach aithne dhuit, gu buadhach
teachd na grèine sear sna speuran dearg is uaine ...
Nì sin taigh tostach, cridhe goirt is sùil làn smuairein,
is i ag amharc cathair fhalamh an fhir air chuantan.   1,220

109.3.5 *The Woman Speaks*

Do not go, my darling. Bide on the shore that you know, | by the tide-lip of the bay where the eddying burn makes music for you, | singing to the sea through the whiteness of sand, with sleep in its crooning; | hazel and birch for shade along it, as it comes from the knowes and the hollows.   1,210

Do what I ask. Do not give way to the ocean fever. Enough for you | are our little bays, our islands and our skerries, and the shingle of the creek | where your first boat went to sea under your steering. | Do you but stay. Do not follow the blind urge of youth.

The heat without rest of the foreign harbours, and their thronging crowds; | the 1,215 lighthouses you never saw before, their beams sweeping | the unknown coasts. And from behind mountains that you do not know the triumphant | coming of the sun, red and green in the eastern sky ... | These things leave a silent house, a sore heart and a mournful eye | looking at the empty chair of the man who is at sea.   1,220

109.4 [DÙNADH: *An Duine agus an Cogadh*]

Saoghal fa leth mac-an-duine,
domhan beò leis fhèin gach urra;
grian is dorchadas na cruinne,
siùil mhara 's grianstad san fhuil ann.
Cia mheud glùn a th'ann ar cumadh?   1,225
Chan innis sgeul, cha lorg cuimhn' iad,
's athbheirear iad uile cuideachd
san naoidhean, is a shinnre cruinn ann.
Thèid e leò gu ceann a thurais,
's bidh pàirt dheth beò an dèidh a shiubhail.   1,230
Chìthear a ghnùis 's e fhèin 'na uirigh;
faodar gur e a ghuth a chluinnear
is ogh' an ogha nach fhac' e 'bruidhinn.
Cùis bhùirt sinn! Ged a tha na h-uile
'nan taighean stòir làn fòtais, usgar,   1,235
dhìleab àrsaidh, shubhailc, dhubhailc,
dh'fhan Clann Àdhaimh fòs 'na struidhear,
ga sgapadh fhèin gu dall, faoin, fuilteach.

Peacadh a thruailleas ùir is adhar,
duin' òg an salachar a' chatha   1,240
'dol às ri reothairt bhrais a latha.

[Brisear

109.4 [EPILOGUE: *Man and War*]

A world apart is each son of man, | a living world in himself is every person; | an earth's sunshine and darkness, | tides and solstices in his blood. | How many generations go to shape us? | No story can tell and no memory trace them. | Yet 1,225 they are all reborn together | in the little child, and his ancestry is united within him. | Along with it he goes to the end of his journey, | and a part of him will be alive after he is gone. | His face will be seen when he himself is in his grave, | 1,230 and it may be that it is his voice that will be heard, | when the grandson of the grandson whom he never saw is speaking. | We are a fit subject for derision! | Though all men | are storehouses full of refuse, gems, | ancient heirlooms, 1,235 virtues and vices, | Adam's Clan still remains a wastrel, | squandering itself blindly, foolishly, bloodily.

It is a crime that corrupts earth and air, | a young man amid the filth of battle, | 1,240 perishing in the headlong springtide of his days.

Brisear an teud – stadar an ceilear –
nuair bu bhinne, àirde sheinn iad.
Sguirear 's gun am port ach leitheach.

Mì-ghnìomh a dhallas grian is reultan,   1,245
a' chuid as bòidhche dhinn 's as trèine
ga h-eadarmhort gun iochd, ga ceusadh.
Na h-òganaich gan cur gu deuchainn
– am feòladair maraon 's an treud iad;
slòigh an domhain ri oidhche èitigh   1,250
a' spealgadh lòchrain càch a chèile.

Ghluais Mochtàr a làmh sa bhruthainn
a shuathadh fallais, a ruagadh cuileig.
Chlisg an *Gefreiter*; sgaoil e 'bhuille.

Bhàsaich àrdan Ahmaid mhòrail,   1,255
ciùineas Obàïd is beò chridh' Òmair,
trò eile le Mochtàr fon mhòrtair.

Bhàsaich am fear a bha ri 'uilinn,
dhubhadh às a shinnsreachd uile;
mhortadh a chlann nach do rugadh.   1,260

The string is snapped, the singing stopped, | when their music sounded its sweetest. | They cease with the melody but half played.

It is a misdeed that blinds sun and stars, | the bonniest and the strongest of us | 1,245 at mutual massacre, slaying and crucifying themselves. | Youth – butcher and flock in one – | being put to the test; | the nations of the world on a foul night | 1,250 shattering one another's bright lanterns.

In the sweltering heat Mokhtâr moved his hand, | to wipe away the sweat, to chase away a fly. | The Gefreiter started, and let loose the shot.

There died the angry pride of regal Ahmed, | the gentle meekness of Obayd and 1,255 Omar's living heart – | they died a second time along with Mokhtâr by the mortar.

There died the man who lay at his elbow. | All his ancestry was blotted out. | His children were murdered unborn.   1,260

Chaidh an domhan beag a bhruanadh,
a dh'fhàs ann fhèin 'na earrach uaine;
a ghin, gun fhios, na bha mun cuairt dha,
is a rinn e 'chumadh le a smuaintean
air na chunnaic e 's na chual' e,   1,265
nuair leig an tuigse air a ghuaillean
a h-eallach duineil, deacair, uasal.
Dà dhomhan iolchruthach, luachmhor,
a dhubhadh às gu bràth mun d'fhuair iad
teachd gu ìre làin, 's a sguabadh   1,270
às an speur le buille thuairmse.

Mort nam marbh is mort nan naoidhean
nach do ghineadh – crìoch dhà shaoghal.

A' CHRÌOCH

There was reduced to dust the little world | that grew within him in his green spring time, | which was created, unknown to him, by everything around him; | which he formed by his thoughts | on all that he saw and heard, | after under- 1,265 standing had laid | its manly, difficult, noble burden on his shoulders. | Two complex, priceless worlds | were blotted out forever before they had attained | the fullness of their being, and were swept | from the sky by a chance blow.   1,270

Murder of the dead, murder of the children | never begotten – the end of two worlds.

THE END

POEMS 1944–1946

(ii)

*110   *Atman*

Rinn thu goid nad èiginn,
   dh'fheuch thu breug gu faotainn às;
dhìt iad, chàin is chuip iad thu,
   is chuir iad thu fo ghlais.   4

Bha 'm beul onorach a dhìt thu
   pladach, bìdeach sa ghnùis ghlais;
bha Ceartas sreamshùileach o sgrùdadh
   a leabhar cunntais 's iad sìor phailt.   8

Ach am beul a dhearbhadh breugach,
   bha e modhail, èibhinn, binn;
fhuair mi eirmseachd is sgeòil uaith
   's gun e ro eòlach air tràth bìdh.   12

Thogte do shùil on obair
   à cruth an t-saoghail a dheoghal tlachd;
mhol thu Debel Iussuf dhomh,
   a cumadh is a dath.   16

---

*110   *Atman*

You thieved in your need, | you tried a lie to get off; | they condemned you, reviled you and whipped you, | and they put you under lock and key.   4

The honourable mouth that condemned you | was blubberish and tiny in the grey face; | Justice was blear-eyed from scrutinising | its account-books, and they ever showing abundance.   8

But the mouth which was found lying, | was mannerly, cheerful and melodious; | I got sharp repartee and tales from it, | though it was not too well acquainted with a meal.   12

Your eye would be raised from your work | to draw pleasure from the shape of the world; | you praised Jebel Yussuf to me, | its form and its colour.   16

Is aithne dhomh thu, Atmain,
  bean do thaighe 's do chòignear òg,
do bhaidnein ghobhar is t'asail,
  do ghoirtein seagail is do bhò.   20

Is aithne dhomh thu, Atmain:
  is fear thu 's tha thu beò,
dà nì nach eil am breitheamh,
  's a chaill e 'chothrom gu bhith fòs.   24

Chan ainmig t'fhallas na do shùilean;
  is eòl duit sùgradh agus fearg;
bhlais is bhlais thu 'n difir
  eadar milis agus searbh.   28

Dh'fheuch thu gràin is bròn is gàire;
  dh'fheuch thu ànradh agus grian;
dh'fhairich thu a' bheatha
  is cha do mheath thu roimpe riamh.   32

Nan robh thu beairteach, is do chaolan
  garbh le caoile t'airein sgìth,
cha bhiodh tu 'chuideachd air na mìolan
  an dubh phrìosan Mhondovì.   36

Nuair gheibh breitheamh còir na cùirte
  làn a shùla de mo dhruim,
thig mi a thaobh gud fhàilteachadh
  trast an t-sràid ma chì mi thu.   40

[Sìdna

I know you, Atman, | the woman of your house and your five youngsters, | your little clump of goats and your ass, | your plot of rye and your cow.   20

I know you, Atman: | you are a man and you are alive, | two things the judge is not, | and that he has lost his chance of being ever.   24

Your sweat is not seldom in your eyes; | you know what sporting and anger are; | you have tasted and tasted the difference | between sweet and bitter.   28

You have tried hatred and grief and laughter; | you have tried tempest and sun; | you have experienced life | and never shrunk before it.   32

Had you been wealthy, and your gut | thick with the leanness of your tired ploughmen, | you would not be keeping company with the lice | in the black prison of Mondovi.   36

When the decent judge of the court | gets the fill of his eye of my back, | I will come aside to welcome you | across the street if I see you.   40

Sìdna Àissa, chaidh a cheusadh
    mar ri mèirlich air bàrr slèibh,
is b'e 'n toibheum, Atmain, àicheadh
    gur bràthair dhomh thu fhèin.   44

*111 *An t-Eòlas Nach Cruthaich*

Fear a' bhreithneachaidh 's an fhiosa,
    am fiosrach balbh nach cruthaich nì,
tearbar am math 's an t-olc leis
    air meidhean cothromach a chinn.   4

Seallaidh e le cinnt an cunntas,
    mar ionnsramaid le gràdaibh mion;
slat thomhais e gun anam fàis ann,
    nach toir nì ùr gu blàths is bith.   8

Chan eil òrd ann, gilb no clàrsach;
    cha snaidh, cha ghràbhail e, cha seinn;
chan eil sguabadh fuarghuth sìn' ann,
    chan eil grìosach ann no greim.   12

Sìdna Âissa was crucified | along with thieves on the top of a hill, | and it would be blasphemy, Atman, to deny | that you are a brother of mine.   44

111 *The Knowledge that does not Create*

The man of judgement and knowledge, | the dumb, well-informed one who does not create anything, | good and bad are segregated by him | on the just scales of his head.   4

He shows with precision his recording, | like an instrument with delicate degrees; | he is a measuring rod without any soul-of-growth in him, | he will bring no new thing to warmth and being.   8

There is no hammer or chisel or harp in him; | he will not carve or engrave or sing; | there is no sweeping of tempest's cold voice in him; | there is no hot ember in him or grip.   12

Chan eil gul ann, fuath no mallachd,
   chan eil beannachd ann no aoibh;
cha mhaoidh e dòrn, cha toir e dùlan,
   cha tig às cagar sùgraidh caomh.   16

Eanchainn gheur gun neul, 's i torrach
   mar thuagh sgoltaidh an làimh threun;
beul a mheasas searbh is milis,
   gun domblas ann, gun mhil leis fhèin.   20

Cluasan èisteachd gach aon bhinnis,
   's nach gluais an spiorad às a thost;
sùilean sgrùdaidh gach aon sgèimhe,
   an ceann cèille marbh nach mol.   24

Mar bhean a phògas fir gu gràdhach,
   is nach àraich 'na staid thruaigh
leanabh leatha fhèin gu 'phògadh,
   b'e sin an t-Eòlas falamh fuar.   28

There is no weeping in him, or hatred or cursing; | there is no blessing in him or rejoicing; | he will not brandish his fist or make defiance; | no kind whisper of sweethearting will come from him.   16

A keen, unclouded brain, as fruitful | as a cleaving axe in a strong hand; | mouth which appraises bitter and sweet, | without any gall or honey in it of its own.   20

Ears that listen to all melodiousness, | but which do not move the spirit out of its silence; | eyes which scrutinise all beauty, | set in a dead head, full of sense, that praises not.   24

As a woman who kisses men fondly, | but who will not rear, in her sad state, | a child of her own to kiss, | such is cold empty knowledge.   28

*112 Còmhradh an Alltain

Na h-aibhnichean mòra,
ge mòrail, mall, leathann iad,
Tàimis is Tìobar,
's an Nìl, ge aost' a seanachas –
na chunnaic mi nam thuras   5
de shruthan mòra 's meadhanach,
Hamìz agus Harrais
is Safsaf Sgiogda eatarra,
Seabùs is Buidìma
is Picentìno eabarach,   10
Meidearda Chruimìri,
Forni, Irno 's Sele leo,
Remel fo Chonstantìna
is Lìri a dhearg ar fleasgaichean –
mas brèagh' iad, is fheudar dhaibh   15
gèilleadh don Allt Bheithe sin;
ge cian iad no ainmeil,
is balbhain gun cheileir iad.

Guthan is cluig
aig mo shruthan mu na clachan domh,   20
cruitean is fuinn,
luinneagan labhar ann;
tiompain is clàrsaichean,
gàireachdaich is cagarsaich,
sùgradh is deasbad,   25

---

112 *The Wee Burn's Talk*

The great rivers, | though they are majestic, broad and slow; | Thames and Tiber, | and the Nile, though aged be its history; | and all that I saw on my journey | of 5 great and middling streams, | Hamîz and Harrash | and the Safsaf of Skikda among them; | Seybouse and Budjîma | and the muddy Picentino; | the Medjerda of 10 Kroumiria, | the Forni, Irno and Sele along with them; | the Rhummel under Constantine, | and the Liri that our youths reddened – | though they be fine, they must | yield to yon Allt Beithe; | though they be far-off or namely, | they are dumb 15 creatures without melody.

Voices and bells | does my wee burn make round the stones for me; | small harps 20 and tunes | and loud ditties in it; | tympans and great harps, | laughing and whispering; | sweethearting and disputing, | 25

feadain gu faramach.
Crònan sgeap mar dhuis
is ceòl brugha troimh an rainich uaith,
cuairteagan is dannsadh,
canntaireachd is caithreaman.   30
Fàilte leis a' bhruthach
is Cumha am beul a' chladaich ann;
glaine, gile, binneas,
sruth glinne is ghlacagan.

An linntean a shàmhchair   35
is sgàthan don chraoibh bheithe e,
an t-àilleagan achrannach,
slatagach, meanganach;
bidh a sgàile thar a bhile,
's am bricein ga fhalach ann;   40
bidh a faileas air 'uachdar
'na lìon duathair is ghathannan,
's is co-cheòl a cheòlain
còmhradh na h-ainnire.

Chan eil guth aig daoine   45
o chaoineadh gu cainnt fhanaideach,
eadar ciùine 's mearan,
beannachadh is mallachadh,
comhairle no searmoin,
eirmseachd is sgaiteachas,   50
nach cluinnear leis na tuilm
feadh nam bulbhag 's nan caiseal uaith.

[Cluinnear

chanters sounding out. | A beehive humming like the drones of pipes, | and fairy-knowe music it sends out through the bracken. | Eddying and dancing, | canntaireachd and bold war-note sounding. | It sounds a Welcome down the brae, | and a Lament at the lip of the shore; | pureness, whiteness and melody, | stream of the glen and the little hollows.   30

In the pools of its tranquillity | it is a mirror for the birch-tree, | the lovely darling | of the intricate twigs and branches. | Her shadow lies across its brink, | and the little trout hides himself in it; | her reflection is on its surface, | a net of shade and sunbeams, | and the speech of the maiden | sounds in harmony with its music.   35 40

There is no tone of voice among men | from lamentation to derision, | between placidity and frenzy, | cursing and blessing, | counselling or preaching | or cutting repartee, | that the knowes do not hear | from it among its boulders and lynns.   45 50

Cluinnear ioghnadh 's mìothlachd,
miodal mìn is masgall ann;
'n àm tachairt ris na creagan   55
bidh gearanaich is talach ann;
brosnachadh is cronachadh,
moladh is achmhasan –
mo shruthan briathrach, bruidhneach,
tha guidhe is atach ann.   60
Tha dàin is duain is ùrnaighean,
sgeòil rùin agus naidheachdan,
tha salmaireachd is aoradh,
tha aoirean is magail ann,
's an ceòl a chuala mac Laèrteis   65
là Cèitein ga ghabhail ann.
Mu Shamhainn uair bidh donnalaich,
ochanaich is casaid ann,
ceumadh is tailmrich
cleas armailt a' faicheachd ann.   70
Là Lùnaist bidh snàth fuaim aige
cleas duanaig aig balachan.

Chan eil eun slèibh no coille
nach tug a ghoir 'na leasain uaith,
's e tiamhaidh, luaineach, ioraltach –   75
tric mar ghairm fheadagan.
Is ann aige air tùs
a dh'ionnsaich iad an gearan ac',

Wonder and displeasure, | smooth fawning and flattery are heard in it, | and when it comes against the rocks | it has girning and vexation in it. | Encouraging 55 and blaming, | praising and reproving – | my wordy, talkative wee burn, | it has supplication and beseeching in it. | There are songs and lays and prayers, | secret 60 tales and newsbearing; | there are psalmody and worshipping, | satires and mockery in it; | and the music that Laertes' son heard | is sung in it on May days. | 65 About Hallowe'en there will be howling | and lamentation and accusing in it, | pacing and [clanging] | like an army marching in it. | And on Lugh's day it will 70 have a thread of sound | like a boy singing a little song.

There is no bird of the wood or hill | that did not learn its cry in lessons from it, | so melancholy, wandering and cunning it is, | often like the call of plovers. | It was 75 from it in the beginning | that they learned their complaining, |

a dh'ùraich ceòl nan Cruimeineach
le cuir agus breabadaich,   80
Taorluath is Siubhal
a' sruthadh a tuill leadarra.
Cantail is cruitearachd,
ruitheannan ceilearachd,
fuinn stàtail mar cheud manach   85
an Laideann 'seinn an Fheasgarain;
saltairt is sitrich
'n àm lighe cleas eachraidh ann;
rothan troma 's drumaichean
's na tuiltean a' greasad air;   90
canain air cabhsairean
an steallraich gach eas' aige.

Cha teirig cainnt no duain dha
's a' ghrian 's an cuan a' solar dha,
len àlach neòil a' cumail fileantachd   95
am filidheachd a choilleagan –
na neòil bheaga is na baidealan
le frasan a' cur dheoch thuige,
neòil shneachda àrda thuraideach,
neòil dhubha oillteil thorannach,   100
neòil earraich luath an iarthuath,
neòil chiara dhùmhail fhogharaidh,
neòil an latha 's neòil na h-oidhche
a' roinn gun ghainne choireal air.

[Tha ceathach

which the music of the MacCrimmons renewed | with cadences and prancing, | 80
Taorluath and Siubhal | streaming from clangorous chanter holes. | Canticles and
crowdering, | rippling runs of melody, | stately tunes like a hundred monks | in 85
Latin chanting Vespers; | trampling and neighing | in time of flood like cavalry, |
heavy wheels and drums | when the spates hurry it on, | cannons on causeys | in 90
the spouting of its every waterfall.

Speech or songs will never fail it | while the sun and the ocean provide for it, |
with their brood of clouds keeping fluency | in the poesy of its lays; | the little 95
clouds and the stormy battlement clouds | sending drinks to it with showers; | the
high turreted snow clouds, | the black awful thunder clouds, | the swift Spring 100
clouds from the north-west, | the dark heavy clouds of Autumn, | the clouds of
day-time and of night-time | giving without stinting tunefulness to it. |

[Tha ceathach, ceò is ceòban   105
a' cumail òran 's oilein ris,]
gach caochan falaich uisge
(mion chuisleannan a' mhonaidh iad),
gach feadain is gach clais
a' cur fala agus sogain ann.   110
Am fraoch a' crathadh driùchda
nuair dhùisgeas a' ghaoth mhochthrathach,
an raineach is an luachair
a' luasgan ris na h-osagan,
is tha luisreadh ùr na mòintich   115
ag òstaireachd mhion chopan da.

Òran buan a' teàrnadh
gach ràidh às na coireachan,
uair le dùrdan dùsail,
uair le bùirich dhoineannaich;   120
ag èigheach 's a' ceasnachadh
's ga fhreagairt fhèin 'na chonaltradh,
a' brìodal chum na tràghad,
a' tàladh 's a' coiteachadh,
a' tilleadh don mhuir chèir   125
o a chèilidh aig na monaidhean,
am beò shruth beag as fheàrr
na gach sàr abhainn thostach leam.

The smirr, the mist and the soft rain | ply it with instructions and songs unceas- 105
ingly; | every hidden runnel of water | (the tiny veins of the moorland are they), |
every rill and channel | send blood and cheer to it. | The heather shaking down 110
the dew | when the early morning wind awakens, | the bracken and the rushes |
rocking in the breeze, | and the fresh plants of the boglands | play the landlord 115
with tiny cups for it.

An eternal song descending | every season from the corries, | at times with a drowsy
droning, | at times with a tempestuous roaring; | crying out and questioning, | and 120
answering itself in its conversing; | crooning down to the shore, | coaxing and
enticing; | returning to the dark sea | from its cèilidh with the moorlands, | the 125
little living stream that I love better | than all the grand silent rivers.

*113   Ed Io Rimasi ad Odorar le Foglie
Agus dh'Fhàgadh Mise le Fàileadh nan Duilleag

M'abhall òg an ceann a' ghàraidh,
    a dh'àraich mi fad bliadhn' an dòchas,
moch is feasgar bhiodh mo shùil air,
    's mi 'n dùil gum biodh a thoradh dhòmhsa.   4

Mi tacan uaith a' gabhail boladh
    duilleach 's toradh nam meur ìosal,
siud ga ionnsaigh fear gun athadh,
    is rùisg e orm m'abhall rìomhach.   8

An t-abhall uain' a chumadh slàn leam,
    nach deach mo làmh ann gu buain ubhail,
rùisg fear eile bun is bàrr e,
    is dh'fhan am fàile mar mo chuid dheth.   12

113   *Ed Io Rimasi ad Odorar le Foglie*
And I was Left to Smell the Leaves

My young apple tree at the end of the garden, | that I tended all year long in hope, | early and evening my eye would be on it, | expecting that its crop would be for me.   4

While I was a little space away from it, savouring the scent | of the leafage and fruit on the low branches, | up to it went a man without scruple, | and stripped my fine apple tree on me.   8

The green apple tree that I kept untouched, | among whose boughs my hand never went to pluck an apple, | another one stripped it top and bottom, | and the scent alone was left as my share of it.   12

*114 At the Quayside

The buyers peer with hands in pockets,
   black against the break of day,
and rienge their wits for jests to cheapen
   our siller won from waters grey.   4
Down from the quay they climb to finger
   what our brown nets swept away,
the hard-won harvest we have wrestled
   from sea and night, from wind and spray.   8

What do they know, or any others,
   of how the midnight wind commands,
and herds the glimmering crests to leeward
   to break in ranks on hidden strands,   12
or how dawn shows the torn horizon
   to staring eyes or frozen hands?
Only the night sea, wudd with winter,
   can give them the mind that understands.   16

We weather foreland after foreland,
   and string the bow of every bight,
where lamps in homes by windless harbours
   shine warm and yellow through the night.   20
We face, unshielded, wind and water,
   and black to leeward as we fight
we glimpse the crouching, thundering forelands
   that bare their fangs there, foaming white.   24

Hour and hour the hammering motor
   echoes through the hold below;
hour and hour the restless forefoot
   soars, then belts the black to snow;   28
the dark sea, wounded, phosphorescent,
   lashes, with icy fire aglow,
the eyes that read it, watching forward
   the sliding waters as we go.   32

Our wives at home are waking with us.
    Listening to the gale they lie.
We listen to its high crests hissing,
    and mark the neighbour's light outbye,   36
red now, green now, lifting, sinking,
    while, unquiet, our steersman's eye
traces the stays to where the masthead
    staggers its arc across the sky.   40

And lights on one bright star beyond it,
    above a cloud rim winking plain
like a beacon on a rampart,
    and of a sudden sees it wane.   44
Down the wind a grey wall marches,
    towering; across us leap again
the streaming spindrift and the fury,
    the squall, the blindness and the rain.   48

And if Fortune chances on us
    in the dark, and swings our keel
into the airt where shoals are swimming,
    we mark them, shoot and round them wheel.   52
Then a foot for purchase on the gunnel,
    numb hands that have lost their feel,
the ebb tide straining, the steep seas snatching
    a backrope like a rod of steel.   56

The buyers outlined on the quayside
    ganting and peering in a line,
the half-awakened early risers
    that wonder if the night was fine,   60
though they can look at dark to seaward,
    and see far out our torches shine,
what can they know of our dim battles
    round Pladda, Arran and Loch Fyne?   64

*115 *Prìosan Da Fhèin an Duine?*

Seall an t-amhsan clis 'na shaighid
   o 'fhaire fo na neòil,
's an t-eun a' luasgan air a shlataig,
   a' cur a bhith air fad 'na cheòl.   4
Their gnìomh is guth gach creutair ruinn,
   ach èisteachd riu air chòir:
"Cha chuir ceann is cridh' air iomrall thu.
   Bi iomlan is bi beò".   8

Cò air bith a chruthaich sinn,
   cha d'rinn E 'n cumadh ceàrr,
is mar thig air tùs gach duine
   air bheag uireasbhaidh o 'làimh.   12
A bheil nì nach biodh air chomas da
   ach cothrom a thoirt dhà,
is a bhuadhan uile còmhla ann
   a' còrdadh 'nan co-fhàs?   16

Ach nì e tric de 'bhuadhanna
   bròg chuagach fo 'shàil,
cuid dhiubh fon chuip, gun srian riu,
   's an dà thrian diubh 'nan tàmh.   20
Bidh an cridhe 'na thìoran aimhreiteach,
   's an ceann aige 'na thràill,
no bidh an corp 'na phrìosanach
   's an inntinn air 'na geàrd.   24

115 *Man His Own Prison?*

See the sudden gannet come as an arrow | from his watching under the clouds, | and the bird rocking on its branch, | putting all its being into its music. | The   4 actions and voices of every creature say to us, | if we would but listen to them rightly: | "Head and heart will not lead you astray. | Be complete, and be alive."   8

Whoever it is has created us, | His modelling was not at fault, | to judge from how every man comes at first | with few defects from His hand. | Is there anything that   12 would not be within man's powers, | were but the chance given him, | with all his qualities together | harmonising in a united growth?   16

But often he makes of his qualities | a lopsided shoe under his heel, | some of them, unbridled, under the whip, | and two thirds of them in idleness. | The heart   20 may be a turbulent tyrant, | with the head under it, its thrall, | or the body may be a prisoner, | with the intellect standing over it on guard.   24

Ceann is cridhe, teine 's coinneal
   a thoirt solais duinn is blàths,
an corp treun 's an t-anam maothsgiathach
   air aoigheachd ann car tràth,   28
fhuair sinn, is dà chois a shiubhal
   gu ceart cunbhalach air làr,
is dà shùil a shealladh suas uaith,
   no 'ruith cuairt nan ceithir àird.   32

An cridhe fialaidh, misneachail,
   na bu chiomach e am fròig;
ùraich cridh' an t-saoghail leis –
   cuir mu sgaoil e – cuir gu stròdh.   36
Biodh do dhruim 's do shealladh dìreach,
   agus t'inntinn geur gun cheò.
Lean gach beò a th'ann mar thiomnadh,
   is bi iomlan is bi beò.   40

Is seall an troichshluagh dàicheil, rianail,
   nach robh riamh ach leth bheò,
is beachdan chàich 'nan gàradh crìche dhaibh
   gan crìonadh ann an crò.   44
Nigh snighe mall an àbhaistich
   an sgàrlaid às an clò,
is thug e breacan ùr an nàdair
   gus a' ghnàthach ghlas fa dheòidh.   48

[Mas seabhag

Head and heart, fire and candle, | to give us light and warmth; | the strong body, and the soul with its delicate wings | a guest in it for a while – | we have that, and 28 two feet to travel | right firmly on the ground, | with two eyes to look up from it, | or to run the circle of the four airts. 32

The generous, spirited heart, | let it not crouch, a prisoner, in a nook; | freshen the heart of the world with it – | unleash it – be spendthrift with it. | Let your 36 back and your gaze be straight, | and your mind keen and unmisted; | follow the witness of every living thing there is, | and be complete and be alive. 40

And see the plausible, orderly dwarf-people, | who were never but half living, | with the opinions of others as a march-dyke round them, | wasting them away in a pen. | The slow seeping of the habitual has washed | the scarlet out of their 44 cloth, | and reduced the fresh tartan of their natures | to the grey customary at length. 48

Mas seabhag bhras no smeòrach thu,
   mìn no ròmach clò do ghnè,
na dèan a' Chruitheachd a nàrachadh
   le nàir' a cridhe 's a crè.   52
Mar thaing don Tì chuir deò annad,
   ma tha do dhòigh 'na Chreud,
no mar fhialachd dod cho-dhaoine,
   bi beò is bi thu fhèin.   56

*116 *Bisearta*

Chì mi rè geàrd na h-oidhche
dreòs air chrith 'na fhroidhneas thall air fàire,
a' clapail le a sgiathaibh,
a' sgapadh 's a' ciaradh rionnagan na h-àird' ud.

Shaoileadh tu gun cluinnte,   5
ge cian, o 'bhuillsgein ochanaich no caoineadh,
ràn corraich no gàir fuatha,
comhart chon cuthaich uaith no ulfhairt fhaolchon,
gun ruigeadh drannd an fhòirneirt
on fhùirneis òmair iomall fhèin an t-saoghail.   10
Ach siud a' dol an leud e
ri oir an speur an tostachd olc is aognaidh.

Whether you are a headlong hawk or a thrush, | smooth or shaggy the stuff of your character, | do not put Creation to shame | by being ashamed of heart and body. | In thankfulness to the One who put breath in you, | if your trust is in His 52
Creed, | or in generosity to your fellow men, | be alive and be yourself.   56

116 Bizerta

I see during the night guard | a blaze flickering, fringeing the skyline over yonder, | beating with its wings | and scattering and dimming the stars of that airt.

You would think that there would be heard | from its midst, though far away,   5
wailing and lamentation, | the roar of rage and the yell of hate, | the barking of [frenzied] dogs from it or the howling of wolves, | that the snarl of violence would reach | from yon amber furnace the very edge of the world; | but yonder it spreads | 10
along the rim of the sky in evil, ghastly silence.

C'ainm nochd a th'orra,
na sràidean bochda anns an sgeith gach uinneag
a lasraichean 's a deatach,   15
a sradagan is sgreadail a luchd thuinidh,
is taigh air thaigh ga reubadh,
am broinn a chèile am brùchdadh toit' a' tuiteam?
Is cò a-nochd tha 'g atach
am Bàs a theachd gu grad 'nan cainntibh uile,   20
no a' spàirn measg chlach is shailthean
air bhàinidh a' gairm air cobhair, is nach cluinnear?
Cò a-nochd a phàigheas
seann chìs àbhaisteach na fala cumant?

Uair dearg mar lod na h-àraich,   25
uair bàn mar ghile thràighte an eagail èitigh,
a' dìreadh 's uair a' teàrnadh,
a' sìneadh le sitheadh àrd 's a' call a mheudachd,
a' fannachadh car aitil
's ag at mar anail dhiabhail air dhèinead,   30
an t-Olc 'na chridhe 's 'na chuisle,
chì mi 'na bhuillean a' sìoladh 's a' leum e.
Tha 'n dreòs 'na oillt air fàire,
'na fhàinne ròis is òir am bun nan speuran,
a' breugnachadh 's ag àicheadh   35
le 'shoillse sèimhe àrsaidh àrd nan reultan.

What is their name to-night, | the poor streets where every window spews | its flame and smoke, | its sparks and the screaming of its inmates, | while house upon 15 house is rent | and collapses in a gust of smoke? | And who to-night are beseeching | Death to come quickly in all their tongues, | or are struggling among stones 20 and beams, | crying in frenzy for help, and are not heard? | Who to-night is paying | the old accustomed tax of common blood?

Now red like a battlefield puddle, | now pale like the drained whiteness of foul 25 fear, | climbing and sinking, | reaching and darting up and shrinking in size, | growing faint for a moment | and swelling like the breath of a devil in intensity, | I 30 see Evil as a pulse and a heart, | declining and leaping in throbs. | The blaze, a horror on the skyline, | a ring of rose and gold at the foot of the sky, | belies and denies | with its light the ancient high tranquillity of the stars. 35

*117 An Lagan

Cò chunnaic an lagan tostach,
   's a' ghrian mochthrath air a shlios,
ag òradh cromadh rèidh an ruighe,
   nach do chaill a chridhe ris?   4

Cò chunnaic riamh an lagan dìomhair,
   's a dhiùltadh a bhith sgìth is fann,
ged bu dian dlùth an Fhiann air,
   'na Dhiarmad le a Ghràinne ann?   8

Cò chunnaic an lagan uaine,
   's e suainte 'na choille chèir,
nach d'fhàg, san tionndadh uaith, fon bharrach
   roinn de 'anam às a dhèidh?   12

Chan eil gaoir no gul san lagan,
   chan eil falachd ann no foill;
sgiath dhomhs' e roimh gach dochar,
   nach leig olc nam thaic a-chaoidh.   16

Chan fhaicear tnùth no gràin san lagan,
   chan fhaicear ciùrradh ann no bròn,
cha tig fuath no leònadh faisg air,
   is coisrigt' ann gach gasan feòir.   20

*

117 The Hollow

Who saw the silent hollow, | with the early sun upon its flank, | gilding the smooth sweep of the lower slope, | that did not lose his heart as he looked?   4

Who ever saw the secret hollow, | and would refuse to be tired and faint – | though close and eager the pursuing Fiann to him – | a Diarmid with his Grainne there?   8

Who saw the green hollow, | happed in its dark woodland, | that did not leave under the birch tops, as he turned away, | a part of his soul behind him?   12

There is no outcry or weeping in the hollow, | there is no feud in it or treachery; | it is a shield to me against all harm, | which will never let ill come near me.   16

Envy or hatred are not seen in the hollow, | hurting or grief are not seen in it, | enmity or wounding will not come near it, | consecrated is each stalk of grass in it.   20

*

B'fhìor dhomh moladh bras a' bhalaich
    a sheinn na facail sin nam cheann;
b'fhìor dhomh, ged tha a 'mhuir cho farsaing
    eadar mi 's an lagan thall.   24

Tha mi an-diugh taobh mara cèine
    fo speur nach fhaic a ghrian sgòth,
ag èisteachd drumaireachd ar làmhaich,
    là fo gheasaibh, blàth, gun deò.   28

Bu mhinig ràmhan strì gad riastradh,
    mhuir ghrianach nam baile geal,
luingeas Àrgois is na Crèite
    is trìreimich na Grèig' o shean.   32

Shalaich cabhlaichean na Ròimhe
    is mòrchuis Chàrtaist cop do stuadh
le fuil, is cuirp is clàran loisgte,
    le sannt, le mort, le geilt is fuath.   36

Cà bheil tuinn uain' as glaine cobhar?
    Ach bu chorrach, luath an sìth
eadar Bheanas is Ragùsa
    is spùinneadaran borb Aildìr.   40

Ge b'e còrsa air am bris iad,
    is truaillte an gile fhuar
an-diugh fhèin, is iad le drillsein
    a' cur gu tìr nam marbh truagh.   44

[Tha fuil

True was the impetuous boy's praise, | that sang those words in my head; | true it was, although the sea is so wide | between me and the hollow beyond it.   24

I am to-day beside a far-off sea, | under a sky whose sun never sees a lowering cloud, | listening to the drumming of our gunfire, | on a charmed day, warm and breathless.   28

Often were the oars of strife tearing you, | sunny sea of the white towns, | the ships of Argos and Crete | and the triremes of Greece long ago.   32

The fleets of Rome | and the arrogance of Carthage defiled the foam of your [billows] | with blood, and corpses and charred timbers, | with greed, and murder, and panic and hatred.   36

Where are there green waves of purer foam? | But unstable and transitory was their peace | between Venice and Ragusa | and the fierce reivers of Algiers.   40

Whatever be the coast they break on, | their chill whiteness is corrupted | even to-day, as, sparkling, | they send the pitiful dead to the land.   44

Tha fuil sa ghainmhich air am bris iad,
   tha fuil 's gach allt a thig 'nan ceann;
tha grìs san oidhche dhiubh ri lasair
   bhailtean air chrith fo chlaidheamh dall.   48

Siud a' mhuir a tha cho farsaing,
   is strìoch fala cùl gach stuaidh;
siud na bliadhnachan air bhàinidh,
   is iad bodhar le ràn nan canan buan.   52

Tha toirm nan stuadh 's nam bliadhna eadar
   mi fhèin is fear a' mholaidh thall.
'Nan dèidh am faighear leam san lagan
   na dh'fhàg mi uair de m'anam ann?   56

*118 Beinn is Machair

Feuch, na dromannan clachach,
fuar, fosgailte, frasach,
a bheir don fhradharc le farsaingeachd ròic,   3
a' sìor àicheadh nam machair,
is nam mìltean ri farpais,
a' sireadh dìon agus smachd anns a' chrò.   6

There is blood on the sand on which they break, | there is blood in each stream that mingles with them; | they shine dull red in the night from the glare | of cities rocking beneath a blind sword.   48

There is the sea that is so wide, | with a streak of blood at the back of every [billow]; | there are the frenzied years, | deaf with the roar of the eternal cannon.   52

The thunder of the [billows] and the years is between | me and the one who made the praise, beyond them. | After them will I find in the hollow | that part of my soul which I once left there?   56

118 [Mountain and Plain]

Behold, the stony ridges, | cold, exposed and rainswept, | a sumptuous feast for the eye to behold, | ever disowning the flat land | and the competing thousands | 3
who seek refuge and discipline in the pen.   6

Beachdaich sìneadh nam bruthach,
lom, fìrinneach, duineil,
eadar fàire neo-chumhang 's na neòil.   9
Nach feàrr an seasmhachd na 'n sonas,
agus sgeanan nan ospag
na saoghal seasgar ga chosnadh air lòn?   12

Air an rèidhlean gun mhùthadh,
far an gèillear don ùine
fo throm speuran gun ùrachadh deò;   15
far a bheil seangain na h-ùrach,
is iad dìcheallach dùmhail
'nam mìltean an smùrach gach còis.   18

Troimh a chèile ag utadh,
a' cur rèis gun cheann uidhe,
driop gun chèill ac' a thrusadh an còrr;   21
is sgaothan sheillean nach cunntar
a' solar sna flùiribh,
agus suaingheasachd dhùsail 'nan ceòl.   24

Siud am baile 'na shiùrsaich,
is corp is anam 'nan cunnradh
feadh nan sàr shràid 's nan cùil ann gach lò;   27
is fa 'chomhair àrd lurach,
glan chomann nam mullach,
gach aon fo choron geal-chuithe 'na òigh.   30

[Tha othail

Consider the stretch of the braes, | bare, forthright, heroic, | between a boundless horizon and the clouds. | Is their permanence not better than happiness, | and the knife-thrusts of squalls not preferable | to a cosy life earned on meadows?   9 12

On the unchanging plain, | where all yields to time | under heavy suffocating skies, | where the ants of the earth | assiduously throng | by thousands in the dust of every hollow.   15 18

Hustling past one another, | running a race without finish, | in a senseless bustle to garner their store; | while swarms of bees beyond count | find provision among flowers, | and their music weaves drowsy enchantment.   21 24

See the city, the harlot, | where soul and body are bartered | in its thoroughfares and backstreets each day, | and high and lovely above it | the pure company of the summits, | each crowned with white wreath like a virgin.   27 30

Tha othail is sùrd ann
an dèidh shochairean 's cùinnidh,
's an sodal làn ùmhlachd don phròis   33
ag amharc on ùpraid
ri àrdan nan stùcan,
ri tost nan coire 's ri dùlan nan sgòrr.   36

An t-allt is luath labhar brasbhinn
leis na bruthaichean casa,
nì an rèidhlean a thachdadh fa dheòidh;   39
is thèid an luaths dheth 's a' mhisneach
gu gruaim bhodaich chrioplaich,
ged a b'uallach le slios e 's e òg.   42

Thèid a cheilearan saora
neo-eismeileach aobhach
'nan sruth eabair feadh raointean is feòir;   45
thèid a bhagartaich ghaisgich
gu mion chagarsaich chaillich,
no gu talach beag smachdaichte fòil.   48

Is e 'na leisgean donn, sàmhach,
dall, domhain a' snàgail,
làn ghlomhar is gàbhaidh is gò,   51
is a chuairteagan crèise
air an truailleadh le brèinead,
ag òl druaip agus dèistinn an t-slòigh.   54

*

There is frantic activity | after profits and cash there, | while servility fawns to pride | and gazes from the tumult | at the loftiness of the peaks, | the silent corries 33 and the challenge of the pinnacles. 36

The fast, loud, free-singing burn | rushing down the steep braes | will eventually be smothered by the plain; | it will lose its drive, and its smeddum | will turn to an 39 old cripple's gloom, | though giddily it raced down slopes in its youth. 42

Its irrepressible warblings, | assertive and joyous, | will become a mire through fields and grass; | and its loud martial bluster | an old wife's feeble whispers, | or a 45 timid resigned plaintive murmur. 48

Now a muted brown sluggard, | blind and burrowing deep, | full of pitfalls, deceit and danger, | its greasy eddies, | polluted and putrid, | will suck the nauseous 51 dregs of the masses. 54

*

A dheagh mhuinntir an t-saoghail,
mur b'e tartar nan daoine
sa bheil gnè nam beann gaothach 's nan sgòrr;
mur b'e an geur stàilinn faobhair
a bhith nur mèinn, bha bhur daorsa
mar chuing na treud a ghreas Maois às a' chrò.

57

60

*119 *Clann Àdhaimh*

Siud bàrca beag le antrom gaoithe sìorraidh
'na siùil chaithte, a' dìreadh cuain gun chòrsa,
's i leatha fhèin an cearcall cian na fàire,
is gul is gàireachdaich troimh chèil' air bòrd dhith.

4

Tha Bròn, Aoibh, Aois is Òige, Sàr is Suarach
a' tarraing nam ball buan a tha ri 'brèidibh;
tha Amaideas is Gliocas, Naomh is Peacach
air a stiùir mu seach is càch gan èisteachd.

8

Fo speur tha uair grianach, uair sgreunach,
– clais is cìrein – fèath is doineann – thèid i,
gu fàire nach do leum saidh riamh no sùilean,
's a lorg 's a h-ùpraid ghuth 'dol bàs 'na dèidh-se.

12

[*Ceangal*

Good people of the world, | without the clamour of those | whose nature is of the windy hills and peaks, | without the blade-sharp steel | in your ore, your enslavement | was as the yoke on the herd Moses drove from the pen.

57
60

119 *Adam's Clan*

Yonder sails a little bark, with the grievous burden of an eternal wind | on her worn sails, climbing an ocean that has no coast, | alone within the distant circle of the horizon, | with a confusion of weeping and laughter aboard her.

4

Grief, Joy, Age and Youth, Eminent and Of-No-Account | are heaving at the everlasting gear that trims her canvas; | Folly and Wisdom, Saint and Sinner | take her helm in turn, and all obey them.

8

Under a sky now sunny, now lowering | – trough and crest – calm and tempest – she goes on | to a horizon that neither stem nor eye yet overleapt, | and her track and her tumult of voices die astern of her.

12

Ceangal

Siud i is brù air a siùil 's i 'deuchainn gach sgòid,
long àrsaidh le sunnd is sùrd is lèireadh air bòrd;
fàire làn rùn nach do rùisgeadh fo cheann a croinn spreòid,
is cop uisge a stiùrach a' dùnadh 's ga chall sa mhuir mhòir.   16

*120 Is E Crìoch Àraidh

Chan eil do shàsachadh a-bhos;
   's e doras taigh do ghràidh an uaigh.
Chan eil an saoghal truagh nam beò
   ach fàsach fògraidh 's iomraill chruaidh.   4

Is e tha 'n sgeul ar là gu lèir
   roimh-ràdh bu chòir a leum ri luaths;
chan fhoillsichear do shùil fon ghrèin
   smior is meud an Leabhair Bhuain.   8

Is deuchainn gheàrr ar beatha bhochd,
   laimrig an aiseig null gar tìr.
A-bhos tha 'n t-olc 's na sìontan borb,
   ach thall tha foirfeachd agus sìth.   12

Envoi
There she goes with a curve on her sails, putting each sheet to the test, | an ancient ship with bustle and cheer and suffering aboard her; | a horizon full of secrets unrevealed under her bowsprit head, | and the foam of her wake closing and losing itself in the great sea astern.   16

120 Man's Chief End
Your satisfaction is not to be had in this life; | the door to the house that you love is the grave. | The wretched world of the living | is but a wilderness of exile and hard wandering.   4

The tale of all our days | is but a foreword to be quickly passed over; | the pith and bulk of the Eternal Book | is revealed to no eye under the sun.   8

Our poor life is but a short trial, | the jetty of the ferry across to our land. | On this side are evil and the savage storms, | beyond are perfection and peace.   12

A mholadh sin don Uile ghlic,
    don Dia tha biothbhuan, math is treun,
a las a' ghrian 's na reultan òir
    os cionn gleann a' bhròin 's nan deur.   16

A mholadh do Aoghaire nan neul,
    a their ris a' Chèitein "Gabh mu thuath";
Buachaill an t-samhraidh measg nan crann,
    foghair is geamhraidh d'A chloinn truaigh.   20

A thulgas an seòl mara mall
    bhos is thall air oir an fhuinn;
is Dorsair tùr nan gaoth, 's dan rèir
    bheir leum is laighe air na tuinn.   24

A sgeadaicheas a' choille lom,
    's a bheir a trusgan donn don ùir;
a roinneas gàire oirnn is deòir,
    breith, bàs, breòiteachd, slàint' is lùths.   28

A thùr dhuinn òige, fàs is aois,
    a shnaidh an saoghal is a sgiamh,
a dh'fhosgail romhainn muir is tìr,
    am magh 's cruth mìorbhailteach nan sliabh.   32

[A thùr

Praise be for it to the All-wise, | to the God who is eternal, good and powerful, | who lit the sun and the golden stars | above the glen of grief and tears.   16

Praise for it to the Shepherd of the clouds, | who says to the Maytime: "Go north-wards"; | to the Herdsman of the summer among the trees, | of autumn and winter for his wretched children.   20

Who rocks the slow tide | hither and thither on the lip of the land; | who is Door-keeper of the tower of the winds, and by them | makes the waves leap and lie down.   24

Who clothes the bare woodland, | and gives its brown raiment to the soil; | who shares out laughter and tears to us, | birth, death, sickliness, health and vigour.   28

Who devised youth, and growth and age for us, | who carved the world and its beauty, | who opened sea and land before us, | the plain and the wondrous shapes of the hills.   32

A thùr ar Bith dhuinn iomadh-fhillt',
   inntinn is colainn, ceann is làmh,
's a thug e dhuinn gu 'mholadh leis,
   's chan ann 'na oidhch' a' meath roimhn là.   36

Gabh gu deònach ri 'lagh glic,
   siubhail A shlighe ceum air cheum;
lean cumadh sìorraidh a' Phuirt Mhòir
   a rinn E dhuinn mar cheòl ar gnè.   40

Cluich an t-ùrlar mall air tùs,
   's gach roinn 'na dhèidh le lùths nad chuir,
air Crùnluath bras do là cuir ceann,
   till air an ùrlar mhall is sguir.   44

An Dia sin as Athair leat,
   'na sheirc a chruthaich sinn gu lèir,
nach binn am moladh Dha o 'chloinn,
   a dìmeas mu na rinn E fhèin?   48

Is e A smuain an t-anam maoth,
   's e 'anail chaomh a' bheatha bhlàth.
Dèan Da moladh sona fìor.
   Meal is mol sàr ghnìomh A làmh.   52

Who devised our being for us so manifold, | mind and body, heart and hand, | and gave it to us to praise Him with it, | and not as a night waning before the day.   36

Accept His wise law willingly, | travel His path step by step; | follow the eternal composition of the Pibroch | He made for us as the music of our nature.   40

Play first the slow Urlar, | and after it each part with vigour in your cadences, | complete the headlong Crunluath of your days, | return to the slow Urlar and cease.   44

That God whom you esteem Father, | who created us all in His affection, | is it not sweet praise for Him from His children, | their contempt for what He Himself fashioned?   48

The delicate soul is His thought; | warm life is His dear breath. | Make a true and happy praise for Him. | Enjoy and praise the excellent work of His hands.   52

*121 Casan Sìoda a' Freagairt

Rinn Casan Sìoda mosgladh air a shocair as a chrùban,
ga shìneadh is a' mèananaich le sealladh dreugain dùr orm.
Dh'imlich e a spògan agus chas e 'shròn le diomb rium,
is thubhairt e mu dheireadh rium: "Nì Math, nach leamh do bhùitich!   4

"Seo mise nam dhubh thràill agad, 's nam gheàrd 's do cheann fod sgèith-sa
gun taingealachd no bruidhinn air no buidheachas 'na èirig,
ach: 'An d'ith an cat na sgadain ud a ghabh a' ghaoth dhaibh fhèin uainn?'
is: 'Cò ghoid an trosg 's am bainne?' – agus, abair e, le speuradh.   8

"Na h-eòin a tha sa ghàradh ud a' togail àl gun obair,
gan reamhrachadh air gròiseidean, is ròic ac' air do chost-sa,
fo fheasgar 's e as dìota dhaibh an sìol a chuir thu mochthrath.
Cò sgapas gus na speuran iad? Gu dè ma dh'ith mi 'n trosg ort?   12

"Thug thu ainm a' mhurtair dhomh, ach cuir riut fhèin an cliù sin.
Fhuair thu cearc no dhà sa ghogail 's iad a' spìoladh ort do fhlùirean.
Ghabh thu fearg na dunach riu, a' mionnachadh gu brùideil
an amhaichean a shìneadh, agus lìnnig thu do bhrù leo.   16

["Mas aithne

121 [Silk Feet's Retort]

Silk Feet stirred slowly from where he crouched, | stretching and yawning, and eyes fixed on me, grim as a dragon's. | He licked his paws and cocked his nose in displeasure at me, | and finally said: "God, how your ranting irritates me!   4

"Here I am, a total slave to you, and keeping guard for you while your head nuzzles under your wing, | and no thanks or mention or acknowledgement do I get in return, | but 'Did the cat snap up all that herring that disappeared with the wind?', | and 'Who stole the cod and milk?' – and what's more, in choice language.   8

"The birds in that garden, work-shy, idly rearing their broods, | fattening them on gooseberries and all gorging themselves at your expense, | their diet in the evening is the seed you sowed that morning. | Who scatters them all sky-high? What of it, if I did eat your cod?   12

"You labelled me a murderer, but give yourself that honour. | You found a hen or two clucking and plucking away at your flowers. | You flew into a blind rage, violently swearing | that you would wring their necks, and you lined your stomach with them.   16

"Mas aithne dhuit na h-iasgairean, bu mhì-chiallach uait an 'leisg' ud.
Their luchd nan cuairt samhraidh riu 'nan aineolas a leithid.
Gach oidhche 's trang ar caithris duinn, 's gur e ar madainn feasgar.
Is mi chumas clos is cadal riut. Cha ghabh mi riut mar bhreitheamh.   20

"Tha mìle luch san taigh agad ri straighlich anns na cùiltean.
Tha seanaid dhiubh sa cheàrnaidh is batàillean slàn fon ùrlar.
Bidh an oidhche ac' air chèilidh, a' cur rèis 's a' streap nan cùirtein,
is millidh iad do shrannraich le an dannsaichean gad dhùsgadh.   24

"Is mi chuireas tost is teicheadh orra. 'S mì 'n Dubh Dhealan obann
a chromas air na deireagain mun teirinn iad 'nan tollaig.
'Ceatharnach sa chistin!' – cha bu mhiste thu mo chogadh
nuair lorg mi oidhch' air truinnsear iad a' dannsadh ruidhle ochdnar.   28

"Fuighleach do bhùird mar thuarastal – nach duairc do shùil an dèidh sin,
's gach cuirm a th'aig na luchainn 's iad cruinn san t-seòmar leughaidh?
Chreim iad leabhar Shomhairle, 's tha 'n comharra 'nan dèidh air;
chaidh am fiaclan mì-nàrach anns na Dàin 's an Craobh nan Teud ort.   32

"If you are a friend of fisherfolk, that 'lazy' was ill-advised. | It's the sort of term applied to them by ignorant summer tourists. | Every night our watch is busy, and the evening is our morning. | I'm the one protects your peace and sleep. I'll take no judgement from you.   20

"There are a thousand mice in your house clattering in the crannies. | There's a Synod of them in the cooking quarters, and an entire battalion under the floorboards. | They spend the night ceilidhing, racing each other and climbing up the curtains, | and they ruin your snoring, waking you up with their dances.   24

"It's me shuts them up and makes them run. I'm the swift Black Lightning | that falls upon the dirty pests before they disappear down their chink. | 'Cateran in the kitchen' indeed! – you were no worse off for my warring | the night I discovered them on a plate dancing an eightsome reel.   28

"Leftovers from your table are my wages – and how ungraciously you view that, | whereas the mice enjoy feast upon feast when they gather in the reading-room. | They've nibbled away at Sorley's book, and have left a mark to prove it; | their shameless teeth have dug into the Poems and the Tree of Harpstrings.   32

"Iain Lom 's Mac Mhaighstir Alastair 's Rob Donn, on ghabh an sùil orr'
is eagach caol an duilleagan, 's is cutach an rainn chliùiteach.
Cuiridh mi geall nach tomhais thu an cron is mò a dhrùidh orm –
fhuair mi an-raoir gu driopail iad ag ithe t'òrain ùir-sa.   36

"Seann chù leisg nan deargan, bheir mi dhuit a dhealbh 's a dhòighean –
miolaran is geòcaireachd 's a shròn a chur sna pòitean.
E fhèin 's a dhrannd 's a chùlagan! – cha dèan e tùrn ri 'bheò dhuit.
Is fheàrr mo spòg na esan slàn – nach mi a shàbhail t'òran?   40

"Ach nach iomadh feasgar sonais agus fois' a thug sinn còmhla,
's tu gam thachas cùl nan cluasan 's mi gam shuathadh riut 's a' crònan?
Gabh rabhadh, agus cuimhnich air na luchainn 's air na h-eòin sin.
A-nis nach leig thu cadal domh? – chan fhiach do chainnt an còrr uam."   44

"Iain Lom and Alexander MacDonald and Rob Donn, ever since they set eyes on
them | their pages have been thin and notched, and their celebrated verses much
abridged. | I wager that you'll never guess the damage that most perturbed me – | I
found them last night furiously munching away at your new song.   36

"As to the old lazy flea-ridden dog, I'll describe him and his ways for you – |
fawning and gluttony and sticking his nose into every pot. | Him and his growl
and molars! – he won't do a useful turn for you in his life. | Better my paw than
his entire bulk – wasn't it me who saved your song?   40

"But have we not spent many quiet, blissful evenings together, | you tickling me
behind the ears and I rubbing myself against you, purring? | Take a warning, and
be mindful of those mice and those birds. | Now, will you please let me sleep? –
your talk merits no more of my time."   44

*122 Na Tuinn ris na Carraigean

A mhuir fo chobhar ris na carraigean,
   an caraich iad led chòmhrag?
Saoghal nan gineal falbhanach,
   an treas' am marbh no 'm beò ann?   4

Am bi cinnt nam marbh a' meatachadh
   na beatha is na h-òige,
is am meòir chnàmha mur buinn luaineach
   gar toirt a-nuas 'nan còrdaibh?   8

Am bi gach smuain a smuainicheadh
   'na ceangal cruaidh mur còmhradh,
is cainnt àrsaidh 'na sean bhuarach dhuinn
   nuair bhios smuain ùr ga tòireachd?   12

Ciod e ma chruthaicheadh an talamh seo
   le cladaichean g'ar cròthadh?
A mhuir, mo mhuir-sa, tha 'n speur rionnagach
   le gaothaibh saor ag ulfhairt òirnne!   16

122 *The Waves against the Rocks*

Sea foaming against the rocks, I will they ever be moved by your fighting? I This world with its transient generations, I is the dead or the living the stronger in it?   4

Will the certainty of the dead I make life and youth weak, I and will their bony fingers be about our wandering feet I to bring us down in their cords?   8

Will every thought that was ever thought I be a hard bond about our conversation; I and will ancient talk be an old hobble for us, I when we are pursuing some new thought?   12

What if this land has been created I to hem us in with its shores? I Sea, my sea, the starry sky I howls over us with its free winds!   16

*123 *An t-Òigear a' Bruidhinn on Ùir*

Seall, a chinne dhaonna, dlùth air,
's gun toir an t-sùil don chuimhne rabhadh.

Seall am fonn a dh'òl ar lotan
air a threabhadh leis a' chanan.   4

Seall na h-achaidhean a shluig sinn,
a' sgeith an duslaich anns an adhar.

Ruidhle aig na cuilbh dhubh' orr'
ri drumaireachd nan gunn' a' tabhann.   8

Air an uisgeachadh le feòlachd,
le fuil òigear oidhch' is latha.

Air an ruamhar, air an riastradh,
air an cliathadh leis a' chasgairt.   12

Seall na bothain is na bailtean
'nan cruachan clachaireachd gun anam.

Seall smùr nam baile pronn san Eadailt,
's nan clachan leagte thall san Aifric.   16

[Duslach mìn

123 The Young Man Speaking from the Grave

Look closely on it, mankind, | and let the eye bid the memory take heed.
See the land that has drunk our wounds, | ploughed by the cannon.   4
See the fields that swallowed us, | spewing their dust in the air.
As the black pillars dance a reel on them | to the drumming of the barking guns.   8
Watered they are with butchery, | with the blood of young men night and day.
They have been dug, they have been torn, | they have been harrowed by the
slaughter.   12
See the cottages and towns, | [soulless] heaps of masonry.
See the dust of the crushed towns in Italy, | and of the villages overthrown in
Africa.   16

Duslach mìn nan taighean marbha,
stùr armailtean air uaigh nan dachaigh.

Bu chòir gun cruinnicheadh gaoth mhòr e
air feadh na h-Eòrpa fad' is farsaing, 20

às an Eòrpa is à Breatainn
ga sguabadh leatha 'na neul gathach.

'S gun sèideadh i sna sùilean cruaidhe
leis nach truagh ar lotan sracte, 24

leis nach truagh ar buain Earraich,
's ar n-uaighean feachda air ar n-aineol,

gan lìonadh le sleaghan duslaich,
gan cur a shruthadh is gan dalladh; 28

ceart mar a thachd an duslach ciar sinn,
's a mhùch e grian òg ar latha.

The fine dust of the dead houses, | the stour of armies on the graves of homes.
A great wind should gather it | through Europe far and wide, 20
from Europe and from Britain, | sweeping it along in a stabbing cloud.
To blow in the hard eyes | that do not grieve for our torn wounds, 24
that do not grieve for us, mown in the Springtime, | or for our campaign graves in strange lands,
to fill them with spears of dust, | to set them streaming and to blind them; 28
even as the dark dust cloud choked us, | and quenched the young sun of our day.

*124 *Meftah Bâbkum es-Sabar?*

Iuchair Bhur Dorais an Fhaighidinn?

Is cuimhne leam an Sùg el-Cheamais,
sa chaifidh dhorcha is sinn a' deasbad,
guth cianail mar ghuth chlag fo fheasgar
a mhol domh strìochdadh don Fhreastal.
"Mo chridhe fhèin, is faoin bhur gleac Ris,   5
's gu bheil gach toiseach agus deireadh
air an sgrìobhadh Aige cheana."

Sgrùd e bas a làimhe 's lean e:

"Do roinn, do mhanadh, is do sgàile,
thèid iad cuide riut 's gach àite.   10

"An rud a tha san Dàn 's a sgrìobhadh,
is gainntir sin a ghlais an Rìgh oirnn.
'S i 'n fhaighidinn le sealladh ìosal
iuchair doras ar dubh phrìosain."

Ghin aintighearnas na grèine lasraich,   15
is ainneart speuran teth na h-Aifric,
gliocas brùite sgìth nam facal.

[A ghliocais

124 *Meftah Bâbkum Es-Sabar?*

Patience the Key to Your Door?

I remember at Sûq el-Khemis, | while we argued in the dark café | a voice,
melancholy as the voice of evening bells, | that counselled me to be submissive
to Providence. | "My heart own, your struggle against It is in vain, | for every   5
beginning and ending | has been written by It already."

He gazed at the palm of his hand and went on:

"Your portion, your destiny and your shadow, | these accompany you in every
place.   10

"What is fated and has been written | is as a dungeon that the Divine King has
locked upon us. | Patience with a downcast look | is the key to the door of our
wretched prison."

The tyranny of the flaming sun, | and the violence of the hot skies of Africa | had   15
begotten the bruised, tired wisdom of these words.

A ghliocais mar chluig mhall' an fheasgair,
chan ann dhuinne do leithid!
Oir sgrìobhadh roghainn fa leth dhuinn,   20
an t-sìth 's am bàs no gleac 's a' bheatha.

Dh'fhalbh na diasan, dh'fhan an asbhuain?
Thuit na bailtean, chinn an raineach?
A bheil tom luachrach air gach stairsnich?
A shaoghail, tha sinn ann ga aindeoin;   25
tha a' ghrìosach theth fon luaithre fhathast.

Na iarraibh oirnn, ma-tà, cur sìos duibh
draoidheachd cheòlmhor fhacal lìomhta,
nithean clòimhteach, sgeòil an t-sìthein,
ceò no òrain airson nìonag,   30
òran tàlaidh caillich sìtheil
a' tulgadh a h-ogha 's ga bhrìodal –
na iarraibh, ach sgal na pìoba.
Beachdan gnàthach, laghach, cinnteach,
òraid dhàicheil à ceann slìogte,   35
nòsan àbhaisteach no mìnead,
suaimhneas turban geal na h-Ioslaim,
faighidinn Arabaich ga shìneadh
fa chomhair Allah fon bhruthainn shìorraidh

Wisdom like the slow bells of evening, | not for us is your like! | For a choice apart
has been written for us: | peace and death, or struggling and life.   20

Are the full ears gone, and only the stubble remaining? | Fallen are the
townships, and up has sprung the bracken? | Is there a clump of rushes on every
threshold? | Oh, world, we are here and live on in spite of it; | the hot ember is yet   25
under the ashes.

Do not ask us, then, to set down for you | some musical wizardry of polished
words, | soft, downy things or tales of the fairy knowe, | mist, or songs for young
girls, | the lullaby of some peaceful old woman | as she rocks her oe and gives it   30
fondling talk – | do not ask that, but the scream of the pipes. | Nice, conventional,
certain opinions, | a plausible oration from a sleek head, | customary ways or   35
smoothness, | the tranquillity of the white turbans of Islam, | the patience of an
Arab prostrating himself | before Allah in the eternal sultriness, |

na iarraibh – tha sinn beò da-rìribh,   40
agus "Is fuar a' ghaoth thar Ìle
gheibhear aca an Cinntìre".
Iarraibh gàire, gean is mìghean,
càirdeas, nàimhdeas, tlachd is mìothlachd –
iarraibh faileas fìor ar n-inntinn.   45

Siribh an annas ar làimhe
a' bheatha ghoirt, gharbh, luath-ghàireach,
oir thairg am Freastal rè ar làithean
roghainn na beatha no a' bhàis duinn.

Blàr-cath' ar toile, leac ar teine,   50
an raon a dhùisgeas ar seisreach,
stèidh togail ar làmhan 's ar dealais;
an talla a fhuair sinn gun cheilear,
is far an cluinnear moch is feasgar
ceòl ar sinnsre is gàir ar seinne;   55
an leabhar far an sgrìobhar leinne
bàrdachd ùr fon rann mu dheireadh
a chuireadh leis na bàird o shean ann –
b'e sin ar tìr. No, mur an gleacar,
rud suarach ann an cùil ga cheiltinn,   60
a thraogh 's a dhìochuimhnich sluagh eile.

do not ask for them – we are alive in earnest, | and "Cold is the wind over Islay | that   40
blows on them in Kintyre". | Ask for laughter, and cheerful and angry moods, | friend-
ship, enmity, pleasure and displeasure. | Ask for the true reflection of our mind.   45

Seek in each new work of our hand | life, sore, rough and triumphant, | for
Providence has offered us during our days | the choice between life and death.

The battlefield of our will, the hearthstone of our fire, | the field our ploughteam   50
will awaken, | the foundation for the building of our hands and our zeal; | the hall
we found without melody, | and where will be heard, early and evening, | the
music of our forebears and the clamour of our singing; | the book where we will   55
write | new poetry below the last verse | put in it by the poets of olds – | such will
be our land. Or, if there be no struggle, | a mean thing of no account, hidden away
in a corner, | which another people drained dry and forgot.   60

195

*125 *Tilleadh Uilìseis*

I

Ràinig mac Laèrteis,
seal mun d'èirich orra 'n là,
Iotaca is tràighean 'òige.

Anns na tràthaibh cianail
mun leum a' ghrian, bha 'n iubhrach àrd   5
dlùth fo sgàile an t-seann chòrsa.

Bha 'n cruinne aosta 'mosgladh,
ag osnaich luchd nan linn a' fàs;
osna airson na grèine
am beul gach dùil roimhn là;   10
's an sgùrr a b'àirde air 'ùr òradh.
    Bu chadal da, 's bha 'n t-eathar
    gu mear a' breabadh cuip o 'sàil,
    a' cur nam bàgh 's nan rubha eòlach.

An ciar nan coille driùchdach   15
's nan dùslainn tiugh thog eòin mun àl
an gearan briste bìgeil:
bha brìdein beul an làin,
is èigh a chràidh aige sa ghlòmainn.

125 *The Return of Ulysses*
I

A short space before day rose upon them, | Laertes' son reached | Ithaca and the strands of his youth.

In the melancholy moments | before the sun leaps up, the high-sided boat | was   5
close under the shadow of the old coast.

The aged world was stirring, | sighing its burden of centuries ever increasing; | a sigh of longing for the sun | in the mouth of every creature before the coming of day; | and the highest peak newly gilded. | He was asleep, while the boat | 10
was prancing, kicking foam from her heel, | weathering the well-known bays and headlands.

In the dark of the dewy woods | and the close-set thickets, the birds above their   15
broods raised | their broken complaint of cheeping. | A sandpiper at the lip of the tide | was calling out its hurt in the half-light. |

Is riamh bu chadal sìthe   20
do Uilìseas, sgìth o 'fhògradh.
    An dèidh gach euchd is faontraidh,
    cleas an naoidhein, rinn e suain
    air a shuaineadh 'na chleòca.

II

Bu chadal do Uilìseas;   25
is dh'fhàg iad sìnt' e air an tràigh,
e fhèin 's a shàibhreas uile còmhla.

Bu chadal. Is nuair dhùisg e
cha d'aithnich e a dhùthaich ghràidh,
oir chàraich a' bhan-dia fo cheò i.   30

B'e seann chù dall nan cartan
a' chiad bheò a dh'aithnich e,
nuair thill a bheò o cheudan dòrainn.

Gun fhuran is gun aithne,
'na chùis bhùirt aig fanaid chàich,   35
fhuair e cùil 'na àras mòrail.

                                                        [III

And still Ulysses slept a sleep of peace, | tired from his exile. | After all his deeds   20
and straying, | like a little child he slumbered | wrapped in his cloak.

II

Ulysses slept; | and they left him lying on the strand, | himself and his riches   25
together.

He slept. And, when he wakened, | he did not recognise his dear native land, | for
the goddess had put a mist over it.   30

The old blind dog full of ticks | was the only living thing that knew him, | when he
brought his life back from hundreds of grievous trials.

Unwelcomed and unknown, | a butt for the mockery of all others, | he found a   35
corner in his lordly dwelling.

III

A' cagnadh 'fheirge, an riochd an dèircich
'na dhùn fhèin, bu ghailbheach
a shùil fhiar fo 'mhailghean air cuirm nan tòiseach.

'Na dhèidh bu labhar sreang a bhogha,   40
is b'fhionnar oiteag a shaighdean
feadh an talla air gruaidhean na dòmhlachd.

Is iomadh misgear uaibhreach a tholladh,
's a leig 'fhochaid dheth 's a ghàire,
's a shleuchd 'na fhuil 's a làmhan dearg mu 'sgòrnan.   45

Is suirgheach maoth a fhuair a leagadh,
beul fodha, 's e 'sgeith lod fala
measg fion, feòl', arain, chuachan is fhear feòirne.

III

Chewing his anger, in the guise of a beggar | in his own dùn, stormy | was his sidelong glance under his brows at the banquet of the chiefs.

And, afterwards, loud was the string of his bow, | and cool was the waft of his   40
arrows | throughout the hall on the cheeks of the throng.

Many an arrogant drunkard was pierced, | and gave over his jibing and laughter, | as he bowed down in his blood with his hands red about his throat.   45

And many a delicate suitor was cast down, | prone on his face, spewing a puddle of blood | amongst wine and flesh and bread, amongst goblets and chessmen.

*126 Ar Blàr Catha

Taobh thall gach rubh' a thogadh leinn,
is cùl gach cnuic a choisich sinn;
a' ruith na dh'fhalaich cromadh
    gach fàire fad' air fuaradh;
màrsal 's dol sìos fo bhrataichean   5
nach d'fhairich gaoth ar n-àirdean,
clach tharraing anns gach àird dhuinn
    is ar màthair gar cur uaipe.
Fad nan linntean taistealach
b'e sin a bha air mhanadh dhuinn,   10
is eadar sinn is còrs' ar n-altraim
    fèath is stoirm nan uile chuantan.

Rangan MhicAoidh is feachd Ghustàvais,
    arm na Frainge, geàrd nan Liuthais,
a liuthad ceum sgìth is leòn is àrach,   15
    's gun leas ar màthar an aon bhuille.
An e gun d'rinn sinn a dearmad,
    's gun d'fhàs i searbh is bochd is cruaidh dhuinn?
Thrèig sinn i 's a làmh, ar leinn,
    'na feum 's 'na teinn gar n-utadh uaipe.   20

[Taobh thall

126 Our Field of Battle

The far side of every headland we ever raised, | the back of every knowe we ever walked; | pursuit of all that was concealed by the curve | of every horizon far to windward; | marching and charging under banners | that never felt the wind of 5 our heights, | a lodestone in every airt for us, | and our mother thrusting us from her. | Through the pilgrim centuries | such was our predestined lot, | while 10 between us and the coast that reared us | stretched the calms and storms of all the oceans.

The ranks of Mackay, the campaigning of Gustavus, | the [army] of France, the guard of the kings Louis, | so many weary steps and wounds and stricken fields, | 15 and no benefit to our mother in one single blow. | Was it that we neglected her, | and that she grew bitter and poor and hard towards us? | We forsook her, and her hand, it seemed to us, | ever in her need and hard straits was thrusting us from her. 20

Taobh thall gach cnuic 's gach rubh' air thalamh,
na còrsaichean ùra gar tarraing,
na dòighean ùra a' sgrios ar dachaigh,
gar ruagadh a thoirt buaidh air aineol.
Falbh dar deòin is falbh dar n-aindeoin   25
gu tàirneanaich nan àrach tartmhor;
buadhach an smùid nan còmhrag thairis,
is smùid an fhògraidh tiugh an Cataibh,
smùid an fhòirneirt feadh gach baile.

Cò dh'fhan a chluinntinn gaoth nan cuantan   30
    feadh luachair nan gort 'na h-aonar?
Tha 'n treabhaiche taobh thall nan cuantan,
    'toirt beath' à gruaim nan coilltean aosta;
tha 'n taigh, bha aoigheil blàth, gun mhullach,
    's a' ghaoth 's an t-uisge ann air aoigheachd;   35
tha 'm baile fuar fo thost na h-uaghach,
    's a dhaoin' air stuadhan fuar' an t-saoghail,
a' fosgladh le iuchair na h-èiginn
    doras seòmar-breith gach gaoithe –
cur is buain is cath is ceannach   40
    air stairsnich seòmar-breith gach gaoithe.

The far side of every knowe and headland on earth, | the new coasts drawing us on, | the new ways destroying our home, | driving us out in flight to seek victory in lands we didna ken; | going willingly and against our will | to the thunder of the thirsty battlefields; | victorious in the smoke of the battles beyond the seas, | while the smoke of eviction lay thick over Sutherland, | the smoke of oppression drifted through every township.   25

Who has stayed to listen to the wind of the oceans | as it sings its lonely song in the rushes of the furrows? | The ploughman is beyond the oceans | winning life from the gloom of the age-old forest; | the house, that was warm and hospitable, is roofless, | and the wind and the rain are guesting in it; | the township is cold and quiet as the grave, | and its people are on the cold waves of the world, | opening with the key of necessity | the door of the birth-chamber of every wind – | sowing and harvesting, battle and buying | on the threshold of the birth-chamber of every wind.   30   35   40

Fuil an ràn nam blàr asainn,
fallas sna coilltean sàmhach dhinn,
clach tharraing anns gach àird dhuinn
    is ar màthair ga cur suarach;   45
'dol bàs a' bualadh dhian bhuillean
an iomall cian na cruinne,
gun bhriathar is gun bhuille
    ga cuideachadh 'na truaighe.

Fàire seachad, fàir' ùr a' nochdadh,   50
gu 'cur ler dùthaich 's leis a' bhochdainn
fo uisg' ar stiùrach, 's ar sealladh romhainn.
Taighean ùr againn gan togail
air oir nam fàsach cian, coimheach –
deanntag is luachair 'nan tomain   55
an Albainn air làr nan tobhta.
An t-arbhar stuadhach ler n-obair
ri luasgan òrbhuidhe fon oiteig
far am b'àrsaidh, aognaidh, tostach
sgàile na ròchoille gun mhosgladh;   60
's am fraoch, 's an raineach, 's a' chopag
a' brùchdadh air ais thar lom nan goirtein,
thar clais is iomair a rinn torrach
fallas ar sinnsre, 's a dhìon on choigreach
glùn air ghlùin am fuil gun obadh.   65

[Is tìom

Our blood flows in the roar of the battlefields; | our sweat flows in the silent woods, | there is a lodestone in every airt for us, | while our mother is left despised; | dying as we strike fierce blows | on the far-off rim of the world, | without a word or a blow | to help her in her pitiful condition.   45

A horizon past, a new horizon showing, | to sink with our land and with poverty | beneath our wake, while we gaze ahead of us. | New houses raised by our hands | on the edge of strange, far-off wildernesses, | while nettle and rush spring in clumps | on the floors of the ruined houses in Scotland. | The undulating wheat through our toil | sways golden-yellow in the breeze, | where ancient, ghastly and silent | lay the shadow of the vast forest not yet awakened; | while heather and bracken and dockens | burst back across the open plots, | over furrow and ridge that were made fruitful | by the sweat of our forefathers, and that were protected from the stranger, | generation after generation, by their blood ungrudgingly shed.   50 55 60 65

Is tìom dhuinn sgur de chathan ciana,
ar cùl a thionndadh ris an iarchuan,
's ar n-aghaidh ris an dùthaich sgiamhaich
a dh'earb ar n-athraichean o Dhia ruinn.

Is i Alba ar clach tharraing,   70
is i Alba ar blàr catha;
's i fhèin a dh'uisgicheas ar fallas,
's i fhèin a gharas teas ar fala;
tha àite do gach buaidh a th'annainn
'na gleanntaichean is 'na bailtean;   75
tha feum air smuaintean 's air tapachd
eadar an stairsneach 's ceann a' bhaile.

**127 Forerunners*

The lonely star standing above the dawn,
    that heralds light to come when all is grey,
proclaims to night the future noon, then wan
    – the shadows challenged – dies in the rising day.   4

Drowned in the surging light they prophesied,
    lost in the later blaze, in flames akin,
how many herald stars have waned and died,
    forgotten in the day they ushered in.   8

It is time for us to cease from far-off battles, | to turn our back to the western sea |
and our face to the bonny land | that our fathers entrusted to us from God.

Scotland is our lodestone, | Scotland is our field of battle; | it is she that our sweat   70
will water, | it is she that the heat of our blood will warm; | there is room for every
quality that is ours | in her glens and her cities; | there is a need for thought and   75
courage | between the threshold and the end of the township.

*128 Grey Ashes

Be canny o trampan on grey ashes;
    they steer an' the air wins the hert o thaim.
In their hidden hert there derns the grieshoch,
    an' oot o the grieshoch is born the flame.   4

Be canny, be canny o grey ashes
    that ligg but reek i the airless bield.
Swing, wund, swing twa points – they are reekan;
    swing three – an' the bleeze rinns owre the field.   8

*129 The White Licht ...

The white licht, wellan up frae springs yont Asia, pales the gowd o the sterns
tae a wae siller, syne consumed i the kendlet crucible o the east,
an ilk limestane lirk o bare Hymettus purples, crimsons then gowden burns,
as the new sun, kythan, glisters alang green watter ablow a rocky coast.

They sterns that dwine frae east tae west,   5
    an' swarf in the surgean Aegean glory,
wane abune flindert craigs, a waste
    o cairns an' soopit stanes, mair weary,
mair yeld than Knoydart's heidlang coast,
    or Rannoch, lang an' braid an' oorie.   10

Sae when the sun westers ayont Aegina, an' doongaun, drains the flush
frae heich upland, heidland, island, an' the nicht ower aa things cups her hands,
ye that whan young rinn on bare rocks an' lauched tae watch green watter flash
alang a heidlang Scottish shore – coont ye this ane o the fremmit lands?

Bonny an' kent afore elsewhere,   15
    new an' acquent, steep, prood, sea-graven,
bare, hard, bonny, tautfeatured land,
    clear, sherp, hertsome, a land for livan.

Bare, hard, bonny – its winds blaw clean
    across clear ridges aff the sea,   20
nae shoggan an' flaffan o fullyerie,
    o reeshlan reeds an' hedges here,

[nae watter-reek

nae watter-reek o laich loanans
   tae dull the thrust o thocht an' ee,
nae braid pleuch-acres o seichan brairds,   25
   nae plains unendan rowed in haar.

Bricht an' hard – a maze sea-fretted,
   kyle an' skerry, stack an' strand,
bricht an' hard – a maze steep-snedded,
   scree an' scaurnoch, strath an' glen,   30
bricht an' hard – wi rocky heidlands
   derk atween lines o bleezan sand,
wi naethin boss in't, mauchy nor mauchless,
   heavy nor dozent, a land for men.
A wee land, bricht an' hard, whaes fowk   35
   soared tae man's heichmaist aince lang syne;
still snaewhite, kythan far frae land,
   their temples vaunt it as they crine.

Oor ain land wi its bitter blufferts,
   its flauchts o licht, its frosty sterns,   40
flashes an' rairs its strengthenan challance –
   what triumphs will answer frae its bairns?

*130   *Oor Jock*

"It's orra, man, the fowk I ken
   wha seem tae gang on burnan grund,
aye breengean oot an' lowpan ben
   lik paper men in a breeze o wund;
     thrang aye, an' maistly thrawn,   5
     ne'er contentit wi their awn;
rinnan aa week, dry days an' drookan,
   lik the bylie's echt-day clock,
wi ne'er a pause for thocht or lookan.
   They're gyte, the bodies," said oor Jock.   10
   "Blint wi sweit an' wudd on winnan,
     shair as daith they'll dee o pechan.
   Life's nae lang eneuch for rinnan –
     better slaw than aye forfochen,"
                  said oor Jock.   15

"It's orra, man, hoo mony fowk
  aye snifter owre what's feenisht fair,
the milk they tint, the crocks they brokk
  echteen simmers syne or mair;
    greetan aye, girnan aye,   20
    derknan the-day wi cloods blawn bye.
Maenan owre the meat they're stechan
  lik a wheen o craikan hens,
sweir an' scunnert wi their brochan,
  het or cauld, lik ailan weans;   25
lookan ahint them aye an' seichan,
  feart afore o what – wha kens?
    They're daft, the gowks, wi aa their bleatan
    o wandert sheep. They'll dee o carean.
    Life's nae lang eneuch for greetan   30
      better lauchs nor tears for sharean,
    better bricht nor black for weiran,"
                said oor Jock.

*131 *Kailyard and Renaissance*

Kailyairder:

Chiels o the Rinascimento,
a thing I'd hae ye aa tak tent o –
forget a while the stoor an' steer med
by thon rampagean Clan MacDiarmaid: 4
Why maun ye fyle, but mense or meanan,
ilk kailyaird that ye e'er hae been in?
Gin ye but sicht a kail-stock rampant,
up gangs yere fit, an' syne ye tramp on't.   8

Oor kailyaird wa's dung doon an' scattert,
oor kailyaird sangbuiks raxt an' spattert
wi ink o infamy an' slander;
it ryses e'en a Yairder's gander.   12

[Whan auld

205

Whan auld Scotland's stern was dwinan,
brichtness, fame, e'en name was tinan,
an' leid an' land had sairly suffert
frae the parchan Soothland bluffert   16
– pair Kintra – whar did sangsters bide in't
hauf sae leal an' hauf sae eident,
keepan the true Lallans lowan,
as whar the kindly kail was growan?   20

Stringan rhymes it was, I grant ye;
twasna Homer, Virgil, Dante;
words eneuch an' thocht fu scanty –
yet the rhymes they strung can haunt ye.   24
They but took a hamely daunder
on Pegasus, an' naethin grander.
Tho the ootcome wasna Spender,
it had hert, was warm an' tender.   28
Twasna sang as maisters med it,
words thrice waled an' finely sneddit,
line wi line in kindness beddit,
lilt an' thocht thegither weddit.   32
Wi the Union an' Culloden
waa'd in war the gates they trod in;
Scotland in a rickle liggan –
was there marble for their biggan?   36

Renaissance Chiel:

Had they waled their stane an' wan it,
there was rowth o honest granite;
gin they trod their gate wi smeddum,
wha daur muzzle or forbid them?   40
They warmed their haunds, nae firean giean,
at oor fire whan it was deean;
grieshoch-rhymsters, rypan cinders,
reengean oot odd bits an' flinders.   44
Tak ony Muse's hand and kiss it;
speir wha't was she used tae visit,
whaes een hae seen, whaes ears hae heard her –
she ne'er cam near a richt Kailyairder.   48
Yon's the reason there's a feck o
Kailyairders answer their ain echo
lik gowks in Spring alang the braes,
lik cribbin parrots an' lik jays.   52

Aye, the rhymes they strung can haunt me.
Thro the nicht in dreams they daunt me
wi their snifteran, snivellan greetan,
till I scraich an' wauken sweitan.   56

Kailyairders! Is't o thaim ye're thriepan?
Dreams o thaim hae gard me, sleepan,
lowp frae bed an' jouk ablow it,
I'se descrive a Kailyaird poet.   60

Croonan the Sangs His Mither Sang
he dovers in his Granny's Chair,
an' rowses Scotia's Bens an' Glens
in fifteen hunner lines or mair.   64

Taen frae a yaird juist no' his ain,
he slorps his cauld kail het again,
tho what wi Briars an' Bonny Broom
for growan kail there's scarcely room.   68

Waff an' wersh an' mim an' mauchy,
thaw-ice, dull an' boss an' bauch, he
Lets Fa' the Tear in ilka season,
an' greets in rhyme, but no' wi reason.   72

This thowless, sornan, thirled North Briton
bewails in words his land doonpitten;
his reid sun dees in Lauder's gloaman,
while reid o dawn fair sets him foaman.   76

His swaiveran gate's o ane that trauchles,
aimless, in slippan-slappan bauchles,
swaiveran, slaiveran, stumblan, mumblan,
while ootbye life's white spate gangs tumblan,   80
an' deif, he disna hear it rumblan.

*132 *Achmhasain*

(trì rainn is amhran)

Na beanntan àrda, saora,
  dh'fhuilingeas gaoth is grian,
gar faicinn mar a tha sinn –
  is achmhasan dhuinn iad.   4

Glinn nan làrach uaigneach,
  far na bhuadhaich am fiadh;
na h-achaidhean fo rainich –
  is achmhasan dhuinn iad.   8

Ar tìr bha uair 'na leòghann,
  bha mòr ri trod 's ri sìth,
'na measan aig sàil Shasainn –
  is achmhasan dhuinn ì.   12

Ceangal

Euchdan ar cinnidh dhuinn is achmhasan fìor,
a cheòl is a bhàrdachd, a chànain 's ar n-òigridh ga dìth;
na h-uillt bhras, is a' ghaoth thig saor o mharannan cian,
samhail misneach ar n-athraichean – achmhasain, achmhasain iad.   16

132 *Rebukes*

(three verses and envoi)

The high, free mountains | which endure wind and sun, | that they should see us as we are – | they are a rebuke to us.   4

The glens with their lonely ruined village sites, | where the deer has conquered, | the fields under bracken – | they are a rebuke to us.   8

Our land which was once a lion, | which was great in war and peace, | a messan at England's heel – | it is a rebuke to us.   12

Envoi

The feats of our nation truly are a rebuke to us; | its music and its poetry, its language which our youth go lacking; | the headlong burns and the wind which comes free from far-off seas, | the image of our fathers' spirit – rebukes, rebukes are they.   16

*133 *Feachd a' Phrionnsa*

(Nuair a ràinig arm a' Phrionnsa ùir Shasainn, agus iad air an abhainn a chur as an dèidh, thionndaidh iad, rùisg gach fear a chlaidheamh, agus dh'amhairc iad gu tostach air Albainn car tacain.)

Nuair a chuir an t-arm an abhainn
's a sheas iad air ciad raointean Shasainn,
thionndaidh iad gun ghlaodh, gun fhacal,
dh'amhairc iad le dùrachd dhainginn
air Albainn, 's rùisg gach fear a chlaidheamh.   5
Bheachdaich iad 'nan tost car tacain,
is gheall iad dhi an neart 's an gaisge.

Sgrìoch na truaillean fon stàilinn,
dh'èigh a' phìob is lean am màrsal.

Tha an còrr againn air chuimhne.   10
Chaidh an gealladh sin a chumail
le ceuman sgìth 's le lotan fuilteach.
Chuir iad Goliat mòr air uidil,
is, aon ri triùir, mu dheireadh thuit iad.

[– Dhùin iad

133 *The Prince's Army*

(When the Prince's army reached the soil of England after fording the river, they turned round, every man unsheathed his sword and they looked silently on Scotland for a while.)

When the army forded the river | and they stood on the first fields of England, | they turned round without either a cry or a word, | they looked with steady, purposeful devotion | on Scotland and every man unsheathed his sword. | They   5
gazed silently for a while, | and vowed to her their strength and courage.

The sheaths scraped under the returning steel, | the pipe cried out and the march continued.

The rest of it is in our memory. | That vow was kept | with weary steps and bloody   10
wounds. | They set great Goliath rocking, | and, one against three, they fell at last.

– Dhùin iad an greis a-bhos le alladh. – 15
Aon chuairt, aon chuairt gheibh sinn air thalamh
a nochdadh an fhaghairt a th'annainn,
a dheuchainn faobhar ar tapachd,
a chosnadh cliù dar tìr no masladh.

Is e bu chòir dhuinn stad is tionndadh, 20
amharc air ar tìr le dùrachd,
le gealladh blàth gun bhòst, gun bhùitich,
is lann ar spioraid theth a rùsgadh,
seann lann lasairgheal ar dùthcha;
's a liuthad bliadhna meirg' is dùsail 25
a mhaolaich i san truaill dhùinte.
B'e 'n dùsal dubh e – seo an dùsgadh.

*134 *Still Gyte, Man?*

"Still gyte, man? Stude I in yere claes
I'd thole nae beggar's nichts an' days,
chap-chappan, whidderan lik a moose,
at ae same cauld an' steekit hoose." 4

"What stane has she tae draw yere een?
What gars ye, syne she aye has been
as toom an' hertless as a hoor,
gang sornan kindness at her dure?" 8

"Though ye should talk a hunner year,
the windblown wave will seek the shore,
the muirlan watter seek the sea.
Then, wheesht man. Sae it is wi me." 12

– They closed their spell in this world with honour. – | One spell, one spell only 15
do we get on earth | to show the temper of the metal in us, | to test the edge of our
courage, | to win fame for our country or shame.

Now is the time when we should stop and turn, | look upon our land with 20
affection and devotion, | with a warm promise without either boasting or threats, |
and unsheath the blade of our hot spirit, | the old flaming-white sword of our
country; | so many years of rusting and slumber | it has been growing blunt, set 25
fast in its sheath. | It was a wretched slumber – this is the awaking.

*135 *Esta Selva Selvaggia*
This Savage Wood

Relief exults, nostalgia sighs
at yesterday shot from our skies
in smoke and splinters, speeches, lies.
  Today's no ground to stand upon –
  unstable fiction balanced on   5
  to-morrow and the day that's gone;
  the hair of midnight, finely drawn
  between last evening and the dawn.

Fearful hope and angry fear
guess at to-morrow, paling there,   10
one man's foul another's fair.

Yesterday? We saw it die
among the shellbursts in the sky,
and heard the snarling headlines cry,
hyenas of a night of fears,   15
scarlet with tracer, pale with flares,
under distorted guiding-stars.
  Man, violent against his will,
  tore himself open, looked his fill
  and saw; and he is shuddering still.   20

*

The swaying landmines lingering down
between Duntocher and the moon
made Scotland and the world one.
At last we found a civilisation
common to Europe and our nation,   25
sirens, blast, disintegration.

The house has buried sister, mother.
Sheer chance – a direct hit. Another
near Bou Arâda buried brother.
None was left, and no one mourned.   30
The telegram has been returned
undelivered, scrapped and burned.

*

[The Bofors

The Bofors got him with his bombs away;
crashed airman, hustled from his burning plane
(*Salopard, voilà ce que tu as fait!*)   35
stumbles dazed to where his stick has strewn
tiles, splintered glass and plaster blotting blood,
pales, stammers: "*Gesù Cristo!* But they should
have struck across the docks. A puff of wind,
a second early! *That* was by my hand?"   40

*

The sergeant from the Folgore
sips his wine and chats away:
"*Ostia!* It was bizarre.
At San Vincenzo, in the square
behind the church, we found them there.   45
Two Fridolins, both some days gone,
near them a girl of twenty-one
shot through the face, two caps, a gun,
two glasses and a demi-john."

"Poisoned the wine she had, I'd say.   50
But one as he began to sway
still had strength left to make her pay."

*

"*Merde!*" says the gendarme "*Ces messieurs indigènes*,
why waste one's time on questioning them, when
science can help. Some electricity   55
applied to the softer parts, and one will see."

*

Chopping sticks below the prickly pears;
turban, hook nose, cheeks hollow with his years.
He drew his lips back, said: "There comes a day
when the *Fransâwi* will be swept away."   60
Jabbing the earth he twisted his cleaver round –
"Just as I grind this cleaver in the ground,
kilêb, kelbât – dogs, bitches – where we find them,
– *hakdha, hakdha* – thus, thus will we grind them."

*

The Irno Bridge; Salerno in the sun,   65
while Capo d'Orso in a bluish haze
watches the cobalt waves against him run.

(You'll find the rest in any guide-book's praise.)
This is the land *par excellence* where you sought
select starred ruins, and the parrot phrase   70
of guides made wearisome the beauty spot.
This is the hell where barking batteries
heap on the old fresh ruins smoking hot.

Here are your newly made antiquities;
new graves and stumps of riddled gables frown   75
from Paestum to the Arno's Galleries.

The Irno Bridge; the Spring wind from the town
sifts rubble-dust across – ghost-walking yet,
sharp dust of murdered homes now ten months down.

This father, hunched up on the parapet,   80
peddles his daughter with sly, beaten eyes;
finding no hirer, begs a cigarette.

And past the Osteria, loud with flies,
trail the *perduta gente* of this world,
"artistic rags" and all. What judge denies   85
peace to these homeless wisps by warblast whirled?

                                *

Ragged and filthy, six years old,
he stumbles on the kerb, and lies
dead still, as if content to hold
this resting pose and never rise.   90
Hands reach down and put him back,
swaivering, on uncertain feet.
"*Poverini!* They are so weak.
Where and how are they to eat?"

                                *

"*Haus kaput – maison finie –*   95
kaput – capito? – familie.
Alles ist kaput. Compris?"

                                               ["*Er hat*

"*Er hat uns belogen* – he told us lies."
"Who wanted war? The poor man dies
in war. He threw dust in our eyes."   100

"Only the great make wars," they say,
"*I pezzi grossi, gros bonnets,
el-kebâr bass* make war to-day."

"*Halûf! Βουλγαρικὸ δκυλì!
Cretini 'e merda! Βρωμεροì!
Τα Μαχαρόνια! Sale Italie!*"   105

"*N'âd dîn bâbak – salauds* – dogs!
Jene Scheissherrn! Wops and Frogs,
they're all the same, myte, like the Wogs."

*

"What crime was it we suffered for?"   110
"They started it. We willed no war."
Listen to yourselves. Beware.

*

Yesterday? We saw it die,
and yet unburied see it lie
rotting beneath a sultry sky.   115

Where the east pales bleak and grey,
to-morrow is it, or yesterday?
Ask the old men. Can they say?

Yesterday made them. On its walls
they write its end; and down it falls   120
in blood and pacts and protocols.

We, having seen our yesterday,
blasted away, explained away,
in darkness, having no to-day,
guess at tomorrow dawning grey,   125
tighten our packstraps for the way.

*136 Truaighe na h-Eòrpa

Tha mùir shnaidhte na h-Eòrpa
shìos 'nan tòrr air a raointean.

Tha an gràbhaladh àrsaidh
air a sgàineadh is gaorr air.   4

Tha dlùth shreathan a tùirean
'nam mion sprùidhlich air aomadh.

Tha muinntir a tallachan
sgapte air faontra.   8

Is luaineach, làn airce,
oidhch' is latha a daoine.

Chaidh geurghuth an truaighe
thar cruaidhghàir a gaothan.   12

Dh'fhalbh bhàrr na h-Eòrpa
trian de 'bòidhchead sèimh aosta.

Seann tèarmann na h-ealain,
cridhe meachair na daondachd.   16

Och, rubha na h-Àisia,
Bàlcan an t-saoghail!

136   Europe's Piteous Plight

The finely hewn ramparts of Europe | are down in a heap upon her plains.
Their ancient carvings | are split and [stained with gore].   4
The close-fitting courses of her towers | are collapsed in small rubble.
The people of her halls | are wanderers dispersed.   8
Without ever rest, full of need, | are the nights and days of her folk.
The shrill voice of their pitiful complaining | drowns the hard roaring of her winds.   12
Gone from Europe | is a third of her tranquil, aged beauty.
The old sanctuary of the arts, | the tender heart of humanity.   16
Och, she is become a promontory of Asia, | the Balkans of the world!

POEMS 1946–1958

*137 An t-Iasgair

Seo mar dh'aithnich mi riamh thu,
fhuair oilein aig sgoil an iasgaich.

An sealladh fir, na sùilean socrach
a sgrùdadh slugan dubh an doininn,
's a leughadh seagh an àrdthuinn obainn,   5
ceann geal troimh dhall na h-oidhche 'nochdadh.

Tha fuaradh 's fasgadh, faire 's fulang
nad shùil 's an ciùine do ghutha;
dh'fhàg caol is cuan, rubh' air rubha
len sruthan cinn 's len gaothaibh uile,   10
dh'fhàg cathadh sguabte iomadh tuinne,
fèath is gailleann is sìontan dubha,
air do ghruaidh an seul, a dhuine.

137 The Fisherman

This is how I ever recognised you, | who were brought up at the school of the fishing.

The man's look, the steady eyes | that would search the black gullet of the storm, | and that would read the meaning of the sudden towering wave, | a white crest 5 showing through the blindness of the night.

Windward and leeward, watching and enduring | are in your eye and in the gentleness of your voice. | Kyle and open ocean, foreland after foreland | with their head tides and all their winds, | the swept spindrift of many a wave, | calm 10 and gale and black tempest, | [all] have set their seal upon your cheek, man.

*138 The Fisherman

This is aye the way I kent you,
that had the fishing for school and learning,
the sea's scholar, the gale's apprentice.

The man's glance, long and steady,
to search the black gullet of the tempest,   5
to read the sudden breaker's meaning,
through the night's blindness palely gleaming.

Windward and leeward, watching, enduring,
are in your eye and the quiet sureness
of the gentle voice that aye is yours, man.   10

Narrow kyle and open ocean,
foam-rimmed foreland after foreland
with head-tides setting, head-winds blowing,
– wind, sea – all have gone to mould you.

Many a wave with spindrift sweeping,   15
gales, calm, black tempest, pale haar creeping
have set their stamp upon your cheek, man.

*139 Bloigh Eadailteach

A bhith leatha o laighe na grèine
gun nì gar faicinn ach na reultan,
aon oidhch' a-mhàin, aon oidhche Chèitein,   3
aon oidhch' a-mhàin; is 'na dèidh sin
na tilleadh grian eile a dh'èirigh
's na glasadh là am bun nan speuran.   6

139 Italian Fragment

To be with her from the setting of the sun, | with nothing to see us but the stars,
| one night only, one night of May, | one night only; and after it | let no other sun   3
return to rise | and let no day break at the foot of the sky.   6

*140 *Tlachd is Misneach*

Ciùcharan nan eun mun chladach,
a' dùsgadh air chionn teachd an latha;
boladh a' bheithe 's na rainich
ag èirigh suas le dealt nan glacaibh;
tùis roid nan còs fo chùirnein lainnir　　　　5
a' smùidrich ri grèin òig na maidne.
Na cnuic fa chomhair Rubha Meall Daraich,
cnuic bheaga, fhiadhaich, mholach, chasa;
a' ghaoth ri osnaich trast am mala,
am muing uaine ga crathadh,　　　　10
's a' mhuir mum bonnaibh ri cagar –
bha sin daonnan mar roinn de m'anam,
'na thobar fionnar sìth' is tlachda;
bha, is bidh 's mi beò air thalamh.

A' mhuir gheamhraidh fon doineann,　　　　15
's i nuallanach, uabhasach a' sloistreadh
druimeach, fuarghlas ri Rubha Loisgte.
A' mhuir earraich ri solas
grian ghaothach a' Mhàirt 's a' mhosglaidh.
Muir na h-oidhche reubte a' losgadh,　　　　20
's an teine sionnachain a' nochdadh
gach sgar an cliathaich na sgotha,

140　*Pleasure and Courage*

The low chirping of birds about the shore, | wakening to meet the coming of day; | the fragrance of birch and bracken | rising aloft with the dew of the hollows; | the incense of the bog-myrtle in the little dales, bog-myrtle beaded and glittering, |　5 steaming in the young morning sun. | The hills facing Rubha Meall Daraich, | little, wild, steep, shaggy hills, | the wind sighing across their brows, | their green mane tossing in it, | and the sea whispering round their feet – | that was always as　10 a part of my soul, | a cool well of peace and pleasure; | was, and will be while I live on earth.

The Winter sea under the storm, | roaring and terrible, surging | in cold-grey　15 ridges against Rubha Loisgte. | The Spring sea gleaming in the light | of the windy sun of March and the Spring-awakening. | The night sea torn and burning, |　20 blazing phosphorescent and revealing | every seam in the skiff's hull, |

fo 'guaillean 's mu 'sàil a' froiseadh;
lasair is sradagan sa chop dhith,
's i 'ruith 's a' tionndadh mar fhiadh air cnocan.   25
Gaoth, frasan, sliabh is tuinn mo locha,
bha sin riamh 'na fhuaran sonais
's 'na èibhleig mhisnich dhomh air choimhich;
bha, is bidh 's mo chuairt a-bhos domh.

*141 *Pleasure and Courage*

The chirp of birds along the water,
wakening to greet the dawning;
the fragrant scent of birch and bracken
born with the dew from little valleys,
rising with the dew, drifting softly.   5
Incense of myrtle in the hollows,
bog-myrtle with clear dewdrops beaded
in the young sun of morning steaming.
The hills of the bay fronting the headland,
wee hills, wooded, wild and headlong,   10
the winds across their summits sighing,
singing about their brows and crying;
their green mane tossing – swaying branches –
the sea about their feet lapping.
That was ever, the shore that reared me,   15
part of my soul, knit in my being;
a cool well of peace and pleasure
it was, and will be for ever.

[The Winter sea

showering under her shoulders and about her heel; | flames and sparks in her
foam, | as she races and turns like a deer on a knowe. | Wind, showers, hill and   25
waves of my loch, | these were always a spring of happiness | and an ember of
courage for me in strange lands. | Were, and will be for all my journey here.

The Winter sea the hard wind scourges,
roaring and terrible, upsurging   20
– cold-grey ridges bristling, foaming –
about the sentinel, sheltering forelands.
The Spring sea flashing and breaking
in the windy sun of March the waker.
The night sea, stemtorn, keeltorn, burning   25
that, phosphorescent, lights the lurching
seams of the hull above it towering,
under stern and shoulders showering;
flames and sparks in the skiff's foam blazing
as she runs and turns to her rudder, racing   30
like a deer on a knowe, her quick heel spurning
the gleaming, windtorn, hurrying summits.
Waves of my loch, wind, rain and heather,
these were a spring of gladness ever,
an ember of courage in strange countries;   35
were, and will be throughout life's journey.

*142 Stoc is Failleanan

Thalla, Eudochais, is beachdaich.
  A' chraobh a leag iad an-uiridh –
seall! – chan fhaic thu 'stoc am-bliadhna
  aig fionmhoireachd nam fiùran uime.   4

Tha ceathach uaine uimpe a' cleith oirnn
  lot na tuaighe a leag a mullach,
oir ghin na freumhan, 's iad air fanachd,
  àlach ghallan far na thuit i.   8

142 Stump and Shoots

Come, Despondency, and consider. | The tree that they felled last year – | look! –
this year you cannot see the stump | for the multitude of shoots around it.   4

There is a green mist about it hiding from us | the wound of the axe that brought
down its crest; | for the roots, which remained, begot | a brood of young sprouts
where it fell.   8

"Sin tè a dhìth air a' choille,
    beàrn san doire nach dùinear" –
ach dh'ùraich i a beatha fhathast
    le failleanan an aghaidh dùile.   12

"Slàn leatha," thuirt sinn, "'s le 'cuid smeòrach.
    Cha chluinnear ceòl a h-eunlaith tuille."
Nuair a thèid bliadhna 's bliadhna seachad
    bidh iad a' seinn as ùr 'na duilleach.   16

Dh'fhan na freumhan an dèidh an leagaidh
    a tharraing beatha on ùir don bhuin i;
A dh'aindeoin choilltearan is tuaighe
    dh'ath-nuadhaich i a h-eòin on duslach.   20

Ar cainnt 's ar cultar, car sealain
    ged rachadh an leagadh buileach,
cuiridh am freumhan 's an seann stoc dhiubh
    failleanan snodhaich is duilleach.   24

*143 Old Stump and Young Shoots

Come, Despondency, gaze on this sign and ponder.
    The tree they felled in the Spring of the year that is gone,
look! seek for the stump – this Spring you cannot find it
    for the young shoots around it, so close have they grown.   4

There is a green mist about it, hiding
    the wounds of the axe that humbled a crest that was tall;
for the same roots bided still, and sent up sunwards
    a brood of slender stems where the old tree fell.   8

["There is one

"That is one lacking from the wood, | a gap in the grove that will never be closed up" – | but it still renewed its life | with young shoots against all expectation.   12

"Farewell to it," we said, "and to its thrushes; | the music of its birds will be heard no more." | When a year and yet a year have passed, | they will be singing afresh among its leaves.   16

The roots remained after the downfall, | to draw life from the soil to which it belonged; | in spite of woodmen and the axe | it has renewed its birds from the dust.   20

Our speech and our culture, | though they should be wholly cast down for a time, | their roots and their old stock will put forth | sappy shoots and leaves again.   24

"There is one that the wood has lost forever;
   a gap in the grove," we said, "that will never close."
But it still renewed its life against expectation
   with saplings, and, brought to earth, with the Spring it rose.   12

"Farewell to it," we said, "and to all its thrushes.
   The music of its birds will be heard no more."
When a year and a year are gone they will yet be singing
   again among leaves we thought no Spring would restore.   16

The old roots bided on after the felling,
   to draw fresh life from the soil from which it grew.
In spite of woodman and axe, this stump we grieved for
   has brought its leaves and its birds from the dust anew.   20

Our speech and culture – Despondency, consider –
   though they be brought low for a time and forgotten by men,
the old stock still has its roots, and the roots will bring us
   shoots and sap, branches and leaves again.   24

*144 *Scots Arcadia*

Walkan heich an gazean far –
   listenan tae the wund in the rashes –
sun an shadow, clood an clear
   shift athwart the hillsides dappled.   4

Listenan tae the burns gang doon –
   listenan tae the wund in the rashes –
watchan Autumn doon the braes,
   a spate o gowd amang the bracken.   8

Watch him rinn alang the glen –
   listenan tae the wund in the rashes –
edge the bramble leaves wi bluid,
   kendle fire on rowan branches.   12

Glisteran rocks wi sun an rain –
   listenan tae the wund in the rashes –
the heather bields the broon muirhen,
   the wae curlew cries lanesome sadness.   16

Birk an hazel, rowan reid –
   listenan tae the wund in the rashes –
bracken, heather; sae 'tis made,
   oor ain Arcadia, wild an tranquil.   20

*145 *We Abide For Ever*

From the dun Grampians to the green Atlantic,
   these glens beneath our living, moving skies
are still a hearth where glows a fire undying,
   home of a handful, not of a folk that dies.   4

These glens and islands, towns by rocky harbours,
   are towers untaken where our fathers were;
surviving adverse centuries, defying
   the siege of history, we yet are there.   8

Since that ill-fated day on bleak Culloden,
   when wind and hail, lead and artillery,
when hireling horsemen facing unslept hunger
   won, but not over souls, their victory,   12

wave upon wave of fate has roared against us –
   a way of life undone in every thing,
e'en to the plaid once worn by kings in Scotland;
   our leaders exiles with their exiled king.   16

The thatch ablaze, red sparks from flaming rafters –
   go, Canada has need of head and hand;
the sombre woods receiving – sick and weary –
   those that the sheep had driven from their land.   20

And more. For war and war in far-off countries
   left blood-stained tartan strewn on hill and howe.
Death, with his sudden, violent tiend to gather,
   stalks through our story, even until now.   24

In spite of blows and weary prophesyings
   we yet go forward, courage not being gone.
Come from a past of tempest and of trial –
   hear, world, and hear mankind! – we yet live on.   28

We are the Gaels that centuries have not shaken;
   we are no broken ghosts, no vanished race.
Our spirit cries in pride from clamorous chanters,
   speaks with a tongue of ancient strength and grace.   32

As long as sun and moon go circling westward,
   while, ebb and flow, pulses the constant tide,
while day from night, while light returns from darkness,
   with speech and melody we will abide.   36

*146 Una Più Crudel del Mare

One More Cruel than the Sea ("Orlando Innamorato")

The sunny wind from off the land
   veered to a greyer, colder air
against the shore, and vexed the sand
   with restless foam. I saw her there.   4

The changing airt, the broken calm –
   her faithless heart was there in them.
In blenching sea and paling sun
   I saw her, never one the same.   8

When can I mind that she was one,
   who, cold and kind, has changed for me
like the waters and the wind?
   She is as cruel as the sea.   12

*147 The Two Neighbours

Two that through windy nights kept company,
two in the dark, two on the sea at the steering,
with aye one another's bow-wave and wake to see,
the neighbour's light away on the beam plunging and soaring.   4

Two on blind nights seeking counsel in turn –
"Where will we head now?" – sharing their care and labours,
spoke across plashing waters from stern to stern,
comrades in calm, fellows in storm, night-sea neighbours.   8

Dark and daybreak, heat and hail had tried
and schooled the two in the master glance for esteeming
the curve of the outgoing net, the set of the tide,
the drift of wind and sea, the airt where the prey was swimming.   12

Two on the sea. And the one fell sick at last,
"for he was weak, the soul, and old". And the other
watched long nights by his bed, as on nights that were past
he watched from the stern for his light, sea-neighbour, in ill a brother.   16

Watched by the peep of a lamp long nights by his side;
brightened his mood, talking their sea-nights over;
followed him to Cill Ainndreis when he died,
and left him at peace in a lee that would feel no wind for ever.   20

*148 *Na Casan air Tìr*

Tha mo chasan air tìr
   is mo lìon air croich òrdail;
tha mo sgoth air a' mhol
   is na sgorraidhean fòipe.   4

Tha na sgorraidhean fòipe,
   is mi gu dòigheil air cathair
mu choinneimh gealbhain mhòir èibhinn,
   is mi 'g èisteachd na gaillinn.   8

Tha mi 'g èisteachd na gaillinn
   ri sgal is toirm orgain,
agus torrann na mara
   air a' chladach san dorcha.   12

Nas mò cha chuir iad orm cùram,
   's cha bhi an stiùireadh gam shàrach;
nas mò cha leugh mi an losgadh,
   's chan iarr mi coltas feadh bhàghan.   16

Cha bhi mi 'n eisimeil an losgaidh
   is a' choltais nas fhaide;
am freastal motar is lìontan,
   an taing na sìne 's luchd ceannaich.   20

[Nas mò

148 *Feet Ashore*

My feet are ashore | and my net is up on orderly crochans; | my skiff is on the shingle, | held up by the props.   4

The props hold her up, | and I am sat comfortably | before a merry big fire, | listening to the gale.   8

I am listening to the gale's | shrieking and organ-thunder, | and to the roar of the sea | on the shore in the dark.   12

No more will they worry me, | nor will the steering trouble me: | no more will I read the burning, | nor seek appearance in the bays.   16

I will be dependent on burning | and appearance no longer, | nor beholden to motor and nets, | or indebted to weather and traders.   20

Nas mò cha tèid làmh dhiom
　　air druim àrcan no ceannair,
's chan fhaic mi rudhadh na grèine
　　trast an speur cùl a' Cheathraimh.　　　24

Iomachar 's an Innis
　　is Rubha Sgibinis àlainn,
an Sgat Mòr is an Coileach –
　　seo soraidh is slàn leibh.　　　28

Tha 'n crann cèill' air an fharadh –
　　nì mo mhac-sa a ghabhail.
Is eòl da camas is caolas
　　nach leig an aois domh bhith 'tathaich.　　　32

Faodaidh esan ri sìontan
　　fad na h-oìdhche bhith 'caithris.
Tha mi fhèin air mo shocair,
　　is tha mo sgoth air a' chladach.　　　36

*149　Ardlamont

Rain from windward, sharp and blinding;
sweet to hear my darling tramping
on her way, the seas unminding,
swinging forefoot wounding, stamping.　　　4

Steep to windward ridges breaking,
huddled down in flocks before her;
light she throws her head up, shaking
broken seas and spindrift o'er her.　　　8

No more will I turn a hand | to cork-rope or bridle-rope, | nor will I see the sun | streaking the sky red behind Kerry.　　　24

Imachar and Inchmarnock | and lovely Skipness Point, | the Great Skate and the Cockerel – | here's farewell and so long.　　　28

The helm's in the loft. | My son will put it to use. | He knows of creeks and of kyles | that age prevents me frequenting.　　　32

Let him stay awake | against the elements all night. | I am now at rest, | and my skiff is on the beach.　　　36

*150 *Fàire*

Inntinn acrach, cridhe tartmhor,
  sealladh dom falamh fad a fhradhairc,
a bheil na shàsaicheas bhur sireadh
  thar fàire idir nas fhaid' air aghaidh?   4

Còrsa ùr – an tuilleadh annas –
  a lòchrain a' fàs fann roimhn ghrèin air:
cainnt eil' air àrdoras nam bùthan;
  speur cinnidh ùir fo smùid an èirigh.   8

Uair is uair, còrsaichean ùra,
  is cùinneadh ùr ga chur a cheannach
blais ùir a dh'fhìon: is sriut de chòmhradh
  nach tuigear deò dheth, taobh a' chalaidh.   12

Taighean solais an t-saoghail,
  a sheòlaidean, a chaoil, a chuantan,
ùpraid a cheidhe, dòmhlachd a chabhsair –
  uisge stiùrach ga chall sna stuadhan.   16

Is ann a tha dà rubha Ghàidhealach,
  's na shàsaicheas sùil, cridh' is inntinn
an taobh a-staigh dhiubh. Dh'fhàg thu, m'anam,
  nad dhèidh am bad as tobar t'ìota.   20

[Gu leòir

150 *Horizon*

Hungry mind, thirsty heart, | gaze that finds empty all that falls within it – | can it
be that what will satisfy your seeking | lies over some horizon further on?   4

A new coast – more novelties – | its beacons growing dim along it before the sun: |
another tongue above the doors of the shops; | the sky of a new nation with the
smoke of their morning rising athwart it.   8

Time upon time, new coastlines, | and a new coinage sent to buy | a new taste of
wine: and a flood of talk, | not a word of it understood, along the side of the
harbour.   12

The lighthouses of the world, | its roadsteads, its straits, its oceans: | the bustle of
its quays, the throngs of its pavements – | these are all wake which is lost among
the waves.   16

There are two Highland forelands, | and enough to satisfy eye, heart and mind |
lies inside them. You have left behind you, my soul, | the place which is a well to
quench your thirst.   20

Gu leòir a dh'imeachd 's a dh'iomairt;
    gu leòir, a chridhe, ded sgrùdadh eirthir.
Is ann mu loch 's fo shlèibhtean t'àraich
    tha fàire t'iarraidh 's tlachd a sheasas.   24

Ach, tha fhios agam, ged chì mi
    Cluaidh 's Loch Fìne mu dheireadh,
tha fàire 'n-sin deas air Arainn
    a bhios gam tharraing uair eile.   28

*151   *The Smoky Smirr o Rain*

A misty mornin' doon the shore wi a hushed an' caller air,
an' ne'er a breath frae East or Wast tie sway the rashes there,
a sweet, sweet scent frae Laggan's birks gaed breathin' on its ane,
their branches hingin beaded in the smoky smirr o rain.   4

The hills aroond war silent wi the mist alang the braes.
The woods war derk an' quiet wi dewy, glintin' sprays.
The thrushes didna raise for me, as I gaed bye alane,
but a wee, wae cheep at passin' in the smoky smirr o rain.   8

Rock an' stane lay glisterin' on aa the heichs abune.
Cool an' kind an' whisperin' it drifted gently doon,
till hill an' howe war rowed in it, an' land an' sea war gane.
Aa was still an' saft an' silent in the smoky smirr o rain.   12

Enough of travelling and bustle; | enough, heart, of your scrutiny of coastlines. |
It is around the loch and below the hills that watched you grow | that you will find
the horizon you are seeking, and pleasure that endures.   24

But I know, although I see | the Clyde and Loch Fyne at last, | there is a horizon
yonder south of Arran, | that will be pulling at me again.   28

*152 *Am Faillean Ùr*
(òran)

Faillean fo bhlàth an gàradh driùchdach leis fhèin,
maise is fàs is fàileadh ùrar nan geug;
siud coimeas mo ghràidh, 's is feàrr a giùlan 's a gnè.
Tha aiteas is bàigh am fàilte mhùirnich a bèil.   4

Càite bheil gin le cridhe dh'fhairich an gràdh,
nach seas air a cheum le spèis ga h-amharc air sràid?
Uil' àillteachd is cruth na Cruitheachd innte a' tàmh.
Tha sgiamh na cruinne cruinn san aghaidh gun smàl.   8

Lainnir is dreòs de òr gach cleirc air a ceann.
A faicinn rim thaobh, a ghaoil, bu gheasachd siud leam.
Sèimh bhruidhinn dhìleas, fhìor is furan gun fheall;
guth ìosal 's e binn, guth bìth mar uisge le gleann.   12

Tha oidhche is là 's gach ràith 'dol tharad nach till,
'cur sèiste rid bhòidhchead òg le falachd gun sgìos.
Dèan gèilleadh don ghràdh, 's na fàg a' bhuaidh aig an tìom,
mun gèill do cheann bàn is blàths do ghruaidh do 'strì.   16

152 [The Fresh Sapling]
(song)

A fresh sapling in bloom in a dewy garden, standing alone, | the grace and fragrant scent of its branches in growth; | yon is a fitting image for my love, and even finer her bearing and countenance. | There is joy and affection in a cheerful welcome from her mouth.   4

Where is one to be found with a heart which ever felt love, | who does not stand rooted to the spot with esteem when seeing her in the street? | All the comeliness and shapeliness of Creation abide in her. | All the beauty of the earth is gathered in the face without blemish.   8

Every lock of her head gleams and blazes like gold. | That she should be seen by my side, love, what enchantment for me. | Gentle speech, steadfast, true, and a greeting without guile; | a low voice, sweet of tone, a tranquil voice like water down a glen.   12

Night and day and every season go past you never to return, | laying siege to your youthful beauty with relentless malice. | Surrender to love, and leave not the victory to time, | before your fair head and the warm glow of your cheeks submit to its strife.   16

*153 The Fresh Sapling

Sapling that grew with dew and sunshine and days,
leafy and slender, fresh the scent of its sprays,
blooming unknown with none to speak in its praise,
where I steal in alone in secret to gaze.   4

Slender she grew and straight, the one that I praise,
a face I look long to, framed in red gold ablaze.
And better than all I've said the spell of her ways,
steadfast and true, with grace around her in rays.   8

When I was down I sought you always, my dear.
Welcome I found there, kindness, solace and cheer.
Gentle and low your slow, soft voice in my ear;
sweet voice like the sound of running water to hear.   12

*154 Edinburgh

A windy toon o cloods an' sunny glints;
    pinnacled, turreted, stey an' steep grey toon;
her soughin' gables sing their norlan' rants
    tae saut an' caller blufferts on her croon.   4

Steeple an' toor an' battlement stand bauld,
    an' gaze ootowre the kindly lands o Forth
tae the braid seaward lift, far, clear an' cauld,
    an' front her airt, the stern, abidin' north.   8

Oh, I hae seen her leamin' frae afar,
    bricht thro the fleetin' blatter o the rain,
an' happed an' hidden, rowed in norsea haar,
    secret an' dour, loom grandly, prood an' lane.   12

Tae stand an' watch frae oot the wooded west
    the heich ranks o her dignity gang by,
an' see it surgein' seaward, crest on crest,
    her lang swell merchan' ridged against the sky.   16

*155 *The Walls of Balclutha*

The pale moon with her healing stream
drenches the world with light and calm;
whitens the rocks and dims the stars
along the eastern sky, and pours
an amber path across the sea.   5
Peace floods down broken crags and scree.
Southward, Orion over Bute
stamps with a restless, angry foot,
leans over Scotland in her sleep
and seems to spurn her, taut to leap   10
out across the sky, and stand
towering above some other land.

Yonder blaze the spangled Pleiades,
clear in the air as over warmer seas.
So Attic steersmen saw them, sure and bright,   15
and shaped their course through the Aegean night.
So from the charred and smoking hill of Troy
they led Odysseus westward on his way.

The moon with tranquil witchcraft stills
the old sounds of the very hills.   20
The daylong roaring of the burns
is lulled and lowered, and it turns
to a fine thread of thin rilling.
The glittering summits, gently spilling
in rocky flanks, go curving, falling   25
chequered with shade and silver light,
still in the stillness of the night.
Thin lines that coil by dip and fold
the pathways go, alive of old,
broken and lost in hillside grass,   30
old echoing ways where no men pass.
Still, still, too still – still without peace
those roads to herried villages.

The rocky ways, grown green at last,
where bards and saints have passed,   35
harper and judge, ambassador,
piper and man of war
swordgirt and plaided, stepping long,
shield behind shoulder slung;
                                                  [monk

231

monk and physician, staid and slow,   40
merchant and galley crew.
The rocky ways, grown green at last,
where peace and war have passed,
shepherd and keeper have them now,
and tall the grasses grow   45
where learning walked and poetry,
music and history;
where kindness passed, and courage stepped
lightly, and laughter leaped
at wit and song. There no men come.   50
Their echoes all are dumb.

Here one who casts his care away
and, singing on a summer day,
by glen and hill goes wandering,
comes suddenly upon a thing   55
and halts before it, looking long,
and leaves half done his summer song.
Hidden in silent hollows, thronged
with slender birch, the homesteads wronged
by greed and haste and hidden fear,   60
look for the men that held them dear.
Gaunt on the hillsides, looming high,
standing gapped against the sky,
torn gables make their hard reproof
to those that see and stand aloof.   65
Drowning the acres won by man,
the brackens, thick where furrows ran
and generations laboured, hint
to those who see indifferent.
The spiked rush under broken walls,   70
on hearth and threshold, bends and thrills
and tosses to the summit wind.
Here it happened. Had they sinned
against the sun, the folk who sang
around these hearths till the rocks rang   75
and dark hills listened in the night?
Had they sinned against the light,
that stood and watched their thatch ablaze,
then turned to walk the world's ways?
Gone are they, with their vanished years?   80
Lost like the smoke from trampled fires?

Those ravaged townships on a thousand hills
are in our being, and their memory fills
our songs and spirit, colouring our mind.
Bitterly gone. All gone. Men of our kind,   85
our kindly race, torn up and cast away.
Foreboding, so, is born with us, a grey
burden from birth. We must be rid of it.
And so the restless fear, felt, and so late,
to lose the past and our inheritance,   90
the colour of our thought, our native glance;
to watch, losing our inborn gait and stance,
our vision fade of what we were, and fall,
beaten without a battle, and lose all.
We fear defeat without a hint of war,   95
to follow on another people's star,
warp ourselves out of being what we are,
to lose our name and nature, thought and mood,
the old, sure ground on which our fathers stood.

We go beneath that burden, and we grope   100
through chilling myths that blench the face of hope.
A trouble to the heart, an old distress,
fable of poverty and bitterness;
the fated withering of our ancient tree,
root and blossom, blight of history;   105
the fated blight that greys our springtime field,
ill, done of old, and never to be healed;
starkness and bleakness innate in our land,
false tale to lame the spirit, hold the hand.
False, false. Black lie of our predestined dearth,   110
veiling the crime that made the mossgrown hearth,
the threshold soft with grass that knows no feet.
Of our own selves, believing, we repeat
that wrong upon ourselves, and hug defeat.

But we are men, and have both thought and will.   115
The same sun rises eastward on us still
as rose on Athens. There is in us yet
the seed that flowered in Attica; and, hot,
that flame – an ember near to glow again –
that flared and lit up Florence. We are men,   120
and hidden in us, restless, with its urge,
the seed of graciousness. Half heard, the surge
of the creative spirit breaks unstilled
upon our rocks. The spirit is not killed.

[Let spring

Let spring but strike its sunlight through our showers, 125
our sprays will vaunt a flourish of new flowers,
new blooming, shaped and coloured by the past.
"Was" will beget "will be" unwarped at last.

*

Orion, straddled over Bute,
rears his restless, angry foot,   130
and round the midnight Ploughshaft creeps
marking the hour, while Scotland sleeps.

*156 [Then Farewell, Tarbert]
(song)

Then farewell, Tarbert, for a while, farewell the hale Kintyre;
farewell the loch, farewell the Sound, farewell the Kerry Shore.
Farewell tie foreland, rock and strand, tie skerry, bight and hill;
though I should trevel twinty lands ye'd stand afore me still.   4

May good luck go for neebor wi the boats that sail from here,
in wind or calm tie hadd yere helm, wherever ye may steer.
The sea would be a store for ye, if thoughts could work their will.
I never watched a settin' sun and didna wish ye well.   8

May good luck hadd yere steerin' hand, and shine, a guidin' light
for aa the fleet, and may ye meet wi Fortune in the night.
A redded net in every stern upon yere homeward way,
and silver high in every howld afore the brekk o day.   12

The sea would be a store for ye, if thoughts could work their will.
I never watched a settin' sun and didna wish ye well.
I'm mindin' o ye every time I look towards the sea.
I never hear the risin' wind but aye I think on ye.   16

If wishin' well could keep from ill, my wish would keep ye safe
from shrouded shores by nerra seas, from shoal, from rock, from reef,
from squall, from hail, from midnight gale, from daybrekk torn wi wind,
and bring ye through the longest night that derkened kyle or sound.   20

When, choked wi storm, the mad Sou'-east leaps down on ye and raves,
when risin' fast below the gusts the Sound is hoarse wi waves,
when aa is blin wi night and rain, and no' a light tie see,
may guidin' Fortune swing yere stem and bring ye tie yere lee.   24

*157 Na Trèig do Thalamh Dùthchais

Na trèig do thalamh dùthchais,
air fearann no air chùinneadh,
air onair no air siùrsachd.

Air mholadh no air ùrnaigh
na trèig do thalamh dùthchais,   5
air ghealladh no air chùmhnant.

Air lagh, air lainn, air dhùlan
na trèig do thalamh dùthchais,
air saltairt no air chiùrradh,
air eagal no air bhùitich.   10

Air chall, air sgìos, air chùram;
air ghràdh, air sìth, air dhùrachd;
air bhàigh, air speuran ciùine
na trèig do thalamh dùthchais.

Air àilgheas inbh' is cùirte,   15
ged bheirte spèis is cliù dhuit,
na trèig do thalamh dùthchais.

Na trèig do thalamh dùthchais,
air fearann no air chùinneadh,
air onair no air siùrsachd.   20

157 Do Not Forsake Your Native Land

Do not forsake your native land | for lands or for wealth, | for honour or for harlotry.

For praise or for prayers | do not forsake your native land, | for promise or for   5
bargain.

For law, for sword, for defiance | do not forsake your native land; | for trampling
or for wounding, | for fear or for threatening.   10

For losses, for weariness, for cares, | for love, for peace, for good wishes, | for
kindly regard, for tranquil skies | do not forsake your native land.

For the imperious wish of position or courts, | though esteem and fame should be   15
your lot, | do not forsake your native land.

Do not forsake your native land | for lands or for wealth, | for honour or for
harlotry.   20

*158 *Seeker, Reaper*

She's a seeker, thon boat. She's a solan's hert.
She's a solan's look. She'll strik doon oot o nowhere.
"Cast off!" she says, "Cast off!" red mad tie stert,
"The loch is wide wi wanderin' watter. Lowse me! Drive me! Go there!"
She's a greed for wind an goin', she's away! an goin' itsel.   5
She'd whiten the world's watter. She'd trail her wake through Hell.
    She's a reaper, she's a river, she's a racer,
    She's a teerer thon. It teks the wind tie pace her.
She's a leaper. She's a gled roar wi the sea afore her face.
She shoothers by her anchor chain, she canna lie at peace.   10
    She wanders at her anchor and feels the slidin' sea.
    Norrard, sou'ard, east an west wilna let her be.
    She bridles at her moorins along the quiet quay;
    She canna lie at peace and be content in any lee.

As she listens tie the lappin' o the herbour watter,   15
lippin' at her shouther, the hale sea's pullin' at her;
as it runs its threids o light along her sunny plankin',
"Up anchor, boys! Come, nightfall! Wester, sun!" she's thinkin'.

The shape o her thoughts is on her in her mould from bow tie stern.
Her drivin' mood speaks oot o her wi the way her shoothers turn.   20
When she clears the dusky herbour where the evenin' windows drowse,
she sets her stern doon and she lifts her questin' bows.
Her motor rings and roars in her, birlin' its whirrin' tunes,
and over she sings and over again, while on the motor drones.

       Heiskir, Haiskir,   25
         the Heids o Ayr,
       Heiskir, Haiskir,
         the Heids o Ayr,
       Man and Canna,
         they ken me there,   30
       I've flung the seas they sent me
         aboot me in the air.

       I ken the spate o Cuan Sound,
         the lurkin' Cairns o Coll;
       Peel and Port Erin   35
         and the bights o Donegal,
       my anchor's felt the groond in ye,
         I've raised ye, left ye all,

I've bucked yere ebb at daybreak,
   and I've seen yere evenin' fall.   40

The rocks o Sleat sprang up and spoke
   tie hear my motor roar;
my bow-wave's run tie brekk itsel
   against the Skerryvore;
Rudha Hunish, Vatersay,   45
   they've felt my wash afore.

I've seen them shine, and then go oot,
   the lights o Stornoway;
I've watched Fife Ness grow faint and fade
   fornent the brekk o day;   50
I ken the oorie, haary east
   beyond the Isle o May.

Eastward's braw and westward,
   aa the ways the rudder tilts;
norrard and sou'ard,   55
   I never found their faults;
windward's a wakener,
   and leeward's a waltz.

Aa night long ye hear it
   chime through the motor's roar,   60
wi an older tune from far-off days
   the loch has heard afore,
when foray's vauntin' high white sails
   came slippin' up the shore.

Miklagarth, Skarp-hethinn,   65
Miklagarth, Skarp-hethinn,
Rómaborg, Skarp-hethinn,
Miklagarth, Skarp-hethinn.
Utan-ferth, Skarp-hethinn,
vestur-ferth, Skarp-hethinn,   70
skíp og haf, Skarp-hethinn,
haf og byar, Skarp-hethinn,
byar og rór, Skarp-hethinn.
Utan-ferth, Skarp-hethinn,
suthur-ferth, Skarp-hethinn,   75
haf og lopt, Skarp-hethinn,
lopt og vindur, Skarp-hethinn,
byar og haf, Skarp-hethinn,

                          [*nes*

nes og nes, Skarp-hethinn.
Gullborg, Skarp-hethinn,   80
vínborg, Skarp-hethinn,
kvennaborg, Skarp-hethinn,
sunnanborg, Skarp-hethinn,
Miklagarth, Skarp-hethinn.[1]

Long is sgioba, long is sgioba,   85
gaoth is gillean, gaoth is gillean,
muir is misneach, muir is misneach,
sgòd an ruigheadh, sgòd an ruigheadh,
seòl is sitheadh, seòl is sitheadh,
creach is iomairt, creach is iomairt,   90
creach is iolach, creach is iolach,
fraoch is frionas, glaodh is frioghan,
gaoth is gillean, gaoth is gillean,
long is sgioba, long is sgioba.[2]

This is the song the motor dirls,   95
   birlin' loud and bright,
and: *The Calf o Man, the Rauchlin,*
   I've seen them loom by night.
I've kent the deep troughs take from me
   the lurchin' Ailsa light.   100

When my gunnel's worn wi raspin' nets,
   and my sides are white wi salt,
when my ropes unlay wi haulin'
   and my steerin's aa at fault;
when my seams are chinked and strakes are crushed, 105
   and the decks are tramped tie spales,

---

[1] *Metropolis, Skarp-hethinn, Metropolis ..., Rome-city ..., Metropolis ... . Outward journey ..., westward journey ..., ship and ocean ..., ocean and fair wind ..., fair wind and calm ... . Outward journey ..., southward journey ..., ocean and sky ..., sky and wind ..., fair wind and ocean ..., point and point ... . City of gold ..., city of wine ..., city of women ..., southern city ..., Metropolis ... .*   [editor]

[2] A ship and a crew, a ship and a crew; wind and lads, wind and lads; sea and spirit, sea and spirit; a sheet stretched hard, a sheet stretched hard; a sail and coursing, a sail and coursing; foray and turmoil, foray and turmoil; foray and outcry, foray and outcry; rage and anger, yelling and bristling; wind and lads, wind and lads; a ship and a crew, a ship and a crew.

when the length o me is sterted
 wi hammerin' intie gales;
when my motor scarce can drive me
 from off some loud lee-shore,   110
then anchor me in Tarbert,
 gie me chain. And no' afore.

Aa the points o Scotland
 wi their wheelin' lights in turn,
I've raised them bright aheid,   115
 and I've sunk them faint astern,
scourin' by tie heidlands
 where new lights burn.

There's a daft song trembles through me
 as my forefoot flings and becks,   120
it echoes hollow in the howld,
 it dirls, runs wild and checks,
it throbs and laughs at hidden rocks
 and aa their brokkin' wrecks,
it beats along my plankin'   125
 and blufferts doon the decks.

Leeward, send me. Windward, send me.
Leeward, send me. Windward, send me.
Steer me, tend me. Steer me, tend me.
Weer me, mend me. Weer me, mend me.   130
Work me, spend me. Work me, spend me.
Risk me, fend me. Risk me, fend me.

The dawn sun, big and scarlet,
 on the foggy Heids o Ayr;
the Badger's Moon dims Pladda light   135
 wi her white, unblinkin' stare;
Barra Soond, Lochboisdale,
 I've whitened watter there.

The blin' shores o Kilbrennan
 in the murky pit o night,   140
they've watched the changin' colours
 o my port and starboard light;
they've heard my capstain drummin' roond
 in loch and kyle and bight.

                                    [Eastward's

239

Eastward's braw and westward,   145
  aa the ways the rudder cants,
norrard's aye good hope for me,
  and sou'ard's aye my chance,
windward's a loud welcomer,
  and leeward's but a dance.   150

Heiskir, Haiskir,
  the Heids o Ayr,
Heiskir, Haiskir,
  the Old Heids o Ayr,
Man and Canna,   155
  they ken me there,
I've pitched the seas they sent me
  aboot me in the air,
I've belted aa the seas I've met
  tie trailin' wisps o hair.   160

When the fleet's a maze o crossin' lights
  along a windy coast,
she'll pass ye lik a dream,
  she'll flit by ye lik a ghost,
her lights stand up astern,   165
  ye take her wash and she is lost.
She's seen, her lights grow big on ye,
  she's level, and she's gone,
while her motor whines and rages
  in her waist tie drive her on.   170
There's no the keel been laid
  that she wilna overhaul;
when ye'd speak tie her abeam,
  she's through the night afore ye call.
She's by ye in a glint.   175
  Was it any boat ye saw?
She'll waltz the hale fleet,
  thon boat, she'll waltz them aa.

She's a solan, she's a tramper, she's a sea-shaker,
she's a hawk, she's a hammer, she's a big sea-breaker,   180
she's a falcon, she's a kestrel, she's a wide-night-seeker,
she's a river, she's a render, she's a foam-spray-waker.
She's a stieve sea-strider, she's a storm-course-keeper,
she's a tide-scour-bucker, she's a quick-light-leaper,
she's a stem-teerer, keel-teerer, seeker, finder, reaper.   185
She's Cast off! Anchor up! deid anchor-weary,

she's a chain-snubber, moorin'-strainer, restless herbour peerie.
She's a skyline-raiser, skyline-sinker, hulldown horizon-crosser,
she's foreland, foreland, on and on, a high-heid-tosser.
She's a glint, she's a glimmer, she's a glimpse, she's a fleeter,   190
she's an overhauler, leave-astern, a hale-fleet-beater;
she's a kyle-coulter, knot-reeler, thrang-speed-spinner,
her mood is moulded on her and the mind that made her's in her.
She's a wake-plough, foam-plough, spray-hammer, roarer,
she's a wind-anvil, crest-batterer, deep-trough-soarer,   195
she's a dance-step-turner, she's a broad-wake-scorer,
she's a sound-threider, bight-stringer, her hert runs oot afore her.
When the big long seas come on lik walls, cold-white-heided,
she doesna flinch a point for them. Straight her wake is threided.

>Though they come from the world's rim   200
>   along wi a livin' gale,
>she'll gap and batter through them
>   and teer her chosen trail.
>She's stieve, thrawn, light, quick,
>   fast, wild, gay;   205
>she'll curtain the world wi hammered seas,
>   she'll drench the stars wi spray.
>They can tower between her and the sky –
>   she never felt their awe;
>she'll walk them aa, thon trampin' boat,   210
>   she'll rise and walk them aa.
>She's a solan's hert, a solan's look;
>   she canna thole a lee.
>I'll coil her ropes and redd her nets,
>   and ease her through a sea.   215
>She's a seeker, she's a hawk, boys.
>   Thon's the boat for me.

159 *Spring Here Northaway*

I tak ma buik and read in't sangs aboot the Spring.
It's aa Sooth winds and Zephyrs, a droll, fremmit thing.
It's fu' o Zephyrs whisperan and wee saft airs o wind;
brockit owre wi rosebuds, a gairden o the mind.
A souchan, seichan, wispy thing, wi silken wafts aa day   5
lispan amang they rosebuds that warm nae livan brae.
It's dandlet and it's fondlet. Almichty God! I fling
the buik frae me and lauch. Ah, no! It's no' oor Spring.

That's the Spring for lassie-boys, a waff Spring for gowks;
a Spring that's spun frae readan, o buiks grown oot o buiks;   10
fancy's season, forman oot o prent, wi fancy's looks.
It wad flaff awa e'en in a lull o the Spring that we ken best,
Spring frae the back o Lewis, oot o the steel Northwest.

Spelteran the deid-time's hardness
   its lourd and foggy air,   15
flingan aa its ice tae flinders
   in glints o frosty fire,
loud and shoutan, swaggeran, vauntan
   in gantan Winter's ear,
rairan in't: "Grey Winter, wander!   20
   Ye'll gang tho ye are sweir.
Rise oot frae aff the land, and foonder
   whar nane will ken or care!"
Young and hard, no' tae be dauntont
   Spring comes rantan here.   25

Winter gowls wi an auld man's anger,
   that naethin' in the warld can please.
Spring cries keen wi a young man's daftness,
   stridean eager owre the seas
that glister back the glint o his een,   30
   and race wi his mood as on he flees.
What can the warld but lout and curtsey,
   laith or no', whan he lets drive?
Aathing cants and rakes afore him,
   shakes itsel and leaps alive.   35

He comes and asks the leave o nane.
He rairs in shrillan wi a run,
and clears a way for the northdrawn sun.

The heich blae wa's o hail
come ramstam doon the loch,   40
and blench the sunlicht pale.

And the tall trees and laich,
there's nane but leans and gies
and streams lik a shiveran sauch.

Thro sunspoke bars he flees,   45
huddlan on the ranks
o snawblae cloods, owre seas

aa steely flauchts and blinks
o caller windy licht.
In owre the steep sea-brinks   50
Spring comes cauld and bricht.

Spring's a riever, a wudd-wind-stripper,
Spring's a waukener, Spring's a whipper
o writhean branch-tips. Spring's a shogger
o bielded shaws, a flail, a flogger,   55
an edge, a spear, a driven dagger,
young thrust that gars grey Winter stagger.

There's nae land-wa' he wilna spring,
nae frozen daith he wilna ding,
nae snaw mortclaiths he wilna fling   60
torn frae the craigs whar lourd they hing.
His mornin challance-sang he'll sing
in Winter's lyart beard, and sting
the warld's bluid tae heat. He'll wring
life back frae frost. Nae dauntont thing,   65
nor Wast-wind-hauntit. No' oor Spring.

160 *Triùir an Earraich*

The Spring Three

Winter's windy sentence
   in the mooth o March the ranter.
March comes wudd and wantons,
   and flegs the dowff auld dranter.
     Gang yere ways, Winter!   5

March is swack and March is swank.
April aye has March tae thank
   for flinderan auld Winter's dure.
March comes hardy, March comes daft,
   March comes bauld wi sturt afore.   10
April follows, wi a waft
   o sun and rain and gentle air.
March dirls "Up!", a daybreak drummer.
April gies a glisk o Simmer.

Frae dawn til nicht they talk.   15
Gowk answers chimean gowk
   through the yellow Beltane Day.
Kendle licht and leam.
   Brindle ilka brae.
Tip the shaws wi bloom;   20
   hap the howes gay
   in green and growth, May.

*161 *Solan*

Hing there, solan,
lik fate up astern;
the watch that doesna wander.
Swing there, solan.
Slip across the wind and turn   5
in a dippin' arc. Hover up thonder.
The height o a man and a man's grip in yere two wings there,
tipped wi black and set wi strength, the stievest in air.

Hing there, solan.
Swing there, solan.   10
Linger at yere ease
in the face o a teerin' breeze, solan.
The eyes in thon heid,
what dim hints can they read, solan,
beneath the flurry o white, the twist o a squall on the watter?   15
Is it the sea puckered wi syle, a stray, shallow scatter
o a brokkin shoal, torn asunder by nets in the night?
Or a gray, green, derk shadda that blunts the surface light,
derkenin' the hue o the loch for half a mile or more,
dullin' its waverin', flauchterin' glints, five faddoms doon oot there; 20
along the lip o the deep channel where the easy eddies are,
forgein' aheid through the slack edge o the spring-tide scour,
oot in the run o Carraig nam Ban –
is thon what ye've seen again, solan?

Between Maol Dubh and Carraig nam Ban, half-daft, half-wild,   25
there are white sheep skelterin' doon oor green field;
a huddle o a brekkin' sea and a rough rant o wind
hoarse over the low plaint o the oot-runnin' tide,
the deep, hollow farewell o the ebb to the shore o either side,
the oot-dreg, the sooth-dreg over the feet o the land.   30
Bright green, derk green, then liftin' intie light,
streakum-stroakum here and there wi wee scuds o white,
the loch's below ye, and, secret in't, thon gray shadda hides,
the solid back o a broad shoal wi its breist against the tide's.

Hing there, solan.   35
Swing there, solan.
Glance doon, solan;
a look lik a lance, solan.
Cant doon, solan, and let yerself drive.

*162 *Smile and Go By*

Out go to everyone
   quick smile and ready laughter,
warm look like the sun,
   a voice like running water.

There is no still pool in him,   5
no linn brooding, quiet and dim.
   It lies but lightly, that warm look.
He curves, and flashes, and runs on.
His mood comes glinting, and is gone,
   twisting, beyond a silent rock.   10

*163 *Feadag Ghòrach an t-Slèibhe*
The Daft Hill Plover

The daft hill plover tumbles,
   and cries his birling cry,
tumbles and climbs and tumbles,
   daft in the wide hill-sky.   4
Alone with his hill-top daftness,
   he runs himself a race,
the windy, daft hill plover,
   daft with wind and space.   8

*164 *The Nerra Boat*

There's no a boat in the hale wide loch can stay wi ye;
there's no a keel that leaves thon wake on aa the sea.
Sheeted in, ye lift lik a bird and leap lik a flame,
till the sea's a smother aroond a runner it canna tame.   4

Black and nerra, stieve and taper tie trevel far.
Long and lean, lean and hungry for wind ye are.
A long white curve from sheet tie peak, yere taut stays cry,
and the tiller trembles beneath the fingers as slant ye lie.   8

Trim and gethered in thegither, ye cant and drive,
and seek aheid more wind tie bring ye right alive.
Ye look aheid for brekkin' seas, and race tie meet   12
the watter black wi the flurry o wind on yere windward beat.

Send yere stem through the hert o the seas that run yere way,
and fling them scattered by your shoothers in bursts o spray.
Teer the watter, green or brokkin, and roar home
a sheet lik a rod, and a lee-gunnel white wi a stream o foam.   16

*165   *Flooer o the Gean*

Flooer o the gean,
yere aefauld white she wore yestreen.
Wi gentle glances aye she socht me.
Dwell her thochts whaur dwalt her een?   4

Flooer o the broom,
gowden abune the thicket's gloom,
I canna see ye as I pu' ye.
My een are fu', my hert is toom.   8

Flooeran slae,
white ye are, untried, in May.
When Simmer's gane, an' hard days rock ye,
yere fruit is black an' bitter tae.   12

Bloom o the whin,
born frae the stabs an' still their kin,
the een that seek her beauty yearn for
a flooer that wounds are dernan in.   16

Flooer o the briar,
the haund that socht ye throbs wi fire.
The hert that socht her tholes its searan
tae see her mood grow sweir an' tire.   20

Flooer o the thorn,
the haund that plucked at ye is torn.
Is anger's edge in ane sae gracious?
Can thon sweet face be sherp wi scorn?   24

[Spray

Spray o the pine,
that never fades nor faas tae crine,
green I pu' ye, leal I ken ye.
I'll weir the green I winna tine. 28

Fior di mento,
la roba vien e va come va il vento.
La bella donna fa l'uomo contento.

Flooer o the mint, 32
lik wund the warld's goods come an' are tint.
Wumman's beauty gies man true content.

*166 *The Crew of the Shelister*

The drollest crew that was ever afloat,
they went to sea in a shelister boat,
wi a twig for a mast, and rigged wi threid,
and a glessack for ballast, or was it a bead? 4

Their boathook was bent from the prong o a fork,
the backrope was buoyed wi crumbs o cork,
the tiller was shaped from the skelf o a match,
and the half o a matchbox lid was the hatch. 8

The flaff o a seagull flyin' by
near cowped their neebor. That isna a lie.
They were near away wi't, and sprung their deck
when they ran agroond on a bladder o wreck. 12

Between the wreck and the side o the pier
they came on watter ableeze, they sweir,
wi burnin' as white as they'd ever seen.
And they crepped away wi the heid o a peen. 16

It answered; and so, at the lip o the ebb,
they shot their net o the spider's web,
in watter two inches deep or more,
so they cleared the ground wi an inch to spare. 20

A thimble o catch, and the hold was full.
The torch they lit was a wisp o wool.
What was the basket was their affair;
they had neither a winch nor a brailer there. 24

248

But what they ringed was no' in my tale.
A cuddy to them was the size o a whale.
Was it syle they struck low in in the bay,
or was it puddocks? I couldna say.   28

167 [Gone and Gane]

This war that's gane – what is gone?
This day that's gane – is it gone?
This gone and gane gangs but on.   3

*168 Madame, a Monte Casino

Quando se parla, se ricorda,
quando non se parla, se ricorda,
quando non se ricorda, se ricorda,
    Madame, a Monte Casino.   4

Quando se vive, se muore,
quando se muore, se muore,
quando non se muore, se muore –
    Madame, a Monte Casino.   8

Quando se avanza, se avanza,
quando se fugge, se avanza,
quando non se avanza, se avanza –
    Madame, a Monte Casino.   12

Quando se rimane, se avanza –
    Madame, a Monte Casino.

Quando se rimane, se ritorna –
    Madame, a Monte Casino.   16

168   Madame, at Monte Casino

When one speaks, one remembers; | when one does not speak, one remembers; |
when one does not remember, one remembers, | Madame, at Monte Casino.   4

When one lives, one dies; | when one dies, one dies; | when one does not die, one
dies – | Madame, at Monte Casino.   8

When one advances, one advances; | when one flees, one advances; | when one
does not advance, one advances – | Madame, at Monte Casino.   12

When one remains, one advances – | Madame, at Monte Casino.

When one remains, one returns – | Madame, at Monte Casino.   16

169 *Fear Breacain Bhallaigh*
[unedited draft]

Latha dhomh 's mi falbh a' ghleannain,
latha dhomh 's mi falbh a' ghleannain,
latha dhomh 's mi falbh a' ghleannain,
thachair orm fear breacain bhallaigh,
latha dhomh 's mi falbh a' ghleannain, 5
thachair orm fear breccin bhallaigh,
dh'fhaighnichd e am b'e a leanainn,
thuirt mi nach b'e siud bh'air m'aire.
Shiubhlainn leis thar chuan, thar bheannaibh,
shiubhlainn leis thar chuain, thar mara, 10
shiubhlainn leis thar chruach, thar bheannaibh,
is cha bu chúram orm e 'm mhealladh.

Shiubhlainn leis thar thuinn, thar bheannaibh,
shiubhlainn cruas is truas gan athadh;
shiubhlainn leis le cuir, le caraibh, 15
shiubhlainn leis le cuir 's le caraibh,
shiubhlainn leis le car, le caraibh,
shiubhlainn leis le car 's le caraibh,
le carthannas, le car 's le caraibh,
le car, le cuir, le cuir 's le caraibh, 20
le cuir, le car, le car 's le caraibh,
le cainnt, le cruas, le cuir 's le caraibh,

169 *Man in Tartan Plaidie*

A day when I was walking the glennan, | a day when I was walking the glennan, | a day when I was walking the glennan, | I chanced on a man in a tartan plaidie, | a day when I was walking the glennan, | I chanced on a man in a tartan plaidie, | he 5 *asked me was it him I'd follow, | I said that that was not my intention. | I'd go with him over seas, over mountains, | I'd go with him over sea, over ocean, | I'd go with* 10 *him over hills, over mountains, | and would not worry that he'd deceive me.*

I'd travel with him over wave, over mountains, | I'd travel hardship and poverty without scruple; | I'd travel with him with twists, with turns, | I'd travel with him 15 *with twists and with turns, | I'd travel with him with a turn, with turns, | I'd travel with him with a turn and with turns, | with charity, with a turn and with turns, | with a turn, with twists, with twists and with turns, | with twists, with a* 20 *turn, with a turn and with turns, | with speech, with hardihood, with twists and with turns, |*

le cainnt, le luaths, le duain, le darach
driop is duain is gruaim is cabhag,
ar marannan, ar muir rim mhaireann, 25
ar mharaichean, ar luing, ar aighear,
ar mharaichean, ar luing 's ar aighear;
gan cheannuidhe, gan iúl caladh,
gan cheannuidhe, gan sgeul caladh,
gan cheannuidhe, gan feum caladh, 30
gan cheannuidhe, gan mhiann caladh,
gan cheannuidhe, gan iarraidh caladh,
gan cheannuidhe, gan tigh'nn ar caladh,
gan cheannuidhe, gan smid mu chaladh,
gan cheannuidhe, gan diog mu chaladh, 35
gan cheannuidhe, gan uiread caladh,
gan cheannuidhe, gan ruigsinn caladh,
gan cheannuidhe, uidheam is acfhainn,
gan cheannuidhe, fo uidheam 's fo acfhainn
gan cheannuidhe, ar uidhe aigein. 40

Shiubhlainn bac is sgeir is cladach,
sgeir is fearann, muir is cladach,
driop is duain is cuan is caisil,
misg is stuamachd, cuan is cathan
[drisg ?] is cuachan, duain is dathan 45
driop is duain, is fuachd is caidreabh,
clach is clóchar, ród is aigean

[magh

---

with speech, with swiftness, with ballads, with oakship | bustle and ballads and
surliness and haste, | on seas, on sea, in my lifetime, | on sailors, on a ship, on gaiety, | 25
on sailors, on a ship and on gaiety; | with no journey's end, no guide to a harbour, |
with no journey's end, no sight of a harbour, | with no journey's end, no need for
a harbour, | with no journey's end, no wish for a harbour, | with no journey's end, 30
no wanting of harbour, | with no journey's end, no chancing on harbour, | with no
journey's end, not a cheep about harbour, | with no journey's end, not a word about
harbour, | with no journey's end, not so much as one harbour, | with no journey's 35
end, no reaching of harbour, | with no journey's end, rigging and tackle, | with no
journey's end, under rigging and tackle, | with no journey's end, going over the seabed. 40

I'd travel sandbank and skerry and shore, | skerry and land, sea and shore, |
bustle and ballads and ocean and bulwarks, | drunkenness and sobriety, ocean
and battles | (?) and goblets, ballads and colours | bustle and ballads, and coldness 45
and friendship, | stone and convent, road and abyss |

magh is cómar, mód is garadh
dragh is dórainn, ceó is raineach,
fleadh is frògan, feòirnein 's talla,   50
lod is còrn is bòrd is basan,
lod is cúirn is múirn is   ;
roimhe gu dòmhnach 's uaidh gach latha,
roimhe gu dòmhnach 's riamh gach latha,
roimhe gu dòmhnach 's siar gach latha.   55

Shiubhlainn réidhleach, cruadhlach, cadha,
beárnan sléibhe, réidhlean 's aisridh,
shiubhlainn coire, doire, darach,
beitheach, bruthach, both is barrach
ceathach, cuithean, loch is   ;   60
shiubhlainn díomhaireachd is glacan
shiubhlainn ríomhachas is raineach;
acarsaid is córsa ascaoin,
acarsaid is córsa carrach,
fiadhaich fosgailte gan fhasgadh,   65
ach caoineadh eadar gaoth is stalla,
ach caoidhrein eadar gaoth is carraig,
ach aodainn chasa ar an sgathadh,
ach aodainn ghlasa ar an sgathadh,
sgathadh glas os cionn nan aitheamh,   70
sgathadh glas os cionn na mara;
fiadhaich mòr 'na mhúr gan fhasgadh,
fiadhaich corr 'na mhúr gan fhasgadh,
fiadhaich dùr 'na mhúr gan fhasgadh,

*plain and confluence, assembly and hideout | trouble and torment, mist and fern, |
feast and merriment, chesspieces and courthall, | pool [of drink?] and horn and*   50
*table and clapping, | pool and horns and joy and   ; | sadly onward and away each
day, | sadly onward and ever each day, | sadly onward and westward each day.*   55
*I'd travel level ground, stony ground, ravine, | mountain gaps, flat land and path, |
I'd travel corrie, grove, oakwood, | birchwood, brae, bothy and brushwood | fog,
snowdrifts, loch and   ; | I'd travel mystery and hollows | I'd travel fine beauty*   60
*and fern; | anchorage and forbidding coastline, | anchorage and treacherous coast-
line, | wild, exposed, offering no shelter, | but only wailing between wind and rock-*   65
*ledge, | only mourning between wind and headland, | only rock-faces sheer and
riven, | only rock-faces grey and riven, | a grey cleaving above the fathoms, | a grey*   70
*cleaving above the waters; | massive and wild, a rampart without shelter, | amazing
and wild, a rampart without shelter, | grim and wild, a rampart without shelter, |*

ach sitheadh gaoith' is tarraing acair,   75
ach ospagan is tarraing acair,
ach uspagan is tarraing acair,
úird is súistean bharr nan stalla
úird is dúirn bharr nan stalla.

Shiubhlainn réidhlean leis is machair   80
is cha bu chúram leam e m' mhealladh;
shiubhlainn eileanan 's thar bheannaibh,
is cha bu chúram leam e m' mhealladh.
Shiubhlainn leis thar chuan 's thar bheannaibh,
iomall domhain, Hel is Hangö,   85
Danmarc agus caladh Baltach,
Tromsö, Runö,
iomall domhain, Hel is Hangö
iomall domhain, ser is Hangö,
iomall domhain, siar thar mara   90
iomall domhain, triall is tarraing,
iomall domhain, siar 's gu Tallinn.

Shiubhlainn bacan leis is bochdainn,
shiubhlainn fearann leis is fortan,
shiubhlainn aisridh, caisil, soc leis   95
shiubhlainn clais is glac is cnoc leis,
shiubhlainn leis le gaoith 's le oiteag
shiubhlainn leis thar roinn is thar oitir,
thar áth, thar árach, tuinn is monadh

[thar síth

---

only violent wind and pulling of anchor, | only sobbing wind and pulling of an- 75
chor, | only soughing wind and pulling of anchor, | hammers and flails down from
the rockfaces | hammers and fists down from the rockfaces.

I'd travel plain with him and machair | and I wouldn't worry that he'd deceive 80
me; | I'd travel islands and over mountains, | and wouldn't worry that he'd
deceive me. | I'd travel with him over ocean and mountains, | rim of the world,
Hel and Hangö, | Denmark and a Baltic haven, | Tromsö, Runö, | rim of the 85
world, Hel and Hangö, | rim of the world, to the east and Hangö, | rim of
the world, to the west over the sea | rim of the world, journey and lure, | rim of the 90
world, west and to Tallinn.

I'd travel hurdles with him and penury, | I'd travel land with him and fortune, |
I'd travel footpath, walls, landend with him | I'd travel furrow and hollow and 95
hill with him, | I'd travel with him by wind and breeze, | I'd travel with him
beyond headland and searock, | over ford, over battlefield, waves and moorland |

thar síth, thar árach, muir is monadh;   100
is mi nach bitheadh fo sprocht leis,
am fear a stiúradh na sgothan,
shuidheadh ar stiúir 's a stiúradh roidean,
shuidheadh ar stiúir 's a steórnadh roidean,
shuidheadh ar stiúir 's a dh'fhóirneadh roidean,   105
sith troimh thuinn 's a mhaistreadh cop leath',
shuidheadh ar rámh san treas tobhta,
sheasadh ri faire shuas 'na toiseach.

Cionnus a bhithinn fo sprocht leis,
's iomadh fealadhá 'na thost ann,   110
is iomadh fealadhá ar ghoil ann,
's iomadh fealadhá fo dhos ann,
is iomadh fealadhá ga loireadh
fo slios is fo ribein, mire 's mort ann,
fo slios is fo ribein, ribe throsg ann,   115
ribe porsk ann, ribe throsg ann
an t-aighear 'na linn is 'na loch ann
is failleanan mu gach stoc ann,
is aiteas mu gach aon *och* ann
is aiteas fo gach aon *och* ann,   120
is aiteas anns gach aon *och* ann,
is annas o gach aon *oich* ann,
is casgairt o gach aon *oit!* ann,
is falacht o gach aon *ochain*.

C'uim nach fágainn tráigh no loch leis   125
c'uim [nach] fuarainn roinn no oitir?

over peace, over battlefield, sea and moorland; | I would not be dejected with him, | 100
the man who could steer the skiffs, | who'd sit at the helm and steer the surges, |
who'd sit at the helm and pilot the surges, | who'd sit at the helm and master [?] the
surges, | rush through waves, and who'd churn the foam with her, | who'd sit to row 105
on the third oarbench, | who'd stand on watch up in her fore-end.

How could I be dejected with him, | and many a jest silent inside him, | and many a 110
jest bubbling inside him, | many a jest hiding inside him, | many a jest getting a
drubbing | under flank and sash, mirth and murder in him, | under flank and sash,
a cod snare there, | a porsk snare there, a cod snare there, | a deep pool and loch of 115
good-humour in him | and young shoots around every stump there, | and gladness
round every alas *there, | and gladness behind every* alas *there, | and gladness in* 120
every alas *there, | and novelty from every* ouch *there, | and slaughter from every*
ow! there, | and feuding from every single alack.*

Why should I not leave strand or loch with him | why should I not weather head- 125
land or sandbank? |

C'uim nach fágainn tráigh is loch leis
c'uim nach fuarainn roinn is oitir?
'S nach caillinn sealladh beinn' is monaidh?
'S nach cuirinn sealladh beinn' is monaidh   130
síos fon fháire le ceud soraidh?
'S nach cuirinn sealladh beinn' is monaidh
díom fon fháire le ceud soraidh,
díom ar fáire le ceud soraidh
díom ar fáire le bláth shoraidh,   135
is mo lámhan ar an togail.
C'uim nach siubhlainn muir is monadh,
ser is siar, miann is soraidh,
er is grian is a dol fodha,
'eólas, m'aineol, stiúir is soraidh,   140
iomall domhain, doimhne, doman,
iomall domhain anaconda,
iomall domhain furibonda,
iomall domhain onda onda.

Shiubhlainn leis thar chuan, thar bheannaibh,   145
shiubhlainn duain is fuaim is facail
shiubhlainn duain is cuan is cadha,
shiubhlainn slighe leis is claisean,
shiubhlainn lighe leis is raineach,
shiubhlainn snighe agus frasan,   150
shiubhlainn ceann gu ceann an atlais,
shiubhlainn is dá thrian an fhaclair,
anuair, ainfhios, annas, aineol;

[uaim

Why should I not leave strand and loch with him | why should I not weather head-
land and sandbank? | And lose all sight of mountain and moorland? | And send the
sight of mountain and moorland | down under the horizon with a hundred bless- 130
ings? | And put the sight of mountain and moorland | away under the horizon with
a hundred blessings | away on the horizon with a hundred blessings | away on the
horizon with a warm blessing, | and my hands raised in salutation. | Why should I 135
not travel sea and moorland, | eastward and westward, desire and blessing, | east
and sun and its setting, | places known to him, unknown to me, helm and blessing, 140
| rim of the world, the deep, transient[?], | rim of the world anaconda, | rim of the
world furibonda, | rim of the world onda onda.

I'd travel with him over ocean, over mountains, | I'd travel songs and sound and 145
words, | I'd travel songs and ocean and defile, | I'd travel a road with him
and trenches, | I'd travel flood with him and bracken, | I'd travel seeping rain and
showers, | I'd travel the atlas from end to end, | aye, and two-thirds of the diction- 150
ary, | storm, strangeness, the unusual, the unknown; |

uaim is fuaim is duain is facail,
duanaire, dáin is saltair,   155
dáin 's iad díreach, dáin 's iad caste,
uaim is fuaim is fead is facail,
uaim is fuaim is fead is aicill.

Shiubhlainn echtraidh agus atlas,
shiubhlainn bárdacht agus bagradh,   160
shiubhlainn cánainean is masgull,
gruaim is grámair, tír is cladach,
breug is fírinn, fríth is caladh,
Greugais, Gáilig agus Danais,
Fraingis, Arabais is Laidionn,   165
grámairean is druim na mara,
tuinn is roinn is caol is faclair
beinn is gleann is cuan is cairtean
shiubhlainn m'aineol is an t-atlas,
druim na mara, druim na mara,   170
moncaidh, annas, anaconda,
anaconda, annas, moncaidh,
craobhan pailme 's lucht nam mogais,
lucht nam burnus, lucht nam mogais,
latha is lasadh, dubhar is doille,   175
beinn is cuan is tuinn ag osnaich,
an sruthadh go [Dhúir?] 's a droma.
Acropolis is pterodactyl
tuinn na mara, druim na mara,
pioramaid is pterodactyl,   180
druim na mara, druim na mara.

alliteration and sound and songs and words, | songbook, poems and a psalter, | 155
poems in strict metre, finely wrought poems, | alliteration and sound and whistling and words, | alliteration and sound and whistling and rhyme.

I'd travel history and atlas, | I'd travel poetry and menace, | I'd travel languages 160
and flattering, | gloom and grammar, land and shore, | falsehood and truth, deerforest and harbour, | Greek, Gaelic and Danish, | French, Arabic and Latin, | 165
books of grammar and the ridge of the sea, | waves and headland and kyle and dictionary | mountain and glen and ocean and maps | I'd travel unknown regions and the atlas, | the ridge of the sea, the ridge of the sea, | monkey, marvel, anaconda, 170
| anaconda, marvel, monkey, | palmtrees and the pantaloon people, | the burnous people, the pantaloon people, | daylight and blazing, dimness and darkness, | 175
mountain and ocean and waves a-sighing, | the streaming to [Duir?] and its ridge.
| Acropolis and pterodactyl | the waves of the sea, the ridge of the sea, | pyramid and pterodactyl, | the ridge of the sea, the ridge of the sea. 180

*170 *The Sun over Athens*

A broad bight and a bonny city,
streets and smoke and the sea curving,
a deed dreams over downcast houses,
a stroke sings about speltered gables,
a sword sighs about splintered doorposts;   5
the guns gaze and gant, thinking,
the night nods in the narrow corners,
the dark dwalms in the droning crannies,
the guns gaze together watching.

The streets stir and the stones are warming,   10
the houses can hear the hidden warning,
the guns gaze together watching.

The sun streams from the sky above them,
a hot hammer, higher than shrillness,
a slight stroke, a strait piercing,   15
sheer shining, shafts and standing,
sure shafts, a sheer hammer.
Good ground and gleaming water
for an era's anchors, ancient shelter,
room for riding and right water   20
for an era's anchors, an ancient roadstead,
for an era's anchors, ancient haven
for an era's anchors, war wanes in it
and wheels elsewhere to whip the water.

A lee and a long one, and a long story   25
looming along it, learning and battles,
through change unchanging, chains go roaring
link and link, linger and tauten,
howl through hawseholes in history's shelter,
hurry through hawseholes in history's roadstead.   30
Drab drift from them as they drag the water,
ships and sheer to their sheering anchors,
grey like gulleys over grey water.
Arrayed like the rocks in ranging colours,
the colour of coastlines creeping by them,   35
grasp the ground and give to leeward.

[Strewn

Strewn like the stones on the stern horizon,
strewn like stones on the stern horizon.
Who am I? Who am I? Who am I? southward.
Who am I? Who am I? Who am I? southward.   40
The sun stands in the sky above them –
history's hill and high marble,
scree and stones and scarred ridges,
highland, haven, headland, island,
a bright and brightness and broad curving.   45
Oil and island, and old fathoms,
oil in aisles, an old harbour,
islands, oars, an old haven.
Hymettus here, Hymettus eastward,
Hymettus hiding hollow and upland,   50
Salamis seaward, Salamis yonder,
Salamis stretched in a smirr from the water;
straying stour, the smoky Piræus,
rough with rubble, rienged by blasting,
a dark door to undeafened ages,   55
soundless strokes the sun hammers.
The sun strides, the sun goes westward,
the sun stands, the sun goes westward,
the sun circles, the sun goes westward;
ancient anchor for ages' thinking,   60
plain and port and pillars between them,
Attica, Attica, Attica rounded.
Hymettus, Hymettus, Hymettus eastward.
The sun circles, the sun goes westward.

The streets are stirring, the stones grow warmer; 65
the houses can hear the hidden warning;
the guns gaze together watching;
the batteries breathe the breath around them,
from bomb and blast, blare and screaming,
shock and shaking, shackled roaring,   70
tearing and tracer, tracks and curving,
sky and scarlet, skirting and climbing,
night and nothing, night and concussion
roaring, recoil, rending and fuming.
The guns gaze together watching.   75

Ancient anchor for ages' thinking,
plain and port and the pillars between them;
history's harbour, history's fathoms.
War watches and wanes above them

war waits and wanes around them   80
war waits and watches near them.

Ancient anchor for ages' thinking,
plain and port and pillars between them;
a lee for learning, a long story,
a long lee, a low island.   85

Ancient anchor for ages' thinking,
the guns gaze together watching.
the sun stands, the sun goes westward.
War wavers and watches in it.

A sword swaivers that swept in the darkness;   90
the houses can hear the hidden warning,
the guns gaze together watching.
Link and link linger and tauten,
chains in the channels of churning hawseholes,
drab like doom drift to leeward,   95
hulls and heel as they hear their anchors,
ships and sheer to their sheering anchors,
strife and steering, stream and hazes,
seas and steering, steering and heeding,
trails and tracks, tracer, skylines,   100
wakes and watching, wan mantles,
smoke in a smirr, smoke in a mantle,
wavering in wisps, wandering outward.
Ancient haven, history's harbour.

History's hill and high marble,   105
plain and port and pillars between them,
a broad bight, a barren hillside,
a broad bight and a bonny city;
streets and smoke and the sea curving.

*171 Cruach Tharsainn 's na h-Oiteagan

An a eucinnt an t-saoghail
  as aobhar dod thalach?
Eadar fàire is fàire   3
  tha fàilte roimh t'astar,
is a dh'oidhche 's a là dhuit
  is slàn duit gun agadh.   6

Gu dè bhiodh tu ach rathail
  leis gach latha tha 'g èirigh?
Siud shuas Cruach Tharsainn   9
  ag amharc 's ag èisteachd,
is tha gaoth fhionnar nan sliosan
  ag iomairt mud cheumaibh.   12

171 [Cruach Tharsainn and the Breezes]

*Is it the uncertainty of the world | which prompts your complaint? | From horizon
to horizon, | a welcome awaits your wandering, | and by day or by night | an*   3
unhesitant greeting.   6

*What could you be but fortunate | with every day that dawns? | Up yonder Cruach
Tharsainn | is watching and listening, | and the cool wind of the slopes | comes*   9
and goes about your step.   12

POEMS 1960–1961

*172 *An t-Anmoch air a' Mhonadh*

Tha 'n solas gam fhàgail,
  's tha càrsan sa Chaol.

Tha 'n dorcha a' teàrnadh,
  is tha an là 'dol a thaobh.   4

Tha mi 'm meadhan a' mhonaidh,
  a' coiseachd an fhraoich.

A' toirt nan ceuman mòr, fada,
  gu bith fada bhon taobh-s'.   8

Aig dà Loch na Machrach,
  agus at air a' ghaoith.

172 [*Evening on the Moors*]

Light is dimming around me | and there's a hoarseness on the Sound.
Darkness descends | and the day slips away.   4
I'm in the middle of the moors, | walking the heather.
Taking big long strides | to get away from this place.   8
At the two Machair Lochs, | and the wind ever swelling.

261

*173 *Miannan an Tairbeartaich*
(*mar gum b'ann le iasgair*)

Gheobh mi rian mar rainn òrain
    air steòrnamh an t-saoghail;
an t-amhsan 's an losgamh,
    is coltas maraon iad;   4
a' mhuc mhara mun Choileach,
    is an goireachan fhaoileag,
is coltas sin uile
    a chuir an Cruithear ar taobh-ne.   8

'S e as fheàrr leam air thalamh
    fuaim a' chapstain 's e 'tionnda',
is an èigh thig gun fhosamh
    o na roithleanan siùbhlach,   12
solas lìn ann an camas,
    b'e sin seallamh mo dhùrachd;
's ar pùt fhèin 'teachd air aghart,
    b'e sin fradharc mo shùilean.   16

Nuair bhios steall fo a h-aistidh,
    nì i 'n t-astar a cheumamh;
's gur e 'n ceòl e nach dona,
    dùrd a motar ra èisteachd.   20
A bhith an ruith an Uillt Bheithe,
    is a' mheadainn ag èirigh,
an clàr uachdar fo reòtach
    agus dreòs air na speuran.   24

---

173 [The Tarbertman's Wishes (as if by a fisherman)]

I will find order like song verses | in the guidance of Nature; | the solan and the burning, | both are appearances; | whales around the Cock of Arran, | and the squabbling of gulls on the water, | all those are appearances | which the Creator has put our way. 4 8

What I like most in the world | is the noise of the capstan turning, | and the relentless din | of the rolling capstan-drums; | a torch-light in a bay | would be the sight of my longing, | and our own net-buoy moving in on us, | would be a delight to my eyes. 12 16

With a full load beneath her hatches, | she'll stride any distance; | and a pleasant music to listen to, | the drone of her motor. | To be in the run of the Birch Burn | at the breaking of day, | the deck glistening with fish-scales | and the skies ablaze. 20 24

*174 Is Aoibhinn Leam An-diugh na Chì

Is fada bhuamsa na nithean
    a bhithinn gan àireamh,
na glinn, 's ceann nan tulach,
    is na rubhachan sàile.   4

Is tìom dhomh nis a bhith 'g àireamh
    nan àite as deise;
Sràid an Dòchais, Sràid Dheòrsa,
    Sràid Seòmar an t-Seilich.   8

Gach sràid is gach caolsràid,
    clach is aol 's leacan rìomhach;
Sràid a' Phrionnsa mu dheireadh,
    is i deisireach, dìreach.   12

*175 Bòd Uile

A' Phutag is Toll Chalum,
    Na Lagain 's Rubha Dubh,
Roinn Chlòimheach 's Rubha Bòdach,
    Baile Bhòid is sguir.   4

174 [A Joy to Me What I See Today]

Far from me are the things | I used to list in praise, | the glens, the hilltop summits | and the ocean headlands.   4

Time now I was listing | the places closest at hand: | Hope Street, George Street, | the Street of the Willow Chamber.   8

Every street and every alley, | stone and lime and elegant slab, | and Princes Street finally, | straight-lined and south-facing.   12

175 [Bute Entire]

Buttock Point and Glencallum Bay, | The Laggans and Blackfarland Point, | Fleecy Head and Bute Point, | Rothesay and stop.   4

*176 Sreathan Mearachdach

Siud i thall an Toll a' Cheiligh
  's i 'na seasamh fad an là,
gun ghlideachamh oiread 's òirleach,
  Flòraidh Mhòr ri beul an làin.   4

*177 An Tìde Àbhaisteach

Glòir agus moladh,
  is coltach an là e,
gaoth an iardheas 'na tacain,
  is na frasan mar b'àbhaist.   4

*178 Cnapadal is Tìrean Ciana Eile

Cùil nan Seamrag 's Bail Ìomhair,
  is na h-Innsean gu buileach;
Àirigh Chreagach 's Meall Mòr,
  an Ròimh is Calcutta.   4

*179 Dà Thaobh na Maoile

Rubha Rèidh is Ceann Bharraigh,
  's iad gun fhasgadh bho dheò:
bithear dall le ca'-mara
  eadar Arainn is Bòd.   4

176 [*Erroneous Lines*]

There she is, over in Cockerel Gap, | standing all day long, | not budging as much as an inch, | Big Florrie at the lip of the tide.   4

177 [*The Usual Weather*]

All glory and praise, | it's a typical day, | bursts of south-west wind, | and showers as usual.   4

178 [*Knapdale and Other Far-off Lands*]

Shamrock Creek and Baliver | and the Indies entire; | Rocky Pasture and Great Mound, | Rome and Calcutta.   4

179 [*The Two Sides of the Moyle*]

[Level Point and Barra Head, | unprotected from the wind:] | you can be blind with spindrift | between Arran and Bute.   4

180 *An Druim-àrcan 's an t-Ìochdar*
[draft]

Cha leig sinn cruit ort no cruaidhchas
  a' togail luaidh' o gach rot
's tu na ràithean gu lèir sin
  an Dùn Èideann air sgoil,   4
an Laideann ga bhruidhinn
  's iad gur cuipeadh mar choin.
Gheibh thusa nad làmhan
  an druim-àrcan, 's dèan boch.   8

Gheibh thusa nad làmhan
  an druim-àrcan, 's bi trang;
's bidh sinn air an ìochdar
  nar n-ìobairtean ann,   12
am beul mòr fo ar glùinean,
  anns a' chrùban gu teann,
is na mill chruinne luaidhe
  'tighinn an uachdar gu mall.   16

Dlùth don chrann ann a toiseach
  nad sgoilear gu ceart
bidh tu dìreach nad sheasamh,
  agus leigidh sinn leat;   20
is fad on Ghreugais ga sgrìobhadh
  gach ìochdar 's sole bheag;
ann a deireadh bidh 'm balach,
  is bithibh a' tarraing a-steach.   24

[Fìor

180   *[The Bow-corks and the Sole]*

We'll keep you from back-hump and peril, | lifting lead from each surge, | since you've spent all those seasons | at school in Edinburgh, | speaking in Latin | while 4 they whipped you like dogs. | You'll get in your hands | the bow-corks, and be glad. 8

You'll get in your hands | the bow-corks, and keep busy; | while we're at the sole | like victims for sacrifice, | the gunnel under our knees, | crouched tight and tense, 12 | as the round lead weights | slowly come to the surface. 16

Close to the mast in her bow, | a scholar indeed, | you'll be standing there straight, | and we'll let you be; | far from the writing of Greek | every bridle-rope and sole- 20 rope; | in her stern will be the boy, | and let both of you haul. 24

Fìor [?] thug thu 'n cutar
  o Tholl na Muice fo 'siùil
tuath air Eilean na Muice
  troimh Chaol Muile 's gach cùil;   28
ach fuaradh no fasgadh
  air Camas a' Mhùir
aig dol fodha na grèine
  nì thu èirigh on stiùir.   32

Rinn deireadh an fhogharaidh
  goid oirnn gun fhios,
gach gaoth agus acain,
  tarraing acair is driop;   36
dh'fhalbh gach leus às an losgamh
  a bhraith na tomain cho tric,
is o gach àrd a bhios neònach
  a' ghailleann bheò, 's i gun tig.   40

Bidh e sgreunach o fheasgar,
  is 'na pheanas air fad
leis na h-ùird is an drumach
  anns an dubhar mu seach.   44
Nuair thèid gach motor 'na steud,
  air an èigh "leigibh às",
leig thusa do sgìos,
  agus cnìodaigh an cat.   48

You took the cutter right [?] | from the Pig Gap under sail, | north of Muck Island, | through the Sound of Mull and each cove; | but windward or leeward | by Rampart Bay, | when the sun goes down | you will rise from the helm. 28 32

The tail-end of the autumn | robbed us in stealth, | every wind and moaning gust, | anchor-hauling and bustle; | all glow has left the burning | which so often betrayed the shoals, | and from every ominous airt | the wild gale descends. 36 40

It will be scowry from evening on, | and an utter penance, | with the hammer-squalls and the downpour | succeeding each other in the dark. | When every motor revs up | at the shout of "let go!", | go take a rest | and fondle the cat. 44 48

*181 Là Fhèill Aindreis, 1960

Is feàrr i na 'ghrian
    air iarmailt ghlain le aoibh,
na 'n t-soillearachd speur
    do Dhùn Èideann 's don tìr mar-aon;   4

Is feàrr i na 'n tìm,
    is chì sinn i fhathast saor,
's i seagh agus ciall
    ar bliadhna, is meud ar raoin;   8

'S gur ionnan 's an là-s'
    a bheir bàrr air gach là 's gach naomh,
crois gheal air ghrunnd gorm
    a' stoirmrich anns a' ghaoith.   12

*182 Ors' a' Bhèist Mhòr ris a' Bhèist Bhig

On as mith thu, ithidh mi thu;
on as mion thu, ithidh mi thu;
ged as clis thu, ithidh mi thu;
nuair nach fhios duit, ithidh mi thu;
o nach mis' thu, ithidh mi thu;   5
gheobh mi ris thu, 's ithidh mi thu;

[chì mi

181 [St Andrew's Day, 1960]

She is better than the sun | bringing joy on a clear day, | or than the brightness of skies, | for Edinburgh and for the entire country;   4

She is better than time, | and we shall yet see her free; | she is the sense and meaning | of our year, the extent of our field;   8

And equal to this day | which excels each day and each saint, | a white cross on a blue ground | cracking in the wind.   12

182 [Said the Big Beast to the Little Beast]

Since you're common, I will eat you; | since you're tiny, I will eat you; | though you're nimble, I will eat you; | when you don't know it, I will eat you; | since you're not me, I will eat you; | I'll catch you exposed, and I will eat you; | 5

chì mi leis thu, 's ithidh mi thu;
on as treis duit, ithidh mi thu;
on as driop e, ithidh mi thu;
o nach tric seo, ithidh mi thu; 10
on 's a-nis duinn, ithidh mi thu,
agus, a-rithist, ithidh mi thu.
'S e mo ghliocas – ithidh mi thu.

*183 Seann Ó Mordha

'S i mo bharail gun iarraidh,
    mur am fiach leibh a h-èisteachd,
mu chùisean na bliadhna-s'
    is gach bliadhna 'na dèidh seo, 4
gum bi a' ghrian gach beò mhadainn
    gun agadh ag èirigh,
is gach feasgar gu cinnteach
    a' dol sìos fo na speuran. 8

Is bidh na mìltean der cinneadh,
    eadar fhir agus mhnathan,
a' falbh uainn, mar bha roimhe,
    air tòir a' chosnaidh gu Sasainn, 12
agus Sasannaich 'nan ceudan
    a-staigh ag èaladh 'na mhalairt –
mar sin ann don bhliadhna-s'
    is tòrr de bhliadhnachan fhathast. 16

I'll see you sheltering, and I will eat you; | *as you've been here a while, I will eat you;* | *to keep me busy, I will eat you;* | *as this is rare, I will eat you;* | *as we're both* 10 *here now, I will eat you;* | *and, once again, I will eat you.* | *My wisest plan is – I will eat you.*

183 Old Moore

It is my opinion unasked for, | if you do not think it worth listening to, | about the affairs of this year | and every year that follows it, | that, every living morning, the 4 sun | will without a doubt be rising, | and every evening will certainly | be going down from the skies. 8

And there will be thousands of our nation, | both men and women, | who will be leaving us, as of old, | to seek for work in England, | and Englishmen in their 12 hundreds | creeping in as a counterpart – | thus it will be with this year | and a heap of years yet. 16

*184 Sgeuma Ghlinn Nibheis

Is don' e, Sgùrr a' Mhàim,
   's chan fheàrr e a Bheinn Nibheis;
tachdaidh iad an gleann
   bho Steall gu Meall an t-Suidhe;   4
"amar sgùrainn" còrr
   "an domhain mhòir" ga mhilleadh,
le falbh is stad chur ann,
   nach do gheall am filidh.   8

Fad nan linntean ann
   bha 'bheinn 's an gleann nar n-anam;
bha 'm fàsach fraoich rir cùl
   ag ùrachadh ar n-aigne.   12
Abhainn Nibheis mhear,
   is mairg a bheir fo smachd i;
is smachd oirnn sin gu lèir,
   is leughaidh sinne 'aimheal.   16

184 [The Glen Nevis Scheme]

Prospects are bad, Sgurr a' Mhàim, | and yours no better, Ben Nevis; | they will choke up the glen | from Steall to Meall an t-Suidhe; | the unique "scouring-trough | of the wide world" destroyed, | its population gone and all farming ceased, | things which the poet did not foresee. 4 / 8

For ages past, | hill and glen have been in our soul; | the heathery wild stretched behind us, | refreshing our spirit. | Wild River Nevis, | woe to them who bring it | under control; | that control is over all of us, | and we shall read its ill-effects. 12 / 16

*185 Na Giomaich is Brest is Dùn Èideann

Cha leugh sibh na rainn seo
    gu ceann leis an tiomadh,
ged a mhùch sinn an èigheach
    mu dhèidhinn nan giomach.   4

Chuir iad sgeul oirnn à Barraigh
    air a' bhraid bha mun chòrsa,
's na co-Cheiltich ga dèanamh –
    's chuir an sgeul bhàrr ar dòigh sinn.   8

Bha sinn an clos, is cho bodhar
    ri gobhar na cairte;
's tha sinn rudeigin dall ann;
    is cha chall na gheobh caraid.   12

Na bithibh a' fàsgadh ar cridhe
    le gach fios mu gach fulang.
A bhith 'gearan mun ghnothach,
    is crosta sin buileach.   16

185 [*The Lobsters, Brest and Edinburgh*]

You will not read these verses | to their conclusion for grief, | though we quelled their protests | about the lobster affair.   4

They sent us a tale from Barra | of the thieving round the coast | perpetrated by fellow Celts – | and their tale irritated us.   8

We kept silent, and as deaf | as the proverbial cart goat; | we are also a touch blind; | and a friend's gain is no loss.   12

Do not come wringing our hearts | with the smallest detail of every wrong. | Complaining of the business | is an utter annoyance.   16

*186 *Monadh Dubh Bhràid-Albainn*

Is Alba seo gu cinnteach,
is Alba seo gun strìochdadh,
is Alba seo gun chìreadh,
   's an cìreadh tu 'n ceò?   4
Is Alba seo 's i rìomhach,
is Alba seo 's i rìoghail,
is Alba nach toir cìsean
   's i cinnteach bho thòs.   8

Seo Alba a' sìor dhìreadh
bho Choireach Bà 'na mìltean
de bheanntan àrda, fìorchas
   gu ìosal nan lòn;   12
gu fàire thall a' sìneadh,
gu sàile 's thun a Crìche,
's a h-àit am measg nan tìrean
   glè chinnteach fa dheòidh.   16

186 *The Black Mount of Breadalbane*

This is Scotland of a certainty; | this is the Scotland that does not submit; | this is
Scotland uncombed – | and would you comb the mist? | This is Scotland ornate; | 4
this is Scotland the royal; | this is the Scotland that does not pay tribute, | and she
certain from the beginning.   8

This is Scotland ever ascending | from Coireach Bà in miles | of precipitous, high
mountains, | stretching out to the low ground of the loanings – | stretching to the   12
horizon over yonder, | to the sea and to her Border, | and her place among the
countries | a certainty in the end.   16

187–188: Gàidhlig is Gèidhlig mu Seach

*187 An Stoirm Oidhche

Is geur a-nochd fuaim na gaoithe,
  is tu 'cluinntinn na géithe.
A-màireach 's a-mèireach
  bidh e fèathail, 's mi éabhach.   4

An déidh na h-ìdhche 's na h-oidhche,
  nuair thig soillse na gréin' oirnn,
nì mi éirigh is ìrigh
  gu h-ìbhinn 's gu h-éibhinn.   8

*188 Na Gealagan

Is iad sin na fir chàlma
  feadh nam bàghan 's nam bèghan,
le lìon ghealag sna sgàilean,
  'nam meàirlich 's 'nam mèirligh.   4

187–188 [Standard and Dialect in Turn]

187 [The Night Storm]

Shrill tonight is the sound of the wind, | as you hear the wun. | Tomorrow and the morne | it will be calm, and I'll be gled.   4

After the nicht and the night, | with the light of the sun, | I will rouse and I'll roose | in good cheer and guid.   8

188 [The Sea-trouts]

Those are the strong men, | about the bights and the bichts, | with a trout-net in the shadows, | thievish and thieftie.   4

*189 Cath Gairbheach

Briseadh madainn là na bàinidh mhòir aig Gairbheach; bu tràth a bhris,
tràth a bhris.

Rinn iad àrach dheth gun iochd, gun och aig Gairbheach, àrd is mith,
àrd is mith.

Thachair ruaim ri gruaim, thachair, an Cath Gairbheach; thachair sin,
thachair sin.

Gu dè rinn Iarrla Mhàirr màilleach an Cath Gairbheach, 's gun e glic,
's gun e glic?

Roinn e Alba 'na dà leth leitheach an Cath Gairbheach; rinn e sin, rinn e sin. 5

Is fada bhitheas cuimhn' againn air Cath Gairbheach; 's fada sin, 's fada sin.

Is fada bhitheas caoidh againn air Cath Gairbheach – thà a-nis, thà a-nis.

*190 "Faodaidh Duine a Theang' a Chumail san Droch Uair" (seanfhacal Lallans)

Gabhaidh cuid againn smuairein
is an smuaintean air Sgàin;

'S cha do thoill i sin bhuapa,
's gur misneach bhuan i nach tràigh.   4

Sin an seann ainm cliùiteach
chuireadh sùrd oirnn 's gach càs,

[Is a thogadh

189   [The Battle of Harlaw]

*Daybreak on the day of the great frenzy at Harlaw; early it broke, early it broke. |
A battlefield they made of it without mercy or pity at Harlaw, noble and peasant,
noble and peasant. | Red anger met sullen gloom at the Battle of Harlaw; they met
indeed, met indeed. | What did the chainmailed Earl of Marr do at the Battle of
Harlaw, none too wise, none too wise? | He divided Scotland in two halves at the
Battle of Harlaw; that he did, that he did. | Long will we bear in mind the Battle   5
of Harlaw; long indeed, long indeed. | Long will we rue the Battle of Harlaw – we
do now, we do now.*

190   [A Man May Hauld His Tongue in an Ill-time (Scots proverb)]

*Some among us will be despondent | as they ponder on Scone;
It did not merit that from them, | for it is a lasting inspiration that will not ebb.   4
That name of ancient renown | would cheer our spirits in every misfortune,*

Is a thogadh bhon chùil sinn
  às ar crùban beag tàimh. 8

Chan fhaigh sinn aon là dheth,
  Dòmhnall Dàsachdach, nis,

Ach tha 'ainm ann a rabhadh
  gu bhith bras le cur-leis. 12

Cluinnear tagradh nach sgleò bhuainn;
  bidh sinn beò, 's coltach ris;

Bidh sinn beòdha is beadaidh,
  's gheobh sinn Bearaig air ais. 16

*191 *Glaistig Phàirc na Bànrigh*

Bu ghlaistig nach truagh mi,
  's bu ghruagach bha dealbhach,
nuair bha 'Ghàidhlig gu buadhach
  gu Tuaidh againn, 's earbsa. 4
Cuairt chrom agam mochthrath
  gu Boglach an t-Sealgair,
's mo laighe chruiteach mus dorchnaich
  air Meall a' Chonaisg làn feirge. 8

And would lift us up from the corner | where quiescent we crouched. 8
Not one day will we draw | out of Donald the Furious now,
But his name is a warning | to be bold and persistent. 12
A claim will be heard from us that will be no empty talk; | we shall be alive, and shall act alive [or shall be like him?].
We shall be passionate and assertive, | and will win Berwick back. 16

191 *The Spectral Woman of the Queen's Park*
I was a spectral woman who was not pitiful, | and I was a maiden who was comely, | when we had Gaelic victorious | to the Tweed, and confidence for days to come. | 4
Bent and stooping I make my way early | to Hunter's Bog, | and I lie down hunched up, before darkness falls, | on Whinny Knowe full of rage. 8

'S a Chalum a' Chinn Mhòir,
  cha bhòst thu aig seanachaidh!
'S a Chalum a' Chinn Mhòir,
  a rinn a' ghòraiche leanabaidh!   12
Ma lìon thu am beul oirnn
  le Beurla nad bheatha dhuit,
bheir mi fhathast an caibeal
  o do Mhairearad Bheannaichte.   16

*192 Òran Nàiseantach

Ho-rò, mo nighean donn, am falbh thu leam?
Ho-rò, mo nighean donn, am falbh thu leam?
Ho-rò, mo nighean donn, am falbh thu leam
  's gun ceannaich mi còta riabhach dhuit?   4

Gun ceannaich mi còta riabhach dhuit,
's e Albannach, sàr sgiamhach dhuit,
air dhathan fraochach, riasgach dhuit:
  gun ceannaich mi còta riabhach dhuit.   8

Tha saoghail 's saoghail ann gu lèir.
Thilginn iadsan trast an speur
is dhèanainn rathad romham rèidh,
  's mo dhèidh air còta riabhach dhuit.   12

[Tha 'n còta

And Malcolm Canmore, | you are no shennachy's boast! | And Malcolm Canmore, | who committed the childish folly! | If you filled our mouths | with English while 12 you were living, | I will yet take the chapel | from your Blessed Margaret. 16

192 [A Nationalist Song]

Ho-ro my brown-haired lass, will you go with me, | ho-ro my brown-haired lass, will you go with me, | ho-ro my brown-haired lass, will you go with me | and I'll buy a brindled coat for you.   4

I'll buy a brindled coat for you, | one Scottish and right elegant for you, | the colours of heather and heath for you, | I'll buy a brindled coat for you.   8

There are worlds and worlds aplenty. | I would cast them across the sky | and make clear a level road before me, | all to get a brindled coat for you.   12

Tha 'n còta laigheadh ort gu caomh
air dhath a' mhonaidh is an fhraoich.
'S e thigeadh gu ceart rid nàdar saor.
    A ghaoil, bidh còta riabhach ort.   16

Chan e 'n lilidh 's chan e 'n ròs
a chuireas lìth air t'aodach còrr,
ach dathan dùthcha 's dreach le nòs
    bheir fraoch nam mòinteach riabhach dhuit.   20

*193   *Furan na Baintighearna bho Chluaidh*

Mhothaich i da beairt, a luathaich
's a raon a' fosgladh dhi gu cuantan;
sìontan fuara sìoda ghuaillean,
bean uasal rìomhach i sna stuadhan.   4

Seòlaidh Albainn i, ma thog Cluaidh i,
's còir air fairge i 's i 'togail bhuainne.
Nì Barraigh iùl di mar bu dual di,
's nì Leòdhas stiùireadh dhi 'na cuairtean.   8

The coat that would lie on you comfortably | is the colour of the moor and the heather. | Well would it suit your free nature. | My love, a brindled coat you'll wear.   16

It's not the lily nor the rose | that'll put their hue on your distinctive dress, | but native colours and a traditional style | which the heather of the brindled moorlands will bestow on you.   20

193   [*The Welcome of the Queen from Clyde*]
She felt her engines at work as they gathered speed | and her road opened out onto the seas; | cold storms the silk for her shoulders, | a grand lady on the waves.   4

Scotland will guide her, if the Clyde built her, | she is good on the ocean as she sets off from us. | Barra will pilot her, as was ever her duty, | and Lewis will steer her in her travels.   8

Chunnaic Loch Seunta tùs a gluasaid.
Dùn Omhain is Tollard os Bòd, fhuair iad
na tuinn a dh'ut i gu mall bhuaipe
is Cille Chatain thràigh-gheal, uaine.   12

Plada 's A' Mhaol 's Àbhann uaigneach,
Allasan 's Maol na h-Ogha gu h-uachdrach –
am furan thall a thà 'na smuaintean,
is cinnteach gum faigh Alba Nuadh e.   16

*194 Ro Fhad' air a' Mhullach

Seo do threis de Choir' Odhar,
　　's tu nad ghobhar air tòrr
air Slia', 's an stailc ort,
　　am fan thu rid bheò?   4
Thig an ceòban gu ciùin ort,
　　thig an ciùran 's an ceò,
thig am feasgar gun fhios ort;
　　och, glidigh 's bi folbh.   8

[Thig

The Holy Loch witnessed the start of her voyaging. | Dunoon and Toward by
Bute received | the waves she slowly pushed aside, | and white-shored, green
Kilchattan.   12

Pladda and the Moyle and solitary Sanda, | Ailsa Craig and the Maiden Moyle
above her – | the welcome yonder that is on her mind, | without a doubt Nova
Scotia will receive it.   16

194 [Too Long on the Summit]

You've had your while at Dun Corrie, | perched like a goat on a hilltop | on Sleea,
in a fit of thrawnness, | will you wait here for ever? | The smirr will gently close in   4
on you, | and the drizzle and mist, | and the evening will creep in on you; | come
on, stir and get going.   8

Thig am feasgar gu clis ort,
  thig an Grioglachan òir,
thig an oìdhche gun ghealach
  a' falach gach fòid.
Bi 'teàrnadh, a bhalaigh;
  och, caraigh, 's bi còir.
Thig an ceathach 's an dubhar;
  glidigh thusa, 's bi folbh.

12

16

*195 Cnocan a' Chait Fhiadhaich

Fhuair an cnocan an t-ainm,
  is dh'fhalbh e fhèin,
's a sheòrsa leis
  chaidh às gu lèir.
'S tha saoghal calldaidh
  gu mall 's gu rèidh
a' dlùthachadh dlùth
  ma dhùthaich 'na dhèidh.

4

8

Tha gach mionaid as tìr,
  san linn seo fhèin,
spiorad cait fhiadhaich
  iadhta nach eug,
spògan, spuirean
  gan cur an streup,
a' spàirn gu fiadhaich,
  fiacaill 's deud.

12

16

The evening will swiftly come on you, | and the Pleiades of gold, | the moonless night will come | and conceal every clod. | Start going back down, lad; | come on, move and be sensible. | The fog and the dark will be here; | stir yourself and get going.

12

16

195 Wild Cat Knowe

The knowe got the name, | and he himself went, | and with him his kind | perished entirely. | And slowly and smoothly | a tame world | is closing in close | about his country after him.

4

8

Every minute in this land, | in this very century, | there is a wild cat spirit, | encircled, which will not die, | paws and talons | thrown into the fight, | struggling wildly, | tooth and fang.

12

16

*196 *Acarsaidean a'* Chutty Sark

Bha gach fear san sgioba 'gabhail mòran eagail,
ri faicinn Ros Neodha 's an loch san dol seachad,
gun robh nì a dhìth orr' a bhiodh 'na lìth 's 'na chneasachd,
bhon bha 'n *Cutty Sark* air acair mu dheas bhuainn.   4

Labhair Suidh' an Easbaig 's Cill Chreagain le chèile:
"Is fadal buan gach faire dhuinn, mur faic sinn fhèin i.
Bhiodh i na bu nàdarra air àrainn a h-euchdan.
Am b'fheàrr dhi bhith 'fuireach bhuainn am Punta Arenas?"   8

'Na tàmh ann an Tàimis an tàrr i fuireach,
a' siaradh air a slabhraidhean, do-cheannsaicht' uile,
ma chaill i Rubha na Cloiche is Cille Mhunna,
is Seann Dùn a h-àbhaiste gu bràth bràth buileach?   12

'S na h-acarsaidean cèine – is cha bu ghann iad –
anns an do chuir a dreuchd i – is cha bu mhall i.
Bu chòir a cur gu dùthchasach le cliù, 's b'e 'n t-àm e,
an Geàrrloch Chluaidh gu h-eòlach air a sàr dhà shlabhraidh. 16

196   [*The* Cutty Sark's *Anchorages*]

*Every man in the crew was greatly worried, | at the sight of Rosneath and the
loch going past, | that they lacked something that would bring them colour and
healing | since the* Cutty Sark *was moored far from us down south.*   4

*Up spoke The Bishop's Seat (Helensburgh) and Kilcreggan together: | "Weari-
some and tedious our watch, if we don't get to see her. | It would be more natural
to have her on the site of her exploits. | Would she rather stay far from us in Punta
Arenas?"*   8

*Will it befall her to be idle away on the Thames, | tugging at her chains, in no way
tamed, | if she has lost The Stone Point (Cloch Point) and Kilmun, | and familiar
Old Fort (Shandon) for evermore?*   12

*And the foreign anchorages – and they were not few – | to which her career took
her – and she was not slow in going. | It is high time she was berthed with acclaim
where her roots are, | in the Gareloch she knows, on her two mighty chains.*   16

*197 An Cnocan Fraoich is Padre Dante

Siud thusa air gach taobh 's mi 'sealltainn bhuamsa.
Mo ghaol, an tulach is a còmhnard torrach;
mo chion, an cnoc ud ìochdar agus uachdar.

Lìon thu mo shùilean domh air an ceud fhosgladh,
is chì mi, nuair a dhùinear iad mu dheireadh,   5
do fhraoch 's do chreagan is t'fhonn ghràinnsear fodhad.

Pàrras no Iutharna cha toir dhìom aon leathad,
càrnan no bruthach dhìot, lèana no glacag,
is tu nad aisling shìorraidh ga mo leantainn.

Bidh sinn nar n-eòlaich fhathast, 's tu nad aisling   10
is mi nam thannasg. Cuirear air an Aog leinn
là bithbhuan nach do smaointich Padre Dante –

nach robh a-bhos an taobh a rinn e glasadh.

197   [The Heather Knowe and Padre Dante]

There you are all around me as I look forth. | *My love, the knoll and its fertile
terraces;* | *my desire, that hill, its uplands and low grounds.*

You filled my eyes the first time they opened, | *and when they finally close for ever
I will see* | *your heather and your rocks and the fertile soil around you.*   5

Paradise or Inferno will not deprive me of one slope, | *nor take one stone-heap or
brae off you, one green meadow or dell,* | *as you follow me, a vision immortal.*

We shall still be acquainted, you a vision, | *I a ghost. We shall prevail over Death,* | 10
on an everlasting day not envisaged by Padre Dante –

who was never in these parts at the break of day.

*198 Na Fiachan Gaolach
no An Nàiseantach do dh'Albainn

(trì rainn is amhran)

Thug mi treis dhuit, thug mi tràth dhuit,
thug mi greis dhuit 's iomadh ràith dhuit,
thug mi treis is gach aon là dhuit,
    's gu là bràth dhuit mo ghrian 's mo speuran.   4

Fhuair mi bith uait air cheann nam bliadhna,
fhuair gach camhanach is ciaradh,
gach là màireach 's mo chian nan cian uait,
    is bheir mi fianais air siud le spèis dhuit.   8

Chan eil san domhan uil' ach t'fhàire;
chan eil 'na rannaibh ruadh' ach t'àirdean;
chan eil sna thùras sinn ach t'àbhaist,
    's bheir mi gu bràth dhuit slàn 's gu lèir siud.   12

Ceangal

Làithean is bliadhnachan, iarmailt is cruinne cè,
na ràithean gan riaghladh 's a' ghrian a' toirt dhaibh an gnè,
fàsach is diasan – is fial bheir thu dhuinn gach seud,
is pàighear na fiachan sin gun iarraidh, gun athadh dhuit fhèin.   16

198   *Debts of Love or The Nationalist to Scotland*
(three verses and envoi)

I gave you a while, I gave you a time; | I gave you a space and many a season; | I gave you a while and each and every day, | and I gave you for ever my sun and my skies.   4

I got being from you to face the years; | from you I got each morning twilight and darkening of evening; | from you I got my every tomorrow and my ages of old; | and I will bear witness to that with loving regard for you.   8

The whole world is only your horizon; | all its regions are only your airts; | all that we devise is only your accustomed wont – | and I will give you all that for ever, whole and entire.   12

Envoi
Days and years, the firmament and the universe, | the seasons as they are ordained and the sun giving them their nature, | wasteland and cornland – generously you give us each treasure, | and those debts will be repaid to you without asking, without hesitation.   16

*199 Ar Cnocan Fraoich

Chan eil gach slios mar bhà. Chuir e oirnne bàire,
    na fhuair uiread àilleachd de shàrach faoin.
'S ann a dh'fhàs a' chopag an àite chroitean,
    's tha làraichean 's iad tostach nar Cnocan Fraoich.   4
'S e a chur an ìre an leigheas dìleas
    air gach gnìomh dubh dìmeas a char da thaobh –
shaltair ainneart obann air gasain mhonaidh,
    's a dhaoine fhèin gan lot air ar Cnocan Fraoich.   8

An dèidh gach fòirneirt, cur-fàs is fògraidh
    tha 'mhisneach is an dòchas 's a' chòir 'nan laoich.
Air fonn, air creagan, air gach aon leathad
    bidh saoghal farsaing, leathann aig Nàisean saor.   12
Ar n-ulaidh chnocain, ar bunait shocrach,
    ri turadh no ri doineann nach bog a-chaoidh –
fraoch no fochann, lom no molach,
    cha deach e fòs a mholadh, ar Cnocan Fraoich.   16

199 Our Little Heather Hill

Not every slope is as it was. The trials, begot by folly, which so much beauty had
to endure, have been a goal driven against us. | The docken has grown in the
place of crofts, | and there are silent ruined village sites on our Little Heather
Hill. | To speak out boldly is the faithful cure | for all the black deeds of despite   4
that have come its way – | sudden violence trampled on moorland heather sprays, |
and its own people were wounded on our Little Heather Hill.   8

After all the violence, laying waste and exiling, | courage and hope and the right
are warriors. | On soil, on rocks, on each and every slope | there will be a wide and
spacious world for a free Nation. | Our treasure of a knowe, our firm foundation | 12
which will never be shaken in sun or tempest – | heather [or] blade of grass,
where it is bare or where it is shaggy, | it has not yet been rightly praised, our
Little Heather Hill.   16

*200 A' Phìob Mhòr Againn

Thug sin bàrr air gach gaoith,
  's air gach taobh às an tàrr iad,
am binneas 's a' ghaoir
  aig a' ghaoith thig bhon mhàla;   4
duis is feadan is gaothair
  ri saothair ceart còmhla,
fhuair iad am bruthach air a' chlàrsaich,
  a' dol an-àird lem puirt-mhòra.   8

Ann am prìomh cheòl na cruinne
  fhuair na Cruimeinich àit dhuinn,
is chuir sinn rìgh air a' pìoban
  anns gach tìr anns an tàmh iad;   12
an t-inneal 's an ealain,
  an deachdadh 's a ghabhail –
am measg na tha 'cheòl ann
  tha seud sònraichte againn.   16

200 [Our Great Pipes]

It has excelled all other winds, | and every airt whence they come, | the melodiousness and skirling scream | of the wind blown from the bag; | drones, chanter and 4 bellows | successfully worked together, | they gained the high ground over the clarsach, | as they soared with their great pibrochs. 8

In the finest music of the world | the MacCrimmons won a place for us, | and we gave a king to all the world's pipes, | whatever the country they occur in; | the 12 instrument and the artistry, | the inspired creation and its delivery – | among all the music there is, | we have a very special jewel. 16

*201 *Rathad Loudaidh 's an Track*

Och, bidh sibh fhèin an oìdhche seo
  ri "dìd ort" leis na rubhachan,
's mo char-mu-thom, 's cha bhàrdachd e,
  ri càraichean 's ri busaichean;
ge aognaidh luaths nan lìnearan,
  's an t-Sìn 'na deagh cheann uidhe dhaibh,
Eilean fo Ghlais no Iomachar,
  is bicheanta na cunnartan.

4

8

Seo bhuam an gearan àbhaisteach,
  's bu Ghàidhlig e mun d'rugadh mi,
'S mas fìor no fealla-dhà seo bhuam,
  gun tàrr sibh às gach udal ann,
's an oìdhche 'teachd sa bheucaich oirbh,
  's e 'sèideadh geal bhàrr shumainnean;
's biodh sgaothan chàr is làraidhean
  gu là a' toirt mo thurais diom.

12

16

<hr/>

201 [Lothian Road and the Track]

Oh, you yourselves will all tonight | be playing keekaboo with the headlands, | while my own dodging – without exaggeration – | will be round cars and buses; | although terrifying the speed of the liners, | and China a good destination for them, | by Holy Isle or Imachar Point, | many are the dangers.

4

8

This is the customary complaint from me, | and it is a Gaelic one that long predates me, | and whether I speak in truth or in jest, | may you pull out of every dangerous tossing, | as the night descends on you among the howling, | and the wind froths white over the breakers; | and let swarms of cars and lorries | keep me off my course till dawn.

12

16

*202 *Abune the Gutted Haddie*

It's sweir, an ye sae thrang wi't;
  ye dwaam fu lang, ma laddie.
Ye'll fin yere rhymes a' roond ye
  abune the Gutted Haddie.   4

The say the causie's shochlie,
  its setts are for the aiver;
ae day, thoch, we maun roose it –
  lik screes, it's Scotland's ivar.   8

Eeno, for that comes efter,
  rise wi the waft that blaws ye.
The heichs an whaups wull sair ye;
  yon's whaur the causie ca's ye.   12

Aboot they braes gang verses,
  whan carses dinna grow them.
they're near the levrocks yonder
  wi a' the howes ablow them.   16

They'll kythe fornent ye thonder,
  gin Willie wi ye's Wullie;
an nivar get yere spleddrach,
  but kep them in a gulley.   20

*203 *Brònach Tadhal Dùn Monaidh*

Brònach tadhal Dùn Monaidh,
  bail' a mhol na ceudan bàrd.
Nuair a chìthear Dùn Monaidh
  is deacair gun *ochain* a ràdh.   4

[Seachd ceud

203 Sad to Visit Dun Monaidh

It is sad to visit Dùn Monaidh, | a town which hundreds of poets have praised. |
When one sees Dùn Monaidh | it is hard not to say *alas*.   4

Seachd ceud is seachd agus mìle,
  cunntas a mhill ar tlachd 's ar fois,
's a dh'fhàg sinn ris anns an ainbheach
  air bheagan meanmainn or toic.   8

Ge brònach tadhal Dùn Monaidh,
  gheobh ar n-Alba saorsa fòs.
Brònach tadhal Dùn Monaidh,
  ach molar e fhathast gun bhròn.   12

*204 Air Suidh' Artair Dhomh Mochthrath

Là 's a' ghrian 'na lainnir,
  air Suidh' Artair dhomh mochthrath,
's mi ag amharc Dhùn Sapaidh,
  is nan glacagan conaisg;   4
a' gabhail beachd air a' mhachair,
  's air na h-achaidhean toiceil,
fonn Loudaidh gun teirce,
  an tìr eararach thorach.   8

"Dèan am beachdachadh sàr mhath;
  chan i 'Gharbhail a th'agad,
sùilean cruthach nam moineach,
  no mol Rubha Bhaltair;   12
ach fonn an cinnich na diasan
  gu fialaidh, farsaing,
tìr gun sgàirneach, gun chruadhlach,
  is i uaine, mìn, maiseach."   16

Seven hundred and seven and a thousand | was a reckoning that ruined our pleasure and our repose, | and left us exposed as dyvours | with little spirit after a wealth of it.   8

Although it is sad to visit Dùn Monaidh, | our Scotland will yet get freedom. | It is sad to visit Dùn Monaidh, | but it will yet be praised without sadness.   12

204 [On Arthur's Seat One Morning]

On a day of glittering sunshine, | when I was early on Arthur's Seat, | I gazed on Dunsapie Rock | and the wee dells of gorse | and took stock of the coastal plain | 4
and the luxuriant fields, | Lothian soil of no scarcity, | the fertile easterly land.   8

"Appraise this as well as you can; | it is not Garvel you have here, | the deep bogs of the hares | or the shingle beach of Walter's Point; | but a soil in which ears of   12
corn grow | generously and expansively, | a land free of scree and hard rocky ground, | verdant, smooth, and lovely."   16

Chunnaic mise, 's bu tric sin,
   nì, le m'fhios, bu mhò maise,
's a thig 'na smuain, is i ealamh,
   chum nan creag-s' air Suidh' Artair;   20
b'e sin monadh Chinntìre,
   is Loch Fìne ga amharc,
A' Gharbhaird ga mholadh,
   cùirn is mol Rubha Bhaltair.   24

Tha siud ann, Cruach Tharsainn,
   agus tlachd dhith gun tomhas;
Cruach an t-Sorchain 's A' Chaolbheinn,
   's iad as caoimhe th'air domhan;   28
na fìor ionaidean garbha,
   Allt a' Ghalbhais is Sgolaig,
a chuireadh sunnd air fear duilich,
   's e 'falbh bhruthach is chnocan.   32

Am fraoch 's an roid chruaiche,
   an luachair 's an roineach,
is na h-ùr bhadain bheithe
   fo na leathadan corrach,   36
an cìob is a' chòinneach,
   gum b'eòlach mi orra;
gum b'e 'n leigheas air eucail
   fàs an t-slèibhe 's a bholadh.   40

[B'e 'n leigheas

I have seen, and frequently, | *something of greater beauty assuredly,* | *the thought of which flies swiftly* | *to these rocks on Arthur's Seat:* | *the plain of Kintyre,* | 20 *beheld by Loch Fyne,* | *praised by Garvel,* | *the stones and shingle of Walter's Point.* 24

The Sidelong Summit stands there, | *giving pleasure beyond measure;* | *Footstool Summit and Narrow Ben,* | *the gentlest on earth;* | *the truly untamed bounds,* | 28 *Altagalvash and Sgolaig,* | *these would cheer a despondent man* | *walking the slopes and hills.* 32

The heather and bog-myrtle, | *the rushes and the fern,* | *the fresh thickets of birch* | *under the steep inclines,* | *the flax and the moss,* | *I have known them all;* | *it was* 36 *ever the remedy for infirmity,* | *the fragrant mountain flora.* 40

B'e 'n leigheas air tinneas,
   ceòl a' ghlinne gun chlos air;
na h-alltain a' teàrnadh
   bho na fàsaichean tostach.   44
Chuireadh cruth an fhuinn fhiadhaich,
   is e liathchreagach, molach,
gleus gu bràth air an fhear sin
   a bhiodh sealan ga choiseachd.   48

'S e sin tolman na h-earba,
   nach eil cearbach 'na siubhal,
's i 'g iarraidh dìdein taobh alltan
   no 'na deannruith ri bruthach.   52
Is binn a ghoireas a' chrotag
   air oiteag nam mullach,
's i 'faicinn Arainn is Ìle,
   is Cinntìre gu h-uile.   56

Bidh caoidh aig a' bhrìdein
   as t-oìdhche san fheamainn,
fon Earrainn Ghoineach gu h-ìosal,
   is cha bu sgìos leinn a ghearan;   60
's e a' goir air bheag furtachd
   anns an dubhar fo chreagan,
gus an èirich an là air
   bho àrd Shlios a' Cheathraimh.   64

It was the remedy for sickness, | the tireless music of the glen, | the streams racing down | from the high grounds happed in silence. | The shape of the wild country, | stone-grey and shaggy, | would forever revive the man | who would walk it a while.   44 48

That hillock is the roe's, | not wrong-footed in her movements | as she takes refuge by a wee brook | or goes tearing down a brae. | Sweet is the plover's cry | in the breeze round the summits | as she sights Arran and Isla | and the whole of Kintyre.   52 56

By night the oyster-catcher | wails in the tangle, | down beyond the Sandy Patch, | his complaint never tiresome to us; | he cries inconsolably | in the shadow of the rocks | till the day dawns on him | from the high Kerry Slope.   60 64

Bho thùs saoghail 's gu suthain,
   fhuair e 'n t-urram air àilleachd,
am fonn chaidh a chumadh
   is a luraiche gharbh air;   68
'na choltas do-cheannsaicht'
   is nì ann e tha calma
is e uaibhreach, garg, rìomhach,
   bho Allt an Lìn gus an Garbhallt.   72

"Chan eil saoi gun a sheis' ann,
   ged thug thu treis mud thìr allail.
Seall an earadheas bhuatsa,
   agus tuairmsich a' ghabhail,   76
far a bheil Garbhallt an Loudaidh,
   's am monadh lom ann ga altram.
Faic Sliabh Allair 's e riabhach,
   's a bhràithrean ciara gun ghainne."   80

"Is ann de t'àbhaist bhith moltach
   mun t-Sloc Dhomhainn 's mun Òrdaig;
mu Chruach Doire Lèithe
   is Cnoc na Mèine cùl mòintich;   84
mu Rubha a' Ghrianain,
   is mu chian Lagan Ròaig.
Cluinnear glaodh bho Dhùn Iubhair
   a bheir an diog às an òran."   88

[Och is och

Since the beginning of time and for evermore, | it has been honoured with the greatest beauty, | the land that was fashioned | with such rough loveliness; | in its untamable appearance | it is a thing of great strength, | proud, fierce and splendid, | from the Flax Burn to Garvald. 68 72

"Every sage has his equal, | though you've been a while evoking your fine country. | Look from you to the south-east | and appraise the lie of the land, | where Lothian's Garvalt stream runs, | nursed by the bare plain. | See gorgeous Allermuir, | and its dusky brothers lacking nothing." 76 80

"You are in the habit of singing | the praises of the Deep Pit and the Thumb; | of Grey Grove Summit | and Mine Hill behind the moors; | of Greeanan Point | and of distant Lagan Ròaig. | But there's a cry from Dunure | that will cut your song short." 84 88

Och is och, an e 'thighinn
 air a' chinneach aig m'athair,
nuair bha imrich an t-Sàthairn
 gus a' Ghàidhealtachd aca?   92
B'ann air là an deagh fhortain
 a thog iad an acair.
Bidh mo bheannachd a-chaoidh air,
 's air an sgaoth rinn a' mhalairt.   96

Chunnaic Eilean na Baintighearna
 dath an cuid seòl bhuaith;
thog iad Rubha Meall Daraich,
 's thug a-mach Toll a' Bhòdaich;   100
chuir iad sgothan air acair
 's b'e sin an dachaigh 's an eòlas.
Sin a' chomain a mhaireas,
 is gur Cainntrich fa dheòidh sinn.   104

Thuirt iad "Slàn le Dùn Iubhair!"
 's thug am furan don Tairbeirt,
do dhùthaich na Gàidhlig,
 a' chàirdeis 's a' gharbhlaich.   108
Bu ghlic a chùm iad san t-seòladh
 an crann spreòid air a' Gharbhail
's gur iad a' Ghàidhealtachd 's a' Ghàidhlig
 an dà nì 's fheàrr a tha 'n Albainn. 112

Och, och, is that an allusion | to my father's people, | when they embarked on their Saturday flitting | and headed for the Gaeltach? | It was on a day of good 92 *fortune | that they lifted anchor. | For evermore I will bless him | and the crowd that made the exchange.* 96

Lady Isle saw | the colour of their sails in the distance, | they raised Oaken Knowe Point | and left the Bute Man's Bay behind; | they anchored their skiffs, | and 100 *made that their home and their country. | That debt persists, | which made Kintyre folk of us in the end.* 104

They said "Farewell to Dunure", | and turned their welcome to Tarbert, | to the land of Gaelic | and communality, to the rough-terrained land. | They were wise, 108 *when they sailed, to keep | their bowsprit aligned on Garvel, | for Gaelic and the Gaeltach | are the two glories of Scotland.* 112

Is mò cumhachd nan sliabh
  na aon riaghaltas maireann;
is fheàrr feartan a' mhonaidh
  na gach oilein tha 'n Sasainn;   116
an Tairbeart dan cosnadh
  an sgoth 's an lìon sgadain,
is treasa gu mòr i
  na Hòmar 's an Laideann.   120

Air cabhsair 's air fireach
  molaidh mise rim bheò sin,
Uaraidh 's an Aisinn,
  Cnoc nan Sgarbh 's Bàgh a' Chòmhraig;   124
bho Shliabh Gaoil riamh gu Claonaig,
  is thar gach taobh ann am bòidhchead,
Sgìre Chalmain Eala,
  am fonn creagach nach còmhnard.   128

Innis Choinnich is Lìte
  's gach druim am Fìobh is gach baile,
's an còrr fhàfann beag, fann,
  a' teachd a-nall bho Shliabh Allair;   132
's e bh'agam Sgolaig 's Allt Beithe
  car treise 'nan aiteal,
's mi 'g amharc raointean is rèidhlein
  mochthrath grèin' air Suidh' Artair.   136

More powerful are the hills | than any government on earth; | greater the virtues of the mountains | than any education in England; | Tarbert, whose livelihood | is 116 *the skiff and the herring-net, | is mightier by far | than Homer and Latin.* 120

On causie and moor, | all my life I will praise it, | Uaraidh and Ashens | Cormorant Hill and Battle Bay; | from Sleea ever to Claonaig, | and surpassing every 124 *region in beauty, | Kilcalmonell Parish, | the rocky, unlevel country.* 128

Inchkenneth and Leith, | every ridge in Fife and every town, | and the wisp of a faint wee breeze | drifting over from Allermuir; | what I beheld for a moment | was 132 *a vision of Sgolaig and Birch Burn, | as I looked out on fields and meadows, | early one sunny morning on Arthur's Seat.* 136

POEMS 1964–1973

*205 *Am Flùr Geal Slèibhe*

Ar leam gur èibhinn 'n àm èirigh ì;
ar leam gur èibhinn 'n àm laighe sìos.
Tha i beusach is tha i ceutach,
am flùr geal slèibhe dh'fhàg èibhinn mì.   4

Tha i màlda is tha i caomh.
Tha i àlainn 's dh'fhàs i saor.
Is e a nàdar, is e a h-àbhaist
gean is gàire, fàilte 's aoibh.   8

Cha ghabh i mìothlachd, is ì gun sgraing.
Tha i sìobhalta bìth 'na cainnt.
Tha 'snuadh 's a lìth ann air ghile dhìthein.
Chan eil mìghean san rìbhinn ann.   12

Is solas lèir i 's gach àit am bì.
Is sona, sèimh i 's is fàilteach ì.
Tha tlàths na grèine san fhlùr gheal Chèitein –
's i 'm flùr geal slèibhe dh'fhàg èibhinn mì.   16

205 *The White Hill Flower*

Methinks she is cheerful at time of rising up; | methinks she is cheerful at time of lying down. | She is virtuous and she is lovely, | the white hill flower that left me cheerful.   4

She is gentle and she is kind. | She is glorious and she has grown up a free being. | Those are her nature, those are her accustomed wont – | a cheerful mood and laughter, a welcome and joy.   8

She feels no displeasure and never shows a grimace. | She is gentle and quiet in her speech. | Her complexion and hue have the whiteness of flowers. | There is no ill mood in the lassie at all.   12

She is a bright light in every place she goes. | She is happy and tranquil, and of a ready welcome. | The gentleness of the sun is in the white May flower – | she is the white hill flower that left me cheerful.   16

*206 *Nationalist Sang*

Ma broon-haired lass, will ye gae wi me?
Ma broon-haired lass, will ye gang wi me?
Ma broon-haired lass, will ye gae wi me
    an' I'se buy a brindled coat for ye.   4

I'se buy a brindled coat for ye,
fu' Scots, fu' fine, fu' fair tae see,
the colour o heather an' muirgerss tae –
    I'se buy a brindled coat for ye.   8

Och, there are warlds an' warlds forbye.
I'd fling them aa acrost the sky,
tae mak a road tae hasten by
    tae buy a brindled coat for ye.   12

The coat that wad kindly sit on ye
's the colour o muirs an' heather tae.
Wi yere freeborn nature 'twad agree.
    A brindled coat'll no happin' ye.   16

It's no' the lily, no' the rose
will gie their hue tae yere wale o claes
but kintra colours a' customs hues
    the heather o brindled moors will gie.   20

Ma broon-haired lass, will ye gae wi me?
Ma broon-haired lass, will ye gang wi me?
Ma broon-haired lass, will ye gae wi me
    an' I'se buy a brindled coat for ye.   24

207 [*Latha san Rainich*]
(òran)

Latha dhomh bhith san rainich,
  hug ò failill ò;
bha a' bhruthainn ann trasta,
  hug ò failill eile,
  hug ò failill ò.   5

Bha a' bhruthainn ann trasta;
bha am fèath air gach glacaig,
is air molan na mara,
is air muir far am faicte.
"Cogaidhean mòra a' tachairt,   10
nas fhaide na Arainn
no biod Chnoc a' Chaisteil.
Cha bhi mac aig an athair;
cha bhi ogh' air a' mhacan.
'S annamh leòntach thig dhachaigh,   15
's a' ghrian lèir air a lathadh."
Latha grèine 's e taitneach,
latha dhomh bhith san rainich.

207 [*A Day Among the Bracken*]
(song)

A day when I was among the bracken, hug o failill o; | the sultry heat was over everything, hug o failill eile, hug o failill o.   5

The sultry heat was over everything; | calm lay on each hollow, | and on the shingle of the sea, | and on the sea as far as eye could reach. | "Great wars befalling, | 10 further away than Arran | or the summit of Castle Knowe. | The father will have no son, | the son will have no grandson. | Few will be the wounded who come home, | and the clear sun will be blotted out." | A day of sun and it pleasant, | a day 15 when I was among the bracken.

208 *Referendum*

Tha daoine beaga an Lunnainn,
   dh'fhàgas guineach gach rann.
Vòt iad, is chuir iad
   a' ghlas ghuib air ar drannd.   4

209 *An Rùnaire Stàit*

Domhan ann fhèin gach duine
   le 'dhubhar is le 'leus.
Ar leam gu bheil an Rosach
   'na fho-dhomhan gu lèir.   4

*210 *Via Media?*
A Middle Path?

Whan the trauchle wad stacher sun an' sterns,
   is't girn an' gie owre?
Or fin' the smeddum whaur it derns,   3
   an' dow an' be dour;
an' in ae glisk, wi aathing stey,
   gang lik stoor?   6

Or plunk the schule? Greet whan it's dule?
   Let the shule faa?
Or fin' ye're pawkie, an' aye be jokie   9
   an' jook aa;
syne lauch an' blether aathegither,
   an' warsle awa'?   12

208 *Referendum*
There are wee men in London | who will cause every verse to be a wounding one. | They voted, and put | a muzzle on our snarl.   4

209 *The Secretary of State*
A world in himself is every man, | with its darkness and light. | Methinks Ross | is an entire underworld.   4

*211 An Ciùran Ceòban Ceò

Dol sìos an cladach madainn dhomh, 's an t-adhar ann gun deò;
bha sìth feadh fuinn is mara ann, is taise bho na neòil.
Cha chluinnte feadh a' chiùinis ach fann chiùcharan aig eòin.
Bha gach nichein tostach, driùchdach anns a' chiùran cheòban cheò.   4

Cha robh àird no iùl ann a stiùireadh neach 'na ròd.
Cha robh àit no ùin' ann, ach aon chiùineas domhain, mòr.
Bha 'n saoghal làn den mhaoithe fo dhraoidheachd is fo chleòc,
is bann sìthe air mo shùilean anns a' chiùran cheòban cheò.   8

Chan fhaicte fonn no fàire. Bha sàmhchair air gach nì.
Bha beithich agus dùslaingean 'nan smùid gun dath, gun lìth.
Bha cnuic is glacan paisgte ann, is chailleadh muir is tìr.
Bha fois is clos is dùsal anns a' chiùran cheòbain mhìn.   12

Chaidh sliosan agus leathadan à sealladh anns na neòil.
Cha robh dath no fuaim ann, no uair, no solas lò.
Bha 'n sileadh mall, rèidh, socrach air cnoc, air glaic, air lòn,
is bha 'm Paiste Beag fo dheataich anns a' cheathach cheòban cheò.   16

211 *The Smirry Drizzle of Mist*

Going down the shore on a morning, when the air was without a breath of wind, | there was peace throughout land and sea and a saftness from the clouds. | Nothing was to be heard through the stillness but a faint chirming of birds. | Everything was silent and dewy in the smirry drizzle of mist.   4

There was no airt or direction to guide one on one's way. | There was no place or time there, but one great, deep stillness. | The world was full of tenderness, under druidry and under a cloak; | and there was a fairy blindfolding on my eyes in the smirry drizzle of mist.   8

Land or horizon could not be seen. Quietness was over everything. | A smoke was rising from colourless, hueless birch groves and thickets. | Hills and hollows were enfolded in it, and land and sea were lost. | There was peace and rest and slumber in the fine drizzle of mist.   12

Hillsides and slopes were lost to sight in the clouds. | There was no colour or sound there, or hour or light of day. | The slow, caressing rain was on hill and hollow and meadow, | and the Wee Patch was in a smoke in the foggy drizzle of mist.   16

Bha na ciothan ceathaich chiùranaich, 's iad dùmhail, dlùth, gun ghlòir,
gu cagarsach, gu cùbhraidh, tais, ùr, gun ghuth, gun cheòl,
a' snàmh mu mhill is stùcan, 's a' dùnadh mu gach còs.
Bha tlàths is tlachd a' tùirling anns a' chiùran cheòban cheò.　　20

*212　Ar Cor an Albainn

A' chaora fon deimheas,
　　's i 'fàs deireasach, fuar,
nì i mèilich mu dheireadh
　　's i 'bualadh bhreaban mun cuairt.　　4

dòigh eile air:

An leòghann bhios fo thàmailt,
　　bheir e ràn gun fhuireach;
bheir e 'n sitheadh garbh às,
　　is marbhaidh e gach duine.　　8

The showers of drizzly mist came closely down, all soundless, | whispering and fragrant, soft and fresh, without voice or melody, | they floated about hilltops and cliffs and closed in about every hollow. | Gentleness and pleasure were drifting down in the smirry drizzle of mist.　　20

212　Our Situation in Scotland

The sheep under the shears, | as it grows miserable and cold, | will bleat in the end | and distribute kicks around.　　4

another way of it:

The lion which is under insult | will give a roar without tarrying; | he will give a rough rush, | and kill every man.　　8

*213 *Eun Maidne*

Is moch a ghoireas eun na maidne
air a' chraoibh fa chomhair an taighe
an Dùn Eideann toiseach earraich.

Tha eun na maidne 'seinn an Suraidh.
Chuala Hòmar a luinneag.   5
Dè dheth? 'S i seo Alba buileach;
Alba an-seo 's an-diugh i.

Dè feum bhith 'leantainn na seann ealain?
'S i 's ealain dhuinn ar tìr nar latha,
is goirear leinn mar eun na maidne.   10

*214 *Bliadhna gun Gheamhradh (Am Paipear Naidheachd)*

Chìthear an aiteal
    na tha 'm paipear ag iarraidh –
mìorun agus gamhlas
    is an geamhradh 'na bliadhna.   4

Chìthear, ach fuireach,
    na tha 'n duine ag iarraidh –
deagh rùn agus rann leis
    is gun gheamhradh sa bhliadhna.   8

213 *Morning Bird*

Early calls the morning bird | on the tree opposite the house | in Edinburgh at the beginning of Spring.

A morning bird is singing in Surrey. | Homer heard its song. | What of it? This is   5
Scotland entirely; | Scotland here and today.

What use is it to follow the old art of poetry? | Our land in our day is the art for us, | and our calling will be like the morning bird's.   10

214 *A Year Without Winter (The Newspaper)*

You can see in a flash | what the paper is after – | ill-will and spite | and winter all year.   4
You can see, if you only wait, | what man is after – | goodwill and a verse accompanying it, | and no winter in the year.   8

*215 *For the* Cutty Sark
Moored in the Port of London

Will the lifts haud the yerds
   in the saft southern air?
Will the hooks haud the groond
   at aa doon there?   4
Hook or hawser, aa that hauds her,
   she'll lift when nane's aware,
an' trail thaim to the Gare Loch
   on her ain, that's shair.   8

She was aye winnan hame
   frae soothward, dawn an' derk.
Her skysails spiered and spied
   efter Clyde, morn an' mirk.   12
Efter aa the knots she reeled,
   her warslean an' wark,
I spay we'll say it again:
   "Weel dune, Cutty Sark!"   16

216 [*Rann Fìrinneach*]

Is fìrinneach a bhios an rann,
   is bheir mi i gu ceann gun athadh –
is tric a phòg mi am beul
   nach do labhair breug fhathast.   4

216 [*A Truthful Epigram*]
This four-lined verse will be truthful, | and I will bring it to a conclusion without
hesitation – | often have I kissed the mouth | that never spoke a lie yet.   4

217 *Sreathan Sìmplidh*

Ealasaid a ghaoil 's a ghràidh ghil,
is fìor ge manntach a' bhàrdachd –
chan fhaighear coire don dàn seo,
's gur àlainn moladh gach nì àlainn.
Nan robh agam alt gu m'àilgheas,   5
dhèanainn rainn a bhiodh 'nan sgàthan
dod bhòidhchead is do t'uaisle nàdair;
ach gabh na rainn sìmplidh seo om làimh-sa.

Is àlainn moladh gach nì àlainn.
Chan fhaighear coire don dàn seo.   10

An là a' glasadh 's mi 'gabhail beachd air.
Air èirigh moch dhomh om leabaidh
chì mi na neòil a' dol seachad,
is gaoth a' Mhàirt gan cur air teicheadh.
Mi 'smaointeachadh 's mo bhas fom lethcheann –   15
feasgar bidh Ealasaid gam fheitheamh.
'S ann mall a bhios an là 'dol seachad.

A chionn a maithe is a maise
tha Foghar mo bhliadhna 'na Earrach.

Tha gaoir gach gaoithe 'na binn bhàrdachd.   20
'S ann 'na Nèamh tha 'n saoghal cràiteach;
's ann 'na chamhanaich gach sgàile.

217 *Simple Lines*

Elizabeth my dear and my white love, | this poetry, though stammering, is true – |
no fault will be found with this song, | since the praise of every lovely thing is
lovely. | Had I the power to joint words together to my satisfaction, | I would   5
make verses which would be a mirror | to your beauty and to your nobility of
nature; | but accept these simple verses from my hand.

The praise of every lovely thing is lovely. | No fault will be found with this song.   10

The day dawns as I watch it. | I have risen early from my bed, | and I see the
clouds going by | with the wind of March putting them to flight. | I am thinking
with my palm to my cheek – | in the evening Elizabeth will be waiting for me. | 15
Slow is the day as it goes by.

Because of her goodness and beauty | the Autumn of my year is a Spring.

The screaming of every wind is sweet poetry. | The painful world is a heaven; | 20
and every shadow is a twilight preceding dawn.

Gheall mi briathran duit is bàrdachd.
Chan fhaighear coire don dàn seo.
Is àlainn moladh gach nì àlainn.   25

218 *Rannghail Leth-èibhinn do dh'Ealasaid*
(car air dòigh "Och, a Naoghais, bi treun" aig Rob Donn)

Ealasaid a' bruidhinn:
Och, a Dheòrsa, bi treun,
is cùm do ghealladh dhomh fhèin.
Gheall thu dhomh bàrdachd is rannan –
biodh t'fhacail is t'aicill 'nan leum.   4

An co-ghealladh:
Cuime nach gabhainnsa misneach,
  's na h-uiread nas miosa na mì.
Air sealltainn dhomh romham 's nam dheaghaidh,
  tha 'm faghart air fanachd nam chrì.   8
Cha bu chneasta leam luaths nan làithean,
  's an dol uainn th'aig gach ràith 's aig gach mìos;
ach dheònaich am Freastal dhomh sòlas,
  caomh leannan 's an òige a-rìst.   12

[Is bruthach

I promised you words and poetry. | No fault will be found with this song. | The praise of every lovely thing is lovely.   25

218 *A Half-humorous Jingle to Elizabeth*
(rather in the manner of Rob Donn's "Och, a Naoghais, bi treun")

Elizabeth speaking:
Och, George, be mighty, | and keep your promise to me. | You promised me poetry and verses – | set your words and internal rhymes leaping.   4

[Promise kept:]
Why would I not take courage, | seeing there are lots who are worse off than I am? | Upon looking before me and behind me, | I find the metal-temper has still remained in my heart. | I used to think the swiftness of the days was indecent, | 8
and the way every quarter and month departs from us; | but Providence has granted me cheer, | a kind sweetheart and youth once more.   12

Is bruthach cas e 's is bòidheach,
　　bhith beò san t-saoghal a-bhos.
Tha cuid a gheibh sunnd is sògh ann,
　　tha cuid a gheibh leòn is lot;　　　　　　　16
ach tha slios againn uile ri 'dhìreadh,
　　's cha chinnteach am fonn fon chois.
Sa chreachann choinnich mi Ealasaid,
　　's is ealamh mo bhuidheachas dhomh.　　20

'S e tha bhuam an irioslachd nàdair;
　　tha gàirdeachas bhuam agus aoibh;
tha eòlas bhuam agus spionnadh,
　　's a bhith cuideachail gun a bhith faoin.　24
'S e tha bhuam càch bhith air banais,
　　is sinne nar caiginn làn gaoil;
pòsadh is pògadh is Pàrras,
　　's mo ghràdh bhith a-ghnàth rim thaobh.　28

Is aotrom, aobhach, fileanta
　　thig filidheachd asam san uair-s'.
Bha mi nam thost rè nam bliadhna,
　　ach is sgiamhach an cuspair seo fhuair.　32
Gheall mi rainn do dh'Ealasaid,
　　ealain is aicill is uaim,
is bidh iad sona, geal-ghàireach
　　mar thoilleadh bean àillidh shuairc.　　36

It's a stey brae and bonnie | to be alive [here] in [this] world. | There are some who find merriment and luxury there, | there are some who find wounds and hurts; | but we all have a slope to climb, | and the going is uncertain underfoot. | 16 On the bare upland reaches I met Elizabeth, | and thankfulness comes readily to me. 20

What I desire is humbleness of nature; | I desire rejoicing and cheer; | I desire knowledge and vigour, | and to be sociable without being silly. | What I desire is 24 that everyone should be at a wedding, | with us as the couple full of love; | marrying and kissing and Paradise, | and my dear to be always by my side. 28

Lightheartedly, joyously and fluently | pours poetry from me at this time. | I was silent for years | but comely is this subject for song that I have now got. | 32 I promised verses to Elizabeth, | art and internal rhyme and alliteration; | and they will be happy and bright with laughter, | just as a beautiful, amiable woman would deserve. 36

Os cionn dùrd na tràchda
    cluinnear nar là 's nar linn
fead nam peilear 's nan slige
    air slighe Hò-Chi-Mình.   40
Cha b'fheàrr bha na fir rè na h-eachdraidh
    len coisichean 's eachraidh is strì –
Napòleon, Attila, Xerxes,
    Eideard a h-Aon is a Trì.   44

Is iongantach leamsa na mnathan
    lem maise 's lem maithe gun chrìoch,
bheir horò air na fearaibh, 's bheir onair
    don cosnadh, don cogadh 's don sìth;   48
don gairge, don gairbhe, don cabhaig,
    don saoghal làn aisith is strì.
Bheirinn riaghladh an domhain do thè dhiubh,
    's bhiodh èibhneas air muir is air tìr.   52

Is fuigheall bheum is chorc sinn,
    na tha beò air an domhan gu lèir.
'S e ar gliocas bhith 'g imeachd gu cruiteach,
    gun fhios ach an tuit oirnn an speur.   56
Mar as gnàthach, 's iad a' chlann nighean
    bheir nigheadh is plasta dar creuchd –
a' mhaighdeann 's a' mhàthair aosta
    's an cinne daonna dan rèir.   60

[Mholainnsa

Above the drone of the traffic | there can be heard in our day and time | the whistle of the bullets and the shells | on the Ho-Chi-Minh Trail. | And men 40 were no better during history, | with their foot-soldiers and cavalry and strife – | Napoleon, Attila, Xerxes, | Edward the First and the Third. 44

A cause for wonderment to me are women, | with their beauty and their unlimited goodness, | for the way in which they give a snap for men and honour | men's wage-earning and war and peace; | men's ferocity and roughness and haste, | and their 48 world full of unpeace and strife. | I would give the governing of the world to any one of the ladies, | and there would be joy on sea and on land. 52

All that are alive on earth | are but the remnants left over by sword strokes and knife thrusts. | The wisest course for us is to go about hunched up | for fear that the sky may fall on us. | As usual, it is the lassies | who will wash and bandage our 56 wound – | the maiden and the aged mother | with the human race obedient to them. 60

Mholainnsa maoithe nam mnathan.
Dhèanainnsa faram is fuaim.
Bheirinn ar riaghladh do rìbhinn,
is sgrìobhainn *Lysistrata* nuadh.   64
Molaidh mi maoithe Ealasaid.
Dòirtidh mi ceilear 'na cluais.
Is i ùrachadh 's fàilte m'ealain,
mo leannan is m'eala gheal chuain.   68

Dh'èirich làn a bòidhchid 's a beusan
a-steach air mo cheutaibh 'na chuan.
Gura h-e is deireadh dom làithean
gean is gàire 's uaill.   72
Bidh ise a' peantadh a dealbhan,
's bidh mise ri rannghail bhuan.
Choinnich mi Ealasaid àillidh,
is choisinn mo mhàrsal buaidh.   76

I would praise the tenderness of women. | I would make a stir and uproar. | I would give the governing of us to a girl, | and I would write a new *Lysistrata*. | 64 I will praise the tenderness of Elizabeth. | I will pour melody into her ear. | She is the renewal of my art and the welcome given it, | my sweetheart and my white ocean swan. 68

The full tide of her beauty and her virtues has risen | up over my senses like an ocean. | The end of my days | is in good humour and laughter and joyful pride. | She 72 will be painting her pictures, | and I will be engaged in eternal versification. | I have met lovely Elizabeth, | and my marching has won victory. 76

*219 *Bratach am Bràigh a' Bhaile*

(trì rainn is amhran)

B'e sin an rìomhadh a thaitneadh,
  's a laigheadh le loinn ort fhèin;
a bheireadh dhuit dùil ri saorsa,
  a bhail' aosta, 's tu òg ler spèis.   4

Seann bhratach shracte,
  a dh'fhairich ceud call is buaidh,
ga nochdadh air do mhullach
  aig bun do speur ghlain, fhuair.   8

A' chrois a bh'aig ar sinnsre
  shuas air mìn chrann caol;
an geal is an gorm,
  is toirm dhiubh anns a' ghaoith.   12

Ceangal

Am baile seo bha iomairteach, is cridhe nàisein ann –
bu làidir a bhuillean uaibhreach, uair, mun d'fhàs iad mall.
An-diugh, an-diugh ma dh'èistear le cluais eudmhoir, thèid mi 'n geall
as ùr, as ùr gum mothaichear do phlosgartaich bhig, fhann.   16

219 *A Banner at the Toun Heid*
(three verses and envoi)

That is the finery which would please, | and which would suit you gracefully; | which would give you expectation of freedom, | oh aged town which is young to the eyes of our affection.   4

An old, torn banner, | which has experienced a hundred losses and victories, | displayed on your crest | at the foot of your pure, cold sky.   8

The cross which was our ancestors', | aloft on a slender, smooth staff; | the white and the blue | roaring in the wind.   12

Envoi

This town which was a stirring place with the heart of a nation in it – | powerful were its haughty heartbeats once on a time, before they became slow. | Today, today if you listen with a zealous ear, I will wager | that afresh, afresh you will notice a small, faint pulsation.   16

220 *An Co-cheòl Iomlan*

Is tlàth air iarmailt
  grian ar latha;
fàs is snodhach,
  fochann 's faillean.   4

Tha dàin is deachdadh
  feadh an adhair –
òran a' mhulaid,
  guidheam, gabh e.   8

Cùm an co-cheòl
  còir sin againn;
bòidhchead a' chumha
  le guth an aiteis.   12

*221 *Orion Over Bute*

I watch Orion over Bute
stamping with his starry foot.
The tiller creaks in the rudder-head.
The lights of the fleet switch green and red.
What land is that which, east away,   5
lies happed in sleep and waits for day?
That land has slept both night and day
two hundred years and more, they say.
It has been a fitful sleep,
nightmare-ridden, never deep.   10
They can tell, who know and care,
the dawn when it will wake is near.

220   *The Complete Harmony*

Pleasant in the sky | is the sun of our day; | growth and sap, | grass shoot and sapling.   4
Poems and creativity | are through the air – | the song of sadness, | I pray you, sing it.   8
Keep that right | harmony with us; | the beauty of the lament | along with the voice of joy.   12

Still Orion over Bute
stamps with his starry, glinting foot.
The autumn Yellow Badgers' Moon   15
glistens on the roofs of Troon;
and round the midnight Ploughshaft creeps
marking the hour, while Scotland sleeps.
Eastern stars will yet grow pale
before the day, when – who can tell? –   20
Scotland will wake with the waking dawn,
and step out from two centuries gone.

That night was forty autumns back.
Near twenty autumns past there broke
the dawn, unmarked, when Scotland woke.   25

What land is that which, east away,
steps ever surer through the day?

*222 Lives o Men (Caller Herrin)

The kyle is haice the nicht.
    The skiffs an' aa the men
wander but lee or licht
    till moarnin comes again.   4

The big seas smoor the bows.
    The kairrie smoors the sterns.
An' they can but jalouse
    whaur the leeshore derns.   8

Herbar's a faur cry.
    This side o't mishanters lurk;
an' mirk is mirker aye
    fornent thaim i the mirk.   12

Nae day was yet sae bricht
    as the morn's i'ts eastern place.
The shoals soom safe the nicht.
    The nicht the kyle is haice.   16

*223 *Tha 'Mhisneach is an Dòchas*
's a' Chòir 'nan Laoich

Courage and Hope and the Right Are Warriors

Hope's a warrior that wins.
He's victor afore the fecht begins.
There flee afore him in his wars
aa the doots an' the despairs.   4

He that hopes has aye cheer.
He that hopes kens nae fear.
Hope is leal an' hope is true.
He that hopes will aye dow.   8

He gangs through aa the warld aboot
bringan the flooer frae the broukit root.
At lee lang last he's come this airt,
sensan afar oor waukan hert.   12

Aye, he has come this gate tae see us,
sensan the virr that's native tae us.
Wha ettles ocht maun tryst wi' him.
We've won oor battle noo he's come.   16

Hope in his forays has come oor gate,
an' we will on, an' no be blate.
"What hae ye frae him?" Div ye speir? –
till the lift louts we bide here.   20

*224 *Howes an' Knowes*

There was never a heich but there was a howe (Scots proverb)

Is't wile me doon frae the heichs abune,
    an' lure me frae ma knowe
tae loanins wi a bield aboot,
    an' hap me in a howe?   4

"The knowes are yeld. The howes hae bield,
    an' sweet the watters rinn
thro gerss an' flooers. An' lown the ooers
    gang dreaman i the sun."   8

"The knowes are yeld. The howes hae bield,
   an' lown ilk field liggs there;
an' aye a calm an' caller waft
   gangs breathan thro the air."   12

The loanins roose the airy knowes;
   the mailins roose the muirs.
Glaur an' stane the blossom hain.
   The yird springs up i flooers.   16

This yird's a hoose for aa oor race.
   A knowe is ilka waa;
an' antrin thochts lik lichtnan flauchts
   licht the thochts o aa.   20

*225 *Alba Cona h-Ingantaib*

Alba le a h-Ioghnaidhean (Dàn Deirdre)

Is sgeulach am maraiche mara
a thill air 'eòlas on aineol,
a shiubhail cuantan gu caladh.

'S ann bruidhneach a thogas e còrsa.
Cluaidh no Lìte sear an t-seòlaid,   5
bidh ioghnaidhean san aithris sgeòil aig'.

Ge-tà, bheir Alba bàrr air 'aithris,
's i a' dùsgadh às a cadal;
's gur dùthaich ùr i gach aon latha,
's i 'nochdadh nìthean a bha 'm falach   10
air feadh na h-eachdraidh, sìth is aisith.
'S i bheir don mharaiche gach annas.

225 *Alba Cona h-Ingantaib*
Scotland With Its Wonders (The Song of Deirdre)

Full of stories is the sailor of the sea, | when he comes back to kent places from places unknown; | when he has travelled oceans and reached harbour.

Full of talk he makes his landfall. | Whether the roadstead be Clyde or Leith in the east, | there will be wonders in his telling of tales.   5

And yet, Scotland will surpass his stories | as she wakens from her sleep. | For, with every day, she is a new country, | as she reveals things which were hidden | 10 throughout history, peace and unpeace. | It is she who will give the sailor all the wonders.

*226 An t-Albannach air Dùsgadh

Ar leam gur cosgarrach an curaidh,
ar leam gur calma an duine,
's gur lionmhor, dìleas a bhuidheann,
an t-Albannach 'na dhùisg a chluinneas
guth a thìre is a bruidhinn.   5

Is binn, binn-ghobach a choille dhosrach.
Is eunach, ceòlmhor uair a mhosglaidh.
Is grianach a mhadainn 's a mhochthrath.

*227 Teirigidh Nàimhdeas: Mairidh Càirdeas

Thig càirdeas an dèidh deasbaid.
Thig aiteamh an dèidh na deighe.
Is math na nàbaidhean mu dheireadh.
Is math na coimhearsnaich mu dheireadh.
Sinn is Sasann – seo na ceilear –   5
sa cheann thall is dà sheis sinn.

An dèidh ar deasbaid thig ar càirdeas.
An dèidh na truaighe is an nàimhdeis
chithear fhathast làmh air làimh sinn.

226 The Scotsman on Waking

Combative is the warrior, I think; | staunch is the man, I think, | and numerous and faithful are his accompanying throng, | the Scotsman awake who hears | the voice of his land and its speech.   5

Melodious, melodious-beaked is his tufted wood. | Full of birds, full of music is the hour of his stirring. | Sunny are his morning and early morn.

227 Enmity Will Pass: Friendship Will Endure

Friendship will come after dispute. | Thaw will come after the ice. | Good are the neighbours in the end. | The neighbours are good at the last. | We and England – let there be no concealing it – | at the very end we are two equals.   5

After our dispute will come our friendship. | After the misery and the enmity | we will yet be seen hand in hand.

*228 *Garvalt Side*

(an auld-farrant sang)

As I cam doon by Garvalt side
upon an early mornin' tide,
the levrocks i the lift sae wide
   were singan oh sae cheery, oh.   4
I luikit syne on ilka haund
an' saw the leaman o the land,
an' syne there cam intae ma mind
   the brichtness o ma dearie, oh.   8

I saw her there that mornin' tide
as gin she stuid there by ma side,
an' aye I thocht as on I gaed
   "The dawn she is o day tae me".   12
She is the levrocks' mornin' tide;
she is the dawn by Garvalt side;
she is the lift sae blithe an' braid
   wi'ts airts tae guide me tae her, oh.   16

For, sterns o nicht an' licht o day,
I see her brichtness whaur I gae
sin' I cam doon thon Garvalt way,
   an' that I tell ye shairly, oh.   20
The levrocks aye sing in the morn,
the muirlands gowd an' purple burn,
I hear't an' see't whaure'er I turn,
   for then I kent her fairly, oh.   24

POEMS 1975–1977

*229 Òran Maraiche

Là an fhèatha 's là nan ceòs
cuimhnichidh mi blas do phòg
's mi a' seòladh air cuan mòr –
    soraidh ò, 'eudail.   4

Rubha na Cloiche – beannachd leò –
na Cinn Gharbha, Eilean Bhòid;
luathaich luaths an einsein mhòir –
    soraidh ò, 'eudail.   8

Dh'fhàg sinn Plada fodhainn fòs;
thùirling ceathach agus ceò;
ris a' Chuan Siar thog i 'sròn –
    soraidh ò, 'eudail.   12

Chì sinn bruthach Chluaidh fa dheòidh,
's Rubha na Cloiche gaolach, còir,
'falbh 's a' teachd air a' chuan mhòr –
    soraidh ò, 'eudail.   16

229   [*Sailor's Song*]

On day of calm and day of swell | the taste of your kiss I'll recall, | as I go sailing the open sea – | cheerio, my darling.   4

Cloch Point – to them adieu – | The Rough Heads (Garroch Heids), the Isle of Bute; | the great engine has gathered speed – | cheerio, my darling.   8

Pladda now we've left behind; | mist and fog have drifted down; | to Atlantic seas she's raised her prow – | cheerio, my darling.   12

We'll see at last the banks of Clyde, | and Cloch Point, lovely and kind, | coming and going on the open sea – | cheerio, my darling.   16

*230 An Iomagain

Soraidh leis an iomagain,
's mi fad' air bhith nam chiomach aic';
ar leam fhèin gur iongantach
 an tinneas tha na h-aoraibh.   4
A-nis on fhuair mi cuidhte 's i,
is eutrom, èibhinn, subhach mi.
On dh'fhalbh i nis air siubhal uam
 is duine mi measg dhaoine.   8

Soraidh leis an iomagain..
Chan fhaic mi fhèin a-rithist i.
Ged chìthear i air iomadh fear,
 cha mhì a bhìos fo 'caonnaig.   12
Gum bi mi chaoidh geal-ghàireach ann
le aighear is le àbhachdas;
gum bi mi 'seinn gu m'àilgheas-sa
 gun sgàile 'teachd air m'aodann.   16

Thug mi oidhchean fada leath',
is mi nam mharbhan caithriseach
a' tionndadh tric, is m'achaine
 gum faighinn saorsa uaipe.   20
Soraidh leis an iomagain;
mo ghuidhe ann gun tilleadh dhi.
Soraidh leis an iomagain;
 cha bhì mi nis ach uallach.   24

230 Anxiety

Farewell to anxiety, | for long I've been her prisoner; | how very strange, it seems to me, | the disease in her constitution. | Now since I am rid of her, | I am merry,   4
light and jocular. | Since she has left me and gone her way | I am a person among people.   8

Farewell to anxiety, | I never again will see her. | Though she'll appear on many a man, | I won't be caught in her strife. | I'll for evermore be bright with laughter, | 12
full of joy and merriment, | and I'll sing to my heart's content | and not a shadow will cross my face.   16

Long nights have I spent with her, | like a wakeful corpse, | tossing and turning, and praying | that I should find release from her. | Farewell to anxiety, | my wish   20
is that she not return. | Farewell to anxiety; | I'll always now be carefree.   24

*231 Sìon a' Chuain

Cluinn geurghuth
   mo ghuidh', a Dhia;
cop is cobhar,
   cobhair iad.

4

*232 Cù is a Choilear

Dhomh tha t'fhacal-sa drùidhteach,
   a rùin, 's mi gun fhois uaith,
on a ghabh mise ùidh ann
   mar chù is a choilear.

4

*233 Do Dhuine a Rinn Cillein

Tha tiùrr air do thràigh fhèin,
   gun chàil fon ghrèin ga do dhìth.
Thig an reothairt a-steach
   is bheir i leatha gach nì.

4

231 [Ocean Storm]
Hear my strident | plea, o God; | through foam and froth, | protect them.

4

232 [A Dog and Its Collar]
*Your word enthralls me, | love, and allows me no peace, | since I was first drawn
to it, | like a dog to its collar.*

4

233 [To One Who has Made a Pile]
*The seaware abounds on your shore, | and not a thing in the world do you lack. |
In will come the springtide, | and sweep it all back.*

4

314

*234 Ar Làraichean

An Sean Lagan 's Allt Beithe,
   tha iad a' feitheamh sheann làithean;
tha iad nas buaine 's nas sìorraidh
   na rìoghachdan stàtail.   4
Air m'fhìrinn 's air m'fhacal
   tillidh fhathast na Gàidheil;
gheibh an tobhta a chuideachd
   is bidh guthan san làraich.   8

Tha 'chuibhle a' dìreadh,
   ged bha sinn ìosal rè fada.
Tha dualchas is còir ann
   's is daoine beò sinn air thalamh.   12
Dùinidh làmh dheas a' cheartais
   le grèim a bhios daingeann.
Bheirear togail mhòr chinn dhuinn
   cho cinnteach rim labhairt.   16

'S ann tha làraichean loma
   sa bheil an tost 'na fhear taighe
fo gach meall, air gach monadh,
   air gach cnoc 's anns gach glacaig.   20
Tha an raineach 's a' chopag
   's iad dosrach 's gach achadh.
Bidh cur agus buain annt'
   aig buanaichean pailte.   24

[Masa mì

---

234 [Our Ruined Townships]

*Seanlagan and Allt Beithe, | they are awaiting old days; | they are more lasting
and more eternal | than stately realms. | On my word and honour, | the Gaels will*   4
*yet return; | each ruin will find its household, | and voices will ring out in the
derelict township.*   8

*The wheel is coming round again, | though we lay low a long while. | Heredity and
right exist, | and we are living persons in the world. | The right hand of Justice will*   12
*close | with a tight grip. | We will have cause to hold our heads high again, | as
certainly as I speak.*   16

*There are ruined sites lying bare | whose man-of-the-house is silence, | by every
hill, on every moor, | on every knowe and in every little hollow. | Bracken and*   20
*docken grow | unchecked in every field. | There will be sowing and harvesting in
them | for numerous reapers.*   24

Masa mì Mac Iain Dheòrsa
' s e an dòchas mo churaidh;
anns gach cunnart is cruaidhchas
  is e mo luaidh thar nan uile.   28
Teichidh an t-eagal
  is an teagamh roimh 'bhuillean;
cuir e gu 'dhùlan,
  nì e cùisean a bhuinnig.   32

Dìridh deatach nan dachaigh
  eadar Cataibh is Àbhann;
o Shrath Spè gu Ceann Bharraigh
  bidh taighean is àiteach.   36
Ged tha làraichean loma
  air gach monadh an-dràsta,
thèid gach duine gu 'ionad
  agus tillidh na Gàidheil.   40

*235 Òran Suirghich

Bi falbh is druid a' chachaileath.
Cluinn, a ghaoil, mo chagar uam.
Nach seall thu frionas m'athar-sa,   3
' s e 'carachadh 's a' casachdaich,
is cùl a chinn ga thachas aig'
  's e 'g amharc air an uair.   6

As sure as I am the son of John son of George, | hope is my champion; | in every danger and crisis, | he is my beloved over all others. | All fear and doubt | will flee 28 *before his strokes; | challenge him to action, | and he'll emerge victorious.* 32

The smoke of the homes will drift up | between Sutherland and Sanda. | From Strathspey to Barra Head | there will be houses and cultivation. | Though there 36 *are empty ruins | on every moor at present, | each person will go to his rightful abode | and the Gaels will return.* 40

235 [Lover's Song]
Be gone now and shut the gate. | Listen, darling, to my whisper. | See my father's agitation, | as he fidgets and coughs, | scratches his nape, | and looks at the time. 3, 6

Bi falbh is druid a' chachaileath.
Thoir do spàgan dhachaigh leat.
Thoir sealladh beag air ais thugam 9
's biodh cuimhn' agad air mhadainn orm.
A-màireach thig gun amharas
an rathad seo air chuairt. 12

*236 Rainn Ghràidh

Guidheam piseach ort is rath.
Teann a-nall 's na teann air ais.
Tha Dia math. Tha thusa math.
Tiugainn, thalla, 'eudail. 4

Na bi fada. Bi am faisg.
Bi rim thaobhsa. Fuirich 's fan.
Tha Dia math. Tha thusa math.
Tiugainn, thalla, 'eudail. 8

Nì mi 'n cridh' annam a bhrath.
Is tu 'n saoghal dhomh air fad.
Tha Dia math. Tha thusa math.
Tiugainn, thalla, 'eudail. 12

*Be gone now and shut the gate. | Be off home on your big feet. | Glance back at me
as you go, | and remember me in the morning. | Tomorrow, come innocently by |* 9
this way on your rounds. 12

236 [Love Verses]

*I wish you prosperity, I wish you luck. | Come over and don't hold back. | God is
good. You are good. | Come, let's go, my darling.* 4

*Don't be distant. Be close by. | Be by my side. Stay and bide. | God is good. You
are good. | Come, let's go, my darling.* 8

*The heart inside me I'll betray. | You are the entire world to me. | God is good.
You are good. | Come, let's go, my darling.* 12

*237 Rainn Ghràidh Eile

Tha gach oidhche 'dol am faide;
  tha gach latha a' dol cì.
Chan eil nas dorra na an cor seo.
   Och, a ghràidh ghil, coitich mì.
    Och, a ghràidh ghil, och, a ghràidh ghil,   5
    och, a ghràidh ghil, coitich mì.

Chan i tha buan grian an t-samhraidh;
  'S dian an geamhradh, fuachd is sìon.
Chan e tha sìorraidh an sonas.
   Och, a ghràidh ghil, coitich mì.   10

Cuir do làmh-sa fo m'uilinn;
  Thoir mo chumasg cràidh gu sìth.
Ceum air cheum bidh sinn a' coiseachd.
   Och, a ghràidh ghil, coitich mì.

*238 Na Faoileagan Maidne

Siud a dhùisg mi moch air mhadainn,
gàir fhaoileagan os cionn an taighe,
's iad air tighinn bhàrr na mara.

237 [More Love Verses]

Every night is dragging longer; | every day is going wrong. | No harder lot there is than this one. | Oh, my white love, urge me on. | Oh, my white love, oh, my white love, | oh, my white love, urge me on.   5

The summer sun won't shine forever; | bitter the winter, cold and storm. | Happiness is not eternal. | Oh, my white love, urge me on.   10

Put your hand under my elbow; | to my pain and turmoil bring some calm. | Step by step we'll walk on forward. | Oh, my white love, urge me on.

238 The Morning Gulls

It was that which woke me early in the morning, | the cry of seagulls above the house. | They had come from the sea.

A' goir: "Dhùn Èideann! Dhùn Èideann!
tha gile sear a' dìreadh speuraibh   5
air chionn èirigh na grèine;
tha dol air ais air na reultan;
tha driùchd air craobhan 's air feur ann,
tha driùchd air craoibh, air flùr, air feur ann.
Tha solais shràid 'fàs fann, is èistear   10
ceud fhuaim na trafaig 'dol nas dèine.
Tha daoin' a' dùsgadh roimhn èirigh.
An cuimhne leò an t-àm a thrèig sinn
's an robh rìghrean an Dùn Èideann,
's cùirtearan air am beulaibh;   15
teachdairean à tìrean cèine;
clàrsach is cruit air ghleus ann;
fìon ga òl is ceòl ga èisteachd?"

A' goir: "Dhùn Èideann! Dhùn Èideann!"

*239 *Beachd is Barail*

Cluinneam uaibh, 's chan ann os n-ìosal,
beachd is barail air an tìr seo
sam biodh reachd is rian aig rìghrean,
riaghladh is rèim aig rìghrean
is comhairlichean an gùin den t-sìoda.   5
Cluinneam uaibhse gu cinnteach.

["Chaill i

Crying: "Edinburgh! Edinburgh! | There is a whiteness in the east climbing the
sky | before the rising of the sun. | The stars are fading. | There is dew on trees   5
and grass; | there is dew on tree, on flower, on grass. | The street lights grow faint,
and there can be heard | the first noise of the traffic growing in intensity. | People   10
are waking and thinking of rising. | Do they remember the time that has forsaken
us, | when there were kings in Edinburgh | and courtiers in their presence; | 15
ambassadors from far-off lands; | great harp and little harp in tune there; |
drinking of wine and listening to music?"
Crying: "Edinburgh! Edinburgh!"

239 [*Thoughts and Opinions*]
Let us hear from you all, and in no furtive tones, | your thoughts and opinions on
this land, | where kings once held sway and order, | kings once had rule and
dominion, | with councillors in gowns of silk. | Let us hear from you all with   5
assurance.

"Chaill i 'n onair, chaill i 'n t-urram
nuair a thriall ar Rìgh do Lunnainn."

"Chaill i cothrom na cùirte,
leth a' chrùin is leth an dùthchais.
Cheangladh i 'na ciomach dùthcha." 10

"An-sin thàin an t-Aonadh dunach
a chuir baoghal ri cunnart,
bliadhna bhuail a' bhuille buileach."

"Thig feabhas air dìth 's air deireas. 15
Chan eil galar gun a leigheas.
Nithear suas gach call mu dheireadh."

*240 A' Chraobh

Tha craobh anns a' ghàradh
    air an leag mi mo làmh gu tric.
Nuair a bhìos mi 'na fochair
    thig uamsa an osna gun fhios, 4
on a bhean mo chiad ghràdh dhi
    gu meachair le 'làimh mhìn ghil,
on a mhol mo chiad ghràdh i
    là sona sa Mhàigh le cion. 8

"She lost all the honour and respect that was her due, | when our king departed to London."

"She lost the prestige of the court, | half the crown and half the patrimony. | She was held in bondage, a slave of a country." 10

"Then came the disastrous Union, | turning danger into crisis, | a year when the decisive blow was struck."

"Deficiency and hurt will give way to recovery. | There is no illness without a cure. | Every loss will be made good in the end." 15

240 [The Tree]
There is a tree in the garden | on which my hand comes often to rest. | Whenever I'm near it, | I cannot help but sigh, | ever since my first love touched it | delicately 4 with her soft white hand, | ever since my first love praised it | with fondness one happy day in May. 8

A meanglain a' luasgan,
   is an oiteag gan gluasad ann;
a duilleach buidh'-uaine
   le sporghail a' gluasad gu mall;   12
a h-eòin 's iad ri ceilear,
   ceòl agus seinn gun cheann;
a feòragan liatha
   ri spòrs an dlùths ciar sa chrann.   16

Tha i bruidhneach, nuair shèideas
   gaoth fhionnar a' Chèitein trìd;
tha sgàile san t-samhradh
   'na h-àrainn fo mheanglain bhinn;   20
tha i ceòlmhor, uain', eunach;
   's i bòidheach, àrd, freumhach brìgh;
bidh boch orm is èibhneas
   nuair thig snodhach 's gach gèig a-nìos.   24

Bidh mi deireasach, brònach,
   nuair a bheanas mo dhòid da rùsg.
Ma tha ealain is ceòl ann,
   sheinn mi le deòir a cliù.   28
Ma bhean mo chiad ghràdh dhi,
   leanaidh mo làmh rithe dlùth.
Ma mhol mo chiad ghràdh i,
   's i a moladh an dàn a b'fhiù.   32

Its branches swinging, | *as the breeze sets them in motion;* | *its yellow-green foliage* | *stirring softly and rustling;* | *its birds at chorus,* | *music and song without* 12
cease; | *its grey squirrels* | *playing in the dusky fastness of the trunk.* 16

It chatters away when | *the cool Maytime breeze blows through it;* | *in the Summer there is shade* | *around it beneath its sweet branches;* | *it is verdant, full of music* 20
and birds, | *lovely and tall, its roots full of sap;* | *I'll rejoice and be glad* | *when the juice comes up every limb.* 24

I feel sadness and hurt | *when my hand touches its bark.* | *If artistry and music exist,* | *I have sung its praise with tears.* | *If my first love touched it,* | *my hand will* 28
closely trace hers. | *If my first love praised it,* | *her praise was the worthiest poem.* 32

*241 *La Scozia Oggi*
(canzone)

L'uomo spera:
  sererò.
Canto finora:
  vanterò.   4

Sonno era
  e lo so.
Canto finora:
  vanterò.   8

Lontana è sera:
  nell' alba vo.
Canto finora:
  vanterò.   12

Terra dura,
  cara sto.
Canto finora:
  vanterò.   16

Terra cara,
  èra ho.
Canto finora:
  vanterò.   20

Questa è l'èra;
  festa fo.
Canto finora:
  vanterò.   24

Il canto spera.
  Cantalo.
Canto finora:
  vanterò.   28

241 *Scotland Today*
(song)

Mankind hopes: | I will hope. | I sing hitherto: | I shall vaunt.   4

It was a sleep | and that I know. | I sing hitherto: | I shall vaunt.   8

Far off is evening: | in the dawn I go. | I sing hitherto: | I shall vaunt.   12

A hard land [am I], | I am held dear. | I sing hitherto: | I shall vaunt.   16

A land held dear, | I have an era. | I sing hitherto: | I shall vaunt.   20

This is the era; | I make carnival. | I sing hitherto: | I shall vaunt.   24

The song has hope. | Sing it. | I sing hitherto: | I shall vaunt.   28

*242 *Aig an Fheurlochan*

Aig an Fheurlochan uaigneach
　　air mo chuairtean san fhraoch,
's mi nam sheasamh car treiseig
　　anns a' bhreithneachadh chaol,　　　　　　4
laigh an làmh air mo ghualainn
　　gu suairc is gu caomh.
Rinn mi tionndadh is amharc,
　　is chan fhaca mi 'h-aon.　　　　　　　　8

Bha na mill is an t-aonach
　　's iad aonranach ann.
Chan fhaca mi gluasad
　　mun cuairt dhomh no thall.　　　　　　12
Cha robh ach osag na gaoithe
　　anns an fhraoch gu mìn, mall.
Labhair caoin ghuth nam chluasan,
　　's cha leig mi 'm fuaim sin air chall.　　16

"'S mi a' bhàrdachd tha fuireach
　　air na tuim 's air na mill.
Is iad m'fhuireachan taighe
　　na cnuic chasa gam dhìon.　　　　　　20
Is tric a bhà mi a' fulang
　　fon uisge 's fon t-sìn;
is tric a thùr mi mo cheilear
　　's na coilltean beithe sin shìos.　　　　24

["Is tric

242 [*By the Grassy Lochan*]

*By the solitary Grassy Lochan, | on my wanderings in the heather, | as I stood
still for a while | lost in contemplation, | the hand lay on my shoulder, | kindly,* 　4
gently. | I turned to look, | and saw no-one. 　8

*The hills and the uplands | stretched there, desolate. | I saw no movement | around
me or beyond. | There was only the breath of the wind | in the heather, light and* 　12
leisurely. | A sweet voice spoke in my ear, | and its sound I will never forget. 　16

*"I am the poetry that dwells | on the mounds and the hills. | They are my dwelling
house, | the steep knolls that protect me. | Often have I endured | the rain and the* 　20
tempest; | often fashioned my birdsong | in those birchwoods below. 　24

"Is tric a ghabh mise fasgadh
anns na Lagain ud thall.
Choinnich mis' thu sa Ghleannan,
ged as fada on àm.   28
Chuir Bòd is an Innis
an lideadh nam cheann;
's gur i Cruach Dhoire Lèithe
dh'fhàg èibhinn mo rann.   32

"Treis air leacainnean Ghairbh-bheinn,
treis an garbh Choire Laoigh;
an Loch Abar nan stùcbheann
is an Dùthaich Mhic Aoidh;   36
am Both Chuideir, san Apainn
is an Raineach nan craobh;
ag iarraidh phuirt do na facail
air feadh Latharna chaoimh.   40

"Ann am Barraigh 's an Uibhist
's ann cluinnear mo dhàin;
am Muile nam mòrbheann
is an Leòdhas an àigh: 44
feadh nan eileanan uile
nì mi fuireach is tàmh –
ann an Diùra 's an Ìle,
san Eilean Sgìtheanach àrd.   48

"Bha uair 's bu leamsa am fearann
eadar Sealtainn is Tuaidh.
An Dùn Èideann nan rìghrean
bhithinn cinnteach à duais.   52

"Often have I taken shelter | in the Laggans out yonder. | I met you in the Glennan, | though that was long ago. | Bute and Inchmarnock have put | their syllables in my   28
head; | and Grey Grove Summit | has enlivened my verse.   32

"A while on the slopes of the Rough Ben, | a while in wild Calf Corrie; | in Lochaber of the high rocky pinnacles | and in Sutherland of the Mackays; | in Balquhidder,   36
in Appin | and in wooded Rannoch; | seeking tunes for the words | throughout fragrant Lorne.   40

"In Barra and Uist | my poems can be heard, | in Mull of the great mountains | and in Lewis the fair: | throughout all the isles | I settle and take rest – | in Jura and   44
Islay | and Skye of the high peaks.   48

"There was a time that mine was the land | between Shetland and Tweed. | In Edinburgh of the kings | my reward was assured. | 52

Bhiodh teudan gan riaghladh
  a chur rian dhomh air duain,
is gum freagradh gach balla
  do dh'aicill is uaim.   56

"An dèidh gach allabain 's ànraidh,
  an dèidh gach tàire bu mhò,
nì mi fanachd gu h-àraid
  aig na Gàidheil fa dheòidh,   60
's chan eil dhaibhsan ach èisteachd
  ri gaoth nan slèibhtean le deòin,
agus cluinnear na facail
  is casadh a' cheòil."   64

*243 Àit air Bith

Tha spiorad san àite
  nì gàire is gul;
nì e seinn 's nì e cagar
  le tatadh 'na ghuth.   4
Tha spiorad san àite,
  rud àrsaidh gun chruth.
Bidh mo thilleadh don àite
  a-màireach no 'n-diugh.   8

Harpstrings would be tuned | to accompany my songs, | and every wall would echo | with vowel-rhyme and alliteration. 56

"After all the wanderings and storms, | after the greatest humiliations, | I will find a special place to stay | among the Gaels, at long last; | they need only listen | with 60 goodwill to the wind in the hills, | and they will hear the words | and the twining music." 64

243 [Anywhere]

There is a spirit about the place | that laughs and cries; | it sings and it whispers | in a caressing voice. | There is a spirit in the place, | something ancient, immaterial. | 4 I will return to the place, | today or tomorrow. 8

*244 [Rann Ionndrainn]

A Dhia nan gràs, sin gàir tha tric na mo chluais,
tuinn Locha Fìne roimh shìn gan iomain gu luath,
nas fheàrr na ceòl pìoba no fìdhle no filidheachd dhuan.
Bidh an cadal gam dhìth leis cho binn 's tha sitir nan stuadh.   4

*245 Vignette

Chailleadh an còrsa 's is neònach coltas an speur.
Tha a' ghaoth 'dol am mòid 's tha na neòil a' slugadh nan reul.
Dùineadh gach aiste 's biodh astar san einsean gu feum
's fasgadh is acarsaid 's caladh is cidhe nar rèis.   4

*246 Lag an Aonaich
(òran san t-seann fhasan)

Ise:

A thasgaidh, a ghràidh 's a ghaolain,
laigh mi leat fon bharrach bhraonach.
Chunna mi san dùn an-raoir thu,
cha b'ann idir nad aonar.
Bha còmhradh tairis nam ban caomh riut,   5

---

244 [Verse of Longing]
Ah, God of grace, that's a roar which is oft in my ears, | the waves of Loch Fyne driven fast before the storm, | better than the music of pipes or fiddle or the composing of verse. | Sleep eludes me, so sweet is the braying of the billows.   4

245 [Vignette]
The coastline is lost and there is an eeriness in the sky. | The wind is swelling and the clouds are swallowing the stars. | Close every hatch and let the engine put speed to good use, | for shelter and anchorage and harbour and quay are all within reach.   4

246 [The Moorland Hollow]
(a song in the old mode)
Her:
My treasure, my dear, my beloved, | with you I lay beneath glistening treetops. | In the dùn last night I saw you, | and you weren't alone, far from it. | The gentle ladies held sweet converse with you, | 5

le pòg am beòil 's am bilean maotha,
is iad gu beuldearg, cùlbhàn, taobhgheal.
Gheibhte le furan gu saor siud.
An cuimhne leatsa lag an aonaich,
fon bheitheach shlatagach 's fo chraobhan   10
is sinn am fasgadh froise 's gaoithe
nar sìneadh san lagan aoigheil
le cion gun chluain, gun chlaoine?

Esan ga freagairt:
A thasgaidh, a ghràidh 's a ghaoil ghil,
laigh mi leat fon bharrach bhraonach.   15
Cha b'ann a' bhòn-raoir no an-raoir e,
ach gu minig, meachair, caoimhneil,
ach gu minig, milis, caoimhneil.
Chuirinn tharad cirb de m'aodach;
chuirinn tharad mo làmh le faoilte.   20
Bu ghoirid leam an oidhch' ag aomadh;
bu luath leam an là ga fhaotainn
'na uinneig an ear an t-saoghail.
Ma bha còmhradh nam ban caomh rium,
le pòg am beòil 's am bilean maotha,   25
cha b'ann orra bha mo smaointean,
is iad cruinn 'nan suidhe taobh rium
ri mànran 's ri gàire aotrom,
ach ort fhèin is tu nad aonar.
Ar ceum a-nochd gu lag an aonaich!   30

---

*kisses from their mouths and their soft lips, | and they red-mouthed, blonde-haired, white-sided. | Gladly and freely you'd get that from me. | Do you remember the moorland hollow, | under the trees and the thickets of birchwood, | as we sheltered   10
close from wind and storm, | lying in the small hospitable hollow, | our love untouched by guile or falsehood?*

He answers:
*My treasure, my dear, my white love, | with you I lay beneath glistening treetops. | 15
Not last night or the night before it, | but frequently, tenderly, fondly; | frequently, sweetly and fondly. | I'd cover you with a tail of my clothing, | I'd put my arm around you warmly. | Too short for me was the night in passing, | too quick I   20
thought the day in dawning, | like a window in the east of the world. | If the gentle ladies held converse with me, | with kisses from their mouths and their soft lips, | 25
not to them did my thoughts turn, | as they sat together round me | in amorous talk and light-hearted laughter, | but to you, and you so lonely. | Let's head tonight for the moorland hollow!*   30

327

*247 Callaidean Shasainn

Bha dealt air a' phoilean
  is bha clos air a' ghaoith,
là Iuchair sa mhochthrath
  an coille dhosrach nan craobh.   4

Ann an iomall na coille
  bha boladh feòir mhaoith.
Bha gach àilean fo norran
  is bha fois air na raoin.   8

Bha na seilleanan mocheirigh
  'solar 's gach taobh.
Bha an lon-dubh a' mosgladh
  's a ghob ri binn laoidh.   12

Bha callaidean Shasainn
  fad seallaidh fo chaoir
le dealt a' mhìn mhochthrath
  air oir nan ùr raon.   16

Bha an saoghal 's e tostach
  fo ortha aig draoidh,
là Iuchair sa mhochthrath
  is gach fochann fo bhraon.   20

247   [The Hedgerows of England]

There was dew on the pollen, | there was a hush on the wind, | early one summer morning | in the lush, dense forest.   4

On the fringe of the forest | hung the smell of fresh grass. | Every meadow was in slumber | and there was peace on the fields.   8

The early-rising bees | were busy all around. | The blackbird was waking, | its beak open in sweet song.   12

The hedgerows of England | were aglow in the distance | as the dew of the soft early morning | tipped the fresh green fields.   16

The world was deep in silence | under some magician's spell, | early one summer morning | and every blade of grass gleaming.   20

*248 Òige na h-Aoise

Thig an òige 's a faghart
    a thadhal na h-aoise.
Aig dol fodha na grèine
    bidh an speur air dhath aobhach.   4

*249 Le Montagnard

Le faîte du mont et sa mine,
la voix du vent sur la colline,
cela va où je vais.
Je regarde, j'écoute et [me] tais.   4

*250 This Warld

This leelang life's a knowe tae sclim.
    It tires the feet o mony.
This warld waivers whim for whim.
    It's a stey brae an' bonny.   4

248   Youth of Old Age

Youth will come with its sword temper | to visit age. | At the going down of the
sun | the sky is a joyous colour.   4

249   [The Highlander]

*The mountain ridge and its aspect, | the voice of the wind on the hill, | those go
where I go. | I look, I listen and stay silent.*   4

251–255: Stanze Irlandesi

*251 [*Quella Donna*]

È quella donna il mio danno, e ben lo so:
fiera e cara e dura. Con cura vo.
Come un morto a porta chiusa sto.
Non avrò pace se tace o dice di no.   4

252 [*Dammi la Mano*]

Dammi la mano stamani, sorriderò.
Baciami tanto, e vanto a tutti ciò.
Tu sei bella, e quello in cuore ho.
Colla speranza pranzo. Cantando vo.   4

*253 *Il* File *e la Morte*

Dante Alighieri trovare non si può.
Andò oltre come altri fecero.
Oggi canzoni – domani silenzio.
Ascolta la gente. Niente. Silente sarò.   4

251–255: *Irish Stanzas*
251 [*That Woman*]

That woman is my ruin, and well I know it: | proud and dear and hard. Full of care I go. | Like one dead I stand at a closed door. | I will not have peace if she is silent or says "no".   4

252 [*Give Me Your Hand*]

Give me your hand this morning and I will smile. | Do but kiss me and I boast of that to all. | You are beautiful and I have that at heart. | I dine along with hope. I go singing.   4

253 *The* File *and Death*

Dante Alighieri cannot be found. | He went beyond as did others. | Today songs – tomorrow silence. | The people listen. Nothing. I shall be silent.   4

254 [*Nel Cuore Cura*]

Nel cuore cura, paura e pensieri,
in strana terra erro per sentieri.
Tu sei cara; fiera e dura, sì –
dammi un bacio. Baciami. Dì "Buon dì". 4

255 *Il* File

So poetare. Tacere non si può.
Parole avevo; cantavo e canterò!
Tesso le rime; ogni tema dorerò.
La voce non tace. Vi piace, sì o no? 4

*

*256 *Aria*

Guardo il cielo
ove tramonta il sole
rosso come il sangue.
Passano i giorni. Mi duole. 4

[Si ride

254 [*In My Heart Care*]

In my heart care, fear and thoughts. | In a land grown strange I wander by pathways. | You are dear, though proud and hard, yes. | Give me a kiss. Kiss me. Say "Good day". 4

255 *The* File

I know how to poeticise. There is no being silent. | I had words; I used to sing and I will sing. | I plait my rhymes; I will gild every theme. | The voice is not silent. You like it, yes or no? 4

256 *Aria*

I look at the sky | where the sun sets | red as blood. | The days pass. It grieves me. 4

Si ride e si ama:
    sempre minaccia la morte.
Cade la foglia d'autunno.
    Oimè, che dura sorte!   8

Vieni a me, speranza.
    Segue l'alba la sera.
Passa l'inverno anche.
    Torna primavera.   12

*257   Skottland til Ola Nordmann

Reis, dikt, og tal til Ola
    i dalen hvor han bor
ved marka den grønn' og gule
    hvor gresset dør og gror.   4
Det tiner og det suser.
    Nordover vender vår
med lov om frukt og roser.
    Så skjer det år for år.   8

Solen står, og bringer
    fornyelse og liv.
Det renner og det synger
    hvor isen før var stiv;   12
og skogens [trær] alle
    får knopper mil for mil.
Reis, dikt, og tal til Ola,
    si vinter sier farvel.   16

One laughs and one loves. | Always death threatens. | The autumn leaf falls. | Ah me, what a hard destiny.   8

Come to me, hope. | Dawn follows the evening. | Also the winter passes. | Spring returns.   12

257   Scotland to Ola the Norwegian

Go, poem, and speak to Ola | in the dale where he dwells | beside the green and yellow field, | where the grass dies and grows. | It thaws and soughs. | Spring   4 returns northward | with a promise of fruit and roses. | So it happens year by year.   8

The sun stands on the sky and brings | renewal and life. | There is a flowing and a singing, | where before the ice was stiff; | and all the wood's trees | bear buds mile   12 by mile. | Go, poem, and speak to Ola. | Say Winter says farewell.   16

258 Våren

Vender vår.
Solen står.
Landet ler.
Ånder år.   4

Gresset gror
hvor bonden bor.
Toner trær.
Vender vår.   8

*259 Steinen på Fjellet

Her blir jeg til luften luter
    en stein på fjellet grå og gammel.
Omkring fjellets [vind] tuter.
    Jeg har set tårer og gaman.   4

Jeg så Håkon. Jeg så Harald.
    Omkring fjellets [vind] tuter.
Jeg så og ser og skal se.
    Her blir jeg til luften luter.   8

258 Spring
Spring [turns]. | The sun stands in the sky. | The land laughs. | The year breathes. 4
The grass grows | where the farmer dwells. | Trees intone. | Spring [turns]. 8

259 Stones on the Mountain
Here bide I till the lift louts, | a stone on the mountain, grey and old. | Round
about the mountain-wind howls. | I have seen tears and merriment. 4

I saw Hakon. I saw Harald. | Round about the mountain-wind howls. | I saw and
see and shall see. | Here bide I till the lift louts. 8

*260 Håpet

Tåken skifter. Håpet er skald.
Vår følger vinter og morgen kveld.
Snøen tiner. Håpet er helt.
De som håper duer til alt.   4

På alle jorden går han omkring,
og viker og sviker for ingenting.
Han setter redsel og tvil i flukt.
Han bøier seg unna for ingen makt.   8

Tåken skifter. Håpet er skald.
Håpet er helt og erobrer bold.
Her i Skotland hos oss han bor;
natten ender og dagen gryr.   12

Hvor han bor gryr det snart.
Han er en skald som synger klart.
Her i landet synger han søtt
og bringer vår blomst fra dens skjulte rot.   16

Håpet har sverd og håpet har sang.
Ingen vei for ham er lang.
Her erkjenner vi ingen tvil.
Håp er den skald vi lytter til.   20

260 Hope

The fog shifts. Hope is a skald. | Spring follows winter, and morning evening. | The snow thaws. Hope is a hero. | They who hope dow for aathing.   4

On all the earth he goes about, | and turns aside and betrays for no thing. | He sets fear and doubt in flight. | He gives way for no power.   8

The fog shifts. Hope is a skald. | Hope is a hero and courageous conqueror. | Here in Scotland with us he dwells; | the night ends and day dawns.   12

Where he dwells it dawns soon. | He is a skald who sings clearly. | Here in this land he sings sweetly | and brings our flower from its hidden root.   16

Hope has a sword and hope has a song. | No way for him is long. | Here we recognise no doubt. | Hope is the skald we listen to.   20

*261 Slutt
(Gaelisk strophe)

Intet du sier. Du tier og ser fra meg.
Munnen som talte og smilte er taus på deg.
Kyss og ord og år alle går sin vei.
Fremtida truer og duer jeg til den ei.   4

*262 Enhver Seiler

Som en som fjerne farer velger
dro han ut på sinte bølger,
la han ut på bitre bølger.
Natt – og skyer stjernene svelgjer;
vinden skifter; stormen følger.   5
Mørket horisonten dølger.

Hver har sitt Vinland over havet.
Bare å seile stiller kravet.
Havn må forlates her i livet.
Hvert øye smerter med bølgenes [støv],   10
og land og ly er ikke lovet.

Skjebnens vær er aldri stille.
Menneskets [seil] er altid fulle.
Vindens røst blir rop for alle.

261 Finished
(Gaelic strophe)

You say nothing. You are silent and look away from me. | Your mouth which spoke and smiled is silent. | Kisses and words and years all go their way. | The future threatens and I am not able for it.   4

262 Everyone Sets Sail

As one who chooses far-off dangers | he set out on angry billows, | he set sail on bitter billows. | Night – and clouds swallow the stars; | the wind shifts, the storm follows. | Darkness hides the horizon.   5

Everyone has his Vineland over the sea. | Only to sail stills the yearning. | Harbour must be left here in life. | Every eye smarts from the billows' dust, | and land and lee are not promised.   10

Destiny's weather is never calm. | Mankind's sails are always full. | The wind's voice becomes a shout for everyone.

*263 An Oidhche Bhuan

Fosgail uinneag an là.
Tha 'n oidhche buan 's an là gam dhìth.
Tha na speuran sgreunach, dubh
is tha gul an guth nan sìon.   4

Chan eil gealach ann no reul;
gaoth is neul is duibhre thiugh;
uisge 's gaoth 'na gaoir on iar,
's i teachd gu dian le caoidh nach sguir.   8

Chan fhaighear cadal no clos.
Tha 'n oidhche fada nochd gun tàmh.
Deònaich grian is madainn dhuinn –
fosgail uinneag an là.   12

*264 "Is Crìon a' Chùil Às Nach Goirear" (seanfhacal)

A' tionndadh san fhànas air 'aisil,
an saoghal iomadhathach sean,
cadal, mosgladh, solas, ciaradh,
oidhche siar is grian sear.   4

263 [The Endless Night]

Open the window of the day. | The night is endless and I long for the day. | The skies are scowry and black | and there's sobbing in the voice of the elements.   4

There is neither moon nor star; | but wind and cloud and impenetrable darkness; | rain and the wind howling from the west, | approaching fiercely with incessant wailing.   8

Sleep or rest is impossible to find. | This night tonight is long and troubled. | Grant us sun and morning, | open the window of the day.   12

264 It's a Tiny Corner from Which There's Not a Cheep (Gaelic proverb)

Turning in space on its axle, | the old multicoloured world; | sleep, stirring, night, dusk; | night to the west and sun to the east.   4

Cainntean 's cinnidhean thar thomhais,
   machair 's monadh, sgùrr is raon,
bailtean bruidhneach, fàsach tostach
   fàire 's fàire 'n domhain aost'.   8

Nuair a thig an là o Lochlann,
   dùisgear moch le bàrdachd nuadh,
a' cur fàilte 's furain roimhe
   or n-àit an-seo sa chruinne bhuan.   12

An Alba chunnaic Aodh MacDhiarmaid
   's i 'ciallachadh rudeigin shìor
le 'seagh fhein am measg nan uile,
   gun fhàire uimpe, sin ar tìr.   16

*265 *Dùdlachd is Earrach Ar Bliadhna*

Is fada, 's fada, 's fad' an oidhche
's i cho dubh ri gual na goibhne.
Is goirid an là geamhraidh doilleir;
is fuar, dian a' ghaoth is goir aic'.
Samhainn 's Nollaig 's reodhadh boillsgeil –   5
is geal na slèibhtean, 's lom a' choille.

Is fada, farsaing an t-sìnteag
gus na h-uain is gu Fèill Brìde.

                                  [Is ann tha

Languages and races beyond measure, | plain and moorland, scaur and meadow, | voluble cities, silent wildernesses, | horizon and horizon of the aged world.   8

When day comes from Norway, | then will be an early wakening with new poetry, | giving it greeting and a welcome | from our place here in the everlasting universe.   12

The Scotland that Hugh MacDiarmid saw, | which signifies something eternal, | with its own meaning in the midst of all, | enclosed by no horizon, that's our country!   16

    265 *[The Darkest-winter and the Spring of Our Year]*
Long, long, long is the night, | and black as the coal of the smithy. | Short is the dark winter-day; | cold and violent the screaming wind. | Hallowtide, Christmas and sparkling frost – | white are the hills, bare is the forest.   5
Long and wide is the leap | to the lambs and St Bridget's Day.

Is ann tha dùdlachd dhubh na bliadhna
a' dùnadh nan àrdan ciara   10
's gaoth an ear le faobhar sgian oirr'
troimh Dhùn Eideann a' sianail,
is fliuch shneachd sgaiteach 'na sgiathaibh.

Thig an t-earrach. Thig an Cèitein.
Uainichidh gile nan slèibhtean.   15
Tha 'n dòchas daonnan 'na èibhleig
ri anuair 's fuachd, 's tha cinnt à Cèitein.
Chì Alba a grian 'na speuraibh.

*266 An t-Ùghdarras agus an t-Eòlas

Càit am facas, càit an cualas
ann an Sasainn bhraonach uaine
no an Lunnainn an uabhair
a h-aon a nì ar ceistean fhuasgladh?

Is faoineas bhuapa gaoth an òraid;   5
is sgleò dhaibh an cainnt 's an còmhradh;
is iad mar mharaichean air còrsa
nach fhac' iad riamh roimhe a' seòladh,
air allaban 's gun iad eòlach.
Stiùirear tìrean len luchd còmhnaidh,   10
's biodh ùghdarras aig an eòlas.

The black wintry depths of the year | are closing off the dusky airts, | as the shrieking   10
east wind | cuts through Edinburgh like a knife, | with stinging sleet in its wings.

Spring will come. Maytime will come. | The whiteness of the hills will turn to
green. | Hope is always a warm ember | against storm and cold, and Maytime is a   15
certainty. | Scotland will see her sun in its skies.

266 [Authority and Knowledge]

Where was ever seen, where was ever heard, | in green, dewy England | or in
London the haughty, | even one who'll succeed in resolving our problems?

All their speechifying wind is vacuous nonsense; | their language and talk is a   5
smokescreen for them; | they are like sailors nearing a coast | they have not seen
before, | adrift in unkent waters. | Let countries be led by their inhabitants, | and   10
let authority be held by knowledge.

*267 [Suas gun Sìos]

Suas gun sìos, buaidh gun bhualadh
  buannachd gun chall, gun dìth;
nì ùr a th'ann san t-seann shaoghal
  buidhinn saorsa le sìth.   4

*268 Uladh

O Shiorramachd Àir gu Àrd Macha ghluais sinn fhèin,
siar nar tàintean bochd cràite gun tug sinn ceum;
is dian a tha làmhach is ràn nam bomba nar dèidh –
a Dhia nan gràs, "is láidir an snaoisín é"!   4

*269 Beannachadh

Rìgh nan reul 's na grèine gile
bhith gad dhìon o dhìth 's o thinneas,
bhith gad dhìon o shìn 's o iomairt,
's tu bhith sìorraidh 'n sìth nad ionad.   4

267 [Up with no Down]

Up with no down, victory with no blows struck, | gaining with no loss or depri-
vation; | it is a new thing in the old world, | winning freedom by peace.   4

268 Ulster

From the shire of Ayr to Armagh we went, | westward in poor worn droves we took
our step; | vehement is the firing and the roar of bombs after us – | O God of grace,
"it is powerful snuff"!   4

269 A Blessing

The King of the stars and the white sun, | may He shield you from want and from
sickness, | may He shield you from tempest and from turmoil, | and may you be   4
eternally in peace in your place.

*270 *Fosgail Uinneag an Là*
Open the Winnock o the Day

Open the winnock o the day.
   The nicht's e'erlastin. Day come kind.
The lift is scowry, black an' wae
   an' greetin's i the voice o the wind.   4

There's nae mune nor stern i sicht;
   wind an' kairrie, mirk on heich;
rain an' wast-wind thro the nicht
   ragean wi an unendin scraich.   8

There's nae sleep nor rest ava.
   Nae ease this leelang nicht I hae.
Grant us sun. Gar mornin daw.
   Open the winnock o the day.   12

*271 "It's a Wee Neuk frae Whilk There's Nae E'en a Cheep" (Gaelic proverb)

Birlan i space wi colours bricht,
   the auld warld roon its axle gaun;
sleep an' wauknan, gloamin, licht,
   nicht tae wastward, eastward dawn.   4

Mair leids an' fowks than ane can tell,
   lawland, muirland, roond they caa;
gabbin cities, desarts still;
   the auld warld's horizons aa.   8

Whan day comes frae Norway's airt,
   we's wauken wi't wi brent-new verse,
giean it welcome frae the hert
   frae oor place i th' eternal universe.   12

The Scotland Hugh MacDiarmid saw,
   signifyin an eternal stand,
wi meanin o'ts ain i the midst o aa,
   wi nae steekan horizons. That's oor land.   16

*272 *Ionndrainn na Sìne*

Cian am-bliadhna 's cian an-uiridh.
Seo an t-àit a bh'ann an-uiridh,
is bliadhn' is bliadhn' is bliadhna buileach.

A Dhia, am faic mi siud tuille,
eagan nan sliabh fon drumach?   5
An t-uisge fiar is an drumach,
an t-uisge ciar is an drumach,
an t-uisge liath is an drumach,
an t-uisge tiamhaidh is an drumach,
an t-uisge cianail is an drumach,   10
is e 'na fhrasan dian dubha,
'oir ga riasladh air a thuras,
a' ghaoth a' sianail is a' tuireadh.
Cha b'ionnan sin riamh is turadh;
cha b'ionnan 's latha brèagh, buidhe;   15
cha b'ionnan is grian is bruthainn
an sileadh neo-lochdach, fionnar.
An t-uisge riabhach 'na thuiltean,
uisge àird an iar 'na dhruma,
uisge nan sliabh is an drumach,   20
eagan nan sliabh fon drumach.

A Dhia, am faic mi siud tuille?

272 *Longing for the Tempest*

Far off this year and far off last year. | This is the place that was there last year, | and year and year and year entirely.

God, will I ever see that again, | the notches of the hills under the downpour? | 5
The slanting rain and the downpour, | the dark rain and the downpour, | the grey rain and the downpour, | the melancholy rain and the downpour, | the lamenting rain and the downpour | and it in vehement, black showers | with its edge tattered 10 on its journey, | the wind screaming and wailing. | Never the same that as dry, warm weather; | not the same as a fine, yellow day; | not the same as sun and 15 sultry heat | the innocent, cool fall of rain. | The brindled rain in its torrents, | the rain of the western airt like a drum, | the rain of the hills and the downpour, | the 20 notches of the hills under the downpour.

God, will I ever see that again?

*273 *Luinneag Thairbeartach*

Is àrd a-mach a thà mo ghaol.
   Thà an Caol càrsanach.
Is fad' o fhearann is o fhraoch
a thà mo laoch gu là uam.   4

Ringeadh sgadain feadh nan tonn,
   treud nan dronn dàsachdach.
Uain' is dearg nan solas ann;
luchd nan lann làimh ruibh.   8

Iomachar 's a' Chleit is Cùr;
   gaoth is stùr bhàirlinnean;
losgadh agus cur mu shùil;
dùrd an duine làidir.   12

Sgibinis is Port a' Chruidh,
   sìos gu ruith Chàradail;
an t-einsean ri fuaim 's ri fonn
feadh nan tonn gàireach.   16

Arainn eagach àrd nam beann,
   ùird gu teann a' teàrnadh uaip';
drumach uisge fiadhaich, fiar
às na ciar àirdean.   20

Is àrd a-mach a thà mo ghaol.
   Thà an Caol càrsanach.
Ringeadh sgadain shìos an Caol –
till, a ghaoil, slàn rium.   24

273 [*A Tarbert Ditty*]

Out on the open sea is my love. | *There's a hoarseness on the Sound.* | *Far from soil and from heather* | *is my lad, away from me till dawn.*   4

Ringing of herring through the waves, | *the herd of the furious rumps.* | *The green and red of the lights;* | *the scaly folk close by you.*   8

Imachar Point, the Iron Rock Ledge and Cour; | *the wind and the stoor of breakers;* | *burning, and shooting round a shoal;* | *the droning of the capstan.*   12

Skipness and Cattle Bay, | *down to the run of Carradale;* | *the engine making noise and music* | *through the roaring waves.*   16

High, craggy, mountainous Arran, | *tight hammer-squalls sweeping down from its slopes,* | *a fierce horizontal downpour* | *out of the murky airts.*   20

Out on the open sea is my love. | *There's a hoarseness on the Sound.* | *Ringing of herring down the Sound –* | *come back to me, love, safely.*   24

*274 Guidhe an Iasgair

Fèath is fàbhar agus fortan,
    pailteas coltais anns gach bàgh,
reòtach air clàr 's air cliathaich
    's margadh fial air teachd an là.   4

*275 The Fisherman's Prayer

Calm an' favour, aye, an' fortune;
    rowth o appearance in ilka bay;
a crannreuch o scales on daick an' gunnel
    an' a muckle mercat at dawn o day.   4

*276 Aubade [1]

Tha driùchd air mullach nan càr
    's tha rudhadh an là san ear.
Dùisg is bi gluasad, a ghràidh.
    Cha bhruadar an là 'na ghreis.   4

*277 Bloigh

Air leathad slèibhe 's an Cèitein ann,
    'n àm dùsgadh eunlaith len èigheach fann,
a' ghrian ag èirigh 's mo chridh' ag èirigh
    's an dealt ag èirigh bho fheur 's bho chrann.   4

274 [*The Prayer of the Fisherman*]
Calm and favour and good fortune, | plenty appearances in every bay, | a frost of fishscales on deck and gunnel, | and a bountiful market at the dawning of day.   4

276 [*Aubade 1*]
There is dew on the roofs of the cars | and the flush of day is in the east. | Waken and be stirring, my love. | Day in its while is no dream.   4

277 *Fragment*
On the slope of a hill when May was there, | at the time of the birds' wakening with their faint calling, | the sun rising and my heart rising | and the dew rising from grass and tree.   4

*278 *Lunnainn agus Alba*

Tha iad ràbhartach, ràiteach
a' smàladh ar misnich
ach a dh'aindeoin an sgeulachd
tha eun anns an driseig.   4

*279 *Irische Strophe*

Tá mé in mo shuídhe o d'éirigh an ghealach a-réir ...
(Amhráin Ghrádha Chúige Chonnacht)

Sie schlafen dort im Dorfe alle nun.
Der Mond steht und geht im Himmel schön.
Ich liebe dich und dichte dies' allein.
Das Gesicht ist weiss – ich weiss nicht was zu tun.   4

*280 *Briseadh na Fàire 'n Albainn*

B'fhada oidhche dhubh nan neul
    trast ar speur 's gach reul ga mhùchadh.
San ear tha solas ar seann là,
    's thà mi 'coimhead mo ghràidh a' dùsgadh.   4

278   [*London and Scotland*]

*With their loud-mouthed prattling, | they are snuffing out our courage, | but in
spite of their story | there's a bird in the briar.*   4

279   [*Irish Verse*]

"A-sitting I've been since the moon rose last night ... "
(from "Love Songs of Connacht")

They are all asleep in the village yonder now. | The moon stands aloft and goes,
beautiful, in the sky. | I love you and make this poem all alone. | [The] face is
white – I do not know what to do.   4

280   *Break of Dawn in Scotland*

Long was the black night of the clouds | across our sky, smooring every star. | In
the east is the light of our old day, | and I am watching my love awakening.   4

281 *Bloigh* Lebensraum

Na muillionan tha 'n Sasainn fheuraich,
' 's mòr à meud iad, uain.
Tha 'd ag iarraidh, mas fìor am beul seo,
' bloigh *Lebensraum* mu thuath.   4

*282 *Leum gu Taobh Life*

Cionnas nach abair mi *Och*
' no *Ochain* no *Och ochain* ì?
Tha 'n samhradh a' boillsgeadh a-steach
' air beinn agus Machair nar tìr;   4
thà sinn air raon an t-samhraidh
' is taod umainn teann air a shnìomh.
Am fuasgail sinn an t-snaidhm le suairceas,
' no uabhar a' chip an spìon?   8

Spùill iad leth an t-saoghail
' is chog sinn rin taobh air a shon.
B'e 'n tràns' e, is dhùisg sinn an Albainn
' air a dearmad glan, ged a chog.   12
Soraidh le cogaidhean thairis
' 's le gleanntaichean falamh 'nan tost;
soraidh le sgrùdadh nan eirthir,
' le eilthireachd, Aonadh is trod.   16

[Thèid mi

281 *A Spot of* Lebensraum

The millions that are in grassy England, | they are proud of size, lamb. | They are seeking, if this mouth speak true, | a spot of *Lebensraum* up north.   4

282 *A Leap to Liffey Side*

How will I not say *Och* | or *Ochain* or *Och ochain i*? | Summer is blazing in | on mountain and Lowland in our country; | we are on the meadow of summer, | and 4 a taut twisted tether around us. | Will we undo the knot with urbanity, | or will we wrench out the haughty pride of the stake?   8

They plundered half the world | and we fought on their side on behalf of it. | It was a trance, and we woke in a Scotland | clean neglected, although we had fought. 12 | A farewell to wars overseas | and to empty glens lying silent; | a farewell to the scrutinising of coastlines, | to emigration, Union, and fighting.   16

345

Thèid mi nam leum gu Life
  a dh'fhadadh cridhe mo chlèibh;
Beinn Eadair is slèibhtean Laighean
  's am Balla Tuath fon ghrèin.   20
B'e 'n t-ùrachadh misnich is toile
  rannt a thoirt an cèin
don eilean mhaiseach, uaine,
  far an do bhuadhaich na Gaèil.   24

I will go with a leap to Liffey | to kindle the heart in my breast; | the Hill of Howth and the hills of Leinster | and the North Wall under the sun. | It would be a   20 renewal of courage and will | to take a rant far away | to the bonny, green island, | where the Gael was victorious.   24

POEMS 1978–1979

*283 *Do Dh'Ùistean MacDhiarmaid*

Domhan ann fhèin gach duine
le 'dhubhar is le 'leus.
Thug thu bàrr orr' uile –
is tu an Cruinne Cè.   4

*284 *[Bigein is Aiteamh]*
(dà rann an amhran)

Craobh earraich air chrith fon bhidein, is ceò sa bheinn.
Sna meangain mu nid tha driop aig seann smeòraich 's greim.
Ged thigeadh uair sgrios air cinneadh gaoil Scòta 's teinn,
tha bigein san nidein 's is fileanta fòs a sheinn.   4

Mo bharail cha cheil air na Ceiltich 's an cuan rin cùl.
Sgaoil an eachdraidh a greim. Thà leinn. Cha suain ach dùisg.
Tha aiteamh sa bheinn. Tha teinn 'dol mun cuairt gu sùrd.
Tha ar latha san ear is ar seasamh air uachdar cùirn.   8

283   *For Hugh MacDiarmid*

A world in itself is every man | with its darkness and its light. | You have surpassed them all – | you are the Universe.   4

284   *[Fledgling and Thaw]*
(two verses in song metre)

A springtime tree trembling under the peak, and mist on the mountain. | In the branches an old thrush makes a busy bustle with a bite of food. | Although destruction and hard straits used to come upon the dear race of Scota, | there is a fledgling in the little nest, and fluent yet will be its singing.   4

My opinion I will not conceal from the Celts with the ocean at their backs. | History has released its grip. Things go with us. It is not slumber but awaking. | There is a thaw on the mountain. Hard straits have gone around to eager activity. | Our day is in the east and we stand on the summit of a cairn.   8

*285 *Na Ràtaichean 's a' Bhàrdachd*

"Cìsean is ràtaichean àrda," ors' esan rium.
"ìocaibh, 's pàighibh," ors' à "air an teas 's na shluig.
Dìobair a' bhàrdachd od fhàrdaich, no creanaidh thu."
Is sìorraidh na dàin, ged bhiodh ràtaichean 'teachd gun sgur.   4

"Prìsean gan àrdachadh àrd agus faradh nam bus
a' dìreadh gach ràith, gun sa bhànca ach tastan tur;
an TV is na pàisdean a' fàs is an caban 'nan sluic.
VAT" ors' à. Dhùisg a' bhàrdachd is chaidil a ghuth.   8

"Bheil e crìostail 's mo spàirn gach là ri pathadh 'na mhuir,
ri ìota nach tràigh, nach sàsaichear aiteal liom,
is na prìsean 's na pàistean, 's gach ràta ag at 's gam ruith?
Ma bhìos tu ri bàrdachd gun stàth, gun can mi *Fuich!*   12

"Deich p airson copan cofaidh is barrachd, fuich!
Trì p airson bocsa mosach leth-fhalamh spung.
Dol sìos air an nota, na rocaidean, ailse, an Ruis;
droch thìde, cion oibre, na robairean, stailcean 's muirt.   16

"A' phrìs chuirear ort airson bothain mar fhail nam muc;
BP a tha coma, air a shocair 's nach abair diog;
EEC is an liotar 's an kilo, 's na Pakidhean tiugh;
Cìopras is Doire, an dolar 's an t-Amin ud.   20

285 *The Rates and Poetry*

"Taxes and high rates," said he to me. | "Fork out and pay for heating and the food you have swallowed. | Banish poetry from your dwelling, or else you will pay dearly for it." | Poems are eternal, though rates should come without cease.   4

"Prices being raised to dizzy heights, and the bus fares | going up every quarter, with nothing in the bank but a meagre shilling. | The TV, and the children growing, with their gabs a bottomless pit. | V.A.T." said he. My poetry wakened and his voice fell asleep.   8

"Is it Christian for me to have to struggle every day with a thirst which is a sea, | with a drouth which will never ebb, and which won't be satisfied by me for an instant? | And the prices and the children and all the rates swelling up and pursuing me. | If you are engaged on useless poetry, I will say *Fie!*   12

"Ten p and more for a cup of coffee, fie! | Three p for a miserable half-empty box of matches. | The pound losing value, the rockets, cancer, Russia; | bad weather, no jobs, the robbers, strikes and murders.   16

"The price you have to pay up for a shack like a pigsty; | an MP who doesn't give a damn, takes it easy, won't say a word; | the EEC and the litre and the kilo, and Pakkies everywhere; | Cyprus and Derry, the dollar and yon man Amin.   20

348

"Brezhnev is Trotski is Mosco 's mo chasan fliuch;
na Sìnich is pop is porno is m'ad à cruth;
gach nìonag cho moiteil 's nach mothaich i aiteal dhuit;
gun dìth air ball coise, 's na coin is na capaill a' ruith.   24

"Tha a' phinnt 'dol an-àird aon là, ged a tha i cus.
An ceann mìosa no dhà 'dol an-àird, 's i 'na h-annas dhuinn."
Chrìochnaich e, 's dh'fhàg e am bàr fo phathadh 's fo chruit.
Rinn mi dìochuimhn' air làn a thàsain 's na rainn seo dhuibh.   28

*286 Cùinneadh Samhraidh

B'e siud an t-òr a b'èirig anuair,
ga thoirt le stròdh, an t-òr ga sgapadh,
òr a' chonaisg 's òr a' bheallaidh
air bruthach, an còs, air lòn, air leacainn
an t-òr dar n-airc ga thoirt seachad   5
madainn 's trath-nòin, is tlachd ga cheannach;
ceò teasa 's luin is bruthainn trasta
air gach cunntaidh 's an t-òr 'na phailteas
air beallaidh 's conasg, 's 'na thoic ga faighinn
's ga cosg air soineann 's turadh tairis.   10

Òr a' chonaisg 's òr a' bheallaidh
far na reòdh an dùdlachd againn,
a' ceannach Iuchair 's eòin dar n-ainnis,
a' fàs gun chosnadh 's ga thoirt an-asgaidh
an glaic, air cnoc, ri oir nan achadh.   15
Òr a' chonaisg 's òr a' bheallaidh
a' teachd òirnn o dhuslach 's talamh;
grian is eòin is ceòl gam fastadh
aig òr a' chonaisg 's òr a' bheallaidh.

[An cùinneadh

"Brezhnev and Trotsky and Moscow and my soaking wet feet; | the Chinese and pop and porn and my hat out of shape; | every lassie too proud to pay you the slightest regard; | and no lack of football or the dogs and the horses racing.   24
"A pint is going up one day, although it is too dear. | After a month or two, going up, novel luxury though it is to us." | He [finished and] left the bar thirsty and bent. | I forgot the whole of his querulous whining and made these verses for you.   28

286   Summer Coinage
[See poem 302]

An cùinneadh Lùnaist òrdha, maiseach   20
feadh phreasan conaisg, feadh dhùslaing beallaidh
ga thoirt gun toilleadh, toic is dathan,
'na dhuais chiùil an cùirt nam meangan
à taigh stòir gun chrann, gun ghlasadh
a dh'fhosgail grian fhial an earraich;   25
's cha druid a' chòmhla gu foghar abaich.
Òr a' chonaisg 's òr a' bheallaidh.

*287 Na Gàidheil sna Bailtean

Na Gàidheil sna bailtean feadh bhalla is chabhsair is chàr,
's a' Ghàidhlig à sealladh 's à claisteachd measg stamhnadh shràid,
an àiteachan aimhleathann taca ri beanntan àrd,
nì mi 'n tàladh 's an tatadh 's an taitinn le rann no dàn.   4

*288 Dreuchd an Fhilidh

Tha mi cinnteach an-còmhnaidh à còmhnadh on Naoinear bhinn
gu lìth chur air còmhradh 's air òrain 'nan caochan still,
gu sìor chur ri ceòl 's gus na h-eòin thoirt à craobhan dìon.
àrd ìosal mo ghlòir, is mi beò, bidh mi chaoidh 'cur dhìom.   4

An fhìrinn gun sgleò, is an deò annam, gheobh sibh i.
A bhith 'strì ris a' cheò, cha chòmhrag no cogadh fir.
Bìgeil nan eòin 'na sòlas, 'na sonas bidh,
's is sìorraidh an smeòrach le mòramhan 's pongan mion.   8

287   The Gaels in the Towns

The Gaels in the towns making their way among walls and pavements and cars, | with Gaelic out of sight and out of earshot in the midst of the confinement of streets, | in places that are narrow compared with high mountains, | I will lure them and fondle them and please them with a verse or a poem.   4

288   The Poet's Calling

I am ever sure of aid from the melodious Muses | to lend colour to speech and to songs gushing like a runnel, | to be ever at music and to wile the birds from their fastnesses in the trees. | High or low my voice, while I live I will ever be laying off.   4

The truth without hazy nonsense while breath is in me you will get. | To be struggling with the mist is no battle or war for a man. | The chirping of the birds is a pleasure and a happiness, | and eternal is the thrush with its crotchets and tiny notes.   8

*289 *Guth Thairis*

Chaidh guth thairis air cùisean ar dùthcha sa chathair mu dheas,
gun fhacal gun dùrd 's gach dùil 'dol air ais sa ghreis.
Tha caban 's iad dùinte is sùilean gun aithn' air neach.
Bhith gan crathadh 's gan dùsgadh on dùsal, b'e rathad ar leas.　　4

*290 *Mòr à Meud*

Och, thà iad bòstail 's cho mòr à meud
le dàil is mòrchuis is sgleò 'nam beul.
An nàisean òg seo 's e àrsaidh, mòrail
tàrraidh e 'n t-òirleach 's an còrr den rèis.　　4

291 *Bàr an Dùn Èideann*

Am ball coise 's na h-eich gan deasbad, 's na gill gan cur;
an deoch is a' bhean 's i 'feitheamh, 's tha prìsean cus;
an cosnadh 's an sgeig, an dibhearsan mun tìde fhliuch,
an cogadh chaidh seachad 's na bleigeardan shom san Ruis.　　4

[An sogan

289 *Letting It Drop*

They have let it drop about the matter of our country in the city in the south. |
There's not a word or a cheep and every expectation has faded out for the moment. |
There are gabs which are shut and eyes which do not recognise a person. | To be
shaking them and wakening them from their snooze, that would be the right way
for us.　　4

290 *Proud of Bigness*

Och, they are boastful and so proud of bigness, | with delay and overweening
pride and hazy nonsense in their mouths. | This young nation, which is ancient
and majestic, | it will make the inch and the rest of the span.　　4

291 *A Bar in Edinburgh*

Football and the horses being argued about and bets being laid; | the drink and
the wife who is waiting, and prices are too much; | making a living and taking the
micky and fun about the wet weather; | the war that has gone and the greasy
blackguards in Russia.　　4

An sogan 's an gean is am measgan àrd ìosal ghuth;
na gloineachan leitheach is leth an tìm air ruith;
an gloc 's e ga bhreithneachadh 'greasad a shìor gun sguir;
na sporain gan creachadh, pinnt eile gun sìn mi dhuit.　　8

Bheil an comann seo 'm fearann na h-eachdraidh is sìol mear Scuit,
fonn Oisein, fonn Deirdre, fonn Henryson, tìr Iain Luim?
Throd an sean ri Eideard, is dhìon am fuil
na coin is na h-eich gan deasbad, 's na gill gan cur.　　12

Mochthrath no feasgar is deimhinn 's is cinnteach siud,
thig mosgladh air fear is fear, air m'fhìrinn dhuibh;
thig smoisleachadh mear, 's cha bhi meas a-rìst no guth
air na coin is na h-eich gan deasbad, 's na gill gan cur.　　16

*292　*Stad a' Bhus*

Nan tigeadh am bus 's mi 'fuireach gu faighidneach ris,
le ticeidean 's le cuibhlichean 's uinneagan 's staidhear air chrith;
fear iomain 'na shuidhe cùl cuibhle 's am faradh 's an driop,
gun nichein ach furtachd is suidheachain 's stadan gu tric.　　4

Tipsiness and good humour and the loud and low confusion of voices; | the glasses half empty and half the time run out; | the clock being studied as it hastens on eternally without ceasing; | purses being plundered, I'll stand you another pint.　8

Is this company in the land of history and the mettlesome seed of the Scots, | the country of Ossian, the country of Deirdre, the country of Henryson, the land of Iain Lom? | Their forebears warred with Edward, and their blood protected | the dogs and the horses being argued about and the debts being laid.　12

Early morning or evening, that is sure and certain, | man upon man will rouse himself, I swear by the truth I tell you. | There will be a mettlesome stirring, and there will be no esteem or mention again | for the dogs and the horses being argued about and the debts being laid.　16

292　*The Bus Stop*

If the bus would come, for I am waiting patiently for it, | with tickets and with wheels and windows and its stair vibrating, | the driver sitting behind the wheel and the fare and the bustle, | and nothing but comfort and seats and stops frequently.　4

An sileadh nan sguireadh gam sguitseadh, bu taitneach sin.
Nan tigeadh 's nan ruigeadh am bus, gum b'aighearach mi,
le sitheadh 's le udal air uidhe 's an lathach ri 'shlios.
Fear iomain is cuibhle – nan ruigeadh e 'n stad seo nis!   8

Cha dioc nas fhuilear, 's ar fuireach 's ar faire gu mion
air ciontaich Lunnainn, 's am bruidhinn a' teachd 'na cioth.
Roimh an tighinn bidh furan is sulas is aiteas or sliochd
do na fir dar fuil o Lunnainn, gach math is mith.   12

293 *An Cruinneachadh no an Tional*

Tha rìl-ràl is hòro-gheallaidh
   an cathair Lunnainn is beòil air chrith
mun Chruinneachadh tha gu bhith againn
   gun chumhachd canton Eilbheis mion.   4

*294 *Tìr-mòr*

Fèidh is caoraich, is craobhan gan cur 's a' fàs;
na h-èisg 's a' chearc fhraoich, is gun daoine gud fhuran ri làimh;
na slèibhtean 's am fraoch is a' ghaoth ri tuireadh gun stàth –
an-dè 's mi air aonach aonranach muladach àrd.   4

If the rain would stop scootching me, that would be pleasant. | If the bus would come, if it would arrive, I would be joyful, | darting and swaying on its way and the mud stuck to its side. | A driver and a wheel – if it would reach this stop now!   8

What one must is more than enough, while we wait and watch closely | the guilty men in London with their talk pouring down in a shower. | There will be welcome and delight and gladness from our race | for the men of our blood coming from London, each gentleman and commoner.   12

293 *The Assembly*
There is staggering confusion and a horoyally | in the city of London and mouths a-quiver | about the Assembly that we are to have | without the power of a minute Swiss canton.   4

294 *Mainland*
Deer and sheep, and trees being planted and growing; | the fish and the grouse, and no people to welcome you at hand; | the hills and the heather and the wind at its unavailing lamenting – | yesterday when I was on a lonely, melancholy, high upland.   4

295 *Canzone Goliardica*

Cantatore
sono io.
Canto finora;
vanterò.   4

Del cantare
il dono do.
Canto finora;
vanterò.   8

Rime fiere
tesserò.
Canto finora;
vanterò.   12

Alla fiera
suonerò.
Canto finora;
vanterò.   16

Mentre respiro
canterò.
Canto finora;
vanterò.   20

*

So che si muore.
Morirò.
Canto finora;
tacerò.   24

295 *Goliardic Song*

A singer I am I. I I sing hitherto; I I shall vaunt.   4
I give the gift I of singing. I I sing hitherto; I I shall vaunt.   8
Proud rhymes I I will weave. I I sing hitherto; I I shall vaunt.   12
At the fair I I will play music. I I sing hitherto; I I shall vaunt.   16
As long as I breathe I I will sing. I I sing hitherto; I I shall vaunt. 20
*
I know that one dies. I I shall die. I I sing hitherto; I I shall be silent. 24

Da folla e foro
   partirò.
Canto finora;
   tacerò.   28

All' ultima sera
   dormirò.
Canto finora;
   tacerò.   32

Notte nera
   guarderò.
Canto finora;
   tacerò.   36

Oltre quel mare
   passerò.
Canto finora;
   tacerò.   40

Caronte fero
   pagherò.
Canto finora;
   tacerò.   44

C'e lo svegliarsi?
   Mai saprò.
Canto finora;
   tacerò.   48

                    *

Il giorno dora
   il cielo, no?
Canto finora;
   vanterò.   52

                              [Andrò

I shall depart | from crowd and forum. | I sing hitherto; | I shall be silent.   28
At the last evening | I shall sleep. | I sing hitherto; | I shall be silent.   32
I shall look at | black night. | I sing hitherto; | I shall be silent.   36
Beyond that sea | I shall pass. | I sing hitherto; | I shall be silent.   40
I shall pay | grim Charon. | I sing hitherto; | I shall be silent.   44
Is there an awakening? | I shall never know. | I sing hitherto; | I shall be silent.   48
                              *
Day gilds | the sky, no? | I sing hitherto; | I shall vaunt.   52

Andrò fuori.
  Sì, andrò.
Canto finora;
  vanterò.   56

Buon è il bere.
  Cosi, berrò.
Canto finora;
  vanterò.   6o

Pieni bicchieri
  vuoterò.
Canto finora;
  vanterò.   64

Buon è 'l ballare.
  Ballerò.
Canto finora;
  vanterò.   68

Buon è 'l cantare.
  Canterò.
Canto finora;
  vanterò.   72

296   *Ritornello*

Quando piove,
sussurra, vien e va e l'aria muove.
Quando piove qua c'è 'l sol altrove
quando piove.   4

I will go out. | Yes, I will. | I sing hitherto; | I shall vaunt.   56
Good is it to drink. | So, I will drink. | I sing hitherto; | I shall vaunt.   6o
Full glasses | I will empty. | I sing hitherto; | I shall vaunt.   64
Good is it to dance. | I will dance. | I sing hitherto; | I shall vaunt.   68
Good is it to sing. | I will sing. | I sing hitherto; | I shall vaunt.   72

296   *Ritornello*

When it rains, | it murmurs, it comes and goes and the air moves. | When it rains here, there is the sun elsewhere | when it rains.   4

*297 [Rann do Shomhairle]

A Shomhairle MhicIll-eathain thallad,
  mo chomhairle dhuit, 's is facal fìor:
crath do mhuing is bi 'sitrich.
  Is tu am filidh 's cha bu mhì.   4

*298 Là Allaban Monaidh

Ris a' bhruthach, leis a' bhruthach,
  's mi a' siubhal feadh nan sliabh;
ris an leathad, leis an leathad,
  cìob is creagan, fraoch is riasg;   4
ris a' mhonadh, leis a' mhonadh,
  feadag 's crotag, fraoch is riasg;
fàrsan farsaing feadh a' mhonaidh,
  fàileadh roide, gaoth is grian.   8

*299 Taigh nan Cumantan

Mañana no 'n-earar, is feithibh ri ràdh a beòil;
domani no 'n deireadh nan seachdain, 's cha dàil ach deòin;
a-màireach no 'm-feasta, no 'n teirinn an dà mhìl' òirnn?
Pàrlamaid Bhreatainn nach deifireach àbhaist is dòigh.   4

297 [A Verse to Sorley]

Sorley MacLean over yonder, | my advice to you, and it is no lie: | shake your
mane and start neighing. | You are the master poet, not I.   4

298 [A Day of Rambling in the Hills]

Up the brae, down the brae, | as I go walking through the hills; | up the slope,
down the slope, | heath and rocks, heather and fens; | up the moors, down the   4
moors, | whistler and plover, heather and fens; | wandering far among the moors, |
scent of myrtle, wind and sun.   8

299 [The House of Commons]

Mañana or the day after tomorrow, and wait for the utterance of her mouth; |
domani or at the end of weeks, and the only delay is will; | tomorrow or whenever,
or will the bimillennium run out on us? | Britain's Parliament, unhurried of custom
and manner.   4

*300 Gum Chur an Aithne

Deòrsa Ciotach mac Iain Dheòrsa,
   sin e mar as eòl dhaibh mi;
nam dhalt' aig Gàidheil 's mi leth-Ghallda;
   fuinn is rainn is dàin mo dhriop.   4

Bhà mi 'm bhalach an Cinntìre
   taobh Loch Fìne, 's thà mi nis
an Dùn Èideann air mo chuairtean;
   sèisean 's duain, is buan mo smid.   8

Ma tha aon a tha san èisteachd
   is e dèidheil air an diog
's air na ceathramhan gan cumadh,
   gu deimhinn, chumainn ranntachd ris.   12

"Tha a' Ghàidhlig rìomhach beairteach",
   às is às gun abair mi.
Air mo shlataig, sìon no soineann,
   is bras mo bhìog mar lon an lios.   16

300   [By Way of Introduction]

Left-handed George son of John son of George, | that's the name they know me by; | fostered by Gaels, and I half Lowlander; | verses and poems and tunes are my craft.   4

My boyhood was spent in Kintyre, | by Loch Fyne, and I am now | in Edinburgh on my journey; | airs and poems, my voice endures.   8

Should there be anyone listening here | who is keen on words | and on the fashioning of quatrains, | I would certainly versify for him.   12

"The Gaelic tongue is rich and splendid", | is what I'll say without demur. | On my twig by storm or sunshine, | bold as the garden blackbird my chirp.   16

*301 M'Oilein is M'Altram

Ciothan is ceathach
  air leathadan casa;
an roid is an luachair
  is an cruadhlach fom chasan;   4
am fraoch is an sliabh,
  an riasg is an raineach;
air feadh mara is monaidh
  chaidh m'oilein is m'altram.   8

Dh'fhàg na tobhtachan làrach
  dubh làrach nam anam;
air ruighe nan aonach
  tosg aognaidh nam bailtean;   12
na dachaighean sgrioste
  ri lideadh 's ri facal;
na ballachan briste
  is smid na cuimhn' asta.   16

Na doireachan 's boladh
  na roide sna glacan;
na leabhraichean, 's eòlas
  na Ròimhe 's nan Aitein;   20
cò aca fon ghrèin
  bu mhò èifeachd air m'ealain,
no an loch is na slèibhtean,
  no a' Ghreugais 's an Laideann.   24

[Am bidein

301 *[My Schooling and Rearing]*

Showers and mist | on steep mountainsides; | bog-myrtle and rushes | and stony ground underfoot; | heather and hill, | the marshground and ferns; | over sea and moorland | I was schooled and reared. 4 8

The ruined dwellings have left | a black imprint on my soul; | on the wilderness slopes | the townships' ghastly gash; | the gutted homes | that speak and tell; | the demolished walls | exuding memory's whisper. 12 16

The thickets and the scent | of bog-myrtle in the hollows; | books, and the learning | of Rome and Athens; | which under the sun | has most affected my art, | the loch and the hills | or Greek and Latin? 20 24

Am bidein 's am bruthach
   is am mullach gun fhasgadh,
is bruidhinn gun sgur
   aig na sruthain le gleannain,   28
no feallsanachd àrd
   agus dràma nan Aitein,
dè as deise dom inntinn?
   Chan eil cinnt a'm cò aca.   32

Gach cainnt is gach cultar
   a chunnaic 's nach fhaca,
aiste is nobhail,
   sonaid is saga,   36
ceòl stàtail na Gearmailt
   is na dealbhan dathte
is cumhachdaiche 'm monadh.
   Is motha e agam.   40

*302 *Summer Coinage*

That's the gold that's requital-money for hard weather
given in a spendthrift way, the gold being scattered,
the gold of the whin and the gold of the broom.
On braes, in howes, on loanings, on slopes
the gold is handed out to our neediness morning and evening,   5
while pleasure is bought with it.
Heat haze and heat-shimmering and sultry heat
across every county, with the gold in plenty on broom and whin,
a wealth that is got and spent on fine weather and gentle sunny weather.
The gold of the whin and the gold of the broom   10

*The pinnacle, the ascent | and the unsheltered summit, | and the ceaseless chatter |
of burns down small glens, | or the lofty philosophy | and drama of Athens – | which* 28
runs deeper in my mind? | I know not for sure. 32

*Every language and culture | I have seen and not seen, | essay and novel, | sonnet
or saga, | the stately music of Germany, | the painted canvases – | more powerful* 36
is the moorland, | and dearer to me. 40

where midwinter froze for us,
buying July and birds for our poverty;
growing without being worked for and given gratis
in hollow, on hill, and on the edge of the fields.
The gold of the whin and the gold of the broom   15
reaching us from the dust and the earth.
Sun ands birds and music are hired
by the gold of the whin and the gold of the broom.
The golden, beautiful coinage of August
throughout whin bushes and thickets of broom,   20
given without being deserved, riches and colours.
a fee for music in the court of the branches
from a storehouse unbolted, unlocked,
which was opened by the generous sun of spring –
and the door will not close till ripe autumn.   25
The gold of the whin and the gold of the broom.

*303 *The Auld Border Wumman*

Nox est perpetua una dormienda

Wull I nae see thaim yet, ma oe, ma ieroe?
    The bairns are grown and gane, and bare's ma shoother.
Is't a leelang nicht i a bed that's nerra?
    Is Heaven a freit, the Carritch a wheen o blether?   4

The gerss dees and grows oot on the loanin.
    The burn? I'd drink its watter i a tassie.
Is't tae be that, a smooran wioot meanan,
    or gang, a ghaist, whaur aince I gaed a lassie?   8

Tae keep a hoose i the mools, when aa is endit,
    whaur nane chap at the dure, nane come tae speir.
Gin I but had ma wull, sweet Christ, I's mand it
    tae luik on Tinto in a thoosan year.   12

*304 *Larochs*

Fu o unease and secret fear
   they turned their heid, and doon cam waas.
Here brent the thack; here brokk the dure;
   here suddent violence made the laws.   4

Thone lanesome laroch abune the howes
   was cantie aince ablow the muir.
The rain's the guest whaur bleezed the fire,
   and silence chaps at the tummlet dure.   8

They brokkin waas that gie nae bield
   war couthie aince wi sang and talk;
and hyucks war eident i the field,
   as doon gaed bere gowd bauk by bauk.   12

Th'unending talk o the burn ablow,
   and the leid o the wind the birks amang;
rashes and dockens and brekkins grow
   whaur hairst was yella and bandsters thrang.   16

Alang the braes the baa o yowes;
   the rinnan rae, the tod, the hare
are nae blate here, whaur heather grows.
   The wae whaups keep the ceilidh here.   20

The tracks grow owre, untrevellt aa;
   heather is broon whaur green was gress;
the wind, the rain, the sun, the snaw,
   the nicht, the day, and naethingness.   24

Mairtinmass and Lammas day
   and seasons hae nae meanan here.
Youth or eild or freend or fae
   are aa ae thing whaur larochs are.   28

Glesca and Embro hae their fowk;
   i faur Cape Breton they are kent.
Here derns a future but a maik.
   They bide, wi naethingness acquent.   32

Aa the moontains o the warld
    tooer atween thaim and their men.
Tae continents they are thirled.
    The reek will ryse frae thaim again.   36

They brokkin waas and fuggie flairs,
    whaur feet will dance again, ding Daith;
whaur aa unguestit gant the dures,
    will ootlast Crouns and Commons baith.   40

Toom laroch in its lanesome lee,
    shenar o cities, bides its day.
Ilk laroch dwauman eternally
    is a strang keep tae lippen tae.   44

*305 The Muirland Man, Hieland or Lawland

A muirland man in a fail hoose;
    match ye his mense, ye wha can.
He was stately and he was crouse.
    He was a king, the muirland man.   4

306 A' Cheòlraidh – Beatha Bun-os-Cionn

Thug mi 'n oidhche caithriseach
    gu camhanaich is fàire,
a' cumadh air an rannaghail
    's an aicill 'teachd 's ga tàthadh   4
gun chlos on Cheòlraidh fhiadhaich
's an norran gnàthach cian uam
mar chomhachag no iasgair
    no ialtag nan sgàile.   8

306 [*The Muses – Life Topsy-turvy*]
I have spent the night unable to sleep | till first light of dawn and sun on the horizon, | fashioning my verse, | and the rhymes coming and bonding it together, | with no respite from the feverish Muses | and my habitual slumber far from me, | like an owl or a fisherman | or the bat of the shadows.   4 ... 8

*307 Airson na Cloinne – Fàilt' air a' Mhadainn

Air a' chiad *mhañana di domani* là,
nuair a dh'èireas grian os cionn nan càrn,
dùisgidh sinn san t-solas is èiridh sinn gu h-obann,
's bidh sinn air ar cois gu sgaradh nan tràth.   4

308 A' Chearc Gheal
[incomplete draft]

O seallaibh an tiugaidh. Tha uighean aic'.
Tha spàistearachd 's casan cama aic'
's gach iteag is gile 's is giobaiche.
    Tha spìoladh aic'.
    Tha spiris aic'.   5
Tha gràcan 's spàgan buidhe aic'.
Tha gogadh is gogail a' mhuineil aic'
's i 'tuireadh mu chuid a' ghuib a th' oirr'
mu dhoras a' bhothain 's b'e 'n uidhe leath';
's i 'sgrùdadh le sùil an-fhurasach   10
feuch duine bhith 'ruigheachd nan uighean aic'.

307 [*For the Children – A Welcome to the Morning*]
On the first mañana di domani day, | *when the sun rises over the stony peaks,* | *we will wake up to the light and rise in haste,* | *and we'll be on our feet till evening falls.*   4

308 [*The White Hen*]
Oh all take a look at the chookie. She's laid some eggs. | *She struts around, on bent legs,* | *her every feather most white and most shaggy.* | *She picks,* | *she roosts.* | *She* 5 *cuckles away on her yellow legsticks,* | *she nods and doddles her neck,* | *griping about the lot of her beak,* | *round the door of the hut which was her goal;* | *as she peers round with a fretting eye* | *lest anyone come near her eggs.*   10

O seallaibh na Buill sna Cumantan
'nan suidhe gu h-urramach, udalach.
Tha bruidhinn ac', tha iorram ac'
tha luinneag ac' 's is cumha i.　　　　　　　15
　　　　Tha bilean ac'
　　　　tha spiris aic'
　　　　tha gràcan aic'
　　　　tha tàsan ac'
　　　　paràda aic'　　　　　　　　　　　20
　　　　paràda ac'
Tha gurraban ac' tha gur aca
cha bhi iad buidheach bhith cuidhteas sinn
ach tachraidh sin uile, 's cha b'fhuilear sin.

309 *An Nàiseantach ga Chomhairleachadh*
[drafts]

Och, cuist a-nis. Bi glic. Nach eil
cuspair ar cinnidh tric fo sgeig?
Is cus leam sin gach lideadh dheth
's chan urra mi an tioma chleith.　　　　　4

　　　　*

Nach cuist thu nis? An tig am-feast
an rud a shireas sibh 's an seas?
Tha cuid as sine dhlighe 's neart
aig mo chuideachd chridhe, 's cridhe mear.　　8

Oh all take a look at the Members in the Commons, | *sitting rocking in self-importance.* | *They talk, they chant,* | *they sing their chorus and it is a dirge.* | 15
They have their bills (?), | *she has her roost,* | *she cackles,* | *they whine,* | *she struts and parades,* | *they strut and parade.* | *They crouch, they hatch,* | *they will not be* 20
grateful to be rid of us, | *but it will all come to pass, as of necessity it must.*

309 *Advice to the Nationalist*
Oh wheesht, now. Be sensible. Is not | *the cause of our nation often ridiculed?* | *It is too much for me, every syllable of it,* | *and I cannot hide my emotion.*　　　　4

　　　　*

Won't you wheesht now? Will it ever come, | *the thing you all seek and will it endure?* | *The older part in dedication and strength* | *lies with the company I love, and a joyful heart.*　　　　8

310 [*Falamh*]

Agam, agad, againn gu lèir.
Thà mi falamh, I'm skint the day,
roinn nan tastan is òl da rèir.
Sin an deachdadh againn fhèin,
leamsa, leatsa, leinn gu lèir.   5

311 *Na Feansaichean*

[editorial reconstruction]

Thug mi gaol dha, thug mi gràdh dha,
don fhearann riabhach fhiadhaich fhàsaich,
don t-sùil chruthaich, don chruaidh, don sgàirneach,
nach tug gin do nighean àlainn,
nach tug gin do bhean no mhàthair,   5
dh'athair no phiuthar no bhràthair,
nach tug duine dh'fhuil no chàirdean,
nach tugadh riamh eadar lànan,
nach tugadh riamh eadar càraid,
do leannan, do leanabh, do phàiste –   10

ach tha feansan fo gach ruighe
far an robh Clann Dòmhnaill 'fuireach.

Tha mo chas air rathad cumant',
air rathad mòr 's a Mhòrachd subhach.

310 [*Empty*]

What I have, what you have, what we all have together. | *I am empty, I'm skint
the day;* | *the shillings get shared and one drinks accordingly.* | *That's the rule of
life we follow,* | *what's mine, what's yours, is ours together.*   5

311 [*The Fences*]

I gave it love, I gave it affection, | *to the wild, desolate, brindled land,* | *to the bogs,
the hard slopes, the scree,* | *such as none ever gave to a beautiful lass,* | *none ever
gave to wife or mother,* | *to father or sister or brother,* | *that no man ever gave to*   5
family or relatives, | *such as was never given between lovers,* | *never given between
a couple,* | *to sweetheart, to infant, to child –*   10

but there are fences below every brae | *where MacDonalds used to live.*

My foot is on a common road | *a high road, while his Lordship makes merry.*

The Summit of the Footstool and the Knowe of the Mine | *the Narrow Ben and the*   15
Summit of the Grey Grove | *they are far from the road, beyond the reach of a cry.*

Cruach an t-Sorchain 's Cnoc na Mèine,   15
a' Chaolbheinn 's Cruach Doire Lèithe,
's fad' on rathad, 's fad' on èigh iad.

A Dhia nam faicinn slios Allt Bheithe
cha bu mhìghean ach bu ghean e.

'S binn a' chrotag os cionn garbhlaich   20
is geur air rathad fuaim a' charbaid.

Far am bi am barrach boltrach
's ann a bhìos na caoraich mholach,
molt is reithe 's reic is lomadh
's cìobair 's cù air sgùrr 's air monadh.   25

Fàsaidh raineach, fàsaidh copag,
fàsaidh feur is fàsaidh croitean,
fàsaidh fraoch is fàsaidh fochann.

Bitear tilleadh chum nan làrach
's bidh na feansaichean air làr ac'.   30

Feansa orr' is caoraich bhàna,
geamair is cìobair 's cìs is fàsach.
An-sin tha feansaichean is àithne.

Far am faicear taighean 's àiteach
tha gaoth is fraoch is caoraich bhàna.   35
Far am bi fraghan, 's taighean 's àiteach
a-nis tha feansaichean mun àite.

God if I could see the hillside of the Birch Burn | it would not be displeasure but would be pleasure.

Sweet is the plover's cry above the rough ground | harsh on the road the noise of 20 *vehicles.*

Where will be fragrant treetops | there will be hairy sheep | wether and ram, selling and shearing | and shepherd and sheepdog on summit and on moor. 25

The bracken will grow, the docken will grow | grass will grow and crofts will grow | heather will grow and blades of grass will grow.

There will be a return to the ruined villages | and the fences will be knocked to the ground. 30

A fence on them and white sheep | gamekeeper and shepherd and tax and wilderness. | Over there are fences and a commandment.

Where will be seen houses and cultivation | there is wind and heather and white sheep. | Where will be room-walls and houses and cultivation | now there are 35 *fences about the place.*

*312 *The Fences*

I gied it luve, I gied it likein,
sic as nane gied tae a luvely lassie,
that nane e'er gied tae wife or mither,
tae faither, tae sister, tae brither,
that man ne'er gied tae bluid or kin,   5
that wes ne'er gien atween a merriet couple,
that wes ne'er gien atween a merriet pair,
that wes ne'er gien tae leman, tae bairn, tae wean,
that I gied tae the brindlet, wild wilderness land,
tae the boghole, tae the hilltap, tae the tummlet rocks.   10
An' there are fences roond the places.

Noo there are fences ablow the gentle slope
whaur Clan Donald uset tae bide.

Ma fuit is on the common roadway,
on the heichroad, wi his Loardship crouse.   15

The Summit o the Fitstule an' The Knowe o the Mine,
The Nerra Ben an' The Summit o the Grey Grove,
they are faur frae the road, they are a faur cry.

Goad gin I could see Allt Beithe hillside,
it wadna be displeisure, it wad be pleisure.   20

Sweet is the whaup abune the reuch groond:
sherp on the road is the soond o the car.

Whaur are the fragrant birk taps,
there are the shaggy sheep,
wedder an' ram, an' sellin an' shearin,   25
an' shepherd an' dog on scaur an' muirland.

Brecken will grow, docken will grow,
gerss will grow an' crofts will grow;
heather will grow an' blade o gerss will grow.

There will be a returnin tae the larochs   30
an' they will hae fences on the groond.

A fence there is an' white sheep,
gamekeeper an' shepherd an' taxes an' a wilderness.
Yonder are fences an' a commandment.

Whaur there will be hooses an' room-waas an' cultivation,   35
wund an' heather an' white sheep,
an' fences aboot the place.

*313   Simmer Cunzie

Thon's the gowd requites hard wather,
   gowd o the whin an' gowd o the broom,
in gowpens owre aa the land thegither,
   makan herts fu' that at Yule war toom.   4

*314   To the Younger Generation

Jimp an' trigg an' gleg an' aa,
ilka day is gled an' braw,
dae ye think the past is fell
an' the mair nations the mair hell?   4

*315   Extempore in Bennett's Bar

I am mair dwaibly nor dwaibly itsel,
   I am mair auld nor auld;
ma neb is blae; the wund is snell.
   What is't? I hae a cauld.   4

*316   The Bard, the Drink an' the Hill

Wad ye raither drink yill i the Cannie Man's
   or watter and gang tae Allermuir?
Wad ye raither hear the juke-box play
   or raither the whaups' overture?   4

POEMS 1980–1982

*317 *Na h-Òrain a Bh'ann 's a Th'ann*

Na h-òrain a bh'ann 's a th'ann, a ghràidh,
na h-òrain a bh'ann gach rann, a ghràidh,
na h-òrain a th'ann nach gann, a ghràidh.   3

Na h-òrain a bh'ann 's gach gleann, a ghràidh,
na h-òrain a bh'ann gun pheann, a ghràidh,
na h-òrain a th'ann gu ceann, a ghràidh.   6

Na h-òrain a bh'ann 's a th'ann, a ghràidh,
na h-òrain a bh'ann nach gann, a ghràidh,
na h-òrain a th'ann gach rann, a ghràidh.   9

*318 *Muir is Tìr,*
no Deireadh Oidhche ri Cladach

Eadar sgeir is sgeir,
eadar iar is ear,
is siud a' ghrian an-ear.   3

---

318 [The Songs That There Were and There Are]

The songs that there were and there are, my dear; | the songs there were, every verse, my dear; | the songs there are a-plenty, my dear.   3

The songs there were in every glen, my dear; | the songs there were, unpenned, my dear; | the songs there are, sung to the end, my dear.   6

The songs that there were and there are, my dear; | the songs there were a-plenty, my dear; | the songs there are, every verse, my dear.   9

318 [Land and Sea, or The End of a Night by the Shore]

Between skerry and skerry, | between west and east, | there goes the eastern sun.   3

Eadar bogha 's tràigh,
eadar cop is càrn,
is siud a' ghrian 's an là.　　　　6

Eadar faoileag 's lon,
eadar slios is loch,
is siud a' ghrian, dèan boch.　　　9

eadar geansaidh 's clò,
eadar iasg is feòil,
is siud a' ghrian gun sgòth.　　　12

Eadar ùir is snàmh,
eadar bùrn is sàl,
is siud a' ghrian tràth.　　　　15

Eadar còinneach 's ceilp,
eadar maois is peic,
is siud a' ghrian a' teachd.　　　18

Eadar bog is cruaidh,
eadar deas is tuath,
is siud a' ghrian luath.　　　　21

Eadar fairge 's fonn,
eadar garbhlach 's tonn,
is siud a' ghrian air lom.　　　24

Eadar ceannair 's làir,
eadar lannan 's càth,
is siud a' ghrian an-àird.　　　27

[Eadar lunn

Between heaver and shore, | between foam and cairn, | there go the sun and the day.　6

Between blackbird and gull, | between hillside and loch, | there goes the sun, rejoice.　9

Between jersey and tweed, | between fish and meat, | there goes the cloudless sun.　12

Between earth and swim, | fresh water and brine, | there goes the early sun.　15

Between moss and kelp, | between fish-hamper and peck, | yonder the sun approaches.　18

Between hard and soft, | between south and north, | there goes the speedy sun.　21

Between ocean and earth, | rough ground and wave, | there goes the glaring sun.　24

Between net-rope and mare, | between corn-husks and scales, | there goes the sun up high.　27

Eadar lunn is feur,
eadar grunnd is speur,
is siud a' ghrian 'na leus.   30

Eadar crann is craobh,
eadar gleann is caol,
is siud a' ghrian 'na caoir.   33

Eadar mogall 's dias,
eadar tobhta 's cliath,
is siud a' ghrian 'dol siar.   36

Eadar oidhche 's là,
eadar àird is àird,
is siud a' ghrian mar bhà.   39

Eadar duileasg 's fraoch,
eadar murabhlach 's naosg,
is siud a' ghrian chaomh.   42

Eadar faitheam 's sgar,
eadar còmhla 's tac,
is siud a' ghrian air ais.   45

Eadar treobhadh 's cur,
eadar cathadh 's dus,
is siud a' ghrian bho thuim.   48

Eadar dubh is moch,
eadar tulach 's loch,
is siud a' ghrian dar toil.   51

Between billow and grass, | between floor and sky, | there goes the sun on fire.   30
Between mast and tree, | between kyle and glen, | there goes the sun aflame.   33
Between mesh and ear of corn, | between oarseat and harrow, | there goes the sun
to the west.   36
Between night and day, | from airt to airt, | there goes the sun unchanged.   39
Between heather and dulse, | between dogfish and snipe, | there goes the gentle sun.   42
Between joint and seam, | between doorleaf and tack, | yonder the sun comes back.   45
Between ploughing and sowing, | between seaspray and dust, | there goes the sun
by the knowes.   48
Between dark and dawn, | between hillock and loch, | there goes the sun of our want.   51

Eadar ringeadh 's buain,
eadar linne 's cruach,
is siud a' ghrian, a luaidh.   54

Eadar putag 's ceap,
eadar ulag 's bleith,
is siud a' ghrian 's ar leas.   57

Eadar tobhta 's being,
eadar cobhar 's beinn,
is siud a' ghrian, ar leinn.   60

Eadar aitheamh 's sgòrr,
eadar tonn is fòd,
is siud a' ghrian 'na dreòs.   63

Eadar ailm is beith,
eadar amhsan 's cearc,
is siud a' ghrian mhear.   66

Eadar stuadh is lòn,
eadar fuarthonn 's crò,
is siud a' ghrian òir.   69

Eadar each is seòl,
eadar peileag 's bò,
is siud a' ghrian chòir.   72

Eadar sionnach 's ròn,
eadar tuinn is tòrr,
is siud a' ghrian, 's is leòir.   75

Between ring-netting and reaping, | between pool and peak, | there goes the sun, my dear.   54
Between oarpin and snare, | between pulley and grinding, | there goes the sun for our good.   57
Between ruin and bench, | between froth and ben, | there goes the sun, we deem.   60
Between fathom and scaur, | between wave and sod, | there goes the sun ablaze.   63
Between elm and birch, | between solan and hen, | there goes the merry sun.   66
Between breaker and lawn, | between cold wave and fold, | there goes the sun of gold.   69
Between horse and sail, | between porpoise and cow, | there goes the kindly sun.   72
Between fox and seal, | between waves and tor, | there goes the sun, and it's ample.   75

373

*319 Hòro, Mhàiri Dhubh

(ath-dhèanamh air seann òran)

Cha dèan mi car feuma ma thrèigeas mo leannan mi,
  hòro, Mhàiri Dhubh, tionndaidh rium,
bean a' chùil dualaich 's nan cuachagan camagach,
  hòro, Mhàiri Dhubh, tionndaidh rium.
A Mhàiri, nan tigeadh tu, thaitneadh tu ruinn;   5
A Mhàiri, nan tigeadh tu, thaitneadh tu ruinn;
A Mhàiri, nan tigeadh tu, b'e do bheath againn thu;
hòro, Mhàiri Dhubh, tionndaidh rium.

Tha 'n latha 'dol seachad, 's e fadalach, fadalach;
is tu bhith gam dhìth a dhìobair mo chadal bhuam.   10

Bu tu, a ghràidh, a thàladh mar leanabh mi,
bu tu sheinneadh ceòl mar smeòrach na camhanaich.

A Mhàiri, 'eudail, na trèig rim mhaireann mi.
A Mhàiri, a rùin ghil, tionndaidh an rathad seo.

319 [*Horo, Black-haired Mary*]
(*a reworking of an old song*)

A useful turn I'll not do if my lover abandons me, | *Horo, Black-haired Mary, turn to me;* | *the lovely-haired woman of twirling locks,* | *Horo, Black-haired Mary, turn to me.* | *O should you come, Mary, you'd be our delight;* | *O should you come,*   5
Mary, you'd be our delight; | *O should you come, Mary, we'd give you great welcome;* | *horo, Black-haired Mary, turn to me.*

The day goes by, so wearily, wearily; | *it's the wanting of you has banished my sleep from me.*   10

It's you, love, who'd lull me to sleep like a baby; | *it's you would make music like the thrush of the dawn.*

Mary, my treasure, don't ever forsake me; | *Mary, my white love, come turn this way.*

*320 *Eich Mhic Nèill*
(òran tàthaidh)

A bhradag dhubh, *a hù o haoi o*, bhrist na glasan, *hù o èile*,
cuiream ortsa an dubh chapall, *hù o haoi o*.

Cuiream ortsa, *hù o haoi o*, an dubh chapall, *hù o èile*,
Càit an d'fhàg thu Ruaraidh 'n Tartair? *Hù o haoi o*.

Càit an d'fhàg thu Niall a' Chaisteil,   5
no Gill-eònain mòr an gaisgeach,
bheireadh am fìon do na h-eachaibh
chuireadh cruithneachd geal 'nam prasaich,
sgaoileadh am flùr air an dealt dhaibh,
chuireadh crùidhean òir fon casan,   10
chuireadh srian an airgid ghlais riu,
diallaidean sìoda sìnte thairis?
Chuireadh iad leus às an adhar,
chuireadh iad crith air an talamh,
sradagan gan cur à clachan.   15
Rèis is ruith is muing air chrathadh,
ruith is ceumadh, rèis is saltairt.
Na h-eich liatha, dhiana, bhrasa,
dh'fhalbhadh raointean, sgaoim cha ghabhadh,
nach iarradh cuip no spuir ach marcach.   20

320   [*MacNeill of Barra's Horses*]
(*a conflated song*)

You wee black thief, *a hu o hey o*, who snapped the fetters, *hu o eile*, | on you I cast the black mare curse, *hu o hey o*.

On you I cast, *a hu o hey o*, the black mare curse, *hu o eile*, | Where did you leave Rorie the Clamorous? *Hu o hey o*.

Where did you leave Neil of the Castle, | or great Gilleonan the hero, | who would   5
give wine to the horses, | who'd fill their manger with white wheat, | who'd
sprinkle flour on the dew for them, | who'd shoe their hooves with shoes of gold, | 10
who'd equip them with bridles of burnished silver. | silken saddles spread across
them? | They would send a blaze through the air, | they would set the earth
atremble, | send sparks flying from the stones. | Racing and galloping, tossing   15
their manes, | galloping, striding, racing and trampling. | The mettlesome, fiery
light-grey horses, | who'd travel the plains, never take fright, | and need neither
whip nor spur but a rider.   20

*321   *Chailein Òig, an Stiùir Thu Mi?*

(ath-dhèanamh air seann òran)

Chrom i 'ceann is rinn i gàire,
   chailein òig, an stiùir thu mi?
nighean rìgh Èireann 's i san àirigh.
   Chailein òig, nighean rìgh Èireann,
   chailein òig, an stiùir thu mi?   5

Nighean rìgh Èireann 's i san àirigh,
giullan bochd is bothan fàsaich,
stairsneach chòinnich 's balla fàil air,
's e fad' às, gun taigh air àrainn,
fad' on bhaile, fad' o àiteach,   10
air aonach fraoich am measg nan àirdean,
os cionn nan cnoc 's thar chromadh fàire;
tughadh luachrach 's leabaidh làir ann;
gun duine 'gluasad, gun sluagh a làthair;
's e ris, gun fhasgadh on àileadh,   15
deò nam beann is allt 's a chànain,
aonranach, uaigneach fon fhànas:
sùilean cruach is cruadhlach 's càthar,
bearraidhean 's creagan is càrnach;
slèibhtean 's fraoch 's a' ghaoth air bhàinidh   20
a tuireadh ri tulaichean àrda,
sèideadh, caoidhrean, caoineadh 's rànail

321   [*Young Girl, Will You Guide Me?*]
      (*a reworking of an old song*)

She turned her head and gave a laugh, | *young girl, will you guide me?* | *the King of Ireland's daughter at the shieling.* | *Young girl, daughter of the king of Ireland,* | *young girl, will you guide me?*   5

The king of Ireland's daughter at the shieling, | *a poor lad and a mountain bothy,* | *with floor of moss and walls of turf,* | *out of the way with no house near it,* | *far from township or habitation,* | *on the heathery moor high up on the summits,* | 10 *above the hills and beyond the horizon;* | *thatched with rushes and a bed on the floor;* | *not a soul passing by, no human presence,* | *exposed, unprotected from the wind,* | *the mountain breeze and the speech of a burn,* | *solitary and desolate* 15 *under vast skies:* | *quagmires, stony ascents and marshland,* | *ridges, crags and rocky escarpments,* | *mountains and heather and the wind demented,* | *its wailing* 20 *up around the high hillocks,* | *heaving, lamenting, howling and shrieking,* |

's fuaim an uillt 'na ghuth gun tàmh ann;
maighich 's fèidh is sprèidh ga h-àrach.

Dh'aithnich mi gum b'i mo ghràdh-sa.　　　　　　25
Thug mi dhi cuireadh 's furan 's fàilte,
's ghabh mi null an taobh a bhà i.
Thug mi brèid dhi, thug mi bràiste,
thug mi làmhainnean da làmhan,
stìom is sgarfa sìoda bràghaid,　　　　　　　　30
usgar daoimein 's leugan 's fàinne.
Shìn mi còrn an òir 's e làn di.
Dh'òl i 'n còrn, a h-aon 's a dhà dhiubh,
dh'òl a trì den fhìon bha càilear.
Dhìrich grìs ri gruaidh na mnà sin.　　　　　　35
Lìon i 'n còrn is shìn e làn dhomh:
"Seo mo phòg is òl mo shlàinte."
Fhuair mi pòg a beòil is mànran,
cion is gean on mheachair mhànla,
mionnan pòsaidh 's còrdadh 's càirdeas,　　　　40
nighean rìgh Èireann 'na cèile mnà dhomh
's Èirinn uile o dhruim gu sàile.
Fhuair mi lùchairtean is pàileas,
Teamhair 's Àileach, faiche 's pàileas,
Connachd, Mumhain 's Ulaidh slàn leath',　　　45
Bòinn is Sionann 's Life làn leath',
pèidse 's pìosan, cìs is càin leath',
cùirt is cùirtearan is tàintean,
nighean rìgh Èireann 's i san àirigh.

[Ghleus mi

and the sound of the burn an incessant voice; | hares and deer, and cattle being reared.

I recognised her as my love. | Greeting, salutation and welcome I gave her, | and　25
over I went to where she was. | I gave her a kertch, I gave her a brooch, | I gave
her a pair of gloves for her hands, | a snood I gave her and a shawl of silk, | a　30
diamond necklace, gems and a ring. | The gold horn I handed her, brimming full. |
She drank the cup and then another, | and again a third of wine so pleasant. | A
glow rose in that woman's cheeks. | She filled the cup and handed it to me: |　35
"Here's a kiss, now drink my health". | I got a kiss of her lips and lovetalk, |
fondness and affection from the kind gracious woman, | vows of marriage, a pledge
and love-bond, | the Irish king's daughter to be my wife, | all Ireland mine from　40
ridge to ocean. | I got mansions and a palace, | Tara and Ailech, plain and
palace, | Connaught, Munster and all Ulster through her, | Boyne and Shannon　45
and the full Liffey by her, | a page and goblets, tax and tribute through her, | a court
and courtiers and herds of cattle, | the king of Ireland's daughter at the shieling.

Ghleus mi ceòl di 's òrain àrsaidh,   50
puirt làn chuir is ruithean dàna;
dh'òl mi fìon oirr' 'na dheoch shlàinte,
fìon 's e dearg 'na dhearbh dheoch phàite.
Dh'fhan i agam na trì ràithean.

Chaidh mi leatha air bòrd air bàrca   55
dhol gu Èirinn thar an t-sàile;
sgioba lìonmhor 's trì chroinn àrda,
siùil gheala, mhìne de lìon an Fhlànrais,
buill is slatan, acair 's càball,
staghan, siùil is stiùir ri 'sàil oirr'.   60
Thog sinn tìr le fortan 's fàbhar.
Ghluais sinn suas o bhruach na tràghad
gu cùirt a h-athar, dùn an àrdrìgh.
Ghabh e rium mar oighre àraid
gus a bhith nam rìgh 'na àite,   65
's a nighean bhith 'na cèile mnà dhomh.

Fhuair mi leatha comhairlichean stàtail,
ridirean, filidhean, bàird leath',
caistealan, baidealan àrda,
tùir is turaidean 'nan àras;   70
Dùn nan Gall is Gailleamh 's Àrann,
Èirinn fo bhuar le 'cluaintean àillidh;
boineidean a-nuas aig càch rium,
modhan 's beiceadh 's freastal m'àithntean,

I plied her with music and ancient songs, | tunes full of twists and audacious 50
runs; | I drank wine to toast her health, | scarlet wine and truly quenching. | She
stayed with me three seasons long.

I went with her aboard a bark, | to go to Ireland across the sea; | a numerous crew 55
and three high masts, | smooth white sails of Flanders linen, | ropes and yards,
anchor and cable, | stays and sails, at her heel a rudder. | We sighted land with 60
favour and fortune. | We headed up from the slope of the shore, | to her father's
court, the fort of the High King. | He took to me as his very heir, | that I might
succeed him in the kingship, | and his daughter be my wife and spouse. 65

Through her I got stately councillors, | knights, master poets and bards by her, |
fastnesses and high battlements, | turreted, multi-towered mansions; | Donegal, 70
Galway and Aran, | cattle-rich Ireland of luscious meadows; | bonnets docked by
all before me, | respect and curtseys and my orders obeyed, |

378

lùbadh ghlùn is dùil ri fàbhar;   75
ollamhan oilein 's aos dàna,
rannan molaidh gun lochd nam làthair;
crùn is cathair, gaisgich 's geàrd leath',
fhuair mi sin, 's gach gin fom làmhan.
Fleadh an-diugh is cuirm a-màireach,   80
fleadh is fèist is rèim is sàibhreas;
manaich 's clèir is cèir is cràbhadh;
cruiteir, fidhleir, pìobair, clàrsair,
cearraiche, seanachaidh 's fear àbhachd,
sgeulaiche is lèigh ri slànadh,   85
cleasaiche 's e clis san làthair,
maor is fiosaiche ri fàistneachd,
torman organ 's còisir phàiste,
capaill rèis gu feum san stàball,
fèist is fialachd gu grian air fàire,   90
is mi nam shuidh' an trusgan cràidhearg
taobh ri taobh 's mo mhaothbhean ghràdhach.
Fhuair mi siud, is rud a b'fheàrr leam,
pòg a bilean, cion is tàladh
air cluasaig uaine nam shuain gu là leath'.   95

Chrom i 'ceann is rinn i gàire,
    chailein òig, an stiùir thu mi?
nighean rìgh Èireann 's i san àirigh.
    Chailein òig, nighean rìgh Èireann,
    chailein òig, an stiùir thu mi?   100

bending of knee and hoping for favours; | *doctors of learning and courtly artists,* | 75
faultless panegyric declaimed before me; | *crown, throne, heroes and guard-troupe*
through her, | *those I got, each one at my bidding.* | *A feast today, a banquet tomor-*
row, | *feast and festivity, power and opulence;* | *monks and clerics, devotion and*   80
candles; | *lute-player, fiddler, piper and harper,* | *gamester, historian and enter-*
tainer, | *storyteller and healing physician,* | *agile conjurer in attendance,* | *officer* 85
and prophesying seer, | *peal of organs and children's choir,* | *racing horses kept*
groomed in stables, | *feasting and revels till sun on the skyline,* | *and I in my seat*   90
in blood-red livery, | *my tender lovely wife beside me.* | *All that I got, and a thing*
more precious, | *a kiss of her lips, and loving caresses,* | *asleep by her side on a*
green pillow till daylight.   95

She turned her head and gave a laugh, | *young girl, will you guide me?* | *the*
King of Ireland's daughter at the shieling. | *Young girl, daughter of the king of*
Ireland, | *young girl, will you guide me?*   100

*322   *Cnoc an Àtha Dhuibh*

(trì rainn is amhran)

Òr a' chonaisg, feur mar shìoda;
   mu 'bhun is binn an sruth:
tha craobhan cruinn 'nan geàrd ann
   mu Chnoc an Àtha Dhuibh.   4

On lochan gus an Dìseart
   tha sìth is gann gun tuig;
is buan Allt a' Bhràghad
   fo Chnoc an Àtha Dhuibh.   8

Tha feur tha mar an sìoda
   is lìth a' chonaisg tiugh.
Is sgeadaichte 's is sàibhir
   Cnoc an Àtha Dhuibh.   12

Ceangal

Feur mar an sìoda is lìth a' chonaisg mar òr,
èideadh an rìgh 's e rìomhach 's a thoic 's a stòr,
badain ga dhìon – is sìtheil cnocan an fheòir
eadar an Dìseart bìth 's an lochan 's na h-eòin.   16

322   *Blackford Hill*

(three verses and envoi)

Gold of the whin, grass like silk; I about its foot sweet-voiced is the stream: I there
are trees assembled together as a guard I about Blackford Hill.   4

From the little loch to the Hermitage I there is a peace that can scarcely be
understood; I eternal is the Braid Burn I under Blackford Hill.   8

There is grass that is like silk I and the thickset hue of the whins. I Apparelled and
rich I is Blackford Hill.   12

Envoi

Grass like silk and the hue of the whins like gold; I a king's clothing of finery and
his hoard of riches; I trees in clumps protecting it – peaceful is the grassy little
knowe I between the still-voiced Hermitage and the lochan and its birds.   16

*323 Gile is Deirge nan Caorann

Thà na caorainn geal is bidh na caorainn dearg.
  Tha 'm blas leamh is searbh, 's is searbh an sgàrlaid leinn
mar èibhlean air slatagan is smuain dhiubh mu shneachd,
  agus beachd bìth mu fhalbhan aig na h-eòin a tha 'seinn.   4

Caorainn gheala 's caorainn dhearga, is eatarra bhon ùir
  duilleach cùbhraidh Iuchair, 's 'na dhlùths na h-eòin 's na nid.
Sgàrlaid 's chan ann milis. Tha ar latha 's a dhruim
  bho ghile gu deirge thruime air a' chraoibh chaorainn sin.   8

*324 [Am Bàrd, an Deoch 's am Monadh]

Am b'fheàrr a' phinnt leanna
  na Sliabh Allair fod chois leat?
Am b'fheàrr an juke-box 's a cheòl
  no puirt mhòra nan crotach?   4

323   The White and Red of Rowan Berries

The rowan berries are white and the rowan berries will be red. | Their taste is wersh and bitter, and bitter is their scarlet to us, | like embers on branches with a thought emanating from them about snow, | and a quiet thought about going with the birds that are singing.   4

White rowan berries and scarlet rowan berries, and between them from the earth, | the fragrant leafage of July and in its fastness the birds and the nests. | Scarlet and no wise sweet. Our day and its zenith ridge | are from the whiteness to the redness of the burden on thon rowan tree.   8

324   [The Bard, the Drink and the Hill]

Would you rather the pint of beer, | than feel your foot on Allermuir? | Would you prefer the juke-box's music | or the pibrochs of the curlews?   4

325 [*Verses in* deibhidhe *metre*]

[incomplete drafts]

Test, men, my cheer. It chafes me
eastward here; west I would hurry
to the island Islay, to sing
my song there while gladly guesting.   4

West of long Kintyre it lies,
best of all isles. Trust, then, nowise
my mood here eastward, dawn's pale child;
it is wan, weary and exiled.   8

Gladly I'd seek the clan of Conn,
lads to stake your life upon
my mind is not Chief of Islay there
    set [fief here?] upon any other   12

Still I long to stand, a guest,
in the land with hillsides buttressed,
there in that place of countries king
where race the hare and the roe running.   16

Yet I yearn to see that isle,
with my fee at Fortune's turnstile
brought on my late way out west,
fought out with fate my close contest.   Test.   20

326 *The Sunday Howffs of Morningside*

An' whaur was Moses i the mirk?
Luikan for matches by some quirk.
Bairns' banter. It wad gar a stirk   3
    lauch till it deed,
the Hermitage fornenst the Kirk
    across Braid Road.   6

At hauf past twal the kirk comes oot.
At hauf past twal whatt aye's afoot! –
the bar dure opens. Drouth an' doot   9
    o sin forgether.
Div they cross owre turn an' turn aboot
    frae ane till the ither?   12

It disna chance in ony nation
but oors. Is't reason for elation
or no? I'm no that shair. Equation   15
   tae mak o't daunts me –
across ae road a confrontation
   fit for Dante.   18

But sic a stieve, thrawn confrontation
isna juist ma nearest notion.
I gang an' seek the liveanan potion   21
   no faur awa,
whaur the volunteer dreams o his ration
   oot by the wa.   24

Holy Corner's abune the brae.
Ablow the brae there liggs they three,
the Hermitage, the Merlin (twae)   27
   the Canny Man's;
an' sowls devout an' drouthy hae
   their pick at aince.   30

I Scotland here there was a day
whan they twae things gaed twae an' twae;
the godly, silent, waff an' wae,   33
   the sinfu seichan;
on weekdays yill an' whisky tae,
   on Sunday skeichan.   36

The law o life alane the Law
o Moses' stane this side the wa;
the Guid Buik an' the Carritch (twa).   39
   There arena monie
wha murn thon's passin sweir an' slaw.
   Or are there onie?   42

It's gane, an' better sae, methinks –
the bairn gants owre the Carritch kinks,
his mammie mumbles owre her thanks,   45
   dovers an' dwaums
an' sits wi folded haunds an' thinks
   aboot the Psalms.   48

[The Canny Man's

The Canny Man's, ma wale o aa –
a hunner knocks hing on the wa,
the Illustrated News, that's braw,   51
    frae 1850.
Newcomers staun an' glim an' aa
    an' tak a shuftie.   54

A bleezan fire at time for mittens.
Nae sinkan ship tae flegg the rattons;
nae play-act place – choice, couthy at aince.   57
    I hae been happy
wi the zeebra's heid, the knocks, the kittens
    an' the puppy.   60
        Och aye, 'n' a drappy.

327 *The Lether*

It's somewhaur yit I dae jalouse.
    Tae say sae is nae whim.
"Be bien at ilka bleeze that lowes.
    Pit yere fitt on the lether an' sclimm."   4

"Mairry amang the debs.
    Be deif tae blether, an' timm
yere gardyloo on the plebs.
    Pit yere fitt on the lether an' sclimm."   8

328 *The Twa Capitals*

Here liggs the Athens o the North
atween the Pentlands an' the Forth.
Gin Allermuir can glisk the Firth,   3
    then we can see
future faur a warld o worth
    here yit tae be.   6

It's comean yit, thoch London's sweir
an' drifts Provincial thru the air
northwards owre Embro. Little mair   9
    can London dae
but that an' rob us. Soothward there
    the Muse is blae.   12

For o the speerit spier ye may.
For thocht or merit whatt can they?
Their nest is herriet. Nocht they hae   15
  that isna dootit;
an' London is a yeld quae,
  that's aa aboot it.   18

Hae we the hodden grey o thocht,
or tartan is't o colour wrocht?
Oor leid we hae, oor land; an' ocht   21
  can mak oor ain.
A bairn wha canna coont tae echt
  can see that plain.   24

The Thatcher wifie, wae or brash,
will hae, or wilna, her stramash.
Her mind – an' her it disna fash –   27
  an' aa that's in it,
's atween High Wycombe an' the Wash,
  Dover an' Thanet.   30

The Commons is't? Whan Scots rise spieran
o Scotland's weel an' hoo's she farean,
they sit, some silent an' some fleeran,   33
  till, cornert, presto,
they cry, some girnan an' some rairan
  "Εἰς κοίρανος Ἔδτω!"[1]   36

Awa! – if thon's their secret hymn.
Awa! – it disna suit oor whim.
Oors is the land forgetsna him   39
  wha sang an' saw that
a man's a man – gie wye tae him! –
  an' aa men aa that.   42

Scotland the word itsel they smoor.
They drift Provincial thru the air.
Scotland an' Embro dinna care.   45
  We hae seen waur,
an' think nae ornament tae gair
  lourd Hampthin glaur.   48

                              [Here liggs

[1] "One leader only!"

Here liggs the Athens o the North
an' yet will rise, a warld o worth.
Whatt thoch the Suddroun deaves the earth   51
    at oor expense?
The London rant's a mint o mirth
    tae fowk o sense.   54

329 *The Haary Toon*

Whan licht is gane it dreams alane
    this eastward toon an' oorie, oh,
o ghaists that mand tae muster then.
    At nichtis noon be wary, oh.   4
There's ghaists aroon that mak nae soon.
    I'll swear the mune is bleary, oh,
an' sweir abune tae blinter doon.
    This haary toon is eerie, oh.   8

Canmore agen an' Donald Bane,
    whan men are ben an' cheery, oh,
gang wi grains the wynds alang.
    Bide ben an' dinna steer ye, oh.   12
An' Rizzio bleeds in Haley Ruid –
    waly, the deed camsteerie, oh!
Bide ben in midnight Embro toon.
    This haary toon is eerie, oh.   16

330 *Wundward Bate*

The bow becks an' the stays sough.
    Oor boat gecks an' gaes, thoch
the rudder cleiks the wave's troch
    an' aheid at her cheeks the spray's reuch.   4

A wundward bate an' I'll bate we're there.
    The bowsprit frets a horizon faur
owre the keenan cauld o the sea's rair.
    Scotland's close-hauled on a lee-shore.   8

Frae whaur sea meets lift the waves rinn
    wi a heedless leesure, fleet they soom:
pint on a leeshore, sheet her in
    for tacks asclent tae sea room.   12

331 The Hert's Aye the Pairt Aye ...

The hert's the compass tae the place
  that ye wad gae whan land ye lea.
The bairn is bauld, the auld are wyce.
  The aefauld instinct disna lee.   4

The moraliser wi his tongue
  wad scaud ye? Haud on. Hae yere whim.
The hert's aye leal. Ye've sangs tae sing.
  He that wad haud ye, heedna him.   8

332 Òran Tàlaidh

M'eudail, mo bhalachan, thig an crodh dhachaigh leat
  thig an crodh dhachaigh leat trast air a' mhòintich.
M'eudail, mo bhalachan, thig an crodh dhachaigh leat
  thig an crodh dhachaigh leat trast air a' mhòintich.   4

Thig an crodh dhachaigh leat, thig an crodh dhachaigh leat,
  thig an crodh dhachaigh leat trast air a' mhòintich.
Thig an crodh dhachaigh leat, thig an crodh dhachaigh leat,
  thig an crodh dhachaigh leat trast air a' mhòintich.   8

M'eudail 's mo bhalachan, thig an crodh dhachaigh leat,
  an crodh imeachd agad 'nam baidnein 's tu mòr ast'.
M'eudail 's mo bhalachan, thig an crodh dhachaigh leat,
  an crodh imeachd agad is slat aig ur Mòrachd.   12

[Thig an crodh

332 [Lullaby]

*My wee treasure laddie, the herd will come home with you; | the herd will come
home with you over the moorland. | My wee treasure laddie, the herd will come
home with you; | the herd will come home with you over the moorland.*   4

*The herd will come home with you, herd will come home with you, | the herd
will come home with you over the moorland. | The herd will come home with
you, herd will come home with you, | the herd will come home with you over the
moorland.*   8

*My wee treasure laddie, the herd will come home with you, | the wandering herd
of your pride in their clusters. | My wee treasure laddie, the herd will come home
with you, | your wandering herd, before the staff of Thy Lordship.*   12

Thig an crodh dhachaigh leat, thig an crodh dhachaigh leat,
  thig iad air ais leat air aisridhean ceòthar.
Thig an crodh dhachaigh leat, thig an crodh dhachaigh leat,
  thig iad air ais leat air aisridhean eòlach.   16

An norran beag cadail air sùil mo bhalachain,
  an norran beag cadail air caitheadh don ghlòmainn;
An norran beag cadail air sùil mo bhalachain,
  an norran beag cadail gu latha 's na h-eòin ort.   20

An norran beag cadail, an norran beag cadail,
  an norran beag cadail gu latha 's na h-eòin ort.
An norran beag cadail, an norran beag cadail,
  an norran beag cadail gu faireachadh deònach.   24

333   *The Green Gairs o England*

Here is the ling, and bracken spreids.
  Sooth awa in England there
in gairdens rosiers hing their heids,
  an' green growes the gerss on the gair.   4

Here is canach an' fugg an' scree
  myrtle an' heather bield an' bare;
there the gerss is tae the knee,
  whaur green growes the gerss on the gair.   8

Here the muir maks o space a rowth;
  thonder the hedges evermair
merch i the kintra tae the sooth,
  whaur green grow[e]s the gerss on the gair.   12

*The herd will come home with you, herd will come home with you, | with you
they'll come back on mist-covered hilltracks. | The herd will come home with you,
herd will come home with you, | with you they'll come back on familiar hilltracks.*   16

*A flutter of sleep on my wee laddie's eyes, | a flutter of sleep at the fall of
the gloaming; | a flutter of sleep on my wee laddie's eyes, | a flutter of sleep till
daybreak and birdsong.*   20

*A flutter of sleep, a flutter of sleep, | a flutter of sleep till daybreak and birdsong; |
a flutter of sleep, a flutter of sleep, | a flutter of sleep till you wake up contented.*   24

Land an' lift are wider faur
   than an hunner horizons northward here;
thonder throng meadows evermair,
   whaur green grow[e]s the gerss on the gair.   16

Here it is boondless, sky an' scaurs –
   lanes an' loanins soothward there.
"Haud!" say the hedges. "Pass wha daurs?"
   whaur green growes the gerss on the gair.   20

Here is the wide an' saikless waste,
   merchless. A chessboard's chequered there.
Ane micht swither an' turn aamaist,
   whaur green grow[e]s the gerss on the gair.   24

334 *White Rowan, Red Rowan*
[draft]

There's a flourish on the gean, and the rowans will be white, and the
                                      rowans will be red.
Pure white vaunts the gean; pure white will lie the drifts; white will
                                      the rowans show.
From the days when the birds return, to the days of Summer Song, to
                                  the days when the birds are fled.
The gean can vaunt its white; long days its leaves are green; dark days
                                  they fall and go.
Snowdrops were white, west is the year's night, white is the gean.   5
The rowans they are red; leaves will drift down dead; the cherry is green
The gean flaunts its foam; gold are whin and broom; summer birds return
The rowans will be red, the birds will all be sped, but gold the thickets burn.

The rowans they are white; the rowans will be red; white was the gean.
The rowans they are white; the rowans they are red; the cherry is green.   10

White rowan, red rowan, show our summer between and our sun overhead,
long days unminding when leafless is the gean, snow is white, holly red.
White rowan, red rowan, cherry green, when is our zenith overhead?
Oh, it is between when the rowans are all white and the rowans they are red.

Envoi

Red will be the rowan; holly berries will be red, when the snow is all white.   15
Rowan white to rowan red, with the sun overhead and small clouds that are white.
Gold burns the broom; the whins are burning gold; snowdrops were white.
White foams the gean; green is the rowan; the rowan will be white –
                                    rowan red, rowan white.

335 *Do Charaid Marbh*

(do Chalum Mac Chaluim Mhic Iain)

[draft]

Ris is leis, b'e sin a lios.
An drochaidh, b'e sin a chabhsair.
Cathadh mara, sin a mheas.

E 'na mheite 's e 'na mhaighstir,
air cuantan cogaidh chuir e fios,   5
cùrsa 's còrsa 's struthan meallta.

Ghabh e seachad air a' Chrios,
ghabh [e] seachad air Albainn Nuaidh,
taighean solais, tuath is deas.

Siar is sear, mu dheas 's mu thuath,   10
rèidio is radar is cairt iùil,
U-bàta is E-bàta luath.
Meite, maighstir, Gàidheal gu chùl.

U-bàta, E-bàta,
E-bàta 's i luath;   15
sgiathalan 'nan dàil o fhàir' a-nuas.
U-bàta, E-bàta,
E-bàta air chuairt.
U-bàta 's i clìceach san t-sìorraidheachd chuain.

335 *To a Dead Friend*

(for Malcolm Johnson)

Windward and leeward, these were his garden. | The ship's deck, that was his causie. | Spindrift, that was his fruit.

*He was a mate, he was a teacher, | he made the acquaintance of oceans of war, | 5
course and coast and treacherous currents.*

He sailed past the Equator, | he sailed past Nova Scotia, | lighthouses, north and south.

*Eastward, westward, to north and to south, | radio, radar and compass, | swift   10
U-boat and E-boat, | a mate and a teacher, a Gael every inch.*

*U-boat, E-boat, | an E-boat so swift, | planes around them swooping down from   15
the skyline. | U-boat, E-boat, | an E-boat patrolling, | a cunning U-boat in the ocean vastness.*

A bhom, a ghunna crios no 'thoirpead,   20
las no bras, 's tu sheas an drochaid.

Cha robh do [sgeul ach?] gann,
is moch a sguir do rann
cho dearbh ris a' Chrann.
Is searbh e na th'ann –   25
tha thu marbh san àm.

*336 [Geal]

'S geal canach an t-slèibhe 's is glègheal sneachda nan càrn.
Tha lainnir na lèige de dh'èiteag na h-aibhne san àth.
'S geal anart na brèide is sèideadh a' chathaidh san là.
'S geal, sneachdagheal m'eudail, an tè thais, chamagach, bhàn.   4

337 [The Caller Wind Blows]

The causie's aith for gangin an' smooth the stanes are,
an' Lothian Road the leelang day gang fey wi cairt an' caur,
fowk breinge aheid wi little heed o ithers, hemmed by waas,
fae screich o day til nicht oot o sicht o knowes an' laws –
    but heich stauns the West Kip, the caller wind blows.   5

It's rallyoch on the ridges o Arran an' Kintail,
it's mochy in the winds, scarce ain minds o ling an' fail,
there's traffic an' there's wa's, ye maun pech, there is nae pause,
fowk hauf-rinn wioot a reason an' gleench wi nae cause –
    but heich stauns the West Kip, the caller wind blows.   10

By bomb, machine-gun or torpedo, | weary or alert you guarded the deck.   20
Your story was but short, | early your song stopped, | as sure as Fate. | It is a bitter
thing | that you are dead at this time.   25

336 [White]

White is the mountain bog-cotton and pure white is the snow on the cairns; |
there is the gleam of a jewel off the river pebble in the shallows. | White is the
cloth of the kertch and the blowing of snowdrift by day. | White, snow-white is
my darling, the gentle fair one of thick curls.   4

*338 Innis Sgeul Dòchais

(trì rainn is amhran)

Innis sgeul dòchais dhomh;
  gabh òran toileachais le sèis;
le fiamh a’ ghàire bi fial;
  cuir a’ ghrian air àird an speur.   4

Innis sgeul dòchais dhomh;
  dòirt sonas à copan làn;
solas aobhach gu h-obann las;
  tairg faochadh is feobhas blàth.   8

Lean air còmhradh sèimh mu dhùil;
  bi ri sunnd mar eun an dos;
teud binnis buail gu bras nam chòir;
  innis sgeul dòchais dhomh.   12

Ceangal
Dòirt o do bhilean gach lideadh a choiticheas cluas;
gabh òran a-rithist ’s a-rithist mu shonas buan;
an dòlas seo iomain om chridhe le boch gu suairc;
sgeul dòchais dhomh innis is innis gu beothail, luath. 16

338   *[Tell a Tale of Hope]*
(*three verses and envoi*)

*Tell me a tale of hope; | sing a song of pleasure with chorus; | be generous with
your smile; | send the sun noon-high in the sky.*   4

*Tell me a tale of hope; | pour happiness out of a brimming cup; | light up a sudden
cheerful flame; | offer soothing solace and warm restoring.*   8

*Engage in calm optimistic talk, | be merry like a bird in a bush; | a melodious
chord strike loud around me; | tell me a tale of hope.*   12

Envoi
*Pour from your lips every syllable that coaxes the ear; | sing again and again a
song about lasting cheer; | this grief from my heart with gladness gently shift; | tell
and tell me a tale of hope, alert and swift.*   16

*339 *Fàire [Aig Tobar an Tighearna]*

Bheum a' ghrian slios nam beann,
    corcar, cròdhearg 's fàire ann,
's an sgàile mu dheireadh 'trèigsinn
    rèidhlean ùrlar nan gleann.   4

Làigh mo shùil air Slia' cas,
    's e 'na bhaideal mu thuath.
Dhùisg cearc fhraoich is rinn i guileag
    air Cruach Bhuidhe fada shuas.   8

Aig Tobar an Tighearna dhomh
    's an là a' mosgladh gu mall,
driùchd air fraoch is dealt air roid,
    's càch 'nan clos 's an fhàire ann.   12

Shoilleirich a bheag 's a bheag
    a' chamhanaich air eagan shliabh.
Dùisgibh, is an leus air leathad!
    Suas a' bheatha, suas a' ghrian!   16

339 *Dawn [By the Lord's Well]*

*The sun smote the flank of the hills, | crimson, blood-red in the dawn, | as the last
shadows fled | the meadows on the floor of the glens.*   4

*My eye rested on precipitous Sleea, | looming like a battlement in the north. | A
grouse-hen awoke and let out a squawk | on Yellow Summit way up high.*   8

*I was at the Lord's Well | as the day slowly stirred, | drizzle on the heather and
dew on the bog-myrtle, | and everyone asleep as dawn broke.*   12

*Little by little the morning twilight | grew bright on the notches of hills. | Wake
up, there is light on the slopes! | Hail to life, hail to the sun!*   16

*340 *Do Shomhairle MacGill-eain*

Nuair bhìos an labharag 'na tost
    ri latha fèatha 's clos air Clàraich,
bidh do bhàrdachd, 's i 'na caoir,
    a' toirt bàrr air maothan màbte.   4

Gach beàrn sa Chuilthionn 'na shuain,
    's gach boglach shìos 'na chluain àillidh;
slànadh agus faochadh tàimh
    gach bioraidh bheò a thà nad dhàin-sa.   8

Nuair a chuisteas ri là luin
    an cagaran 's a dhuilleach àlainn,
gabh-sa fois is suaimhneas smaoin,
    's an sin cluinneadh gaoth a' Bhràigh' thu.   12

341 *The Hermitage o Braid*
(three verses and envoi)

There is scarce a tree that shogs;
    aa is lown an aa is staid;
there are gloomy heidlang crags
    i the Hermitage o Braid.   4

340   [*For Sorley MacLean*]

When the prattling wood turns silent | on a peaceful day, and a calm descends on the Clarach, | your poetry, like a blazing flame, | will bring a maimed bud to flower.   4

Every breach in the Cuillin happed in sleep, | and, below, each swamp a bright verdant pasture; | a healing and a restful respite | for every white-hot sting found in your poems.   8

When on a day of prattling they turn to silence, | the dear whispering wood and its lovely foliage, | find quiet rest and tranquillity of thought, | and then let the Braes wind hear you.   12

What Culdee fasted there,
   schuled by Ee while ermies gaed?
Spier o Dysart, gif ye care.
   Tis a Hermitage lik Braid.   8

Mirk o crags an' lown air
   here's a hame that silence made;
the Braid Burn disna row there;
   quate is the Hermitage o Braid.   12

Envoi

It kens nae herm the hermitage there o Braid;
eternal its term, whilst ermies were gethered an' gaed.
Derk shaddas cled braes an' the days scarce kythe there for shade.
The Culdees are gane an' alane rinns the burn whaur they prayed. 16

*342 An Lonan Iuchair

An cluinn thu feochan an fheòir 's an t-achadh fon ghrèin?
An cluinn thu an smeòrach ri 'ceòl mear maidne air gèig?
Dè dhuinn latha sòlaimteachd reòta 's an latha gun eun
's an t-Iuchar is Ògmhìos nan ròs a' leantainn a' Chèit?   4

342 [*The July Prattler*]
Do you hear the breath of wind in the grass as the sun warms the field? | Do you hear the thrush at its bright morning song on a branch? | What do we care for a day of frozen solemnity devoid of birds, | when July and June of the roses follow from May?   4

*343 *Ballade*

Dictes moy ou, n'en quel pays
est Flora la belle Rommaine ...
mais ou sont les neiges d'antan?

François Villon (rugadh 1431)

Innis dhòmhsa no cò 'n tìr
   am bheil Deirdre mhìn. Bheil fhios?
Chaidh i às an t-saoghal a-mach.
   Càit an deach i? Cà bheil i?   4
Na bàird a bh'ann – feith agus èist –
   às am beul cha chluinnear smid.
Big a th'aig a' Bhàs fo smachd.
   Ach cà bheil sneachd an uiridh nis?   8

Ùistean dealanaich MacDhiarmaid còir,
   filidh a bhà seachd mòr seach mi,
a-rithis chan fhaigh neach an còrr
   'chainnt a bheòil is e fo lic.   12
Soutar agus Edwin Muir,
   an ealain rinn den t-saoghal lios.
Cà bheil iad? Iarraibh an leac.
   Ach cà bheil sneachd an uiridh nis?   16

Sidney Mac a' Ghobhainn bàn,
   cha chluinn thu 'ghàire blàth a-nis.
Ged a shirte siar is sear,
   cha lorgar e le fear sam bith.   20

343 [*Ballade*]

Tell me in what land | is sweet Deirdre. Is it known? | She has gone from the world. | Where did she go? Where is she? | The poets of yesteryear – stop and listen – | from their mouths not a sound is heard. | All chirping is under Death's command. | Ah, where now is last year's snow?   4   8

Good Hugh MacDiarmid the thunderbolt, | a poet ten times greater than I, | never again will one hear | speech from his mouth, now that he lies in the grave. | Soutar and Edwin Muir, | their art made a garden of our world. | Where are they? Ask the gravestone. | Ah, where now is last year's snow?   12   16

Fair Sydney Smith, | you will not hear his warm laugh now. | Though he should be sought east and west, | he will be found by none at all. | 20

Dh'oidhche 's a là chan fhaicear e,
  ged a chìte e gu tric.
Den Mhìle Rìoghail bhiodh a thlachd.
  Ach cà bheil sneachd an uiridh nis?   24

Rìghrean, ridirean suaithneis, clèir,
  feallsanaich gheur; am math 's am mith,
ìslean 'nan ginealaich, beairteach 's bochd
  dh'fhalaich an sloc a tha fon lic.   28
Curaidhean, gealtairean, balbhain, bàird,
  ìosal is àrd cha d'fhuair iochd.
Chaidh iad ris a' Bhàs a ghleac.
  Ach cà bheil sneachd an uiridh nis?   32

Envoi (Ceangal)
Bhà iad iomraiteach 'nan là.
  Tha iomradh orra 's cliù a-nis.
Cà bheil iad? No dè do bheachd?
  Ach cà bheil sneachd an uiridh nis?   36

344 [*Gile*]

Cathadh làir, cathadh mara
  gile chneas na mnatha sin;
èiteag aibhne, èiteag mhara,
  sneachd air gèig a h-amhach ris.   4

*Night or day, he'll not be seen, | though he was once a common sight. | He would
draw pleasure from the Royal Mile. | Ah, where now is last year's snow?*   24

*Kings, knights of leisure, clerics, | sharp-witted philosophers; the gentry and the
peasantry, | generations of common folk, the rich and the poor, | the pit under
the tombstone has hidden them all. | Heroes, cowards, mutes, poets, | lowly or*   28
*powerful, not one was spared. | They went to wrestle with Death. | Ah, where now
is last year's snow?*   32

Envoi
*They were renowned in their time. | Their fame and repute survive today. | Where
are they? What do you think? | Ah, where now is last year's snow?*   36

344 [*Whiteness*]
*Ground-drift, spindrift, | the whiteness of that woman's skin; | river-pebble,
sea-pebble, | snowy branch her throat exposed.*   4

345 [Aubade 2]

There is dew on the roofs of the cars
and the flush of day in the east.
Wake and be stirring, dear.
No dream is the day and its haste.   4

*346 Ròsan an Lethbhaile

[ath-dhèanamh air òran le Eòghan MacColla, Bàrd Loch Fìne]

Air fail ithil ò ro, ho-rò, cuim an ceilinn e?
Air fail ithil ò ro, ho-rò, cuim an ceilinn e?
Gu bheil mo shaogh'l 'na bhruadar. Is dual dhomh bhith deireasach,
's mo ghràdh air bheagan dòchais air Ròsan an Lethbhaile.   4

Air fail ithil ò ro, Ròsan an Lethbhaile,
Air fail ithil ò ro, Ròsan an Lethbhaile.
Gu bheil mo shaogh'l 'na bhruadar. Is dual dhomh bhith deireasach,
's mo ghràdh air bheagan dòchais air Ròsan an Lethbhaile.   8

Chan e cruas na gaoithe an-raoir chùm nam chaithris mi,
is idir chan e fuachd chuir o ghluasad le fadal mi.
Gu bheil ceann fàth mo smuairein 's mo smuaintean 'son fada nis
an riochd caileige tha bòidheach tha 'n Còmh'l nan slios badanach.   12

346 [Rosie of Half-town]
[a reworking of a song by Evan MacColl, the Loch Fyne Bard]
Air fal ihil o ro, horo, why should I hide it? | Air fal ihil o ro, horo, why should I hide it? | I'm living in a dream, and fated to be hurt | since there is little cause for hope in my love for Rosie of Half-town.   4

Air fal ihil o ro, horo, Rosie of Half-town, | Air fal ihil o ro, horo, Rosie of Half-town, | I'm living in a dream, and fated to be hurt | since there is little cause for hope in my love for Rosie of Half-town.   8

It's not the harshness of the wind that kept me awake last night, | and neither was it the cold that forced weary inaction on me. | The root cause of my dejection and my pensiveness for a long time now | is in the shape of a bonnie girl in Cowal of the thicketed slopes.   12

Fhir thàinig thar Loch Fìne, nach inns thu dhomh, guidheam ort,
am faca tu 'n tè bhòidheach a leòn thun a' chridhe mi?
Am faca tu 'n tè uasal, tè uallach, tè lurach i?
Am faca tu mo ghràdh-sa, 's gur bàs dhomh mur faigh mi i.   16

Tha cuailean tha bòidheach air Ròsan an Lethbhaile.
Tha gruaidhean mar na ròsan air Ròsan an Lethbhaile.
Thà i uasal, còir agus thà i bòidheach, ceanalta.
Ghluaisinn leath' gun stòras. 'S i Ròsan an Lethbhaile.   20

Is coibhneil, ciùin do dhòighean, Ròsan an Lethbhaile.
Is daoimean agus òr thu, Ròsan an Lethbhaile.
Is binne leam do chòmhradh na 'n smeòrach 's i ri ceileireachd.
Is gile thu na 'n neòinean, a Ròsain an Lethbhaile.   24

Mo dhùrachd rid bheò dhuit, Ròsain an Lethbhaile.
Dhùraiginn do phòsadh, a Ròsain an Lethbhaile.
Tha mi sunndach, beòdha an-còmhnaidh 's mi gun deireas orm,
is dùil agam ri pògan o Ròsan an Lethbhaile.   28

Is gnàth mi 'coimhead Chòmhail, Ròsain an Lethbhaile
on tha thu ann a chòmhnaidh, a Ròsain an Lethbhaile.
Tha bàt' agam ga seòladh 's cha mhòr an loch seo eadarainn,
's gun dàil bidh mi 's tu còmhla, Ròsain an Lethbhaile.   32

Man who has crossed Loch Fyne, won't you tell me, I pray you, | did you see the bonnie woman who has cut me to the heart? | Did you see the noble woman, the proud one, the lovely one? | Did you see my own darling? – I will die if I cannot find her.   16

Rosie of Half-town has curls so bonnie, | Rosie of Half-town has rose-flushed cheeks, | she is noble and virtuous, bonnie and good-natured. | I'd go with her penniless, Rosie of Half-town.   20

Your manner is kind and gentle, Rosie of Half-town, | you are diamond and you are gold, Rosie of Half-town, | sweeter to me is your talk than the thrush's warbling chorus. | You are whiter than the daisy, Rosie of Half-town.   24

My goodwill for life to you, Rosie of Half-town, | my wish would be to wed you, Rosie of Half-town. | I'm ebullient and cheerful always, and content | when expecting kisses from Rosie of Half-town.   28

I gaze often towards Cowal, Rosie of Half-town | since it's there that you dwell, Rosie of Half-town. | I've a boat for the sailing, and this loch is not wide between us, | and without delay you and I will be together, Rosie of Half-town.   32

*347 *Mo Robairneach Gaolach*
(òran tàthaidh)

Hò nan tigeadh mo Robairneach gaolach,
bìrlinn aig' agus ceatharnaich dhaoine;
le bhàta 's le sgioba 's iad sgiobalta aotrom;
b'aighearach mise nan tilleadh a' ghaoth e.   4

Tha do bhìrlinn a' tighinn mun iomas seo 'n-dràsta,
timcheall an rubh' agus buidheann mo ghràidh innt'.
'S tu leagadh a cùrsa air dùthaich nan àrdbheann;
's tu b'urrainn a stiùireadh air cùl nan tonn àrda.   8

Mo chruit is mo chlàrsach, mo dhàn is mo dhuan thu;
m'fhaidhrean is m'fhaidhir is m'aighear is m'uaill thu
led sgiath 's led chlaidheamh is dag air do chruachainn;
's tu sheatadh, 's tu leumadh, 's tu cheumadh, 's tu ghluaiseadh. 12

'S ann tha mo Robairneach soideanach, suairce,
leannan tè maisich cho math 's a tha gluasad,
aotrom, aigeannach, aighearach, uallach;
dh'òlainnsa sgailc air an spailp de dhuin' uasal.   16

347   [My Dear Bonnie Laddie]
(a conflated song)

Ho were my dear bonnie laddie to come, | bringing a galley and some champion men; | with his boat and his crew, and they smart and agile; | I would be glad were the wind to return him.   4

Your galley approaches these parts [?] at this moment, | rounding the point with the company I love. | It's you'd set her course to the land of the high hills; | it's you who could steer her behind the high billows.   8

You're my lute and my harp, my song and my poem; | my fairgift, my fairing, my bliss and my pride, | with your shield and your sword, at your haunches a pistol, | you would set, you would leap, you would step and you'd swagger. 12

My bonnie man's sturdy and jovial and gentle, | a fair woman's lover as good as they come, | light, spirited, cheerful and boisterous; | a long draught I'd quaff to that dashing young noble.   16

348 *Is Trom Mi 'Siubhal Slèibhe*

Is trom mi 'siubhal slèibhe
airm mo mhic na mo làimh 's a sgiath nam làimh eile
Is trom mi 'siubhal slèibhe.   3

Is sgìos leam a' ghrian 's i 'g èirigh
airm mo mhic na mo làimh 's a sgiath nam làimh eile
Is sgìos leam a' ghrian 's i 'g èirigh   6

Is bàs dhà, a Rìgh na Fèinne ...   7

Leagadh am faillean bheuman ...   10

Dh'fhàg mi fo lic nam dhèidh e ...   13

Mi 'g amharc is e cha lèir dhomh ...   16

An tuisleadh-s' air sliabh rèisg dhomh ...   19

Is crom mi 'siubhal slèibhe ...   22

348 *[With Heavy Heart I Walk the Moorland]*

*With heavy heart I walk the moorland, | my son's weapons in one hand and his
shield in the other, | With heavy heart I walk the moorland.*   3

*Wearisome to me the sun and its rising, | my son's weapons in one hand and his
shield in the other, | Wearisome to me the sun and its rising.*   6

Death has claimed him, O King of the Fianna ...   7

The fierce-smiting sapling has now been felled ...   10

I left him behind me under a gravestone ...   13

Though far I should look, it's not him I'll see ...   16

My step is stumbling, through grassy moorland ...   19

I am stooped as I walk the moorland ...   22

*349 A Mhnathan a' Bhaile Seo

A mhnathan a' bhaile seo, bhaile seo, bhaile seo,
  a mhnathan a' bhaile seo, 's mithich dhuibh èirigh.
Dh'èirich mi mochthrath 's dhìrich mi 'n cnocan,
  is sheinn mi am port dhuibh gu brosnachadh èirigh.
  A mhnathan a' bhaile seo, 's mithich dhuibh èirigh.   5

Dh'èirich mi mochthrath 's dhìrich mi 'n cnocan,
  is sheirm mi am port dhuibh gu brosnachadh èirigh.
Tha deireadh na Dùbhlachd is toiseach Bliadhn' Ùir' againn.
  'S moch rinn mi dùsgadh is sùrd orm èirigh.
  A mhnathan a' bhaile seo, 's mithich dhuibh èirigh.   10

Tha Oidhche na Callainn 's a' bhliadhn' air dol tharainn.
  A mhnathan a' bhaile seo, 's mithich dhuibh èirigh.

Seo toiseach na bliadhna is dosan gan riaghladh,
  is port feadain cianail, 's gaoth dhian ga shèideadh.
A mhnathan a' bhaile seo, bhaile seo, bhaile seo,   15
  a mhnathan a' bhaile seo, 's mithich dhuibh èirigh.
  A mhnathan a' bhaile seo, 's mithich dhuibh èirigh.

349 [*Women of This Township*]

*Women of this township, this township, this township, | women of this township,
it's time you were rising. | Early I rose and ascended the hill, | and struck up my
tune to incite you to rise. | Women of this township, it's time you were rising.*   5

*Early I rose and ascended the hill, | and struck up my tune to incite you to rise. |
The end of December and a New Year are on us. | Early I woke and was eager to
rise. | Women of this township, it's time you were rising.*   10

*Hogmanay night and the year have gone past us. | Women of this township, it's
time you were rising.*

*It's the start of the year, there's a tuning of drones | and a chanter's sad air blown
by a vigorous wind. | Women of this township, this township, this township, |*   15
*women of this township, it's time you were rising. | Women of this township, it's
time you were rising.*

*350 *Marbhrann dom Mhàthair*

B'fhada i o Earra-Ghàidheal
  nuair a rinn am bàs a tathaich;
b'fhad' o 'càirdean i 's o 'daoine
  nuair a chaochail i air aineol.   4
Spiorad beò an colainn chràitich,
  bana-Ghàidheal, bana-Cheathrach,
b'fhad' o Ìle bhà Catrìona
  's o Loch Fìne. B'fhada, b'fhada.   8

'S fad a mhaireas beàrn nam chridhe,
  's bean na misniche 'na laighe.
O nach fhaic mi rìst a h-aghaidh,
  bhà i laghach. Sìth da h-anam.   12

351 *Somebody –*
The Beginnin o an Auld Sang

Hey, hey, for somebody,
ho, ho, for somebody,
I wad waak a winter nicht
for a sicht o somebody.   4

Gif somebody wad come again,
gif somebody wad mand the main,
and the auld Stewarts back again!
I hain ma hert for somebody.   8

[Gif somebody

350 [*Elegy on My Mother*]

Far she was from Argyll | when death came to call on her; | far from her family and from her people, | when she died in alien country. | A living spirit in a   4 pain-wracked body, | a Highland woman, a Kerry woman. | Far from Islay was Catriona | and from Loch Fyne. Far, far.   8

Long will there remain a void in my heart, | now that the brave woman lies at rest. | As I will not see her face again, | she was kindly. Peace to her soul.   12

Gif somebody wad board his craft,
gif he wad come wi wind frae aft,
I wad dance is I war daft
   and aft I'd beck tae somebody.   12

Gif somebody wad raise the coast
we'd hae the something we hae lost.
Tae simmer wad turn winter frost,
   gif tae us crossed owre somebody.   16

Like bird on gairden beuch, I'll sing,
a gowd sun gild the heich o ling,
and swords frae belts will ready hing,
   bring they but news frae somebody.   20

Breezes, blaw the air frae aft,
speed him tae us, winds that waft.
Ootowre the sea ma een gang aft
   for a kindly lift for somebody.   24

Oh, gif France wad speed the keel,
the wind wad dance aboot her heel;
and aince he sees the land that's leal,
   weel I'se welcome somebody.   28

Mony a day I wes in gloom
haudden by Whigs ablow their thoom,
but yet in merriment I'll soom
   somewhere wi ma somebody.   32

Gif he but come, the sun will sclimm;
aa Scotland's his, her aa tae timm.
Throne and croon and coort for him –
   somethin' for ma somebody.   36

Hielandmen and Lawlandmen
will come tae cast the German doon.
'Twad e'en be sicht tae een are blin –
   he's nae be lown, oor somebody.   40

Law will ligg the Whig sae bland,
that gied a foreign king the land;
and London town will kiss the haund
   some day o ma somebody.   44

Wife and man, we're aa wi him.
Scotland's day the east will sclimm,
owre the sea if he but come.
    Someane is ma somebody. 48

Gif somebody the king sould be,
I wad dance the feet aff me.
We socht a gift that nane could gie.
    Peace there will be wi somebody. 52

*352   *Cuideigin*

(òran Gallda is cruth ùr Gàidhlig air a chur air)

Haoi, haoi, do chuideigin,
hò, hò, do chuideigin,
Shiùbhlainn oidhche gheamhraidh fhad'
ach am faicinn cuideigin. 4

Nan tigeadh cuideigin air sàil',
nan tilleadh e o fhad' o làimh,
's na Stiùbhartaich air ais mar bhà,
    dh'fhàiltichinn roimh chuideigin. 8

Nan tigeadh cuideigin gu tràigh
is clis a rachainnsa 'na dhàil.
Ged bhitheadh neimh sa chopan làn
    dh'òlainn slàinte chuideigin. 12

[Thig e

352   [*Somebody*]
(*a Lowland song given a new Gaelic form*)

Hey, hey for somebody, | ho, ho, for somebody, | I would walk a long winter
night | that I might catch sight of somebody. 4

If somebody would come by sea, | if he returned from far away, | and the Stewarts
were back as formerly, | I would welcome somebody. 8

If somebody would come to shore, | to meet him I would briskly go. | Though with
poison the cup should flow, | I'd drink the health of somebody. 12

Thig e òirnne, thig an là,
air luing mhòir is gaoth mu 'sàil.
Bidh 'n geamhradh fuar 'na shamhradh blàth,
    an là a thilleas cuideigin.   16

Bhà mi dubhach iomadh là
fo chuing Chuigse 'dol o stàth.
Bidh mi subhach beò gu bràth
    an àiteigin le cuideigin.   20

Nan robh cuideigin 'na rìgh,
dhannsainn fhèin na casan dìom.
Bha guidh' againn a bhà gar dìth
    's bidh sìth againn le cuideigin.   24

Thig na Gàidheil, thig na Goill
a leagail Ghearmailtich lem foill.
B'e 'm fradharc air ais do shùilean doill,
    is cha bhi moill' air cuideigin.   28

*353   Dh'Fhalbh Mo Leannan Fhèin

(mo dhòigh fhèin air òran eòlach)

Dh'fhalbh mo leannan fhèin.
    Dh'fhalbh mo chèile lurach.
Misneach mhath 'na dèidh;
    dhomhsa b'fheudar fuireach.
    Dh'fhalbh mo leannan fhèin.   5

He will come on us, come the day, | *on a great ship, wind at her heel.* | *Cold winter will turn to summer warmth,* | *the day that somebody returns.*   16

I was in gloom many a day, | *aimless under Whigs' hard sway.* | *For ever I'll be alive and gay* | *somewhere with somebody.*   20

If somebody were the king | *I would dance the feet off me.* | *A prayer we had that needed granting,* | *and we'll win peace with somebody.*   24

The Gaels will come and Lowlanders, | *to smite down German treachery.* | *It were sight restored to eyes gone blind,* | *and somebody will not delay.*   28

353   [My Love has Gone Away]

(my own version of a well-known song)

My love has gone away; | *gone my lovely spouse;* | *good cheer follow her;* | *for me there was only waiting.* | *My love has gone away.*   5

Dh'fhalbh i bhuam an cèin;
   chan eil feum san tuireadh.
Thog i oirre 'n-dè:
   B'fhaid an-dè na 'n-uiridh.
    Dh'fhalbh mo leannan fhèin.   10

Osna 's fada thèid;
   faide na 'n èigh gun cluinnear;
osnaich na mo bheul;
   's fad' an èigh nach ruig i.
    Dh'fhalbh mo leannan fhèin.   15

Mi air mullach slèibh,
   's mi leam fhèin 's mi cruiteach,
sgìth gu grian o ghrèin,
   's chan eil èis air mulad.
    Dh'fhalbh mo leannan fhèin.   20

Sgìth ri gaoith 's ri neul,
   sgìth ri grèin 's ri turadh:
cà bheil i a-rèist?
   'S fhìor dhomh sèis na luinneig –
    Dh'fhalbh mo leannan fhèin.   25

Misneach mhath 'na dèidh –
   bheir mi ceum le bruthach.
Tillidh i o chèin:
   's ann is fheudar fuireach.
Dh'fhalbh mo leannan fhèin.   30
Dh'fhalbh mo chèile lurach.
Misneach mhath 'na dèidh;
dhomhsa b'fheudar fuireach.
    Dh'fhalbh mo leannan fhèin.

She left me to go far; | *there's no use in lamenting;* | *she set off yesterday;* | *longer that day than last year.* | *My love has gone away.*   10

It's far a sigh will go; | *further than a shout is it heard;* | *sighing in my breast;* | *it's a far shout that won't reach her.* | *My love has gone away.*   15

I'm up on a hill summit, | *solitary and crooked,* | *tired from sun to sun,* | *there's no respite from sorrow.* | *My love has gone away.*   20

Weary by wind and cloud, | *weary by sun and dry weather:* | *where then can she be?* | *How true the song's refrain –* | *My love has gone away.*   25

Good cheer follow her – | *I'll head down the brae.* | *She'll return from far away;* | *there's nothing to it but waiting.* | *My love has gone away;* | *gone my lovely spouse;* | 30 *good cheer follow her;* | *for me there was only waiting.* | *My love has gone away.*

*354 Nìonag a' Chùil Duinn, Nach Fhan Thu?

(seann òran air 'ath-nuadhachadh)

Nìonag a' chùil duinn, nach fhan thu?
Fhios as tìr gur tu mo leannan.
Nìonag a' chùil duinn, nach fhan thu?

Thà mi cho deònach air do phògadh
　's thà na laoigh òg' air deòl a' bhainne.　　　　　5

Nuair a dhìreas mi a' ghuala,
　bidh mo ghruagach tigh'nn fom aire.

Nuair a theàrnas mi an gleannan,
　bidh mo leannan dhomh nas fhaisge.

Gach aon cheum a bheir mi 'mhòintich,　　　　　10
　bidh do phògan rium a' fantail.

Nuair a ghoireas eòin a' Chèitein,
　bidh fonn do bheulain ann an caithream.

354　[Girl of the Lovely Brown Hair, Won't You Stay?]
(an old song revamped)

Girl of the lovely brown hair, won't you stay? | It's no secret here that you're my lover. | Girl of the lovely brown hair, won't you stay?

I'm as hungry for your kisses | as young calves are for suckling.　　　　　5

When I climb the mountain's shoulder, | into my thoughts comes my lassie.

When I go down the little glen, | I sense my lover ever closer.

Each step I take across the moors, | your kisses are waiting for me.　　　　　10

When the birds of May cry out, | the tune of your pretty mouth is in their happy din.

*355 Cruinneag na Buaile
(Òran do Nic Fhraing an Gleann Comhann)
[ath-dhèanamh air seann òran]

O, chruinneag, è, chruinneag,
  ò, chruinneag na buaile;
ò, chruinneag mo chridhe,
  leat a ruithinn am fuadan.   4

Gur ann thall anns a' Chàrnach,
  an gleann àrd nan sruth fuara,
thà 'n rìbhinn as bòidhche
  dh'fhàg fo leòn gu Là Luain mi.   8

Tha thu cumadail, fìnealt',
  's tu cho dìreach ri luachair,
o do mhullach gud shàiltean,
  gun chron, gun fhàilteam ri 'luaidh ort.   12

'S ann a ruithinn don Fhraing
  le Nic Fhraing a' chùil dualaich.
'S tu nach bitheadh fo mhìghean
  's ceòl na fìdhle nad chluasan.   16

['S tu nach

355 [The Lass of the Cattlefold
(A Song to Rankin's Daughter in Glencoe)]
[a reworking of an old song]

Oh, lassie, eh, lassie, | Oh lass of the cattlefold, | Oh lass of my heart, | With you
I'd run away in hiding.   4

Way over in Càrnach, | in the high glen of cold streams, | lives the bonniest of
maidens | who's left me wounded till Doomsday.   8

You are elegant and shapely, | and as straight as the rushes, | from your top to
your heels | no fault or blemish to mention.   12

I'd run off to France | with the lovely-haired lass Rankin. | You would not be
downhearted | at the sound of the fiddle.   16

'S tu nach bitheadh fo mhìghean
   's ceòl na fidhle nad chluasan.
Bheirinn ceòl dhuit is èibhneas;
   bheirinn fìon dhuit an cuachan.   20

Bheirinn èibhneas dom chruinneig,
   bheirinn luinneagan 's duain dhi.

Bheirinn treiseag air fasgadh,
   bheirinn tacan air fuaradh,   24
gus nach bitheadh fios aca
   is sinn fada air fuadan.

356 *Musa Caledoniae*
The Caledonian Muse
[draft]

The muse that gaes on rallyoch ridges
– fords o burns her journey stages –
that greets the licht by muirland edges,
that bields by nicht on scaurnoch ledges,
she's nivar thrang wi sangs on pages.   5
In coorts o kings she wan her wages,
gowd in the haas whaur noo there lodges
forgetfulness, sae memory rages.
Great herp and crowd mang lords and lieges.
She's deep, as deep as nae man gauges;   10
she'll thriep sae ilkane glisks and fidges;
she sings frae scaurs o peers and pages,
o Scone's, Dumferline's, Embro's ages,
o coonselors and saints and sages.
See but her een! The stievest budges.   15
In wind and rain the screes she trudges.
Hear but her voice! It nivar ages.

*You would not be downhearted | at the sound of the fiddle. | I'd give you music
and pleasure; | wine I'd pour for you in goblets.*   20

I would give my lass pleasure, | songs I'd give her and ballads.

For a while I'd sail leeward, | for a time I'd sail windward, | so that they could not   24
find us | while we were far away eloping.

The ling, bogmyrtle, birk her badges,
heidlang corrie depths she gauges.
That he has heard her wha alleges   20
what bard wha laich in glennans lodges?
Her singing's nane o the drone o gudges,
nor scaldachan o birds in cages.
She'll nae abide the mant o drudges.
She disna haunt green loanin edges,   25
whaur rivers rinn mang sauchs and sedges.

She is the Ane that's mair nor Nine.
Wha steeks his ear tae her maun tine
hert and tongue an hairns; syne
be exiled frae the sets ingyne.   30
Gif ye'd be leal and her wad hear,
hear but the wind frae Allermuir
or from Schiehallion, and the air
and words will reach ye, sae, for shair,
ye will be hers for evermair,   35
and verse and melody will gar
ye sing like the mavis on the gair.

357 [*Dùrachdan Nollaige, 1982?*]

Nuair a thig oirbh an Nollaig
    guma sona a bhìos sibh,
agus rè na Bliadhn' Ùire
    mòran sunnd is toil inntinn.   4

*When Christmas comes on you | may you be happy, | and through the New Year |
much joy and contentment.*   4

411

POEMS 1983

*358 *Dùrd a' Ghlinne*

Fonn ciùil bu bhinne dùrd a' ghlinne,
  e dùint' an grinneas chraobh;
duilleach 's feur is guth nan eun,
  là buidhe grèine caomh.   4

*359 *[Am Bàta Dubh]*
(seann òran air a chur ris)

Chì mi bàta steach sa chaolas
ceathrar ga h-iomram 's fear a' taomadh.
  Hò rò na haoi bhill ò.

Ceathrar ga h-iomram 's fear a' taomadh,
bean 'na toiseach a' sìor chaoineadh.   5
  Hò rò na haoi bhill ò.

Bean 'na toiseach a' sìor chaoineadh,
bean 'na deireadh a' sìor ghlaodhaich,

358 [The Hum of the Glen]
The sweetest music is the hum of the glen, | enclosed in an elegance of trees; |
foliage and grass and the voice of the birds, | on a gentle golden sunny day.   4

359 [The Black Ship]
(an old song expanded)
I see a boat inside the straits, | four at the rowing and one man baling, | ho ro na
hoovi lio.
Four at the rowing and one man baling, | a woman at the prow ever wailing, | ho   5
ro na hoovi lio.
A woman at the prow ever wailing, | a woman at the stern ever shouting, |

beum air stiùir is sùrd air gaoir aic',
is i crom fo throm na gaoithe,   10
falt a cinn a' falbh le gaoith aic',
gach aon atach 's gach aon ghlaodh aic',
èigh is gul is guth air faobhar.
Fliuch a h-èideadh, reubte h-aodach,
deòir le 'gruaidh 's le fuachd a h-aodainn.   15
Dìosgan ràmh is sgreuchail fhaoileag,
dìcheall làmh san iomram daonnan.
Bàta dubh ga cur tron chaolas
fad' a-mach o chladach fhaochag,
àrd a-mach o chlachan maoraich,   20
o mhol, o chreig, o sgeir, o mhaoil i,
fad' o thràigh, 's o bhàgh 's o fhraoch i,
fad' o thiùrr, o ùir 's o raointean,
fad' o shlèibhtean, feur is craobhan,
's an caol fosgailte 'na raon di.   25
Buillean diana liaghan caola,
iomram gun fhiaradh, gun aomadh.
Bàrr nan tonn mar lomain chaorach
suas ri guaillean 's air gach taobh dhi,
sèideadh fuar air uachdar caolais,   30
's i 'triall gu fasgadh 's caladh 's caomhnadh.
C'às a tha a' chuideachd fhaontra
a tha cuidhteas cuid is daoine?
C'às a thugadh leò, an saoil sibh,
an t-iomram teann an aghaidh gaoithe,   35
a' farpais ann ri dùilean baoghail?

[An do chuir

beating the rudder with vigorous cries, | stooping under the force of the wind, | the hair of her head wild in the wind, | she gives every order and every shout, | calling and weeping, voice close to breaking. | Soaked her clothing, torn her garments, | tears down her cheeks and down her cold face. | The creaking of oars and the shrieking of seagulls, | hands constant in utmost exertion of rowing. | A black boat being steered through the channel, | far out from winkle seashore, | way out from shellfish rocks, | from shingle, crag, skerry or mull, | far from beach, | from bay, from heather, | far from tangle, soil and fields, | far from mountains, grass and trees, | the open kyle her plain to travel. | The powerful strokes of slender oarblades, | no straying or veering in the rowing. | The crest of the waves like the fleece of sheep | up to her shoulders and on every side of her, | a cold wind blowing on the channel's surface, | as she heads for shelter and haven and safety. | Where are they from, this vagrant company | so bereft of wealth and men? | From where, do you think, have they engaged | in this strenuous rowing against the wind, | pitted against the perilous elements? |

413

An do chuir iad Sruth na Maoile
a dhol an caraibh Arainn gaothair
o Dhiùra ciar nam fiadh 's nam fraochbheann?
An do theich o chreich 's o fhaobhar,
o thughadh 'na lasair 's falachd aosta?
Am fuigheal aisith 's chlaidheamh caol iad?
An ann de Chloinn Dòmhnaill an fhraoich iad,
de Chloinn Nèill no 'threubh 'ic Mhaoilein,
an ann on Roinn de Chloinn Mhic Aoidh iad?
Am fàiltich càirdean 's dàimh a-chaoidh iad?
Dh'fhaighnichdinn diubh sin, nam faodainn,
aig iomram 's gul is guth na gaoir ac';
a' ghaoth 'na cuip 's a' mhuir 'na baoibh ac',
caoineadh 's glaodhaich, ràmhan 's taoman,
madainn sgreunach mach sa chaolas,
a' sealltainn dhòmhs' o sgòrr an aonaich
bàta dubh is cumha 's caoidh innt',
ceathrar ga h-iomram 's fear a' taomadh.

40

45

50

*360 Mìos a' Ghearrain

Is dian an latha railleach 's a' ghaoth 'na sùist,
ag iarraidh ar lathadh on earadheas aognaidh, dhùr.
Is fiar iad na frasan gan sgapadh o aonach 's sgùrr.
Liath air gach dath. Chaidh guth thairis air faochadh dhùinn.

4

Did they weather the Run of the Moyle | going past the coast of windswept Arran | from dusky Jura of the heather-hills and deer? | Have they fled from plundering raid and swordblade, | from thatch set alight and from ancient feud? | Are they remnants of slender sword and warring? | Are they from the house of Clan Donald of the heather, | from the clan of MacNeil or the sept of MacMillan, | are they from the land of the clan of Mackay? | Will friends and relations ever give them welcome? | All this I would ask them if it were in my power, | as they row to the sound of weeping and crying; | the wind like a whip and the sea as a witch to them, | wailing and shouting, oarwork and splashes, | a scowry morning out in the channel, | as I observe from the upland summit | a black boat loud with lament and mourning, | four at the rowing and one man baling.

40

45

50

360 [The Month of February]

The day is ferocious and stormy with a flailing wind | seeking to numb us from the ghastly grim south-east. | Blown askance are the showers that scatter from upland and scaur. | All colour is washed grey; our hope of respite is gone.

4

Is fiadhaich an latha, is lasan na gaoithe dùisgt'
ag iarraidh gach fasgaidh 's a' crathadh nan craobhan rùisgt',
a' sianail feadh cathadh geur mara 's ri aodann stùc,
a' siabadh sneachda 's a' dalladh am faobhar shùl.   8

Is cianail an caithream tha 'm faram o ghaoith gun tùr,
dianshèideadh callain a' casadh o chraos nan dùil;
is tiamhaidh an tabhann don chlaistneachd, 's gach aon an cùil
'na ghiall aig a' Ghearran, 's an t-adhar 'na bhaoibh 's 'na bhrùid.   12

B'e mo mhiann a bhith tamall taobh aibhne feadh raointean fhlùr,
's a' ghrian 'na lasair air latha bhiodh maoth, 's e ciùin,
an ciarbhadan mheangan, 's fonn tairis aig sgaoth a' chiùil,
seach sgian an latha raillich is gaoth 'na sùist.   16

361 [Killiecrankie]

[unfinished draft]

The Hieland men cam doon the brae
    and, wow, but they war vaunty oh
we focht, we fell, we ran oor ways
    frae the braes [o Killiecrankie oh.]

They cleft, they shore wi braid claymore   5
    their eldritch war wad daunt ye oh
an' we's be mindfu aa oor days
    o the braes o Killiecrankie oh.

Aa ways fae there tae win awa
    were smaa and they war scanty oh   10

[Clan Donald

Fierce is the day, with the fury of the wind aroused | seeking out every shelter and shaking the leafless trees, | shrieking through sharpened spindrift and round the high cliffs, | sweeping the snows across and blinding the edge of vision.   8

Sad is the din in the clangour of this senseless wind, | a fierce noisy blowing twisting down from the jaws of the skies; | mournful to the ear is the howling as all hide away, | held hostage by February and the brutish hag in its air.   12

If I could but be by a river in flowery meadows a while, | with the sun blazing down on a day that was peaceful and mild, | and from cool latticed branches sweet songs from the musical flock, | instead of this knife-stabbing day of flailing winds and storm.   16

Clan Donald met us in the widd
  we met nae guid I'se grant ye, oh
some rinns, some gaes, some faas, some stays
  on the braes [o Killiecrankie oh.]

Sic wes that war, aa ye wha hear   15
  an' nevar fleer nor taunt me, oh
for I hae wandert weary ways
  frae the braes [o Killiecrankie oh.]

There it was aith tae chance wi daith
  wi's bitter braith an' gantin oh   20
an' hunners ligg wi cloven claes
  doon the braes o Killiecrankie oh.

*362 *Dùthaich nan Craobh*
(mo dhòigh fhèin dheth)

A bhith 'fàgail na dùthcha,
's a bhith 'càramh nan siùil rith',
's a bhith 'stiùireadh ar cùrsa
  do dhùthaich nan craobh.   4

Rìgh, gur mi tha fo smuairein
is mi 'seòladh nan cuantan,
's mi ag ionndrainn na gruagaich –
  's i mo luaidh, 's i mo ghaol.   8

362   [*The Land of Trees*]
(*my own version*)

To be leaving the country | *and setting the sails to her,* | *and steering our course* |
to the land of trees.   4

Lord how sadness weighs on me | *as I travel the seas,* | *how I long for my lass,* |
she's my dear, she's my love.   8

Tha 'n cuan is e farsaing
eadar mise 's mo leannan,
stiùir ruighinn, buill tharrainn,
   siùil gheala is gaoth.   12

Thig t'ìomhaigh thar mhara,
t'ìomhaigh annamh, a leannain,
a dh'oidhche 's a latha
   tro lasan na gaoith.   16

Thig grian is thig latha,
thig reultan, thig gealach,
thig mise dhuit dhachaigh
   le aiteas is faoilt'.   20

Ma phòsas tu, mun till mi,
fear as feàrr leat na mise,
na gabh pòitear no misgeir,
   's na gabh idir fear faoin.   24

There's a vastness of ocean | between me and my lover, | a solid rudder and tackle, |
white sails and a wind.   12

Over the sea comes your countenance, | your countenance beyond compare, my
darling, | by night and by day | through the blasts of the wind.   16

Come sun and come daylight, | come stars and come moon, | to you I'll come
home | with joy and delight.   20

Should you wed before then | one you'd rather than me, | take no boozer or
drunkard | and above all no fool.   24

363 [*Is Mear a Bhreabas i Sàil*]

[unordered drafts]

Is mear a bhreabas i sàil,
   'ruith leis air sàile gaothar,
na tuinn 'na dèidh fo chop
   ri 'deireadh 's an loch fo chaoraich   4
mheara luatha nan ceòs
   'nan dreòs o fhuaradh 's 'nan loman
a' mèilich is [a'] roid
   air lèana 'n locha fon oiteig.   8

I 'ruith is clàr cha fhliuch
   air àirde thuinn, 's gach beic dhi
deas, tuath, iar is ear
   ga feitheamh 's an loch ga leadairt.   12
Cho beadaidh ris an làir
   air là na rèis 's i 'beiceadh.
A' ruith ron ghaoith air sàil'
   a sàil is mear a bhreabas.   16

*

363 [*Prancing She Kicks the Heel*]

Prancing she kicks the heel, | running to leeward on a windy sea, | a trail of waves in a froth | against her stern, and the loch overrun with sheep, | mad, fast, wide-   4
hipped, | like a blaze from windward, a fleece, | bleating and darting | on the meadow of the loch whipped up by the breeze.   8

In her run not a plank she'll soak | on the crest of waves, and her every dip, | north south east and west, | still ahead of her, as the loch is battered / as the loch batters her. | Impatient as a mare | frisking on the day of the races; | running before the   12
wind out to sea, | her heel she kicks as she prances.   16

'S math an cuspair bàird
  bàta dubh ga moladh.

Chan eil a leithid air muir
  aig luaths, aig cumadh, 's i socrach.   20

Ri brosnachadh chan fhèith
  siùil gheala nuair a thogas

Stuadhan 'na dèidh ri sàil
  ga leagail 's an àird ga togail.   24

*

'Dol ris 's a slinn fo chop
  giùig oirre ri fuachd fhuaraidh,
is clis a bhreabas i sàil
  ruith leis air sàile uaine.   28

Is mear a fhreagras i stiùir
  is siùil air fairge ghleannaich
fo ghaoith a nì den t-sàil'
  àrdain is gleannain [   ]   32

a' coiseachd ann thar dhronn
  nan tonn 's gan cur 'nan ceathach,
is mear a bhreabas i 'sàil.
  Cà bheil air sàile seis di?   36

*

[I 'ruith

It is a fine bardic theme, | the praise of a black boat.
She needs no incitement | when the white sails are hoisted.   20
Billows chase at her heel, | throwing her down and lifting her.
She has no peer on the water | for speed and mould when calm.   24

Going out, her shoulder in foam, | flinching at the cold to windward, | nimbly she
kicks the heel, | running leeward on a green sea.   28

With mad excitement she responds to rudder | and sails on a deep-valleyed sea, |
driven by a wind that turns the waters | into [   ] peaks and glens.   32

walking over the backs | of the waves and sending them up in a smoke, | prancing
she kicks her heel. | Where is her equal on the sea?   36

I 'ruith 's na tuinn a shad
   a' falbh gu fasgadh bhuaipe,
am bàta dubh fo shiùil,
   'na h-ioghnadh air muir uaine.   40

An loch gu lèir mu 'sàil
   ruith leis air sàile ghleannaich,
on chùrsa cheart cha chrom
   fo throm na gaoithe greannaich.   44

Leis is ris a lios
   's i clis gu fasgadh 's fuaradh,
cathadh mara a mios
   is tric a bhlais i cuach dheth.   48

364   *I 'Ruith Leis*

Is mear a bhreabas i sàil
   'ruith leis air sàile gaothar.
Is mear a bhreabas i cop,
   's an loch 'na lomain chaorach.   4

As she runs, the waves she's hit | *move away from her to leeward,* | *the black boat under sail,* | *a wonder on the green waters.*   40

The entire loch about her heel | *as she runs leeward on a sea of valleys,* | *she'll not veer from her proper course* | *under the weight of the surly wind.*   44

Windward and leeward her garden, | *as she flits before the wind or against it,* | *spindrift is her fruit,* | *often she's tasted a cup of it.*   48

364   [*Running Before the Wind*]

Prancing she kicks the heel, | *running before the wind on a blustery sea.* | *Prancing she kicks up froth,* | *as the loch is whipped into fleece.*   4

365 [Dùghall a' Seòladh]
[drafts for "Mochtàr is Dùghall"]

Dh'fhàg e còrsa 's sheòl e siar uaith
gus an robh gach donn is liath dheth,
gach buidhe, uaine agus riabhach,
gach creag is craobh, gach fraoch is riasg dheth,
gach rèidhlean 's bruthach, tulach 's sliabh dheth   5
gorm am bun an speur is cian uaith,
gus an deach iad às fon iarmailt
's a dh'fhosgail buaine a' chuain siar dha.
Còmhla sheòl na luingeas liatha,
a' gabhail air fhiaradh 's air fhiaradh;   10
U-bàta 's E-bàta gan iarraidh.
Thàinig orra, 's iad san fhiaradh
trast an domhain an oidhche 'ciaradh

*

cùl fàire thall chailleadh a' ghrian air
an dorcha aognaidh sgaoil a sgiathan   15
trast an domhain an oidhche 'ciaradh
a thug na dathan is an sgiamh dheth
thar na sàile aon sgàile a liath i
's na reultan òir 'nan dreòs san iarmailt
a dh'oidhche is a là 'dol siar dhaibh   20

['tionndadh

365 [Dougall Sailing]

He left the coast and sailed from it westward | till its every brown and grey, | every yellow, green and brindled patch, | its every rock and tree, heather and moorgrass, | its every flat stretch and brae, knoll and upland, | all were blue on the skyline and far from him, | till they disappeared under the skies | and the immensity of the Atlantic opened before him. | The grey ships sailed in convoy | criss-crossing the ocean, | sought out by U-boat and E-boat. | As they moved aslant, | there came on them | the darkening of night across the world.

beyond a faraway horizon line he lost sight of the sun | the eerie darkness spread its wings | night fell across the world | and wiped out its colours and its beauty | drawing one great grey shadow across the ocean | while the stars blazed golden in the sky | by night and by day they made their way westward |

'tionndadh deas is tuath, 's mar fhianais
Dùghall ann 'na shaighdear rianail
sa chuan shìorraidh, 's tìr air iarraidh
sgaoil na sgàilean air sàil' an sgiathan
gach dath ga dhubhadh aig dubhar 's ciaradh   25

*

Sheòl iad fàire 's fàire 's fàire
sheòl iad làithean agus là dhiubh
thionndaidh sear gu fearann 's fàilte.
Lean iad sear aig briseadh latha
agus thog iad còrsa aineoil   30
còrsa allta thall na h-Aifric
agus caolas caol Ghiobraltair.

Bha Dùghall an-sin is e 'na òigear
ga thoirt gu h-èasgaidh gu beul a' mhòrtair
ceann uidhe a shlighe 's cha b'fhios 's cha b'eòl da   35
fiosaiche ris cha robh còmhla.
's e dearbh à saoghal am baoghal còmhraig.
Ghiorraich a bhàs air ged a b'òg e
is dùnadh shùl is e làn sòlais
a bheag 's a bheag mar a sheòl i   40
dhùinte a là mar dhùinte còmhla
's ceann uidh' a rathaid faisge na 'n còrsa.

*

*turning to north and south, and witnessing it all | was Dougall, a private | in the
infinite ocean, longing for land; | the shadows spread their wings on the ocean |
every colour blotted out by darkness and dusk.*   25

*They sailed one horizon after another | they sailed forever and a day | they turned
east to land and welcome. | They persisted eastward at break of day | and set their
course on an unknown coast | the strange coast of Africa yonder | and the narrow   30
straits of Gibraltar.*

*Dougall was there, a youth | being brought eagerly to the mouth of the mortar |
the endpoint of his journey, unknown and unsuspected by him | there was no   35
soothsayer beside him | he was sure of his life amidst the danger of battle. | His
death closed in on him even though he was young, | and the closing of eyes, though
he was full of the joys of life | little by little as she sailed | his day was shut as one   40
would shut a door | the end of his road nearer than the coastline.*

Gealach cha d'èirich. Bha 'n speur 'na chriathar
mhìltean reul 'nan leus, 's b'e 'n sgiamh e,
grian fodha mar nach robh i riamh ann.   45
Chaidil cuid 's iad cuidhteas fiamh ann
's na luingeas cogaidh bhith gan iadhadh.

Chaidh air tìr 'n Aildìr an Dùghall –
ghiorraich e rithist air ceann a chùrsa
am fearan sgìth, is sgrìobhadh dùnadh   50
air a rann am beanntan Thùnais.
'S ann a bha e taingeal sunndach
's e 'teachd on mhuir gun d'ruigeadh ùir leis

am fiathachadh nach gabh diùltadh
don truagh, don t-sàr, don tràill, don phrionnsa,   55
a bheirear am bothan bochd 's an lùchairt
air sàil, air tìr, do sgìos, do lùths ann,
cuireadh falbh, ge searbh, a-null e.
Bha 'n cuireadh deiridh feitheamh ri Dùghall
gach madainn is gach feasgar dhlùthaich   60
air, gun fheum an guidhe no 'n dùlan.
Bha 'n Gefreit fon adhar dhùmhail
'ìomhadh a' mhortair gus am b'ùr e.

No moon rose. The sky was a sieve | of a thousand stars burning, and it was a sight of utter beauty | the sun gone down as if it had never existed | Some slept, no 45 longer troubled by the fear | of warships encircling them.

Dougall landed in Algeria – | he drew even closer to the end of his course | a tired little man, and the ending of his verse | was written in the hills of Tunis. | But he 50 was thankful and happy | to have reached dry land after being at sea

the invitation that cannot be refused | given to poor and to powerful, to slave and to prince | that is given in poor hut and palace | on land, on sea, to the weary and 55 the strong | the call to cross over, however bitter. | The final call was awaiting Dougall | every morning and evening drew closer | to him, all entreaty or defiance 60 useless. | Under the sultry sky the Gefreiter | was polishing the mortargun till it gleamed as new.

366 *[Och-òin mar a dh'Fhalbh Sinn]*
[draft]

Och-òin mar a dh'fhalbh sinn
togail siùil ri croinn àrda.
'Dol sìos o Chluaidh 's an speur fo ghruaim
  's a' mhuir ri fuaim ghàbhaidh.
Och-òin mar a dh'fhalbh sinn.   5

Arainn ris is Manainn leis
  's mo chridhe deas gu sgàineadh.

Briosgaid chruaidh is tarrainn bhuan
  's am meata duairc gar smàladh.

Slat is seòl 's a' ghaoth mar cheòl   10
  's mo làmhan reòta, cràiteach.

Seòl is slat is ròpa chas
  is driop gun stad is spàirn ann.

Cathadh mara 's sneachd gar dalladh
  's an caiptean chaill na h-àirdean.   15

Roinn stalla 's i dlùth 's na h-àirdean dùint',
  neòil dhùmhail 's gaillean làidir.

Gach cunnart cuain gu tiugh mun cuairt
  's gur fada bhuainn Astràilia.

Falbhaidh sprochd is nì mi boch   20
  an latha thogas Àbhann.

366 *[Alas that We Set Out to Sea]*

Alas that we set out to sea | hoisting sails up high masts. | Heading down from the Clyde, the sky overcast | and an ominous sound from the ocean. | Alas that we set out to sea.   5

Arran to leeward and Man to windward, | and my heart on the verge of breaking.
Hard biscuit and constant hauling, | and the gruff mate crushing our spirits.
Yard and sail, the winds that wail, | and my hands painful and frozen.   10
Sail and yard and twining rope, | endless bustle and struggling
Snow and spindrift blinding us, | and the captain who's lost his bearings.   15
A craggy point close but the airts are closed, | dense clouds and a heavy storm.
Every danger of the ocean tightening round, | and a long way off is Australia.
All gloom will lift and I'll rejoice | when we set our course on Sanda.   20

A' ghaoth 'na smùid is dithist air stiùir
   's i 'ruith an cùrsa ceàrr oirnn.

Gun fhios gun eòl gun chinnt air chòir
   an tog sinn còrsa sàbhailt'.   25

Tha 'ghaoth an ceann 's an stiùir cho teann –
   is seo mo rann sa Ghàidhlig.

Further couplets of undetermined position:

An cuan fo 'sròin gu fìor bhun-sgòth
   's i 'seòladh mach o Àbhann.

Fo chrannaibh loma, lùbte, nochda   30
   'ruith chon na taoibh o thàinig.

Na tuinn ag èirigh gus an speur
   aig dèine 'n doininn dhàna.

Is mion sa chuan am bàrca luath
   ged bhiodh i uair glè stàtail.   35

Riofadh shiùil ge rag na dùirn
   is neart is lùths air t'fhàgail.

Riofadh shiùil, buill tharraing 's stiùir
   is blàths is lùths air t'fhàgail.

Fàire, fàire, fàire, fàire,   40
   fàire anns gach àird oirnn.

The wind in smoke, two men at the helm | as she takes us in the wrong direction.
Not knowing, not kenning, in no way certain | if we'll raise a friendly coastline.   25
The wind's in command and the steer's so tight – | this is my rhyme in Gaelic.

The sea at her prow meets a bank of cloud | as out she sails from Sanda.
Under bare, exposed, bending masts | she runs to the side she came from.   30
The waves are heaving up to the sky | so fierce is the daring tempest.
Tiny on the ocean is the speedy bark | though once she seemed so stately.   35
Reefing sails though fists are stiff | and you're drained of strength and vigour.
Reefing sails, tackle and helm | and you're drained of warmth and vigour.
Sealine sealine sealine sealine | a sealine all around us.   40

367 *Homer* [revised]

They say that you were blind. Yet, from the shore
    you saw the long waves cresting out at sea;
before the climbing dawn, from heaven's floor
    you saw the dark night flee.   4

You saw the swordmen; Helen without flaw.
    You saw the spearmen by the Skaean Gate.
Hector, Achilles, Priam – those you saw –
    Odysseus homeward late.   8

Demodocus still sings within the hall,
    Telemachus still sails and seeking goes,
and Deienera tells of Ilium's fall,
    and Ajax faces foes.   12

The torrents swirling in the springtime thaw,
    the shady slopes of Ida many-pined,
the curving flash of falling swords you saw.
    They lie. You were not blind.   16

368 *The Smoky Smirr o Rain* [revised]

A misty mornin' doon the shore wi a hushed an' caller air,
an' no a breath frae East or Wast tie sway the rashes there,
a sweet, sweet scent frae Laggan's birks gaed breathin' on its ane,
their branches hingin beadit in the smoky smirr o rain.   4

As I gaed doon by Laggan shore on a misty moarnin' aa,
the warld was turned a mystery in the mist o rain sae smaa,
for time an' airt in aa that place tie ken o there war nane,
as reek o haze ilk wye did steek in the smoky smirr o rain.   8

The day was hushed an' doverin' as the fog o rain cam doon.
Owre shore an' watter hoverin' it drifted frae abune.
Nae waft o air tie steer it was there; the lift was lown,
an' rallyoch winds gied owre their virr in the smoky smirr o rain.   12

The hills aroond war silent wi the mist alang the braes.
The woods war derk an' quiet wi dewy, glintin' sprays.
The mavies didna raise for me, as I gaed bye alane,
but a wee, wae cheep at passin' in the smoky smirr o rain.   16

Rock an' stane lay glisterin' on aa the heichs abune.
Cool an' kind an' whisperin' it drifted gently doon,
till hill an' howe war rowed in it, an' land an' sea war gane.
Aa was still an' saft an' silent in the smoky smirr o rain.   20

A blessin', a caressin' was the rain upon my face.
Deep dwaamed the silence. Calm lay deep an' kind owre aa that place.
Nae cry o whaup cam frae the lift, an' lift an' yirrd war ane,
as I gaed doon by Laggan in the smoky smirr o rain.   24

As I turned frae Laggan Roaig, I brocht back wi me
a history o mystery an' mist on land an' sea,
o muted mavies, waveless shores an' gairs in haar their lane
as I cam back frae Laggan shore in the smoky smirr o rain.   28

Aa licht was faint, horizons tint, asclent the rain cam doon.
The day was derk, the braes war mirk an' misty heich abune
an' strand an' land war dernin an' the mavies made their maen
as beuchs an' branches bieldit thaim in the smoky smirr o rain.   32

369   *We're Nae Awa tae Bide Awa*

I was fleean fair. The fire was reid.
   The pints war on the table,
and if I'd been hingan by a threid,
   I was hingan by a cable.   4

Gif ye come ben by yon toon street,
   and meet in wi a bonnie laddie,
gif he spiers at ye "Will ye hae a pint?"
   say "Aye, man, that's my hobbie."   8

This is the sang. It isna lang.
   Tae sing it is ma notion.
They sang it aa as they gaed awa
   tae sail across the ocean.   12

370   *Fragment*

On a hill-land brae in May to be,
with hillbirds making faint melody,
the sun arising, my heart arising,
and the dew arising from grass, from tree.   4

371 [*Thèid na Fèilltean Seachad*]

[unfinished draft]

Fèill Brìde is Fèill Eòin
Nollaig Mhòr 's a' Challainn
mar choin a' ruith bhàrr èill
thèid na fèilltean seachad.   4
Là buidhe Bealtainn bric
an Inid is an Carghas
mar ruith le gleann aig fiadh
na bliadhnachan a' falbh bhuainn.   8

Mar shèideag gaoithe làidir
na ràithean a' dol tharainn.

An Lùnastal 's an Dùlachd
ùine is uair 'dol às bhuainn.   12

An-dè 's an-diugh 's gach là
a-màireach is an-earar
gach là a' falbh 'na leum
mar each rèis aig marcach,   16
Samhradh agus Geamhradh
Earrach air chall is Foghar
mar shruth 'na steall le eas
gach feasgar is madainn mhoch dhuinn.   20

371 [*The Festivals Go Past*]

*St Bridget's Day, St John's, | Christmas and New Year, | like dogs running off the
leash, | the festivals go past. | Yellow speckled Beltane, | Shrovetide and Lent, | like*   4
a deer's dash down a glen, | the years go from us.   8

As a gust of strong wind | the seasons pass over us.

Lammastide and Midwinter | time and hour slipping by us.   12

*Yesterday, today and every day, | tomorrow and the day after, | every day going
in a sprint | like a horseman on his racehorse, | Summer and Winter, | Spring lost*   16
*and Autumn, | like a stream gushing down a waterfall, | our every evening and
morning.*   20

372 *The Sain*

"That rhyme" the spaewife said tae me
  "will daunton doom, will bield frae ill."
Never the sain tae sing made she.
  I ken it no? I seek it still.   4

Had I that sain tae bring ye bien
  frae ern an' main, I'd sign ye wi't
and sing on ye that seldom sain
  on bluid an' bane, on haunds and feet.   8

Nae gloamin' gane wad ye doonspeed
  tae ligg amang the deid yere lane.
Frae murnin', maen, ill thocht an' deed
  I'd sing on ye that seldom sain.   12

But noo there's nae the charm or spell
  will shield frae ill, frae harm, frae wae.
It comesna near me, inch or ell.
  I can but call on Christ an' pray.   16

I can but say tae God my prayer.
  I kenna aye whaur gangs yere gate.
The sain's a freit. I gie it owre.
  The sain is tint an' blint is fate.   20

373 *The Toper's Night*

The *deoch* – I am cheery wi't,
  be it eerie efter gloamin'.
There's loch o't. I'se no weary wi't.
  Fules may fleer at it. It comes foamin'. 4

Drink it doon, boys. No fear for ye.
  Gie the gear o' ye. It comes roamin'.
It comes roon tae ilk fier o ye.
  Gif ye spier at me, I am homein'.   8

The day daws. Aa clear is it.
  We maun steer an' aa gang roamin'.
The gray waas shine sheer in it.
  Frae here maun we an' skail homein'. 12

374 *[The Rosyns and the Waste]*
[draft]

The rosyns blossom faur awa,
  faur awa they lowe aa reid
in peacefu' places faur awa
  graceful the lilies lift their heid.   4

Here is the wide an' saikless waste,
  aamaist o man aa unaware.
Soothbye, in garths wi guestin graced,
  lily an' rosyn blossom there.   8

The waste aa wild, on ilka side,
  streetches as faur as ee can faa.
Rosyn an' lily in aa their pride
  blossom in gairdens by the waa.   12

Tae me the waste! The maist I mind
  's by gair an' strand tae wand my way,
sooth in the sunny suddron land
  let blossoms dover through the day.   16

It's faur tae whaur the lily grows
  an' the rosyn lowes aa reid,
an' the lang day dovers sunny, clear.
  It's faur frae here, indeed.   20

375 *[The Airts Eternal]*

The west sae mild, the east sae snell,
  the north sae shrill, the south wi sun,
the airts eternal, winds and clime,
  are there sin' time has e'er begun.   4

376 *A Nor'-Sea Day*

It's a Nor'-Sea day wi haar, dear.
  It's lown. The wind is wee.
I see nor sun nor star, dear,
  luikan aye for ye.   4

It's a Nor'-Sea day wi haar, dear.
  The foghorns blare on Forth.
Whaure'er I luik I see ye,
  East, West, Sou' or North.   8

The lift's but sun or sterns, dear.
  Aa derns. The caurs gang slaw,
an' melancholy, dronean,
  on Forth the foghorns blaw.   12

The blin' haar comes ben driepan,
  creepan frae the sea.
Ilk gate's a guess for aa, dear,
  ilk waa a mystery.   16

The licht is waff an' smoorit
  wi haar frae aff the sea.
Be bricht. Be crouse an' kind, dear,
  an' aye hae mind o me.   20

377 *[The Airts]*

Nor's auld, cauld east,
Sou' blaws virr, smirry's west.
  Nae snaw-blaw, sou'-west!   3

North is old, cold east,
South blows vigour, smirry's west.
  No snow-blow, south-west!   6

378 *Cha Tig Mòr, mo Bhean, Dhachaigh*
(ath-dhèanamh air seann òran)

Cha tig Mòr, mo bhean, dhachaigh,
   cha tig Mòr, mo bhean ghaoil;
cha tig Mòr, mo bhean, dhachaigh
   bho chlachan nan craobh.   4

Thig Màrt is thig Foghar,
   thig todhar, thig buain,
ach cha ghluais mo bhean dhachaigh
   bho chlachan nan stuadh.   8

Thig blàth air a' ghiuthas,
   cinnidh duilleach air gèig,
cinnidh gucag air luachair,
   ach cha ghluais mo bhean fhèin.   12

Thig grian is thig gealach,
   thig madainn le faoith',
thig oidhche, thig latha,
   ach cha charaich mo ghaol.   16

378 [*Mòr, My Wife, Won't Come Home*]
(*a reworking of an old song*)

Mòr, my wife, won't come home, | *Mòr won't come, my dear wife;* | *Mòr, my wife, won't come home* | *from the wooded enclosure.*   4

March and Autumn will come, | *manuring and harvest will come,* | *but my wife will not stir* | *from the gabled enclosure.*   8

Blossom comes on the fir. | *Leaves sprout on a bough.* | *Buds sprout on the rushes,* | *but my wife will not stir.*   12

Sun comes and moon comes, | *morning comes and its babble,* | *night comes and day comes,* | *but my love will not move.*   16

Eiridh grian anns na speuran,
   èiridh eòin bhàrr nan geug,
èiridh ceò bhàrr nan slèibhtean,
   ach chan èirich i fhèin.   20

Laighidh grian, laighidh gealach,
   laighidh balachan sgìth,
ach cha laigh i nam leabaidh,
   's i 'na laighe sa chill.   24

Fosglaidh Earrach na ràithean,
   fosglaidh blàthan as ùr,
fosglaidh còmhla air doras,
   ach chan fhosgail i sùil.   28

Bha mi uair agus shaoil mi
   a saoghal bhith buan,
ach cha ghluais i dhomh dhachaigh
   bho chlachan nan uaigh.   32

Thig Foghar, thig Earrach,
   's lom mo leac is gur fuar.
Cha dùisg caoineadh do mhàthair –
   dèan ba-bà a-nis, uain.   36

Sun rises in the skies, | *birds will rise from the boughs,* | *mist will rise from the hills,* | *but she will not rise.*   20

Sun sets, moon sets; | *a tired wee boy lies down;* | *but she won't lie in my bed,* | *in the kirkyard she lies now.*   24

Spring opens the seasons, | *blossoms open anew,* | *a doorleaf will open,* | *but she'll not open her eyes.*   28

There was once that I thought | *she would live on eternally,* | *but from the graveyard enclosure* | *home for me she'll not come.*   32

Come Autumn, come Spring, | *bare and cold is my hearth.* | *Sobbing won't wake your mother –* | *now sleep my wee lamb.*   36

379 *Is Fada Thà Mi 'm Ònar*

Hì hoireann ò, hi-rì ho-rò
is fada thà mi 'm ònar
hì hoireann ò, hi-rì ho-rò.

Nuair bhà mi leis na caileagan
    gum feuchainn blas am pòige,   5
ach nise their iad uile rium,
    "Sheann duine, 's mòr do dhòchas".

Hì hoireann ò, hi-rì ho-rò.

Nan tigeadh arm na Frainge oirnn,
    cha bhithinn las 'nan còmhdhail –   10
ach 's bòsta seann duin' agam sin,
    's mi glagach, brùite, breòite.

Dh'fhalbhainn slèibhtean 's mharbhainn fèidh
    air garbhlach fèin 's mi 'm òigear;
bhuailinn beum is ghearrainn leum   15
    is dhèanainn feum an còmhrag.

Ach nise 's seann fhear crùbain mi –
    mo dhùrachd gun till òige –
is riumsa their na caileagan
    "Bi 'fanachd bhuainn led bhòstan!"   20

379 [*I'm a Long Time Alone*]

Hì hoireann ò, hirì horò | I'm a long time alone | hì hoireann ò, hirì horò.

When I was with the lassies | I was one to taste their kisses, | but now what they all   5
say to me's | "Old man, you live in hope!" | *Hì hoireann ò, hirì horò.*

If the armies of France came on us | I'd not be slack against them – | but that's an   10
old man's bluster, | I'm doddery, frail and broken.

I'd trek the hills and kill the deer | in rough terrain when younger; | I could strike
a blow and cut a leap | and be of use in combat.   15

But now I'm just a stooped old man – | my wish that youth would come again – |
and what the lassies say to me's | "Keep from us with your boasting!"   20

380 [Natur's Child]

He was aye lauchan an' cheery,
  he was camsteerie an' wild.
They said "He's glaikit, the cratur".
  He was natur's child.   4

381 [Thàin' Trath-nòin]
[drafts]

Dè do bheachd air èirigh
lainnireach na grèine?
No dè do bharail air a laighe,
's latha seachad 's lèirsinn?   4
Is ann mar sin dhomh fhèin e
a-nis, bhon chiar mo speuran.
Mo ghrian bhoillsgeach theich ro oidhche,
's oillt an deaghaidh èibhneis.   8

Rim mhadainn b'aotrom, mear i,
mo chas, air fraoch nan leathad.
Fàire òg mo là bu deònach.
Thàin' trath-nòin 's is sean mi.   12
O mhochthrath gu tràth feasgair
na cnocain is na creagan –
Slia' mo luaidh cha tig a-nuas
's cha tèid mi suas am-feasta.   16

Chan fhaic mi thu, a Chaolbheinn,
a-nis on dh'fhàs mi aosta.
An àite chnuic an tàmh 's a' chruit
's ceum tuisleach chasan caola.   20

381 [Evening has Come]

*What think you | of the glittering sunrise? | Or what are your thoughts on
the setting of the sun | when daylight and sight decline? | That is my lot | now,* 4
*since my skies have grown dim. | My radiant sun has fled before the night, | and
joyfulness has given way to dread.*   8

*Light and sprightly in the morning of my life | was my foot on hillslope heather. |
Willing my youthful dawn of day. | Evening has come and I am old. | From*   12
*the first morning light till the evening hours, | the knowes and the rocks – | my
beloved Sleea will not come down to me, | and I will never again ascend it.* 16

*I won't see you, Narrow Ben, | now that I have grown old. | Instead of the hills,
resting and stooping, | and the faltering step of thin legs.*   20

382 *Air Leathad Slèibhe*

Air leathad slèibhe 's an Cèitean ann,
'n àm dùsgadh eunlaith len èigheach fann,
a' ghrian ag èirigh, 's mo chridh' ag èirigh,
's an dealt ag èirigh bho fheur 's bho chrann.   4

B'e 'n sòlas àraidh bhith 'n làthair shliabh
is dreòs na fàire an-àird a' triall,
eòin an fhàsaich rin ceòl beag tràthail
air lòn 's air àilean a-bhàn, 's air riasg.   8

Tùis is boladh aig roid nan còs,
aig fraoch air cnocain mholach chòrr;
fonn ciùil aig osnaich chiùin na h-oiteig,
's i 'dùsgadh mochthrath air monadh 's sgòrr.   12

Guileag chrotaig, 's i moch air sgèith
os cionn a' mhonaidh, a' dol na sèis;
cùirnein solais air chùirnein solais
an driùchd air fochann, air roid, air gèig.   16

Air leathad slèibhe 's an Cèitean air,
'n àm dùsgadh eunlaith len èigheach mear;
driùchd air gèig ann, air flùr, air feur ann,
'na smùid ag èirigh ri grèin san ear.   20

.

382 [On a Hill-land Slope]

On a hill-land slope with Maytime come, | when birds are wakening and faintly chirping, | the sun rising, my heart rising, | and the dew rising from grass and tree.   4

It would be a deep comfort to be among the hill-lands | as the blaze of dawn was climbing the sky, | with the birds of the wilderness making small morning music | down on meadow and plain and on moorgrass.   8

Incense and fragrance of bog-myrtle in small hollows, | and from the heather on shaggy enchanted knowes; | a melody playing in the gentle sigh of the breeze | that wakens early on moor and summit.   12

The cry of a plover, on morning flight | above the moor, swelling into a chorus; | bead of light upon bead of light | on dew-covered grass and myrtle and branch.   16

On a hill-land slope in Maytime bloom, | when the birds are wakening and brightly chirping; | dew on its branch and flower and grass | rising like smoke with the sun in the east.   20

383 Whan Ye Gang Awa, Jamie

(for the men of 1914–1918)

> Whan ye gang awa, Jamie,
>   faur across the sea, laddie,
> whan ye gang tae Germanie,
>   what'll ye bring tae me, laddie?   4

I'se bring ye a silken goun, lassie.
I'se bring ye siller shoon, lassie.
Silken goun and siller shoon
ootfrae a fremmit toun, lassie.   8
>   Whan ye gang awa, Jamie, etc.

I'se bring ye a gowden kaim, lassie,
diamant ring the same, lassie;
gowden kaim an' ring the same,
I'se bring them hame tae ye, lassie.   16
>   Whan ye gang awa, Jamie, etc.

The barrage creeps alang, lassie.
On Flanders Daith is thrang, lassie.
The Scots amang he aye was thrang,
but my gift tae ye will gang, lassie.   24
>   Whan ye gang awa, Jamie, etc.

A gift for ye, it's shair, lassie,
I'se bring ye frae owre there, lassie.
Shells may flare an' cannon rair,
but I'se be here frae there, lassie.   32
>   Whan ye gang awa, Jamie, etc.

I'se bring ye ma ain sel, lassie,
back frae the yetts o hell, lassie.
My ain sel frae the yetts o hell,
I'se bring that tae yersel, lassie.   40

> Whan ye gang awa, Jamie,
>   faur across the sea, laddie,
> whan ye gang tae Germanie
>   bring back yersel tae me, laddie.   44

384 *I'm Wearan Awa, Jean*
(for Allermuir)

I'm wearan awa, Jean,
like snaw-wreathes in thaw, Jean,
I'm wearan awa
   tae the land o the leal.   4
There's nae trouble there, Jean.
Aathing is fair, Jean,
an' happiness is shair
   i the land o the leal.   8

I'm wearan awa, John,
like snaw-wreathes in thaw, John,
I'm wearan awa
   tae the land o the leal.   12
There aa is fair, John.
We'se baith be there, John.
We'se be thegither there
   i the land o the leal.   16

I'm wearan awa, Jean,
like snaw-wreathes in thaw, Jean,
I'm wearan awa
   tae the land o the leal.   20
Tinto may be heich, Jean,
Rannoch Muir be dreich, Jean,
For thaim I will seich
   i the land o the leal.   24

I'm wearan awa, John,
like snaw-wreathes in thaw, John,
I'm wearan awa
   tae the land o the leal.   28
Tinto will be wi us there.
Rannoch wilna lea us there.
And Allermuir they'll gie us there
   i the land o the leal.   32

385 *Beam Sea in Biscay*

(a song for liner passengers)

We're rolling in a beam sea in Biscay, oh,
We're rolling in a beam sea in Biscay, oh.
Give her steam. Oh, give her steam.
We're rolling in a beam sea in Biscay, oh.   4

I wish I was in Frisco, oh,
or even Nome Alaska, oh,
or steaming down the good Gulf Stream.
We're rolling in a beam sea in Biscay, oh.   8

She rolls and she is frisky, oh.
I dose myself with whisky, oh.
When I am seen my face is green.
We're rolling in a beam sea in Biscay, oh.   12

To eat a bite is risky, oh.
I treat myself to whisky, oh.
To me it seems she doesn't steam.
We're rolling in a beam sea in Biscay, oh.   16

You know what I would ask you, oh –
take me back to Glasgie, oh.
My face is green. Oh, give her steam.
We're rolling in a beam sea in Biscay, oh.   20

We're rolling in a beam sea in Biscay, oh,
We're rolling in a beam sea in Biscay, oh.
Give her steam. Oh, give her steam.
We're rolling in a beam sea in Biscay, oh.   24

386 *Over the Isles to America*
Null Thar nan Eileanan dh'Ameireaga
(ruidhle)

Null thar nan eileanan dh'Ameireaga gun tèid sinn.
Null thar nan eileanan dh'Ameireaga gun tèid sinn,
Null thar nan eileanan dh'Ameireaga gun tèid sinn;
null rathad Shasainn agus dhachaigh rathad Èireann.   4

Saoil thu 'n tèid mi leat thar a' chuain bheucaich?
Saoil thu 'n tèid mi leat thar na mara cèine?
Ghaoil, gun tèid mi leat thar a' chuain bheucaich,
null rathad Shasainn agus dhachaigh rathad Èireann.   8

Null anns an eilthireachd dh'Ameireaga gun tèid sinn.
Null sinn nar n-eilthirich! Dh'Ameireaga gun tèid sinn.
Null anns an eilthireachd dh'Ameireaga gun tèid sinn,
null rathad Shasainn agus dhachaigh rathad Èireann.   12

Saoil thu 'n tèid mi leat thar a' chuain bheucaich?
Thèid mi cuide riut, 's cha bu ruith ach leum sin.
Ghaolain, thèid mi leat fada gu tìr chèin ann,
null rathad Shasainn agus dhachaigh rathad Èireann.   16

386   [*Over the Isles to America*]
(*reel*)

Over the isles to America we'll go; | over the isles to America we'll go; | over the isles to America we'll go; | over England way, and home by way of Ireland.   4

Do you suppose I'll go with you over the roaring ocean? | Do you suppose I'll go with you over foreign waters? | My dear, of course I'll go with you over the roaring ocean, | over England way, and home by way of Ireland.   8

Over in exodus to America we'll go. | Over as emigrants! To America we'll go. | Over in exodus to America we'll go, | over England way, and home by way of Ireland.   12

Do you suppose I'll go with you over the roaring ocean? | I'll go along with you, aye, jump at the chance to do so. | My darling, I'll go with you away to far-flung country, | over England way, and home by way of Ireland.   16

Null anns an eilthireachd nar n-eilthirich gun tèid sinn.
Null sinn nar n-eilthirich! San eilthireachd gun tèid sinn.
Null anns an eilthireachd nar n-eilthirich gun tèid sinn,
null rathad Shasainn agus dhachaigh rathad Èireann.   20

Togail bhailtean ann 's gleann air ghleann ga lèirsgrios.
Far am biodh na laoich, caoraich ann a' mèilich;
cìobairean is coin sa choirre bhiodh na fèidh ann –
Null rathad Shasainn agus dhachaigh rathad Èireann.   24

An saoil thu fhèin an tèid mi leat thar a' chuain bheucaich?
Saoil thu 'n tèid mi cuide riut air druim na mara èitigh?
Thèid mi leat. 'S tu leanas mi ged chreanadh mi gu geur air,
null rathad Shasainn agus dhachaigh rathad Èireann.   28

Mo ghealladh seo, is bheir mi dhuit e – fuireach na do dhèidh ann
cha dèan mi. Thèid mi cuide riutsa, 's chan e ruith ach leum sin.
Beannachd bhuam le tìr nan cnoc. Is soraidh e 's cha trèigsinn;
null rathad Shasainn agus dhachaigh rathad Èireann.   32

Dùthaich chan eil againn san eilthireachd gun tèid sinn.
Null sinn, ged theirinn e! Dh'Ameireaga gun tèid sinn.
Dùthaich chan eil againn. Nar n-eilthirich gun tèid sinn,
null rathad Shasainn agus dhachaigh rathad Èireann.   36

[Sgur air cur

Over in exodus as emigrants we'll go. | Over we go as emigrants! In exodus we'll go. | Over in exodus as emigrants we will go, | over England way, and home by way of Ireland. 20

Building of towns there, while glen upon glen is ravaged. | Where the fine people lived, there now the sheep go bleating; | shepherds and their dogs in the corrie where the deer were – | over England way, and home by way of Ireland. 24

Do you think yourself I'll go with you over the roaring ocean? | Do you think I'll go along with you on the back of the raging waters? | I'll go with you. It's you I'll follow though it should cost me dearly, | over England way, and home by way of Ireland. 28

To you I'll give my promise now – staying here behind you | is out. I'll go along with you, aye, jump at the chance to do so. | My farewell to the land of the hills – a goodbye, not desertion; | over England way, and home by way of Ireland. 32

No country do we have, in exodus we'll go. | Over we go, though I should say it! To America we'll go. | No country do we have. As emigrants we'll go, | over England way, and home by way of Ireland. 36

Sgur air cur is buain, is buailtean gun sprèidh annt';
Fògradh agus ruaig air tuath 's màil gan èigheach;
thèid sinn bho na glinn gu Innseanaich an cèin ud,
null rathad Shasainn agus dhachaigh rathad Èireann. 40

Null thar nan eileanan, etc.

387 *Soraidh an Sgoileir*

Seo slàn agus soraidh
le fàsach a' mhonaidh;
Dhia, cha b'fheàrr leam mar shochar
    na na cnocain fam chòir; 4
na tha de sgòrr is de dh'aonach
eadar òrdag 's a' Chaolbheinn,
a' mhòinteach 's am fraoch
    air an aotrom a' bhròg. 8
Mi 'dol bhuaith sin gu Sasainn,
    's chan ann luath a bhios m'astar,
gus na duain anns an Laideann
    is gu eachdraidh na Ròimh, 12
is gu Hòmar 's gu Greugais.
Seo mo shoraidh, a shlèibhtean.
Gus an till mi bho chèin ruibh
    seo nam dhèidh "soraidh ò". 16

An end to sowing and reaping, the cattlefolds lie empty; | banished and fleeing
tenantry, as rent payments are called for; | from the glens we will go to the Indians
far yonder, | over England way, and home by way of Ireland. 40
Over the isles, etc.

387 [The Scholar's Farewell]

Here's farewell and goodbye | to the vast mountain moorland; | God, no favour I'd
ask | but the hills in my sight; | all the scaurs and bare uplands | between Thumb 4
and the Narrow Ben, | the heather and moors | where the shoe treads light. | I 8
leave that for England, | and my pace won't be hurried, | for verses in Latin | and
the history of Rome, | and for Homer and Greek. | Farewell, then, my hills. | Till I 12
return from afar, | here from me's "cheerio". 16

George Campbell Hay:

A Review

"A STEY BRAE AN' BONNIE"

A Short Biography

Tarbert

Born on 8 December 1915, in the Renfrewshire parish of Elderslie, George was the second child of Catherine Campbell and the parish minister John MacDougall Hay. Catherine Campbell, though native to Cowal, had close connections with Tarbert, Loch Fyne, through her mother Jessie MacMillan. Her father had been a farmer on Islay before following a religious calling into the Free Kirk ministry; at his death, Catherine moved to Tarbert, where she met John MacDougall Hay, the son of a local fishing merchant. He was then studying for the Church of Scotland ministry, having already distinguished himself at Glasgow University and spent some years teaching. A prolific journalistic writer, MacDougall Hay is chiefly remembered for his extraordinary first novel *Gillespie*, published the year before George's birth. Recognisably set in Tarbert, the book dismayed some by its harsh portrayal of greed, pettiness and brutality in the fishing community. It received enthusiastic reviews, however, on both sides of the Atlantic, but this success stalled with the outbreak of war in Europe, and the book did not receive further recognition until its republication some fifty years later.

In October 1909, a few months after MacDougall Hay had assumed his charge in Elderslie, he and Catherine Campbell were married, and in 1911 they had their first child, Sheena. George, their second, had only just turned four when his father died of tuberculosis. The small family moved back to Tarbert, where Catherine's aunts lived together at "Ingleside", on the south side of the village towards the pier. There the young boy put down his cultural and emotional roots, drawing nourishment from various springs: his attraction to the boats moored below the house; his admiration for the ring-net fishermen, no doubt heightened by the loss of his father; his passion for the hills of North Kintyre, stretching from the Heather Knowe directly behind the house to Skipness; and above all, his early curiosity for Gaelic and the associated (and increasingly submerged) place-names and traditions of Kintyre.

The poet and social historian Angus Martin has given an eloquent account of Hay's boyhood and of his formative relationships with his great-aunts and with the fisherman Calum Johnson (see Martin 1984: 48–71). What follows are some of Hay's own reminiscences of that period, in an interview with Martin recorded in 1980.

> *AM*: You said that you acquired a good deal of your Gaelic from your aunts.
>
> *GCH*: I did indeed, yes.
>
> *AM*: Was that your primary source in Tarbert?
>
> *GCH*: Uh-huh.
>
> *AM*: And how did you go about that?
>
> *GCH*: Och, when I was about six, I started asking them what was the Gaelic for this and what was the Gaelic for that, and so on, and that's how I learnt Gaelic.
>
> *AM*: How was it that your interest in Gaelic was stimulated at such an early age? Was it through your mother's influence or was it an external influence in the village?
>
> *GCH*: I think it was my mother's influence ... I think so.
>
> *AM*: So although she wasn't perhaps a fluent speaker, she –
>
> *GCH*: Oh she had some Gaelic, she had some Gaelic.
>
> *AM*: And what was your aunts' reaction to your interest?
>
> *GCH*: They were encouraging.
>
> *AM*: Did you accompany that aural learning –
>
> *GCH*: [laughs] By reading the Bible, yes.
>
> *AM*: The Bible?
>
> *GCH*: The Bible, aye, and then sermons; they were on the shelves, you know, in Ingleside. I just found my way to them, you know, and then the MacLean Bards [A. M. Sinclair 1898, 1900].
>
> *AM*: Did you visit [your aunts] frequently?
>
> *GCH*: Oh yes! Whenever I was on my holidays I went down to Ingleside.
>
> *AM*: Were they talking Gaelic in the house naturally?
>
> *GCH*: Ach, an odd word – like Tarbert, you know.
>
> *AM*: So although they were fluent they werena conversant in Gaelic habitually?
>
> *GCH*: They weren't, no. They weren't speaking it because they'd been brought up in the old tradition: "the Gaelic language is a terrible thing", you know – the old tradition; it's gone. And they thought: "This boy's keen on Gaelic; we'll spoil him, we'll teach him some Gaelic". But they didn't speak it to themselves – but my sister heard them singing a waulking-song in Gaelic to one another. I didn't hear it, I was on the hill.
>
> *AM*: So perhaps in private they would have their wee lapses.
>
> *GCH*: Perhaps, yes. You know the Tarbert people, they're very careful.
>
> *AM*: And what was your mother's reaction to your interest?

GCH: Oh she was the Argyllshire way, she'd come out with an odd word in Gaelic, you know.

AM: But did she encourage you to visit your aunts?

GCH: She did, yes.

AM: You mentioned one word in particular that you remember having got from your aunts.

GCH: "Croidhe" [for "cridhe"]. And "eisge" for "uisge".

AM: Can you remember any other words or phrases that you associate with your aunts?

GCH: "Thig a-steach anns an teine is blàth thu-fhèin" – come in to the fire and warm yourself. (SSS October 1980)

The MacMillan sisters' house, Ingleside, and Heatherknowe, the Hays' own house, were almost adjacent, on the slope south of the harbour on the road to the old pier. At the bottom of the brae, across the road, was the boatbuilder Dougie Leitch's shed, and it was here that George met some of the Tarbert fishermen, and in particular Calum Johnson.

GCH: Well, Ingleside and Heatherknowe were above the Earrann Ghoineach [the Sandy Stretch]. You know Dougie Leitch's shed, the boatshed, at the bottom of the big brae, they were above that. And Calum had his boat out moored off it, the "Liberator". And, in front of Dougie Leitch's shed there used to be a log where they sat down and talked, and I don't remember when I met Calum first, but he used to go round and sit on the log and talk, you know, and I was small and I sat down beside him and talked to him, and I got to know him that way; and his boat was out there, and I said "Oh I'll go to the fishing" to him, so I went to the fishing with Calum – and that's how I got to know Calum Johnson. He was a very independent man, and he had a son called Malcolm, and his wife was from Shetland. And I used to sit and talk to him and I got to know him well, and when I went out to the fishing with him I got to know him very well.

AM: Now at that time, would I be correct in saying that there would be no Gaelic openly used – or habitually used – in Tarbert?

GCH: There was Gaelic openly used, but not habitually.

AM: So it was possible, then, to hear conversation in Gaelic?

GCH: It was, yes. ... among the older men and women, yes.

AM: How frequent would that be?

GCH: Pretty frequent. ... Dougie Leitch used to keep his shed, and it was a boat-harbour shed, he used to build boats there during the winter, and the fishermen used to come in for a blether, and stand and talk, and whittle away with their knives on bits of wood, you know, and they used to be talking away and, as I told you before, I never asked a question, and I never listened, I just remembered [?] something I heard, you know, and they used to come out with this and that, and I can remember it all. And I heard many a thing in Dougie Leitch's shed. (SSS October 1980)

As good an illustration as any of the way Gaelic might have surfaced in conversation in George's presence can be found in a short story by Hay about a night spent "at the plash" (poaching) around the West Shore:

> "He's mogullt, he's mogullt," whispered the Beadle in ecstasy. "Come on, we'll lift her."
>
> With loving care, as a mother dandles her child, and leaning overboard till I thought he was going to share the meshes with his prey, he brought the net aboard. Suddenly he gave a wild shout, that must have been heard over "seven hills and seven glens," returning, as is usual in those circumstances, to his langue de cœur.
>
> "Dhia, tha fear cho mòr agam ris a chunna mi riamh!"
>
> "Cum greim bàite air a' mhoisein," bellowed Did-Ye-Get-Yer-Tea, who had caught the infection, tumbling over athwart in his eagerness. "An e bradan a th' ann?"
>
> "Och, no, no; it's a cock-sparra," said the Beadle sarcastically. (Hay 1940a: 40)

The language shift away from Gaelic in Tarbert was a relatively recent development. Unlike the south end of Kintyre, with its linguistically divided community in Campbeltown, Tarbert had not had to accommodate any strong Scots-speaking settlement. Ayrshire farmers and fisherfolk who resettled in Tarbert in the eighteenth and nineteenth centuries

> were encompassed entirely by it and became as Gaelic as their native neighbours. The process of conversion was no doubt a rapid one, as, indeed, it had to be to overcome initial alienation in overwhelmingly Gaelic communities. (Martin 1984: 33)

Hay's paternal great-grandfather, William Hay, probably came to Tarbert from Dunure in the 1830s. He married a local woman, and they and their family are listed in the Census of 1841. In 1881 and 1891 their son George, "steamboat agent and fish merchant", is listed as a Gaelic speaker, as is his wife, mother of John MacDougall Hay. The language was apparently lost, however, as swiftly as it had been absorbed into the family: not one of George Hay's seven children is credited with Gaelic (Census records 1881: 17, 1891: 22).

Published census statistics indicate a Gaelic colouring in Tarbert village of 69 per cent in 1881, but 49 per cent (including only twenty-five monoglots) in 1891. By 1921, around the time that Hay's curiosity for the language started manifesting itself, that proportion was down to 26 per cent, and as Hay's own reminiscences suggest, competence in Gaelic as reported in census returns did not imply regular use of the language (*Accounts* 1882: 213, *Accounts* 1893: 116, HMSO 1922: 268 and 297).

Edinburgh

Intriguingly, in another conversation with Martin, Hay admitted his reluctance actively to ply the fishermen with questions:

> I never asked a question, never. I wouldn't. They do now; I mean, you do, but I never did. It was different then, you know; they wouldn't like you to ask a question. ... I wish I'd asked him more questions, Calum Johnson. (SSS 1979)

Such reticence in male company – it was not manifested towards his aunts, nor towards another informant, Annie MacDougall (see Martin 2001) – is perhaps not surprising in a boy at the threshold of adulthood, in particular one with no fully established identity in the village. Catherine Hay later recalled that the Laws, the Bruces and the Hays – all from Ayrshire stock – "were always a bit detached from the rest of Tarbert" (Reid 1972), but George Campbell Hay's experience was one of actual estrangement as he was plucked at the age of 10 out of his childhood environment and sent to school in Edinburgh, "that east-coast mausoleum of a place" (Source 46, letter 8, summer 1935). As the son of a deceased minister, he received a full scholarship to attend John Watson's School, then in 1929 he moved on to Fettes College. His removal from Tarbert, while necessarily loosening his social bonds within the village community, seems to have nourished an intense emotional dependency on the place and a notably uncomplicated, idealised identification with North Kintyre; the physical wrench of the separation also became a poetic leitmotiv, from "Soraidh Slàn le Cinntìre"[19], apparently first drafted at the age of 12, to "Soraidh an Sgoileir"[387], his last extant draft.

Hay's few references to those years are unenthusiastic – in a 1960 draft evoking the late summer nights spent at the bow-corks, "An Druim-àrcan 's an t-Ìochdar"[180], the fishermen welcome the youth back with protective affection "after all the seasons spent at school in Edinburgh, speaking Latin, and being whipped like dogs"; and in 1941, army life is said to compare favourably to "that piece of Forever England, Fettes College" (Source 37, 2 June 1942). But the times seem to have been cheerful enough, and have been fondly evoked by Robert Rankin, Hay's closest friend at Fettes (see Rankin 1984). Already in those years, he recalls, George showed "his phenomenal powers of learning other languages":

> I do not think he ever needed to consult a Latin or Greek dictionary. ... I remember playing a game with George, in which I opened the Homeric dictionary at random and asked him the meaning of a word. I was never able to catch him out. A few years later we played the same game with Maceachan's Gaelic dictionary, and with the same results. (Rankin 1984: 2)

Prof. Rankin has further written that

we may have disagreed with the "public school" system, but I do not think we disliked Fettes, except perhaps during the first two years, because of the fagging system. I remember George being quite prepared to go and visit there after we left. ... I would say that, particularly during our last two years, we had quite a lot of freedom, and the company was in the main congenial ... I think he would appreciate too that he got an extremely good classical education; things were not so good on the scientific side, but that would not worry him. Like other schools, it has improved greatly over the years and there is now no fagging, no floggings by prefects, no early morning school before breakfast, etc., etc. I get the impression also that Scottish accents are now more generally acceptable than they used to be. (Letter to editor, 12 August 1991)

However anglicised the school may have been, Hay made clear his own allegiance to Gaelic and to the Highlands in some of his contributions to the school magazine, *The Fettesian*. Mostly submitted under the pseudonym "Ciotach" ("left-handed"), they included the "Lament for Ruaraidh Mòr MacLeod"[3] which Hay retained a while in his adult corpus, and a nostalgic "Innse Gall" ("Hebrides"), as well as translations from Irish poetry (56:6, July 1934; 57:1, November 1934). His review of the Irish biography *Twenty Years a-Growing* comments with lucidity that

> the Gael has till now only been revealed to the world through a series of interpreters of varying sympathy and sincerity ... But in this novel the Gael himself speaks out; for it was written by an islander without any self-consciousness, and without any of the posing which is so annoying in ... worshippers of the mythical "Celtic Gloom". (56:6, July 1934)

Alien perceptions of the Highlands are satirised in "A Scene in the Highlands (which appeared in a Sassenach magazine)" (55:4, April 1933), while the melancholy short story "Home" (56:6, July 1934) evokes an exile's return to his native township, Baliver, now lying in ruins (a township of this name had existed west of Tarbert).

Following George's departure to John Watson's, the family had moved to Edinburgh, but to Tarbert they returned in holiday time, and as the boy reached his mid-teens he joined Calum Johnson's crew on the "Liberator".

AM: Were you out quite frequently with Calum Johnson?
GCH: In September, mostly; my holidays, you know. ... August and September.
AM: Were you out every night the boat would be out?
GCH: Very near it.
AM: And that would be from quite an early age.
GCH: Sixteen on.

AM: So you were old enough not to cause your mother any concern about going overboard, or –

GCH: Oh no, she never worried. I was on the hill, all the time, she never said the word "hill" to me yet – and you know, it's a rough hill, you know the hill yourself. I went out to the fishing, she never said the word "fishing", I don't believe she said the word "fish" to me at all, no.

AM: Did Calum Johnson know anything about your own fishing connections on the Hay side?

GCH: He would, but he didn't say anything about them, you know Tarbert.

AM: [What was] your range of experience when you were out with Calum?

GCH: The bowcorks, and I was steering till sunset.

AM: Was Gaelic used aboard the boat?

GCH: An odd word, "toman o mackerel", and so on.

AM: How extensive was Calum Johnson's Gaelic?

GCH: I think it was very extensive, but I think, in the summer, you know, in the holiday time, they used to speak English a lot – or speak Tarbert or English – and I came down in the holiday time, so I didn't hear them speaking as much Gaelic as they spoke really during the winter, you know.

AM: I suppose to some extent his facility in the language would be diminishing year by year, through –

GCH: I think he was thinking it over all the time. ... I think so.

AM: That of course would have been his first language.

GCH: It was, yes.

AM: How many of the older people at that time would have been proficient in that sense in Tarbert?

GCH: Well I don't know because I was in Heatherknowe and I was always on the hill, I was hardly ever in the village, and I only ever met the people down by Dougie Leitch's shed, and so on, and I don't know one side of Tarbert, because I was very careful too, and I suspect there was a lot more Gaelic going on in Tarbert than I ever knew, from Tarbert, I mean. I was always on the hill, or I was across the road, into a boat and away down the West Shore again. [Laughs.]

AM: So you'd be on the hill all during the day, then at sea at night.

GCH: [Laughs.] Sea at night, yes.

AM: You wouldn't have been sleeping much, then.

GCH: Oh I was sleeping normally, aye.

AM: Were you going all on your own to the hill?

GCH: Uh-huh.

AM: You werena meeting many people on the hill, no?

GCH: On the hill? No, you'd never meet anyone.

AM: So the West Shore in your time was totally uninhabited?

GCH: Totally, aye. (SSS October 1980)

Oxford

Hay and Rankin both won scholarships in 1934 taking them on to the next rung of the English educational ladder: the universities of Oxford and Cambridge. Hay seems to have enjoyed his years at Corpus Christi College, in Oxford; his main memories some forty years later were of drinking and piping sessions with Christopher MacRae, a fellow Gael from Kintail. One friend remembered him as

> certainly the most colourful of an interesting bunch of fellow first years, at Corpus. You suggest that he was a pretty wild customer. I do not know that he was ever involved in anything nefarious, although I doubt if the dons had him listed as one of their most admirable students. He had a totally individual approach to study, as indeed to everything else. He hated philosophy, but loved language, and languages. ... His regard for authority was slender. His memory for words and phrases, in I do not know how many languages, was to me unique. ... He consumed a fair amount of malt whisky, as a student, but I do not recall this seriously impairing his faculties. He always claimed that it improved his playing of the pipes. (John Dunlop, letter to R. A. Rankin, 30 May 1991)

Another contemporary recalls that

> he had quite a small sitting-room into which he would crowd many Scots and a few others drinking whisky and trying to talk against a background of bagpipes ... He was very convivial – perhaps too convivial. He was pretty idle with regard to the official curriculum and got no way near as good a degree as his abilities deserved. (J. O. Urmson to editor)

The late Arnold Jennings, a fellow Classical scholar who counted George among his very best friends, has written that

> I knew George Hay as above all always cheerful, a jolly chap. His being rooted in a genuine strong tradition different from ours made a great appeal to me, and I loved to hear him singing Gaelic songs. He was very convivial – a social drink was always offered you. His refusal to be impressed by pretentious people of any kind appealed to me. (Letter to editor, September 1992)

This last trait was noted by his school friend Robert Rankin, who recalled that

on occasion he could be extremely vituperative, particularly to people
he thought were being pretentious and putting on airs, but his abuse
(not of the four-letter kind) often missed its mark as his victims were
usually not well enough educated to understand his allusions. (Rankin
1984: 11–12)

And an anecdote from another friend, Ronald Daffern, picks up on the same
lack of deference to "authority":

during a walking-tour in Lochaber in Summer '36, after spending the
night on the floor of what George called a bothy, [we were] woken the
next morning by a tall and well-dressed man – a gamekeeper? the
landlord? – who strode in and demanded "And who might you be?" to
which George commented "That is an example of the Indignant Sub-
junctive". (Letter to Robert Rankin, 15 July 1991)

The Oxford classical degree in Greek and Latin was divided into the five-
term course of Honour Moderations (Mods), followed by seven terms of
Literae Humaniores (Greats). The nature of the work set in Mods is of
particular interest in view of Hay's extraordinary ability for calquing literary
voices in his poetry:

You did Latin prose and translation, e.g. leading articles from *The
Times*, or speeches in the House of Commons, into Ciceronian Latin;
similarly Greek prose; English poetry into Latin and Greek verse; you
read an *immense* amount of Greek and Latin literature (the whole of
Homer and Virgil to begin with), some of it in very great detail; trans-
lation of passages you had not seen before from Greek or Latin into
English; and one or two papers in "special subjects". (Jennings, letter
to editor, September 1992)

Greats, however, consisted of Ancient History and Philosophy, the latter of
which Hay particularly detested.

Philosophy was not for him: his cast of mind and mental powers were
not suited to it. I suspect that he never really knew what philosophy
was about: he certainly heartily disliked it. (Jennings, op. cit.)

He hated philosophy, but loved language, and languages. I still bear a
nose bent by him, following his strong objection to my persisting in
discussing philosophy with a fellow student, in his rooms. He inflicted
the damage, although I was twice his size and weight. Peace was re-
stored by suitable applications of Glenlivet (to which he had first intro-
duced me) taken internally. (Dunlop, op. cit.)

Undoubtedly Hay's interests during his four years in Oxford strayed far
beyond the subjects of his academic study. As he expressed shortly before
his final exams:

Greats are drawing nigh – shadow of the evening snoops across the
sky. 'S mòr m'eagal nach dean mi euchd no tapachd. Fada bhuaithe!

Mar tha 'n donas sa chùis, tha mi air tuiteam eadar an long 's an laimirig – no eadar fichead long 's fichead laimirig. Between greats, Irish, Welsh, Icelandic, Anglo-Saxon, Swedish, Danish, Modern Greek and the need to learn German ... – tha mo cheann bochd dìreach na bhrochan. However I'll get a degree of kinds, tho I dare say I'll be in some disgrace. (Source 54, May? 1938)

I'm afraid I won't be performing any great feats. Far from it! The damned truth of the matter is that I've fallen between the ship and the pier – or between twenty ships and twenty piers. ... – my poor head's in a stew. ...

As predicted, he left Oxford with an inglorious fourth-class degree.

Hay had started learning Old Icelandic in the summer of 1936, then Danish a year later "los cur seachad na h-ùine", "to pass the time" (Source 46, 26 July 1937). A letter in Norwegian to Mrs Fanny MacTaggart in 1942 gives an insight into his easy acquisition of new languages:

You ask where and how I learnt my Norwegian. I have to say it wasn't "the direct method" I used. First I learned Old Norwegian/Icelandic ... from books, as the development of Gaelic could not be understood without a knowledge of the language that has given us so many words and expressions. Then I learnt Danish partly by reading, partly on board an old coal steamer going east to Copenhagen. The results when I went ashore were funny enough, for on board the ship they spoke pure Bornholm dialect, and some of their expressions weren't as re-fined as they might have been. Then I sought other places between Larvik and Mandal on board another [Icelandic] freightship, and when I saw your lovely country and heard the manly Norwegian pronuncia-tion, its tone so reminiscent of that to be heard at home in Argyll, "The Danish", I thought, "can have their Himmelbjerg and their glottal stop, but here is a country and people worth knowing". And then I preferred to forget my Danish and learn Norwegian. (Source 42, 25 October 1942; transl. A. Kruse)

During his last term, he ambitiously began compiling a Gaelic lexicography, evidence for which remains in some of the notebooks held by the National Library of Scotland (see NLS MSS 26723–7, 26738, 26746–7).

The idea is to give all the references, as nobody now can tell the status of a Gaelic word from a dictionary. It has to be done sometime, and I can only hope my efforts will save labour for somebody ... Examples must come from Old Irish, Bardic usage and Keating as well. (Source 54, May? 1938)

Hay's holidays during those years were spent on hill-walking excursions in the Highlands, and sailing trips on the Clyde and along the west coast (on yachts like "The Corrie"), as well as the time spent in Tarbert, hunting, plashing and, come autumn, ring-net fishing on the "Liberator". Arnold Jennings remembered being invited on a cycling and walking tour of the Highlands:

> Included in George's scanty luggage for this trip was a knife with a two-edged blade some six inches long. He explained to me that such a knife was a useful thing to have with you, and could come in handy in many ways. When I asked for an example (as I, a town-bred chap, could not think of any), he said "Well, skinning a deer, for example."
>
> On a Sunday evening we were walking up a long glen which contained but one house, at the top end of the glen. George was hoping they would put us up for the night, which they did. Next morning first thing I found George with an enormous smile, obviously very pleased with something. He told me that on the Sunday evening he had asked the crofter if he knew any Gaelic songs: the man had said no, he didn't, but George had been suspicious. On the Monday morning he had repeated his question, and in reply the man had sung to him a great number of Gaelic songs, but "he didn't want his wife to hear him singing songs on the Sabbath". (Jennings, op. cit.)

Robert Rankin has said that Hay was "the leading spirit" on these walking tours, which "always had some literary or historical objective" (Rankin 1984: 4).

At some point in his time at university, Hay befriended Douglas Young, an unmistakable landmark in the small Scottish community in Oxford – "an exceedingly tall fellow with a shovel-beard", as he was described in 1940 by the poet William Soutar – "his leanness, longness and fringiness gave one the initial impression of a BBC announcer who had partially metamorphosed into an aerial" (Soutar 1988: 158). A gifted Classical scholar and by all accounts a man of charisma, Young's physical and intellectual attributes had earned him the nickname "Dia" or "God" during his first degree in St Andrews (see Young 1970: 12). In Oxford his political views veered to the left and to Scottish nationalism. Young was to become one of the foremost spokesmen for the Scottish Renaissance poets of the 1940s, as well as a political celebrity, and he was probably responsible for introducing Hay to the work of Hugh MacDiarmid. Young himself, however, later attributed his own poetic beginnings to the urging of his younger friend:

> Ye first inciteit me tae sclim
> oor Scottish Helikon,
> an shared ma ilka ploy an whim
> in Gaelic poetry or in Scots;
> forbye kept me on
> the anely course for patriots.
>
> ("Tae Deòrsa i the heather, back-end o 1940", Source 37;
> revised as "To a Friend on a Campaign", *Poetry Scotland* 3:26)

Another poem by Young evokes Hay at an Oxford party:

> Deòrsa, the peat-fire
> that smoulders darkling,
> with sudden rapture
> flaring and sparkling.
> ... Wrapped in the breacan waves
> blue-green, the Bright of Eye
> lives in an older realm
> than our drab narrow Scotland of dull slaves.
> ... Heart-whole he sits, and still,
> and smokes and drinks his fill;
> sits still and smile serene,
> oblivious of the Dean.

("Lines on a Gaelic poet at an Oxford party", Source 37)

This perception of Hay as one holding on to the values of an older age is one which emerges in other accounts and in Hay's own work. In one letter to Robert Rankin, he quotes an old Gaelic verse and comments:

> It's an entirely different world of thought and outlook from any to be found now, and from their songs one feels that the "old men" must have been a bloody fine race. ... The ideal in the line "Leòghan, leanabh agus rìgh" ['lion, child and king'] isn't barbarous or anything like it. What they admired was a man who was gentle and even soft but fierce and wild when the occasion called for it. (Source 46, December 1936)

Whether by temperament or conscious emulation, there is much of Hay himself in that description. Both the testimonies of his contemporaries and Hay's own letters suggest that to a modest reserve he could add bursts of exuberance; one friend, for example, recalled an incident at a College Bump Supper (celebrating a boating victory):

> Someone spilled beer over me, and I unwisely mentioned this to George. "Nobody is going to spill beer on a friend of mine!" he said, and searched furiously for the man who did it, an oarsman well above George in height. (Dunlop, op. cit.)

Hay's friendship with Young seems to have been the relationship within which he most discussed his literary activity and his politics. Both men left Oxford in 1938, and what survives of their voluminous correspondence from then until the end of the war (Source 36) provides a vivid picture of his preoccupations and activities over those years, supplemented by his letters to Kenneth MacLeod and Robert Rankin (Sources 44 and 46), and the diary he intermittently kept between 1938 and 1941 (Source 5).

The National Movement in the 1930s

In the course of the 1930s, Scotland experienced a pronounced resurgence of political and cultural nationalism, and once back in Edinburgh Hay threw himself into the service of the cause. His nationalist sympathies apparently went back a long way. He once commented that it was "hurt racial pride" that had made the nineteenth-century Gaelic poet William Livingston a nationalist, and added: "a very sufficient reason, and I myself was one of that kind ages before I further developed into one of the statistical variety" (Source 37, February 1940). Stirrings had already been felt at the tender age of 11:

> The wild west wind comes o'er the sea
> Crying "Sound the pibroch! Up! To arms!
> Alba'll e'ermore in freedom be,
> Sons o' the moors and the glens and tarns
> For Gael can conquer Sassenach"
> She cries.

("The Winds o Alba", Source 20, 5)

His anglicised schooling may have helped fan the flames, but Hay's teenage years in any case coincided with the growth of a vocal nationalist movement whose very marginality in the world of conventional party politics seemed to encourage a compensatory flamboyance. The 1920s had seen the steady demise of the pre-war Home Rule All Round policy, what with the irrevocable collapse of the Liberal Party, open hostilities between the fledgling Labour Party and ILP, and the labour movement's entrenchment behind British class politics after the failure of the 1926 General Strike.

The scuppering of Barr's Home Rule bill in 1928 signalled the end of the road for the Scottish Home Rule Association, and precipitated the formation of the National Party of Scotland (NPS). Cross-party lobbying was deemed to have failed, and the home-rule cause was henceforth to be put directly to the electors as another contestant in the political arena. The new party had a gifted orator in John MacCormick, and he was to become the prime mover in the national movement for the next twenty years. Although party membership grew to 8,000 within three years (Hanham 1969: 157), electoral recognition did not come so easily, and one of the leadership's principal concerns was to attract mainstream moderate opinion and consolidate the party's financial base. Intent on distancing the NPS from the colourful radicals who seemed to make the headlines, MacCormick made a determined effort to steer the party away from the literary-intellectual circles that had been prominent in the Home Rule movement, and attempted to keep the anti-imperialist fundamentalists at bay and to impose discipline within the ranks. He courted Liberal and Unionist opinion, and especially sought rapprochement with a small Unionist splinter group, the Scottish Party, "an élite pressure group" for Home Rule rather than an organised political group (Finlay 1994: 157).

In 1934, as Hay's career at Fettes College was drawing to a close, the NPS – having rid itself (temporarily) of its most vocal fundamentalists and ditched its commitment to Scottish independence – absorbed the Scottish Party into its leadership, and turned itself into the Scottish National Party. The new arrivals brought money and prestige to the party, but inevitably the initial ideological peace was short-lived, and divisions and incoherence obstructed any real political advance. In spite of lingering economic depression, a renewed surge of home-rule sentiment and the dramatic collapse of Labour organisation in central Scotland (after the suicidal secession of the ILP), the SNP remained totally marginalised throughout the decade.

The recession which had gripped the Scottish economy by the early 1930s lingered longer than in the rest of Britain, despite attempts to reduce the country's dependence on the stricken industries of steel and shipbuilding and to encourage new light industries in the Central Belt. Labour minister Tom Johnston, writing about the "real bellows which blow the fires of Scots nationalism" such as "the almost perpetual preponderance of our unemployment figures vis-a-vis England and Wales", recorded that

> In the period 1932–1937 there were 3,217 new factories started in Great Britain, but Scotland got only 127 of them, or one in every 25; and during the same period we closed 133 factories, so we actually lost on balance. We had serious emigrations of our healthiest stocks of citizenry; we had 300,000 houses without water-closet; our maternal mortality was 50% higher than in England and Wales, our infant mortality was 25% worse; our army rejects were 6% higher; control of some of our banks was moving south to Lombard Street. (Johnston 1952: 65)

The clouds of economic depression lifted temporarily at the approaching prospect of war, with the renewed upturn in steel and shipbuilding. The issue of war also raised particular fears and hopes in the nationalist movement, highlighting divisions in the ranks, and it eventually served as catalyst for a dramatic split in the SNP.

When Hay returned to Edinburgh, the questions which had long divided the party – on the degree of national autonomy it was campaigning for, and the best way of attaining it – had hardened into factional disputes. The party was plagued by "uninspiring leadership, poor discipline, low morale, declining branch activity, increasing financial pressures, and last but not least, the stigma of being nothing more than an inconsequential fringe group in Scottish politics" (Finlay 1994: 206). It has been estimated that membership had sunk to below 2,000 (Webb 1977: 61).

MacCormick appeared to be moving back to the old SHRA tactic of lobbying the British parties. His devolutionary stance and political flirting was anathema to many activists, including those who had recently resurrected the collapsed Edinburgh branch, and he provoked further alienation by his authoritarian style of leadership. Nevertheless, MacCormick's "moderate" policies gained ground, and plans for a National Plebiscite and the calling of a National Convention were only stalled by the outbreak of war. But the formulation of SNP policy on the war effort added yet another faultline to the over-accidented terrain of nationalist politics. By the time Hay returned to Edinburgh, two distinct factions were discernible in the party, with the "fundamentalists" – for outright independence, by electoral opposition to other parties – tending also to be firm anti-conscriptionists.

In 1937, the Annual Conference of the SNP passed a motion declaring itself "strongly opposed to the manpower of Scotland being used to defend an Empire in the governing of which she has no voice" and pledged that "all male members ... of military age [would] refuse to serve in any section of the Crown forces" until the party's programme had been fulfilled (Finlay 1994: 243). "This was a pretty strong resolution", wrote Young,

> but no way out of the ordinary for a national movement if one reflects on the history of national movements in general. It struck me that, if one was to be serious at all about self-government for Scotland, it was only proper to be serious about the most serious aspects of the question. Accordingly the question of Scotland's position in a war was of more importance than the incidence of infantile mortality, overcrowding in slums, electrification of railways, construction of road-bridges over the Forth and Tay ... and all the other stock-in-trade of nationalist platforms. (Young 1950: 56)

The nationalist anti-conscription movement had its pacifists, most notably the veteran SHRA campaigner Roland Muirhead, but most of its activists based their stance on opposition to London government, only strengthened by Westminster's decision not to enforce conscription in Northern Ireland. Adherents of Wendy Wood's Anti-Conscription League defended their "constitutional right as a citizen of Scotland, to refuse all military service under the British Government" since the Treaty of Union had been violated (Source P26, September 1937: 11); slogans declaring "We will fight no more in England's wars – èirich Alba" were "stencilled all over the capital", while (rather more cryptically) "1715, 1745, 1938 – third time's lucky" was "to be found adorning many Scottish towns" (Source P33 I.1, June–August 1938). The Scottish Neutrality League, set up in June 1939 by Arthur Donaldson (a future leader of the SNP), demanded the cessation of conscription in Scotland, arguing that the country should claim neutrality like Ireland or Switzerland, since "our only risk of war comes from our connection with England and her overgrown, wobbly Empire" (Source P26, November 1938: 14). The meticulous case later defended in court by Douglas

Young included both the argument that the Treaty of 1707 precluded the right of Parliament to conscript Scots for foreign service, and also the fall-back position that in any case the numerous violations of the Treaty invalidated the authority of Westminster in Scotland (Young 1942).

As German aggression increased and war became ever more likely, subsequent Party Conferences overrode the 1937 policy, and Arthur Donaldson and members of his league (now the United Scotland Movement) were expelled from the party. The bulk of the SNP, however sympathetic to the anti-conscriptionists' arguments, supported the war effort, but Young and Hay resolutely stood by the stance which they had taken while still in Oxford. One friend remembers:

> During the last 18 months of our course at Oxford many undergraduates took it for granted that there would soon be a world war, and would speculate on what they would do. George made it clear that as a loyal Scot he would take the view that it was no part of his duty to fight the Englishmen's war for them. When someone said he might not be allowed the choice, he said he would go up into the hills and lie low there, and "if they came to get me, I would shoot them", and to me, with a cheerful smile, "and if it was you that came to get me, I'd shoot you too". (Jennings, op. cit.)

There was nothing frivolous about Hay's stance, however. The wayward path on which his convictions took him did not lead to quite as dramatic a showdown as envisaged in his quip or in the poem "Teisteas Mhic Iain Deòrsa"[82], but it was nevertheless to prove a steep and lonely road.

In the Vanguard

Much of Hay's diary and correspondence on his return to Scotland is taken up with the worsening international situation, his own political activities and the divisions in the nationalist body. He finds the movement deplorably ragged:

> The pity is that any Scotsman who thinks, or is alive or revolutionary, is strongly for Scottish self-government; but they are nearly all side-tracked into being Communists, Labour men, Liberals and God knows what. If they had eyes in their heads they would see that under the present dispensation nothing will be done for the good of the people … Surely they can at least see how thin the cloak of Parliamentary representation is wearing, and notice the Fascist posturings of those on high. (Source 5: 5, 1 December 1938)

In December 1938, Hay met the patriot activist Wendy Wood. Having "imagined her a targe", he was surprised to find her "one of the most charming and vital people I have ever seen" (Source 5: 6). He joined her newly formed "Comunn airson Saorsa na h-Alba" (League for the Independence of Scotland), dedicated to "undertak[ing] the education of the people by propaganda [and] to the re-establishment of the Scottish State" (Source P26, November 1938: 11). For five months the League was given its own supplement in the *Scots Independent*, before the SNP finally asserted its control over the paper. In the course of its brief existence the Comunn launched a campaign advocating native production for native markets, announced that it had "accepted a pact of peace between the IRA and Scotland", sought to launch a National Plebiscite on the issue of self-government, and organised protest meetings at the Rosyth naval yard, following the eviction of Scots hands by the Admiralty (see Source P26, January–July 1939). Its involvement at Rosyth is mentioned in a revealing letter from Hay to Young, where he expounds at length on the needs of the party:

> The people have to be moved in the right direction, and what is more have to be given some real impetus, and even in Scotland the only impetus is that of emotion. … Opportunism is necessary. … I mean merely that favourable circumstances must be exploited at once and fully, before they no longer exist. And they can even be created. And for doing this one must have neither doubts or scruples. Unfortunately opportunists of this kind are born not made. An example. You know about Rosyth of course – neglected since the war and now the recipient of doubtful favours. A mass eviction of 400 by the Admiralty and the arrival of swarms of English hands (as if there were no such thing as a Scottish shipyard hand unemployed). What an opportunity, and what an air of brotherhood there must be about the place! The Comunn airson Saorsa na h-Alba alone took the chance, and they have left the place a boiling pot of racial hatred (it will be given a stir frequently). Thus the emotion is supplied. If one has doubts or scruples these things can't be done. If such things aren't done nothing will be attained. (Source 36, "Friday" April 1939)

Writing to Kenneth MacLeod in early December 1938, around the time of meeting Wendy Wood, Hay is excited by the many signs that "Scotland is awakening", including "the most startling thing of all, … that even some Glasgow Clan Societies have started agitating for more Gaelic at their meetings":

> Things will seem very different in Gigha, but even in a comparatively quiet city like Edinburgh it grows clear that the future holds for us a Major War … and almost certainly a social revolution with all the bitter struggles of Communism and Fascism. The most discreet paper cannot hide the fact that our government eyes Germany with a longing admiration, and that it has already gone far in the way of imitation. If anything happens it will be Fascist heads that I will be breaking, and there must be plenty of those among the Highland landlord families.
>
> It is only honest for me to say that the prospect attracts me. Meanwhile Scotsmen must be prevented from marching in case of a war to give their lives on behalf of the future Bank of England and the

armament firms, and to ensure that the natives of Kenya Colony and India continue to suffer slavery, hunger and death in our glorious Empire. Scotland has bled enough already.

This will seem feverish to you, and not like my old self, and it may displease you. The old self is still there, but when one sees the field being cleared for a struggle before one's eyes (though the process may take years) one must come to a decision and be ready to act on it. Am fear as cruaidhe dòrn 's as luaithe buille, is esan bhios an uachdar [He will win who is hardest of fist and swiftest to strike]. (Source 44, early December 1938)

We have no record of Kenneth MacLeod's response, but a letter from Hay soon after is more tempered:

Your first letter redoubles my confidence in you. I like my friends to tell me when they think I am being a damned fool, and I value very much those who do so. But don't worry; we won't break any heads. We won't even indulge in repetition of the Lewis Deer Drive, although I think it would greatly benefit our poor country. Years of propaganda are needed, for the Scottish people is distressingly dùsalach [lethargic]. (ibid., 13 December 1938)

Hay had first contacted the elderly minister in October 1938, presumably feeling in need of some validation from a Gaelic authority as the bulk of his poetry increased. Kenneth MacLeod, then ministering in Gigha, was known to Catherine Hay's aunts, the MacMillan sisters, and the two men had briefly met in Tarbert. Hay can have had little enthusiasm for the romantic, Twilight interpretations of Gaelic culture promoted in MacLeod's popular book *The Road to the Isles* and in his musical collaboration with Marjory Kennedy-Fraser, *Songs of the Hebrides*. Indeed, when six years later Sorley MacLean's satire on the MacLeod poetic style was published in *Dàin do Eimhir agus Dàin Eile*, Hay's feelings were mixed:

I feel rather uncomfortable when I envisage him reading that satire in Somhairle's book, for it will hurt him. Though I agree with Sam. Why doesn't he write some prose, for his Gaelic prose is the best going, I imagine. (Source 36, 17 July 1944)

Certainly the minister's deep knowledge of Gaelic tradition and the excellence of his Gaelic prose could not be disputed. Hay tentatively sent him a few poems, "only a small sop out of the seid [wisp out of the bundle]":

I would be seven times grateful if you would tell me plainly whether I should burn these productions and their fellows and dance on the ashes, or give way further to my infamous itch for stringing words together. (Source 44, 2 October 1938)

A week later, having received "an exceedingly kind and encouraging" reply, the young man sent off a bulkier selection, revealing in his letter his attraction to the compactness and discipline of classical bardic poetry. Hay visited MacLeod in Gigha, and continued a lively correspondence with him, on various matters beyond literature, including his political enthusiasms. The December letter quoted above thanking MacLeod for his honesty goes on at length to express Hay's "great aversion" to the Normans ("with [them] came that worship of successful inhumanity from which all, Irishman, crofter and Saxon ceorl have suffered in time"), as also his enthusiasm for modern Greek poetry, in particular "the songs about the Klephts, or the outlaws who fought the Turks. ... The Gaelic language is waiting with open arms for poetry like that" (ibid., 13 December 1938).

Again in that same letter he could tell MacLeod that "Gaelic originals and translations now amount to about forty". An approach to Gaelic and nationalist publisher Aeneas Mackay proved fruitless, but from the end of 1938 Hay's poetry began to appear in various periodicals: *An Gàidheal*, *The Scots Magazine*, *Scots Independent* and Hugh MacDiarmid's *The Voice of Scotland*. Hay was also considering applying to the McCaig Trust for funding towards publication, and he asked MacLeod for a note of recommendation, adding cautiously that he would "neither take it on the nose nor on the mouth" should the minister have any reservations about endorsing his application (ibid., c. May 1939).

Hay's caution was not ill-founded: "Coinneach MacL. has actually sent me my bundle of utterances, tho without any note of recommendation. There is no answer to that but silence" (Source 36, 24 October 1939). Religious sensibilities, it seems, had been ruffled by one satirical poem, "Na Griogaraich" (preserved in Source 59), "an epic on how the MacGregors, having returned to their place of origin, stole their progenitor's tongs and coal, so that there ensued drifting of snow and freezing in the very seventh circle" (Source 44, 2 October 1938). "He *is* a meenister, and could hardly act as an under-midwife to the Griogaraich", Hay noted wryly (Source 36, op. cit.). There was no such understanding to be had from Hugh MacDiarmid when word eventually reached Whalsay of the minister's "appalling hardihood":

> George Campbell Hay is a young poet but he is the greatest promise of renascent Gaelic poetry Scotland has had since the glorious outburst round the time of the '45 ... and the efforts of a creature like you to hinder his coming to the fore are reminiscent of the efforts of the misguided gentleman who tried to stay the incoming tide with a whalebone besom. I propose in other quarters to expose your disgraceful cretinizing manoeuvres – and to show in detail the despicable tactics by which you, and the rest of the Old Gang with whom you are associated, have blocked the interests of the Gaelic language and literature at every possible point on behalf of your horrible little religious and political prejudices and because you know only too well that the emergence of work of real literary calibre ... will speedily put paid to your

account and blow the gaff on the ridiculous over-estimation so long bestowed on your own pitifully silly stuff and nonsense, and the work generally of all the self-appointed trustees and censors of Scottish Gaeldom who have so monstrously betrayed that trust. (Source 44, 8 April 1940)

MacLeod countered vituperation with amiable calm (ibid., 25 April 1940). Pointing out that "only a very small part of your letter really applies to me", he reasserted "his strong personal liking" for Hay and his full appreciation of his work, but insisted that he could not make himself "responsible for anything that would jar on the genuine religious feelings of my fellow-Gaels, such as their attitude of reverence towards the Deity". "Na Griogaraich" aims its mild scurrility at clan pride rather than Presbyterian piety, but it does depict God as a grumpy geriatric intent on sleeping undisturbed through the Sabbath (see Source 59: 18–21).

By then Hay had made the acquaintance of the composer Francis George Scott, who had already set "To a Loch Fyne Fisherman"[20] to a solemn melody for baritone, and by Spring 1940 was working on more lyrics sent to him by Hay (probably Poems 62, 70 and 71). Writing to MacDiarmid, Scott enthused:

> I herewith give warning that George Campbell Hay will be the next star in the Scottish firmament and unite in himself both Gaelic and Scots traditions. ... I am finding something pretty new in his rhythm sense (no doubt Gaelic) and in less than a week I had finished music to three of his lyrics. ... For a lad of 24 he amazes me by the maturity of his judgements of people and literature. I like him immensely, and his work, though tentative at times, has a real classical sanity about it, and ... a rhythm that stirs me right over into music. (Lindsay 1980: 203)

Much of Hay's correspondence with Young in this period is taken up with politics, and also with their various plans for publication. Young seems to have entertained doubts about the anti-conscription stance, for in one letter Hay sets about rebutting his "immense change of front":

> You say that as we are placed we should fight for our pluto-democracy, wretched as it is, against the much worse Nazi Germany. Firstly brethren, I see the pluto on occasions, but never the democracy ... The House of Commons is now a farce ... Public opinion is powerless in big issues. The people and the government were almost as clearly divided over Spain as were the opposing forces in Spain itself. We know what was the outcome and we should remember it, for people with short memories are easy to stampede into enthusiasm.
>
> ... Such pretences as there are of democracy, and such civil rights as are left will automatically disappear with the declaration of war, perhaps never to reappear. ...
>
> It would only be another Empire and Markets Balance of Power

War ... and one can't go and fall into line in such an affair. ... How would Germany dare immobilise vast bodies of troops in a hostile Britain, especially when there was an empire to be dealt with? It's quite preposterous. Of course if she takes our possessions and markets there will be starvation – in England. It will be an interesting thing for Ireland to watch. ...

Really, to fall into line and fight a war although it were against the deil himself would be very much the worse of the two evils. You know yourself that from the Nationalist's and from the genuine left-wing point of view the enemy is between here and the Channel, and needs more careful watching every day.

As for nationalism being too strong a drink for Scotsmen to swallow, I think that is doubtful; and over-caution is a fatal error, for it creates apathy. You can't lead people on by walking back to meet them. I know that there are more than a 100 people who think Scotland, even at the present juncture, comes first. ... What's more the children are coming into the movement, and every meeting brings more members.

The general body of the country is still fairly rotten, and ready to behave in the usual conditioned reflex way, but we will not improve that by following suit. In the last war ... there were 1,191 Socialist objectors, of whom 805 belonged to the ILP. A mere nothing, but they were at the time our only true Socialists, and the value of their example is no mere nothing. They were ready to assume the responsibilities as well as the honours of being in the vanguard, and if nationalists do not do the same nationalism will retreat. But if they don't shrink, nationalism will be raised to a higher and more serious plane.

... It is the duty of all nationalists to have some definite plan of construction for otherwise he would be an anarchist and not a nationalist, but at present the place for such plans is in the background ... for God's sake don't let anyone say "We'll win self-government, and then we'll &cet.". One must say "We'll win self-government, and then you, the Scottish people, shall decide what is to be done with the country".

... What we need at present is pure nationalism. ... A lot of the Central Belt and the South receive nationalism with joy, and Comunn airson Saorsa na h-Alba finds recruits that are even more advanced than itself, which is saying a lot! (Source 36, 15 May 1939)

By October, after a summer out in the West, Hay was active in the Young Scottish Nationalists, set up in April by the Edinburgh branch of the SNP (Source P26, June 1939). The group's main activities seem to have been canvassing and selling *SIs* around Midlothian, as well as decorating Arthur's Seat and the Castle Rock with appropriate slogans. Wendy Wood, meanwhile, had repaired with her partner MacAindreis to an abandoned croft where they were to spend the war years, partly to renew their energies after years of strenuous peripatetic activism, but also to demonstrate the viability of a Highland crofting life, "crofting and fishing [being] the only natural Highland industries, and the Highlands ... the only real Scotland" (Wood 1946: 14).

Early in 1939, Hay had made contact with the newly appointed Professor of Celtic in Edinburgh, James Carmichael Watson. He sent Watson the Gaelic lexicography begun in Oxford and began attending classes in Middle Irish at the young professor's house (Source 5, 4 January 1939). He was not long in gaining Watson's confidence:

> The late Prof. MacKinnon left behind many tomes of interleaved Gaelic dictionaries, with his additions and annotations. They are to be prepared for publication under a grant of £100, and Watson asked me if I would be willing to undertake it. As they say at home "I could herdly refuse the sowl" – so that's that, and it couldn't be better. With regard to my own [lexicographical] work he pointed out rightly that it was premature to compile a dictionary with hardly anything properly edited, and the spelling in chaos. He suggested that I should annotate two minor poets such as Eachann Bacach and Mairearad Ni'n Lachainn, which flattered me vastly. It seems as if the good Gaelic doesn't intend to play a nasty trick on me after all. (Source 46, 14 February 1939)

That autumn, Hay enrolled at Moray House College to train as a classics teacher, with the intention of obtaining a post in the Highlands. With Britain's declaration of war against Germany, the SNP came under pressure to clarify its position, and in December it agreed to support the Government, but urged that "the definition of conscientious objection should be enlarged to include objections based on profound political conviction" (Webb 1977: 58). For MacCormick and what he termed "the sane element in the Party", the situation regarding the war was "well in hand, and we were able to march in step with Scottish public opinion", but a minority disagreed with this shifting of policy, and, in MacCormick's eyes, "the malcontents were noisy and troublesome" (MacCormick 1955: 97). Hay's own frustration at the SNP erupts in a letter of 21 August 1940:

> We are continuing our activities here (mainly the S.I.) ... but the muckle deil knows what's to be done about our Glasgow Führers ... Their main concern seems to be to appear orthodox and respectable ... They do no fundamental thinking about the why and whither of this war, and will hardly be able to say the proper things to hungry, unemployed and bewildered millions after the war. ... Do they even know how strong or otherwise Nationalism has become? I dare say their only criteria are sales of the S.I. and increase in party membership. ... If they would find out what is being said in Youth Hostels and Schools they might be surprised ...
>
> They express no will ... They compromise and yield, and discuss after the manner of a debating club when they should be thrawn and

sure of themselves. As they do not lead, people will never follow them, and as they do not stand their ground people will never range themselves behind them.

Another example of their timorousness is their fear of being called romantic. Montrose jeered at a party composed of "poets" and suggested we wanted one made up of "business men". We have business men, and to spare, and look at the results. Everyone knows by now that they are fond of statistics, returns and wool prices, and that's all to the good as far as it goes. But if they do not display some soul or spirit … the romantic creature that lurks within the greater part of Scotsmen (and of human beings) will feel cold and draw away. … As far as they are concerned the Gaelic language doesn't exist, nor kilts, nor pipes. They ought to study the romantic nature of pre-1914 Ireland, and of the '16 people. … They do not offer the necessary pageantry; nor do they offer the necessary enemy. In real fact England browbeat Scotland into political captivity, and ruined her, and was glad to do it. The English treat us with disdain but all they do is to yelp, and be silent again, like a kicked dog. They might cultivate the retentive memory and the revengeful spirit, by which Ireland kept her fire alight, and Scotland once did … However, no talking will put misneachd [energy] into bodachs. They are typical, stinking Whigs, and that's the truth of the matter. (Source 36, 21 August 1940)

At the end of April, Hay had appeared before a local tribunal to explain his stance against conscription. "I was no sooner in than out, and the tribunal avoided any real discussion of nationalism", Hay recorded (Source 5; 21v). "Will appeal as a matter of tactics." To Young he wrote:

I told them in my appeal that I was ready to do agricultural work and serve against parachute troops and other invaders of Scottish soil. The point is that I am ready to mitigate the effects of the war on the Scottish people, and a parachutist may be regarded as a kind of bomb. … Of course my willingness applies only to Scotland, and the English can look after themselves as far as I am concerned. There are about 40,000,000 of them and they should be able to make a shape at it. Nor has my attitude to the war changed, like that of so many people recently. (Source 36, second half of May 1940)

The Difficult Road

In July, Hay took up duty at Holyrood Palace with the Local Defence Volunteers, and attended his appeal tribunal which, predictably, upheld the Local Tribunal's decision. Hay was clearly beginning to feel the pressures of his political defiance and uncertain future, and his morale seemed to be wilting. His diary entry for 23 July provides a rare record of dejection:

Who am I, and what have I done so far? Not much. I was a scholar, and am a B.A. of Oxford. We can cross that out. I can sail and look after a boat up to 15 or 20 tons, I could make a hand at the ring-net fishing, I can use a rifle moderately accurately; I can play the pipes and the recorder, and sing about 200 songs, mostly Gaelic; I can speak Gaelic, Danish and English, and read also Swedish, Icelandic, Irish, Modern Greek, Greek, Latin, French, and with a lot of dictionary thumbing Welsh and Spanish; I can also draw moderately well. Have I done anything? – written some poetry in English, Scots and Gaelic, had a few articles and sketches published, 3 or 4 lyrics set to music by F. G. Scott, translated poetry from Modern Greek, Icelandic, Welsh and English into Gaelic, and from Irish and Gaelic into English (And tr. 2 Middle-Irish tales to Sc. Gaelic); composed maybe 15 melodies, half of which are passable, and edited part of Prof. Alec [sic] MacKinnon's lexicographical remains in preparation for the press. What a mixture-maxture, and it amounts to very little. But never mind, I have good friends, and have seen good days by hill and sea, and may see them again yet. Yet I am not very pleased with myself. Well, give over this introspection. (Source 5: 26r)

More and more of Hay's fellow objectors were deciding to abandon their protest and joining up –

"since Scotland was in danger" etc. As if Scotland weren't in continuous danger from her gluttonous Southern neighbour. What weak-kneed, weak-minded windbags! (Source 36, 1 August 1940)

He himself received a notice of medical examination at the beginning of August, which he disregarded, then a notice giving him four days to reply – "liable to summary arrest and detention. Now the real business begins" (Source 5: 26v). Obligingly, Hay explained his position:

thuirt mi riu nach robh smachd no reachd aca air Albannach 'sam bith, bho'n rinn iad stròicean caola de Chumhnant an Aonaidh. ... Ma leigeas iad leam fanaidh mi an so a dhà no trì de sheachduinean, air eagal gun toir na Gearmailtich ionnsaigh air an dùthaich so 's gun téid aca air a ràdh gun do ruith mi air falbh 's gun do thréig mi mo phost. B' urrainn daibh mo mharbhadh na'm b' àill leo. Ach ma bhìos e soilleir nach tig na Gearmailtich air an trò so bheir mi a' Ghàidhealtachd orm, oir tha àite no dhà agus deagh Albannach no dhà air a bheil mi eòlach an sin. Codhiù, tha mi cinnteach à aon nì – cha strìochd mi do mhuinntir Lunnainn. (Source 46, c. 20 August 1940)

I told them they had no authority or power over any Scot, since they'd made shredded strips of the Act of Union. ... If they leave me alone I'll stay here another two or three weeks, in case the Germans attack this country and they accuse me of running away and abandoning my post.

They could kill me if they wanted to. But if it becomes clear that the Germans won't appear this time round I'll take to the Highlands, since there are one or two places there where there's a good Scot or two that I know. Anyway, I'm sure about one thing – I won't submit to the London lot.

The same letter, describing German bombing raids on Edinburgh and Leith, reveals a chilling ruthlessness:

Ach feumar aideachadh gu bheil na Sasunnaich a' faotainn a' chuid as miosa dheth, 's bu chòir gum faigheadh. Ghabh iad d'an ionnsaigh fhéin a h-uile sògh beairteas cliù is urram a bhuineadh do na trì rìogh-achdan, agus anis gabhadh iad gach bomb peileir agus slige-spreadhaidh. A dh'innseadh na fìrinn, cha n-eil truas agam riu. Cha robh iad fhéin ach mosach riamh, agus cha n-eil anns na h-uachdarain aca ach seann-daoine leibideach d'am bu chòir a bhith sa chill. Is iomadh Albannach tapaidh òg a fhuair bàs obann air tàillibh nan seann chullach ud, agus is e mo dhòchas is mo dhùrachd fhéin nach bi e 'na bhàs gun éirig. (ibid.)

But it has to be admitted that the English are getting the worst of it, and it's only right that they should. They took for themselves every resource richness honour and glory that belonged to the three king-doms, so now let them have every bomb bullet and explosive. In all truth I've no sympathy for them. They've never been anything but mean-minded, and their ruling class are just worthless old fools who ought to be in the grave. Many's the brave young Scot who met a sudden death on account of those old eunuchs, and I just hope and pray that it won't have been a death without its price.

Some time in October, Hay took to the hills of Argyll. Contact was main-tained with the outside world through agents in Glasgow, and proselytising did not cease: a letter to the *Scots Independent* in January urged the party to articulate a policy for the Gaelic language now that it was perceived as a "level-headed and prosaic" body rather than a rag-bag of "fushionless ro-mantics" (Source P26, 164: 6), and in the May issue, reporting the wartime banning of Gaelic in Canada, Hay advocated more radio time for the language in Britain (ibid., 168: 4). The *Scots Socialist* was also the recipient of articles, in both English and Gaelic (8: 4, March 1941; 11: 2–3, June 1941, by "Ciotag").

Early on 3 May 1941, raids were carried out on the homes of nationalist radicals throughout the country, possibly in reaction to the first broadcastings of the German "Radio Caledonia". The raids aroused some protest, but the SNP hastily pointed out that the action had been directed not at its own members as such but at extremist fringe groups (Source P26, 169: 1, June 1941). Those targeted by the CID included Roland Muirhead, the pacifist Honorary President of the SNP, Arthur Donaldson (who was imprisoned), the Rev. John Mackechnie (Gaelic scholar and activist, and Gaelic columnist to the *Scots Independent*), Douglas Young, and the Hays in Edinburgh

(*Scots Socialist* 11: 1, June 1941). That same day, Hay himself was intercepted at Arrochar:

Saturday [3 May]: a boiling hot day, which I passed lying in the sun up the glen. As I was walking down the track in the evening singing to myself a man jumped out of the heather and walked down behind me. He was wearing a natty blue lounge suit which struck me as queer at the time. I made myself a meal then went off to Arrochar to meet the YNA people who were coming by bus. On the way down I met another man wearing an immaculate blue lounge suit. He was over six feet high, with a hard determined mouth pulled down to one side and a pair of piercing grey eyes. It surprised me when a man of his age and appearance asked about the hostel. He turned back with me and we walked down together. He spoke with the faint trace of an Argyllshire accent, and I asked him if he belonged to these parts. "No," said he "I'm working here just now, but (looking at me) I come from Edinburgh." Worse and worse. As we walked across the field something kept jingling in his pocket. Worse still. I halted and said I thought I would turn back now. Damned all hope of that. He fixed me with his eyes and said in a hoarse frantic voice "You'd better come with me, Hay." My freedom was at an end. (Source 5: 31r)

Hay's diary provides a racy and at times amusing account of his arrest and subsequent dealings with the authorities. Although he feared that the prosecution might claim that he intended helping the enemy, he was in fact tried for refusing to submit to medical examination:

My case was called first, and I climbed a flight of steps, popping up through the floor of the courtroom like Mephistopheles in a play. I was wearing my oilskin and had on my heavy boots which made a tremendous din. The judge had bleary blue eyes and looked like some melancholy fish. An advocate or some other species of local corbie got up from the table before me and in an oily obsequious manner, making delicate gestures with his right hand, gave the sad fish a history of my crimes, consulting whiles a cardboard file stuffed with papers. ...

The cod (I had decided by now he was a cod) asked had I anything to say. I said that I had explained my attitude to two tribunals and no heed was paid to it. They intended to force me into service and I intended that they wouldn't, so I had put myself out of their reach. That was all. The cod got exasperated. The tribunals had seen no reason for exempting me and I must submit to their decision. "My attitude is unchanged." But the tribunals had turned me down! "Well, these are still my opinions," said I, and clamped along to the head of the stairs. I was just beginning to clatter down the stairs when they called me back. They had still to sentence me. It was 10 days or a fine ... I chose the 10 days. (ibid.: 35v)

On his release from Saughton only a few days later, however, Hay yielded. On 19 June he reported to Earl Shilton, by Leicester, for service in the Royal Army Ordnance Corps. As he later explained to Kenneth MacLeod:

B'e sin m'fhacal, agus rinn mi na b' urrainn mi a chum fanachd ri m'fhacal. Bha mi trì ràithean fo'n chàrn an Earraghaidheal – cuid de'n ùine "fon chàrn" am fìor dharìribh. … Leis na chunnaic mi de na meadhonan a chleachdas trusdairean an CID a chum a' chrìoch a tha uapa a thoirt amach 's a chum daoine nach àill leo a chur amach air a' chéile gu bràth bràth cha strìochdainn dhaibh Hitler ann no as. Ach bha iad ag cumail faire air an taigh re nan ochd mìos ud 's a' lorgadh mo mhàthair nuair a bhiodh i amuigh, agus ged nach cuireadh a leithid ormsa cha robh e ag còrdadh rithe, rud a tha nàdurra gu leòir. Air an aobhar sin ghèill mi dhaibh ged a thug mo chridhe car 'nam chom nuair a rinn mi sin. (Source 44, letter 17, 1942?)

That was my word of honour, and I did all I could to keep to my word. I spent three seasons "under the cairn" in Argyll – part of the time quite literally "under the cairn". … With what I've seen of the methods used by the CID rascals to achieve their own ends and to divide people they don't like, never but never would I yield to them, Hitler or no Hitler. But they were keeping watch on the house during those eight months and tailing my mother when she went out, and although that kind of thing wouldn't bother me, she didn't like it, which is natural enough. For that reason I gave in to them although my heart was in my throat when I did that.

He interpreted his enlisting in the RAOC as an intentional slight, and he was to note that "you certainly meet a lot of political bad boys in the Ordnance" (Source 36, 2 June 1942). Life "in the khaki hordes" he found "startlingly like life in a boarding school except it's not so bad" (ibid., c. July 1941). He deplored the docility he perceived in most English privates, but was glad to note that "most of my compatriots … haven't the faintest trace of the spirit of subordination and are incredibly outspoken for poor bloody privates" (ibid.). In August, Hay was moved to Catterick where he was engaged in clerking work in the Depot. He applied for a transfer to the Intelligence Corps, but, predictably, this was rejected. A meeting with Sorley MacLean gave him "a rest from English speech and English inanity" (ibid., 9 September 1941). MacLean's own decision to join the British army had not been without its moral dilemmas: he admitted to Young that he felt

unhappy and diffident in not being on same side as yourself and Deorsa [Hay] … who were the bravest and most unselfish men I knew, … circumstances and my own judgement [having] put me by the side of those I hated and despised. (NLS Acc. 6419/38b, 11 September 1941)

Of his meeting with Hay, he reported:

With Deorsa I had two splendid afternoons and evenings when we talked Gaelic poetry the whole time. ... I had never before had such a full talk with him and I felt I knew him better than ever before ... [He] looked splendid physically and was very cheerful. Politically Russia seems to have come to mean a great deal to him and, as far as I can see, he is reconciled to the fight against Hitler both because of the Russian business, and because he now regards the Nazis as the greatest curse to small nations. That is at any rate my reading of his remarks but actually we talked poetry chiefly. (ibid., 7 September 1941)

Hay's change of opinion was perhaps not as decisive as MacLean suggests, to judge from a letter to F. G. Scott:

Not a very glorious business, but I said I would defy them and I did my poor best. ... I'm not in a frame of mind conducive to creation. After all I damned well said I wouldn't let them get the better of me. But here I am in khaki. Yet the Germans are a very pestilence in their doings and perhaps one should be in khaki. On the other hand the English have been just as bad even recently, not on such a scale it is true, but that doesn't count. A curse on both their houses! I say, but it is not an attitude easy to express in action for "they" are both pretty powerful. Anyway, here I am in khaki and in some mental confusion and all that can be done is to wait and thole. (9 November 1941, courtesy of G. N. Scott)

"Wait and thole" seems to have characterised his attitude to army life throughout the war, with his mind firmly set on Scotland and on the work which would need to be done there once the war was over, but his initial despondency at his own isolation and surrender surfaces poetically in the verses he added to "Final Lyric to Nationalists Who Refuse English Conscription" (see "Is Duilich an t-Slighe"[64]). "Sguabag 1942"[85], however, strikes a more characteristic note of optimism: "This is no time for lamenting or sighing, it is a time for incitement and activity", Hay declaims, in the expectation that the winds of war will sweep aside the dead wood of the old order.

Hay continued to follow political developments back home with avid interest. The first of these was the dramatic split in the SNP at its 1942 conference, where Douglas Young was elected Chairman and John MacCormick quit the party to found the home-rule pressure group Scottish Convention. Young was an unlikely figurehead for the fundamentalists, as he had always tended towards the devolutionist position and even argued for a federal Britain, but he was seen above all as the best-known and most articulate of the anti-conscriptionists. At the time of his election he was on bail pending the result of a highly publicised appeal in the High Court. Hay of course welcomed the parting of ways: "The young enthusiasts have kicked out the old wrigglers ... Enter the Scots – exeunt Britti Septentrionales panourgoste [exit the North Brits and the mischief-maker]" (Source 36, 19 August

1942). Young for his part did not have long to celebrate: days after his election, his appeal was rejected and he was incarcerated in Saughton for eight months.

Africa

At the beginning of November 1942, Hay boarded ship on the Clyde for the week-long journey to North Africa, as part of Operation Torch, planned to set off a decisive pincer advance on Rommel's desert army. The Americans disembarked at Oran and Casablanca, while joint British–American troops landed at Algiers. 1st Army forces advanced on Annaba (Bône) and proceeded to cross the border into Tunisia, where Rommel's Afrika Korps had retreated under pressure from the 8th Army in Libya. The Germans reacted swiftly, overrunning Vichy France and pouring troops into Tunisia. By the end of the year, Allied attempts to seize Tunis had stalled, but the fighting continued until the spring, with towns like Bizerta caught in the crossfire. Rommel attempted to push out eastwards, in March 1943, unsuccessfully, and was recalled by Hitler. Finally in May, German and Italian forces capitulated.

Hay gave a description of his duties at this time to Young in a "screed with a purpose", sent as part of a renewed effort to obtain a transfer to the Intelligence Corps:

> Since I was taken into the Army I have pursued the occupations sometimes of an office-boy, sometimes of an amateur charwoman, sometimes of an unskilled stevedore. Since I came over here my chief profession has been loading and unloading lorries, though latterly I have been advanced to filing away forms in number order. (Actually these few days I am supposed to be ruling lines on sheets of paper.) … For five months … I had a fairly sensible job, as Ordnance jobs go, that of looking after the Oxygen and Acetylene supply. … I kept the records, scrounged the transport and the labour, kept the French who were doing the filling in trim, and often loaded and unloaded the lorries alone with the driver. … For well over a month I was on my own. Ultimately I handed over this job to one sergeant, one lance-corporal, one clerk, two storemen and one Pioneer. So I can't be inefficient, even if you discount ten odd languages. In my opinion this glorious career will take some explaining. It's gone on long enough to become shocking, and now I'm going to have it explained. (Source 36, 4 August 1943)

The only explanation eventually forthcoming was an explicit rejection by the War Office and by the Intelligence Corps. Hay's persistence was out of a desire "for a comeback, rather than personal benefit": "I'm about as good a Christian as the old Ossian … As the Arabs say: 'He who does not remember good and ill, Is not a man of worth'" (ibid., 24 December 1943).

On top of his normal private's duties, Hay was acting as unofficial interpreter for his unit in French, Italian and Arabic, the last two of which he had been steadily acquiring since his arrival in North Africa. Frustrated by the tedium of mindless routine and papershifting – "la vie routinière, moutonnière, paperassière" (ibid., 21 July 1943) – his unflinching preoccupation with the state of Scotland turned to dark anxiety, expressed in such poems as "Épreuve de Doute". It was fuelled by news from home of continuing Bevinisation (the forcible removal of Scottish women down to armaments factories in England), continued talk of emigration drives, relentless appropriation of Highland estates by English firms; even Tom Johnston's plans for a North of Scotland Hydro-electric Board Hay seemed to view as further exploitation of the Highlands for alien benefit:

> When I think of Scotland now I do so with anxiety and bitterness, because I think that the maiming or extinction of the Scots as a nation is intended. ... I think of her as a nation against whom a white war, biological and economic, is being waged under cover of this bloody war against Germany. (ibid., 2 December 1943)

News that he was to be sent to a new unit where he would be "instructing Italian prisoners in the mysteries of the RAOC" did not lift his spirits overmuch:

> Resolute ignorance is the only path to salvation ..., and indifference to the whole business the only reasonable attitude. Schweik's the stuff to give them. The one overriding consolation is that ... I have great opportunities for proselytising, for it appears that the further away from home Scotsmen are, the more recipient they are. So, after all, I should be grateful. (ibid., 20 December 1943)

But if Scotland was uppermost in his mind, Hay was not blind to his environment outside army precincts. He had quickly warmed to the Maghreb:

> Africa is admirable, and there is a general air of life and a tolerance in small details (probably due to poverty) which are lacking in industrialised N.W. Europe. There is none of the ugliness which is the rule by the Clyde or the Tyne; there is more of natural good manners and less of convention and there are also some very bizarre smells to be dodged here and there. ... They show qualities here which would greatly benefit Western Europe, but W. Europe having all the machine guns doesn't worry about unmaterial qualities. She peers thru the sights and sees nothing beyond but phosphates, cork, cheap labour and what not. (ibid., 20 April 1943)

> The war seems to have left us behind here. ... We used to rub shoulders with the folk, work with them, barter with them and visit their houses, but now we languish on a muddy slope girt by a barbed wire Great Wall of China. We might as well be in Britain. So you see it

doesn't do to get too far from the front line. ... Your correspondent is doing almost nothing but reading what French books he can lay hands on (and an odd Arabic one), blethering to the prisoners – his Italian having improved by leaps and bounds – and wondering when the hell he is going to get out of the place. I made a lot of friends and acquaintances of all sorts and conditions in the town nearby where we lay last winter, and it is pleasant to have to stop and speak to someone you know every twenty yards, but for all that I would like to move on. Though I would always want to come back and see the dockers, old white beards mounted on donkeys, serious country folk in striped hooded burnouses, fat pale shopkeepers in tarbushes and pantaloons, ragged beggars chanting "Er-rabbi yerahmek", shoeshine boys screeching in chorus ..., cafetiers, mirailleurs who clap their hands in rhythm and chant monotonously things not fit for mixed company as they march along, and all the rest of the infinite variety. (ibid., 2 October 1943)

Although I'm over a year here I've not fallen out with North Africa yet. With French, Italian and Arabic I can always find a welcome and interesting company whenever I go, and as for the average common soldier abroad, and particularly the front line one, all that has been said is true. They are the salt of the earth. Among the Italians there are some good sorts, but an awful lot have the servile characteristics of crawling to their superiors and bullying those to whom they calculate it is safe to do so – e.g. the down and out class of Arabs. I've had to pull them up quite frequently for buggering Arabs about ... Those unpleasant characteristics may be due to Fascism, or equally to their many years of military service. (ibid., 14 December 1943)

In Africa, Hay's "tempo of production", he could report, had increased, kickstarted by his easy fluency in French, which gave him the opportunity to spread the evangelical net wider:

Such things [as "Épreuve de Doute"[99]] will win a lot a sympathy and goodwill if they get round. Primarily I wrote my French things because I felt the urge, but there's that thought in it too. ... Such efforts can be our British Council. (ibid., 23 October 1943)

Hopes of a published collection were still being entertained. Hay's mother, Douglas Young and the Rev. John Mackechnie held copies of his poems. Mackechnie had made a hasty selection of Hay's work for submission to the McCaig Trustees, and he was to act more or less as Hay's Gaelic agent until their acrimonious break in 1945.

MacDiarmid loyally maintained his support. In January 1943, now working in an ammunitions factory in Glasgow, he wrote to Young (still in Saughton Prison):

I have not heard of or from Hay for a long time now, but Scott's settings of some of his lyrics were included in the recent Edinburgh concert and scored a great hit. They are really magnificent. I'll be glad to add my urging to yours that he should put a volume together and if he agrees and so wishes I'll be very pleased of course to supply a preface. I've mentioned this to [William] MacLellan too as a volume he ought to publish if he is really going to ... establish himself as the progressive Scottish publisher we've been praying for ever since the end of the last war. (Bold 1984: 599)

But Hay did not take up the offer of a recommendation from the doyen. A year later, when a book was finally in the offing, he would tell Young:

If there are to be tunes at the hinter end I don't think we should bother with a foreword at the front. I think the awesome mixture should be delivered point blank between the eyes without any "halts" or "who goes theres". Besides I can never reconcile myself to English forewords for a book mainly Gaelic. (Source 36, 4 January 1944)

The serious planning of a collection started in early November 1943, when Young was able to inform Catherine Hay that the McCaig Trust had promised £50 towards publication. She and Young were to be responsible, Hay decided, for selecting the non-Gaelic material:

As for what English and Lallans to include, I have complete confidence in my mother and you. ... She has had plenty experience in books and publishers with my father's work, and I think taking an active part will give her very great pleasure. (ibid., 20 December 1943)

My mother says something about me making English translations from my Gaelic poems. It's too late in the day for that at present. I've made translations of a few at odd times in one place or another, but they've probably gone up the lum long since. It's not indispensable, is it? (ibid., 24 December 1943)

As the McCaig Trust is greasing the slips, if not actually doing the launching, over half – say 6/10 – must be Gaelic. Some French (is the Norse thing suitable?) and the rest Scots and English should complete it. The nature poetry might as well go in together. ... That would get the hill and sea, boat and bealach, adolescent stuff under sail together. ... The English will come in its proper place, "second by a long interval", and then it will be verse and half of it in Scots. It had better come after the French indeed. I think "Dom Mhàthair is do Albainn" [To my Mother and to Scotland] is the thing. When I think of you [Young] and Somhairle [MacLean] and Grieve [Hugh MacDiarmid] and F. G. Scott I tell myself I'm ungracious, but I think you and the others will ... understand. ... Ideally I'd prefer it 10/10 Gaelic? Possibly also the McCaig folk will want it so. (ibid., 4 January 1944)

The "awesome mixture" was simplified a month later to Gaelic poems only, when Hay's last suspicion proved correct. At this time Young was again suggesting a collaboration, about which Hay was enthusiastic:

The Omnium Gatherum is a good idea, and now is the time for poly-glot books when chance has made Scotland itself so very polyglot. Yes, why not dedicate it to the whole constellation? "All one body we". It's time Edwin Muir got a chance to gambol since Chris Grieve has been dealing him such dunts. (ibid., 18 February 1944)

A note of anxiety is felt a few weeks later:

I'm in a bit of a haze about what really is happening to my work. MacK. [Mackechnie], I know, is getting published a good amount of the Gaelic, and that's O.K. You also propose a joint production or "omnium gatherum" to be published by MacL. [William MacLellan], and that's also O.K., though I'd like some idea of what's to go in it. [...] I think we'll see how things go with the Gaelic book and the joint one, and then I'll take stock of the material left and see what I want to do with it. I'm not in any great hurry. (ibid., 29 March 1944)

Three weeks later, he writes:

On the matter of the book. Let them [MacLellan and Mackechnie] go ahead with it as it stands, though give a look at the proofs. ... Gaoth air Loch Fìne [Wind on Loch Fyne] will do for the title. There's no point in making a song and dance about it and taking it too seriously. It might as well be launched as it stands, and once it's off the slips we can fix up the "Gallimawfry". From the universal, and the Scottish, point of view it seems to me that the republication of my father's books is far more impor-tant than the publication of anything of mine. (ibid., 18 April 1944)

Hay's reservations about his own work were also confessed to Sorley MacLean:

Doubts assail me at times as to whether ¾ of my stuff is worth publishing. A lot of it may be bonnie verse, but is not new or signifi-cant. (Source 48a, 28 December 1943)

It's not a book that will show much advance or development on the past in the way D[àin] do E[imhir] has done. My only hope is that it revives a few genres and some technique that was valuable in the past. But I feel in the trim for a forward jump one day. (ibid., 22 February 1944)

He also amusingly reported to MacLean the difficulties caused by the book title itself:

There are two artists disputing the dustwrapper among themselves, and I hear that they at least agreed upon one thing, "that the title won't do, because they can't paint wind". ... They can paint a row of cat's arseholes for all I care. I'm not interested in the least. (Don't tell anyone, tho. It might hurt their feelings.) What I suggested, partly out of devilment was that they should stick a bloody great St Andrews Cross all over each cover, and have apothegms such as "Cuir amach an Sasannach is thoir astaigh an cù" ["Kick out the Englishman and bring in the dog"] done in a flowing romantic Twilight script round the borders of each page. (ibid., 12 May 1944)

In early May, Hay told Young that there was no point sending out the proofs to him in Africa and that he had instructed Mackechnie "to go ahead on his own". Further, to satisfy the family lawyer, he made his mother "my 'literary executor' as it were, and her wishes will decide or otherwise the publication of any of my work", though "she had better coopt Mackechnie, as a Gaelic speaker and scholar" (ibid., 3 May 1944). By June, MacLellan had apparently "let [Hay and Young] down in the matter of the joint book", but that was perhaps no bad thing:

> If we were to combine your work and mine, which are both Protean, the resultant variety would be labyrinthine, and the public might hold up their hands in despair. They must be treated after the Arabs' precept "Give men the dose of truth (or anything else) that they've the capacity for". So I think we should carry on separately till I get back. ... When this present book is out I'll take stock of the situation, and plan another, but piano piano. (ibid., 5 June 1944)

Ironically it was the free hand Hay himself had allowed Mackechnie which in part precipitated the crisis. Hay was shocked when he finally received the proposed contents of the book, as he reported to Sorley MacLean:

> MacK had included some political rants which he counted as clever, and which I would term smooth doggerel of a kind which serves a purpose in certain circumstances. (Source 48a, 18 July 1944)

By this stage Hay clearly felt he was losing control over his own work. Having heard, "wrongly I hope", that Young and MacLellan had again discussed his work and the possibility of its inclusion in a polyglot book, his first letter from Italy warns in an uncharacteristically curt tone that

> any future projects will be formed by me, and by me only. ... I will not have arrangements made without my knowledge and without my consent, and I think it would be best if you refrained from having anything to do with my work. ... If any liberties are taken ... by anyone whatsoever I will take legal action. (ibid., 21 June 1944)

He struck a more conciliatory note a few weeks later, assuring his friend that he was not "unconscious or unmindful" of all his help

> but to avoid friction and confusion (and friction over questions of taste is unavoidable) it seemed to me that the only thing to do was 1. to let MacK. finish this book, it being in Gaelic 2. to give authority for the

future to one single person [Catherine Hay]. ... It's been most unfortunate that the book should have caused contention, and at one period I was considering scrapping it and refunding everybody out of my credits. (ibid., 17 July 1944)

Some of the contention was due to "some ghastly confusion about F. G. Scott's settings", and Hay admitted that

the trouble is in a great part due to myself, who, having other preoccupations, said "Go ahead, go ahead". I then woke up with a start to find that all sorts of things had been, or were being, arranged for me, and that things were in a tangle. (ibid., 23 July 1944)

Hay's move to a new unit at the turn of the year had been delayed by an attack of conjunctivitis which kept him in hospital for five weeks and cost him his new job as interpreter. When he did rejoin the unit in February 1944, he was given the duties of interviewing new recruits and producing an Italian news bulletin. Now "when I'm finished for the day, I'm finished" (ibid., 18 February 1944), and there was time aplenty for reading and letter-writing. He had received the new fruits of the Scottish Renaissance which were tumbling out of William MacLellan's press: the Renaissance flagship *Poetry Scotland*, collections of poetry by Sydney Goodsir Smith and Douglas Young, and above all Sorley MacLean's *Dàin do Eimhir agus Dàin Eile*, of which he had said years before, at the news that funding for publication was assured: "The life in these poems is hot enough to break-up even the thick casing of dead-ice that has lain over Gaelic literature so long" (ibid., 19 December 1941). Not that Hay was short of reading material:

Sometimes I feel I'm interested in too many things, and reflect that I'd be hard put to make Somhairle's comhchur [synthesis] of them. Between the French intellectuals of [the literary journal] *Fontaine*, Sufi mystics, ill-assorted odds and ends of Italian literature, the works of Anatole France, Berbr poetry, Tunisian proverbs, and what's going on in Scotland, Ireland, Wales, and so on, it's a braw mixture, yet nothing in variety to the types I meet on the streets and roads. But when I think again, I thank the Lord for diversity. (ibid., 18 April 1944)

Italy

In June 1944, Hay's unit moved to Italy, where the Allies had finally broken through the Gustav Line at Monte Cassino, and pushed back German troops beyond Rome and up to the Gothic Line. Hay's unit remained in the south of Italy, in the region of Salerno and Naples, and his job became one of "instructor and interpreter all in one" (ibid., 20 December 1944). The move to Italy coincidentally signalled the start of a period of extraordinary poetic activity, the "forward jump" predicted by Hay in February. Ideas sown in

Algeria here came to fruition, and over the next eighteen months Hay produced some of his finest work, including his poems on war and on Arab themes. In July he informed his mother that new poems were on their way to her, including

> three first installments of a poem which I realise with stupefaction is likely to run to something near 1,000 lines. I visualised it at first as being of about 2–300 when the idea first occurred to me in Africa. Talk about the Muses dragging one along by the scruff of the neck. They too must have joined the women police and have taken a course in ju-jitsu. (Source 23: 4, 5 July 1944)

Over the months of July and August, he wrote 700 lines of "Mochtàr is Dùghall"[109], from the solemn introduction and the keening to the tale of war-scarred Ahmed and the enthralling account of Omar's Sahara journey. During that same period he compiled a Gaelic collection of Tunisian proverbs and riddles (some of which he inserted into "Mochtàr is Dùghall"), made extensive translations of modern Croatian poetry (from Italian versions), and translated Petrarch. Original poems over the autumn and winter months included "Atman", "Còmhradh an Alltain", "Prìosan Da Fhèin an Duine?", "Bisearta", "Beinn is Machair" and "An Lagan", then in the spring of 1945 "An t-Òigear a' Bruidhinn on Ùir", "Meftah Bâbkum es-Sabar?" and "Tilleadh Uilìseis"[110–25].

Meanwhile the *Gaoth air Loch Fine* book continued to be a source of dissatisfaction, as Hay expressed to Young:

> Myself I have thought all along that certain things marked out for the book had their heart in the right place, but were far from being poetry ... In fact I'm postponing and reviewing the whole goddam situation, which will give myself and everyone else a well-earned rest. (Source 36, 20 December 1944)

However well earned, the rest was not appreciated by all concerned, judging by Hay's remarks to Young a few weeks later:

> My attitude to MacLellan is not much different from F. G. Scott's now. My only desire is to get the abortion cancelled, pay the creature his costs and be quit of him ... He was silly enough to show some resentment, polite of course, at my mother's intervention, whereby he damned himself in aeternitatum. There was one [Mackechnie] who wasn't even polite ... ες κόρακας an dithisd aca [to the crows with the two of them]. (ibid., 10 January 1945)

In March, Hay explained to Robert Rankin:

> As for the book, MacLellan doesn't give a damn and is slow-motion, and MacK is rather an autocratic gentleman. He saw fit to show impatience with my honourable parent and bark at her over the phone, so I cut the ground from under his feet by taking the thing right out of

his hands; for which I received some extremely abusive letters which I am going to preserve and hang in asbestos frames. Between them they made a proper mess, from which I have cut clear, and I'm now preparing something more worthwhile. ... first of all I'll get all the material together, then I must edge MacLellan into a settlement for the mess he helped to make, then I'll look around. (ibid., 6 March 1945)

Difficulties were not resolved until Hay returned to Scotland on leave in late August, and gave the book "glan deas" ("fresh and new") to MacLellan (Source 46, 27 January 1946). He heard no more of it until his altogether more troubled return to Scotland the following summer.

Politically, the news from home was encouraging, with the SNP making deceptively good showings at the polls in the special circumstances of the war-time electoral truce. Douglas Young, now well known for his stance against military and industrial conscription, had taken 41 per cent of the vote at a by-election in Kirkcaldy in February 1944. In April 1945, Robert MacIntyre, a conscientious objector, won Motherwell and became the first SNP Member of Parliament; a day after his election, the renowned nutritionist John Boyd Orr won a Scottish Universities seat on an independent nationalist ticket. The advances were encouraging, and for Hay seemed to herald "a new phase of expansion which will require harder work than ever":

The way I saw it a long time ago is this. The choice was "Combattre ou disparaître" ["fight or disappear"] and I was damned determined there would be no disappearing. ... Things have moved quicker than [I thought], and we are no longer crying in the wilderness. But it is when we get self-government that the real work will begin, for self-government is only the means to an end – the end being to make Scotland a prosperous country without slums or unpeopled wastes, and with plenty of spirit and life. ... If it's [a big task] so much the better. No one in Scotland need suffer from frustration or feel that there's nothing worthwhile to do in this world. ... Don't think the political activity is "useless". On the contrary, it's necessary, and being Scotsmen, and awake, we can't do otherwise. (ibid., 19 April 1945)

Hay himself had been sounded out about submitting his candidature for South Argyll in the post-war election, but, as he told Young, his vocation lay elsewhere:

Would my energies not be better concentrated on Gaelic, which is Scotland's most obvious mark of individuality and one of the hottest red embers under our heap of cinders? I think myself that Gaelic and writing are my sectors. (ibid., 10 January 1945)

Greece

In the spring of 1945, Hay was promoted to the grade of corporal, then sergeant. Promotion had not been won by conformity, however. On the preparatory course which he had undergone before his transfer to the Education Corps, the "almost complete neglect of Scotland in lectures on history and current affairs" led him "into some brulzies" (ibid., 26 November 1945):

> the machine of government expounded was English. No one was aware that [Scottish] questions and problems existed, and they were frowned on (if you were too insistent about them, it was immediately decided … that your kit was in an untidy condition). Indoctrination, in short, and English indoctrination for Englishmen. (Source 8: 29)

The new post did have its consolations, however. In the New Year, Hay could announce:

> The Fates have been kind to me and sent me where I very much wanted to be sent, namely to Greece. This HQ is situated on a little headland called Kavouri, half-way between the Piraeus and Sunium, a very pleasant ακροτήριον overgrown with small pinetrees and girt with skerries. … Unfortunately it is this brigade's turn to serve in the more inaccessible parts, and next week we are going to Kavalla, over against Thases and damned nearly in Thrace. About half of the place-names round it are Turkish, and the map shows a magnificent vast marsh near it, whereas the mountains are some miles away. Not an enticing place from what I can judge. (Source 36, 2 January 1946)

In Macedonia, Hay spent much of his spare time frequenting the locals. Rural Greeks he liked, for predictable reasons:

> An taobh am muigh de na bailtean móra tha na's leòir de chruadal s de àrdan annta. Agus seòladairean na b'fheàrr sna bàtaichean beaga cha n-fhaca mi riamh. (Source 46, 27 January 1946)

> *Outside the big cities they have much more hardiness and pride. And I've never seen better navigators in small boats.*

In a short story written soon after, he paints a sympathetic portrait of the men of Kavalla:

> Winter and the war that's gane, poortith and the cauld, send the men o Kavalla … alang the braes and doon thro the howes efter firean tae warm their weans or tae sell for breid. And sae it is – on thae days aboot the gait-tracks o Gamila … ye may meet aa the gairit claes that are seldom tae be seen on the causeys o the toon, and hear the tales that the world, wi a weel-stechit wame, has nae patience for. The down dyvour, the herrit and hapless, stacher alang they tracks, booed doon by the wid they aiblins hae pluckit wi their bare hands. Aften I didna ken whar tae pit ma een as they had telt me hoo they passt their

months and years o war. It's nae that they mak a puir moo o't. There is smeddum eneuch amang thaim in spite o the fanklet threid o their fortune. And there are nae sornars amang thaim. They hae nevar as muckle as asked a cigarette frae me, and aften and aften they hae offert me ane. ... Siccan men ye wad meet on Gamila. Men wha had felt aa the wecht o the war, some wha had gane doon an' ithers wha had stood straucht. The factories o Germany, the hames soopit bare by the Bulgarians – on Gamila I heard it aa. (Hay 1977: 22–4)

These were troubled sectarian times, however, particularly in Macedonia, and all the more so in the run-up to the general elections of 31 March. On election day itself, Hay records, British troops were kept indoors, and Kavalla registered an abstention rate of 48 per cent (Source 8: 19v).

Macedonia is still the old uneasy Macedonia one used to read of. You don't hear any talk of IMRO [the International Macedonian Revolutionary Organisation], though χομιταδζης [Bulgarian-Greek guerilla] is a common Greek noun yet, but factions abound. KKE [Communist Party of Greece] and the Χιτες [right-wing paramilitary group] (what Brits [call] the "royalist X organisation") are present, as they are everywhere in Greece, and there are also the Ὀχρανιτες, the Macedonian autonomists ... The Armenian element, who "played the worst of roles under the occupation" according to a Greek acquaintance, are mostly Ὀχρανιτες. And of course there are the Bulgars, ... gazing greedily over the frontier towards the plains and coastlands where they committed so many atrocities. (Source 36, 2 February 1946)

In this volatile, factional climate, Hay's associations with local people could not easily have been politically neutral, and the consequences were to be disastrous. In late May or early June he was struck by "nervous trouble" and sent home by way of several hospitals, finally ending up in Carstairs Military Hospital. According to his mother, "in both Carstairs and Lochgilphead ... they found it impossible to get him to talk of what brought on his breakdown in Salonika" (Source 44, 3 June 1947). Medical records relating to his admission to the District Mental Hospital in Lochgilphead in November 1946 offer some clues:

he was suspect in the army because of his leftish views, suspect by the Greek lefts because of his nationalism, and suspect by the Greek rights because of his left views. It is reported that his life was in danger for a time because of this. (Quote courtesy of Dr A. K. Zealley)

Limited insight is offered by a letter written by Hay from hospital a few years later. He had "not been very well when it was written", according to his mother (Source 36, October 1950), and he turns to his subject out of the blue:

Salonica seems to have attracted far too much attention to my mind ...
I was right in the middle of it, and it was pretty horrible, although, to

my observation, a nationalist overseas becomes very much habituated to that sort of thing … For myself, I had pretty much given up hopes of my life, although I hoped to be able to present something of the event, in spite of that, and something of Scotland overseas … At any rate I shall never forget Greece, neither Kavóuri nor Kaválla nor Salonica. It's very like Scotland in many a way. (ibid.)

Over thirty years after the event, Hay gave a more precise account of this crucial episode:

I was an education sergeant and I was sent to Macedonia. And there had been the civil war in Greece, and the right-wing were on top. I was left-wing in my sentiments. In Macedonia I used to hob-nob with working-class people (I spoke Greek) and the right-wing people noticed this, and I was in a place called Kavalla, and they got a notion I was a communist, and that was death in Greece at that time – I mean, the right-wing were on top. There was a terrific to-do, knives and carabines and all the rest – and that's the origin of my getting my pension. … I wasn't shot. I missed it narrowly. (SSS November 1980)

Whether precipitated by one traumatic incident or by an accumulation of war experiences, the onset of mental illness was to have profound effects on Hay's life and on his literary career.

Envoi

The seriousness of his condition does not seem to have been immediately apparent, as he made plans for his future:

Probably I'm a bit optimistic, but I hope to find [a livelihood] as a teacher in Edinburgh, then take my mother down to Tarbert and those parts. It's ages and ages since she saw her native land of Islay, to mention only one place. (Source 36, 20 June 1946)

In regard to the publication of his poetry, things were moving, and on 4 July Hay could tell Young that "MacLellan appeared here last night with the *Fuaran Slèibh* proofs, in good spirits and full of projects" (ibid., 4 July 1946). Hay was discharged from Carstairs at the end of that month as partially disabled, and repaired to Tarbert with his mother. Although he had withdrawn from his teacher-training course in 1940, he was awarded a Teacher's Special Certificate in Classics effective from the end of August; his hope was to find a post in a Gaelic-speaking district, but he was informed that his first posting would be in Campbeltown – "not exactly the sort of place I would relish" (ibid., 15 September 1946).

Upon his discharge from Carstairs he had approached Oliver & Boyd with a manuscript of Scots, English and French poems which they accepted. MacLellan, meanwhile, was "still evasive enough about the Gaelic book", but Hay continued working on "Mochtàr is Dùghall" and preparing a second

Gaelic collection, as well as compiling the Gaelic section of an anthology of Scottish poetry for Nelson Publishers (ibid., 15 September 1946 and 27 August 1946). He had rented the old family house, Heatherknowe, over the winter, intending to spend most of his time writing:

> I've been pretty busy down here, both in English and Gaelic tho not in Scots, I'm ashamed to say. Very soon I should have my Gaelic magnum opus completed … which runs to little more than 1,200 lines or so. In addition I've managed to write a poem or two, and one or two articles, as well as trying to get Gaelic into the columns of the Campbeltown Courier, which is a trifle which might be important as there is a small Gaelic revival in Tarbert and Campbeltown. (ibid., late November 1946)

But "Mochtàr is Dùghall" never did reach completion: at the end of November, Hay was admitted to Lochgilphead Hospital. In his mother's words:

> He went to Tarbert for some months and he was so happy rolling in and out of boats and climbing the hills, but I could sometimes see that he was not feeling well. Towards the end of November the crash came and though I wanted to try and take him round here [Edinburgh] it just didn't work out. I often think now that that was all for the best as he is happier in his beloved Argyll and among those kindly Gaelic speakers. They are awfully kind to him. … [The young doctor in Lochgilphead] is hoping to get George to consent to having a course of [insulin] any time now. He has been very very ill but there is a definite improvement, and he is becoming interested again in what people are doing and reading, especially in Gaelic. (Source 44, 3 June 1947)

That spring, while Hay was in hospital, progress with *Fuaran Slèibh* had again stalled, as his mother reported:

> Mr. McLellan tells me by phone that George's translations … are lost. It is fortunately a blow which George is spared knowing about… After a week's intensive work I have managed to piece together a good many of them from scraps here and there, but there are several of which there is no trace. (Source 36, 11 March 1947)

These poems remained untranslated in the final product, but Sorley MacLean produced a translation of "Cinntìre"[26] which Hay praised in the foreword for its elegance and depth of understanding ("snas agus tuigse"). Hay's return to Tarbert that autumn set off another spate of activity, and more additions were made to *Wind on Loch Fyne*, including in late November the formidable "Seeker, Reaper"[158].

Eight years before, Hay had written that "thoughts do come when one is very tired; the last flicker before the flame dies, or the sudden increase in the heat of the sun just before it goes under a cloud" (Source 1: 44v), and there is something astonishing about Hay's creative energy at this time, in the ambitious sweep of poems like "Seeker, Reaper"¹⁵⁸ or "The Walls of Balclutha"¹⁵⁵; in his collected song settings, a copy of which he sent to F. G. Scott; in his attempt to gather his prose writings, including recently written short stories and a long essay on the importance of Gaelic song as "An untapped source of Scottish history" (Source 22: 128–63); in the anthology of Scotland he compiled, illustrating aspects of culture and literature, language, custom, and social and economic history (NLS Acc. 10651). The conclusion to "Mochtàr is Dùghall"¹⁰⁹⁴ drafted in Greece was finalised, but Dougall's story remained incomplete. In Edinburgh he saw "most of the Makars of the day, some of whom are a bit solemnly serious" (letter to Mrs F. G. Scott, 6 December 1947). His condition did not allow him much respite, however, and he was returned to Lochgilphead Hospital at the New Year and submitted to insulin treatment, with little success (Source 46, A. F. MacLean, 9 March 1948).

In March 1948, *Fuaran Slèibh* at long last came off the press. That same month, Hay was transferred to the Royal Edinburgh Hospital, where his sister Sheena had been detained since the late 1930s, and from which he would only be discharged some twelve years later. By September, *Wind on Loch Fyne* was ready for launching. In spite of poor sales in an unfavourable market, reviews were glowing. An early encomium came in a BBC broadcast by Alexander Scott:

> His language is always idiomatic, always "the tongue of the people in the mouth of the scholar". ... Campbell Hay is a poet of wide range and great technical dexterity, and he has a heart that feels and a mind that understands. ... There is in his work that sense of the past which is essential to the interpretation of the contemporary scene. (Transcript in Source 23: 51–7)

Hugh MacDiarmid called *Wind on Loch Fyne* "the most distinguished volume of Scottish poems that has appeared for a quarter of a century", containing "quite a number of lyrics that cannot be omitted from any real representative anthology of modern Scottish poetry". The two collections, wrote MacDiarmid, pursuing an idée fixe, demonstrated the closeness between Gaelic and Lallans writers, which would "prove in the long run that the cultivation of Lallans has been merely a stage in the breaking away from English and return to Gaelic" (*National Weekly* I.4, 9 October 1948). MacDiarmid also quoted from a review by Austin Clarke in the *Irish Times*:

> In the best sense of the word, George Campbell Hay is an academic poet. He has identified himself so closely with Gaelic poetry that there is a timelessness in these poems of nature, as in his lyric "the Glen" ["An Gleannan"⁸] ... He captures too the exact mood of the ironic love poems common to Scotland and Ireland ... To have mastered a tradition, as I think this poet has, is an important advance.

The reviewer for the *Inverness Courier* (8 October 1948), presumably not a devotee of MacDiarmid's Renaissance, found that all the poems in *Wind on Loch Fyne* – "even in Scots!" – had merit, "and many have distinction", while the *Times Literary Supplement* (on 13 November 1948) noted the "concern with the whole European tradition". Veteran fellow poet Lewis Spence praised Hay's "imagination and craftsmanship":

> His verses are infused with a fine sense of the power of the sea ... Most of the poems are couched in a species of musical Highland Scots, very graceful after some of the crunching sounds made by the brogues of the Makars ... [He] has the gift of minting the rarer phrases of poetic proverb ... Some of the rhythms in "Seeker, Reaper" are victorious indeed, the finest of their sort since Swinburne's mighty line. (*SMT Magazine*, November 1948)

The echoes detected in "Seeker, Reaper" by Robin Lorimer were not of Swinburne, but of Greek and Gaelic; he admired its "train of thrilling modulations" leading to "grandiloquent, Aeschylean sophistications":

> Hay's verse is polished and finely articulated. His language is terse and lucid: it pinpoints: it has sword-blade poise and flexibility. ... Even his English poetry reveals characteristically Gaelic motives: the desire for precision and completeness, and for perfection of technique in preference to innovation; ... the ascendancy of the formal discipline; the presentation in multiple image of accumulated detail. ... The central fact about Hay's poetry is that it is Gaelic poetry; even in English he works still within the framework of the Gaelic literary tradition. (*Scots Review* 9: 8, December 1948)

This "central fact" was sensed, with less sympathy, by another reviewer of *Wind on Loch Fyne*:

> As far as one can judge ..., the chief tributary into [the] Scots and English poems is Gaelic, and that – for a Scottish poet – is perhaps the most dangerous influence of any. ... The rhythms and techniques of most of the English poems show little awareness of the best of contemporary English poetry. ... It would be a pity if Mr. Campbell Hay should fail to develop to its utmost a most promising talent, because he has uncritically accepted the dogma of a clique. Even the contemporary English poets have something to teach him. (*The Scottish Educational Journal*, 5 November 1948)

Following on this flurry of interest, Catherine Hay approached Oliver & Boyd on the matter of Hay's prose writings, which he had intended to collect before his readmission to hospital:

> I am not suggesting submitting it ... at present I dare not trouble George about it. I am so anxious to keep him from being forgotten till such times as he can write again. (NLS Acc. 5000/509, 18 January 1949)

But there was little evidence to sustain hopes of a recovery. One friend from happier days who saw Hay around this time was fellow Fettesian Alistair MacLean, now himself a psychiatrist:

I went to see George last month, at Morningside. He is much worse than I ever saw him and answered my Gaelic overtures with English abuse. … He called me Alistair and/but spontaneously said he knew who I was; I do not know the specific reason for his hostility. His *Fuaran Slèibh* and *Wind on Loch Fyne* are not long published and have got very good reviews. He is being hailed in some quarters as the greatest Scots poet living and fit to rank with the greatest of all time. … It was very depressing seeing him; he himself was not depressed however. (Source 46, late 1948/early 1949)

Even Catherine Hay's brave optimism was being eroded:

For a little it seemed to me that there was an improvement. He had got ground parole and he was writing quite a lot though no one could say what, and my hopes soared in consequence. I have not seen George for six months or longer, and I feel it hard. … He absolutely refuses to see any of his friends here but they tell me he is quite happy. … My hopes, Mr Scott, are dying …. I went to Crail for a fortnight's rest … in the hope that the sea and the quiet of a garden would bring some balm to a sorely stricken heart. But I'm an old woman now and my grief is for the tragedy of youth, and for my happy laughing boy. (Letter to F. G. Scott, 26 June 1949, courtesy of G. N. Scott)

A year and a half later, Hay's mother made another approach to Oliver & Boyd, this time proffering *O na Ceithir Àirdean*, a small manuscript of translations and original poems. Hay had at least partly planned the book in 1946, and two-thirds of its original poems (as well as a good number of its versions) had already been published, principally in *An Gàidheal* and MacDiarmid's *Voice of Scotland*. The manuscript was initially turned down as commercially unviable, but once again the McCaig Trust agreed to subsidise publication and guarantee against loss, and old friends rallied round to bring the project to fruition (see NLS Acc. 5000/569). By October 1950 the galley proofs were being "carefully gone over both by George – who got the greatest pleasure out of the job – and by Sam MacLean" (ibid.). John Lorne Campbell supplied the basis for a publicity blurb and this was then turned into Gaelic by Kenneth MacLeod. It appeared in both languages on the book's jacket:

[*Fuaran Slèibh*] was hailed by a distinguished critic as "unquestionably the most important volume of Gaelic poetry for a century and a half", and another has said that "Hay must be rated as the best poet in Gaelic since the death of Alasdair Mac Mhaighstir Alasdair two centuries ago". This new volume gives fresh proof of the vigour and versatility of his genius as a Gaelic poet. … Scholars will appreciate the subtle craft of Mr. Hay's versification; all Gaelic readers will respond to the tragic depth of the poems inspired by his war experiences and the nostalgic intensity of his evocation of the winds and waves of Loch Fyne and the birch and bracken of the hillsides of Kintyre.

Around this time, Catherine Hay could inform Douglas Young that George was employing "a good deal of time writing – mainly in Gaelic … I am trying my best to type it all out but it is rather difficult (partly owing to difficult writing)" (Source 36, 23 October 1950). Hay himself wrote:

> Times have permitted me to do quite a lot of writing, although scattered, which is often the post-war manner. (Odd lines from air-raids and barrages, and so forth.) Quite a lot of the songs from Bràigh Chinntìre [Kintyre] have come to my memory … (ibid.)

The contents of that letter suggest that Hay was not well; but a year later Catherine Hay had more encouraging news:

> The prospect of having *O na Ceithir Àirdean* published has helped George a lot and thrice of late I have been able to take him for a run into the countryside round about. Last Friday we saw the SEA so it was a red-letter day. It may not have had the beauty and glamour of the western seas but it yet gave us both much pleasure. (Source 44, 26 November 1951)

O na Ceithir Àirdean finally appeared in 1952. An unsigned advance notice of 5 April in the Dingwall paper *The North Star*, written in fact by Sorley MacLean (letter to editor, 15 October 1991), praised Hay's "lovable genius", his "sympathetic imagination", the "wonderful poem of bombed Bizerta[116], so haunting with its wistful, questioning rhythms":

> [He] is of course, an amazing linguist and an even more amazing virtuoso in poetic technique … but the highest distinction of his work is not ultimately in its virtuosity but in its exquisite flavour, which seems a delicate blend of the old and the new in Gaelic, for, however far he ranges, he remains fundamentally and proudly a Gaelic poet, conscious of the great poetic traditions of Scotland and Ireland, … and of the past and present of Scotland.

And a young Iain Crichton Smith, in one of the earliest assessments of the "nua-bhàrdachd" (non-traditional twentieth-century Gaelic poetry), wrote with insight:

> Courage: that is one impression from Hay's poetry. Courage, love of his homeland, and a respect for tradition. … Hay is probably more in the true tradition of Gaelic poetry than MacLean in his emphasis on nature, his preoccupation with "eternal" themes, the strictness of his forms. Nevertheless, there is a lack of passion. Sometimes he is as if immured in marble. At his best, however, his qualities of disciplined integrity and meditative power are fine. (Smith 1953: 202–4)

Smith was to pay further tribute several years later, during Hay's period of silence:

> A neart do bhàrdachd dh'ionnsaich mi
> misneachd a thug neart dhomh fhèin,
> oir feumar balla trom air son
> aibhnichean boillsgeanach ...
>
> Oir chunna tu an saoghal mar thà e,
> muir ri creig, 's an t-iasgair geur
> a' cothachadh le inntinn làidir,
> ach, àm is àm, lasraidh troimhn speur
> solas a sheallas neochiontas
> toirt maitheanas don dorch' 's don bhàs.
>
> (from "Airson Deòrsa Caimbeul Hay", in *Gairm* 24 (Summer 1958): 308)

From the power of your poetry I have learnt | a courage which has given power to me in turn, | for it takes a heavy wall to withstand | swelling rivers ...

For you saw the world as it is, | sea against rock, and the keen-eyed fisherman | struggling with strong mind, | but time and again, across the sky there flares | a light which reveals innocence | bringing forgiveness to darkness and to death.

The Silent Years

It is apposite that Hay's long, silent years of slow recovery coincided with a protracted period in the political wilderness for the SNP. The year 1950 had been the annus mirabilis of John MacCormick's Scottish Covenant, with its National Assembly attracting 1,000 delegates, and signatories of its call for a Parliament heading for the 2,000,000 mark, but the momentum evaporated in the face of central government opposition, and the Covenant played no role in the 1951 election (Harvie 1981: 107). The Stone of Destiny adventure in the winter of 1951–2 provided a colourful finale to the home-rule agitation of the inter-war years.

On the Gaelic front, however, Hay would have been cheered by the appearance in 1952 of an accessible, popular, all-Gaelic periodical, the cheerfully innovative *Gairm*. The need for such a vehicle to stimulate the development of Gaelic prose writing had been a repeated preoccupation of his during the 1940s (Source 36: 23 June 1943, 22 August 1943, 25 January 1944, 5 March 1944, 20 December 1944, 26 November 1945; and Hay 1944), and it is sadly ironic that when Derick Thomson's and Finlay J. MacDonald's *Gairm* did make its appearance, Hay was no longer in a position to contribute. On receipt of Hay's subscription for 1954, however, the editors requested material and were sent the magical "Sahara Journey", extracted from "Mochtàr is Dùghall"[109.2.3]. Three years later the magazine featured a short Kintyre poem[171], and an intriguing alliterative poem "The Sun in Athens"[170] appeared in *The Saltire Review*, while in 1956 Mac-Diarmid's *Voice of Scotland* published a rambling, allusive essay by Hay on cultural and literary affinities (Hay 1956).

Return

Whether or not he was writing much during these years in hospital, to the outside world his voice remained muted until 1960. In that year he was discharged, a happy development

> made possible by a multiplicity of factors, with improved drug management only one part of the explanation. He undertook certain work in the University Department of Psychiatry latterly, and this "rehabilitation" is almost certain to have been associated with improved general wellbeing, itself contributed to by a more satisfactory range of drug treatments. Further, the early '60s saw an acceleration in the pace of discharge of patients who had formerly been regarded as of "long-stay nature". What was changing in those days was not so much practical things as attitudinal things. (Dr A. K. Zealley, letter of 7 January 1992)

Hay found employment on an informal basis in the Printed Books Department of the National Library of Scotland, under its Welsh keeper, David Myrddin Lloyd. His main responsibility was in the field of Scandinavian literature, but in addition "most questions concerning Gaelic or Irish printed books come my way, which is very pleasant" (Source 46, 31 December 1960).

Contact was renewed not only with the outside world through work, kirk and ceilidh – "The Tìr nam Beann ceilidhs are a regular haunt of mine, and I go to the Tolbooth Gaelic Church on most Sundays" (ibid.) – but also with the inner world of his Muses:

> At present I am writing a lot, most of it in Gaelic and some in Scots, and in two or three years I think I should have another Gaelic book ready. *Gairm* and *An Gàidheal* are going to publish some of the Gaelic things, but I really have more than I know what to do with. (ibid.)

Gairm did indeed publish a long poem of allegiance to Kintyre ("Air Suidh' Artair Dhomh Mochthrath") and some Tarbert ephemera (as did *An Gàidheal*), but the bulk of the shorter poems were published by the now weekly *Scots Independent*, between December 1960 and May 1961. In March 1961, Hay was in Tarbert, and noting down overheard or long-remembered snippets of Tarbert speech (see Sources 12 and 13). But by

May he was on the run, to the alarm of his friends, Hugh MacDiarmid among them:

> Also wonder if George Hay has turned up again. I met him in Edinburgh after his enlargement and had several letters, mss, etc. from him afterwards, and had hoped he was all right, but his disappearances since have been a grief and worry to me and I do hope he is back again and in good shape. (Source 36, 9 June 1961)

The demands of regular employment may have been too heavy for his impaired stamina; in addition his fierce independence of spirit was unabated and he resented the restrictions and controls placed on his life by a regimen of regular treatments and hospital visits. In the course of his 1961 disappearances, "planned to avoid being roped into hospital" (Source 49: 102), George spent a month in Dublin and some time in Inverness and Fort William. He later told a friend that during his time in Dublin sleeping rough, he had been taken in and fed by a religious organisation, but "he couldn't take the religion, and baled out" (Source 24: 76). At Fort William, in May, he ran into Sorley MacLean, and was taken back down to Edinburgh with the help of two schoolfriends (psychiatrist Alistair MacLean, and Robert Rankin). George resented the interference, subjecting MacLean to "such a torrent of abuse" on the train journey south that the doctor had to withdraw from the compartment (Rankin 1984: 12).

In October he was readmitted to the Royal Edinburgh Hospital, and only discharged in May 1963. After undergoing a serious intestinal operation the following year (Source 49: 105), Hay was to spend four further spells in the Royal Edinburgh in the mid- to late 1960s. During this period, he did some translation work for the Psychiatry Library of the hospital, and was co-opted onto the editorial board of the hospital's community paper, the *Morningside Mirror*, to which he contributed the odd review and several of his old poems and translations. Similarly, in 1965, he dug up some old poems (two of them previously unpublished) for inclusion in the forthcoming *Oxford Book of Scottish Verse*, following a request from co-editor Tom Scott. That anthology was picked up soon after publication by a young Campbeltown boy, Angus Martin. Discovering in its pages, "with a thrill of association which I can recover still", a poem about two old Tarbert skippers "The Two Neighbours"[147], Martin made contact with its author (Martin 1984: 49). The friendship which ensued was to be the richest of Hay's later years.

From 1968 to 1970, Hay appeared in *Catalyst*, organ of the newly formed "1320 Club". The Club had been set up in 1967 in the expectation that "a breakthrough was going to occur on the Scottish political scene very shortly and that independence was not far off" (*Catalyst* I.1: 1). Such optimism was given credence by a dramatic rise in SNP membership, sweeping gains by the party in municipal elections and Winnie Ewing's spectacular election victory in Hamilton. The SNP leadership itself had reservations about an

organisation gathering such seasoned mavericks as MacDiarmid, Wendy
Wood and Oliver Brown, and eventually banned the organisation, but mean-
while the Club organised symposia on the legal and constitutional aspects of
independence, prepared a constitution and a defence policy for the new
Scotland, and continued to produced its lively journal. Hay's nationalist
verse was given great prominence in *Catalyst*, from wartime "classics" like
"Ar Blàr Catha"[126] to more recent shorter pieces.

Hay was in regular touch with the magazine's editor, poet (and then
student in Celtic) William Neill. They met mostly in Milne's Bar, the
Saturday Mecca of the Scottish poets, but Hay seems to have kept his
distance from that literary set. Neill recalls:

> George was, as far as I could see, very little involved with other Makars.
> He sat in the company of people who combined an interest in Scottish
> literature (and language) with an interest in Scottish politics. Since
> being Scot Nat at that time was not popular with many of the minor
> Scottish literati ... we were rather a fringe group. ... George himself
> was rather quiet, drinking only two pints of heavy per session. The
> company which admired him were, for the most part, outcasts from
> the rather smart central group. (Letter of 18 February 1992)

Another writer, at the time a young "small-time newspaper man", who met
George in Milne's in the late 1960s, confirms that

> he did not, as I remember, mix with or talk much to the other poets. I
> never saw him ensconced with the leading lights in the Victorian wood-
> panelled, stained-glassed-windowed cubicle [known as "the Kremlin"]
> which formed an enclave in the bar's big room. ... I remember him as
> being small, florid-faced, with wispy thinning sandy hair, and specta-
> cles. I think he had a walking stick. He talked about Tarbert Loch
> Fyne, his father and the novel *Gillespie*. ... George was by no means
> short of talk, although he was hesitant and shy with it. ... As someone
> who hardly knew him, I was immediately respectful of a poet, scholar,
> linguist, and, of course, a patriot. (Jeremy Bruce-Watt, letter of 21
> February 1992)

Hay also attended events organised by "The Heretics", a nationalist cultural
group founded by Willie Neill and the late Stuart MacGregor, and was even
once persuaded to read in public, "but he suffered from stage-nerves and
preferred others to read his poems" (W. Neill, op. cit.).

The new exposure given to Hay's poetry, albeit low-level and of a limited
selection only, led to important developments. The *Catalyst* pieces aroused
the interest of the Edinburgh publisher Gordon Wright, who, upon discov-
ering *Wind on Loch Fyne*, decided to include as much of the book as
possible in a new anthology. Selection of the Gaelic poems was left to Hay
himself (G. Wright, letter of 21 February 1991): he chose nine from *Fuaran
Slèibh* and four only from *O na Ceithir Àirdean* (including neither "Bisearta"

nor "Meftah Bâbkum es-Sabar?"). Wright's anthology *Four Points of a Saltire*, also featuring the poetry of Sorley MacLean, Willie Neill and Stuart MacGregor, became a landmark in the reappraisal and in the sheer availability of both Hay's and MacLean's work.

In 1969, Hay made friends with a new visitor to the hospital day centre, Elizabeth Kirk. They grew close, and Hay's romantic interest surfaced in several poems of the period (Poems 216–18). The two were in touch for ten years or so; Ms Kirk remembered him as a kind but private man, talkative at Centre meetings and among friends, but who could retreat into complete silence before strangers, and who shunned all public exposure. He had never lost the stravaiging habits of his youth and would frequently go wandering the Pentland Hills; occasionally he would also take his sister out of hospital for short breaks.

Although Hay's poetic output increased as his mental ill-health receded, his boundless optimism was not matched by mental stamina, and as a result longer-term projects tended to run aground. Plans for a collected edition had been instigated by Gordon Wright shortly after the publication of *Four Points of a Saltire*, and in June 1972 Hay informed the publisher that half the manuscript was ready. By this time George had also signed a contract with Robin Lorimer of Southside Publishers, allowing the inclusion of his work in a projected anthology of five modern Gaelic poets. This was to be edited and introduced by the youngest of the contributors, Donald MacAulay, who wrote to Hay:

> As you must know, your poetry has had a very definite influence on the work of the rest of us – quite apart from its direct contribution to Gaelic verse. I think the poems I have chosen illustrate both these facets. (Source 23, 15 September 1971)

The contract also granted Southside first option on Hay's next book, but on this occasion the option was turned down, and the way seemed clear for the publication of Hay's collected poems by Gordon Wright. Hay, however, does not seem to have ever completed his manuscript, and without explanation declined to sign the contract prepared by Wright (G. Wright, letters of 21 February and 3 July 1991; R. L. C. Lorimer, conversation of 3 March 1991). Shortly after, in 1973, he was admitted briefly into hospital.

A period of poetic silence then ensued, although in a feat of sustained effort Hay produced a complete Gaelic typescript (Source 21) in 1973–4, which added more recent material to the poems of *Fuaran Slèibh* and *O na Ceithir Àirdean*. In February 1975, he wrote to David Morrison, editor of the Wick-based *Scotia Review*:

> I seem to be written out and haven't produced anything for over a year except reviews for the Scotsman. Maybe the Muse will return, and if that proves to be the case, I will certainly send Scotia Review the wale of the outcome. … I was working on my collected poems and have got

the Gaelic part complete, but I don't seem to be able to get round to the Scots and English. Maybe it is too early to be thinking of collected poems anyway as I am only 59. (NLS Acc. 7309/1)

Hope's a Warrior

The Muse was not long in returning: the autumn 1975 issue of *Gairm* published the first of a stream of poems, both original and translations, which continued – bar a silent spell in 1979 – until Hay's death. In 1976 the Lorimer anthology, *Nua-bhàrdachd Ghàidhlig*, finally appeared, having been delayed by financial difficulties and the takeover of Southside by Canongate Publishers. The bilingual volume became the canon of modern Gaelic poetry in schools and universities, and gave Hay's reputation a new boost, but it appeared too late for Catherine Hay to witness: after years of ill-health, she died in June 1975, aged 92. Hay's elegy to "the woman of bravery" (see Poem 350 "Marbhrann dom Mhàthair") strikes a poignant and very Gaelic note of lament for her death in foreign surroundings, "far from her family and from her people".

The later 1970s were a highly productive time for Hay: Gaelic material went mostly to *Gairm*, except for the political verse which was sent to the *Scots Independent* (along with some Italian and Norwegian effusions), and also to *Carn* (the Dublin-based journal of the Celtic League); Scots poems (old and new) appeared in *Lallans*, *Akros* and *Chapman* (to which Hay also sent his magisterial thirty-year-old "The Walls of Balclutha"[155]); and *Scotia Review* followed up an appreciative essay by Willie Neill with a finely varied selection by Hay of old and new, original and translated work, in Scots, Gaelic, English and French (issue 17, Summer 1977). "I am ever sure of aid from the melodious Muses", Hay sang in "Dreuchd an Fhilidh"[288], on a triumphant wave of creativity. In 1978 he envisaged busy times ahead:

> This year I'm translating a book from Irish into Scottish Gaelic for the Gaelic Books Council, and that'll take up pretty well the whole year, and next year will be taken up with reading for the big projected historical dictionary of the Gaelic language. And then four years at my collected poems. Have sparet! … I'm writing a lot …, and I foresee a very busy six coming years. My heid's full of Tarbert lore, and I sometimes sit by the fire going over it for hours on end. (Source 24: 1, 22 February 1978)

Hay had agreed to translate the medieval Irish tale "Trí Truagha na Scéaluidheachta" ("The Three Sorrows of Storytelling") for the Books Council the previous April; he planned to have it finished by the end of 1978, but that year was not an easy one for him, and in early 1979 he had to admit that the task was beyond him.

He had new plans, however, which he enthusiastically unveiled to Angus Martin, by now a regular visitor and correspondent:

The month of May I hope to spend in Tarbert. I mean to scout around for a house, either to rent or to buy. In fact, a Council house would do. My intention is to return to Tarbert for the rest of my life, for it's beginning to be unbearable to be away from it. The flat here I'll sell, or else give to Sabhal Mòr Ostaig [the fledgeling Gaelic College in Skye] for an Edinburgh HQ. ... I'm thinking of years recording the Gaelic of Kintyre, Knapdale, Cowal, Gigha, Islay and Colonsay, and Jura. I'll start from scratch with my 100 per cent War Disablement Pension, some blank notebooks, typing paper and my typewriter. And a few books. Most of the books and furniture I'll leave in the house for the [Ostaig] people. (ibid.: 5, January 1979)

With the writing commitments I have before me I can't leave Edinburgh until May, as I want to have the decks clear for the upheaval and the flitting and start from scratch with a clean slate in Tarbert. To Tarbert I am going, even if I live in a but-and-ben with a paraffin lamp and get my water from a well. Time and time again in Gaelic and Scots and English I have written nostalgic poems, and either you mean it or you don't mean it. I have always meant it. As for gifting the house here, once again, either you mean it or you don't mean it. You know Sabhal Mòr Ostaig as well as I do, and they may never want a place in Edinburgh, though my opinion is that they should have one, and one in Glasgow too. If they don't want the flat, I'll give it to the SNP. Either you mean it or you don't mean it. ... Let me put your mind at rest ... To my mind I'm more like a millionaire than a penniless poet. ... I have a 100 per cent War Disablement Pension of £57 a week, and there are thousands if not millions who work themselves to the bone and get through a lifetime on less. There are people who go on bitter strikes for less. If you take a good, realistic look at it, I think you will see and agree I'm a rich man. That money is paid to me by people working in coalmines and factories and on the deck of skiffs, and I intend to make my contribution in return, which is writing. I have spent years sitting and thinking and my head is full of things to write, and maybe the sitting and thinking are over for good. (ibid.: 6, 31 January 1979)

For all his optimism and sense of purpose, the years ahead were to be difficult. Hay did not leave for Tarbert in May, but that month he was recorded by Angus Martin (at the time preparing his second book, *Kintyre: The Hidden Past*), recalling Tarbert words and expressions and reminiscing on his own early experiences. His fondness for the village bursts out in the comments that punctuate his anecdotes: "Oh, it's some place! A laugh all the time, something original all the time", "Tarbert's more romantic than

Campbeltown", "Ho, Tarbert's a laugh – Parahandy was nothing to Tarbert!", "You could hear anything in Tarbert, by God aye!", "Oh, they were wild people, God knows they were!"

Magnum Opus

It was in the course of further recorded conversations with Martin that Hay mentioned "Mochtàr is Dùghall"[109], with an almost mischievous (but probably ingenuous) casualness. Speaking about his breakdown in Salonica, Hay agreed that it had brought his scholarly career to an end.

> AM: But it was after the war mainly that your poetic ability surfaced?
> GCH: Well, "Mochtàr is Dùghall" is from the war.
>
> AM: What was that?
> GCH: "Mochtàr is Dùghall" – do you want to take it home with you and look at it? (SSS November 1980)

Out came the typescript, and a rapid look was enough to suggest the importance of the work. Martin took an extract to Derick Thomson, founder-editor of *Gairm* and Professor of Celtic at Glasgow University, and by December Hay had given Thomson permission to publish his abandoned magnum opus. He attempted to complete the work, and again entertained plans for a collected or selected edition of his poems (Source 24: 12). The war poem was previewed in the arts and affairs journal *Cencrastus* in summer 1981, through the agency of literary scholar John Burns. Burns lived in the same Morningside street as George, and had first approached him early in 1979 partly to discuss his own studies on Neil Gunn.

> From then on I saw him quite often, and spent many afternoons sitting in his flat more or less just keeping him company. Sometimes he would be quite talkative, other times not. Depending on his health he was interested in what was happening on the literary scene ..., and was working away on poems and songs, and on a couple of review pieces ... I was very much aware of the fragile nature of his health so I never really quizzed him about his past ... I do know that in times of illness his mind often went back to the war and to things he had seen. He once said, though, that although war was a terrible thing, it often brought out rare qualities in people. (Source 24: 76–7)

Burns later recalled Hay in terms shared by other friends of the period: a man of great courtesy, but also withdrawn, who would lapse into long silences and was loath to discuss himself or his poetry. He had not lost the old independence of mind: his social worker Bill Cook remembered that when they first met at hospital, in 1979,

> he was not a happy man ... as he felt people were interfering with his life, and I can recall he was quite hostile initially. He did not think that

he required any assistance, although his house and his living conditions were poor. (Letter of July 1991?)

His sojourn in hospital that year was brief, but he was taken in again in 1980, after a severe bout of alcohol abuse:

> For more than a year I was drinking a quarterbottle of rum in the morning, a quarterbottle in the afternoon and a quarterbottle at night, with pubs in addition and hardly any food or sleep. I was told I was lucky to have come through alive. Everything went to pot – house, correspondence, writing, friends – everything. (Source 24: 8, 12 June 1980)

Hay's resistance to being helped lessened, and in April 1982 he moved to a hospital hostel, and offered his flat to the Social Work Department for use as a group home for discharged patients. That March, "Mochtàr is Dùghall" had finally been released to the public, in a rather spartan format. In spite of Hay's efforts, the poem was still more or less as it had been abandoned thirty-five years before: the section on Dùghall was very fragmentary, and only half the poem was translated; but for all that, the quality and originality of the work shone irrepressibly through, and the book did much to revive the reclusive poet's reputation. In *The Scottish Review*, Iain Crichton Smith would call it "a glittering artifact" whose "sustained power of description can hardly have been surpassed by any Scottish poet this century" (Smith 1986: 112). One can only speculate what impact Hay's magnum opus would have had on the Gaelic world had it been completed and published in the immediate post-war years. Would the depth of his imaginative engagement with Islamic North Africa and the broad eclecticism of his work have been as startling to his public and as liberating to younger poets as the passionate syntheses of Sorley MacLean's poetry? The most public accolade came in November 1983 when, at the National Mod, Hay was awarded "Gaeldom's premier literary prize", An Comann Gàidhealach's Gaelic Writer's Award. Only five months later, Hay's name was again to be in the papers, for an altogether sadder reason.

He had returned to his own flat in December 1982, and started work on his Collected Poems: "There's a mass of material. Writing a lot, almost all in Gaelic, and there are my 50 melodies to be recorded" (Source 24: 54, 6 December 1982). But the attempt at preparing a collection did not get very far. "Leigidh às mo sheisreach, on tha 'm feasgar 'teannadh dlùth", it announces, quoting a Gaelic song ("I shall unyoke my ploughteam, since evening is fast approaching"), but the effort stalls after several poems. More sustained were the annotated revisions to his old collections (see Sources 29, 30, 32, 33).

In January 1983, in a move which took his friends by surprise, Hay returned to his native place. Poetic inspiration surged:

The Muse hasn't forsaken me here, neither in Scots nor in Gaelic. ... I have now 53 melodies, the latest of them for "The Smoky Smirr o Rain"[151] ... Have been to the fishing for a day, and I brought them good luck. Trawling, not ring-net, alas! (Source 23: 103, 2 March 1983)

"Plenty of Gaelic to be found in Tarbert", he noted (ibid.: 104), and he was said to have veritably "held court" in Tarbert's Columba Hotel, being consulted on all kinds of matters Gaelic (Rankin 1984: 11). Unable however to find permanent accommodation or to afford any more rent, Hay came back to Edinburgh at the end of August and spent another brief sojourn in hospital. Whether his return to the city was touched by disillusionment can only be a matter for speculation. His friend Angus Martin has written that

George never fully explained to me why he returned to Edinburgh after his stay in Tarbert. ... The ostensible reason was that he couldn't get into a council house; but I doubt if that was the whole truth. He may have been disappointed. It's hard to say how his mind worked. He was drinking a lot while in Tarbert ... and it may well be that he never fully came to an understanding of what he was really doing there. Yet he may have sensed the futility of his presence there. ... Obviously the place has changed. The fishing has lost its character, and the boats are different boats in most ways. There's no Gaelic; and the old men are all gone. What could have remained, other than the physical existence of the place? ... The question is: did Tarbert fulfil his expectations? Did he – did he even want to – address himself to that question? Was he happy there? – another question. Was he happy anywhere? – yet another question. George was an enigma. I didn't understand him. Who did, in the post-war years? (Letter of 11 December 1989)

Still Hay composed, and he seems at this stage to have again tried to add to "Mochtàr is Dùghall"[365], but over the dark winter months his courage ran low: his social worker recalled that "right at the end he wasn't interested [in help] and I have the feeling that he had just decided that enough was enough" (Cook, letter of July 1991?). On 26 March 1984, Bill Cook called round to the Maxwell Street flat and found Hay's body, lying dead since the night before.

"Scotland has lost a most rare poet and patriot", wrote Sorley MacLean, acclaiming his poetry as

the work of a virtuoso in language and in metrics; of a man of a great heart, intensely obsessed with the suffering and aspirations of his own compatriots and of human beings in general. (*The Scotsman*, 30 March 1984)

Surprisingly, despite urgings from Robin Lorimer, Gordon Wright and other friends for a thorough search, the clearing of Hay's flat brought little to light in the way of literary manuscripts. It was not until almost a year later that these surfaced, bringing Hay's name once again into the columns of *The Scotsman*: "£3 Auction Buy Reveals Gaelic Treasure", it announced.

> The literary papers of one of the leading Gaelic poets of this century were sold at an Edinburgh auction recently for £3, the price of the old suitcase in which they were contained. (ibid., 14 March 1985)

Alerted that the contents of Hay's flat were to be sold off, antiquarian bookseller Donald MacCormick had attended the auction, and discovered an old suitcase full of notebooks and loose papers with drafts dating from the 1930s down to the 1980s. The find was sold to the National Library of Scotland in February 1985; Hay's collection of printed books (much of it annotated) was sold to the Library in July, and three months later further notebooks were deposited by Hay's estate.

In addition to Sorley MacLean's *Scotsman* tribute, and others in the same paper by Ronald Black (7 April and 9 June 1984) and Iain Crichton Smith (Smith 1984), assessments of Hay's work were given by Derick Thomson and Iain Crichton Smith in *The Scottish Review* (issue 35), by Donald Meek in *Chapman* (issue 39), and by John Burns in *Cencrastus* (issue 18), while *Gairm* later featured a lengthy reappraisal by William Gillies (Gillies 1986). Fascinating for their biographical detail were Angus Martin's painstakingly researched chapter on the "Bard of Kintyre" (Martin 1984), and Robert Rankin's frank and sympathetic portrait in *Chapman* (Rankin 1984). In October 1985, a plaque commemorating "Sàr Bhàrd an Tairbeirt" ("The Great Tarbert Poet") was unveiled by Martin in Tarbert Academy, and the event was accompanied by an exhibition of watercolours by the Tarbert-born architect Archie MacAlister, inspired by Hay's poetry.

A special limited edition of the long poem "Seeker, Reaper"[158] was published in 1988 by the Saltire Society, introduced by Martin and again illustrated by MacAlister. Two years later, MacAlister released a recording of this poem and others from *Wind on Loch Fyne*, read by Tom Fleming and Simon Donald, with evocative musical explorations by the late Francis Cowan. Some of Hay's own musical settings were aired for the first time in February 1990 by Anne Lorne Gillies at a benefit performance in Edinburgh for the Scottish Poetry Library, devised by composer and pianist Ronald Stevenson. Hay's importance was further brought to public notice by the BBC Scotland film *Seeker, Reaper*, a vivid elegiac dramatisation of his life and poetry by Paul Murton, starring Peter Mullan, which was premiered at the Edinburgh International Film Festival in August 1993.

THE POETIC CRAFT

Aspects of Form and Language

In everything, yes, form and form alone
ennobles what the poet spirits say,
stamps it as great and genius' very own.

Yes, form I worship, cost it what it may.
That's understood. Bear this in mind from me –
with form my verses become poetry.

(G. C. Hay, from the Norwegian of Henrik Ibsen)

Manifesto

In his "envoi" for *Fuaran Slèibh*[108], dispatching his book out into the world in the classical fashion, Hay speaks of spending his greatest energies on poems in Gaelic, chipping away at them and polishing them ("gan snaidheadh 's gan lìomhadh"). This makes explicit what his entire poetic output bears witness to, namely that he saw poetry not as a fruit of spontaneous outpourings, but as a demanding trade requiring the development and perfection of technical skills. Some extant drafts give us an insight into the painstaking labour involved (see as an example the various versions of "Na Baidealan"[67], given in the commentary). His fascination with the intricacies of poetic technique is also evident in his notebooks of the war period: in Source 7, for example, as well as notes on classical Arabic metrics, we find page after page of lines and phrases lifted from his readings of French, Arabic and especially Italian poetry, illustrating tricks of technique. If further confirmation were needed, Hay's article on "Gaelic and Literary Form", which appeared in Hugh MacDiarmid's periodical *The Voice of Scotland* in 1939, confirms how deliberate was his cultivation of those formal qualities which so characterise his work. The article is presented as something of a manifesto for the future of Gaelic poetry, but is of more interest as a blueprint for Hay's own practice.

"The most obvious failing of formlessness and dispensing with workmanship in poetry", Hay writes by way of introduction, "is ... that in formlessness there is no variety" (Hay 1939: 14). The main thrust of the article is that Gaelic poetry should not abandon its traditional technical strengths for indiscriminate borrowings.

> It would be safe to make it a general principle that if the borrowing of a literary form ... involves the jettisoning of any fundamental native characteristic, the borrowing will either have a bad effect or, if the native tradition is strong enough, none at all. And the fundamental characteristic of Gaelic poetry is ... a highly developed technique. ...
>
> Most people must be conscious of how horrid are the results in Gaelic of borrowing simple-minded English technical forms. ...
>
> Certainly not every poem which has been composed with great technical care or according to strict rules has been successful. But floods of versification subject to neither care nor rule of any kind have been one of mankind's greatest afflictions – and here and there murmurs have been heard that versification in Gaelic is "too easy" and that not enough is required of the versifier.
>
> It is when much is required of the composer and when he makes a successful response to the demands, that poetry reaches its highest degree of attainment. Such a remark might sound ridiculously untrue in relation to English poetry, where the tendency has been to shake off the trammels and set the spirit (good, bad or indifferent) free to work its will. But Gaelic seems to set no limits to developments in technique, and has not even yet exerted all its strength in this direction. (Hay 1939: 15, 15–16, 17)

Although Hay singles out some contemporary perpetrators of "horrid" borrowing (John MacFadyen, K. W. Grant, Angus Morrison), there is a broader line of attack implicit in his argument. It is now generally accepted that the nineteenth century saw a decline in both the metrical and the expressive range of Gaelic poetry which continued, with some notable exceptions (see for example Meek 1995 and MacMillan 1968), until the emergence of Sorley MacLean and Hay. MacLean himself had decried the trend in a talk to the Gaelic Society of Inverness in 1938, choosing one of the most popular of the "Victorian" poets to make his point:

> The technical inferiority of nineteenth- and twentieth-century Gaelic song is manifested in a flabbiness of rhythm, a lack of the clear, definite outline of the older song, and that is accompanied by an insignificance and worthlessness of matter and a lack of sincerity and realism unknown in the older poetry ... Indeed, Neil MacLeod's poetry is symptomatic of the rapid decline in the backbone of Gaelic poetry. It is sentimental, pretty-pretty, weak and thin, only sometimes attaining splendour in its occasional realist moods ... (MacGill-eain 1985: 32, 46)

Hay too bemoaned the poverty of content in most recent Gaelic poetry. "It is time that we had truth again, as well as romance, in Gaelic", he wrote to Young in February 1940 (Source 36), and in an accompanying review of Sorley MacLean's contribution to *Seventeen Poems & 6d.* (a collaboration with the Edinburgh poet Robert Garioch), he asks:

How long ago was it that the last Gaelic poetry that really meant anything was produced? At the time of the evictions? Long since anyway. But from these poems it looks as if we are getting out of the rut at last. ... [Mr MacLean] has avoided our continual lyricism, which at present looks like becoming as maudlin as the Lowland lyric once was. He follows neither the [romantic] "Och mo nighean donn" nor the [nostalgic] "far an d'fhuair mi m' àrach òg" persuasion. Nor ... has he wandered off into a drawingroom Tìr Nan Òg at the heels of the Clàrsach Society and the Kennedy Frasers. (Source 36, February 1940)

However, it was the technical flaccidness of much modern Gaelic poetry which seemed to preoccupy Hay in his article, that "weakness and flabbiness of rhythm due largely to the overdoing of artificial metrical stresses" identified by MacLean (1985: 46). It may well be that more discipline in ornamentation and metrics would tend to filter off cliché and the easy option in lyrical expression; he may also have felt that until he (or any other Gaelic poet) had something new to say – as MacLean clearly had – then his poetic energy should concentrate on rearticulating the old themes in a more artistically challenging way.

Through a combination of factors, which must include his remarkable powers of memory, the intellectual nature of his acquisition of Gaelic, and maybe above all his schooling in the Classics (which gave him not only a solid grounding in the poetic technique of the West's most influential tradition, but also, and more importantly, a heightened sensitivity to the technical skills nurtured by all poetic traditions) – through all these, Hay was more than normally aware of the literary qualities and traditions of Gaelic, in a manner that sets him apart from his poetic peers. Sorley MacLean himself, speaking of that "burden" of unattainability which the old songs of the sixteenth and seventeenth centuries place on the modern Gaelic poet (because they remain "the supreme hermaphrodite of words and music"), has suggested that

[Hay] felt the burden more lightly, in that the music he seems to have most often at the back of his mind is the word music of the Bardic Schools, a more sophisticated, less intense, more attainable music than the "out of this world" music of Cairistìona, Little Sister, Girl over yonder ... and scores of others. (MacGill-eain 1985: 115)

As we shall see, the "old songs" exerted their power over Hay too, but undoubtedly the Bardic Schools were exactly what he looked back to in much of his earlier poetry. As he explained to Kenneth MacLeod in an early letter,

The compactness and art of the bardic poetry has always attracted me, and I sometimes feel that Gaelic poetry needs discipline – it's too easy at times to go on rhyming and rhyming like a bó-bhàrd [lower rank of bard]. Welsh cywydd [a couplet form with elaborate alliteration] is strict, and yet they still turn out perhaps the finest lyrics in Britain – or Europe. (Source 44, 10 October 1938)

In his *Voice of Scotland* article, Hay suggests ways of adapting the art of the medieval bards for modern purposes:

> For models of high artistic skill one inevitably turns to the work of the bardic schools. Dàn Dìreach metres can be adopted [sic] by substituting a system of stress for the syllabic system, and by disregarding the rules about classes of consonants. There would remain a regulated system of alliteration and of comparatively richer internal rhyming. The Welsh cywydd is suggestive with its consonant sequences ... Or again, it would be interesting to see what effects would be produced in Gaelic by the Icelandic system of triple groups of alliteration within each couplet.
>
> But these are matters of detail, and the main point is that Gaelic's attainment in mere technique is high, and could be vastly higher. It would be foolish to throw away these possibilities for a heroic couplet or two. (Hay 1939: 17)

By the time Hay wrote his "manifesto", he had already composed such intricate lyrics as "An Gleannan"[8], "Siubhal a' *Choire*"[7] and "Do Bheithe Bòidheach"[22], as well as the more expansive "Cinntìre"[26] and "Tiomnadh"[36]. One may speculate whether Hay's composing had been based from the start on such a clear policy, or if his initial impetus was a more intuitive attraction towards certain models; at any rate his article clearly enunciates what he had in fact been doing ever since the adolescent "Aisling"[5]. The intricacy of "An Gleannan"[8], Hay's earliest surviving nature lyric, can serve as an example of his reapplication of centuries-old ornamental complexity: in that poem, three and even four vowel-rhymes bind most couplets, in addition to the terminal rhymes between couplets; there is much consonantal rhyme, and there can be little doubt that Hay intended an alliterative sequence like the one in "cluain nam fiadh, còrr am fàrdach" (c-m-f c-m-f), on the Welsh cynghanedd model.

In the poem "Cinntìre"[26], we can observe all the more clearly what we might call Hay's "neo-classicism", since in its expression that poem is so reminiscent of bardic verse. As prescribed in Hay's article, the syllabic count which characterised bardic metrics has given way to the accentual (i.e. the stress metrics of the near-totality of post-bardic verse), with a steady four-beat rhythm. Yet, as in most of his lyrics built on the four-line *rann*, one feels that he has purposefully kept a check on line length (here keeping to seven or eight syllables) so that the suggestion of bardic syllabic verse adds to the feel of concision and restraint (an effect reinforced by the occasional accentual irregularity, such as l. 16 "a' mhuir a' teannadh gu tràigh"). But it is principally in the richness of ornamentation that the bardic influence is clearest: in the first two verses, for example, on top of a final rhyme linking the couplets, one finds three assonances (vowel-rhymes) in all but the first couplet, alliteration in five lines, and further consonance. For all their accomplishment, these verses are not exceptional; their level of ornamentation is sustained throughout the poem. Nor is it something Hay reserves only for pieces with the poise of "Cinntìre": witness the marvellous juxtapositions of "Brìodal Màthar"[37], the exhilarating cadences of "Siubhal a' *Choire*"[7], or indeed the richness of the romantic "Òran"[28], with its demanding eighteenth-century rhyme scheme.

Hay's attachment to bardic verse also led him to pastiche, in his recreations of the seventeenth-century "trì rainn is amhran" hybrid (where three syllabic quatrains led to a summing-up verse in song metre). Hay was later to use the form for nature and even political themes, but his earliest attempts are elegant, even ironic, treatments of courtly love, perhaps in a deliberate effort to counter the sentimentality of much Gaelic love song. Predictably, although the metrics of these poems are predominantly accentual, the syllabic influence can be strongly felt (for example in the first verse of "An Gaol Cha d'Fhiosraich Mi"[63]).

Of course, not all of Hay's poems are ornamented to the same degree, and it is notable that the peaks of embellishment appear mostly in the early poetry. Significantly, too, most of Hay's poems of this early period, say up to 1940–1, have antecedents in Gaelic tradition: his nature and sea poems, for example, though not necessarily following specific models, powerfully exploit the prodigious store of vocabulary and imagery available in the literary tradition. A lyric like "Siubhal a' *Choire*"[7] gathers the expressive power of language diffused in a host of maritime songs, and in its compactness is arguably the most accomplished Gaelic poem of the type.

Hay's talent from the start is virtuosic and eclectic. While in this period he may be serving his apprenticeship, testing his own capabilities and finding his own voice, it is clear from his *Voice of Scotland* manifesto that he is also consciously extending the poetic field, hoping to modernise Gaelic poetry by re-energising its traditional strengths. The role-playing talent which he deploys to this end is impressive, and operates both in the formal domain of metre and diction and in a deeper, less tangible sense. Maurice Lindsay, for example, has said of Hay:

> He has a rare gift of ... "bodily grasp", "the ability to penetrate into the being of others, into that profound being which they are most unaware of themselves". All poets must possess this gift to some extent, of course, but in Hay it is particularly marked. Because of it, his poems about old folk, "The Auld Hunter"[32/33], a Gaelic piece, or ... "The Old Fisherman"[70], have made many elderly people wonder how a young man can so sensitively understand feelings which he himself can never have experienced. (Lindsay 1948: 23)

This comment, however true, underplays the mechanics of Hay's craft and his ability to penetrate into the varied streams of literary tradition. The Gaelic poem mentioned, "An Sealgair agus an Aois"[32], no doubt owes much to Hay's easy empathy with older people and to his own passion for the hills and the hunt, but in its articulation its greatest debt is to the voices found in Gaelic poetry. The poem's last verse strongly echoes the seventeenth-century MacDonald poet, Iain Lom, but overall the poem is in a tradition best exemplified by the long Lochaber poem "Òran na Comhachaig" ("The Owl's Song").

Time and time again Hay uses traditional voices, both literary and popular, with an ease once described as chameleon-like (Gillies 1986: 336). At times the results amount to stylistic exercises or pastiche, as in his courtly love poems, the love songs in a more popular vein ("Òran a Rinneadh ann an Ainm Fir Eile"[79], "Òran"[28], "Song"[34], "Garvalt Side"[228], "Lag an Aonaich"[246]), mothers' songs ("Brìodal Màthar"[37], "Òran Tàlaidh"[332]), or that amusing slapstick addition to the canon of Ossianic lays, "Ùrnaigh Oisin as Ùr"[27]. At other times, the intent is more serious, and tradition is used as a suitable vehicle for the poet's (often political) message, such as in "Grunnd na Mara"[68], "Alba Ghaoil Ò"[75], "Soothwards Owre the Sea"[69], "An Cnocan Fraoich"[104], "Aig an Fheurlochan"[242], or "Nationalist Sang"[206]. While occasionally models are clearly identifiable (as in "Alba Ghaoil Ò"[75]), often it is a much more subtle question of tone, as in the understated, wonderfully laconic delivery of "Tilleadh Uilìseis"[125].

Clearly the reworking of tradition to the modern poet's own ends, often into gems of technical richness, was part of Hay's apprenticeship. His interest in the craftwork of poetry and his technical ability never deserted him – one of his last poems, the tiny but exquisite "Dùrd a' Ghlinne"[358], might as credibly have been written before the war. Neither did his facility for tapping into seams of tradition dissipate: towards the end of his life he produced a variety of rewritten or expanded songs, including some breathtakingly skilful recreations of waulking-songs (in particular "Chailein Òig an Stiùir Thu Mi?"[321] and "Am Bàta Dubh"[359]). This interest had already manifested itself (albeit with less discipline) during his hidden years – represented here by "Fear Breacan Bheallaigh"[169]. In his one notebook from this period (Source 9), litanies of verse in various forms of Gaelic, Irish and Norse roll from one page to the next, in a bewildering amalgam of poet and tradition, as if Hay's poetic energy in a period of creative abeyance were channelled into reprocessing the masses of raw material he had so thoroughly absorbed in the 1930s.

In the war years, however, as his own voice clearly emerged in innovatory developments, he found less need to ground his poems in tradition, and we find technical structure and ornament loosening their hold somewhat, and the poetic technique becoming less easy to isolate from the poem's total impact. This development, a tendency rather than a clear progression, can be felt in "Atman"[110], which moves with a more organic rhythm and altogether less ornament than its contemporary "An t-Eòlas Nach Cruthaich"[111]. And if "Prìosan Da Fhèin an Duine?"[115] was written in a fairly traditional setting (reminiscent, for example, of Màiri Mhòr MacPherson's "Eilean a' Cheò"), "Ar Blàr Catha"[126] uses traditional stress metres with much more flexibility and in novel combinations. Then in the dramatic narrative of "Tilleadh Uilìseis"[125] Hay lets go for the first and last time (in Gaelic) of traditional form and rhythm. The artistry of that poem is of a different order from that of Hay's lyrics, yet the tools are traditional enough – for all its variations in pace, the melody of the narrative is grounded on a bass-line of final ò-rhymes, with recurrent "aicill" binding the poem. (Aicill, a vowel-rhyme linking the final stress of one line to a stress inside the next, remains to this day the most characteristic ornament of Gaelic poetry, and was used by Hay to Gaelicise imported forms, such as in "Bisearta"[116].)

The Ulysses poem explores a very flexible approach to poetic narrative, but in the year preceding its composition Hay had been developing a more traditional form which he had advocated years before, in his *Voice of Scotland* article, as "suitable for sustained narrative" (Hay 1939: 17). This was the so-called "caoineadh" (keening) metre of much Gaelic folk poetry: lines of equal stress built up in paragraphs, bound only by the same final rhyme. In his article, he wrote:

> In this unornamented recitative there may lie the seeds of a narrative form of verse, for certainly some of our finest poetry is to be found in it, just as the finest poetry of modern Greece is her Klephtic ballads and Murologia [keens] composed in the long unembellished lines of the "political metre". (ibid.: 18)

Sorley MacLean has recorded that Hay shared his "obsessing admiration" for the anonymous songs of the sixteenth and seventeenth centuries "which we both regard as the greatest thing in all Gaelic poetry" (Source 36, 7 September 1941), and this is confirmed by George himself in a letter to John Lorne Campbell written while on the run, c. April 1941:

> A réir mar a chì mise e, is ann de'n chuid as fheàrr de'n bhàrdachd againn na h-òrain luadhaidh ud agus òrain eile a rinneadh 'san aon mheadrachd shimplidh riu – "caoineadh lom" theagamh gum bu chòir a ràdh rithe, gun uaim no comhfhuaim sam bith innte ach aig ceann gacha sreath. Cha n-fhaigh thu eadar Dallán Forgaill [6mh linn] agus luchd rannghail ar latha-ne bàrdachd a bheir barr air Cumha Nic Raonaill –
>
> > Dh'fhosgail mi doras bhur seòmar,
> > thàinig bhur fuil thar mo bhrògan,
> > is teann nach d'òl mi fhìn mo leòir dheth.
>
> … Cha ghabhadh bàrdachd 'sa' Ghàidhlig a bhith na bu shimplidhe a thaobh ealain, ach, sud agad e, cuiridh i crith 'nad fhuil nach cuir "Moladh an Leómhain" fhéin air cho snasda saothaireach dlùth-thoinnte 's gu bheil e. (Source 23: 1–2)

The way I see it, among the greatest glories of our poetry we must count the waulking-songs and other songs composed in the same simple metre as them – "bare keening-metre" we should maybe call it, with no alliteration or rhyme at all except at the end of each line. Between Dallán Forgaill [sixth-century poet] and the versifiers of our own day you'll not find poetry to surpass Nic Raonaill's Lament – "I opened the door of your room, I your blood flowed over my shoes, I I stopped myself from drinking my fill of it". … No poetry in Gaelic could be simpler artistically, but, that's the thing, it shifts your blood in a way that even [Mac Mhaighstir Alastair's] "In Praise of the Lion" can't for all its elegance, craft and tight construction.

John Lorne Campbell, the recipient of the letter, had first contacted Hay to comment on his long essay "Scottish Gaelic Poetry", serialised in the *New Alliance* (Hay 1940–1). There, Hay remarks that

> the tone of heroic literature is often quiet, restrained and almost matter-of-fact, and time and time again that is the tone of Gaelic poetry. … It is in this quiet way that the deepest things are expressed. … It is in this unworked simplicity that poetry reaches its greatest height in any language. (ibid., III: 10)

Elsewhere, we find Hay bemoaning

> the trend in all modern English poetry [which] militates against the simple, bald style in which much of the greatest poetry is written. … Personally I favour the bald hard poetry high above any other. (Source 36, 24 October 1939)

And some years later, he would praise the poetry of the French Résistance for being "laconic and hard without any striving after those effects" (ibid., 14 February 1944). Appropriately, Hay's retelling of Ulysses' return, particularly in the violent finale, captures the hard, laconic tone of heroic tales, but Hay's general partiality for the "bald hard poetry" may surprise in a poet so noted for his formal sophistication. Yet, apart from his direct imitations of the Gaelic folk-song style such as "Grunnd na Mara"[68] or "Luinneag"[15], there are echoes of the popular voice in the passionate utterance of a piece like "An t-Òigear a' Bruidhinn On Ùir"[123] or the understated emotion of "A' Bhean a' Bruidhinn"[109.35].

During the war, Hay set about exploring the potentialities of the "keening metre", in accordance with the blueprint set out in his *Voice of Scotland* manifesto. "Mochtàr"[109.2] triumphantly proved the metre's narrative possibilities, and Hay proceeded to use it for more discursive purposes in "Meftah Bâbkum es-Sabar?"[124], "Ar Blàr Catha"[126], "Feachd a' Phrionnsa"[133] and the later sections of "Mochtàr is Dùghall". Although the tone of these poems is still highly polished rather than "bald and hard", the craft is less in the regular application of ornament than in the subtle ebb and flow of patterns of rhythm and sound in a way more organic to the meaning of the poem. It is hard to imagine a better traditional vehicle for the sustained, magical description of Omar's Sahara journey[109.2.3].

Hay's magisterial control of his material and his sense of the appropriate form is well exemplified by the two poems "Na Tuinn ris na Carraigean"[122] and "Meftah Bâbkum es-Sabar?"[124]. While both can be said to address the same basic theme, the first does so with the concision of the embellished lyric, whereas the "caoineadh" metre of the second allows far more elbow room to explore the fundamental philosophical issue through narrative and rhetoric. Both poems illustrate the success of Hay's two-pronged strategy of turning to bardic poetry and to the folk tradition for further poetic developments.

This success, however, is strictly in relation to his own work, for Gaelic poetry since the war has developed along significantly different paths from those envisaged by Hay. While the class of poet that we may for convenience generalise as the township bards has continued to compose in the metrical forms of the sung tradition, the urban-educated poets since Hay and MacLean have radically transformed – and are still transforming – the character of Gaelic poetry with unpredictable heterogeneity, for the most part shedding traditional technique.

It may be that a retrogressive policy such as Hay's could never provide a sufficiently modernising impulse for future poets; perhaps it presumed a literary education in Gaelic which too few could attain; certainly it vastly underestimated the inspiration which younger poets would find in the varied currents of English-language poetry. Yet if Hay's influence on the development of literary form in Gaelic has been minimal, his own practice has proved how effectively the old traditions could be reinvigorated to address the twentieth century.

Aspects of Language

A happy development in the social and cultural life of Scotland over the last decades has been the greater acceptance and even nurture of the variety of Scotland's indigenous cultures and minority ethnicities. The monolith of official English monolingualism has been severely dented by the advance of Gaelic in public life and the increasingly assertive voice of Scots, as well as the recognition of community languages in the civic arena. Links have been reforged between Gaelic and Scots cultures, as evidenced by such initiatives as the "Scotsoun" poetry recordings, Gaelic–Scots drama productions, and – from the very heart of the educational establishment – the Scottish Consultative Council on the Curriculum's schools anthology *The Kist/A' Chiste*. Yet Hay remains an almost unique figure in his straddling of all three major languages of Scotland.

Each of these languages carries its own burden of associations both literary and sociocultural, its history of dominance, suppression or coexistence, and it would be fascinating to know what led Hay to compose in one language rather than another. Poetic models, conscious or not, must have played a role, as well as considerations of target audience, but one suspects that a more subtle psycholinguistic process might also have operated in the choosing of Gaelic, English or Scots as a poetic medium. Unfortunately, we have little insight from Hay himself on this. Towards the end of his life, in an interview, he agreed that the selection process was "automatic" – what conditions might contribute to his choice of language he simply "couldn't say" (SSS October 1980). His responses to personal questioning in those years were reluctant, but it may be that even in more loquacious times he would have had little to add. We know, however, that in 1979 he envisaged writing

> a prose article on my own position as regards Scotland's assembly of languages [which] shouldn't be meagre, as I have plenty to say on the subject and have never yet published anything about it, and it is a matter I have been thinking about all my life, being one third Lowland and two thirds Highland. (Source 47/1, 29 January 1979)

Regrettably, the article never materialised.

Hay himself ascribed his curiosity for languages to the stimulation of his environment in Tarbert. He remembered words being discussed and compared there:

> Tarbert's like that. When I was wee. They discussed. They had a great personal regard for language – Gaelic and Scots and English. They thought that way. That's how I learned all my languages, I think. (SSS op. cit.)

The language shift away from Gaelic in Tarbert was a relatively recent development, and although Gaelic was clearly in terminal decline as a communal tongue, its legacy was still very much present in the significant number of Gaelic words and idioms that modulated Tarbert English. Douglas Young recalled Calum Johnson's "normal conversation … as sheer poetry, in a mixture of Gaelic, Lallans and Biblical English" (Source F: 334). Johnson, of course, was a native Gaelic speaker, but many Gaelic remnants were to be heard in the speech of "people who have no Gaelic beyond a few phrases like Là maith" (NLS MS 26747: 1). Hay's list of these words amounted to "about 140" in 1938 (Source 44, 10 October 1938); only a quarter of that list has survived (NLS MS 26747: 1–3), but further examples of dialect words, phonetics and idioms were written down by Hay in the early 1960s, following his release from hospital (see Sources 12 and 13). Three letters by him from this same period survive in the public domain, and all three are greatly exercised by the transference of idiom and poetic technique across linguistic boundaries, in particular between Gaelic and Scots.

To Robert Rankin, Hay conveys fragments of Tarbert tradition and adds:

> Some time, when I have a longish holiday, I am going to type out

everything I can remember from Tarbert – stories, proverbs, Gaelic dialect, Gaelic usage in English …, Gaelic words used in English … and Scots, of which there is quite a lot …. As far as I can make out it will run, in the end, to 30 or 40 pages of typescript, and phonetics of some kind will have to enter into it, if only to indicate that "summer" [samhradh] is sevrav, etc. … (Source 46, 9 December 1960)

Writing to another fellow Fettesian, Angus MacIntosh (by then a distinguished scholar in linguistics), Hay speculates about "fields of Gaelic idiom which either disappeared or shifted over into Scots, [or at least] left a certain tendency in Scots idiom formation". In his recent translating of "about two hundred of Henderson's Scots proverbs into Gaelic", he found that

amusing things happen … – "Nae sooner up than his heid in the aumry" becomes "Cha luaithe air a chois na a cheann san amraidh", and the resulting contrast between "cas" and "ceann" could almost make one believe that the proverb was originally phrased in the Gaelic of Lowland Scotland. (Source 54, 31 December 1960)

And soon after, in an excited communication to Douglas Young concerning "that old friend of mine, Homer" and his use of various "old Indo-European tricks" of technique, we find Hay burrowing into the tiny recesses of poetic craft. Much of the letter is taken up with an examination of "word-rhyme" ("[an] ancient technique on which I could write a lengthy thesis were time available"). Hay mentions its occurrence in Persian, Provençal and Norman French poetry, then turns to an example closer to home:

The old distich: "Duke of Atholl, king in Man, / and the wisest man in aa Scotland" – has "man" recurring in the Gaelic internal rhyme position (aicill), and offers word-rhyme in the form of a pun … Thus "man" rhymes with itself, and also forms a bardic deibhidhe rhyme with "Scotland". (A deibhidhe rhyme is "fling", for example, rhyming with "running" …) The aicill there I take to be a Broad Scots hint that Broad Scots still remembered the Old Gaelic poetry and the Old Scotland of Scone, and it's really a hint left for us among others. The prophecy couplet about Prestonpans goes:- "Between Seton and the sea, / many a man will dee that day" – and is very highly ornamented, as if by a Gaelic professional bard (which I am quite certain is another hint left for us). … Average dàn dìreach [classical bardic poetry] can show nothing more intricate than that (at first glance) homely Broad Scots couplet … These two couplets are the Hidden Scotland alright, and to my mind are very important indeed. … [They] are really volumes of history left for us to study and understand, such can be the subtle, hinting nature of the Scottish mind. (Source 36, letter recorded 17 January 1961)

The mnemonic, proverbial role of technique had always intrigued him – those playful, sometimes accidental felicities of rhyme and alliteration by which phrases gain and retain popular currency. He explored this both in his translations – for example the Arabic riddles which he turned into Gaelic (Source 34: 38v–40), mostly featured in *O na Ceithir Àirdean*, or the Gaelic renderings of Scots proverbs mentioned above – and also in the vocal play of many of his own short verses, from the French "Hypocrite"[94] (with its final cynghanedd sequence) to the Gaelic "Sìon a' Chuain"[231].

But for all Hay's interest in the linguistic particularisms of Tarbert, dialect features little in his poetry. Some of the poems set in Tarbert – "The Three Brothers"[14], "Then Farewell Tarbert"[156], "Solan"[161], "The Nerra Boat"[164], "Seeker, Reaper"[158] – are written in local speech, which Hay would describe as "neither Scots, English or Gaelic, but all three" (letter to Mrs F. G. Scott, 6 December 1947). Also initially written in dialect were the Scots poems "Lomsgrios na Tìre"[29] and "Tìr Thàirngire"[13], but these were then shifted into a delocalised, more literary Lallans.

In his Gaelic poems, Hay gives no place to dialect until the later part of his career, from the 1960s on. His avoidance of it in earlier years reflects a concern that a modern literary standard should be developed and main-tained, capable of addressing educated Gaels throughout Scotland. In an article written in Algeria, he had stressed the central role played by the poets in the maintenance of Gaelic language and identity:

> ma sgrùdar ar n-eachdraidh fad an dà linn so chaidh, chìthear gur i a' bhàrdachd a sheas inbhe is maireannachd na Gàidhlige, oir as aonais obair nam bàrd air beul a luchd-labhairt is na comhchruinneachaidhean bàrdachd 'nan làmhan bha i air sgaradh 'sna ceudan frithchainnt is air dol 'na patois suarach gun ìomhadh, gun snas, gun mheas. Is i a' Ghàidhlig prìomh dhaingneach ar cultuir Albannaich agus is iad na bàird le'n cuid rann a thug tilleadh as an luchd séisdidh a bha an rùn daingneach dheireannach ar cinnidh a thoirt a nuas 'na chruach chlach. (Hay 1944: 104)

> *Studying our history in the last two centuries, one can see that it is poetry which defended the status and survival of Gaelic, for if the work of the bards had not been on the lips of its speakers or poetry collections in their hands, the language would have split into hundreds of dialects and become a mere patois without polish, elegance or status. Gaelic is the foremost stronghold of our Scottish culture and it is the poets with their verses who kept at bay the besiegers intent on reducing the final stronghold of our nation to a heap of stones.*

This inherited responsibility for the integrity and status of the language must have influenced Hay both in his general avoidance of the colloquial in poetic register, and in his eschewal of dialect. Particularism would not have accorded well with the bardic voice which he assumes in order to treat great themes. When in later years he did wish to lay more emphasis on his distinctive linguistic locality, he was consistent in clearly signalling any departures from standard Gaelic.

The Gaelic poems actually written in dialectal phonetics are few. Most of the "Tarbert poems" – incorporating fishing terminology or other words surviving only in English speech, or even with no specific dialectal input – function as reconstructions of the oral traditions which once were or might have been, when Tarbert was still home to a flourishing Gaelic community: verses such as existed throughout the Gàidhealtachd, about the geophysical reality of Kintyre, its place-names and boundaries, its weather. Verses such as "Bòd Uile"[175] or "Sreathan Mearachdach"[176] were clearly not conceived as "nature poems", comparable, say, with "An Gleannan"[8], but rather are on a par with the small rhymes, proverbs and epigrams that flourish in strongly oral cultures, serving as mnemonics of experience and wisdom – poetry as a repository of popular tradition. Whatever impulse drove him to such activity in later life – the realisation of the passing of time and the loss of tradition, the decline in his own stamina, the need to root his identity and his craft more specifically in Tarbert – these small productions were evidently considered by him a valid exercise of his poetic skill. However artistically trivial some of them may be, they are of no small significance in any evaluation of the man and his work.

It has been remarked that, whatever language he writes in, "[t]he central fact about Hay's poetry is that it is Gaelic poetry" (Robin Lorimer; see p. 487 above). This is true not only in relation to the themes he chooses, or the general "ethos" of his poetic style – that "precision, definiteness, completeness" which W. J. Watson identified as the "principle which informs and pervades all Gaelic artistry" (1918: xxvii) – but also in the formal discipline of his work. Sometimes it is a matter of deliberate imitation in the application of ornament, such as the aicill rhyming of "Kintyre"[35] ("These on my mouth, I walk / among grey walls and chill ..."), or the runs of internal rhyme in "The Fresh Sapling"[153] echoing the Irish amhrán style of its Gaelic original. This last highly rhythmical form, which he frequently deployed in Gaelic in the later 1970s, he was also to essay in Italian, Norwegian and German ("Stanze Irlandesi"[251-5], "Slutt"[261], "Irische Strophe"[279]).

One critic, reviewing *Wind on Loch Fyne*, complained that "[t]he rhythms and techniques of most of the English poems show little awareness of the best of contemporary English poetry" (*The Scottish Educational Journal*; see p. 487 above). Certainly there is no evidence of Hay ever revealing much interest in or regard for English literature, and his English poetry is particularly susceptible to Gaelic influence. Hints of this preponderant influence include the subtle suggestion of amhrán in "To a Loch Fyne Fisherman"[20], the richness of assonance and consonance in "At the Quayside"[114], the song rhythms of "We Abide For Ever"[145] or "Old Stump and Young Shoots"[143], and the descriptive accumulations of "Seeker, Reaper"[158]. The feeling that Gaelic is never far from the surface is reinforced by Hay's use of Gaelic titles for Scots or English poems such as "Lomsgrios na Tìre"[29] and "Còmhradh nan Rubha"[78]. If one looks, too, at those Gaelic poems which he transposed (usually in the same creative fire) into Scots or English, one finds Gaelic metres very close to the surface in "Old Stump and Young Shoots"[143], "The Fresh Sapling"[153] or "Pleasure and Courage"[141]. The Scots versions, by contrast, of "An Oidhche Bhuan" and "Is Crìon a' Chùil Às Nach Goirear"[(270–271)], although very close to the meaning of the originals, have a much stronger poetic identity, arguably bettering their Gaelic models. The "caoineadh" metre transposes well in the short poem "The Fisherman"[138], but does not avoid monotony in "The Walls of Balclutha"[155] (though the metrical model here may rather be Fergusson's couplets). One finds a greater versatility in Hay's Scots usage, from the "bricht an' hard" images of "The White Licht"[129], to the delicate lyricism of "Flooer o the Gean"[165], the exuberant energy of "Seeker, Reaper"[158], the rhythmic modulations of "Solan"[161], and the impatient colloquialism of the Habbie Simson stanzas of "The Twa Capitals"[328].

Songs

The severing of poetry from the song tradition in Gaelic does not go back much further than the First World War, and all major Gaelic poets since Hay have to some extent been concerned with freeing their poetry from what was felt to be the tyranny of Gaelic music, usually drawing on English-language influences to do so. Hay, as we have seen, deplored the overinsistence of latter tradition on romance and nostalgia and its over-reliance on hackneyed metrical forms, but he remained much closer to the song tradition than any of his peers or successors. This, as also his bypassing of English influences, may partly be explained by the greater linguistic choice open to him and his awareness of other European traditions, which allowed him other channels for experimentation: in addition, for example, to the crossovers from Gaelic already mentioned, he brought the Homeric hexameter to bear in the grand lines of "Fàire M'Òige"[86], and Italian metrics were adapted to Gaelic, Scots and English ("Bisearta"[116], "An Cnocan Fraoich is Padre Dante"[197]; "Flooer o the Gean"[165]; "Esta Selva Selvaggia"[135]).

The proximity of Hay's work to Gaelic song is manifest both in his use of explicit song-forms (in pieces like "Luinneag"[15], "Òran"[28], "Alba Ghaoil Ò"[75], "An Cnocan Fraoich"[104], "Òran Nàiseantach"[192] / "Nationalist Sang"[206], "Latha san Rainich"[207], "Garvalt Side"[228]) and in the sheer musicality of so many of his lyrics, that rhythm "that stirs me right over into music", as F. G. Scott exulted (Lindsay 1980: 203). Some of these lyrics were in fact written to a melody or subsequently set to music by Hay. He was, of course, an adequate (self-taught) piper, and by his mid-twenties had acquired a vast repertoire of songs – "about 200 … mostly Gaelic" (Source 5: 26r). By then he was already composing, in a manner he explained to Douglas Young when sending him some specimen tunes:

I haven't made words of my own for most of them yet. When I come across a Gaelic poem I like, I naturally hunt for the tune. If I can't find it I start singing the poem or delivering (gabhail) it in a singing voice. Finally a tune emerges ... Of course some are awful and have to be dropped; some come into one's head all at once and they are usually passable. Strange methods! (Source 36, February 1939)

Hay's early musical notebooks (Sources 17 and 18) contain mainly traditional tunes, but in late 1947 he made at least two copies of his collected melodies (Sources 19 and 58), one of which he gave to F. G. Scott. Of the twenty-five tunes included, seven were for his own original poems, and are given in Appendix 3.

"Brang air na Sasannaich"[74] and, later, "Latha san Rainich"[207] were also composed to original melodies, now lost. In the early 1980s, Hay drew up a list of forty-four melodies "all unrecorded and not written down" (Source 11: 90–1). These include settings for the following poems, in addition to the 1947 set: "Òran Nàiseantach"[192], "Air Suidh' Artair Dhomh Mochthrath"[204], "Aig an Fheurlochan"[242], "Garvalt Side"[228], "Ritornello"[296], "Òran Tàlaidh"[332], "Chailein Òig an Stiùir Thu Mi?"[321], "Eich Mhic Neill"[320], "Cruinneag na Buaile"[355], "Ròsan an Leth-Bhaile"[346], "Is Trom Mi 'Siubhal Slèibhe"[348], "Soraidh an Sgoileir"[387]. In 1983, "The Smoky Smirr o Rain"[151] was added to the list (Source 23, 2 March 1983).

Translations from Other Literatures

For reasons of time and space, the present edition of Hay's work has limited itself to presenting his original verse. It would clearly distort our view of him as a poet, however, not to mention his considerable work of translation from a variety of literatures into Gaelic, Scots and English.

That this aspect of his work was important to Hay is clear from its prominent inclusion in his published collections. Almost half of *Wind on Loch Fyne* consists of translations from Irish, Gaelic, Italian, Greek and Croatian verse (this last from Italian versions), with Welsh and Norwegian also represented. The translated component of *O na Ceithir Àirdean* is even greater, with Gaelic versions of mainly Italian, Croatian (again from the Italian), Arabic and Greek verse, plus the odd piece from Icelandic, English, Spanish, Welsh and Finnish (from English). The offering in *Fuaran Slèibh* is much slimmer, but includes Gaelic versions of Greek, French, Italian and Arabic verse (the latter translated from English), plus English versions of two Gaelic songs.

Hay's translating activity had early beginnings: in 1932, still at Fettes College, he was turning Irish verse (love songs from Connaught) into English. During his time in Oxford, he turned his attention to popular Greek poetry, in particular the ballads of the Klephts. In these songs of guerillas who had fought the Turkish invaders, he no doubt heard echoes of the fugitive MacGregors or of cattle-raiding Dòmhnall Donn of Bohuntin. "The Gaelic language is waiting with open arms for poetry like that!" he would enthuse to Kenneth MacLeod (Source 44, 13 December 1938). Gaelic versions, then Scots ones, resulted. Over the next few years, the collection grew, and various plans for publication were entertained with Douglas Young, himself a keen translator who devoted much of his energy to bringing Gaelic poetry (including the work of MacLean and Hay) to Lowland attention.

Such translating activity accorded well with the ideals of Hugh MacDiarmid's Scottish Renaissance programme, intent throughout the 1920s and 1930s both on increasing mutual awareness between Scotland's own linguistic groupings (in the main acquainting non-Gaels with Gaelic literature) and equally on reforging links with the rest of Europe. MacDiarmid had blazed the trail with his translations from Russian and German, and more recently his renditions of two eighteenth-century Gaelic "classics", "The Praise of Ben Doran" by Duncan Bàn MacIntyre and Alexander MacDonald's "Birlinn of Clanranald" (see MacDiarmid 1940: 43–58, 65–85).

Hay's own pedagogical intentions are clear from a letter of c. 30 September 1940:

> The latest idea is for making part at least of European literature accessible in Gaelic, if only by excerpts. I'm going to translate things from the Scandinavian languages, Modern Greek, Welsh and perhaps Spanish. I'm sure Somhairle [MacLean] could produce an anthology of French verse and prose some day, and of course John his brother is a classical scholar. There is also Calum [MacLean] and Hector MacIver … but it can't be done till the war is over. There will be the publishing difficulty … [but] in any case we will have done something practical for Gaelic and broken the ring of clergy, Comunn Gàidhealach Britons and academicians who would like to preserve the Gael in a kind of intellectual Red Indian Reserve, where their folklore will not be contaminated by reading the tales of any other nation and they will be aesthetically and morally catered for by the soiree and the Kirk. The poor Gael is a claim for scores of vested interests … who would all like to make and keep him a parochial private cretin for themselves. They won't manage. (Source 36)

In a letter to MacDiarmid of 1939, Hay declared himself

> all for the "minor literatures" and the "backward races" whose literatures have not been etherealised out of life. Our contacts might as well be with the Icelandings or with those grand rascals the Serbs as with Bloomsbury or the Seine. (Source P33 II.1: 1)

In the event, it was not with the "grand rascals" but with their neighbours, the Croats, that Hay made literary contact during the war, through an Italian anthology (Salvini 1942); sixteen poems ensued, in English and in Gaelic. Apart from the Arabic riddles and proverbs, however, most of Hay's translations during this period were from Italian literature, many of these produced not in a lull of original inspiration but in the thick of creative ferment, in the period of "Mochtàr is Dùghall", "Atman" and related works. Some pieces parallel the Irish/Gaelic dánta grádha (courtly love poems) which Hay had adapted for modern consumption years before. A quite different affinity was found in the rakish sonnets of Cecco Angiolieri, that

> turbulent child of 13th-century Sienna, … a man of human heart, … a
> sincere and warm nature, … a poet whom the countrymen of Burns,
> above all others, should understand. (BBC script, Source 8: 11)

Hay's Scots versions of Angiolieri probably count among his most successful translations (see France and Glen 1989: 53–4).

Hay's translating activity continued, at a lesser rate, into the 1970s, occasionally from Norwegian, but most often travelling the short distance from Irish to Gaelic. By this time there was no lack of enthusiastic translators to ensure that the barriers round the reserve, so severely breached in the 1930s and 1940s, would not be re-erected (see MacThòmais 1990).

"OUT OF THE MIDST OF LIFE"

Recurrent Themes in Hay's Poetry

For poetry is not made by jugglers with words, but by men who have hearts, brains and bodies, who speak to men and for them. They speak out of the midst of life, like ... the poets of the French resistance, not from outside it. ... The poets in widely different countries are declaring that they are men among men, and people among the people.

(Hay 1946–7, I: 52, 58)

1 Voyage

Tha bàta fodhainn gu 'cur a shiubhal,
... 's chan eil, a ghràidh, air thalamh uile
làn shàsachadh no fìor cheann uidhe
do mhiann an fhalbhain anns an duine.

There is a boat under our feet to set sailing, ... and there is not, dear, on all the earth, full satisfying or a true journey's end for the love of wandering in man.
("Mochtàr is Dùghall", ll. 1,202–6)

Maritime Verse

As a sea-faring nation, the Gaels have acquired a copious maritime vocabulary and developed a long, varied tradition of maritime verse. In the alliterative runs of the old tales, in the praise of medieval Hebridean princes, the cameo evocations in waulking-songs, in ambitious set pieces like the eighteenth-century "Birlinn Chlann Raghnaill" and in a host of popular sailors' songs, a rich seam of imagery has been formed and exploited to paint with vivid strokes the "hundreds of shifting shapes" of the western seaboard and the vessels that have criss-crossed its Channel.

Given Hay's passion for ring-net fishing and yachting and the abundance of poetic models, it is not surprising to find him turning to this theme in his earliest extant excursions in Gaelic verse. The setting of "Aisling"[5], for example, has antecedents stretching far back in Gaelic song tradition, and were it not for the "merry drone" of the engine, the "darach cridhe" could be one of the Hebridean galleys that navigate so many old songs – and which Hay so skilfully evoked years later in his recreated waulking-song, "Am Bàta Dubh"[359]. The terms in which Hay describes the boat in "Aisling" character- ise his poems on this theme: she is a fighter, defiant against the living force of the sea, hurling her engine-song like a battle-cry, exultant in the struggle.

The depiction was brought to perfection in the short lyric "Siubhal a' Choire"[7]. This lyric, using a stanza-form first essayed in the English poem "For the Corrie"[4], was honed down through several drafts to a terse eighteen lines which convey the exhilaration of the struggle with extraordinary conci- sion and aural suggestiveness. There is no direct model for the verse-form of the poem, but it uses the tight self-contained lines of the waulking-song tradition, and its vivid onomatopoeic language is also drawn from a vast traditional store, distilled to splendid effect. (The 1983 drafts "I 'Ruith Leis"[364], while evidencing that Hay never lost his facility and felicity of language in maritime verse, serve to highlight the compactness of "Siubhal a' Choire".)

If language is tightly harnessed in "Siubhal a' Choire", words are let loose in the long Scots poem "Seeker, Reaper"[158], written on Hay's return to Tarbert after the war, when he was once again "rolling in and out of boats" (Catherine Hay, Source 44, 3 June 1947). Prefigured by the adoles- cent "The Hind of Morning"[1], the poem is a gloriously exuberant paean to a cocky, irrepressible fishing boat. In a whirlwind of soundmusic, incantated place-names proclaim the champion vessel's wide dominion, and Norse and Gaelic chants evoke her reiving forebears on the turbulent western sea- board. The composition of the poem appears to have been astonishingly rapid, and much of its strength derives precisely from its apparent sponta- neity, the suggestive, restless cadences of its metres and the instant evoca- tiveness of its accumulated images.

Its very exuberance, however, gives "Seeker, Reaper" an allegorical edge: when Hay told his publisher that the poem expressed the vaunting of the younger fishermen, and the "wild dynamism of the Highlands, [which] is still there, but to our impoverishment seldom expressed" (NLS Acc. 5000/ 465, 2 December 1947), he was invoking a moral quality which Gaeldom and Scotland had to regain were they to be complete and alive – it is the lost fire mourned in "Sgairt Mo Dhaoine"[77], the prodigality and passion praised in "Prìosan Da Fhèin an Duine?"[115], the ebullient individuality extolled in a letter to Young:

> our compatriots need reminding that they don't belong to a plodding, painstaking, borné species. … We need to restore the tradition of the out-of-the-ordinary and plain daftness. (Source 36, 20 April 1943)

There is clear allegorical intent in the short poem "Alba"[62], but the poem's power is mostly fuelled by its unattenuated literal vividness (an expository fourth verse was dropped from the final version). This is no joyous, luminous picture of a fishing boat heading home as in "The Kerry Shore"[71], but a dark depiction of human struggle against fierce odds, of heroic persistence in the face of raging elements, death beckoning at every lurch and land only a dim, ghostly promise. If the poem on one level is an appeal for political commitment, the fishing crew's predicament is drawn in hard, clear outlines, precariousness and danger held in one menacing laconic line: "nothing is here but the sea when her seams fail".

The Fishermen

In poems like "Alba"[62] or "At the Quayside"[114], Hay depicts the actuality of ring-net fishing with the authenticity of personal experience, and the exhilaration of his sailing poems gives way to a darker tone, underlining the risk and danger inherent in the fishing trade. The burden of anxiety borne by the fishermen's families, too, is evoked in the early poem "The Three Brothers"[14], and given a place on the canvas of Dùghall's life in the lyric "Bean an Iasgair"[109.33]. There is an underlying sense of heroism in Hay's perception of the fishing community, and a strong idealisation in his portrayal of the Tarbert fishermen.

Thus in an early poem, "To a Loch Fyne Fisherman"[20], the eponymous fisherman is one "who keeps to the old ways" (in an early title of the poem), who is constant in a world of transience and superficiality, no broken branch adrift, but – in a very old Gaelic image of praise – solid as an "ancient yew". In men such as Calum Johnson, Hay admired an older way of life, one of shared values marked by individual dignity and communal rootedness, at odds with the trends of modern urban society. Its traditions are signposts of identity, nurtured and handed on from generation to generation, and inherently valuable by virtue of their distinctiveness from mainstream mass culture:

> If a man still insists on having the tiller of his boat of rowan wood, or on making three sunwise circles with her before he leaves the harbour, he adds something to the diversity of life and harms no one, not even himself. He is unusual in that he has some opinions of his own that didn't come out of a newspaper, and is to be admired for that. (Hay 1946–7, I: 49)

Much later, he would comment on that particular practice:

> When they lifted anchor in the old days, in a crowded harbour, they would do a sunwise turn before they set sail. So I was told. God knows, they must have collided with one another, some of them! Oh they were wild people, God knows they were! (SSS 1979)

By contrast, what Hay deplored in the English privates with whom he trained was that they were "derivative men with little or nothing of their own":

> Their decency can't carry them far, for they have no values, principles or convinced attitudes, and they have no traditions. As a Tarbert man once told me in horror about his English pals in the last war, a lot of them neither know nor care who their grandfathers were. (Source 36, 19 August 1942)

He was to find a culture much more congenial in Arab North Africa, which by both its affinities and its alienness stimulated him to the imaginative heights of "Mochtàr is Dùghall"[109], and drove him to explore ideals of human living in a remarkable series of poems.

Men and Mannikins

In "Atman"[110], the first of these, an Algerian peasant is whipped and imprisoned for stealing in time of need. Hay contrasts judge and criminal, and finds kinship with the latter. "Is aithne dhomh thu, Atmain", he twice iterates – "I know you" – the first time indicating personal acquaintance, but then in admiring recognition of the type: "I know you – you are a man and alive". Atman is a "man" because he has known joy and anger, love and hatred, the sweet and the bitter; materially poor, he is rich in stories and repartee and in love for his locality; above all, he has "felt life and never shrunk before it". This is the quality of "manhood" Hay had admired in the Tarbert fishermen rediscovered, and the poem marks a moment of revelation, as the poet's experience of brotherhood transcends the cultural boundaries of his youth.

In contrast to Atman, the heartless judge can never be fully a "man", or fully "alive"; he is merely honourable and "decent", defending the letter of the law from a position of privilege and power. This model of stunted humanity was attacked more forcefully in "An t-Eòlas Nach Cruthaich"[111], where Hay denounces sterile knowledge, that fruitless acquisition of experience which measures and judges but does not give. Evil is not condemned here, nor maliciousness or cruelty, but parsimony of spirit, lack of conviction, hollowness of heart. In "Prìosan Da Fhèin an Duine?"[115], Hay makes explicit the philosophy which underlies the previous two poems. Drawing inspiration from the gannet in headlong rush and the small bird in full musical flow, Hay's urging is to heed the example of all living things: with unmisted mind and a generous heart, to live one's potential to the full, to "be complete and be alive", "be alive and be yourself". Hay's negative type, again, is pitiable rather than wicked, a spirit stunted by excessive reasonableness, its spontaneity stifled by other people's opinions, its individuality drained to an undifferentiated grey.

There are clear points of intersection between the qualities praised by Hay and those he admired in Gaelic culture; one critic has remarked that "praise of the spendthrift, of the passionate, is of course in tune with the ideals of Gaelic poetry", and that Hay's "courageous, generous, spirited man [is] a typical Highland paragon" (Smith 1984). Indeed, years before, Hay had said of Gaelic poetry:

It seems to blaze up, or burst out with a natural abandon, and whether it be praise or cursing, sorrow or joy, it is always satisfying. ... It is the expression of a people who were impatient of external restraint in deed or word, of men who never forgot a favour or an ill-turn, and of a society where personal affection and the individual played the most important part. ... Therefore upon these mewed and cautious times, when everything can be calculated and is held to have its price, and when people seem to exist for the benefit of statisticians, it blows like the wind from the Atlantic, clearing clouded skies and restoring its dignity to humanity. (Hay 1940–1, I: 6, 7)

It is not difficult to see where this line of thought leads to in the political sphere: as one critic has commented, "Prìosan Da Fhèin an Duine?" is a poem in praise of difference, "which can as easily be the difference between cultures and languages as that between individual personalities" (Whyte 1990: 125). Such difference is celebrated to wonderful effect in "Mochtàr is Dùghall"[109], but "Meftah Bâbkum es-Sabar?"[124] provides the clearest expression of Hay's philosophical thinking in his nationalist verse.

Around the time Hay composed these last poems, he returned to the theme of the Tarbert fishermen in "At the Quayside"[114]. In that poem, he set up an antithesis of human types (heroic fishermen and ignorant dealers) very reminiscent of poems like "Dleasnas nan Àirdean"[106], "Atman" and "Prìosan Da Fhèin an Duine?". The quayside buyers with their cheap jests resemble the judge in "Atman" as they pass sentence on men whose experience of life is beyond their ken.

The consistency in the development of Hay's thinking from his native Tarbert to the wider community of his wartime experience is felt again in another fishing poem, the post-war portrait "An t-Iasgair"[137], perhaps an elegy for Calum Johnson. There the fisherman is praised not simply for his tracking skills (won and inherited through generations of hard experience) but for his manliness and gentleness, and a wisdom born of endurance. Storm and calm have both left their mark upon his cheek, just as Atman has tasted both the bitter of life and the sweet. Both men are (male) archetypes of authentic living.

The Integrated Being

Still in the flush of composing "Prìosan Da Fhèin an Duine?"[115] (Source 23: 8), Hay had begun writing a long polemical article "Poetry in the world or out of it?", which aimed its fire at the French poet André Gide and his recent

advocacy of "the poetic word as mere sound and tone" (Hay 1946–7: I, 52).
Years before, Hay had written admiringly of Sorley MacLean that

[he] has his feet on the real earth. He sees it as the Via Dolorosa of the
common people of Europe, and for them he speaks out of a full heart.
(Source 36, February 1940)

In his blast against Gide, Hay attacks elitist, hermetic conceptions of art,
and, drawing on the ideas of the philosopher-politician Benedetto Croce, he
elaborates a key duality of "fragmentary" versus "integrated" being:

Such poetry is the fragmentary speech of fragmentary beings. The
inhabitants of the towers are not whole men. The dust and mud of the
common earth have never soiled their feet and given them the strength
that was Antaeus's, and is every integrated being's. Have they ever
sweated, wept, blessed, cursed, hungered, thirsted, loved, hated, feared,
exalted or thought as men? Do they speak as if they have ever lived
wholly at all? (Hay 1946–7, I: 52)

Poets are to be judged essentially by the fullness of their humanity, by the
extent to which they have experienced life as Atman has, as Calum Johnson
has, and by the extent to which this informs their art. They are expected to
portray "life, sore, rough and triumphant", and paint a "true reflection" of
the mind of their people (see "Meftah Bâbkum es-Sabar?"[124]). For the
individual to lead an integrated life, and for the poet's work to be integrated
into the communal life, however, demands that there should be shared
values and hopes at all levels of society:

Life is one and poetry is part of it. You cannot separate literary and
social problems completely, for it is only in certain types of society that
widespread culture is possible, and a people without certain values in
common from the highest to the lowest, or rather from the richest to
the poorest, cannot be really civilised. (Hay 1946–7, II: 57)

At the start of his military career, Hay had been dismayed by what he saw
as the cultural hollowness of the English privates he met, which he attrib-
uted to the fact that "for centuries they have had no folk culture or traditions
shared by all the people":

They've been thoroughly urbanised, even the country folk with a few
exceptions. I was trying to see what are the values that have been taken
from them to leave them such toom masses of bone and muscle. Well,
for their thoughts and opinions they are dependent on certain physical
equipment – books, newspapers, magazines, wireless sets and cinema
tickets. They have become derivative men with little or nothing of
their own, except that decency which ... is as much a common human
attribute as a pair of legs. ... The English race has been atomised.
Each individual is on its own, having no spiritual links with others, the
only connections being the chance that throws them together ..., the

convenience of the moment; or conventional arrangements like marriage and the household ... Derivative, rootless, traditionless, scattered into units wriggling like flies in the cash nexus (who are the spiders?), once they enter a state of je-m'en-foutisme [don't-give-a-damnism] and cynicism they are a terrifying phenomenon. (Source 36, 19 August 1942)

"Beinn is Machair"[118] elaborates the association in Hay's thought of integrated existence with rural communities, and of the fragmentary life with urbanisation. The entirety of "Mochtàr is Dùghall"[109], however, is a broad canvas of integrated living, celebrating the spiritual thread that links each generation to the next through speech and history, the mystery of kinship passed on by heredity and maintained by living tradition. Both Mokhtâr's society and Dougall's are of the type where "widespread culture is possible". In "Dùghall", Hay explicitly muses on the meaning of cultural identity for Scottish Gaels[109.3.2], but the Arab section of the poem – where Mokhtâr learns of his ancestry through storytelling – is a more successful, if unexplicit, meditation on the theme. In Arab Africa, Hay thrilled to the recognition of shared inheritance and strong communal bonds, the possibility of integrated living and of art in the midst of life, which he knew from the old Gaelic world passing away in Tarbert.

Horizons

Another theme at the heart of "Mochtàr is Dùghall" is the pursuit of new horizons, physical and metaphysical. In each generation of Mokhtâr's family, the protagonist sets out on a quest: Ahmed to fight the colonial oppressor, Omar to satisfy his thirst for adventure, Obayd in search of spiritual truth through renunciation of the world. Mokhtâr, of course, embarks on a journey not of his own choice, "to the mouth of the mortar" (ll. 1,035–6). Each individual is driven by an inner spur to chase after "the deer of the spirit", attaining only ever the briefest glimpse of it (ll. 729–46). The variety of manifestations which this same urge can take is celebrated as an expression of humanity's infinite variety and infinite potential: "What is man? What can he not be?" asked Pindar, and towards the end of the poem Hay answers: "a world apart is each son of man, a living world in himself" (ll. 1,221–2).

This questing theme recurs persistently, in an imagery congenial to Hay, as the urge to set sail for new horizons. It is treated with a harsh pessimism in the early Scots poem "Tìr Thàirngire"[13], which may be a deliberately ghoulish subversion of the fey preoccupations of the Celtic Twilight. The allegorical "Clann Àdhaimh"[119], though certainly an agnostic vision, is not necessarily pessimistic: though the bark of humanity is battered and worn, her wake in the vastness of ocean insignificant and the horizons she follows ever elusive, the boisterous, colourful, fully living motley crew aboard her give the quest a celebratory tone. More emotionally revealing is the searching note struck by "Fàire"[150], composed on Hay's return from war. In the earlier "Fàire M'Òige"[86] he had evoked with happy contentment the skyline of Argyll peaks which circled his youth, but in "Fàire" he honestly acknowledges the spur of discontent, and explores the conflict between his need for rootedness and the undeniable lure and excitement of new coasts, a conflict dramatised in the "A' Bhean a' Bruidhinn"[109·3·5] lyric of "Mochtàr is Dùghall".

The patriot in Hay regrets and fights the lure of foreign shores, which through the centuries has drained his country of so much young blood – in "Ar Blàr Catha"[126] and "Na Trèig do Thalamh Dùthchais"[157] he argues that loyalty to the wellbeing of Scotland must become the new lodestone. Sailing for new horizons must become a communal, national quest, rather than a merely individual one; indeed, he assures us, the wonders of a new Scotland will eclipse all the magical tales of the wandering sailor ("Alba Cona h-Ingantaib"[225]). In a Norwegian poem from the 1970s, he writes that "enhver seiler", everyone sets sail: "only to sail stills the yearning ... harbour must be left here in life ... and land and lee are not promised" ("Enhver Seiler"[262]). These lines may refer to the small bark of individual lives, but they were composed at a time when the Scottish ship of State seemed set to sail the uncharted seas of self-government. Throughout his adult life Hay was preoccupied with the national question; through his life's journey, from Tarbert to Edinburgh, Bizerta to Kavalla, Lochgilphead to Morningside, Scotland remained his lodestone. How this primary commitment in his life manifested itself in his poetry is examined in the next section.

2 Scotland

I speak for a blue and very ancient land,
which pulses in my blood, glances blue from my eyes;
its hills embrace my heart, close-set tendrils that bind,
more close and stronger far than love's unlasting embrace ...

(G. C. Hay, from the French of G.-E. Clancier)

The national question exercised Hay's poetic energies more than any other single theme. The intrusion of political themes in the poet's work should not surprise. As he made clear in his war-time essay "Poetry in the world or out of it?" (Hay 1946–7), any artistic distancing from the lot of common humanity was anathema; furthermore, most of the poets in any way linked to MacDiarmid's movement were socially committed. Yet few committed their poetic expression to the cause of political nationalism as explicitly as Hay.

He clearly saw his writing as a form of activism, primarily in the service of Gaelic, as "An Ceangal"[108], his poetic "mission statement", testifies; and if he composed the overwhelming bulk of his political verse in Gaelic it may be because in that culture the tradition of bardic poetry as a social function to the community (whether township, clan or nation, whether actual or notional) still held considerable credibility and offered plentiful example. In the burst of poetic activity which followed his discharge from the Royal Edinburgh Hospital in 1960, Hay sent an accompanying note to the *Scots Independent* in which he explained that since time immemorial there had never been a Gaelic poet who was not also a nationalist – "nach robh bàrd Gàidhealach riamh nach robh 'na Nàiseantach, bho linn na Féinne fhéin" (Source P26, 375: 4). That claim is too simplistic to be accepted without demur, but it clearly indicates one of the sources from which Hay drew legitimation for his propagandising voice. It also suggests that he wished to reclaim the agenda of nationalist politics for the Gaelic community, rather in the way that Sorley MacLean had reinterpreted the Gaelic experience in Marxian terms. Both poets found their voice at a time of great ideological ferment; as radicals and anti-imperialists writing in Gaelic, both were faced with the problem of articulating a new political focus for a marginal culture which had to a large extent found itself a niche in the British imperialist worldview. For Hay, Scottish nationalism was the faith that could rescue Gael and Lowlander alike from their imperialist devils. This meant asserting again and again to his Lowland audience the central place of Gaelic in the national life; for his Gaelic audience, he had to reclaim the highly militarised rhetoric of Gaelic solidarity and redeploy it in a Scottish civic context rather than a British regimental one. This reinterpretation is particularly evident in the long poem "Ar Blàr Catha"[126].

Propaganda

Some of the nationalist poems, like "Ceithir Gaothan na h-Albann"[65], centre on the emotional bond tying poet to country, with Scotland presented as something of a Greater Kintyre, mother of Gael and Gall; others, such as "Meftah Bâbkum es-Sabar?"[124], approach nationalism from a more philosophical angle. But the bulk are openly propagandist; the political commentary can be crudely satirical as in "The Scottish Scene" sequence[38–54], or pithy and more subtly barbed as in the quatrains from the 1970s.

Much of this poetry is unashamedly partisan: most of the poems were sent for publication to the *Scots Independent*, while in the late 1960s the nationalist magazine *Catalyst* promoted Hay as something of an official bard. It is often verse written to arouse feeling and promote action, rather than to stimulate thought or explore the issues of being human. The problems raised by such necessarily one-dimensional poetry, in artistic terms, were not lost on Hay. In 1940 he wrote:

I have done the most awful things for my country's sake, even to turning out a goodly amount of doggerel. Still I think Fletcher [of

Saltoun] would have said "Let me write the nation's doggerel" today, instead of "ballads", and he would have been right. But the process of production is pretty painful. (Source 36, 28 April 1940)

And when it came to planning the contents of his own books, his criteria were stringent enough:

Myself I have thought all along that certain things marked out for the book had their heart in the right place, but were far from being poetry. ["Is Duilich an t-Slighe"[64]] is poetry in my estimation ... and "Alba Ghaoil Ò"[75] may just be poetry, but definitely "Brosnachadh"[103] isn't. (Source 36, 20 December 1944)

Similarly, "['Brang air na Sasannaich'[74]] is very nearly doggerel" (ibid., 5 June 1944). Consequently, a good number of political poems were excluded from the collections.

The line of sensibility demarcating "is poetry" from "may just be" and "definitely isn't", however, must be as elusive as that distinguishing one person's erotica from another's pornography. It was of Hay's major national-ist poems, after all, not his discarded doggerel, that one otherwise sympa-thetic critic has bluntly said: "This theme of nationalism recurs constantly in his poetry, but it is not one that has created great verse: it is too exhortatory, too external, too much like poster-poetry" (Smith 1986: 109). It is interest-ing that the one poem Hay approves of as poetry in the letter quoted above is "Is Duilich an t-Slighe": that poem began its life as a rallying-cry to fellow anti-conscriptionists, but was given greater emotional depth by verses added after Hay's capitulation to the authorities in 1941 – the admission of per-sonal vulnerability and inner conflict mark it off from Hay's prescriptive poetry.

In Praise of Difference

The excisions made to *Fuaran Slèibh* have rather obscured the develop-ment of Hay's political verse in the 1940s. Having tended towards the flippantly satirical in English and the denunciatory in Gaelic, his nationalist poetry during the war years takes on a more reflective, existentialist tone – it identifies a moral choice needing to be made at both the personal and the political level between atrophy through inaction, or survival by active strug-gle. The nationalism increasingly postulated is one of positive assertion of difference and of communal creation, at some remove from the reactive nationalism of "hurt racial pride" which Hay acknowledged as the initial source of his own politics (Source 36, February 1940). It is the political concomitant of the philosophical message of "Prìosan Da Fhèin an Duine?"[114]: "Be complete and be alive, be alive and be yourself". In that view, political discourse should primarily be concerned with the search for communal identity, rather than attachment to any specific ideological model. To adopt Hay's own imagery, he is far more concerned with seeing the ship set sail, colours hoisted, than with the arrangements on board or indeed with the precise destination, since horizons are elusive and winds blow off course.

Two poems of a formally similar nature, "Bail' Ìomhair"[105] and "Achmhasain"[132], can serve to illustrate this shift in discourse. The first, from early 1944, denounces the plundering, murderous Imperial Capital; the second, two years later, rebukes the Scots for neglecting their responsibility, for failing to take up the heroic challenge expressed in "Dleasnas nan Àirdean"[106] and "The White Licht"[129]. Undoubtedly, at great geographical remove from both Scotland and England, Hay had found new perspectives on the national question: "Mochtàr is Dùghall"[109] successfully explores issues of cultural identity and difference, but obliquely, through the prism of its Arab portrayals, and it is noticeable that when he came to address the Scottish aspect directly, through the story of Dùghall, inspiration faltered.

The growth in thinking, and the link with other less overtly political poems, is evident in "Meftah Bâbkum es-Sabar?"[124], arguably the best of Hay's nationalist poems. This is not a political poem in any simple didactic sense: it is concerned with individual and communal attitudes to life, and with the role of the poet in society. The national community it depicts is one which lives its life to the full, "sore, rough and exultant", passionate and defiant, self-asserting and creative, and shaping its own destiny; within this community, the poet is called to portray life truthfully in all its diversity. Consonant with his consistent rejection of pessimism, Hay refuses the quietist stance advised by an Arab, for "Providence has offered us during our days the choice between life and death".

The café scene which opens the poem gives a strong human focus to what is a poem of ideas. The discussion may or may not have taken place, but primarily is a very effective poetic construct: the melancholy words spoken by the poet's Arab companion are gleaned from traditional Arabic texts. In the rhetorical section of the poem, behind the artist's plea not to be asked for "some musical wizardry of polished words", for mist and fairy mounds and lullabies, but for "the true reflection of our mind", there is an attack on the feyness of the Celtic Twilight and the preponderance of romance in modern Gaelic verse, and also more generally on those ivory-tower poets who fail to link their art to the lot of humanity:

> Such poetry is the fragmentary speech of fragmentary beings. ... The social problems of today are the problems of any poet who is not alone in an ivory tower far off the highways of humanity ... (Hay 1946–7, I: 52; II: 57)

In "Meftah Bâbkum es-Sabar?", Hay makes use of an Arab theme for an essentially Scotocentric discourse. The debate of ideas is not fundamentally one pitting Arab against Scot, or Islamic against Western thought: the fatalism it rejects is one which many Gaels would recognise as part of their own religious tradition (a parallel drawn explicitly in Hay 1947b), and which Hay identified as peculiarly Scottish in "The Walls of Balclutha"[155], a long, eloquent piece centring round the image of cleared townships. Hay has explained that, historically, the abandoned townships of the West Shore were not casualties of the Clearances:

> Down here about the mouth of Loch Fyne there were a few evictions, but mostly the people left of their own accord, drawn by the flourishing herring fishing of the growing Tarbert, the young ones often yielding to the pull of the world's horizons and the lure of the square-riggers. … Grey, pathetic assemblies of tumbled walls and gable ends, they are not entirely forsaken, for they are still remembered with affection by the descendants of their inhabitants. (Hay 1947a: 259)

Nevertheless these ruins play a prominent symbolic role in his poetry. They evoke the despoiling and misappropriation of the Highlands (among Hay's earliest and latest poems are protests at landownership in Scotland), and are reminders of the scars inflicted on the Scottish psyche. In "The Walls of Balclutha", their legacy of fear and foreboding is in us from birth, draining us of self-belief, making us cling to myths of defeat, the "black lie of our predestined dearth". The way out of this debilitating fatalism is to exercise thought and will, to be "men" (in the moral sense used in "Atman"[110]) – not through heroic battle, but by releasing the "seed of graciousness", "the surge of the creative spirit" through which the legacy of the past can be transformed into a worthwhile future. This echoes the vision of "Meftah Bâbkum es-Sabar?", where communal endeavour is seen in terms of creative acts linking past and present: the writing of new poetry in the old bardic songbooks, the hall echoing to the old music and the new. Both poems express Hay's passionate rejection of indifference and defeatism, his belief in struggle and action, found also in his prose writings of the period:

> Are we doomed or dying out, the broken ghosts of a vanished race? … How much longer have we to listen to … facile, half-informed defeatism about our language and our culture and ourselves? We are not dying or doomed, melancholy or inert or backward gazers. It is the present and the future that we are mostly thinking about … We are not dying, and never will die while there is a Europe and a Scotland as part of it. (Hay 1947c: 104)

The appeal to "thought and will" lies at the heart of "Feachd a' Phrionnsa"[133], where we are urged to follow the moral example of the Prince's army. Years before, Hay had celebrated the values promoted in Gaelic poetry as "steadfastness in the face of odds, loyalty to a manifestly losing cause, and independence. … That sort of thing is called Quixotism today ..." (Hay 1940–1, I.6: 7). Culloden may have been "the disaster that brought about our temporary decline" (Source 46, letter 37, 6 March 1945), but the integrity and commitment of those who accepted the challenge – irrespective of the success of their cause – is applauded and held up as an inspiration. In the modern-day struggle to be a complete and living national community, however, the only sword needing to be unsheathed is that of the spirit, the "old flaming-white sword of our country". The poem ends on the evangelical tone of much of Hay's nationalist verse and with one of its recurrent images, of slumber and awakening.

Military imagery is subverted further in the long poem "Ar Blàr Catha"[126], which moves on a similar pattern of elaborated historical example then exhortation (mirroring the call to reflection and action, thought and will). It is time to call a halt to military adventurism and colonial expansion, and redirect all that enterprise and energy to the new – civic – field of battle, the Scotland which is still to be created and in which there will be room for every quality. "Thought and courage" are needed to stop the flow out of the community, and a refusal to be lured any further by shifting horizons.

Later Poems

In all these major poems, Hay finds ways of discussing the national question that do not mention England, and where the emphasis is not on oppression but on building the future through active transformation of the past. Few if any of Hay's numerous later political poems assert themselves as authoritatively as these works of the mid-1940s. The theme is approached from an impressive range of angles, however, and there are some notable successes such as "Cnocan a' Chait Fhiadhaich"[195], "Na Faoileagan Maidne"[238] and the succession of quatrains tracking the political advances of the 1970s. Notable in the later poems is the insistence on Hope as a personal and political force. It is personalised as a warrior-hero in the Norwegian "Håpet"[260], the Scots "Tha 'Mhisneach 's an Dòchas 's a' Chòir 'nan Laoich"[223], and again in the Gaelic "Ar Làraichean"[234], a poem with strong echoes of Màiri Mhòr MacPherson, spokeswoman of the crofter's struggle.

These poems can have the simplistic fervour of Hay's earlier nationalist preachings and lack the ambition and complexity of his major work; perhaps their imagery is too traditional, too rural and antiquarian, to successfully sustain a theme of future dynamic broached so repeatedly. Yet in their indeflectable optimism, they bear witness to a spirited, resilient idealism.

3 War

Here lies the cherished life that mothers gifted, crushed.
Here a man is less than nothing among such myriad dead.
Yet each of them was a world, and who knows but this scattered dust
lived hot days of grandeur in their wars unwritten, unread.

(from "Soldier's Graveyard", by Franc Alfirević,
transl. G. C. Hay)

Gaelic song has a rich store of imagery with which to celebrate the warrior. At the time that Hay was sailing for Algeria, the most formidable traditional Gaelic poet of the century was composing a twenty-two-verse celebration of the 8th Army's victory at El-Alamein which could have issued from the mouth of a bard centuries before. In it he acclaims "the nobles of the athletic feats ... the Gaels of my country in the vanguard as usual", "powerful hardy men under the emblem of Scotland, the noble blood of the roughbounds, red as scarlet; renowned pursuers, agile and courageous, who would smite to kill in the violent handslaughter", "the seed of the warriors heroic throughout history, clothed in the plaid that was the uniform of their nation" (see MacMillan 1968: 47–52).

The ethos of Gaelic tradition perpetuated by its bards was deeply militaristic, with praise of the warrior a constant, whether in panegyric verse to chiefs, in battle-incitements, in pan-Gaelic Jacobite verse or in much of the popular song tradition. Following on the post-1745 "pacification" of Gaeldom, British military policy successfully capitalised on this heroic reflex in its creation of Highland regiments, within which, as the shock-troops of the Empire, the Gaels could still affirm their ancestral valour and racial solidarity. This grafting of Gaelic (and Scottish) militarism onto the hide of British Imperialism was one which Hay resisted both in action (in his anti-conscriptionist stance) and in his poetry. "People of the islands, dearly have you paid for the greatness of Britain!" he exclaims in "Grunnd na Mara"[68], elaborating on the familiar voice of feminine lament.

It is natural enough that, having tackled some of the political issues of the war in his poetry, Hay should eventually have come to deal with its human reality; yet there is little in his previous writing to suggest that from his pen would issue arguably the harshest indictment of war by any Scottish poet. His resistance to conscription had clearly not been on pacifist grounds – this was the fiery youth who could cite the proverb "He will win whose fist is strongest and whose blow is swiftest" (Source 44, December 1938), and who could say of the English "let them suffer every bomb, bullet and explosive" (Source 46, c. 20 August 1940). As a trainee soldier in Catterick he had described the war as merely a springtime storm which would scatter the dead wood of the old order ("Sguabag 1942"[85]), but four years later in "Esta Selva Selvaggia"[135] the spring wind of which he writes blows across pulverised towns, sifting the "sharp dust of murdered homes".

The actuality of war was first evoked by Hay in 1944, in the eerie silence which opens "Mochtàr is Dùghall"[109]: two soldiers lie dead on the dusty slopes of a Tunisian mountain, the Arab and the Gael made brothers by a chance hit, all difference between them annulled in their morbid concord. Their killer was "no cheerful, eager warrior" of the kind so often celebrated in Gaelic tradition, but a man driven to insanity by fear, exhaustion and thirst, and bitter disillusion.

The terrible irony of this fraternity of the dead is pursued in the fragmented multiple images of "Esta Selva Selvaggia": the civilisation now uniting Scotland, Europe and the world is that of "sirens, blast, disintegration"; Italy is strewn with "newly-made antiquities": "graves and stumps of riddled gables". The documentary of destruction is completed with a series of multilingual soundbites where protestations of innocence vie with racial taunts, while Hay's voice-over warns: "Listen to yourselves. Beware."

The anonymous dead soldier given a voice in "An t-Òigear a' Bruidhinn on Ùir"[123] bids "the eye give warning to memory", and Hay's poems of the war are all marked by powerful, indelibly visual images, delivered particularly effectively in the couplets of Gaelic popular tradition. "Truaighe na h-Eòrpa"[136] dramatically evokes the destruction and human misery in terms of epic, antique culture, and one senses the despair of the classical humanist before such a devastating assault on European civilisation.

The change in Hay's voice over the war years from political passion to passionate humanity is complete in "Bisearta"[116], one of the most powerful of all Second World War poems and arguably Hay's finest single piece. In this hypnotic meditation on Evil, the intelligent heart perceives what the senses cannot: the horror of saturation bombing, the terror of war for ordinary people paying as ever the "old accustomed tax of common blood". Written in a metre adapted from Italian religious poetry, "Bisearta" swells and contracts like the fire on the horizon, pulsating like a heartbeat and burning with angry compassion. The soldier's stance in the poem in some ways typifies Hay's position in the war: following on the trail of the North African and Italian campaigns, Hay was more of an onlooker than a participant. The French "Stances de Simple Soldat"[94-8] and "Esta Selva Selvaggia" may offer insights into army life, but his is not essentially a soldier's poetry. Neither does it address, like the war poems of some of his contemporaries, the issue of "the necessary choice" (Sorley MacLean, in Henderson 1990: 11). Hay no longer concerns himself with whose war is being fought; his indignation is no longer targeted at "mòrachd Bhreatainn" (Britain's greatness) nor at the depredations of Nazism, but at "deagh shìbhealtachd na h-Eòrpa" (the goodly civilisation of Europe, "Mochtàr is Dùghall", l. 52), and more fundamentally (as explored in "An Duine is an Cogadh"[109.4]) at the responsibility borne by all Adam's Clan for war. Consequently, his poems on the war have no moral ambiguity but a resonant moral clarity.

In "Mochtàr is Dùghall", Mokhtâr's great-grandfather Ahmed joins the forces of the Emir of the Faithful against the colonising French, and in an unsettling foreshadowing of Hay's own fate returns from the war physically unscathed but mentally scarred. There are no prose writings by Hay, at least in the public domain, which reveal his reaction to the devastation witnessed in North Africa and Italy, but one remarkable poem, "An Lagan"[117], is unique in expressing a self-awareness, a consciousness of being scarred by war. It was composed in 1945, while Hay was in Italy, but incorporates in a wilfully dislocated fashion a much earlier paean to Seanlagan, the haven Hollow of peace and tranquillity in Kintyre. An ocean of "frenzied years" separates the boy and the man, so terribly vast that the poet fears he may never again find that part of his soul he left in the Hollow. The theme articulated is one of loss, loss of innocence, of serenity, the tempering of idealism by experience, processes that for Hay, as for many of his generation, were brought to bear in exceptionally traumatic circumstances.

Hay's idealism survived the trauma of the war, but the difficulty of connecting the arcadian past with the troubled present may have contributed to his blockage in recreating the story of Dougall – drawing from his own story and that of his people – and completing "Mochtàr is Dùghall". Echoes of that dislocation are still heard in "Latha san Rainich"[207], a song from 1968 which presents the contemporaneous realities of an idyllic day in Kintyre and the terror of nuclear war, without elaboration, as if all explanation evaded the poet. Yet the spiritual comfort of the Hollow endured, celebrated in poems such as "Tlachd is Misneach"[140] and "Scots Arcadia"[144]. That powerful balm in Hay's life inspired the most intimate and sensual moments in his writing, and this is examined in our last section.

4 Kintyre

The Bruce used to refresh his spirit by coming to Tarbert to hunt. ... And some of the Jameses did the same, for this land weaves its own enchantment. It is not only the hunter's instinct and the wandering instinct that give the powerful impulse to frequent these serene, solitary, wild, Arcadian places. Their untamed, unsoiled, tranquil charm, their quiet, untroubled lonely beauty lure you, and in them you are face to face with the old earth itself. ... The bights and creeks and forelands, the burns singing seaward through a curtain of birch and oak and hazel, the kent hills tumbling sheer to the shore, mantled with the foliage of the native trees, "the green mane of the knowes", precipitous and hardly to be passed for fallen rocks, the kindly old names given them by the generations that are long gone but never forgotten, have a power to draw the heart and to lift it, so that they cannot be seen without an upsurge of affection. We belong to them and they are part of us.

(Hay 1948: 340)

Place, People and Tradition

Hay's intense attachment to Kintyre was from the start a mainspring of his poetry. From "An Gleannan"[8] of 1936 to the small "Dùrd a' Ghlinne"[358] of 1983, from "Na Baidealan"[67] to "Mìos a' Ghearrain"[360], that environment inspired him to lyrics of a rare beauty. It is Kintyre which made Hay a nature poet and a poet of place.

As with his verse of the sea, a theme which sprang from personal passion was also one for which there is a vast lexicon in Gaelic and a rich seam in Gaelic literature. His earliest surviving nature lyric "An Gleannan", an intricate, masterfully compact lyric, typifies many of Hay's nature poems in its sense of both sacredness and sensuality. The tone of such pieces takes us back almost 1,000 years to the delicate lyrics of the Irish hermits, or the nature verse incorporated in medieval Irish tales or in later heroic ballads. Sometimes the allusion can be explicit, as in the reference to Diarmid and Gràinne in "An Lagan"[117]; in another poem, "Do Bheithe Bòidheach"[22], something as simple as the use of "binn binn" awakens echoes of chirruping birds long gone, like the sixteenth-century blackbird of Derrycarn.

That these associations were not merely literary models, but at a deeper level a prism through which Hay interacted with his natural environment, is suggested in the article quoted above by the description of Seanlagan, the haloed haven evoked in "An Lagan" and "Scots Arcadia"[144]:

> Seanlagan, the Old Hollow, above a clean, white shore and at the foot of an amphitheatre of gracious, sheltered slopes, where the roe-deer go calling in the fresh stillness of the morning – a wild land's quiet and secret sanctuary, "the green Hollow, the dewy Hollow", a secure and innocent bield like the Gleann Ruachtaigh of the old Irish poem – "A land whose men fear no red rout on hill or vale. Glen like Dallán's secure glen, with its fairy-forts of Manannan." (Hay 1948: 340)

The "kindly old names" invoked in Hay's article are the ones he recites as a litany in "Kintyre"[35], as "a flame to warm, a sain against all ill", the names of hills and hollows, of creeks and headlands, of intimate landmarks like the Paiste Beag of "An Ciùran Ceòban Ceò"[211], and also the names of deserted settlements:

> Meall Daraich, or the Oaken Knowe; Alld Beithe, the Birch Burn; Seanlagan, the Old Hollow; Airigh Fhuar or the Cold Shieling – they are names that evoke the old Arcadian life of grazing cattle and peat fires, fish-oil cruisies, spinning-wheels and a song from every open doorway. (Hay 1947a: 259)

There is more than deep nostalgia here: Hay's sense of place and history, of the human associations in every feature of the natural environment, and his awareness of the emotional, atavistic power of place-names, places him at the heart of Gaelic tradition, in line with all Gaelic poets before him. A praise poem like "Cinntìre"[26] makes clear that his apprehension of place is as historical-intellectual as it is sensual-emotional: the peninsula's roots run deep in history, back to the Lordship of the Isles, further back to the very first arrival of Gaelic and Christianity in Scotland, and even further into Irish legend. The eighteenth-century poem "Moladh Chinntìre" ("In Praise of Kintyre") spoke of the peninsula as the nurse of Lowlands and Highlands (Watson 1918: 183), and in Hay's poetry too Kintyre is not only the cradle of Gaelic Scotland, but at times a paradigm of modern Scotland: in the litany of images evoking "Scotland of the Lowlanders and Highlanders" in "Ceithir Gaothan na h-Albann"[65], in the blue ramparts of Arran in "Épreuve de Doute"[99], in the windswept peaks of "Dleasnas nan Àirdean"[106] or in the Heather Knowe[104 & 197 & 199] (a motif from Irish song, but also the hill behind the Hays' house in Tarbert). Indeed, Hay's imagery for Scotland is primarily rural: reflecting his dislike of cities, urban Scotland is poetically mute.

The obvious symbolism of "An Cnocan Fraoich"[104], "Dleasnas nan Àirdean" or "Beinn is Machair"[118] marks them well apart from the bulk of Hay's nature verse: in clear affinity with Gaelic poetic tradition, Hay's treatment of nature as a theme is very literal. Again and again he celebrates the natural environment for its own sake, not as an allegory or as a metaphor of interior landscape. In "Do Bheithe Bòidheach"[22], "Na Baidealan"[67], "The Smoky Smirr o Rain"[151] and "Ionndrain na Sìne"[272] to cite but a few, the physical reality of Kintyre is evoked in clear sensual outline and precise detail. Hay's stance in these poems is the realist one of traditional Gaelic poetry, succinctly summed up by Sorley MacLean:

> To the modern Gaelic poet the sea gives spiritual messages; to the older Gaelic poet the sea gives no message. It is either a power to be conquered or enjoyed by man, or a ruthless force that destroys precious lives. (MacGill-eain 1985: 32)

"Còmhradh an Alltain"[112], in its circular exploration on a grand scale of a very limited theme, is particularly reminiscent of the great Gaelic nature poems of the eighteenth century, although it may also owe something in its scope to Sorley MacLean's ambitious symbolist poem on the woods of Raasay, "Coilltean Ratharsair", which Hay read in 1944. (MacLean's poem may also have influenced Hay's use of the forest as a symbol for the historic Gaelic nation in "Mochtàr is Dùghall"[109], ll. 1,110–28, although the image is a recurrent one in the seventeenth century.) Whether there is a direct influence or not, both poems typify their respective authors' vastly different approaches and qualities: Hay's prodigiously fertile imagination in celebratory description, MacLean's more cerebral psychological and cultural exploration through symbol.

Nostalgia

Towards the end of his life, Hay was to say of his poetry:

> Time and time again in Gaelic and Scots and English I have written
> nostalgic poems, and either you mean it or you don't mean it. I have
> always meant it. (Source 24: 6, 31 January 1979)

The poetic expression of "cianalas", or longing for the homeland, had be-
come a staple theme of songmakers, particularly among exiled Gaels, and
was increasingly typified by sentimental cliché and lack of realism. Many
emigrant songs understandably romanticised the golden days of youth spent
in a happier land among kindlier folk. The burden of those associations,
though discernible in Hay's prose writings, is sidestepped in his poems,
partly by his greater inventiveness and avoidance of poetic cliché, and also
by his technical discipline. It is significant that in his best poems the nostal-
gic theme is brought to bear in a metrical setting quite removed from the
conventional one for songs about the homeland, in forms which carry their
own discipline. The terse couplets of "Luinneag"[15], for example, convey the
aching physicality of longing, while "Cinntìre"[26], with resonances of both
highly formalised bardic verse and the more passionate popular tradition, is
finely poised between emotional lyricism and restraint.

In other poems, sentimentality is sidestepped by an oblique approach to
the theme. In "Còmhradh nan Rubha"[78], for example, the conventional
voice is inverted: there, conversing headlands long for the return of the
fishermen at war. "Tiomnadh"[36], ostensibly concerned with the nature of the
afterlife, is essentially a poem of longing for the hard, living winds of
Kintyre, with which no Otherworld can compare (a motif already broached
in "Cuimhne Nach Tèid Às"[23] and "Cinntìre").

Conflict

The dislocation and alienation in Hay's life brought about by his schooling is
a leitmotiv of his poetry (see, for example, "Kintyre"[35], "Leaving the Land"[18],
"Luinneag"[15], "Cinntìre"[26]), and it was explored more fully in some later poems.
"M'Oilein is M'Altram"[301] explicitly wonders which, native environment or
acquired schooling, has had most influence on the poet. The answer given
there is the same one proclaimed twenty years earlier in "Air Suidh' Artair
Dhomh Mochthrath"[204]: "Tarbert of the skiff and net is mightier by far than
Homer and Latin". Composed at an important juncture in his life, when he
emerged from twelve years' residence in hospital, that poem is an apologia for
Hay's cultural allegiance, a renewed declaration of love for Kintyre. Although
themes of conflict sustain the poem – Lothian versus Kintyre, Lowland versus
Highland, natural environment versus formal education – the facility with
which these are resolved suggest a lack of real conflict in the poet's mind.

Hay's attachment to his home country is notably uncomplicated, and this lack of conflict in his cultural identity and in his portrayal of his native place is in stark contrast to the other modern Gaelic poets of his generation and the next (Derick Thomson, Iain Crichton Smith and Donald MacAulay in particular, Sorley MacLean to a lesser degree), who make of their physical and emotional exile a strongly ambivalent poetic theme. Hay's idealisation of Tarbert must be attributable in part to his low level of social involvement in its community. His acquisition of Gaelic, his most fundamental act of engagement in the heritage of North Kintyre, was in itself a social estrangement from his peers, for whom the language was something to be heard only intermittently in the mouths of people at two generations' remove. He was relatively untouched by the social strictures of small-town presbyterianism (alluded to only in the epigram "An t-Sàbaid"[11] and the opening of "Mochtàr is Dùghall"[109]) – by contrast a veritable *bête noire* of some of his fellow poets. Neither did he witness in his community the heartbreaking, apparently unstoppable decline of Gaelic, his experience being one of reappropriation, not relentless loss: "We came from Carrick in Ayrshire and we're at the Gaelic again", he wrote in a backcover (NLS MS 26786), and he had little sympathy for the deep pessimism of some native speakers regarding the future of the language (cf. comments in interview, SSS 1979).

Single-minded optimism was Hay's fundamental attitude to life and the recurrent note in his poetry. He praises the beauty of Kintyre and the heroism of its fishermen, rather than explore the possible shortcomings of its small communities; he proclaims the renascence of Gaelic, rather than bemoan its decline; he urges wholehearted dedication to the Scottish cause as if the practical implications of such a stance were uncomplicated. His poetry is not one of doubt or of cynicism. Again and again he renews his belief in the rationality and goodness of human beings, and in the power of his art to help and inspire his people. Wrought through episodes of great darkness, his is a poetry of hope and of sanity.

Commentary
to the Poems

Sources 1–59 are manuscripts, sources A–J are published collections, and sources P1–P33 are periodicals. (For full details see Appendix 1.)

Source codes are followed by page or folio number, except periodicals which are followed by issue number then page number.

Information on the copy-text (primary source) for each poem is given in **bold italics**.

Date lists refer to poem lists compiled by Hay. (For full details see Appendix 1.)

Unless specified otherwise, all translations of poetry or of prose extracts are by the editor.

POEMS 1932–1938

1 *The Hind of Morning*

26: 30–1, 1932. 3 lines.
P27: XXX.5: 374, Feb. 1939.
B: 9, 1948.
H: 79, 1970.

Date: 1932. List 3 (although the later List 8 dates the poem to 1933).

2 *Homer*

P13: LVI.2: 128, Dec. 1933.
B: 1, 1948.
P18: May 1967: 3.
H: 79, 1970.

Date: 1932. List 3.

Hay expanded the poem in 1983: see Poem 367 "Homer [revised]".

l. 1 **Ida**: a mountain dwelling of the gods.

3 *Cumha Ruaraidh Mhòir*   *Lament for Ruaraidh Mòr MacLeod*

P13: LVI.2: 131, Dec. 1933 (signed "Seòras Ciotach").
39: typescript by Douglas Young, late 1930s.

Date: 1933 (List 3). **39** specifies "Fettes, Easter".

Title: the name of a pibroch (MacDonald 1895: 108). Sir Roderick MacLeod of Harris and Dunvegan, praised by poets for his lavish hospitality, died in 1626.

l. 2 **dread**: handwritten insertion by Douglas Young, presumably at Hay's instigation, to replace the earlier "sore".

l. 15 **Patrick**: Pàdraig Mòr MacCrimmon, hereditary piper to Sir Roderick MacLeod; pibroch compositions attributed to him include the lament for Sir Roderick and the famous "Lament for the Children".

4 *For the* Corrie

39: typescript by Douglas Young, late 1930s.

Date: September 1935 (**39**).

l. 5 **heads**: handwritten insertion by Young.

l. 9 **roaring**: deleted by Young, with the suggested replacement "snoring" in the margin.

l. 15 **out**: corrected to "at" by Young.

5 Aisling

55: 1936.

46: letter of 14 Nov. 1936 (signed "Ciotach").

P14: XXXV.1 (Dàmh. 1939): 12 (signed "Eilean A' Chòmhraig").

Date: 1935 (List 3).

Robert Rankin and Alistair MacLean, the recipients of **46** and **55** respectively, both accompanied Hay on a sailing trip on the Clyde estuary in August 1936. In **55** Hay comments: "Pretty tiresome, but I think a chappy's going to publish it"; the poem, however, was rejected, as Hay reports in **46**:

> Cha do chòrd m' òran-sa ris na daoine dan tug mi e. Ach mo thogair. Nach ann orm tha mi-nàire a bhith goid na mara bho Choinneach MacLeòid, agus sealbh cho daingeann àrsaidh aig' orra! Ach mas le Coinneach a' mhuir is leams' i cuideachd.
>
> *My song didn't please the people I sent it to. Too bad. How shameless of me to steal the sea from Kenneth MacLeod, when it's been his closely held domain for so long! But if the sea's Kenneth's, it's mine, too.*

l. 22 **bid**: glossed in **55** "Tarbert: creaking", presumably related to standard Gaelic *bìd*, "chirping".

6 Na Geamairean

54: letter of Sept. 1936.

Date: September 1936 (**54**). Hay composed and sent the verses to Angus MacIntosh as an apology for not joining him in Barra. The text is incomplete:

> 's mar sin aghaidh, ach fòghnadh sin, oir tha na rainn mu dheireadh làn mhionnaichean, 's bidh 'd a' cur nàire air Miss Johnson, mas ann gum faic i seo.
>
> *and so on, but let that suffice, for the last verses are full of curses and they'll embarrass Miss Johnson [the landlady] should she happen to see this.*

7 Siubhal a' Choire

17a: 18v (1936). Three lines and chorus.

17b: 38v (1936). Six lines and chorus.

19a: 8 (1936?). Three lines and chorus.

19b: 1v (1947). Six lines and chorus.

46: letter 18 (Dec. 1936). Seven three-line verses. See Rankin 1984: 7.

58: 1V, 1947. As **19b**.

A: 12, 1947.

21: 4, 1974.

J: 119, 1976.

29: 12, c. 1983.

Date: 1936 (List 3, and **46**).

Sources **17a**, **17b**, **19a**, **19b** and **58** are all song settings. An early version (**17b**) runs:

> Chunna mi 'n Coire, haoi ò, deas 's i fo h-uidheam horò.
> Madainn moch air uchd na cruaiche

feadh nan glac 's nam badan uaigneach
chunnaic mi bàt' air àrd nan stuadhan
    Hò è 's i 'n Coire a bh' ann

Tè dhubh àrd nì gàir 'na gluasad
'n tè dhubh chaol nì caoir le tuairgneadh
's chuimhnich mi mar ghabh mi 'n cuan innt'
    'S i 'n Coire i fhèin a bh' ann.

I saw the Corrie, hey o, fine in full rigging, horo. | Early one morning on the brow of the hill | among the solitary hollows and thickets | I saw a boat high on the waves | Ho e, the Corrie it was. | A tall black one who makes a din as she goes, | the narrow black one who makes a blaze as she buffets, | and I recalled how I had sailed the sea on her. | The Corrie herself it was.

Text **46**, published with translation in *Chapman* magazine, includes the following extra verse in second position.

Dh'fhuar sinn roinn gach rubha fhuasaich,
gleusta, gasta rinn i gluasad,
shìn gach ball gu teann fon fhuarghaoith.

Its third and fourth verses are a version of lines 4–9, as follows:

Shìn i 'ceum ri cèin thar chuantan,
shìn i 'taobh ri taobh nan stuadhan,
thug i sìnteag rìoghail uallach.

Thog i 'ceann ri deann nan cruachan,
thog i sèitreach, sèist gun suaimhneas,
thog i gaoir fo ghaoith gun ghruaimean.

8 *An Gleannan*

59: 6, 1940?
A: 9, 1947.
21: 1, 1974.
29: 9, c. 1983.
Date: 1936 (List 3).

9 *Òran don Oighre*

P33: I.4: 14, March–May 1939.
Date: 1936 (List 3 and List 8).

P33 includes a note to the periodical's editor (Hugh MacDiarmid):

The Gaelic of my home place, Tarbert, Loch Fyne, diverges very widely from the so-called "standard" Gaelic, wherever that may be spoken, but I think the things I enclose conform fairly well to the literary norm. A for *è* (he) is an exception, but it is to be heard from the Mull to Cape Wrath, and in printed books the rhyme demands it hundreds of times.

Hay referred to this and its companion piece in *The Voice of Scotland* as "two of the feebler efforts" (Source 36, letter of 7? March 1939).

l. 3 **calamh**: Tarbert form of *caladh*.

10 [*What Song Is Ours*]

3: 84v, 1930s; eleven lines.
20: 9, 1938–9?

Date: 1936, Oxford (**20**).

Typescript text **20** is headed "Former Follies" and holds other early fragments. This draft is glossed: "done in another style", possibly a reference to "Lòmsgrios na Tìre" (Poem 29).

Text **3** lacks ll. 1–8, 11 and 14 but includes the following:

> the rocks that have seen   speak they cannot
> and the silent hills   hide the knowledge
> deaf to our questing,   quiet, abiding.
> Here you may go   and none will know ye.

Hay mentions the poem in a letter of 6 December 1947 to the wife of the composer F. G. Scott:

> Did he [her son George] ever think of experimenting with the Anglo-Saxon metre – lines of four stresses with the position of the stress varying? It can be very impressive I think. I tried it once, and have often meant to return to it. If I remember rightly it went something like this:–
>
> > Whát is our sóng   but an álehouse chórus,
> > cúrsing the shéep   gréy on the híllside &cet.
>
> But it should have the alliteration too. It can be very effective in a sombre way.

11 [*An t-Sàbaid*]

P14: XLIII.1: 7 (Dàmhair 1947).
C: 65, 1952.

Date: 1936, Tarbert (Source 33); but this ascription is from the 1980s, and the absence of the quatrain from any lists may cast some doubt on it.

ll. 3–4: the MacDonald forces headed by Alastair MacColla and the Marquess of Montrose inflicted a decisive defeat on the Campbells and their Covenanter allies at Inverlochy on Sunday 2 February 1645.

12 [*Dùrachdan Nollaige, 1936*]

46: letter of December 1936.

13 Tìr Thàirngire   The Land of Promise

40: late 1930s.
37: late 1930s.

B: 8, 1948.
30: 8, c. 1960 and c. 1982.
H: 86, 1970.

Date: December 1937, Oxford (**37**); and List 3.

Title: in the Irish "Betha Brenainn" ("The Life of Brendan"), the *tír táirngire* is the Paradisal land revealed to Brendan in a vision, and which he finally reaches after sailing westwards in a boat of hide for seven years.

ll. 25–8: the macabrism is one found in both Scots balladry and Gaelic folk poetry, but may also owe something to the "dreary, dreary paganism" of modern Greek keens which Hay had been reading and was soon to translate (Source 47, 13 December 1938).

14   The Three Brothers

37: folder (1), 1937.
B: 4, 1948.
30: 4, c. 1960.
H: 78, 1970.

Date: 1937 (List 3).

Text **37**, Douglas Young's copy-text for *Scottish Verse 1851–1951* (pp. 288–90), includes an account by Hay dated February 1937 of the events which inspired the poem:

> In the winter about ten years ago these three brothers left Ayrshire in their skiff with their week's wages in their pockets, although the sky to south was all dirty and haary. It must have been south of the Cumbraes that the gale came on them, but they never put back. They held on past Garroch Heads, through the tide-rip there, and across the wide, open Inchmarnock Water between Bute and Kintyre. They reached Kintyre after running across a huge sea which must have often broken aboard over the gunnels of their undecked skiff. But for all their hardihood they were drowned not a mile from [sic]; for a "bare squall" leaped down on them from a gully in the hills and "took the mast out of her and flattened her". At least that is what must have happened.
>
> What certainly happened is this. Their folk and their friends were sitting talking round the fire, when between midnight and one in the morning there came three heavy knocks on the door. They thought that this was someone playing a trick, and one ran to the door and opened it quickly. But there was no one there. They could hear the wild noise that the gale was making out on the loch, and they were so uneasy at this unknown knocking that they had no taste for sleep. And so they sat on, without even so much as saying why. About break of day they heard a great wailing from the point near the house, and tho they were willing to think it was the crying of a bird none of them thought so.
>
> Next day there was a heavy sea on the shore and they couldn't use the boats, but they went along the shore-tracks and at the point of the ebbing stone they came upon a skiff which they knew well enough, drifted ashore and grinding her backs on the rocks. Her net was twisted round the stern thwart and the rudder-head, half overboard, and her mast was snapped and her sail rent. A calm day followed and the boats went out with the long lines; and by noon they lifted up three from the place where the tide had carried them.

In his own edited version of the story, Young explains: "The language is Tarbert English, that is: precise and anxious English with a Southern Highland voice, and outcroppings of Scots and Gaelic". Although the poem underwent some changes, the Tarbert idiom was retained in **B**.

ll. 35–6 **rubh'**: headland. **cèinteach**: dialect form of *caointeach*, the Otherworld female whose wailing presaged death.

15 *Luinneag*

59: 7, 1940?
19: 2r, 1947. Two verses and chorus.
58: 2r, 1947. As **19**.
A: 17, 1947.
57: 17, c. 1960?
21: 9r, 1974.

Date: 1937 (List 3).

ll. 4–5: a traditional motif; cf. "Chan e fuaim na gaoithe an-raoir chum an cadal uam", from the song "Ròsan an Lethbhaile" by Eòghan MacColla (for Hay's version see Poem 346), and "Tha 'ghaoth an iar cho caithreamach. / 'S i chum an-raoir nam chaithris mi", from an eighteenth-century song which Hay set to music (see Source 19: 4r).

l. 8 **mu Gharbhail**: texts **21** and **57** change this to the definite form "mun Gharbhail", which is also used in "Air Suidh' Artair Dhomh Mochthrath" (Poem 204).

16 *Fada–Geàrr*

P14: **XXXIV.3: 47, Dùdl. 1938.**

Date: 1937, from letter of 11 May 1937 (Source 46): "I'm sending you ... two *ranns* to Alasdair [MacLean, schoolfriend] expostulating with him for denying the need of an accent".

The pairs of words underlined in translation are distinguishable in Gaelic only by vowel-length.

l. 16 **rac**: the word occurs in Mac Mhaighstir Alastair's "Birlinn Chlann Raghnaill", and is glossed in MacLeod 1933: 64.

17 *A' Chas air Tìr*   *Feet Ashore*

39: late 1930s.

Date: Summer 1937 (**39**), although dated 1936 in List 3.

Title: cf. the Gaelic proverb "Is math a' chas air tìr" ("Good is the foot ashore").

l. 14: although the poem was discarded, this line was redeployed by Hay. It appears in a fragment from c. 1946 (Source 7: 24v), and finally finds its place in the poem "Edinburgh" (Poem 154).

18 Mi 'Fàgail na Tìre   *Leaving the Land*

P27: XXX.2: 122, Nov. 1938.
44a: letter of Nov. 1938.
39: late 1930s.
44b: letter of 26 Sept. 1940.
B: 1, 1948.
H: 77, 1970.
15: 7, 1983.

Date: 1937 (**44b**, List 3 and List 8).

Title: a quote from the eighteenth-century song "Cumha Choir' an Easain" (see Watson 1918: 119).

l. 9 **Sleea**: Sliabh Gaoil, the Hill of Love. "They generally call Sliabh Gaoil *Slia'*" (**44a**).

19 Soraidh Slàn le Cinntìre

18a: 7, 1936?; first verse (3/4 tempo).
59: 30, 1940?
18b: 1v, c. 1947; first verse (2/4 tempo).
19: 1v, c. 1947; as **18b**.
58: Musical MS: 1v, 1947; as **18b**.
5: 36v–37r, 1982.
15: 1–2r, 1983.
24: 67, letter of 5 Oct. 1983.

Date: 1938 (List 3), but the song has earlier origins. **18b** and **58** (featuring first verse and melody) date the song to Spring 1936. In the 1980s, Hay associated it with much younger days: "I made a start on a Gaelic song at the age of twelve: Soraidh slàn le Cinntìre ..." (NLS MS 26752: 14). In **5** he dates the piece to 1928, and he introduces text **15** as "òran a rinn mi 's mi nam bhalach gam chur don sgoil a-mach an Dùn Eideann" ("a song I composed as a boy when I was sent away to school in Edinburgh").

20 To a Loch Fyne Fisherman

P33: 1.4: 15–16, March–May 1939.
D1: 25–8, 1939.
B: 5, 1948.
F: 288, 1952.
H: 84, 1970.

Date: 1938 (List 3).

This was the first of Hay's lyrics to be set to music by F. G. Scott, in June 1939. It was described by Hugh MacDiarmid as "one of the very best of contemporary Scottish lyrics" (Source P19, I.1).

l. 1 **Calum**: Calum Johnson was the skipper on whose fishing boat Hay worked in the 1930s.

21 'S Leam Fhèin an Gleann

P33: I.4: 13, March–May 1939.

Date: 1938 (List 3).

This is the other of the "feebler efforts" mentioned in Source 36 (see Poem 9 "Òran don Oighre").

Title: the name of a pipe-tune (see Comunn 1936, Book 6: 162).

22 Do Bheithe Bòidheach

59: 10, 1940?
A: 10, 1947.
57: 10, 1960?
21: 2, 1974.
J: 116–17, 1976.

Date: 1938 (List 3).

l. 13 **binn binn**: the word, given such prominence, has resonances of much older nature poetry, from early Irish lyrics such as those of Mad Sweeney (see Murphy 1961), to later pieces such as the Ossianic "Lay of the Blackbird of Derrycarn" (c. 1600), which begins "Binn sin, a luin Doire an Cháirn!"; or another Ossianic lyric preserved in the sixteenth-century *Book of the Dean of Lismore*, beginning "Binn guth duine i dTír an Oir" (see Ó Tuama and Kinsella 1981: 40–3, and Ross 1939: 82).

23 Cuimhne Nach Tèid Às   A Memory that will not Fade

39: late 1930s.
P27: XXX.5: 373, Feb. 1939.
B: 6, 1948.
H: 84, 1970.

Date: Summer 1938 (**39** and List 3).

l. 9 **Lethe**: in Latin mythology, the river of which the dead drank to lose all memory of their past life.

24 The Fisherman Speaks

39: late 1930s, typescript by Douglas Young.
44: letter of 26 Sept. 1940.
B: 10, 1948.
H: 80, 1970.

Date: Summer 1938 (**39** and **44**). **B** and **H** have the footnote: "1938 – when the Loch was alive with herring, and the men, 'unemployed', were set to mending the road that runs along its shores".

A letter of September 1938 (Source 46) describes the social circumstances of the period:

Thug mi dà sheachduin ann an Tairbeart, oir cha b' urrainn domh gun dol

ann, ach cha robh móran r'a dheanamh. Bho roinn na Maoile gu ruig ceann
Loch Fìne tha 'mhuir làn do sgadan cho briagh garbh sultmhor 's a bh' ann
riamh. Tha Caol Bóide loma-làn dhiubh, us bha 'd 'gam faotainn aig an Sgeir
Bhuidhe s an Dubhchaollinne, s bha sùil aibhiseach a' sìneadh amach bho
Dhruim an Dùin agus Iomachar ann an Arainn cha mhór gu ruig an taobh eile
de'n Chaolas. Ach codhiù se beag iarraidh orra tha sa chùis, no se 'm bacadh a
rinneadh air aon luchd sgadain a b' fhiù s a b' fhiach saothair a chur air tìr, cha
dean am pailteas ud bonn feuma do mhuinntir an àite – ach amhàin fear no
dhà us bàta mór le motor làidir aige. Is truagh a bhith faicinn beairteas sa
mhuir cho goireasach fagus, agus bochdainn air tìr; na h-iasgairean ri obair air
na rathaidean mar phrasgan dreamasgail Ghallda. Ach tha Breatann mór us
saoibhir, 's nach math a bhith ad Bhreatannach! Bidh an tsaorsa agad co-dhiù
– 's e sin, saorsa gu màl a phàigheadh 's do dhùthaich fhàgail.

*I spent a fortnight in Tarbert, for I couldn't not go, but there wasn't much to do.
From the Moyle up to the top of Loch Fyne the sea is full of herring as beautiful
thick and plump as ever was. The Kyles of Bute are bursting with them, and
they could be found at the Sgeir Bhuidhe and the Dubhchaollinne, and there
was a huge shoal stretching out from Druim an Dùin and Imachar in Arran
almost to the other side of the Sound. But whether it's because of low demand,
or it's the efforts that were made to prevent a single herring load worth the
trouble getting to land, all that abundance won't do an ounce of good to the
local people – except one or two who have a large boat with a strong engine.
It's a crying shame to see such wealth in the sea so near and handy, and yet
poverty on land; the fishermen put to work on the roads like a pack of Lowland
rabble. But Britain is great and prosperous, and what a joy to be British! You have
freedom, at least – the freedom, that is, to pay rent and leave your country.*

Hay's short story "The lamp itsel' will tell ye" takes up the same theme:

The latter days of desolation had come on the entire business. True, herring had
never been so plentiful for years. From Brown Head in Arran to above Otter
they were there. All day and every day the solans worked in swarms along the
bights, and herring had been got with splash-nets inside the very harbour.

Here was wealth for the taking, one would have thought; but it could ben-
efit nobody. In the recent bad seasons boat after boat had been sold, many of
them to become yachts, and there were not more than seven pairs in the har-
bour. The men were away on yachts or coasters, or (most bitter thing of all)
working on the roads as navvies. All the cunning and the wisdom that had
accumulated through generations stood the people in no stead, and the most
uncannily certain tracker of the wandering shoals was no better than the big-
gest fool in the fleet once it was a matter of picks and wheelbarrows. (Hay
1940b: 62)

25 *Looking out from Kintyre*

P27: XXX.5: 374, Feb. 1939. Five verses.
B: 13, 1948.
H: 81, 1970.

Date: 1938 (**B** and List 3).

P27 has verses 1–4 and the additional penultimate verse:

> The Marxist covenanter, gospel-mad,
> that spits before your feet for dogma's sake,
> the ministerial monster, seemly clad,
> the sheep that bleat, the herd that is their stake.

26 *Cinntìre*

59: 2–3, 1940?
P14: XXXIX.1: 9, Dàmhair 1943.
A: 15–16, 1947.
21: 6–8, 1974. Copy-text of translation.

Date: 1938 (List 3).

After the loss of translation proofs for *Fuaran Slèibh* in 1947, Sorley MacLean provided a translation for publication, which Hay praised for its elegance and sensitivity ("snas agus tuigse", Source A: 7). Hay's own translation in **21** seems based on MacLean's.

l. 25: a traditional motif; cf. the lament *Is daor a cheannaich mi an t-iasgach*.

ll. 41–2 **Iain Mòr**: John MacDonald of Islay (fl. c. 1400), son of John I, Lord of the Isles. His sept of the MacDonalds extended their sway to Dunyveg and the Glens of Antrim (a song to one of his most celebrated descendants, Alastair MacColla, refers to North Kintyre as "Dùn nan Ultach", "the Ulstermen's Fort" – see Watson 1918: 212).

l. 47: in the Irish tale "Oidheadh Clainne Lir", the children of the god Lir are turned into swans and spend 300 years wandering the Mull of Kintyre (see Dillon 1994: 63–8). **Sruth na Maoile**: the North Channel, between Ulster and Kintyre.

27 *Ùrnaigh Oisein as Ùr*

44: 1938?; four quatrains shorter.
37: folder (2), 24 Oct. 1939; translation only.
59: 8–10, 1940? Two quatrains shorter.
A: 51–3, 1947.

Date: 1938 (List 3).

The poem remained untranslated in *Fuaran Slèibh* (**A**). **37** is the translation of a version similar to **44** but even shorter. I have adapted it to the final text.

Title **Oisean** (Ossian): in Gaelic legend, the warrior-poet son of Fionn MacCumhaill. He outlives all his contemporaries, and (in the late medieval ballads ascribed to him) vaunts to St. Patrick the virtues of the old pagan order. For examples of the dialogue ballad 'Ùrnaigh Oisein', see Ross (1939: 124–35) and J. F. Campbell (1872: 40–7).

ll. 1–4: a traditional verse.

l. 19 **Thalla laoghaibh**: a homophonic play on "halleluia".

l. 53 **Chriosostom**: St John Chrysostom, fourth-century Doctor of the Church.

28 Òran

44: 1938?
59: 7–8, 1940?
P22: 3: 34, 1946.
A: 22, 1947.
19: 6, 1947?
58: Musical MS: 5v, 1947?; first verse only.
H: 98, 1970.
21: 12, 1974.

Date: 1938 (List 3).

The metre is that of Duncan Bàn MacIntyre's "Òran Coire a' Cheathaich".

l. 26 **e**: I have corrected the feminine *i* of **A**, in accordance with **21** and other occurrences of "fàileadh".

29 Lomsgrios na Tìre   *The Destruction of the Land*

P27: XXX.5: 372, Feb. 1939.
39: typescript by Douglas Young, 1940?
P33: 2.2: 1, Dec. 1945; "First four verses".
B: 14, 1948.
H: 87, 1970.

Date: 1938 (List 3). (**39**, like the later List 8, dates the poem to 1937, but also places publication a year early to February 1938.)

There are substantial linguistic differences between **P27** and **P33/B**, explained by Hay's note to **P27**: "The dialect of the above poem is not properly Lowland Scots, but represents what the people of Tarbert speak when they are speaking English". In the later version, the linguistic register has been shifted into a more distinctive Scots; some of the changes effected are seen in Douglas Young's annotations to **39**. See Poem 10 "[What Song Is Ours]" for an earlier treatment of the same theme.

l. 2 **Priam**: the last king of Troy.

l. 6 **a lass wi a bricht face**: Helen of Troy, famed for her beauty. Married to the king of Sparta, she eloped with Priam's son Paris. This led to the siege and destruction of Troy by the Greeks (see Homer's *Iliad*).

l. 25 **"Keppoch is wasteit"**: "'s a' Cheapach 'na fàsach" from Iain Lom MacDonald's song "Murt na Ceapaich" of 1663 (see Mackenzie 1964: l. 978).

30 [Rann Aoire air Bàta]

44: letter of 26 Oct. 1938.

Date: 1938?

Presumably by Hay. Having quoted one sailing song and mentioned picking up the tune of another over a crackly wireless, Hay writes: "How do you like this – *I gun ùrlar* [etc. ...]".

31 *Do na Daoine Muladach Nach Gabh Òran ach Òran Gaoil, 's e Fìor Bhrònach*

44: letter of c. 1 Nov. 1938.
59: 25, 1940?
Date: 27 Nov. 1938 (**59**).

In a letter of 20 December 1944, Hay thinks the poem "quite amusing, but … a wee bit kind of clever" (Source 36).

32 *An Sealgair agus an Aois*

39a: Hay typescript, c. Nov. 1939.
39b: typescript by Douglas Young.
59: 10, 1940?
E: 80–1, 1946.
A: 19, 1947.
57: 19, 1960s?
H: 109, 1970.
21: 16, 1974.

Date: 2 Nov. 1938, Tarbert (**39b**, and List 3).

The old hunter lamenting the loss of his vigour and his livelihood, and the personification of Age as an obstructor, are both found in Gaelic tradition, most notably in the Lochaber poem "Òran na Comhachaig", a dialogue between an owl and an old hunter composed c. 1600. That poem fascinated Hay, who wrote to Robert Rankin from North Africa (Source 46, 25 January 1944): "The Owl has come into my mind at intervals, and I always reflect what a unique poem it is. I've never met anything quite like it." It was an enthusiasm he passed on to his friend, who after many years of research wrote the definitive study of the song (see Rankin 1958; also Watson 1918: 249–59).

ll. 13–16: note the following verse from Iain Lom MacDonald's "Cumha Mhontròis" of 1650: "Nan tachrainn is tu fhèin | Ann am boglachan Beinn Èite, | Bhiodh uisge dubh na fèithe | Dol troimhe a chèile 's ploc" (Mackenzie 1964: ll. 695–8).

In 1983, Hay wrote the following quatrains which he may have envisaged adding to this poem and its English version (Source 15, 3v):

> Bha mi uair 's bu choingeis còmhla
> cnoc is còmhnard, lòn is learg.
> Thàinig an aois gu h-obann, grìsfhionn
> is sgob e dhìom siud. Mìle mairg!

> I was a time when it was equal,
> level or steep where heather grows.
> Age came upon me sudden and sallow
> and snatched that from me. A thousand woes!

33 *Age and the Hunter*

39: typescript by Douglas Young.
A: 19, 1947.
H: 109, 1970.
21: 17, 1974.

Date: 5 Nov. 1938, Edinburgh (**39**, and List 3).

See commentary to Poem 32.

34 *Song*

44: letter of c. 1 Nov. 1938; one verse only.
39: typescript by Douglas Young; two verses only.
P22: 3: 34–5, 1946.
A: 23, 1947.
G: 582–3, 1966.
H: 99, 1970.
21: 13, 1974.

Date: 1 Nov. 1938, Tarbert (**39**, and List 3).

An English version of Poem 28 "Òran". (Both **44** and a letter to Tom Scott in connection with **G** indicate that the Gaelic version is the original.)

ll. 9–16: this verse, derived from ll. 21–4 of "Òran", seems to have been the first composed. It is first found in **44**:

> Here's a translation, much expanded, of *Fìon ad bheul-sa* into "Tarbert" –

> > Rudd the mooth lik the wine o' Flanders,
> >   rudd and tender, an fine wi' pride;
> > white the thrott that throbs wi' her singin,
> >   white the neck that the ringlets hide,
> > lik a burst o' sun on brokkin watter
> >   when the West wunn scatters the seadrift wide,
> > lik the driftin snow that the wunn is blowin,
> >   whusperin up on the hullside.

35 *Kintyre*

44: letter of 14 Nov. 1938.
P32: 23.3: 25, Sept. 1939.
B: 2, 1948.
15: 9r, 1983.

Date: List 3.

After text **44**, Hay writes: "Damn it, I saw Lagan Ròaig and Airidh Fhuar then, and I near grat".

36 Tiomnadh

59: 1–2, 1940?
A: 13–14, 1947.
57: 13–14, 1970?
21: 5–6, 1974.
29: 13–14, 1983.
Date: 1938 (List 3).

l. 13 **Tìr nan Òg**: The Land of the Young, paradise of Gaelic mythology.   **Abhalon**: paradise of Arthurian legend.

ll. 19, 23 **bios**: the relative future ending in independent position is attested in several dialects of the north and east peripheries of Gaeldom, but limited to use with certain pronouns (see Gleasure 1986). The only other use of it by Hay that I have come across is in a contemporary letter (September 1938): "Bíos mi gabhail neònachais ..." (Source 46, letter 28).

l. 23 **Tìr fo Thuinn**: Land under the Waves, inhabited by the drowned.

ll. 49–50: in his revision of c. 1974 (text **21**), Hay changed the gender of *lios* to masculine. Needing a new rhyme to replace *innt'*, he changed l. 50 to "Cha toir do Bhreannan sìth".

ll. 51–2: St Brendan is said to have sailed seven years in a coracle in search of the Land of Promise of the Saints.

l. 52 **lunn**: could refer to the middle part of an oar (see Dwelly).

37 Brìodal Màthar

59: 25, 1940?
A: 11, 1947.
H: 108, 1970.
21: 3, 1974.
Date: 1938 (List 3).

l. 7 **Oscar**: a hero of Gaelic tale and song, the son of Ossian.

POEMS 1938–1940

38–54: The Scottish Scene
[A Satirical Sequence]

Date: 1938–9 (Source 44 and Source 5). The first mention in Hay's diary is on 15 December 1938 (Source 5: 9v), when Hay visits Wendy Wood "to leave 'The Scottish Scene' and a Gaelic pamphlet". Then on 1 January 1939 (ibid.: 11v):

> Car fad amach anns an oidhche thàinig Wendy Wood is MacAindreis a-staigh. ... Mhol iad dhomh cur ris "The Scottish Scene". ... Rinn mi suidhe agus sgrìobh mi a dhà no trì de na duanagan.
>
> *Pretty late on in the night Wendy Wood and Mac Aindreis came in ... They encouraged me to add to "The Scottish Scene". ... I sat down and wrote two or three of the ditties.*

On 15 February 1939, Hay informed Kenneth MacLeod that he was sending him the sequence (text **44**) "though I don't know whether it'll please or annoy you".

The title may be an allusion to "Scottish Scene, or the intelligent man's guide to Albyn" by Lewis Grassic Gibbon and Hugh MacDiarmid, published in 1934.

38 *Gather, Gather, Gather*
44: typescript of entire sequence with letter of 15 Feb. 1939.

39 *Renaissance*
44: typescript of entire sequence with letter of 15 Feb. 1939.
P26: May 1939: 9, signed "Sròndearg Mac na Bracha" ["Rednose son of the Malt"].

40 *International Repercussions*
44: typescript of entire sequence with letter of 15 Feb. 1939.

41 *The Soccer Scene*
44: typescript of entire sequence with letter of 15 Feb. 1939.

42 *The Proper Procedure*
44: typescript of entire sequence with letter of 15 Feb. 1939.

36: letter of early Feb. 1940.
P26: May 1940: 9.
P24: No. 3?: 12, 1946?

l. 8: in **P24** "divert the Cart to Kelvinside".

43 The Scottish Chelsea
or "Ged as fad a-mach Barraigh ruigear e"

44a: letter of 14 Nov. 1938.
44b: typescript of entire sequence with letter of 15 Feb. 1939.

44 Life's Little Compensations

44: typescript of entire sequence with letter of 15 Feb. 1939.
36: letter of early Feb. 1940.
P26: Apr. 1940: 9.
P24: No. 3?: 12, 1946?

l. 5 **Farming and grazing are**: post-war this became "Our aviation is" (**P24**).

l. 9: in the earliest version (**44**) "Shipbuilding, mining and so forth", and post-war
(**P24**): "Our shipping, railways and so forth".

Text **44** has the additional (final) verse:

> On his account (oh, saving grace!)
> there is no reason for alarm;
> our Secretariat is a place
> "where one can not do any harm".

45 Our Culture Still Counts

44: typescript of entire sequence with letter of 15 Feb. 1939.

46 Tìr nan Òg   The Land of the Young

44: typescript of entire sequence with letter of 15 Feb. 1939.

Title: paradise of Gaelic mythology.

47 How to Deal with "Revelations"

44: typescript of entire sequence with letter of 15 Feb. 1939.

The poem imitates the verse form of Walter Scott's "MacGregor's Gathering":

> The moon's on the lake, and the mist's on the brae,
> And the clan has a name that is nameless by day;
> Then gather, gather, gather, Grigalach!
> Gather, gather, gather, Grigalach!

(See MacQueen and Scott 1966: 435–6).

48   Nature Notes

44: typescript of entire sequence with letter of 15 Feb. 1939.
22: 141v, 1946?

49   Buffalo Bill in Gaiters

44: typescript of entire sequence with letter of 15 Feb. 1939.
P26: June 1939: 9, signed "Sròndearg Mac na Bracha Mhic Eòrna"
["Rednose son of the Malt son of Barley"].
22: 141v, 1946?

This is the piece Hay thought Kenneth MacLeod might have found particularly objectionable. In a letter of late February–March, he writes:

> I am very much afraid that I have offended you either by my long silence, or else by my (I admit) very cynical "Scottish Scene", or probably by both. ... "The Scottish Scene" is not to be taken very seriously. It may be that you think it irreverent in places, but surely you yourself dislike those who turn their churches into recruiting offices as soon as ever the international situation becomes strained. It's bad for the church, for it disgusts the public.

Hay's next letter takes up the theme (with an apposite quatrain; see Poem 58 "[Rann Comhairle]"):

> An e gu bheil an t-Easbuig Sasunnach gad fhàgail car mì-thoilichte? Siuthad a dhuine, 's na gabh air an t-sròin e, oir cha robh mi a' dèanamh cuspair cuimsichidh de do shròin fhèin no de shròin Albannaich air bith, ach de shròin mhóir dheirg nan "luirgneach Lunnainneach" is nan gille-ruith aca.

> *Are you unhappy about the English Bishop? Come on, man, don't take it personally ["on the nose"], for I wasn't out to lampoon your own nose or any Scottish nose, but the big red nose of the "London longshanks" and their lackeys.*

l. 20 **wait till the crisis**: glossed "colloquial English for wait till the week-end" (**P26**).

50   'S Leam Fhèin an Gleann   The Glen Is Mine

44: typescript of entire sequence with letter of 15 Feb. 1939.
Title: the name of a pipe-tune (see Comunn 1936, Book 6: 162).

51   An Informative Volume Bound Tastefully in Blue

44: typescript of entire sequence with letter of 15 Feb. 1939.

52   Am Fiann air an Uilinn   The Fiann on Their Elbows

44: typescript of entire sequence with letter of 15 Feb. 1939.
36: letter of early Feb. 1940.
P26: Nov. 1940: 8.

Title: **Am Fiann**: The "Fenians" of Ossianic song and story, a heroic band of mercenaries led by Fionn MacCumhaill; originally Irish, they became the most popular figures of Gaelic legend. (See J. F. Campbell 1872 for Scottish examples of Ossianic tales and ballads.)

53 *Is Coma Leam Cogadh no Sìth*   *War or Peace, I Care Not*
44: typescript of entire sequence with letter of 15 Feb. 1939.
36: letter of early Feb. 1940.

Title: the name of a pipe-tune (Comunn 1961: 304).

l. 1 **war**: changed to "push" after the outbreak of war (**36**).

l. 3: changed to "we'll have more Polands to defend" after the outbreak of war (**36**).

ll. 13–16: this verse was dropped in **36**.

54 *Our National Building*
44: typescript of entire sequence with letter of 15 Feb. 1939.

St Andrew's House by the Calton Hill in Edinburgh was officially opened in 1938.

✻

55 *[Banaltram nam Bàrd]*
P14: XXXV.3: 46, Dùdl. 1939.
59: 4, 1940?
A: 26, 1947.
21: 14–15, 1974.

Date: 1939 (List 3).

The "trì rainn is amhran" structure practised in eighteenth-century Ireland combines three quatrains in syllabic metre with a verse of stressed song metre, and was described by Hay as "the Gaelic equivalent of the sonnet" (see Poem 322 below).

56 *An Gaol a Bh'ann*
39a: c. Nov. 1939.
39b: typescript by Douglas Young.
34: 33v, 1945?
A: 25, 1947.
H: 94–5, 1970.
21: 14, 1974.

Date: 1939 (List 3).

Possibly inspired by a Greek lyric translated by Hay as "Dìochuimhne" (see Source C: 60).

57 *Love Is Forgotten*
3: 83v–84, 1939?
39: typescript by Douglas Young.

Date: List 3.

This poem post-dates its Gaelic version: "*Love is forgotten* (of which I don't think much) and *The Hunter and Age* are translations from my own Gaelic" (Source 36, letter of 19 December 1941).

Text **3** includes drafts of a further verse:

> Pour out some salve impassionate
> that shall consume their quiet distress
> give the nursed flame of inward hate
> for this heartbreak of friendliness.

58 [*Rann Comhairle*]

44: typed letter, undated.

Date: c. April 1939. Hay had sent Kenneth MacLeod his satirical "The Scottish Scene" in mid-February and had not heard from him since. He suspected the collection had offended the minister, in particular the attack on jingoistic clerics (see Poem 49 "Buffalo Bill in Gaiters").

59 *An Dèidh Tràghaidh Thig Lìonadh*   After Ebb Comes Flood

1a: 67 (incomplete draft), 1939.
1b: 36v–37, 1939.
39: typescript by Douglas Young.
P19: I.1: 8, March 1940.
B: 18, 1948.

Date: September 1939 (**39** and **B**). Britain and France declared war on 3 September, following Germany's invasion of Poland.

l. **4 in blooms a frieze**: Hay and Young shared doubts about this, Young glossing "Jeeze!" in **40**, and Hay writing in mid-October 1939: "God help me, I've thought of nothing to string up instead of my *blooms a frieze* yet!", then in early February 1940: "owing to my laziness the *blooms a frieze* are to come out in all their horror" (in the forthcoming **P19**).

All texts bar **B** have additional lines between the first and the second verses. The version in **40** and **P19** runs:

> Craobhan crom thar iomall fairge,
> trom a fairm air feadh na coille;
> fonn fiadhaich an fhàsaich luraich,
> sian do ghàirthonn mu do dhoirean.[1]

> We saw the black rocks drowned, our shore ablaze,
> a hem of foam round sunshot forest ways.

---

[1] Trees stooping over the edge of the sea, | heavy its uproar throughout the wood; | wild land of the lovely wilderness, | the cry of your loud waves (is) about your groves. (**P19**)

60 *A Ballad in Answer to Servius Sulpicius Rufus*

36: letter of mid-Oct. 1939.
B: 10–11, 1948.
30: 10–11, 1982.

Date: 1939 (**36** and **B**).

The poem was prompted by Douglas Young's poem on the outbreak of war: "Leaving Athens, 2nd September 1939" (see Young 1947: 28–9). In notes to **B**, Hay quotes Young's stanza: "More likely home to ruins. That old jurist | Servius Sulpicius Rufus, as a tourist | among the wrecks of Greece serenely pondering, | wrote to his Cicero what seemed the surest | anodyne for his grief. And in our wandering | we have a consolation, not the poorest." Young's poem quotes from Rufus' letter (written in 45 BC to comfort Cicero on the death of his daughter), and comments: "The carcass of ancient cities lying | may teach a man the smallness of his dying ...".

Texts **36** and **B** provide notes by Hay. These are included below.

l. 6 ***Nos homunculi***: "We little men". Servius Sulpicius Rufus wrote: "Are we little men to be indignant if any of us short-lived beings dies or is killed, while in one single place so many remains of towns lie overthrown?". [**B**]

l. 17 ***Teamhair 'na féar***: refers to the line *Tá Teamhair 'na féar agus féach an Traoi mar tá* ("Tara is grass, and see how Troy is"). [**36**]

The line is from an Irish quatrain translated by Hay in Source 36:

> The world o'erwhelmed them, and swept like chaff by the blast
> Alexander, Caesar and all their people have passed;
> the grass hides Tara, and see how Troy doth lie,
> and the English themselves, it may be that they will die.

l. 18 **Durlus o Guaire**: Guaire, or Guaire Aidhne, King of Connacht, who died in AD 663, was famed for his generosity, and it was usual for poets to call their patrons a Guaire or an *athGhuaire* ("a second or a re-Guaire"). He lived at Durlus. [**36**]

l. 20 **Sycharth o Owen**: Sycharth was Owen Glendower's place, praised by many Welsh poets as a hospitable house. [**36**]

l. 21 **Emain an' Tailtiu**: Emain Macha was the palace of the Ulster kings, near Armagh, and Tailtiu is Teltown where the great fair or gathering of all Ireland was periodically held (very reminiscent of Olympia). [**36**]

l. 22 **MacEwen's Kerry keep**: the MacEwens had a castle near Kilfinnan (at Eilean Ardgadain) in Kerry Cowal. Only the site is left. [**36**]

l. 26 **kains**: taxes and tributes. [**36**]

l. 27 **Lia Fàil**: the Irish Stone of Destiny, used in the installation of Scottish kings at Scone until its removal by Edward I of England in 1296.

l. 28 **Canmore**: Malcolm III, king of Scots (r. 1058–93).

l. 29 **Carnaborg**: Carnaborg was a fastness of the MacLeans in the Treshnish [Islands, off Mull]. It is wonderfully steep and strong. [**36**] **Duntuilm**: a seat of the MacDonalds of Sleat, in Skye.

l. 30 **Mingarry**: seat of the MacIans of Ardnamurchan.

l. 33 **Dia**: "God", the nickname acquired by Douglas Young during his time at St Andrews University, and consistently used by Hay (see Young 1970: 12).

Text **36** has an extra verse before the envoi, and another appended:

> They ettle tie ding doon the Canongate,
> that smellt sae sweet, some day. Aye, aye; we'll see.
> The Calton Jyle, frae whar it stood o' late,
> a wheen o' clerks rule us by their decree;
> the Crystal Palace (fuich! eh michty me!)
> flew up in sperks. (Praise Goad, I hear ye cry.)
> But wha wad dee servin' his enemie?
> They lived afore they deed, an' sae maun I.
>
> Realms hae come smertly doon, lik ony wean
> that rinnin' on a rough rodd in the nicht
> an comhair a shròine, striks its fit t'a stane,
> an comes a spledrach. It gaits up a'richt,
> the wean; the empire passes frae oor sicht –
> braid empires, lik deid jeelyfush they lie.
> (We maun stan' oot, an folla oor awn licht.)
> They lived afore they deed, an sae maun I.

Both verses are mentioned in a letter of 4 January 1944 (Source 36):

> the verse "Realms hae come smertly doon, lik ony wean" contains some nonsensical – or grotesque – simile about a jellyfish, and a horrible flat line "It gets up aa richt". Better without it. What about "They ettle tae ding doon the Canongate"? It's a doubtful case. But I'm fond of the bit about the "wheen o clerks".

61   *1918–1939*

16: 4v, 1983.

Date: 1939, Edinburgh (**16**).

62   *Alba*   *Scotland*

39: c. Nov. 1939?
P29: 2: 17, Spring 1946.
B: 24, 1948.
D3: 100–2, 1949.
H: 76, 1970.
30: 24, 1983?

Date: 1939? (**39**). Note the entry in Hay's diary from March 1940 (Source 5: 20v): "Visited F. G. Scott [in Glasgow] and spent a long time thrashing out the final form of *The blaffering wind*".

Text **39** has a fourth verse appended:

> Scotland is wind-headed, and hell storms;
> but her we would spin, scattered sticks on the tide.
> Up wind! while the red ember of hope warms,
> for over this weary water our goal bides.

63 An Gaol Cha d'Fhiosraich Mi

3: 83v, 1939? Gaelic and English quatrain.
39: c. Nov. 1939.
37: 1940? Translation only.
59: 3–4, 1940?
44: letter of 26 Sept. 1940.
A: 27, 1947.
21: 15, 1974.

Date: 1939? (**39**).

ll. 9–12: the poem may have originated in this verse, drafted in **3** as a quatrain:

> Och nach gabh thu truas rium,
> och, nach duilich leat mo chor,
> thus' a' càradh do chùil bhàin,
> mise 'dol bàs air do shon.

In **37**, Hay appends a version of the English quatrain to his prose translation:

> And have you not a shred of pity
> or mercy, then, for me to spare?
> Good Heavens! I for you am dying,
> and you are doing up your hair!
>   — but that's a little too flippant.

There is a Scots version of the poem by Douglas Young (see Young 1947: 32, "Lass wi the Keekin-Gless").

64 Is Duilich an t-Slighe

39: typescript by Douglas Young; verses 1–6 only.
C: 42, 1952.
32: 42, 1960s?
33: 42, c. 1983.

Date: 1939, Edinburgh (**33**). That ascription can only refer to the early six-verse version of the poem, entitled in **39** "Final Lyric to Nationalists Who Refuse English Conscription", and which in late April 1940 Young reports having set to music (Source 36). The subsequent four verses must have been added after Hay's apprehension and enlisting into the British army in May 1941.

Note Hay's comment on 20 December 1944 (Source 36):

> I have thought all along that certain things marked out for the book had their heart in the right place, but were far from being poetry. "Is tiamhaidh dùsgadh a' mhochthrath" is poetry in my estimation, though there are several good reasons for not publishing it at the present juncture ...

65 Ceithir Gaothan na h-Albann

48a: 1942–3?
A: 33, 1948.

21: 21, 1974.
J: 120–1, 1976.

Date: early Spring 1942 ("toiseach an Earraich an Cataraig", **48a**). The poem thus properly belongs with Poems 83 to 85.

66 *The Waukrife Corp*

39: 1940?

Date: 1940? The poem post-dates List 3 (c. Summer 1939), but the typescript **39** must pre-date Hay's flight to Argyll in the autumn of 1940.

Title: handwritten insert by Douglas Young.

67 *Na Baidealan*

3: 80v–81, 1939–40; incomplete draft.
20: 19, c. 1940; four verses.
59: 22, 1940?; four verses.
44: letter of 26 Sept. 1940; four verses.
34: 33v, 1945.
A: 18, 1947.
21: 16, 1974.
J: 118–20, 1976.

Date: 1940? (**3** and **44**) and 1943?

The source texts offer a clear picture of the development of this poem. The earliest draft (text **3**) is as follows:

> Neòil mhiarailteach gan càrnadh suas
> gan snìomh   cuairt
> advance   gu mòrdhail   air màrsal mar gum b' ann le tàir,
> 's an tàirneanach 'nan cridh' a-staigh.
>
> Sgaoilidh rompa an duibhre oillt,
> 's an dealan boillsgeach ast' anuas;
> is slaodar leò an t-uisge trom   darkening thick hiding
> mar churtan dall lom a' chuain [changed to nan stuadh]
>
> Neòil mhiarailteach an sud gu h-àrd
>
> turaidean rìoghail, torran tr
> baidealan bagraidh
>
> Arainn (am plath) sa chith na suainich
> glòir uamharra de ghlòiribh Dhè.

This becomes (texts **20**, **59** and **44**):

> ### Neòil air Fuaradh
>
> Neòil iongantach an sud gu h-àrd
> is ruaim ghàbhaidh 'nan gnùis bhorb;

turaidean treuna, bàbhan còrr,
baidealan bagraidh, ceò is colg.

Neòil mhiarailteach gan càrnadh suas
's gan snìomh an cuairteagan cas,
ag imeachd mar gum b' ann le tàir,
's an tàirneanach 'nan cridh' ag at.

Snàgaidh rompa an duibhre oillt,
's an dealan boillsgeach ast' a-nuas;
slaodar leò an t-uisge glas
mar chùirtean dallaidh trast' nan stuadh.

Cuan is cladaichean gun dath,
gan dubhadh as le steall nan speur,
is Arainn bheàrnach bhuainn fo chleòc –
glòir uamharra de ghlòiribh Dhè.

The revision of the poem to its final three-verse form may date from Hay's time in Africa. This is suggested by the poem's appearance in Source 34, and by a letter of 27 January "1943" (but possibly of 1944) in which Hay sends his mother "four of the old poems revised" for *Fuaran Slèibh* (Source 23: 4).

68 *Grunnd na Mara*

36: letter of early Feb. 1940. Ll. 22–33 omitted.
A: 34, 1947.

Date: 1940? (**36**).

The poem may have been intended as part of the political sequence "Dealbh na h-Eòrpa" (see Poem 77 "[Sgairt Mo Dhaoine]"). "Thonder They Ligg", a Scots version by Douglas Young, was included in *Fuaran Slèibh*.

ll. 1–2: from the eighteenth-century lament "Ailein Duinn shiùbhlainn leat", attributed to Anna Campbell of Scalpay.

l. 17: a reference to the proverb "Thèid an osna nas fhaide na 'n eubh" – "the sigh goes further than the cry" (see Meek 1978: 163).

l. 35: **mòrachd Bhreatainn**: possibly an allusion to the John MacFadyen poem of that name which earned the bard a prize at the 1900 mod (see MacFadyen 1902: 256–9).

69 *Soothwards owre the Sea*

36: letter of 17 Feb. 1940.

Date: 1940? (**36**).

In his letter, Hay describes the song as "a vulgar ballad for the times, to the tune I made for *The Lowlands o' Holland*". (The tune can be found in Source 17: 24.)

70 The Old Fisherman

44: letter of 26 Sept. 1940.
P29: 2: 17, Spring 1946.
D2: 2–3, 1946; three verses.
B: 12, 1948.
56: 3 Sept. 1969.
H: 89, 1970.
30: 12, 1983?

Date: Spring 1940 (**44**).

In **30** and List 11, the poem is dedicated to Calum Johnson (1878–1944), on whose skiff Hay served his apprenticeship in ring-net fishing.

71 The Kerry Shore

39: 1940?
44: letter of 26 Sept. 1940.
D2: 10–12, 1946; three verses.
B: 7, 1948.
H: 90, 1970.

Date: 1940? (**44**). The poem, like Poem 70, is probably one of those mentioned in a diary entry of 14 April 1940 (Source 5, 21): "Looked in at F. G. Scott's [Glasgow] ... The three poems I sent him had struck a spark, and lo! three songs."

72 Fuar Fuar   Cold Cold

36: letter postmarked 23 April 1940.
P8: No. 2: 37, March 1946.
B: 29, 1948.
H: 89, 1970.
30: 29, 1982?

Date: 1940 (**36**). At the foot of his typed letter, Hay inks in: "Here's a verse. No more has come"; verse 1 follows, then verse 2 ("two, only the last to come"), and verse 3 appears at the top of the page with the comment: "Fini! It shows you only have to take the trouble."

Title: the poem's title and structure echo a ninth-century Irish lyric on winter (copied down by Hay in Source 2: 28v), starting: "Fuit fuit | fuar inocht Mag Lethon Luirc, | árda in snechta nás an sliab | nocha roichenn fiadh o cuid" (see Greene and O'Connor 1967: 134–6).

73 Am Maraiche Gàidhealach sa Chogadh

5: 3, 1940? Early draft.
20: 18, 1940?

Date: 1940? (suggested by calligraphy and paper type of **20**, and by poem's theme).

74 [*Brang air na Sasannaich*]

37: c. June 1940.

Date: 1940? The poem must pre-date a postcard of 16 July 1940 (Source 36) in which Hay writes: "The tune I had in mind for *Cuiridh sinn brang* explains the versification".

Hay later described the song as "very nearly doggerel" (Source 36, 5 June 1944).

ll. 13–16: a reference to conscription. Note Hay's explanation of his own stance in a letter to Kenneth MacLeod (Source 44, fragment 17):

> b'e mo ghuidhe gun cuirte as do'n dithisd aca [Sasannaich is Gearmailtich]. A bharrachd air sin cha bu toigh leam ruith gu h-umhal d'an ionnsaigh air a' cheud fhead a dhèanadh iad, cleas a' mheasain.
>
> *My prayer was that the two of them [English and German] would be destroyed. What's more I had no wish to run to them obediently at their first whistle like some lapdog.*

75 *Alba Ghaoil Ò*

37a: folder 2, typescript and hand, c. June 1940.
37b: folder 2, translation typescript, 1940?
36: First verse and melody.
P26: No. 215: 5, July 1944.
A: 29, 1947.
19: 2v, 1947. As **36**.
58: Musical MS: 3, 1947. As **36**.
21: 17, 1974.

Date: 1940 (**37a**).

Hay's immediate model for this song was Sìleas na Ceapaich's Jacobite "Òran do Rìgh Seumas" of 1714 (see Ó Baoill 1972: 16–18), itself part of a larger complex of songs which Hay mentions in a paper on Gaelic song groups (Source 22, 121–2).

76 [*Alba Àrsaidh*]

37: Spring 1940?

Date: 1940. (Reference to a paper by Young on medieval Latin poetry suggests that **37** dates from Spring 1940.)

Hay specifies that the verse was composed to his own melody for Eachann Bacach's "Òran do Lachann, Triath Cholla". Despite Hay's stated intention to complete the song, no further verses have survived.

77 [*Sgairt Mo Dhaoine*]

7: 39v–40r, 1946.

Date: 1940, from mention in letter postmarked 30 September 1940 (Source 36; see below).

Although text 7 was considered for insertion into Poem 109 "Mochtàr is Dùghall", the lyric was originally intended for a long political piece, "Dealbh na h-Eòrpa", the only surviving evidence for which is the letter to Young of September 1940:

As for "Dealbh na h-Eòrpa", I'm glad you like it. There is a great deal of scurrility in it, although scurrility is in accordance with genuine Gaelic tradition which is to give your aversions the full benefit of what you think, and then a bit more air sgàth an fhasain [for the sake of fashion]. The first part dealing with those that sit on the seats of the mighty was to be scurrilous for a contrast to the later parts showing what they had done to Scotsmen, which were all to be after the manner of "Tha iad ann an grunnd na mara" [see Poem 68] ... Both were to get their just deserts in fact, as were the intermediate British muinntir na h-Alban [people of Scotland] who get them in one of the lyrics "Sgairt mo dhaoine 's am mòrachd". It will be finished if I'm spared.

78 *Còmhradh nan Rubha*   The Talk of the Headlands

4: 53v, 1940? Incomplete draft.
36: letter of 1 Aug. 1940.
44: letter of 26 Sept. 1940.
P27: XXXIV.1: 80, Oct. 1940.
B: 6–7, 1948.
H: 90, 1970.

Date: 27 July 1940 (**36**). (**B**, however, gives 1939.)

79 *Òran a Rinneadh ann an Ainm Fir Eile*

36: letter of 28 Aug. 1940.
44: letter of 26 Sept. 1940.

Date: 1940 (**36**).

Hay tells Young in **36**: "meanwhile there is a moan on the back of this page written sub persona amici cuiusdam [using the persona of a certain friend] who made a great to-do when his girl took a tirravee".

Text **36** has an extra couplet:

> Corp is anam a bhith 'n aisith,
> mo leannan bhuam cho grad air teicheadh.

Body and soul at war with each other, | and my lover fled so suddenly from me.

80 *Cuimhneachan do Ealasaid agus Anna NicMhaoilein*

44: letter of 26 Sept. 1940.
P14: XLII.6: 77, Màirt 1947.
C: 3, 1952.
21: 40, 1974.
24: 57–8, letter of 10 Dec. 1982. Translation.
13: 14r, 11 Dec. 1982. Translation.
33: 3, 1983.

15: 4–5, 20 Oct. 1983. Translation.

Date: September 1940 (**44**).

Ann MacMillan (Black by marriage) died on 25 January 1940, and her elder sister Elizabeth on 21 September 1940. In a letter of early February (Source 36), Hay wrote to Young:

> The younger of my two great-aunts died 12 days ago, and of course I have been in Tarbert from then almost till now. Loss of a personality is a bewildering thing – and she was one – and I am sorry that I cannot fully believe in spirits. Ach beannachd leatha, bha i laghach. [But a farewell blessing on her, she was a good person.]

And to MacLeod in September (**44**):

> The first poem is a (very poor) tribute to my two great-aunts. The elder of them died in Tarbert last week and to my sorrow I could not get away to her funeral. ... There we have lost two great personalities, and a link with the old world. Oh well. "Marbhaisg air an t-saoghal chruaidh!" ["A curse on the cruel world!"]

The sisters, like Catherine Hay's own mother Jessie MacMillan, were native speakers of Tarbert Gaelic. Although they did not normally converse in the language, they did much to nourish Hay's boyhood curiosity in Gaelic.

l. 1 **Cill Aindreis**: note the corrected version given in **24**: "this should be *Cill Ainndreann*, an old *-nn* genitive of *Ainndrea*: (Saint) Andrew. However there is *Sloc Aindreis* at the head of the harbour." Both forms had already been noted by Hay c. 1960 in Source 13: 6.

81 *Aonarain na Cille*

59: 26, 1940?
A: 21, 1947.
H: 105, 1970.
21: 11, 1974.

Date: 1940–1? The poem must pre-date April 1942, when according to a letter of 23 July 1944 (Source 36) Hay first heard a musical setting of it by Margaret Brown (artist, and wife of the Scottish Socialist polemicist W. Oliver Brown).

For the Scots version by Douglas Young, "Guestless Howff", see Young (1947: 31) or Source G: 286.

82 *Teisteas Mhic Iain Deòrsa*

3: 85–6, 1940?; lines 2–8 missing
59: 4–6, 1940?

Date: 1940? from contexts **3** and **59** and theme of poem. The third last and second last verses suggest a time around Hay's flight to the hills of Argyll in October 1940.

Note the following outburst in a letter to Kenneth MacLeod, c. April 1939 (Source **44**):

Molaidh mi 'n dreathann donn, is gabhaidh mi mo phort reasgach fhéin, is gus an téid mo thachdadh chan abair mi facal sìobhalta ri Sasunn. Sasunn – tha am facal e fhéin 'na phurgaid thilgidh dhomh, dìreach mar a tha e do na h-Innseanaich, do na h-Arabianaich, do na h-Éiphitich, do na h-Iùdhaich, do mhuinntir Bhurma, Kenya is iomadh àit' eile.

I'll praise the wren and stick to my own stubborn tune, and till I'm throttled I won't say one civil word about England. England – the word itself is a purgative to me to be spat out, just as it is to the Indians, the Arabs, the Egyptians, the Jews, to the people of Burma, Kenya and many another place.

ll. 21–4 **Uallais**: William Wallace, patriot, executed in London in 1305. **Ghilleasbaig**: Archibald Campbell, 2nd Earl of Argyll and Chancellor of Scotland, killed at Flodden in 1513. **Màiri**: Mary Queen of Scots, executed in England in 1587. **Cùil Fhodair**: Battle of Culloden, 1746. **Dàrien**: the Darien Venture, a doomed attempt to establish a Scottish merchant colony in Panama, 1698–1700.

Please note that Poem 103 "Brosnachadh" belongs to the period pre-October 1940.

POEMS 1942–1944

Please note that Poem 65 "Ceithir Gaothan na h-Albann" dates from Spring 1942.

83 *Casan Sìoda*

20: 23, 6 March 1942.
48a; 1942–3?
P3: No. 3: 2, 1942.
A: 28–9, 1947.
21: 34–6 (1974).

Date: March 1942 (**20**). In a letter of 13 March 1942 (Source 36), Hay encloses the "results of recent inspiration", including "an address, not serious, to a cat".

Title: Mrs Elizabeth MacPherson, daughter of the Rev. John Mackechnie, has kindly informed me that Casan Sìoda was the name given by Hay to the family cat on one of his visits to the Mackechnie household.

l. 24 **bheir e Inbhir Lòchaidh dhuit**: in 1645 the MacDonalds routed the Campbells and their allies at the battle of Inverlochy.

See Poem 121 for the cat's reply.

84 *Rabhadh*

20: 20, 11 March 1942.
A: 24, 1947.
H: 104, 1970.
21: 11–12, 1974.

Date: March 1942 (**20**). In a letter of 13 March 1942 (Source 36), Hay encloses the "results of recent inspiration", including "a reprimand, serious, to a woman (not an ATS)".

l. 7 **cursta**: one of the uncommon words which Hay attributed to his great-aunts, the MacMillan sisters (see Martin 1984: 54).

85 *Sguabag 1942*

20: 21, 1942?
A: 31, 1947.
21: 19, 1974.
29: 31, 1983?

Date: 1942, Catterick (**A**). Hay was based in the Yorkshire military camp from mid-

August 1941 until his departure for North Africa in November 1942.

Title: **Sguabag**: "Sweeper", the name of a strong Spring wind; Dwelly's dictionary specifies: "Trì là Sguabag, three days, the 7th., 8th., and 9th. of April". A rhyme noted by Hay (Source 23: 20) speaks of "Sguabag, Sguabag, màthair Fhaoillich fhuair, a mharbhadh caoirich is caoil uain" ["Sguabag, Sguabag, mother of cold End-Winter, who would kill sheep and young lambs"].

Hay commented to Sorley MacLean (Source 48a) that he had become disgusted with the poem's "dòchas faoin" ("shallow optimism") after reading a report on the famine in Greece. "Chan eil ann ach gliongartaich fhacal, co dhiubh is briagh am fuaim no nach eadh" ("it's all just word-clinking, whether the sound of it is pretty or not").

86   Fàire M'Òige

P14: XLI.1: 7, an Dàmh. 1945.
22: 133v, 1946?
C: *1–2, 1952.*
21: 39, 1974.
33: 1, 1983.

Date: 1942. From Hay's mention of the poem in a letter of 27 January 1943 (Source 23: 4), the poem must pre-date Hay's departure to North Africa in November 1942.

A letter of 8 April 1942 (Source 36) refers to metrical experiments which must have given birth to the piece:

> Then I was trying my hand at assimilating hexameters to Gaelic. Clearly stress would have to take the place of quantity, for you can only get two long vowels together in compound words like "ògmhìos" (and then in speech the stress of the word often robs one vowel of its length).
>
> Instead of two longs, and a long and two shorts, we must have a stressed syllable separated from the next stressed syllable by one unstressed or by two unstressed syllables. As Gaelic verse can't carry on for hundreds of lines beginning each line with a stressed syllable, an anakrusis [extra syllable(s) preceding the first foot of a line] must be permissible, but it shouldn't be too regular or run for a number of lines continuously.
>
> The final disyllabic word of one line will rhyme with its fellow in the next line, and one vowel rhyme will be continuous over blocks of lines, maybe of 3 or 10 or 36 or any number, just as the matter of the verse (still in the womb of time of course) falls into blocks. Thus a speech by someone would make a natural block of rhyme (the terminology isn't elegant, but I don't think it's obscure).
>
> Lines so long would be bald without internal rhyme. The 3rd foot can rhyme with the 5th or with the 4th, or the 2nd with the 4th. That allows for plenty of variety and room to move at ease.
>
> Some day of course this magnificent invention will be used for the Gaelic Odyssey, Aeneid, Theokritos, Argonautica of good old Apollonios Rhodios (whom I esteem more than is fashionable), Hesiod, Lucan and anything else that goes on six feet.

l. 7 **beinn sheilge Dhiarmaid 's na Fèinne**: Sliabh Gaoil in Knapdale had acquired Fenian associations. In a post-war article, Hay mentions Sliabh Gaoil "where Diarmaid was killed by the magic boar" (1948: 340).

87 [Duilleach an Fhoghair]
A: 28, 1947.

Date: 1942. In a letter of 2 June 1942 (Source 36), Hay tells Young:

> I haven't written much. Only another Trì Rainn is Amhran which I enclose with its translation. An invitation, not to the Valse, but (I suppose) by general-ised delicate and poetic hints Au Lit [to bed]. However it's very noble in tone indeed, including as it does night and day, spring and autumn, the rising of the sun and the setting thereof. Not novel images, but satisfactory.

The following year, in North Africa, Hay composed a French version (see Poem 91).

88 Skottland til Nordsjøfarerne
B: 78, 1948.

Date: 1942 (**B** and Source 42).

On 19 October 1942, Hay wrote to Mrs Fanny MacTaggart (recently appointed Scottish Representative of the Norwegian Government Information Services, and organiser of the Norwegian Exhibition mounted in Edinburgh that November), to suggest producing a Norwegian pamphlet on the Scandinavian influence on Scottish place-names and Gaelic (Source 42). He ends his letter:

> Jeg vedlegger et dikt som jeg skrev for noen tid siden til de Nordmenn som tilsøker Skottland "nordsjøveien", og jeg ber dem om å huske at, selvom det finnes noen feil i språket, ordene kommer fra hjertet.
>
> *I enclose a poem that I wrote a while ago to the Norwegians who visit Scotland "the north-sea way", and I ask you to remember that even if there are a few mistakes in the language, the words come from the heart.* [Translation by Dr Arne Kruse]

In a letter of 4 August 1943 (Source 36), listing his linguistic credentials in a bid to be transferred to the Intelligence Corps, Hay mentions that the poem may have been read at the winding-up dinner of the Norwegian Exhibition – "it was mentioned in the papers anyway".

89 Deux Vers
34: 4v, 1943–4.
B: 74, 1948.

Date: July 1943, Algeria (**34**).

Translated from the Gaelic (see Poem 81 "Aonarain na Cille").

90 *Le Revenant du Marin Parle à sa Mère*

36: letter of 21 July 1943.
34: 3v, 1943–4.
B: 73, 1948.

Date: July 1943, Algeria (**34**).

This is a version of the second section of Poem 68 "Grunnd na Mara". Sending it to Young along with "Trois Vers et Envoi", Hay comments: "Two more examples of how to pass your time in the Ordnance Corps" (**36**).

l. **4 aveugla**: the meaning intended may be *s'aveugla* ("blinded itself"), as suggested by Young in his copies of the poem.

91 *Trois Vers et Envoi*

36: letter of 29 Sept. 1943.
34: 4, 1943–4.
P33: III.3: 12, March 1947.
B: 74, 1948.
30: 74, 1982?

Date: July 1943, Algeria (**34**).

Translated from the Gaelic (see Poem 87 "[Duilleach an Fhoghair]").

92 *Le Gaël Réfléchit*

48a: letter of Aug. 1943.
36a: letter of 4 Aug. 1943.
34: 3, 1943–4.
P19: V.1: 10–11, Jan.–Feb. 1944.
36b: letter postmarked 21 Sept. 1946.
B: 71, 1948.
P18: Dec. 1967: 13.

Date: July 1943, Algeria (**34**).

In **36b**, Hay tells Young that the poem is "rather irregular metrically, but to the point".

93 *L'Écosse M'Accompagne*

48a: letter of Aug. 1943.
36: letter of 4 Aug. 1943.
34: 8, 1943–4.
P19: V.1 (Jan.–Feb. 1944): 10.
B: 72–3, 1948.

Date: 31 July 1943, Algeria (**34**).

In his letter (**36**), Hay tells Young that this poem and Poem 92 "were well received here".

94–98: Stances de Simple Soldat

94 *Hypocrite*
36: letter of 4 Aug. 1943.
B: 77, 1948.
Date: 1943 (**36**).

95 *L'Essentiel*
36: letter of 4 Aug. 1943.
34: 3ᵛ, 1943–4.
B: 77, 1948.
Date: 1943 (**6**).

l. 4 **système D**: Le système D – le système débrouillard, l'habitude de se débrouiller. [**B**]

96 *Crime et Punition*
B: 77, 1948.
Date: 1943, by inference.

97 *Le Capitaine*
B: 77, 1948.
Date: 1943, by inference.

98 *"Ne t'en fais pas, c'est pas la peine ..." (chanson populaire)*
6: 9, 1943.
36: letter of 18 Oct. 1943.
34: 3ᵛ, 1943–4.
P33: IV.2: 32, Dec. 1947.
Date: 15 August 1943 (**6**).

For some months, Hay had been unsuccessfully applying for a transfer away from the Ordnance Corps to a post more suited to his linguistic abilities (he was at this time fluent in Norwegian and French, and proficient enough in Italian and Arabic to be unofficial interpreter for his unit). All approaches, however, were turned down by the War Office. It was in this context that Hay sent Young his little verse, in disguise:

> Les Arabes, j'ai remarqué, ont de jolis dictons en vers, et j'en ai traduit un. ...
> L'auteur s'appela [sic] Deòrsa ou quelquechose de la sorte, je crois.

> *The Arabs, I've noticed, have neat little epigrams in verse, and I've translated one. ... The author was called Deòrsa or something like that, I think.*

*

99 *Épreuve de Doute*

36a: letter of 23 Oct. 1943. One extra verse.
34: 5v–6, 1943–4. As **36a**.
36b: letter postmarked 21 Sept. 1946.
P33: 3.1: 18–19, Sept. 1946. Two verses omitted.
B: 75–6, 1948.

Date: 27 October 1943, Algeria (**34**).

Hay writes in **36a**:

> Such things, if the language is correct, and the verse sincere, will win a lot of sympathy and goodwill if they get round. Primarily I wrote my French things because I felt the urge, but there's that thought in it, too. The same goes for the Norwegian poem. Such efforts can be our British Council.

The preoccupations of this poem are elaborated in a monologue sent to Young on 2 December 1943 (Source 36), of which I quote only extracts:

> Such is the state of Scotland today that anything, everything will turn the thoughts of a Scotsman abroad towards her in a questioning way. After the exile, the return. After the return – what? ... To speak frankly, when I think of Scotland now I do so with anxiety and bitterness, because I think that the maiming and extinction of the Scots as a nation is intended, and that it is being forwarded – consciously or unconsciously – by some Scotsmen, mostly bought or snared by vanity.
>
> [Scotland] is a storehouse of that force of the future, Water Power ... Her coasts are a complex of actual and potential naval bases and easily protected anchorages for all kinds of shipping ... She is the natural terminus for the Transatlantic Air Route ... Three such reasons are enough to condemn any small nation to unwelcome attention from its greater neighbours, even to attacks on its existence.
>
> And so we find the attempts to devitalise and mongrelise our people, to divest us of youth, vigour, labour power, industries, everything ... The attack is many-sided ...
>
> Those instances, and others like them, are the kind of news from home that makes Scotsmen overseas anxious and bitter. And that is why their constant prayer is that their countrymen and countrywomen at home should become awake to the peril now, and fight against it. ... It rests with the Scots at home to see to it that we do not come back to such a ruined remnant of our country, I think that some of us would rather die abroad than have such a homecoming.

Hay postscripts: "But I'm not always as pessimistic as that".

The extra penultimate verse in texts **36a** and **34** runs:

> Car on a vu – on verra –
> d'avachis, serfs bien soignés
> d'encasernés lâches, las,
> de peuples morts, surveillés.

For one has seen – one will see – | spent listless men, well-tended serfs, | weary, cowardly garrisoned folk, | peoples dead and under watch.

l. 13 **regard:** editorial correction of Hay's "regarde" (a recurrent error in his French).

100   *Fhearaibh 's a Mhnài na h-Albann*

34: 5, 1943–4.
A: 30, 1947.
21: 18, 1974.

Date: 27 November 1943, Algeria (**34**).

This poem may have been Hay's response to a request from the composer F. G. Scott for "a Gaelic thing on National Anthem lines to make music to" (Source 36, 23 November 1943).

101   [*Rann fo Chraoibh Orainse*]

6: 40r, 1944? (cutting of published story "Fo Chraoibh Orainse").

Date: 1943–4?

The source is a cutting of a short story by Hay, "Fo Chraoibh Orainse", published in the short-lived periodical *Alba Nuadh* (see Source 48a, letter of 21 March 1944).

The story tells of an uneventful nightguard, during which the narrator takes his companion Gilleasbuig to task for his attempt at a soldier's homesick plaint in traditional style; he is then challenged by Gilleasbuig to explain his own feelings for North Africa:

"Gu dearbh fhèin" orsa mise "cha b' e so mo dhachaidh no mo dhùthaich, oir gheibh thu sin eadar an dà Ghalltaobh 's chan ann eadar Tùnais is Oràn. Chan iad na dubh chuileagan aingidh seo cuileagan còire Chinntìre, aig a bheil de mhodh 's gun eòl daibh sgur. Chan e is chan iad, ach chan urrainn mi gun àicheadh gur toil leam cothrom fhaotainn air eòlas a chur air cinnich eile – air na beachdan is na barailean a thig iad a mach leo, air an creideamh is an dòigh air an aor iad Dia, air an taighean 's am biadh, air gach cànain a sgileas iad, gu ruig is air na chuireas iad umpa eadar burnus is eile. A h-uile sochair a dh' fhaodas tu ainmeachadh, air a' cheann thall fàsaidh tu sgìth dhith le bhith 'ga shìor mhealltainn ... Nach iad làithean bruthainneach Aildiri is Tùnaisi a dh'fhàgas am blas air Tobar na Crìche Gile an dèidh seo, is nach iad leathadan odhar sgreaganach Djebel Harr a chuireas sgiamh eile ris an sgèimh a bh' air Sliabh Gaoil mun d'fhalbh sinn thar mara. Bheir mi dhuit rann an èirig do ranntachd, anns an abair mi ris na h-Albannaich: ..."

"Without a doubt", says I, "this is neither my home nor my country, for you'll find that between the two Gall regions[1] *and not between Tunis and Oran. These vicious black flies aren't the kind flies of Kintyre who have enough couth to know when to stop. But I can't deny that I like to get the chance to discover other peoples – the thoughts and opinions they express, their religion and the way they worship God, their houses and their food, every language they are skilled in, and even what they wear, whether burnous or whatever. Every pleasure you could name, you'll finally grow weary of through constant enjoyment. See how the sultry days of Algeria and Tunisia will enhance the taste of the White Rim Well after this, and how the brown parched slopes of Djebel*

---

[1] Professor William Gillies suggests that this refers to the two "Gallaibh", Caithness and Galloway.

Harr will add a new beauty to the beauty we saw in Slea before we went overseas. I'll give you a verse in exchange for your rhymes, in which I'll tell the Scots: ..."

102 Athair nan Cluas

36: letter of 10 March 1944.
34: 2v, 1944.
A: 50, 1947.
21: 37–8, 1974.

Date: 6 March 1944, Algeria (**34**).

Title: Bû Udnîn, "the Father of the Ears" – an Algerian Arabic nickname for the donkey. [**A**]

103 Brosnachadh

59: 16, 1940?
P26: 214: 5, June 1944. Two verses only.
P22: 2, 32–3, 1945.

Date: 1940? **59** was typed by Hay on his own typewriter, and thus must pre-date his disappearance in October 1940.

Hay himself was not involved in the poem's publication. John Mackechnie, who was acting as Hay's agent for his planned collection *Gaoth air Loch Fìne*, was also columnist to the *Scots Independent* and used the poem to advertise the book which was "now in the press" and would feature his own English versions (**P26**). It was Mackechnie who sent Maurice Lindsay "Brosnachadh" for publication in *Poetry Scotland* (**P22**). Lindsay's correspondence to Young reveals that Hay initially objected to publication (Source 36, 10 February 1945). He clearly had reservations about the poem: after postponing his book, he admitted to Young that some of its contents "were far from being poetry" and that "definitely 'Brosnachadh' isn't" (Source 36, 20 December 1944), and he described the song to Sorley MacLean as "graceless doggerel full of ducktailed jostling words' (Source 48a, 14 May 1945). Maurice Lindsay rated the poem more highly and quoted it in full in an article on "The poetry of modern Scotland" (1947: 24–5) as an illustration of the unsentimental, hard-edged quality of the new Gaelic verse.

104 An Cnocan Fraoich

34: 1–2r, 1944 (minimal legibility). Extra verse.
36: letter of 12 March 1944. Extra verse.
48a: with letter of 21 March 1944. Extra verse.
P26: 242: 5, Oct. 1946.

Date: 10 March 1944, Algeria (**36**).

In his letter (**36**), Hay says of his "latest Gaelic outburst":

It's not very high and solemn poetic or Pindaric, being rather of the street ballad variety or at best of the Seán Clárach [Irish bard, died 1754] type. It goes to the tune of "An Cnuicín Fraoigh" ... There you have an example of what the vin rouge d'Algérie can do when taken in the right spirit.

The verse omitted from **P26** goes:

> Nuair a dh'èigheadh sàmhchar an dèidh an àir,
> ghlèidh iad an seann nàimhdeas 'nan cridhe na chaoir,
> is iad ga àrach mar rogha bhlàiths –
> bhà iad an rùn bàis duinn 's dor Cnocan Fraoich.
> Is mar thoradh air a' ghràin chaidh gach baile thogail slàn;
> chuireadh coigrich ann an àite nan Gàidheal caomh.
> Is e sgeul nan làrach 's nan raointean bàn
> mar a b' fheudar dhaibh bhith 'fàgail a' Chnocain Fhraoich.

When peace was proclaimed in the wake of the slaughter, | they kept the old enmity in their hearts like an ember, | tending it well like a choice source of warmth – | they intended death for us and our Heather Knowe. | And because of this hatred every township was rebuilt; | foreigners were installed where had been kindly Gaels. | The story which the ruins and the untilled fields tell, | is of forced departures from the Heather Knowe.

105 [*Bail' Ìomhair*]

34a: 10, 1944; handwritten.
34b: 10, 1944; typescript pasted over 34a.
Date: 15 March 1944, Algeria (**36**).

Title: as cited in List 8. The township of Baliver in South Knapdale was deserted in the course of the nineteenth century (it is marked as ruins on the Ordnance Survey map of 1867–8, sheet CCI). It was the subject of a melancholy short story by Hay at Fettes College ("Home", in *The Fettesian* 56.6, July 1934: 432–4).

106 *Dleasnas nan Àirdean*

3: 87, c. 1939? One verse only.
34: 4ᵛ, 1944.
A: 32, 1948.
21: 20, 1974.
Date: 10 May 1944, Algeria (**36**).

The poem may have originated in the nature verse of text **3**:

> Tha sìor shèideadh mu 'creachann,
> tha sìor cheathach mu 'sliosan,
> is fiar fo na casan
> a h-aisridhean snigheach;
> cha trèig a' ghaoth tuath
> a guaillean car tiota
> ach bidh sgal aic' a' greasad
> an sìor shneachda na chithean.

> The wind ever blows about its summit, | the mist ever drifts about its sides, | treacherous under the feet | are its dripping paths; | the north wind does not forsake | its shoulders for one instant | but howls as it drives | the eternal snow in drifts.

See also Poem 118 "Beinn is Machair" for a development of the central image.

107 [Rinn Sibh Cuan ...]

34a: 12, 1944; handwritten, only partially legible.
34b: 12, 1944; typescript pasted over 34a.

Date: 15 May 1944, Algeria (**34b**); but the first and fourth verses are from 1939 (**34a**).

The poem may have had its origins in Hay's planned political sequence "Dealbh na h-Eòrpa", mentioned in a letter of late September 1939. (See commentary to Poem 77.)

108 An Ceangal

34: 9v, 1944.
A: 54, 1947.
H: 110–11, 1970.
21: 84, 1974.

Date: 24 May 1944, Algeria (**34**).

l. 1: I have emended Hay's published translation of this line, which corresponded to an earlier version of the poem.

POEMS 1944–1946

(i)

109 *Mochtàr is Dùghall*

Sources are listed for each section of the poem. Typescript **48** was the copy-text for the 1982 edition of the poem (published by the Celtic Department of Glasgow University).

Date: The writing of the poem began soon after Hay's move to Italy in June 1944 and progressed steadily through the summer. By early July he realised "with stupefaction" that the poem was likely to run to 1,000 lines (Source 23: 4). Having finished the story of Omar by the end of August, Hay seems to have done little more to the poem until his move to Greece in early 1946: in Kavalla he wrote the final section of the poem and the story of Obaïd. By November 1946 the poem seemed to have reached more or less the form in which it has survived to this day: the imminent completion announced in a letter of late November (Source 36) was stalled by ill-health, but slight additions were made in the autumn of 1947. Although Hay's hopes of adding to the poem in 1981 came adrift, drafts for the "Dùghall" section do survive from 1983 (see Poem 365).

Notes were provided by Hay in text **48** for the initial part of the poem, and his correspondence with his mother gives further glosses. These are indicated below by their source.

109.1 [FOSGLADH]

34: 18v–19r, June 1944.
52: 1–2, 1946–7.
48: 1–2, retyped 1981; with translation.

l. 27 **Gefreite(r)**: German infantry soldier.
l. 33: "The war is shit! The Führer, shit!"
l. 34 **Sieg Heil**: "Hail Victory", Nazi military salute.
l. 36 **diumàr** (jumar): a plant common on the mountains of North Africa. From its short stem pointed leaves spread out fanwise. Its root is eaten. [**48**]   **debel** (jebel): mountain.
l. 38 **Rùimi** (Roumi): "Roman", i.e. a Westerner, non-Arab.
l. 47 **marbat** (marabout): a holy man, or his descendant and the tender of his shrine. [**48**]

l. 49 **tàileab** (taleb): a lettered man. Every schoolmaster is a taleb, but not every taleb a schoolmaster. Literally a "seeker" (after knowledge). [**48**]   **iomàm** (imam): a religious functionary in a mosque, who usually delivers the Friday *khotba*, or sermon. [**48**]

109.2 MOCHTÀR

109.2.1 *Bean Mhochtàir is Mnathan an Dùair*

34: 19v–20v, June 1944.
52: 2–4, 1946–7.
48: 2–4, retyped 1981; with translation.

l. 53: a common Arabic saying – *Kull shi fi yedd Allah.* [**48**]

l. 55 **dùar** (douar): a native village. [**48**]

l. 58: *el-barud*, or gunpowder, is used as a synonym for warfare. *Yetkellem el-barud* – the powder speaks, war is afoot. [**48**]

l. 60 **Tiorailliùr** (Tirailleur): a North African infantry soldier. [**48**]

l. 75 **Càifir** (Kaffir): an Unbeliever, a godless man, blasphemer. [**48**]

ll. 83–4: the Moslem has five obligatory prayer hours a day, and before every prayer he must perform ablutions. The prayer hours are *El Fejr*, or daybreak; *Ed Dhor*, or midday; *El Asr*, half way between midday and sunset; *El Maghrib*, or sunset; *El 'Isha*, when the afterglow has faded from the sky. [**48**]

l. 86 **Iblis**: Satan. [**48**]

l. 90 **Muaidìn** (Muezzin): the man who calls the Muslims to prayer with the formula: "Come ye to prayer! Prayer is better than sleep." [**48**]

ll. 94–5: according to the Moslems Mohammed was the last and greatest of the Prophets, who included Moses (*Mussa*), Abraham (*Ibrahim*) and "our Lord Jesus Son of Mary" (*Sidna Aissa ibn Miriam*). [**48**]

l. 99 **càid**: chieftain.   **sìch** (sheikh): chief.

l. 102 **Rinneadh ionnlaid** (His ablutions were performed): an Arabic saying of a man who has died. Ablutions are performed before prayer and on the dead. [**48**]

Note the couplet quoted in Source 6: 16r (with 102 drafted on the opposite page):

> El-mît – Am Bàs [Death]: Tawwada – ma silla sh,
>   hezz qshâshu – ma willa sh.
> He made his ablutions – he did not pray | he took away his belongings – cha do thill e [he did not return].

ll. 104–15: the passage derives from a religious lament by the Tunisian oral poet Amor Ben Yûsef, copied out by Hay in transliterated Arabic and French (Source 6: 16r–17v), and which includes the following lines:

> Sâmur el-qelb srej   towweg dukhkhâna, ...
> Jâwer Sidi Frej   u nsû jeyyâna.
>
> Sâmur el-qelb ugedd   'ala bwey hanîni;
> beddel dârhu menjedd –   ma 'âd ijîni
> sag erhîla tsegged: ya horg eknîni.

Sâmûri waqqdd   nârí mash'ûla,
fâged baba 'l-akbâd   qoffodh merhûla, ...
Jâwer nâs eb'âd   wa tegga zûlho.

Lâ temmen chi l-ayyâm   Râhi h'azzâna.

Lâ temmen chi l-ayyâm   Choûma r'orriya
Râhi mouch dâr douâm   Nâsek wîn hiya

The hearth of my heart is kindling, it is spewing its smoke ... | Sidi Frej is his abode, his coming (every evening) has been forgotten ...

The hearth of my heart is all ablaze for my beloved father; | no more doubt, he has changed house, he will no longer come to me | he has raised camp and gone his way, o burning of my heart ...

My hearth is ablaze, its flame burns in me | I have lost the father of his heart's darlings, he has packed his belongings ... | He bides among strangers, his shadow has vanished.

Place not your trust in the days, they are source of trouble.

Place not your trust in the days, they are sinister deceivers, | this world is no lasting abode. See: where are your parents? (Translated from the French)

109.2.2 Ahmad

6: 23v–24r, 26r, July 1944; ll. 196–225.
34: 21–22r, July 1944.
23: 5, July 1944; translation of ll. 194–225.
48: *4–6, 1946–7, except ll. 119–50 retyped 1981; with translation.*
52: 4, 1946–7; ll. 119–50.

l. 124 **Abd al-Cadar** (Abd el-Qader), AD 1808–83: self-styled Emir of the Faithful, who proclaimed a *Jehad*, or Holy War, against the French shortly after they had captured Algiers. He built a fortress at Takimdent, of which nothing remains today. He fought the French for more than ten years, and finally he was obliged to be continually on the move with a sort of nomad court and capital called his *smala*. The French treated him with generosity, and he came to terms with them in the end. He has descendants alive today. [**48**]

l. 128 **burnus** (burnous): a hooded cloak.

l. 131 **a lann Innseanach**: swords wrought of Indian iron are cited by Hay as a common motif of old Arabic poetry, and comparison is drawn with the "Spanish blades" of Gaelic verse (Source 6: 45r).

l. 147 **smala**: see note to l. 124.

l. 148 **Aimìr nan Dìleas** (the Ruler or *Emir* of the Faithful): see note to l. 124.

l. 161 **saibhlean siùbhlach** (moving granaries): *mtamir er-rahala* – a nomad kenning for flocks. [**48**]

l. 189 *tâh as-sûr*: "the wall has fallen".

l. 190 **mùr Thakideimt** (the rampart of Takidemt): see note to l. 124.

l. 192 **Còirneil Iussuf** (Colonel Yussuf): a European who was seized by the

Barbary corsairs, went over to Islam and attained a high position in the Sultan's army. When the French landed he took their side, and captured the fortress of Bone (the barracks there are named after him Caserne Yussuf). He subdued the countryside around there in a rather merciless manner. Finally he reached the rank of general. [**48**]

l. 210 **tobar Zemzem**: The well of Zemzem is near Mecca, and pilgrims bring back its water which is sprinkled on the dead. [**23**]

l. 215: Keening is very common at funerals outside the big towns, and sounds pretty terrible. "Roaring and sighing" a Scots fellow described it once. [**23**]

l. 222: the "witnesses" (*shuahed*) are the two stones, one at the head and one at the feet. [**23**]

109.2.3 *Òmar*

34: 22v–28, July–Aug. 1944; ll. 226–693.
23: 5, July 1944; translation of ll. 226–32.
20a: 40, Aug. 1944, translation of ll. 633–93.
35: 15r, March 1946; ll. 694–703.
20b: 42–42A, translation of ll. 226–78 (*Sahara Journey*).
20c: 41, translation of ll. 666–93.
48: 6–16, 1946–7; with translation.
P15: 10: 155, Winter 1954; ll. 291–331 (*Turus Fàsaich*).

l. 230 **Deaha** (Jeha): a popular daft character about whom scores of stories are current. If an Arab messed his work I used to ask him if he was related to Jeha, and that always caused a laugh. [**23**] **Harùn na Còrach** (Harun *er-Rashid*, the Just): the capricious sultan who appears in the 1001 Nights, and is another popular favourite for yarns. [**23**]

ll. 263–6: an Arabic epigram translated by Hay as "A Chur Cùram air Fògradh" ("To Banish Anxiety"); one of many such verses and riddles translated into Gaelic by Hay (Source 34: 38v–40), several of which were published in *O na Ceithir Àirdean*.

l. 285 **siomùm** (simoom): hot desert wind.

l. 288: an Arabic saying; Hay quotes it in his essay "Poetry in the world or out of it?" (1946–7, II: 52).

l. 313 **luingeas Tharsis** (ships of Tarshish): these prestigious ships, of which Solomon had a fleet, are frequently referred to in the Old Testament, e.g. 1 Kings 10:22, Isaiah 23:14, Psalms 48:7. I am grateful to Sr Bernadette Byrne O.S.B. for explaining the reference and pointing out the mistaken identification in Hay's translation with Tarsus in southern Turkey. See also Black & Rowley 1962: 492.

l. 314: in the *Iliad*, the Greek fleet left for Troy from the port of Aulis.

ll. 326–9: from a line by the sixth-century poet Hassân Ibn Tâbit, noted by Hay in Source 7: 18r, and translated: "Nous le boirons pûr et mêlé, puis nous chanterons dans les demeures de marbre" ("We shall drink it straight and mixed, then we shall sing in the marble abodes").

l. 334 **an Sudàn**: Mali (former French Sudan).

l. 395 **Tuargach** (Touareg): nomadic Berber people of the Central Sahara region, considered by Arabs to be only lukewarm adherents to Islam. Culturally homogeneous but politically disparate, Touareg tribes were organised around an aristocratic warrior caste, whose principal activity was the quasi-institutionalised *rezzi* or herding raid (rather like the Gaelic *creach*). Trans-Saharan trading caravans were also the object of pillaging, or alternatively of hired protection. European exploratory initiatives into the heart of the Sahara in the course of the nineteenth century led to large-scale colonisation by the French in the early 1900s. While the tall, veiled Desert Pirate became a central figure in French literary exoticism, the pacification and opening-up of the Sahara precipitated the breakdown of traditional Touareg society.

l. 400: an expression noted down by Hay: "Allah yen'al lahiti; gum mallachd Dia m' fheusag" (Source 6: 17v).

ll. 430–2 **Hoggar**: a mountainous region in southern Algeria, in the heart of Touareg country. **Tamanrasset**: an oasis settlement in the Hoggar, and an *oued* (river-bed) running west into the Tenezruft. **Tenezruft**: one of the Sahara's two expanses of utter barrenness, it separates Touareg country from the territory of the Maures. **Imusharh**: the aristocratic warrior caste of the Touaregs.

l. 439 **raspars**: included in Hay's contribution to the *Historical Dictionary of Scottish Gaelic*, explained as "overbearing behaviour (Kintail)". In earlier notes (c. 1960), the word is attributed to Calum Johnson, and given as "rospars" with stress possible on either first or second syllable (Source 12: 2r).

ll. 477–8: the *tagelmoust* veil, worn by the male Touaregs, and removed only for sleeping.

l. 481 **Sidi Ocba**: the Islamic general who took part in the conquest of North Africa and attempted to quash Berber resistance; he was killed in battle at Sidi 'Okba, near Biskra, in AD 683.

l. 564 **Bàrdo Thunais** (the Bardo of Tunis): the winter residence of the Beys of Tunisia.

l. 601 *Ya Rabbi, Rabbi!*: "O My Lord, my Lord!"

ll. 646–9: Henri Lhôte, in a contemporary study of the Hoggar Touaregs, states that
for drink they take only water ... and milk; in the last fifty years they have grown accustomed to drinking green tea in the Arab manner, flavouring it with mint or certain aromatic plants of the Hoggar. (Translated from Lhôte 1944: 237)

Before l. 694: editor's asterisk.

109.2.4 *Obàïd*

35: 15–17v, March 1946; ll. 704–820.
20: 44A, March 46; ll. 798–820.
23: 7, March 46; translation of ll. 798–820.
7: 37–38r, 1946; ll. 840–960.
48: 16–23, 1946–7; *with partial translation.*
P33: IV/2: 26–9, Dec. 1947; ll. 729–97 with translation.

ll. 729–30: from the Greek poet Pindar's 8th Pythian ode:

Creatures of a day! What is a man? What is he not? A dream of a shadow is man. But whenever Zeus-given brightness comes, a shining light rests upon men, and a gentle life. (Race 1996: 337)

ll. 750–4: an Arabic riddle noted elsewhere by Hay (Source 6: 15r):

El-qalb: Ala idoqqfî sandûq
        ihûm ala el-gherb û esh sherq
        mâ yelqâsh emnîn itûq.
Il bat dans une caisse | rôde de l'ouest à l'est | et ne trouve pas où sortir.

The Heart: it beats about in a box | goes from west to east | and finds no way out.

ll. 794–6: from a poem by the Croatian Antun Nizeteo, read by Hay in the Italian anthology *Poeti Croati Moderni* (see Salvini 1942: 210, "Un Segreto Istante"). Hay's Gaelic and English versions of modern Croatian poems were published in *Wind on Loch Fyne* and *O na Ceithir Àirdean*.

ll. 798–820: Hay tells his mother in **23**:

Here is the next instalment of the well-known pair. I'm afraid Obayd may get a bit sententious, but he must say his piece. ... We'll clearly have to be careful with Obayd, or he'll sound like extracts from MacCheyne's sermons. I've got my eye on him.

l. 804: Hay's notes on Arabic sayings and customs (Source 6: 17v–18r) include:

"Quand tu veux t'assurer de la fidélité de quelqu'un, souris lui au visage et placez la nourriture entre vous deux" (Dicton) Khan el-ma u el-meleh – il a trahi l'eau et le sel.

"To be sure of someone's loyalty, smile to his face and put food down between the two of you" (Proverb) Khan el-ma u el-meleh – he has betrayed the water and the salt.

ll. 813–14: Arabic epigram translated by Hay in Source 34: 40r.

l. 846 **Antar**: warrior-poet (fl. AD 600) who became a hero of popular legend and the subject of a celebrated chivalric romance, the *Sîrat Antar*.

l. 847 **gàita**: Spanish (and North African?) bagpipes.

l. 850 **durc**: note the alternative reading "dagger" preferred by Ronald Black (Black 1999: 363).

l. 872 **den**: editor's emendation; **48** has *don*.

ll. 953–8: based on an anonymous early sixteenth-century Italian poem urging the citizens of Florence to repent, which includes the lines:

O popolo della Italia meschinello,
i' veggo la tua rovina tanto crudele,
che morte chiamerai zucchero e mele.
Se tu sapessi quello che à seguire,
gli uomini desiderrebbon di morire
per non sentire tanta crudeltate.

O mean-hearted people of Italy, | your fall as I see it will be so terrible | that death will be called by you sugar and honey. | If you knew what is to befall, |

even the men would wish to die | so as not to witness such barbarity.

Hay came across the poem in his reading of Savonarola (see Piccoli 1927: 136), and noted the "sugar and honey" motif (Source 7: 36).

ll. 961–70: based on an Arabic riddle, "The New-born Boy", recorded by Hay in Source 6: 15:

> Le Nouveau-né. Anla dnhîf, û frahnna bîh
> lâ jûna mâshi lâ anla sâqîh
> jâna min bled, lâ trâb fîh
> bahnna sha û el-adhâm fîh.
> Jâ bi-hedhâna wa stakenn [?]
> qâd bi-hedhâna wa staken.

C'est un hôte à qui nous avons fait fête [He is a guest that we feasted] | he hasn't come walking on his legs | come from a country where there is no earth | we have sacrificed for him a ewe and eggs | he came to our side and rested in peace | he settled at our side and put himself in security.

109.2.5 *Deòir Ìblis*
48: 23–4, 1946–7.

109.2.6 *[Turas Mhochtàir]*
48: 24, 1946–7.

l. 1,048 **Saghuan**: Jebel Zaghouen, mountain south of Tunis.

109.3 DÙGHALL

Drafts in Source 7 include the following outline for the "Dùghall" section:

Opening lyric:-

> 1 Ciod e a th' annainn ...
>
> 2 Folachd – An Gàidheal [Lineage – The Gael]
> Lyric   Sgairt mo dhaoine 's am mòrachd [see Poem 77]
> Folachd
>
> 3 Àrach [Rearing]   Outside   -in: cèilidh, pipes, yarns
>
> 4 Hill
>
> 5 The Sea
> Lyric
>
> 6 Love
>
> 7 War – sailing – thairis.

Drafted fragments include the following verse (Source 7: 39r, and Source 48):

> Cha dùin mi mo shùilean
> eagal t' ùrshliosan fhaicinn,

cha leig mi steach thu dom smuaintean
air neo is uaigneas leam caidreabh,
Eadúch nan tiugh choilltean
bi dom chuimhne nad fhàire
cuairtich m' inntinn, tulg m' ionndrainn
le mo shùilean a thàladh.   plus rann toisich

*I shan't close my eyes | for fear of seeing your fresh flanks, | I shan't allow you
to enter my thoughts | for then no company will relieve my loneliness, | Edough[1]
of the thick woodlands, be my memory's skyline, | encircle my mind, shift my
deep longing | by enticing my eyes.   plus an initial verse*

Other fragments for "Dùghall" in Source 7 link with the following stray lines on war
(Source 20: 45):

Gliocas an Iar, sgian sa ghreallaich
na cnàmhan ris a dh'easbhaidh arain,
na luingeas luchdaichte san aigein,
's na fir gan tulgadh san t-seòl-mhara.
Sgeilm mu onair – is olc am manadh
a' bhòilich 'ud don òigear thapaidh.

Mas àrd a bàrr leagar an darag
's bidh crìonaich na coille maireann.

Is sinn a' choille thèid a lomadh
thoirt sùigh do sheann rùsg a' mhosgain.
B' ùrar ar bàrr is bu dosrach
's tha 'n tuagh ga geurachadh mur coinneamh,
le sean fhir shanntach an domhain.

Siogalam-siùbhlach de inntinn
air siùdan eadar moit is cìocras.
Tha a marcaich fhèin air muin gach tìre
le gaol air a bhith 'm beul na sgìreachd
snotadh is snoigeas is dìmeas

càrnadh corp is brochan fala

*The wisdom of the West, a knife in the guts | the bones that show through for
lack of bread, | the laden ships on the ocean bed, | and the men tossed around
by the tide. | Idle talk about honour – it is an ill omen | all that vain bluster for
the spirited young man.*

*Though high its top branches, the oak will be felled | and the woodland will
wither away completely.*

*We are the woodland that will be stripped bare | to bring sap to the old putre-
fying bark. | Fresh and luxuriant were our topmost branches | and the axe is
being sharpened in front of us | by the covetous old men of the world.*

*A see-saw of the mind | swaying between pride and greed. | Every country has
its own rider on its back | ? | snorting and suspicion and contempt.*

heap of corpses and brochan of blood

---

[1] Jebel Edough, above Annaba (Bône), where Hay was posted in Algeria.

109.3.1   [*Sa Mhadainn eadar Cadal 's Dùisg*]

52: 25, 1946–7.
48: 25, retyped 1981; with translation.

Title: cited in List 34.

109.3.2   [*Folachd is Àrach*]

7: 38v, 1946; partial drafts.
48: 26–7, 1946–7; with partial translation.

Title: taken from the plan for "Dùghall" drafted in Source **7**.

l. 1,163: **of the watch and the sudden dive**: editor's emendation; **48** has "of the long wings falling in a rush".

109.3.3   *Bean an Iasgair*

48: 27–8, 1946–7.
P9: 6 Dec. 1947: 4.
C: 44, 1952.
32: 44, c. 1961.
21: 71, 1974.
33: 44, 1983?

(All sources include translation.)

109.3.4   *A' Mhuir*

7: 38v, 1946; draft.
20: 44, 1946; draft.
48: 28–9, 1946–7; with translation.

109.3.5   *A' Bhean a' Bruidhinn*

48: 29, 1946–7; with translation.

109.4   [DÙNADH: *An Duine agus an Cogadh*]

20a: 43a, 1946?; ll. 1,261–71 omitted.
20b: 43, Feb. 1946 and Sept. 1947; ll. 1,265–71 in draft.
48: 30, 1946–7; ll. 1,258–73 only, and full translation.
P15: 76: 330, Autumn 1971; ll. 1,221–51 only.
21: 75–6, 1974; ll. 1,221–51 only.

Title: "An Duine agus an Cogadh" is the title of texts **P15** and **21**.

ll. 1,221–57: since Hay's typescript (**48**) lacked the page bearing these lines (perhaps mislaid by Hay after he sent **P15** to *Gairm* in 1971), the poem was published without them, but with a complete translation. Presumably unaware that he still had copies of the missing Gaelic text among his papers (**20a**, **20b** and **21**), Hay later attempted to reconstruct the passage (see a 1983 draft, Source 20: 163).

l. 1,251: after this line, the translation in **48** includes the following passage:

These two saw the fighting of battle. May God never let anyone who is close to me see such a thing, aye, even a moment's glimpse of it, even though it should be in sleep and in a dream.

No equivalent Gaelic text survives, except the following draft (Source 7: 39r):

Chunnaic thu bhith cur a' chatha,
's nar leigeadh Dia a leithid fhaicinn
do ghaolach dhomhsa, seadh, car aitil,
ged a b' ann am bruadar cadail.

Although the missing page in **48** (containing ll. 1,221–57) may have included a version of these lines corresponding to the translation, it is equally possible that the paragraph was discarded by Hay and only remained in the translation through oversight.

POEMS 1944–1946

(ii)

110 Atman

34: 12v–13, 1945?
P10: 3, Spring 1946.
22: 132v and 130v, 1946?
C: 11–13, 1952.
H: 102–3, 1970.
21: 46–8, 1974.
J: 128–31, 1976.

Date: 11 August 1944, Italy (**34**).

l. 15 **Debel Iussuf**: Sliabh Ioseiph [**P10**]; beinn an dùthaich Aildiñ [**C**]. Mount Joseph, Algeria.

l. 36 **Mondovì**: baile beag margaidh san Ailgèir [**P10**]. A small Algerian market town.

l. 41 **Sìdna Àissa**: ar Tighearn Iosa (Arabais) [**C**]. Our Lord Jesus – to the Moslems Jesus was one of the prophets [**21**].

111 An t-Eòlas Nach Cruthaich

34: 41, 1944–5.
20: 39, 1944–5?
22: 137v, 1946?
C: 16–17, 1952.
21: 48–9, 1974.

Date: 1944, from a letter of 29 November 1944 (see Poem 115 "Prìosan Da Fhèin an Duine?").

The idea derives in part from a Croatian poem by Božo Lovrić, read by Hay in an Italian anthology (Salvini 1942: 37, "La Donna e il Saggio"):

> The woman who does not bear a child | accursed is she in her seed. | But equally, the wise man | who has known good and evil | and is drained of creativity | seems to me like a king | who has lost his kingdom | but still wears his crown | and still holds his sceptre: | a mendicant rogue. | Accursed is intelligence, | that clear, brilliant intelligence | which is incapable of creating, | which deludes others | and leads to ruin. | Accursed the woman | who loves but does not bear a child.

l. 6 **gràdaibh**: *degrees*, tomhas teas agus fuachd. [**C**]

112   Còmhradh an Alltain

34: 32–3, 1944.
20a: 27–8, 1944?
20b: 31–4, 1946? Translation.
20c: 29–30, 1947? Partial text.
21: 41–5, 1974.
33: 4–7, 1983?
P2: 27–9, 1948.
C: 4–9, 1952.

Date: 31 October 1944, Italy (**34**).

ll. 7–14 **Hamîz, Harrais, Safsaf, Seabùs, Buidìma, Meidearda, Remel**: aibhnichean an Aifric mu Thuath (an Aildirì is an Tùnaisi) [**C**]. Rivers in North Africa (in Algeria and Tunisia).   **Cruimìri**: ceann-dùthcha an Tùnaisi [**C**]. a region in Tunisia.   **Sgiogda** (Skikda no Philippeville), **Constantìna**: bailtean an dùthaich Aildirì [**C**]. Towns in Algeria.   **Picentino, Forni, Irno, Sele**: aibhnichean deas air Salerno san Eadailt [**C**]. Rivers south of Salerno in Italy.   **Lìri**: abhainn fo Chassìno, eadar Nàpol is an Ròimh [**C**]. River below Cassino, between Naples and Rome.

l. 30 **canntaireachd**: cantering, vocalised pipe-music.

l. 65: ceòl nan Sìrein a chuala Uilìseas [**C**]. The sirens' music heard by Ulysses.

l. 71 **Là Lùnaist**: Lugh's Day, 1 August.

l. 81: two of the variations in a pibroch.

l. 86 **am Feasgaran**: seirbhis fheasgair na h-Eaglaise Caitligich (Vespers sa Bheurla) [**C**]. Vespers, the evening service in the Catholic Church.

ll. 105–6: these lines disappeared from the poem in **C**, though they are present in all previous sources. All extant translations include them.

113   Ed Io Rimasi ad Odorar le Foglie
Agus dh'Fhàgadh Mise le Fàileadh nan Duilleag

34: 34, 1944–5.
22: 153v, 1946?
C: 10, 1952.
21: 45, 1974.
33: 10, 1983.

Date: 12 November 1944 (**34**).

Title: seanfhacal Eadailteach [**C**]. An Italian proverb.

114   At the Quayside

34: 34–5, 1944.
36: letter of 27 Aug. 1946.
P?: unidentified periodical; cutting in Source 1: 3v, Oct. 1946.
B: 16–17, 1948.
H: 82, 1970.

30: 16–17, 1982?

Date: 16 November 1944 (**34**).

The central opposition in the poem may owe something to a scene in John MacDougall Hay's *Gillespie*, between buyers and fishermen:

> The half-dozen buyers on the Quay were in a flutter, running about like hens, sharing their empty stock. ... Standing on the Quay and looking down upon these fishermen in their loaded boats, one caught a look of pathos upon their rugged faces, tawny with sweat thrashed out of them in a fifteen-mile pull in the teeth of the tide. ... The spectacle was compelling in its beauty, in its suggestion of prodigal seas and of the tireless industry and cunning craft of man; and at the same time sad with the irony of circumstance – niggard dealers haggling, shuffling, sniffing in the background. (1914: 192–3)

l. 36 **neighbour**: the partner boat; ringnets were shot by pairs of boats.

115 *Prìosan Da Fhèin an Duine?*

23: 6, letter of 29 Nov. 1944.
20: 39, 1945?
34: 35, 1944–5.
A: *38–9, 1947.*
H: 105–7, 1970.
21: 24–6, 1974.

Date: 23 November 1944 (**23** and **34**).

Hay tells his mother in **23**:

> Here is the Gaelic poem I sent to Crombie S [Saunders, editor of *Scottish Art and Letters*] along with the English one. As you'll see, this poem, "Atman" and "Knowledge That Does Not Create" are really a group, and their ideas all lie in the same direction. But there's no harm in their being published separately, especially as there may be one or two more on this theme, or themes related to it. Let me know if it strikes you as sermonising in tone or not. It's impossible for me to tell, and sermonising or moralising is a deadly trap to fall into.

l. 1 **shaighid**: editorial emendation of text **A**'s "saighead", in line with text **21** and Hay's consistent palatalisation of the feminine dative.

ll. 3–4: Note the following in an essay by Benedetto Croce, read by Hay sometime "over the last four months" of 1944 (Source 36, letter of 20 December 1944):

> L'uccello – scrisse una volta il De Sanctis ... – canta per cantare, ma nel cantare esprime tutta la vita, tutto l'esser suo, tutti i suoi istinti, i suoi bisogni, la sua natura: appunto come l'uomo a cui, per cantare, non basta essere artista, ma deve essere uomo. (Croce 1959: 88)

> *De Sanctis ... [once] wrote that the bird sings for song's sake but in singing expresses all its life, all its being, every instinct and every need, its whole nature. So a man, if he is to sing, must be a man as well as an artist.* (Croce 1949: 134)

Hay's reading of Croce is clear from his own essay of December 1944 "Poetry in the world or out of it?" (see Hay 1946–7, Part 1: 52).

l. 56 **bi thu fhèin**: an unusual, perhaps incorrect, construction.

116 Bisearta

34: 40v, 1945.
E: 78–9, 1946; with Scots version by Hugh MacDiarmid.
C: 39–40, 1952.
21: 68–9, 1974.
J: 122–5, 1976.
33: 39–40, 1983.

Date: 16 January 1945 (**34**). Texts **C** and **21** give "1943", but "Bisearta" must have been mainly composed in Italy, where Hay came across the unusual metre used in the poem.

In **33**, Hay explains that the metre used is from an Italian medieval religious poem, of which he quotes a verse. The poem in question is "Pro Itinerantibus" by the fifteenth-century Dominican preacher and civic leader Girolamo Savonarola. The poem begins:

> In su quell' aspro Monte,
> Dove contempla la Magdalena
> Andian con dolci canti
> E con la mente santa e serena ...

> (Piccoli 1927: 53)

Up this arduous mountain, | Where contemplates the Mary Magdalene, | Let us go with hymns, | And with a spirit saintly and serene.

Savonarola's poems were read by Hay in late 1944 (Source 36, letter of 20 December 1944, and Source 7: 58v).

The description of the fire may owe something to Hay's father's depiction of a fishing fleet ablaze in *Gillespie*:

> It had a rhythmic movement which fascinated the eye. Its flat, jagged head oscillated backwards and forwards slowly, like the head of a snake. This was the main sheet of flame, whose splendour and terror mesmerised. It took a hundred fantastic shapes – now like the chain mail of warriors tearing at each other with bloody hands in a cauldron; now like witches with streaming hair of flame [...]. In greater gusts of the wind the wall swayed, bellied, and broke, and great golden balloons hovered in the air. (1914: 355)

Title: Tunisia was trapped in Allied–German crossfire in the last months of the North African campaign (November 1942 to May 1943), with the last of the German resistance based around Bizerta and Tunis.

> For six uneasy months German command and French administration co-existed, while Tunisian towns and villages were bombed in a war which Tunisians could not by any stretch of the imagination regard as their own. (Calvocoressi 1989: 394)

117 An Lagan

59: 14, 1940?; eight verses, entitled "Seannlaggan".
34: 36, 1945.
A: 42–3, 1947.

21: 29–31, 1974.

Date: 11 February 1945, Italy (**34**), but the first section of the poem dates back in part to 1937 (see Lists 3 and 34: "Cò Chunnaic an Lagan Dìomhair").

The original poem to Seanlagan (**59**) is as follows:

> Cò chunnaic an lagan dìomhair,
> 's a' ghrian mochthrà air 'shlios,
> a' soillseachadh clàr an ruighe,
> nach do chaill a chridhe ris?
>
> Cò chunnaic an lagan uaigneach,
> 's e suainte an glac nam meall,
> nach b' àill leis bothan cois an t-srutha,
> fois gun sàr aig' suthain ann.
>
> Nuair a leum a' ghrian 's a shnàmh i
> os cionn Bàrr nan Damh na dreòs,
> 's a dhòirt i tein' air d'uchdan preasach,
> thug mi searc dhuit thar gach fòid.
>
> Chan eil ciùrradh ann no leònadh,
> chan eil bròn no caoineadh ann,
> b'e sin slànachadh air gach dòrainn
> a bhith tàmh fa chòir do bheann.
>
> Cha chluinnear gaoir no gul san lagan,
> chan fhaicear falachd ann no foill,
> sgiath dhomhs' e roimh gach dochair,
> nach leig olc am thaice chaoidh.
>
> Air dhèinead fheachd san t-saoghal bhrònach,
> air dheòir 's air ainiochd dhaoine thruagh,
> bidh thus' aig sìth fo dhìon 'nan [sic] tulach,
> 's tu 'd ultachan 'nam broilleach uain'.
>
> Mi 'm shuidh gu h-àrd air a' chreachainn,
> 's mo shùil ri Cearaidh thall a ghnàth;
> bidh àillteachd fhathast is loinn san lagan,
> a-màireach, ged nach fhaic mi à.
>
> *Ceangal*
>
> A' ghaoth-sa bhith sèideadh thar slèibhtean Ròaig gach là,
> tuar a' bhraoin is na grèine ruith chèile feadh sgòrr is chàrn,
> beul maiseach a' Chèitein, 's a thrèigsinn gu falbh na thràth:
> 's mo laigh as tìr chèin ud, 's mi-èibhinn 's is aimheal à.

ll. 7–8: Hay twice mentions the Fenian associations of Sliabh Gaoil in articles: it is the Hill of Love "where Diarmaid was killed by the magic boar" (1948: 340) and "where Grainne heard the ominous cry of the heron on the morning of the day that Diarmaid was killed there" (1947a: 260).

118 Beinn is Machair

34: 30v–31, 1945.
C: 14–15, 1952.
33: 14–15, 1983.
Date: 12 February 1945, Italy (**34**).

119 Clann Àdhaimh

34: 44v, 1945.
P22: 3: 33, 1946.
A: 20, 1947.
21: 10, 1974.
Date: 16 February 1945 (**34**).

The poem may owe something to the "Ship of Fools" theme, current in European literature at least since Sebastian Brant's satire "Das Narrenschiff" of 1494. Although the philosophical concerns of Hay's poem link it essentially to his other works of the period rather than to satirical models, he would also have been aware of the two misogynist satires by the Bard MacIntyre in the sixteenth-century Book of the Dean of Lismore, describing a mysterious ship of drunken, wanton women (see Watson 1937: 218–33).

120 Is E Crìoch Àraidh

34: 29v–30, 1945.
A: 36–7, 1947.
21: 22–4, 1974.
Date: 18 February 1945 (all).

Title: "It is the chief end ...", a quote from the Gaelic catechism.

121 Casan Sìoda a' Freagairt

35: 1, 1945–6; extra verse.
A: 48–9, 1947.
21: 36–7, 1974.
Date: 25 February 1945 (**35**).

l. 28: an extra verse follows in **35**:

> Tha bean nam poit an conas rium 's cha b' e mo chomain dith e.
> Is mi ghlanas dith na truinnseirean, 's i fhèin gan cur fom smigeid.
> Is tric a thog i iad mar dh'fhàg mi iad, 's a chàrn i orra 'n dinneir,
> gun uiread is a h-aparan dhol thairis orra idir.

The woman with the pots quarrels with me, which is hardly what she owes me. | It's me cleans up the dishes for her, when she sticks them under my nose. | Often has she picked them up exactly as I left them, and piled on the dinner | without giving them so much as a wipe of her apron.

l. 32 **na Dàin**: Sorley MacLean's collection *Dàin do Eimhir agus Dàin Eile* was published in 1943 and received by Hay in February 1944 (Source 36). **Craobh nan Teud**: a poem in MacLean's book dedicated to Hay.

l. 33 **Iain Lom**, **Mac Mhaighstir Alastair**, **Rob Donn**: Iain Lom MacDonald, Alexander MacDonald and Rob Donn Mackay, major Gaelic poets of the seventeenth and eighteenth centuries.

122   *Na Tuinn ris na Carraigean*

35a: 2, 1945.
35b: 44, 1945.
P14: XLI/4: 35, Jan. 1946.
22: 128v, c. 1946?
P29: 4: 25, Autumn 1949.
C: 18, 1952.
21: 50, 1974.

Date: 1945 (from context **35**, and absence from List 34).

123   *An t-Òigear a' Bruidhinn on Ùir*

35: 3, 1945.
P14: XL/11: 87, Aug. 1945.
A: 40–1, 1947.
21: 27–8, 1974.
J: 126–9, 1976.

Date: 30 March 1945 (**P14**).

l. 14: I have emended Hay's published translation of this line, which corresponded to an earlier version.

124   *Meftah Bâbkum es-Sabar?*
Iuchair Bhur Dorais an Fhaighidinn?

35: 3v–4, c. 1945.
41: letter of 24 Aug. 1946; extracts only.
P26: 257: 2, Jan. 1948.
C: 22–5, 1952.
J: 132–7, 1976.
21: 54–6, 1974.
33: 22–3, 1983.

Date: May 1945, Italy (**35**).

l. 1 **Sùg el-Cheamais** (Sûq el-Khemis): baile beag an Tùnaisi [**C**]. A small town in Tunisia.

ll. 5–7: a North African saying found in Hay's notes (Source 6: 17v) and included in a draft of his short story "The dancers at Ras El Hamra" (Hay 1945):

Ya qalbi, 'alesh etkhemmem? Mektub 'andhu mzemmem. "My heart, why be anxiously thinking? He has your lot written and stored up for you." So we felt, listening to the wind over Ras El Hamra. (Source 22: 19)

ll. 9–10: a saying found among Hay's notes (Source 6: 17v):

Dans les couches laborieuses de la population la croyance est ferme en cette "part de bien" (rizq) que la Providence attribue à tout homme. Qasmek ma' khialek u ajlek, wain temshi mohadhinek – ta part avec ton ombre et l'heure de ta mort, où tu vas, sont à ton côté.

In the labouring strata of the population there is a firm belief in that "portion of goods"... which Providence allots to every man. Qasmek etc.– your portion, with your shadow and your hour of death, wherever you go, are at your side.

Note however Hay's reluctance to accept stereotypes of Arabic culture. In his article "Caifidh Mòr na h-Òigridh, 1942", which draws parallels between Arab and Gaelic storytelling, he writes:

Caifidh na h-Òigridh, Caifidh an Dòchais, Caifidh an Ama-Gu-Teachd – sin agad an seòrsa tiotail as mò aig na h-òsdairean Arabach am bailtean beaga is mòra Aildiri is Thùnaisi; ach a dh'aindeoin sin, bìtear a' cumail a-mach gur nì nach gabh atharrachadh an gnè nan Arabach an dèidh a th' aca air a bhith ag ràdh, "Tachraidh na thachras – kull shì fi yedd Allah (a h-uile nì an làimh Dhè)". Ma tha iad buailteach gu "lùbadh leis a' chùis a bhith mar tha e", nach eil seanfhacal againn fhèin a their "An rud a tha san dàn, 's e thachras"? (1947b: 98)

The Cafe of Youth, The Cafe of Hope, the Cafe of the Future – that's the kind of name most favoured among publicans in towns big and small throughout Algeria and Tunisia; yet in spite of that, people still maintain that the fondness of Arabs for saying "What must be will be – kull shì fi yedd Allah (all things are in the hands of God)" is something inherent in their nature and can't be changed. If they do tend to "bow to existing circumstance", do we not have our own saying which goes "What's fated must be"?

ll. 11–14: the North African poem on which this is based is quoted in Hay's notes (Source 6: 19v):

> Wa Quila fi Es-Sabir (and it is said of patience):
> Bena Allah le-l-akhiara baitan samawuhu,
> momum wa ahzanu wa hiyatanuhu edh-dhorr;
> wa edkhalahum fihi wa eghlaqa babahu,
> wa qala lehum "Miftahu bikum es-sabru".

He built a house for us of which the walls are affliction and evil, and entered us in and shut the door, and said to us "The key of your door is patience" (Meftah babkum es-sabr).

l. 19 **dhuinne**: a revision by Hay of text **C**'s "duinne". Hay's tendency in later years, particularly evident in Source 21, was to lenite the prepositional pronouns of "do" and "de" even after "s" or "n".

ll. 41–2: the saying is very close to a verse in the Irish Annals of Tigernach, in the entry for c. AD 625 (see *Revue Celtique* 17: 178). My thanks to Dr Thomas Clancy for pointing this out.

l. 46: the line echoes the traditional phrase "cluinneamaid annas do làimhe" used to formally invite bards to declaim (see Watson 1918: 120, 293). Hay himself used the expression in his short story of 1944, "Fo Chraoibh Orainse" (see Poem 101).

125 *Tilleadh Uilìseis*

35: 4ᵛ–5 and 43ᵛ–44, 1945–6.
A: 44–5, 1947.
21: 31–4, 1974.

Date: 23 May 1945, Italy (**35**).

Title: Ulysses (in Greek tradition Odysseus), king of Ithaca, a Greek hero who returned to his island after twenty years of war and wandering. His wife, harassed by suitors, has agreed to marry the man who can wield her husband's great bow. Disguised as a beggar, Ulysses succeeds in the challenge and massacres the assembled suitors. See Homer's *Odyssey* (books 13–22).

l. 30 **a'bhan-dia**: Athene, daughter of Zeus and protector of Ulysses/Odysseus.

126 *Ar Blàr Catha*

35: 5ᵛ–7, 1945.
P33: II/3: 2–5, March 1946.
22: 162ᵛ–161ᵛ, 1946?
C: 26–9, 1952.
21: 57–60, 1974.
33: 26–7, 1983.

Date: 2 December 1945, Italy (**35**).

Note the following from a war-time article by Hay (1942):

> Several generations of Scotsmen have fought and pioneered to gain those "colonies and dependencies", and on some few individual Scots they have conferred benefits. But on Scotland as a nation they have brought depopulation and casualty lists, wars and far-off distractions and neglect at home; and it is as a nation that we think today ...
>
> We have helped to enslave others for long, and in doing so have come near to enslaving ourselves. We have won dependencies, and reduced our own land to a place among them. We have sweated to develop Africa and Asia and have hewn farms from the forests of Canada, leaving Assynt and the Gorbals, the bracken-covered townships and the vennels, to become a shame and a danger to us as a nation. We are going to give up such folly.

ll. 13–14: in 1631, Mackay troops, led by the 1st Lord Reay, joined the Protestant army of Gustavus Adolphus of Sweden in the Thirty Years' War. Scots mercenaries had long been part of the Royal Household Guard of France, and their status in the *Maison du Roi* was formalised by Louis XIV; Jacobite regiments were also recruited to the French army under Louis XV.

127 *Forerunners*

35: 7v, 1946.
36: letter of 27 Aug. 1946.
22: 145v, 1946?
B: 15, 1948.
P17: Oct. 1968; first verse only ("The Morning Star").
H: 81, 1970.

Date: 9 January 1946, Greece (**35**). The poem seems, however, to have had much earlier beginnings, in the following verses from the late 1930s (Source 2: 37v):

> *An Réalt Aonarach* [*The Solitary Star*]
>
> The solitary star, convenient to the dawn,
> that heralds the light to come in no uncertain way,
> proclaims to night the midday sun – thereupon,
> the shadows vanquished, yields to approaching day.
>
> Absorbed in the dawning rays they prophesied,
> lost in the later light, in seams astray,
> how many prophet souls have justified
> the prognostications they made concerning the day.

128 *Grey Ashes*

8: 4r, 1946; three lines only.
35: 8v, 1946.
36: letter of 27 Aug. 1946.
B: 28, 1948.
H: 79, 1970.
30: 28, 1980s.

Date: 10 January 1946 (**35**).

129 *The White Licht ...*

35: 7v–8, 1946.
20: 26, letter to Catherine Hay of 13 Jan. 1946.
B: 30–1, 1948.
P22: 4, 37–8, 1949.
H: 92–3, 1970.
30: 30–1, 1980s.

Date: 10 January 1946 (**35**).

l. 5 **Hymettus**: mountain in Attica, east of Athens.

130 *Oor Jock*

8: 4r, 1946; five lines only.
35: 9, 1946; eight lines remaining.
B: 25, 1948.

H: 88, 1970.
30: 25, 1980s.
Date: 12 January 1946, Greece (**35**).

131 *Kailyard and Renaissance*

35: 9–10, 1946; includes four extra lines.
B: 26–8, 1948.
30: 26–8, 1980s.

Date: 13 January 1946, Greece (**35**).

Title: the parochial literature of the Kailyard was a great *bête noire* of Hugh MacDiarmid's Scottish Renaissance movement.

l.27 **Spender**: the English poet Stephen Spender (1909–95)?

l. 44: this line is followed in **35** by:

> Scotland mine, kind fate defend her
> frae the like o draggin' Spender;
> but soop her clean, as wert, o asses
> biggin Kailyairds on Parnassus!

l. 75 **Lauder**: Harry Lauder, music-hall comedian (1870–1950), author of "Roamin in the Gloamin".

132 *Achmhasain*

35: 12, 1946.
37: folder (2), 1946.
P26: 236: 5, April 1946.
20a: 118, 1946? revised c. 1969.
20b: 94, 1969.
56: Feb. 1969; see P6 2/2: 4, Spring 1969.
21: 77–8, 1974.

Date: 3 February 1946, Greece (**35**).

l. 11 **measan** (messan): "Perhaps you had better gloss *messan*. It is a Gaelic word, borrowed by Scots, and means a lap-dog or a pet dog" [**56**]. The word was inserted in 1969, replacing "galla" ("bitch").

133 *Feachd a' Phrionnsa*

35: 12v–13, 1946.
P33: III/1: 14–15, Sept. 1946.
P14: XLIV/6: 82, June 1949.
C: 20–1, 1952.
H: 100–1, 1970.
21: 52–3, 1974.
33: 20–1, 1983.

Date: 1 March 1946, Greece (**35**). The poem may have been prompted by the impending bicentenary of the battle of Culloden (4 April).

Note the following reference to the '45 in Hay's unpublished essay "An untapped source of Scottish history":

> and the last campaign, which rocked the throne of Britain – *Bliadhna Theàrlaich* or the '45, culminating in military defeat and spiritual victory. If, as Goethe says, "what is to live in song must go under in life", the people who met their most crushing setback in arms on Culloden Moor are indeed likely to live in literature for ever – and live in life too as a resurgent people in their own country. (Hay 1946a: 128)

134 Still Gyte, Man?

8: 4r, 1946; two lines only.
35: 13v–14, 1946.
36: letter of 27 Aug. 1946.
B: 29, 1948.
P22: 4: 34, 1949.
H: 83, 1970.

Date: 30 March 1946, Greece (**35**).

135 Esta Selva Selvaggia   This Savage Wood

8a: 4, 1945–6; embryonic draft.
8b: 25v–26, 1946.
35: 40v–43 and 37v, 1946.
P29:3: 16–19, Spring 1947.
B: 20–4, 1948.
30: 20–4, c. 1983.

Date: March–April 1946? The poem was sent for publication on 12 April (Source 8: 23v).

Title: from Dante's *Inferno* [**B**]. See Canto 1, 4–6:

> Ahi quanto a dir qual era è cosa dura
> esta selva selvaggia e aspra e forte
> che nel pensier rinova la paura.

Ah, how painful it is to speak | of this wood, so savage and harsh and brutal, | and the very thought of which rekindles my fear.

l. 29 **Bou Arâda**: town in north Tunisia, 50 km west of Zaghouan.

l. 33 **Bofors**: anti-aircraft gun.

l. 35: "Bastard, there's what you've done!"

l. 41 **Folgore**: an Italian division, destroyed in Africa, reformed as the Nuova Folgore to fight against the Germans in Italy. [**P23** and **B**]

l. 43 **Ostia!**: "(by the Sacred) Host!" [**B**]

l. 46 **I Fridolin**: Italian nickname for the Germans. [**B**]

l. 53: "Damn it! These native gentlemen ..."

l. 60 **Fransâwi**: A Frenchman. [**B**]

ll. 65–86: this passage is in the terzina scheme of Dante's entire *Commedia* (tercets of interlocking rhymes: aba, bcb, cdc etc.).

l. 66 **Capo d'Orso**: a promontory on the north-east tip of Sardinia weathered in the silhouette of a bear.

l. 84 **perduta gente**: the "lost people" of Dante's *Inferno*. Cf. the Gaelic "Cho caillte ris an Diabhul"– as lost as the devil. [**P23** and **B**] See *Inferno*, Canto 3, 1–3.

l. 93 **Poverini!**: poor little things! [**B**]

ll. 95–7: "House destroyed – house finished – destroyed – get it? – family. Everything's destroyed. Get it?"

ll. 101–3: note the following quotes from Hay's notebook (Source 7, 12r):

El-kebâr y 'amlu el-harb, mush i enha. Fi-sh-shâm keînn kullhum ki-wahed. (Hussein Dey)
Noi siamo ignoranti, e non abbiamo voluto la guerra. Sono stati i signori a farla. I signori sono istruiti, non vogliono star tranquilli. (Sant Antonio)
Se dichiarano la guerra ancora una volta i popoli dovrebbero ammazzare i governi ed' abbracciarsi ... (Salerno)

The big shots make war, it'll never end. In wickedness [?] they are all as one. (Hussein Dey) Transl. Y. Dutton.
We're uneducated folk, and we never wanted war. It's the masters who waged war. The masters are educated, they won't stay at peace. (Sant Antonio)
If they declare war one more time, the people should kill off their governments and embrace each other. (Salerno).

ll. 102–8 **I pezzi grossi**: the big knobs. [**B**] **gros bonnets**: big shots. **el-kebâr bass**: only the great. [**B**] **Halûf!**: pig! [**B**] Βουλγαρικό σκυλί! (Boulgarikó skulí): Bulgarian dog! [**B**] **Cretini 'e merda!**: filthy cretins! [**B**] Βρωμεροί (Bromeroí): stinkers! [**B**] Τα Μακαρόνια (Ta Makarónia): the Macaronis. [**B**] **N'âd dîn bâbak!**: curse the faith of your father! [**P23**] **salauds**: bastards. **Jene Scheissherrn!**: Shits, all of them!

ll. 104–9: note Hay's remarks in a letter of 7 March 1945 (Source 36):

The most depressing thing of all is this. You meet individual Frenchmen and Arabs, and individual Italians and Greeks who are charming, or fine men, or put it how you like. You become friends with them, exchange addresses and so on – you know "Après la guerre vous devez faire une visite chez moi. C'est obligatoire ça", or "Ba'd et trad lâzem tjûz 'alîna, ya khûya", or "Verrai vederci dopo la guerra, nevvero?" or "Μετά τόν πόλεμον θά φιλοξενῶ σε στο σπίτι". I can hear them all saying it. Then you observe that the Frenchman loathes the Arab and detests the Italian, that the Arab hates the Italian and the Frenchman, that the Italian thinks the Arabs are animals while the Greek has it in for the Italian. "Je ne peux pas les voir, ces Macaronis-là", "Non possiamo vederli, quei Francesi. Ce l'hanno con moi!" Yet all the individuals are too damned good to get knocked over the head for the sake of old feuds. It's very distressing.

He had previously remarked on English xenophobia (Source 36, 3 May 1944):

I can't imagine a more cosmopolitan place than the seaboard of North Africa. You have to study people individually and figure out what they are … You certainly find a vast number of pleasant people wherever you go, though curiously enough the average English soldier in his ignorance seems to find nothing but crowds of "dirty bastards", who are much inferior to him in every respect, wherever his masters order him to go.

136 *Truaighe na h-Eòrpa*

22: 128v, 1946?
P33: III/1: 16–17, Sept. 1946.
P14: XLV/3: 46, March 1950.
C: 19, 1952.
21: 51–2, 1974.
J: 122–3, 1976.
33: 19, 1983.

Date: 1946? (from first mention in List 8, and thematic links with Poem 135 "Esta Selva Selvaggia").

l. 4: I have emended Hay's published translation of this line, which corresponded to an earlier version.

POEMS 1946–1958

137 *An t-Iasgair*

26: ix, 1946?; three lines only.
35: 21v, 1946.
36: letter of 27 Aug. 1946.
22: 136v, 1946?
P14: XLII/1: 6, Oct. 1946.
20: 35, 1947?
C: 30, 1952.
P18: Spring 1972: 20.
21: 61, 1974.
33: 30, 1983.

Date: August 1946, Tarbert (**35**).

l. 13 **a dhuine**: a common phrase, but one which may have had a particular reso-
nance for Hay, being one of the Gaelic expressions still heard in Tarbert English
(see the words and phrases listed in NLS MS 26747: 1).

138 *The Fisherman*

35: 19v–20r, 1946.
20: 35, 1947?
B: 15, 1948.
H: 80, 1970.
30: 15, c. 1983.

Date: August 1946, Tarbert (**35**).

As indicated in **30**, this is an adaptation of Poem 137 "An t-Iasgair".

139 *Bloigh Eadailteach*

7: 39, 1946.
20a: 48, 1946?
20b: 126, 1975?
P1: 11/31: 8, Aug. 1976.

Date: 1946. Text **7** is among drafts for Poem 109 "Mochtàr is Dùghall".

The piece is based on three lines of Petrarch's First Sestina (Le Rime XXII):

> Con lei foss'io da che si parte il sole
> e non ci vedess'altri che le stelle,
> sol una notte, e mai non fosse alba!

rendered thus by Hay in his English version of the sestina (**B**: 65):

> Were I but with her from the setting sun,
> and nothing else to see us but the stars,
> one night, one night never to know a dawn!

140 Tlachd is Misneach

35: 21v–22r, 1946.
22: 136v, 1946?
C: 31–2, 1952.
21: 62–3, 1974.
33: 31–2, 1983.
Date: August 1946, Tarbert (**35**).

141 Pleasure and Courage

35: 19, 1946.
B: 18–19, 1948.
H: 85, 1970.
30: 18–19, c. 1983.
Date: August 1946, Tarbert (**35**).

As indicated in **30**, this is an adaptation of Poem 140 "Tlachd is Misneach".

142 Stoc is Failleanan

35: 21r–20v, 1946.
36: letter of 15 Sept. 1946.
P14: XLII/3: 38, Dec. 1946.
C: 33–4, 1952.
P18: March 1968: 4.
21: 63–4, 1974.
33: 33, 1983.
Date: 12 September 1946 (**36**).

In **33**, Hay appended the dedication "Do Tholl a' Cheiligh", and in Source 32 the poem is glossed: "Ghearr iad na craobhan uile aig Toll a' Cheiligh etc.?" ("They cut all the trees at Toll a' Cheiligh etc.?").

143 Old Stump and Young Shoots

35: 22v–23, 1946.
36: letter of 15 Sept. 1946.
P19: 7/7: 7, Oct. 1946.
B: 33, 1948.
H: 93, 1970.

Date: 14 September 1946, Tarbert (**35**).

As indicated in **36**, **B** and **J**, this is an adaptation of Poem 142 "Stoc is Failleanan".

144 *Scots Arcadia*

35: 23, 1946.
P33: III/3: 17, March 1947.
B: 2–3, *1948*.
H: 91, 1970.
30: 2–3, c. 1983.
15: 10r, 1983; first verse only.

Date: 22 September 1946 (**35**).

145 *We Abide For Ever*

35: 23v–24, 1946.
20a: 25, 1946?
20b: 57, 1946?
P19: 8/6: 95, Oct. 1947.
P26: 74: 8, May 1977.

Date: October 1946, Tarbert (**35**).

l. 30: the line alludes to two poems in the anthology *Modern Scottish Poetry* (Lindsay 1946). In one poem, G. S. Fraser takes MacDiarmid to task for his Celticist concerns:

> What a race has is always crude and common,
> And not the human or the personal:
> I would take sword up only for the human,
> Not to revive the broken ghosts of Gael.
>
> (ibid.: 115)

This last phrase was quoted by Hay in an article of the same period:

> We want a Scotland where there is no rotten and rotting defeatism about the Highlands, where no poet can talk of "the broken ghosts of Gael" and where our Gaelic heritage is not left to moulder in obscurity. The Gael is not broken, nor is his culture a dying culture, sorely though it has been tried, and here is the answer in Gaelic to the premature bewailers of his disappearance: ... [quote from Poem 124 "Meftah Bâbkum es-Sabar?"]. (Hay 1946b: 17)

The second poem is a warmer tribute to MacDiarmid by Maurice Lindsay, who praises the doyen for his refutal of romantic perceptions of Scotland:

> You have put that contemptuous nonsense back in its place,
> and are no longer concerned with the rotting shielings
> and the dreary, crumbling dust of a vanished race ...
>
> (Lindsay 1946: 134)

Hay was to cite the offending phrases again the following year in a spirited apologia:

"We haven't noticed it, but can it really be so? Are we doomed or dying out, the broken ghosts of a vanished race?" (Hay 1947c: 104).

146 *Una Più Crudel del Mare* One More Cruel than the Sea

35: 24v, 1946.
20: 53, 1940s?
P19: 7/9: 11, Dec. 1946.
10: 39r, 1981.
Date: October 1946, "above Seanlagan" (**35**).

Title: from the eighteenth-century reworking by Francesco Berni of Matteo Boiardo's fifteenth-century chivalrous epic *Orlando Innamorato* (Book I, Canto XXIX, verse 6), read by Hay in July 1945 (Source 7: 58v). Since Boiardo's text and Berni's version are substantially different, I have dropped Boiardo's name from the title: in the medieval poem, the dame is more cruel than a bear.

147 *The Two Neighbours*

35: 26v–27r, 1946.
20: 69, 1946–7?
P17: 56/127: 215, March 1948.
G: 299, 1966.
Date: 4 November 1946 (**35**).

This poem was to have been included in *Wind on Loch Fyne*, but it was taken out by Hay in view of its impending publication in Source P17, and to allow the late addition of Poem 158 "Seeker, Reaper" (NLS Acc. 5000/448, and letter from Catherine Hay to F. G. Scott). The poem was set to music by F. G. Scott.

Title: glossed in **35** "MacCaig and Calum". Archibald MacCaig and Calum Johnson worked at the ring-net fishing as "neighbours" (i.e. as a boat pair). Hay worked on Calum's boat "Liberator" most Septembers in the 1930s; MacCaig's boat was the "Seònaid" (see Martin 1984: 56). Calum Johnson died on 25 April 1944.

148 *Na Casan air Tìr*

C: 43, 1952.
21: 70, 1974.
33: 43, 1983.
Date: **33** has "An Tairbeart '46", but the poem's absence from both Source 35 and List 8 suggests that 1947–8 is a more likely date.

l. 2 **croich (crochan)**: the Gaelic word "crochan" was used in Tarbert English for the "stance" or net-pole, on which nets would be hung to dry. (See Martin 1981: 126; and Hay's notes for the *Historical Dictionary of Scottish Gaelic*.)

l. 7 **gealbhan**: the normal word for a hearth-fire in Tarbert Gaelic, according to Hay, "teine" being used of bigger conflagrations (SSS 1979).

ll. 15–16, 17–18 **losgadh**: the "burning" (in Tarbert English), the sea phosphorescence that reveals the presence of herring at night.   **coltas**: "appearance", a sign of the presence of herring. (See notes to Poem 173.)

l. 29 **crann cèille**: the term is found in the sixteenth-century poem "Caismeachd Ailean nan Sop", and glossed as "helm" in Sinclair 1898: 24–6.

149 Ardlamont

B: 3, 1948.
H: 91, 1970.

Date: Autumn 1947? The absence of any other sources suggests that this poem was one of the late additions to *Wind on Loch Fyne* sent to the publisher in October 1947 (see NLS Acc. 5000/465).

150 Fàire

20: 46–7, 1947.
C: 35–6, 1952.
H: 96–7, 1970.
21: 64–6, 1974.
33: 35–6, 1983.

Date: 20 August 1947, Lochgilphead (where Hay had been hospitalised since November 1946) (**20** and **C**).

33 has the dedication: "Do Chalum MacIain, For Malcolm Johnson".

151 The Smoky Smirr o Rain

P12: 16 Oct. 1947: 4.
B: 9, 1948.
P22: 4: 36, 1949.
P18: Feb. 1969, 7.
H: 77, 1970.
30: 9, c. 1983.

Date: 1947? From the absence of references to the poem, it is unlikely that it long pre-dates its first published appearance. It may have been one of the late additions to *Wind on Loch Fyne* sent to the publisher in October 1947 (see NLS Acc. 5000/465). The poem was set to music by F. G. Scott.

See Poem 368 for Hay's expansion of the poem in the 1980s.

152 Am Faillean Ùr

19: 1, 1947; first verse and melody.
58: Musical MS: 1, 1947; as **19**.
C: 39, 1952.
32: 39, 1960s?
21: 67, 1974.
33: 39, 1983.

Date: 20 October 1947, Tarbert (**19** and **32**). The melody is dated 1937 (**19**).

153 The Fresh Sapling

50: 23, 1947.
20a: 51, 1947.
19: 1, 1947; first verse and melody.
58: Musical MS: 1, 1947; as **19**.
11: 19, 1976.
20b: 130, 1976–7.
P25: 17, 55, Summer 1977.

Date: c. November 1947. The poem post-dates its Gaelic model "Am Faillean Ùr", and was sent to Maurice Lindsay for publication (**50**) on 27 November.

154 Edinburgh

P12: 14 Nov. 1947: 4.
B: 32, 1948.
30: 32, c. 1961.
H: 76, 1970.

Date: 1947? From the absence of references to the poem, it is unlikely that it long pre-dates its first published appearance. It may have been one of the late additions to *Wind on Loch Fyne* sent to the publisher in October 1947 (see NLS Acc. 5000/465).

l. 16: this line, initially used in Poem 17 "A' Chas air Tìr", also appears in a Scots fragment of c. 1946 (Source 7: 24v).

155 The Walls of Balclutha

8: 26v, c. 1946; five-line draft.
20a: 58, 1947; ll. 102–32.
20b: 59–61, 1947.
P12: 26 Dec. 1947; ll. 34–51.
47: folder 7, 1947?; published in Chapman 21, March 1978.
20c: 79, 1972; ll. 102–9 and 115–26.
P26: 14: 12, May 1972; as **20c**.

Date: October 1947, Tarbert (**20b**). Hay seems to have lost or forgotten about the poem, found one page of it (**20a**) in 1972 and then rediscovered the entire text in 1977–8.

Title: from MacPherson's *The Works of Ossian* (1765). In "Carthon", Fingal mourns the destruction of Balclutha, the great stronghold by the Clyde:

> I have seen the walls of Balclutha, but they were desolate. The fire had resounded in the halls; and the voice of the people is heard no more. The stream of Clutha was removed from its place by the fall of the walls. The thistle shook, there, its lonely head: the moss whistled to the wind. (Gaskill 1996: 128)

In his serialised essay on "Scots Gaelic poetry", Hay wrote:

> I used to revel in MacPherson, having been taken in by him; now I don't believe him, but I still like him. He was a true Scotsman, a man of great influence abroad who did no good to his own country. (Hay 1940–1, 1: 7)

ll. 7–12: the image may derive from nights at the fishing, but a creative spark could also have been struck by a war-time diary entry of October 1940:

> It was about five on a fresh morning with a clear starry sky. All over the sky to S.W. was a great orange reddish low, pulsing, burning brighter & fading, & very pale grey smoke going up through it like a curtain. Over it a fleecy cloud about the size of a fist drifted up from the S.W. growing bigger and turning pink and orange. East of it straddled Orion, not standing quite square, but with his westerly foot raised a little off the ground, as if he were about to stamp and say "To hell with all that folly". Small wonder the low was a rich colour. At the time burning whisky was running down the streets and people were scooping it up, some with buckets it is said. A distillery was burnt out, and three blocks of tenements wrecked. (Source 5: 29v)

This may have led to the draft in **8**:

> Small wonder [   ]
> Orion striding over Bute
> spurns the earth with his northward foot
> To wake that flame that, smothered, still
> is sleeping somewhere in the Gael.

ll. 34–51: published (**P12**) under the title "Ways Grown Silent".

ll. 102–9, 115–26: Hay seems to have rediscovered the stray page **20a** with these lines (and a handwritten draft of ll. 110–14) in 1972, and revamped them under the title "Renascence" (**20c** and **P26**).

ll. 129–32: this last paragraph of sheet **20a**, unused for "Renascence", seems to have formed the basis for Poem 221 "Orion Over Bute".

156 [*Then Farewell, Tarbert*]

19: 1, 1947; first verse and melody.
58: Musical MS: 1, 1947; as **19**.
20a: 49, c. 1947; first verse.
20b: 76, 1977.
P1: 13/37: 82, April 1978.

Date: October 1947, Tarbert (**19** and **58**). Although there are no early texts of the entire poem, the absence of any drafts in Hay's notebooks from the 1970s makes it unlikely that the song was substantially expanded for publication in 1977 (**20b** and **P1**).

This may be the song referred to by Hay in a letter of 6 December 1947 to Mrs F. G. Scott:

> I sent a couple of songs to the BBC, one in the language of Tarbert, which is neither Scots, English or Gaelic, but all three. God knows whether they'll find anyone with tastes low enough to sing it. It's all about catching herring. Maybe the Fishery Board would like it for their "Eat More Herring" campaign.

l. 5 **neebor**: the sister-boat; the ring-net method of fishing required boats to work in pairs.

157   *Na Trèig do Thalamh Dùthchais*

7: 33, c. 1946?; three lines only.
P33: 4/2: 20–1, Dec. 1947.
C: *37–8, 1952.*
21: 66–7, 1974.

Date: 1947, Tarbert (Source 33).

158   *Seeker, Reaper*

9a: 4v, 11–13r.
9b: 5, 1947?
20: 59v, 61v, 60v, 1947; ll. 1–40 missing.
58: 1947.
B: 34–40, 1948.
30: 34–40, emendations from c. 1961 and c. 1983.
7: 44v, 1972; four lines.

Date: November 1947 (NLS Acc. 5000/448, letter of 26 November 1947). In his letter to Ainslie Thin of Oliver & Boyd Publishers, Hay writes: "I am enclosing a poem which I wrote a few days ago for your consideration. It has to my mind more drive in it than most of the work in the book." Composition of the poem had been rapid, according to Catherine Hay:

> Personally I've been specially interested in the reaction to "Seeker, Reaper". This poem, like many of the more recent ones, was done straight onto the typewriter without notes, or a note of any sort, and commenced and completed in a matter of hours. (ibid./509, January 1949)

On hearing that "Seeker, Reaper" had been accepted for *Wind on Loch Fyne*, Hay wrote:

> It is pleasant news to hear that "Seeker, Reaper" is to be included, for I wouldn't like the age, melancholy and death of "Calum Thonder", "The Old Fisherman" and "The Two Neighbours" to be the over-riding notes sounded by the Loch Fyne poems. There are young fishermen too, who like their vaunt about a boat that is "a hawk and a tramper". The old wild dynamism of the Highlands is still there, but, to our impoverishment, seldom expressed. (ibid./448, 2 December 1947)

Text **58** gives some clarifications of stress-fall, included below.

Title: the poem may have been prompted in part by a Loch Fyne skiff, the "Sireadh" ("Seeking"), noticed by Hay in the 1930s (Martin 1988: 8). Hay himself found it "hard to say" whether or not the title of his poem derived from that skiff, but agreed that "Sireadh" might have had a suggestive function (SSS, November 1980).

l. 3: ... rídd mád tie stert [**58**].

l. 9 **afore**: **B** has "before"; I have changed it to the reading in **58** (in line with the correction made in **30**) for consistency with the five other occurrences.

l. 22: she séts her stérn doón ... [**58**].

ll. 63–4: the first line originally read "when the low long ships from Norway", but was changed when the Norse passage was temporarily deleted (see note below). On examining the galley proofs, Catherine Hay wrote:

> the original ... I think refers to a definite incident and the following verse with Norse words seems to bear this out. George, I think, was alluding to the time when the Norse under Haakon were claiming all the Western Isles. In his desire to add Kintyre to these, he sailed down the west of Kintyre, rounded the Mull, then slipped up the shore to Tarbert where he landed. He then had his ships drawn across the isthmus to West Loch Tarbert, thus encircling Kintyre and adding it to those other possessions round which he could sail his ships. (NLS Acc. 5000/484, 3 May 1948)

In 1972, Hay again changed l. 63, to "when Norway's sails o ridd and white" (**7**).

ll. 65–84: This passage was deleted at Oliver & Boyd's suggestion (NLS Acc. 5000/484, 1 December 1947). In accepting the deletion, Hay commented:

> I don't think the loss of the Norse will be a serious one, for most of the readers wouldn't be able to pronounce it or get the rhythm. With the Gaelic it's a different story. (ibid./448, 2 December 1947)

Three weeks later, however, he asked that Oliver & Boyd reinstate the Norse passage after all.

l. 65 **Miklagarth**: the "muckle city" was Constantinople, successfully attacked and forced into trading links by the Vikings early in the tenth century. **Skarp-hethinn**: "parched hide", the name of a hero in the Icelandic *Njals Saga*.

l. 188: she's a skýline-raiser, skýline-sinker, hulldówn horízon-crósser [**58**].

l. 194: in **30**, this line is preceded by two new lines drafted in **7**:

> She's a glisk, she's a glint, she's a glimpse, she's a glimmer;
> She's a seeker, she's a reaper o the silver-shoal-swimmer.

l. 196: she's a dánce-stép-túrner, she's a bróad-wáke-scórer [**58**].

l. 198: When the bíg long seas come ón lik wálls, cóld-whíte-heíded [**58**].

159 *Spring Here Northaway*
58: 1947 (see Source 20: 65–6 for carbon copy).
10: 37–9, 1981.

Date: 1947; **58** was sent to F. G. Scott in late November or early December (letter to Mrs Scott of 6 December 1947).

Title: Hay added a couplet to the title in **10**:

> The rallyoch ranter frae the northwest
> skirls awa an' blaws his best.

160 *Triùir an Earraich* *The Spring Three*
58: 1947.

Date: 1947; text **58** was sent to F. G. Scott in late November or early December (letter to Mrs Scott of 6 December 1947).

161 *Solan*
20: 67, 1947.
40: Folder 35 (published in Akros 11/32, Dec. 1976).

Date: 1947 (from paper and typeface of **20**, stylistic affinities with Poem 158 "Seeker, Reaper", and biographical circumstances).

The poem is in the dialect of Tarbert, Loch Fyne. [**40**]

162 *Smile and Go By*
P12: 9 Jan. 1948: 4.

Date: 1947?

163 *Feadag Ghòrach an t-Slèibhe* *The Daft Hill Plover*
20a: 69, 1947?
P12: 22 Jan. 1948: 4.
20b: 91, 1970s.
20c: 96, 1970s.
10: 36r, 1981.

Date: 1947? The poem must pre-date Hay's entry to hospital at the beginning of 1948.

Title: a Gaelic air (MacDonald 1895: 51).

164 *The Nerra Boat*
20a: 70, 1947.
20b: 76, 1977.
P1: 13/37: 81, April 1978.

Date: 1947; the poem must pre-date Hay's entry to hospital at the beginning of 1948, and is cited in List 20 with poems of October 1947.

165 *Flooer o the Gean*

P19: 9/1: 15, April 1948; seven verses only.
G: 583–5, 1966.

Date: 1947; the poem must pre-date Hay's entry to hospital at the beginning of 1948, and is cited in List 20 with poems of October 1947.

The poem was inspired by the popular Italian *stornello* rhyme, an example of which Hay noted down during the war (Source 7: 19r):

> Fiore di pepe
> io giro intorno a voi, come fa l'ape
> che gira intorno al fiore della siepe.

> *Flower of the pepper, | I circle round you, as the bee does | which circles round the flower of the hedge.*

(Further examples can be found in Warrack 1925.)

ll. 29–34: these two verses may have been added in the 1960s; they are metrically closer than the other verses to the Italian models.

166 *The Crew of the Shelister*

20a: 49, 1947–8?
20b: 56, 1947–8?
22: 65–70, 1947–8?; with story.

Date: 1947–8? The story and poem were broadcast by the Home Service on "Children's Hour", 2 September 1948.

l. 2 **shelister boat**: in the preliminary to his story Hay explains:

> On the West coast of Scotland – especially in Argyllshire – children make little boats from the broad, green flags of the shelister, or the wild iris as they call it in England. The shelisters aren't hard to find, for they grow thick on the damp, grassy patches at the head of the little bays that face the south and the sun. (**22**: 65)

l. 10 **neebor**: the neighbour boat:

> "Some of you go and fell a big shelister, and I will see to building you a boat, and a neighbour boat to go with her, since you must always fish in pairs in these parts." (**22**: 67)

ll. 15–16 **burnin', crepped**:

> And so they set out at sundown, one summer evening, sailing along the lip of the tide, watching the bright "burning", which is what they call the summer phosphorescence in the sea away west on Loch Fyne side. To startle the fish, they "crepped the anchor", as we say. That is, they brought it down with a loud bang on the gunnel. And so they went, banging away with the anchor and watching the "burning" for signs of fish. In the end, close on midnight, they saw fish glowing below them, out went the pigmy fathoms of spider's web over the stern, and in half an hour the hold was full and the torches lit. (**22**: 68)

l. 27 **syle**: tiny immature herring.

167 [*Gone and Gane*]

5: 36v, 1982.
15: 1r, 1983.

Date: 1948 (**15**).

In both sources, the verse is used to head Hay's attempted Collected Edition.

168 *Madame, a Monte Casino*

P33: V/3: 15, June 1949.

Date: 1949? Catherine Hay wrote to F. G. Scott on 26 July 1949:

> For the first time a letter came from him a few days ago. ... [He] said that he'd been too busy writing poems to find time for letter writing and he mentioned that he had sent a war poem to Mr. Grieve [Hugh MacDiarmid, editor of Source P33].

The absence of the poem from any extant sources or lists suggests that it was a recent work rather than one dating from the war.

With no surviving glosses by Hay, this poem is the only obscure work in his corpus. "Monte Casino" may be an error for "Monte Cassino", an unlikely mistake for Hay or MacDiarmid to make; or a pun may be intended (*casino*: "brothel" or "shambles"). The poem is signed "Denostene", presumably a misprint for "Demostene", the Athenian orator (384–322 BC) who dedicated much of his political life to resisting the rise of Macedonian power.

169 *Fear Breacain Bhallaigh*

27: 91–3, endpages and backpaste, 1950?

Date: 1950?, from the very distinctive calligraphy that Hay employed at this period (see his letter of October 1950, Source 36). Catherine Hay wrote to Young:

> He employs a good deal of time writing – mainly in Gaelic, but I don't know what the quality of this may be. I am trying my best to type it all out but it is rather difficult (partly owing to difficult writing) and I can do very little at a time. (Source 36, 23 October 1950)

In the accompanying letter, Hay himself wrote:

> Things have permitted me to do quite a lot of writing, although scattered, which is often the post-war manner. (Odd lines from air-raids and barrages, and so forth.) Quite a lot of the songs from Bráigh Chinntíre have come to my memory ...

The poem is an expansion of a traditional song; Hay returned to this kind of composition in the 1980s.

ll. 1–13: these lines are found in MacPherson (1868: 128–9).

ll. 15–23 **le**: Hay seems to writes "lè".

170 *The Sun over Athens*
P23: IV/11: 31–3, Summer 1957.

Date: 1957? There is no firm evidence to date this poem. It must however post-date December 1947 when Hay cited "[What Song Is Ours]" as his only attempt hitherto at using the Anglo-Saxon alliterative metre, which "The Sun over Athens" imitates (see commentary to Poem 10).

171 *Cruach Tharsainn 's na h-Oiteagan*
P15: 23: 253, Spring 1958.

Date: 1957–8?

POEMS 1960–1961

Dates: since more precise dating is not possible from the sources, the poems have been ordered by date of publication. The majority, however, probably date to the latter part of 1960, judging from Hay's comment at the end of the year that he was writing a lot ("most of it in Gaelic, some of it in Scots") and in fact had "more than I know what to do with" (Source 54, 31 December 1960).

172 *An t-Anmoch air a' Mhonadh*
43: folder 9; published in Gairm 34, Winter 1960.

l. 2 **càrsan**: the hoarse sound of rising sea and wind [Hay's notes for the *Historical Dictionary of Scottish Gaelic*]. **sa Chaol**: An Caol – Caol Bhranndain [**43**]; Kilbrannan Sound.

173 *Miannan an Tairbeartaich*
(mar gum b'ann le iasgair)
25: 126, 1960; two lines only.
43: folder 9; published in Gairm 34, Winter 1960.
In **43**, Hay glosses the dialectisms and the fishing terms.

l. 2 **steòrnamh**: steòrnadh – agus mar sin air aghaidh. [**43**]

l. 3 **amhsan** (evsan): sùlair [**43**]. **losgamh** (losgadh): teine-sionnachain. Gheibhear sgadan "san losgamh" anns an fhoghar. ["Burning": the phosphorescence by which herring can be caught in the autumn.] [**43**]

l. 4 **coltas**: comharraidhean air sgadan agus, corr uair, air rionnaich, is e sin: a' mhuc-mhara, an t-amhsan, na faoileagan ag obair air uachdar an uisge, ùilleadh èisg air an uisge, "leus" anns an losgadh, agus eile. ["Appearance": signs betraying the presence of herring and sometimes of mackerel, i.e. the whale, the gannet, seagulls busying on the water, fishoil on the water, a glow in the phosphorescence, etc.] [**43**]

l. 6 **goireachan**: faoileagan 'nan sgaoth a' goirsinn 's ag obair air uachdar na mara. [**43**] Further explained to Angus Martin as "a loud noise of birds playing in the water ... Ma grand-aunt was looking out the window and she said 'The birds are making a goireachan on the water'" (SSS 1979).

l. 10 **roithlean**: a capstan-drum. Theirte "An Duine Làidir" ris a' chapstan corr uair – 's e "An Duine Iarainn" a bh'aig Seonaidh Caimbeul air. Tha roithlean a' ciallachadh "a child's hoop" cuideachd. [**43**]

l. 13 **solas-lìn**: an solas a lasas iad air bòrd nuair a bhios an lìon ga thoirt a-staigh. Is e solas leictreach a th'aca a-nis. ["Netlight": the torch lit on board when the net is being hauled in. Now an electric lamp.] [**43**]

Formerly a paraffin lamp known as the "flambeau" (see Martin 1981: 154).

l. 15 **pùt**: am pùt mòr air an druim-àrcan, leitheach slighe eadar an dà cheann deth. Theirear "bù" no "bùi" ris cuideachd, agus ri buoy sam bith. [**43**]   **teachd air aghart**: a' dlùthachadh ri cliathaich a' bhàta, mar a bhios an lìon ga thoirt a-staigh. [**43**] The large buoy halfway down the net-rope "moves forward", that is, moves in on the boat as the net gets hauled in.

l. 17 **steall**: tòrr, mòran. [**43**]

l. 22 **meadainn**: madainn. [**43**]

l. 23 **reòtach** (reòdhtach): lannan sgadain air bàta no air aodach duine gu tiugh. [a frost: herring scales lying thick on the deck or on clothes.] "Tha reòtach oirre (uirre)": tha i còmhdaichte le lannan sgadain. "Is ann tha reòtach an sin": tha lannan sgadain gu tiugh air a' bhàta sin. [**43**]

174   Is Aoibhinn Leam An-diugh na Chì

25: 159, 1960.
43: folder 9; published in Gairm 34, Winter 1960.

Title: from the sixteenth-century poem "Òran na Comhachaig" (The Song of the Owl of Strone), a favourite of Hay's. (See Rankin 1958: 141, or variant in Watson 1918: 256.)

l. 5: perhaps a conscious echo of a line from Alexander MacDonald's nature poem from the 1740s, "Allt an t-Siùcair": "'S tìom dhomh sgur d'an àireamh ...".

l. 8: Theireadh cuid gu maith cumanta Sràid Seòmar An t-Seilich ri Sauchiehall Street, ged a dh'aidicheadh iad gum b'e Sràid Talla An t-Seilich a bu cheirte. [**43**] Hay's note defends his particular Gaelic rendering of "Sauchiehall" as "Sauchiechamber".

175   Bòd Uile

43: folder 9; published in Gairm 34, Winter 1960.

Title: the long vowel of Bòd (and Bòdach) is consistently given by Hay as close (/oː/).

Hay appends the following topographical notes:

l. 1 **A' Phutag**: Buttock Point. Ceann tuath Eilein Bhòid [north tip of Bute].   **Toll Chalum**: Glencallum Bay, aig ceann deas an eilein [at the south tip of the island].

l. 2 **Na Lagain**: The Laggans, beagan mu thuath air Rubha Dubh. Fìor dhroch acarsaid leis na balbhagan mòra a th'air a' ghrunnd. [A terrible landing-point, due to the boulders on the sea-floor.]   **Rubha Dubh**: Blackfarland Point mu choinneimh Thaigh na Bruaiche [opposite Tighnabruaich].

l. 3 **Roinn Chlòimheach**: aig ceann deas an eilein, faisg air Rubha Nan Eun [on the south tip of the island, near Birds Point]. [OS Roinn Clùmhach, on the south-east coast].   **Rubha Bòdach**: air cladach tuath an eilein, mu choinneimh baile Chaol An t-Snàimh [on the island's north shore, opposite Colintraive].

618

176 Sreathan Mearachdach

43: folder 9; published in Gairm 34, Winter 1960.

Title: Tha an ceathramh am mearachd a chionn gu bheil a leithid de nithean agus lìonadh is tràghadh ann. [The quatrain is in error because there exist such things as ebb and flow.] [**43**]

Hay glosses the dialectal features:

l. 1 **Cheiligh**: Choilich. [**43**]

l. 3 **glideachamh**: glideachadh. [**43**]   **oiread**: uiread. [**43**]

l. 4 **Flòraidh Mhòr**: corra-ghritheach. [**43**]

177 An Tìde Àbhaisteach

25: backpaste, 1960.
43: folder 9; published in Gairm 34, Winter 1960.

l. 3 **na tacain**: tha sin na chomharradh air gailleann a bhith tighinn [a sign of impending storm] [**43**]. See Martin (1981: 176) for an associated Gaelic saying remembered by Hay.

178 Cnapadal is Tìrean Ciana Eile

43: folder 9; published in Gairm 34, Winter 1960.

179 Dà Thaobh na Maoile

25: 73, 1960.
43: folder 9; published in Gairm 34: 138, Winter 1960.

Title: note the Gaelic proverb "Tha dà thaobh air a' mhaoil", "the mull has two sides" (Nicolson 1996: 397).

l. 1: **Rubha Rèidh**: a prominent landmark in Gairloch. Its light could be seen from anywhere on the Minch (my thanks to Iain Fraser).

180 An Druim-àrcan 's an t-Ìochdar

25a: 192–5, 1960.
25b: 197–8, 1960.

Date: context **25**.

The entire poem is inscribed in margins. What I have termed **25a** is a jigsaw of lines (single, couplet, quatrain or verse) spread over four pages; **25b** is a complete, verse-numbered draft.

Title: **druim-àrcan**: the back-rope, or floating-rope of the net, lined with corks. **ìochdar**: the sole (bottom of the net) or sole-rope, laden with lead weights.

ll. 1–8: Hauling in the bow-corks had been Hay's job on the "Liberator" in the 1930s. In 1979, explaining his limited knowledge of netting terminology, Hay told Angus Martin: "I was on the corks on the bow ... I was an amateur. They put me in the corks of the bow to keep me safe" (SSS 1979).

l. 2 **rot**: uncertain reading.

l. 22 **sole bheag**: presumably a rope connected to the sole. Hay himself was unsure of its exact meaning, claiming in 1979 that he knew nothing about it, but in a dialect word-list of 1938 he associates the term with *crìoch*, "the joins in a net" or "the edge along the sole" (NLS MS 26747: 3).

ll. 25–32: in 1980, Hay recalled his own duties aboard the "Liberator" as "the bowcorks, and steering till sunset" (SSS, October 1980). I cannot decipher the second word of the verse.

l. 26: **Toll na Muice**: unidentified.

l. 27: **Eilean na Muice**: this may be the isle of Muck, although its usual form is plural: Eilean nam Muc. There is also a tiny island of that name off Erraid on the south-west tip of Mull (OS Landranger sheet 48).

l. 30: **Camas a' Mhùir**: unidentified.

ll. 37–8: from the month of August, shoals could be located by catching their movement in the sea-phosphorescence or "burning".   **losgamh**: dialect form.

l. 43 **drumach**: Tarbert for "a downpour". Hay remembered mentioning the word to Kenneth MacLeod, who suggested a derivation from *trom* ("heavy"), "but I think it's ... a drum, you know, battering on the decks and so on" (SSS 1979).

l. 48 **cnìodaigh**: dialect form of *cnìodaich*.

181   *Là Fhèill Aindreis, 1960*
P26: 352: 2, 10 Dec. 1960.

182   *Ors' a' Bhèist Mhòr ris a' Bhèist Bhig*
P26: 355: 2, 31 Dec. 1960.

A note to the poem, presumably by Hay, explains:

> We think that the reader will be able to deduce that "the big beast" is England, and the little one Scotland. The fact conveyed is, of course, a very elementary one, but it is useful to recall elementary facts, and poetry is very often the place for them.

Note the Gaelic proverb: "A' bhèist as mò ag ithe na bèist' as lugha, 's a' bhèist as lugha 'dèanamh mar a dh'fhaodas i" – "the big beast eating the wee beast, and the wee beast doing what it can" (Nicolson 1996: 2).

l. 13 **gliocas**: *glocas* in **P26**; my thanks to Ronald Black for pointing out that the rhyme scheme demands this correction.

183 Seann Ó Mordha

P26: 356: 4, 7 Jan. 1961.
56: letter of 3 March 1969; published in Catalyst 2/3, Summer 1969.
P18: April 1969: 5.
21: 83, 1974.

Hay wrote to Dodo Neill in **56**:

> I had some hesitations about sending the above to you, hailing as you do from
> Kent, but I really think you will understand and forgive. It was published ...
> about ten years ago, but I think it says something which will bear repeating. If
> you don't like it, scrap it. ... The verses ... are in the style of Iain Lom in a way ...

And in his next letter, of 7 March 1969:

> Lo and behold, what I feared has happened. "Old Moore" has vexed you, and
> I am deeply sorry. What you say about some of the English people who settle
> in Scotland doing more for their country of adoption than do many Scots is
> perfectly true. What "Old Moore" is getting at is the considerable number
> who come up here feeling they have a mission to take over. They do exist, you
> know. They feel they have a sort of "Imperial Mission" within G.B. Don't
> publish "Old Moore", and let's forget the whole thing.

The poem may have been prompted by successive reports during December 1960 in
the *Scots Independent* on emigration figures for the 1950s, such as the following:

> If these figures [of jobs gained and lost in Scotland, 1949–59] are accurate –
> and they are probably too favourable – we have had a net loss of jobs in the
> last ten years of at least 35,000. We can see why in this period ... something
> like 200,000 people have had to emigrate from Scotland – and that is net
> emigration, the English and others who came in having been offset by addi-
> tional Scots forced out. (Source P26: 353, 17 December 1960)

Title: *Old Moore's Almanack* – an annual pamphlet of predictions and horoscopes.

184 Sgeuma Ghlinn Nibheis

P26: 357: 3, 14 Jan. 1961.

On 6 October 1960, the North of Scotland Hydro-Electric Board announced plans
for a £4 million scheme in Glen Nevis involving the flooding and damming of the
natural basin above the Glen, below the Falls of Steall; the electricity generated
would be exported to finance further electrification of the Highlands. (See *The Scots-
man*, 7 October 1960, leader and feature articles, and subsequent letter columns.)

ll. 4–8: a reference to the satirical piece "Gleann-Nibheis" by The Ardgore Bard (see
MacPherson 1868: 45–6):

> Gleann-Nibheis, gleann nan clach,
> gleann sam bi' n gart anmoch;
> gleann cumhang, gleann fàs,
> gleann dubh, fada, fiadhaich, gnàd,
> sam beil sluagh a' mhì-ghnàis –
> gleann ris na chuir Dia a chùl,
> amar sgùrainn an domhain mhòr.

Glen Nevis, the stony glen, | *the glen of evening gloom;* | *a narrow glen, an* *empty glen,* | *a long, black, wild, ugly glen,* | *home of a graceless people –* | *a* *glen that God turned His back on,* | *the dregs-basin of the world.*

185 *Na Giomaich is Brest is Dùn Èideann*

P26: 358: 2, 21 Jan. 1961.

The *Scots Independent* of 17 September 1960 (340), renewing its call for Government protection of the Moray Firth, Minch and Clyde fishing waters and for the establishing of a thirteen-mile fishing limit, featured a report headed "French Lobster Poachers Cause Unemployment":

> The islanders blame the French for the fact that Barra has the heaviest unemployment rate among the Scottish islands ...: "There are twenty French fishing vessels in the area between Barra Head and the butt of Lewis all the time ... [and] some six French vessels fishing regularly on the west side of Barra ... As the fleet sometimes lifts 2000 lobster-pots three times a day in an area 6 miles by 5, you can see how much damage they are doing to our stocks."

The unwillingness of the Scottish Office to take protective action in line with other fishing countries was for years a source of discontent, and seems to be the butt of Hay's satire.

ll. 9–10 **cho bodhar ri gobhar na cairte**: ràdh Ileach [an Islay saying]. [**P26**]

186 *Monadh Dubh Bhràid-Albainn*

P26: 359: 2, 28 Jan. 1961.
20: 93, 1969.
P6: 2/3: 18–19, Summer 1969.
21: 80–1, 1974.

187–188: Gàidhlig is Gèidhlig mu Seach

P14: LVI/2: 16, Feb. 1961.

Hay accompanies the poems with the following notes on Tarbert Gaelic (fragments of which can be found in Source 25: ix, 49, 61, 113):

> "Is crìon a' chùil as na goirear", agus tha na rannan sin a' tighinn bhuamsa as leth Tairbeart Locha Fìne. Thuirt Òbanach rium bho chionn ghoirid gun robh facal mu seach aige den Ghàidhlig 's den Bheurla nuair a chaidh e don sgoil air tùs. Air dòigh a tha car coltach ri sin, bha a' Ghàidhlig riaghailteach agus Gàidhlig Na Tairbeirt le chèile am beul nan daoine. Corr uair theirte *èirigh*, corr uair *ìrigh*, ged nach cuala mi neach riamh ag ràdh ach *ìdhche* (oidhche). Theirte *lèabag* no *leòbag*, mar bu trice *leòbag*, agus theirte *riunnaich, riunnaigh* no *reannaigh*. Fad a bheatha slàn thuirt an aon fhear *Bègh*[1] *A' Chòmhraig* agus *Bàgh Osda* (Ascog Bay). Tha Bàgh Osda thall sa Cheathramh (an Còmhal),

[1] Hay writes "bèagh", and in Poem 188 "bèaghan". These forms lead to confusion of the intended /ɛ:/ with /ia/.

agus, mar sin, gheibheadh e *bàgh* gu riaghailteach, a chionn nach robh e cho eòlach, dùthchasach. Theirte *na balaich* a cheart cho tric ri *na balaigh*, ach is ann annamh a chluinneadh tu *a bhalaich* an àite *a bhalaigh*. A rèir coltais, tha an cleas ceudna aca an Ile. Mhìnich Ileach dhòmhsa mar so e: "Their sinn *dh'èirich mi* mun àm a chaidh seachad, ach their sinn *irich!* mun àm so làthair." Tha dà shreath de òran Ileach a chluinnear mar so:-

> Le ùilleadh na muic-mhara
> chaidh na balaigh air an daoraich. (Corr uair *daoraigh*.)

Agus bho Ileach faodaidh tu cluinntinn:-

> gun chrodh laoigh, gun chaoraigh agam.

An cuid de na sgeulachdan Ìleach, a chruinnich Iain Og a tha air ainmeachadh air an eilean sin, gheobh thu *èiridh*, 's e clò-bhuailte, an àite *èirich*. Bha *oineach* aig bàird an Dàin Dìrich mu'n do bhuail iad air *eineach* a ràdh, agus, cosuil riutha, tha *ceileach* againn an àite *coileach*. Chan ann nar n-aonar a tha sinn, tha fios. An àiteachan air tìr-mòr san Taobh Tuath their iad *go'ail* no *gabhail*. Tha *gabhail* sa Ghàidhlig riaghailtich, agus tha e beagan nas spaideile.

Mac Iain Dheòrsa

"It's a wee nook from which there's not even a cheep", and the following verses come from me on behalf of Tarbert Loch Fyne. An Oban man told me recently that when he first went to school he constantly switched between Gaelic and English. In a fairly similar way, people spoke both standard Gaelic and Tarbert Gaelic.

Hay then gives examples from Tarbert and Islay speech.

189 *Cath Gairbheach*

9: 10v–11r, 1948?
P26: 360: 2, 4 Feb. 1961.

The poem has its origins in a draft from c. the late 1940s (9):

> *Rechtaireacht An Chath Ghairbhigh (1411)*
> [*The Declamation of the Battle of Harlaw*]

> Briseadh madainn latha shalaigh san Chath Ghairbheach,
>   sin na bh' ann, sin na bh' ann.
> Gu dè rinn Iarla Mhàirr anns an Chath Ghairbheach?
>   Gu dè a rinn? gu dè a rinn?
> Roinn e Alba na dà leth 'n Cath Gairbheach –
>   rinn e sin, rinn e sin;
> Gad is slad nan Gaoidheal san Chath Ghairbheach,
>   sin na bh' ann, sin na bh' ann.
> Fuair mi Rolf is Rollo 'n dèidh 'n Chath Ghairbhich,
>   fuair mi sin, fuair mi sin,
> fuair mi maith is saith sa Chaisteal an dèidh 'n Chath Ghairbhigh,
>   fuair mi sin, fuair mi sin;
> fuair mi slaoighteireacht an dèidh 'n Chath Ghairbhigh,
>   fuair mi sin, fuair mi sin.

Nuair a bha sinn san Chath Ghairbheach,
Nuair a bha sinn san Chath Ghairbheach,
  bha mi thall,
  bha mi aig an àm,
bha mi thall ins an Chath Ghairbheach.

The dawn of a dirty day in Harlaw, | *that's what it was, that's what it was.* |
What did the Earl of Marr do at Harlaw? | *What did he do, what did he do?* |
He split Scotland in two halves at Harlaw – | *that he did, that he did;* | *the*
thrashing (?) and the plunder of the Gaels at Harlaw | *that's what it was,*
that's what it was. | *I found Rolf and Rollo after Harlaw* | *that I found, that I*
found, | *I found the noble and the base in the castle after Harlaw* | *that I found,*
that I found, | *I found villainy after Harlaw,* | *that I found, that I found.*

When we were at Harlaw, | *When we were at Harlaw,* | *I was over yonder* | *I*
was there at the time, | *I was over in Harlaw.*

Title: The battle of Harlaw (in Aberdeenshire), fought ostensibly over control of the
earldom of Ross, pitted the invading army of Donald, Lord of the Isles, against the
forces of the Duke of Albany, Regent of Scotland. The battle was inconclusive, with
both sides claiming victory, but the Hebridean army was forced to retreat, and Donald
agreed to keep the peace. Later historians interpreted Donald's aggression as an
attempt to claim the kingship of Scotland, and the battle came to be viewed as an
archetypal Highland–Lowland, Celtic–Norman confrontation.

l. 4: Alexander Stewart, earl of Marr, led the Regent's army at Harlaw.

l. 5: perhaps an allusion to the traditional Gaelic claim to half of Scotland (with the
House of the Harpstrings near Pitlochry marking the centre of the dividing line),
which some bards seemed to associate with Harlaw (e.g. see Mackenzie 1964: 148).
Another tradition links the division of the Scottish kingdom with the earl of Marr's
defeat by a Hebridean army twenty years later at Inverlochy. The perspective of
Hay's poem, casting Marr as the instigator of the territorial split, is odd.

190 *"Faodaidh Duine a Theang' a Chumail san Droch Uair"* (seanfhacal Lallans)
P26: 361: 4, 11 Feb. 1961.

Title: "A man may hauld his tongue in an ill-time" (see Henderson 1876: 51). On 31
December 1960, Hay wrote (Source 51):

> Recently I translated about two hundred of Henderson's Scots Proverbs into
> Gaelic, and found that they made very racy Gaelic indeed. Some time this
> year I'll try and get the best of them, especially the rhyming couplets, pub-
> lished ... in the cause of Scottish solidarity.

l. 10 **Domhnall Dàsachdach**: fear de na rìghrean Gàidhealach Albannach roimh
àm Chaluim A' Chinn Mhòir. [One of the Gaelic kings of Scotland before Malcolm
Canmore] [**P26**]. Donald II, grandson of Kenneth MacAlpine (see Skene 1867: 21).

l. 14 **cur-leis**: glossed by Hay as "perseverance" in his copy of Aonghas MacCoinnich's
Eachdraidh na h-Alba (NLS MS 26755: 251)

l. 16: the issue of the national allegiance of Berwick was brought to public attention in June 1959 by Wendy Wood's Scottish Patriots. Shortly before, the Town Council had successfully applied for a new coat-of-arms from the Lord Lyon of Scotland. On the premise that the Tweed waters are legally Scottish and that the Scottish–English border traditionally runs in the middle of the Royal Tweed Bridge,

> we ... considered it advisable ... to have someone caught on the English side of the supposed borderline to bring the matter to more public notice. So two young men undertook to saw down the sign in broad daylight and (if they could get so far) to carry it to the border bridge ... It had been arranged that in Court they should refuse to recognise English Law on Scottish territory, the new Coat-of-Arms over the Magistrate's head signifying the power of the Court as being of a Scottish Burgh. (Wood 1970: 207–8)

See also *The Scotsman* of 1 and 2 June 1959.

191 Glaistig Phàirc na Bànrigh

P26: 362: 2, 18 Feb. 1961.
56: letter of 7 March 1969; published in Catalyst *2/3, Summer 1969.*
21: 82, 1974.

Title: **Glaistig**:

> The Glaistig was a tutelary being in the shape of a thin grey (*tana glas*) little woman, with long yellow hair reaching to her heels, dressed in green, haunting certain sites or farms. ... She is said to have been at first a woman of honourable position, a former mistress of the house, who had been put under enchantments and now had a Fairy nature given her. (J. G. Campbell 1900: 155)

Pàirc na Bànrigh: the Queen's Park behind Holyrood Palace, at the foot of Arthur's Seat, Edinburgh.

l. 6 **Boglach an t-Sealgair**: Hunter's Bog, at Arthur's Seat.

l. 8 **Meall a' Chonaisg**: Whinny Knowe, by Arthur's Seat.

ll. 9–16: The decline of Gaelic among the rulers of Scotland is associated with the reign of Malcolm III (1054–93) and the Normanising of the Scottish court through the influence of his English wife, Margaret.

l. 12 **a' ghòraiche leanabaidh**: The "childish folly" was being swayed too much by his wife. [**56**]

192 Òran Nàiseantach

9: 26r, 1948?; fragments of two verses (page torn).
P26: 365: 3, 11 March 1961.
P6: 1/4: 23, Autumn 1968.
11: 27, 1978?
20: 147–8, 1978?
43: folder 24; published in Gairm *120, Autumn 1982.*

The song was written to a tune of Hay's composition (**11**, **20**, **43**). For a traditional model, see A. M. Sinclair (1892: 217).

ll. 9–12: this verse and another were drafted with the chorus in the late 1940s (**9**).

193 *Furan na Baintighearna bho Chluaidh*
P26: 366: 3, 18 March 1961.

ll. 9–14: these lines track the liner's course from the Holy Loch down the Firth of Clyde, past Bute and Arran into the North Channel.

194 *Ro Fhad' air a' Mhullach*
P14: LVI/4: 44, April 1961.

The poem is in Tarbert dialect, with verbal ending *-igh* for standard *-ich*, *folbh* for *falbh*, and *oìdhche* for *oidhche*.

195 *Cnocan a' Chait Fhiadhaich*
31: backpaste, 1960–1.
P26: 368: 3, 1 April 1961.
56: letter of 24 Feb. 1969; published in Catalyst 2/3, Summer 1969.
21: 82–3, 1974.

Title: see Appendix 2: A Glossary of Lochfyneside Place-names.

196 *Acarsaidean a'* Chutty Sark
P26: 369: 2, 8 April 1961.

Title: **Cutty Sark**: the clipper was built in the Denny Brothers' shipyard at Dumbarton, and launched in 1869. It was first used in the tea-trade with China, then went on to set successive records in the wool-trade with Australia. The ship was opened to public viewing in 1957, berthed in a purpose-built dock in Greenwich. (See Hackney 1974.) The anchorages mentioned in the poem are in the upper Firth of Clyde, around the Holy Loch and the Gare Loch.

l. 8: Punta Arenas: a town in the southern tip of Chile.

197 *An Cnocan Fraoich is Padre Dante*
P26: 370: 3, 15 April 1961.

The poem is in the terzina form of Dante's *Commedia* (three-line verses rhyming aba, bcb, cdc etc.).

198 *Na Fiachan Gaolach no An Nàiseantach do dh'Albainn*
P26a: 371: 3, 22 April 1961.
20a: 92, 1969.

20b: 120, 1971.
P26b: 7: 13, Sept. 1971.
21: 74, 1974.

ll. 1–4: a strongly traditional verse. Note that a version of it appears in a song written down by Hay in the late 1940s, beginning:

> *Oich iù agus hiùraibh eile,*
> *oich iù agus hiùraibh eile,*
> *oich iù agus hiùraibh eile,*
> *mo rìbhinn chaoimhneil 's ann leatsa thèid mi.*

> Nuair a bha mi 'm chaileig ghòraich,
> thug mi cion agus ceist don òigear,
> air an d'fhàs an cuailein bòidheach,
>   mo ghille bòidheach, mo ghiullan eutrom.

> Thug mi treis dhuit, thug mi tràth dhuit,
> thug mi bliadhna is thug mi là dhuit,
> thug mi gaol dhuit, thug mi gràdh dhuit,
>   thug mi bàigh dhuit 's mo cheann sna speuran.

Oich iù agus hiùraibh eile | ... | ... | My kindly maiden, it's you I'll follow.

When I was a foolish girl | I gave regard and esteem to the youth | on whose head grew bonnie curls, | my bonnie boy, my lively laddie.

I gave you a while, I gave you a time, | I gave a year and I gave you a day, | I gave love, I gave affection, | I gave you fondness, and my head in the clouds.

Three more verses follow (Source 9: 21v–22r).

199   *Ar Cnocan Fraoich*

P26a: 372: 3, 29 April 1961.
P6: 2/4: 20, Autumn 1969.
21: 78–9, 1974.
20: 97, 1976–7?
P26b: 73: 8, April 1977.

The poem was composed to the Irish tune "An Cnuicín Fraoigh" (**P6**).

Title: An Cnocan Fraoich – is e sin, Alba. [The Heather Knowe – i.e. Scotland.] [**P26**]

I have used the title in **P6** and **20** to avoid confusion with the 1944 poem "An Cnocan Fraoich" (Poem 104).

200   *A' Phìob Mhòr Againn*

31: backpaste; first verse and fragments.
P26: 373: 2, 6 May 1961.

l. 10 **na Cruimeinich**: the MacCrimmons were hereditary pipers to the MacLeods of Dunvegan from the sixteenth to the eighteenth centuries.

The development of piping in Scotland and the predominance today of the Highland bagpipe throughout the world are due very largely to the musical genius of one family, the MacCrimmons. (MacNeill 1983: 162)

201 Rathad Loudaidh 's an Track

P21: Autumn 1961: 9.

Title: **Rathad Loudaidh**: Lothian Road, in central Edinburgh.   **An Track**: an lìne chùrsa a ghabhas na luingeas mòra, 's iad a' togail gu cuan no 'tighinn a-staigh bhon Chuan Siar, eadar ceann a deas Eilein Bhòid agus Creag Ealasaid. [The course taken by the ocean liners as they head out to sea or come in from the Atlantic, between the south end of Bute and Ailsa Craig.] [**P21**]

202 Abune the Gutted Haddie

20: 72, 1960–1?
P28: 4 Nov. 1961: 5.

Date: The poem pre-dates February 1961 (List 30).

Title: **The Gutted Haddie**: a hillock on Arthur's Seat, Edinburgh.

l. 6 **aiver**: carthorse [**P28**].

l. 19 **spleddrach**: a sprachling fall, a tumble [**P28**]. Elsewhere, Hay explains it as Tarbert for a "cropper", as in "to come a spleddrach" (Source 37, letter of mid-October 1939).

203 Brònach Tadhal Dùn Monaidh

P26a: 404: 4, 9 Dec. 1961.
20: 119, 1972.
P26b: 12: 6, Feb. 1972.
21: 79, 1974?

Title: **Dùn Monaidh**: "Mound Fortress", a kenning for Edinburgh. In **P26a**, Hay cites its use in Bishop Carswell's translation of Knox's *Book of Common Order* (see Thomson 1970: 1).

l. 7 **anns an ainbheach (as dyvours)**: dyvours – debtors, bankrupts [**21**]. Hay had heard the word in Tarbert (Source 23: 84).

204 Air Suidh' Artair Dhomh Mochthrath

25: frontpaste–iv, 1960–1; eleven verses only.
43: folder 10; published in Gairm 38, Winter 1961.

Date: context 25.

Hay glosses in **43** that most of the places mentioned are between Tarbert and Skipness, and provides topographical details. Place-names from the Tarbert locality can be consulted in Appendix 2.

Title: **Suidh' Artair**: Arthur's Seat, the hill in the centre of Edinburgh.

l. 2 **mochthrath**: Hay's submission to the *Historical Dictionary of Scottish Gaelic* includes the use of the word as an alternative to "madainn", as in "mochthrath math dhuit".

l. 3 **Dùn Sapaidh**: Dunsapie Rock in the Queen's Park, Edinburgh.

l. 11 **moineach**: maigheach, geàrr [**43**]. Tarbert dialect.

l. 34 **roineach**: raineach [**43**]. Tarbert dialect.

l. 73: a Gaelic proverb.

l. 79 **Sliabh Allair**: Allermuir Hill, in the Pentlands.

l. 87: the Hays came to Tarbert c. the 1830s, from Ayrshire, probably Dunure (see Martin 1984: 49).

l. 91: refers to the Gaelic proverb (noted by Hay on frontpaste of NLS MS 26771):

> Imrich an t-Satharn mu thuath,
> imrich an Luain mu dheas;
> is mur robh agam ach an t-uan,
> 's ann Di-luain a dh'fhalbhainn leis.

The Saturday move to northwards, | the Monday move to south; | and if all I had was the lamb, | it's on Monday I'd set off with it.

l. 97 **Eilean na Baintighearna**: Lady Isle, beagan mu thuath air Inbhir Àir [just north of Ayr]. [**43**]

POEMS 1964–1973

205 *Am Flùr Geal Slèibhe*

20a: 99, 1969.
P15: 67: 228, Summer 1969.
20b: 100, 1970s.
21: 75–6, 1974.

Date: 1964, Edinburgh (**21**). The translation used (**20b**) dates from 1971.

206 *Nationalist Sang*

P6: 1/4: 23, Autumn 1968.
P18: Sept. 1968: 8.
20: 148, 1977–8; carbon copy of text sent for publication.
11: 26v, 1981.

Date: 1968?

As with its Gaelic model, "Òran Nàiseantach" (Poem 192), Hay wrote the poem "tae ma ain tune" (**20**).

207 *[Latha san Rainich]*

56: letter of 20 Feb. 1969.
20: 95, 1969.
21: 81–2, 1974.

Date: 1968, Edinburgh (**21**).

Hay explains in his letter (**56**): "It's about the shadow of atomic war, and is really a song, for I composed it complete with tune".

l. 12 **Cnoc a' Chaisteil**: in Cowal near Loch Ascog (Loch a' Chaisteil) and like Arran forms part of North Kintyre's horizon. [**21**]

208 *Referendum*

56: letter of 17 Feb. 1969.
20: 94, 1969.

Date: 1968–9?

209 *An Rùnaire Stàit*

56: letter of 20 Feb. 1969.
20: 95v, 1969.

Date: 1969.

ll. 1–2: These lines were used again by Hay in the eulogistic Poem 283 "Do Dh'Ùistean MacDhiarmaid". The central image had been elaborated years before in Poem 109 "Mochtàr is Dùghall" (ll. 1,221 ff.).

l. 4 **an Rosach**: William Ross, Secretary of State for Scotland under the Labour Government of 1966–70. His term in office was marked by spectacular electoral gains for the SNP, but Ross remained implacably hostile to any legislative devolution of power. (See Pottinger 1979.)

210 *Via Media?* *A Middle Path?*
40: folder 30, letter of 26 Feb. 1969; published in Akros 3/11, Aug. 1969.

211 *An Ciùran Ceòban Ceò*
20a: 131v, 1969?; partial draft.
20b: 105, 1969.
51: 28 Feb. 1969.
P15: 67 (Samhradh 1969), 227–8.
20c: 106, 1971.
21: 72–3, 1974.
20d: 107–8, 1975?
J: 138–9, 1976.

Date: 25 February 1969 (**20b**).

The poem is "a Gaelic counterpart" (**21**) to "The Smoky Smirr o Rain" (Poem 151). It is in amhrán song metre, marked by lines of equal stress with the same end-rhyme and each containing internal rhyme.

212 *Ar Cor an Albainn*
20a: 95v hand, 1969.
20b: 92 typescript, 1969.
P18: April 1969: 5.
P6: 2/3: 18–19, Summer 1969.

Date: 1969?

213 *Eun Maidne*
P6: 3/3: 13, Summer 1970.

Date: 1970?

214 *Bliadhna gun Gheamhradh (Am Paipear Naidheachd)*
P31: 11: 37, Sept. 1970.

Date: 1970?

215 *For the* Cutty Sark *Moored in the Port of London*

38: with letter of 6 July 1970; published in Scotia 10, Oct. 1970.

Date: Spring 1970? The poem was sent to David Morrison, editor of *Scotia*, in an-swer to a request for some Gaelic pieces. "I haena written muckle i the Gaelic they past months, but I hae a wee thing aboot the Cutty Sark ... Aiblins it'll suit *Scotia*" (NLS Acc. 7309/1).

Title: Built in the Denny Brothers' shipyard at Dumbarton in the 1860s, the famous clipper has lain berthed in Greenwich for public viewing since 1957.

l. 7: Hay has "Gairloch", but it is clear from "Acarsaidean a' *Chutty Sark*" (Poem 196) that the loch in the Clyde estuary is intended.

216 *[Rann Fìrinneach]*

53: 1970–1?
20: 154–5, 22 March 1971.

Date: 1971? Hay first met Elizabeth Kirk c. 1970.

Typescript **20** is headed "Do dh' Ealasaid mu Ealasaid", "To Elizabeth about Eliza-beth".

217 *Sreathan Sìmplidh*

53: 1970–1?
20: 154–5, 22 March 1971.

Date: 1971?

218 *Rannghail Leth-èibhinn do dh'Ealasaid*

53: 1970–1?
20: 156–9, 27 March 1971.

Date: 1971?

Title and ll. 1–4: Rob Donn Mackay's song (Gunn and McFarlane 1899: 67) opens:

Ho ro! a Naoghais, bi treun!
Is cum do ghealladh rium fhèin;
Cho liutha 's a tha tabhairt ort comhairl',
Bhi 'g amharc mun tabhair thu leum.

l. 37 **tràchda**: < Gàidhlig Eireannach "trácht": traffic. [**20**]

l. 53 **fuigheall bheum is chorc**: the phrase is from Iain Lom's lament "Cumha Mhontròis" of 1650 (see Mackenzie 1964: l. 706).

l. 64 **Lysistrata**: the comedy by the Athenian Aristophanes in which he portrays the women of Athens as refusing themselves to their husbands until the husbands put a stop to the Peloponnesian War (5thc. BC). [**20**]

219 *Bratach am Bràigh a' Bhaile*

7: 26v, 1946; one verse and fragments.
20: 121, 1971.
P26: 8: 14, Oct. 1971.
21: 80, 1974.
Date: 1971?

220 *An Co-cheòl Iomlan*

23: 9v, 1971; draft of first two verses.
20a: 164, 1971.
20b: 91, 1973?
21: 72, 1974.
Date: 11 July 1971 (**20a**).

221 *Orion Over Bute*

20a: 109, 1972; two lines lacking.
20b: 110, 1972.
40: Folder 19(i), 1972; two lines lacking.
53: 1972?; two lines lacking.
P26: 22: 7, Jan. 1973.
Date: 10 February 1972 (**20**). See notes to Poem 155 "The Walls of Balclutha" for the likely genesis of this poem.

Texts **40** and **53** are dedicated "to Hugh MacDiarmid on his Eightieth Birthday" (11 August 1972), and signed "Dunureman" (the Tarbert Hays are thought to have come from Dunure in Carrick). Akros Publications had requested submissions for a celebratory collection of poems in tribute to MacDiarmid.

222 *Lives o Men (Caller Herrin)*

7: 45, 1972.
2: 90, 1972.
20: 98, 1976?
P16: 7: 19, Mairtinmas 1976.
Date: 4 March 1972 (**2**).
Title: a reference to the chorus of "Caller Herrin" by Lady Nairne (1766–1845):

> Wha'll buy my caller herrin'?
> Oh, ye may ca' them vulgar farin' –
> Wives and mithers, maist despairin',
> Ca' them lives o' men.

(MacQueen and Scott 1966: 415–16)

l. 1 **haice**: hoarse [**2**]. Perhaps prompted by the Tarbert usage of "càrsan" ("hoarseness") in both Gaelic and English to refer to the sound of rising sea and wind.

223 *Tha 'Mhisneach is an Dòchas 's a' Chòir 'nan Laoich*

Courage and Hope and the Right Are Warriors

7: 45, 1972; three verses only.
2: 88v–89, 1972.
20: 78, 1972.
P26: 13: 10, April 1972.

Date: 4 March 1972 (**2**).

Title: a quote from Hay's own poem "Ar Cnocan Fraoich" (Poem 199, l. 10).

224 *Howes an' Knowes*

7: 44v, 1972; third verse lacking.
2: 89v, 1972.
20: 132, 1977?
P25: 17: 50, Summer 1977.

Date: 5 March 1972 (**2**).

Title: preceded in **2** by a quote from Poem 106 "Dleasnas nan Àirdean":

> Is e tuairgneadh nan àrdan
> a bheir sàmhchar don ghleannan.

> *It is the buffeting of the heights | that gives tranquillity to the glennan.*

225 *Alba Cona h-Ingantaib*

Alba le a h-Ioghnaidhean (Dàn Deirdre)

2: 90v, 1972.
P26: 17: 9, Aug. 1972.
20: 125, 1973?
21: 77, 1974.

Date: 2 July 1972 (**2**).

Title: The "Song of Deirdre" in question is the song of farewell to Scotland spoken by Deirdre in the pre-Christian Irish tale *Longes Mac n-Uislenn* ("The Exile of the Sons of Uisliu"). Versions of the story survived in oral tradition in Scotland into the twentieth century, but the literary tale was also preserved in collections such as the fifteenth-century Glenmasan MS. The song as preserved in that source opens:

> Inmain tiar an tiar ut thoir
> Alba cona hingantaib

> *A dear land, that land in the east | Scotland with its wonders.*

Hay's poem may have been provoked by a romantic piece in the June issue of the *Scots Independent*: "Deirdre's Farewell to Alba (to the tune of the Mingulay Boat Song)".

226   An t-Albannach air Dùsgadh

2: 91, 1973.
20: 123, 1973?
21: 76, 1974.
P26: 64: 8, July 1976.

Date: 20 February 1973 (**2**).

227   Teirigidh Nàimhdeas: Mairidh Càirdeas

2: 92v, 1973.
20: 124, 1973?
21: 76–7, 1974.
P26: 28: 5, July 1973.

Date: 24 March 1973 (**2**).

228   Garvalt Side

2: 93, 1973.
20: 122.
P25: 17: 51, Summer 1977.

Date: 21 July 1973 (**2**).

POEMS 1975–1977

229 *Òran Maraiche*

10: 8–9, 1975.
43: folder 18; published in Gairm 92, Autumn 1975.
Date: 1975.

l. 2 **ceòs**: "hip, buttock"; billowing seas or swelling clouds?

ll. 4, 8 etc. **soraidh ò**: expression heard by Hay from Tarbertman Dougal "Moore" MacAlpine:

> I said "Cheerio" and he said "Soraidh ò", and there you are. A word's enough. It's the only known Gaelic for "cheerio" in existence, I expect. (SSS 1979)

230 *An Iomagain*

10: 11r, 8v, 13; 1975?
43: folder 18; published in Gairm 92, Autumn 1975.
Date: 1975.

231 *Sìon a' Chuain*

30: 67, c. 1960; two lines.
10: 9v, 13r; 1975.
43: folder 18; published in Gairm 92, Autumn 1975.
Date: 8 August 1975 (**10**).

232 *Cù is a Choilear*

10: 13r, 1975?
43: folder 18; published in Gairm 92, Autumn 1975.
Date: 8 August 1975 (**10**).

233 *Do Dhuine a Rinn Cillein*

10a: 13b, 1975.
10b: 12v, 1975.
43: folder 18; published in Gairm 92, Autumn 1975.
Date: 8 August 1975 (**10**).

Title: the expression is from Iain Lom MacDonald's lament "Cumha Morair

Hunndaidh" of 1649, where he refers to "daoine beaga a rinn cillein" (see Macken-
zie 1964: l. 607).

234 *Ar Làraichean*
10: 17–18, 1975.
P15: 93: 50–2, Winter 1975–6.
Date: 1975.
l. 25 **Mac Iain Dheòrsa**: Hay's patronymic; see note in Poem 301 "Gum Chur an
Aithne".

235 *Òran Suirghich*
10: 18, 1975.
P15: 93: 52, Winter 1975–6.
Date: 1975.

236 *Rainn Ghràidh*
10: 8–9, 1975.
43: folder 18; published in **Gairm** *94, Spring 1976.*
Date: 1975.

237 *Rainn Ghràidh Eile*
10: 10, 1975.
43: folder 18; published in **Gairm** *94, Spring 1976.*
Date: 1975.

238 *Na Faoileagan Maidne*
10a: 10, 1975.
10b: 21v, 1976?
20: 126, 1976?
P15: 94: 129, Spring 1976.
P1: 11/31: 7, August 1976. Translation only.
Date: 1975.

239 *Beachd is Barail*
10: 10v, 1975.
P26: 63: 8, June 1976.
Date: 1975.

240 A' Chraobh

10: 12, 1975.
43: folder 18; published in **Gairm** *94, Spring 1976.*
Date: 10 June 1975 (**10**).

241 La Scozia Oggi

10: 18v, 1975–6; verses 2–7.
20: 142, 1976?; verses 2–7.
P26: 70: 8, Jan. 1977.
Date: sent for publication on 2 January 1976 (**10**).

242 Aig an Fheurlochan

25: 73–9, 1960; draft of five verses and three variant verses.
20a: 111–12, 1976?
20b: 113–14, 1976.
43: folder 19; published in **Gairm** *99, Summer 1977.*
Date: 1960 (verses 1–4 and 8) and 1976? (verses 5–7).

Text **25** is written entirely in top and bottom margins. The three discarded verses are as follows:

> 'S math mo chòir air an fhearann
>   eadar Sealtainn is Tuaidh,
> 's math mo chòir aig gach àite
>   eadar Àbhann 's Taobh Tuath.
> Thug am Bùta dhomh sealladh
>   gu Maol Ghallabha uair;
> chaidh an uair sin seachad
>   's tha mi 'tathaich nan cruach.
>
> Treis air Làirig na h-Èilde
>   treis ag èirigh sa Chrò;
> treis ri taobh Abhainn Tatha
>   treis an Arainn nan sgòrr;
> treis an Diùra 's an Uidhist
>   a' cumadh ur ceòl;
> treis a' dèanamh nan duanag
>   mu Dhruim Uachdar an fheòir.
>
> Ge fada an èigh e
>   gu Dùn Èideann san ear
> bidh mise ann romhad
>   is bidh mo chomhairle leat
> air mòrshliabh Loudaidh
>   a' dèanamh fhonn is gam meas
> gheibhear mise ma shirear
>   feadh nam fireach gu ceart.

Good is my claim on the land | between Shetland and Tweed, | good is my claim on every place | between Sanda and the North country; | from the Butt I could view | the Mull of Galloway once, | that time has gone by | and I now haunt the hills.

A while on Lairig na h-Eilde, | a while ascending Kintail, | a while by the River Tay | a while on mountainous Arran. | A while in Jura and Uist | giving form to your music; | a while composing ditties | around grassy Drumochter.

Although it's a far cry | to Edinburgh in the east | I will be there before you | and my council will follow you | on Lothian's great hill | making tunes and appraising them | I will be found if needed | among the moorlands indeed.

l. 19 **m'fhuireachan taighe**: Hay's notes for the *Historical Dictionary of Scottish Gaelic* include the entry: "Fuireachan: àite còmhnaidh, taigh, togail, bothan; 'am fuireachan àite sin shìos'".

He may have only heard the word used in Tarbert Scots: "Thon fuireachan o a place doon thonder. (Hamish about Dougie Leitch's shed at the Earrann Ghoineach, August 1960)" (Source 12: 1).

243 Àit air Bith

10: 21–2, 1976.
20: 115, 1976?
43: *folder 19; published in Gairm 99, Summer 1977.*

Date: January 1976 (**10**).

244 [Rann Ionndrainn]

10: 20r; 1976?
20: 115–16, 1976?
43: *folder 19; published in Gairm 99, Summer 1977.*

Date: 1976 (List 10).

245 Vignette

10: 20r, 1976.
20: 116, 1976.
43: *folder 19; published in Gairm 99, Summer 1977.*

Date: 1976 (List 10).

246 Lag an Aonaich

10: 22, 1976.
20: 114–15, 1976?
43: *folder 19; published in Gairm 99, Summer 1977.*

Date: 28 February 1976 (**10**)

247 Callaidean Shasainn

10: 21v–22, 1976.
20: 115, 1976?
43: folder 19; published in **Gairm** *99,* **Summer 1977.**
Date: 2 March 1976 (**10**).

248 Òige na h-Aoise

20: 126, 1976.
P1: 11/31: 8, Aug. 1976, 8.
Date: 1976?

249 Le Montagnard

10: 21r, 1976.
P25: 17: 53, Summer 1977.
Date: 1976.

l. 4 **me**: editorial emendation.

250 This Warld

10: 20r, 1976.
P25: 17: 53, Summer 1977.
Date: 1976.

l. 4: see l. 13 of Poem 218 "Rannghail Leth-èibhinn do dh'Ealasaid".

251–255 Stanze Irlandesi

10: 20v, 1976.
20a: 136–7, 1976.
20b: 138–9, 1977–8.
P26: 77: 8, Aug. 1977. Stanzas 251 and 253.
Date: 14 April 1976 (**20a**).

Hay explains in **20b**:

> Queste stanze sono nel metro irlandese che si chiama "Amhrán", o Canzone.
> Ha rim' al mezzo e si trova anche nel Gaelico Scozzese.

> These stanzas are in the Irish metre called "Amhrán" or Song. It has internal
> rhyme and is also found in Scots Gaelic.

Titles 253 and 255: *file*: l'irlandese per "poeta" [the Irish for "poet"]. [**20b**]

256 Aria

10: 20, 1976.
20: 136, 1976.
P26: 77: 8, Aug. 1977.

Date: 14 April 1976 (**20**).

257 Skottland til Ola Nordmann

10: 19r, 1976?
P26: 64: 8, July 1976.

Date: 1976?

Title: **Ola Nordmann**: the Norwegian national character; cf. the English John Bull [**P26**].

l. 13 **trær**: editorial correction of Hay's "trærne".

258 Våren

10: 19v, 1976?
20: 134, 1976–7?

Date: 1976?

Hay may have had in mind an old Irish metre, used in a ninth-century poem about winter which starts:

Scél lem dúib: | dordaid dam, | snigid gaim, | ro fáith sam.

(See Greene and O'Connor 1967: 98)

I've news for you: | stag bellows, | winter snow, | summer's gone.

ll. 1 and 8 (transl.) **turns**: editorial correction of Hay's "returns".

259 Steinen på Fjellet

10: 19r, 1976?
20: 134, 1976–7.
P26: 72: 9, March 1977.

Date: 1976?

l. 1: see l. 20 of the Scots poem "Tha 'Mhisneach is an Dòchas 's a' Chòir 'nan Laoich" (Poem 223). The idea crops up in a Norwegian–Scots draft (Source 9: 12v, 1960–1?), which includes the following:

skalder og barder skulle forstå hverandre, som de gjorde før …

> Her er vi kvar til luften luter,
> som de Galater
> Till the lift louts
> and aa erd's levrocks ablow it

we will bide here singan lik levrocks
but no soarin' awa' frae the ground we ken.

the skald and the bard should understand one another, as they did of old ...
Here we are till the sky caves in, | as Gaels   (transl. A. Kruse)

ll. 3 and 6 **vind**: editorial correction of Hay's "vinder".

260 *Håpet*

2: 101v, 1976; verse lacking.
11: 4r, 1976.
20: 74–5, 1976.
P26: 67: 8, Oct. 1976.

Date: 10 May 1976 (**11**).

l. 1 **skald**: the court-poet of medieval Icelandic/Norse society. Like his Gaelic counterpart the *filidh*, the skald specialised in panegyric and cultivated intricate metrical technique.

261 *Slutt*

2: 102, 1976.
11: 5, 1976.
20: 74–5, 1976?
P26: 67: 8, Oct. 1976.

Date: 10 May 1976 (**11**).

262 *Enhver Seiler*

2: 102, 1976; partial draft.
11: 4v, 1976.
20: 133, 1976–7?
P26: 75: 10, June 1977.

Date: 10 May 1976 (**11**).

l. 6 **Vinland**: Vineland, in Norse legend the land beyond the western sea; identified historically with Newfoundland.

l. 10 **støv**: editorial correction of Hay's "støvet".

l. 13 **seil**: editorial correction of Hay's "seiler".

263 *An Oidhche Bhuan*

11: 1–2, 1976.
20: 135, 1976–7?
43: folder 20; see Gairm 105, Winter 1978–9.

Date: 1976.

264 "Is Crìon a' Chùil Às Nach Goirear" (seanfhacal)

11: 3, 1976.
20: 140–1, 1976–7?
P15: 97: 35, Winter 1976–7.

Date: 30 May 1976 (**11**).

265 Dùdlachd is Earrach Ar Bliadhna

11: 6, 1976.
20: 80, 1976.
P26: 69: 8, Dec. 1976.

Date: 23 July 1976 (**11**).

l. 8 **Fèill Brìde**: St Bridget's Day, 1 February, traditionally the start of Spring.

266 An t-Ùghdarras agus an t-Eòlas

11: 7–6v, 1976.
20: 80, 1976.
P26: 68: 8, Nov. 1976.

Date: 23 July 1976 (**11**).

267 [Suas gun Sìos]

20: 127.
P26: 68: 8, Nov. 1976.

Date: 1976?

Title: the verse was published without a title, but its translation was headed "The ballot not the bullet – a victory with no defeated".

268 Uladh

20: 127.
P26: 68: 8, November 1976.

Date: 1976?

ll. 1–2: The Presbyterian settler and the Irish Gael driven west to "Hell or Connaught". [**P26**]

l. **4 is làidir an snaoisín é**: from an Irish quatrain; snuff brings tears to the eyes [**P26**]. For the quatrain in question, see Ó Rathile (1925: 24).

269 Beannachadh

11: 1v, 1976.
P25: 17: 53, Summer 1977.

20: 135, 1977?

Date: 1976.

270 *Fosgail Uinneag an Là*   *Open the Winnock o the Day*

11: 8v, 9, 16; 1976.
P25: 17: 53, Summer 1977.

Date: 1976.

A Scots version of Poem 263 "An Oidhche Bhuan" ("frae ma ain Gaelic", **P25**).

l. 3 **scowry**: (Gaelic "sgreunach") inclement, overcast and windy. [**P25**]

271 *"It's a Wee Neuk frae Whilk There's Nae E'en a Cheep" (Gaelic proverb)*

11: 9v, 10, 17–18; 1976.
P25: 17: 54, Summer 1977.

Date: 1976.

A Scots version of Poem 264 "Is Crìon a' Chùil às Nach Goirear" ("frae ma ain Gaelic", **P25**). The poem was published with title in Gaelic and Scots.

272 *Ionndrainn na Sìne*

11: 8, 14–16; 1976.
20: 129, 1977?
P25: 17: 51–2, Summer 1977.

Date: 1976.

l. 5 etc. **drumach**: see note in Poem 180 "An Druim-àrcan 's an t-Ìochdar".

273 *Luinneag Thairbeartach*

11: 11–12, 1976; extra verse 1978.
43: folder 19; published in Gairm 101, Winter 1977–8.

Date: 1976.

l. 1 **àrd amach**: fad amach air a' mhuir. [**43**]   A note from the early 1960s attributes the expression to "Dougall Moora, August 1960" (Source 12: 2r).

l. 2 **an Caol**: Caol Bhreannain [the Kilbrannan Sound]. [**43**]   **càrsanach**: Hay heard "càrsan" used in Tarbert (pronounced "cèrsan") to signify "the hoarseness in the rising wind" (see Poem 172). "I put it in plenty of poems, *cèrsan*, it's very romantic ..." (SSS, October 1980).

l. 9: **Iomachar**: am prìomh rubha air còrsa an iar Arainn [the main headland on the west coast of Arran]. [**43**]   **a' Chleit**: sgeir fhada fo làr air còrsa iardheas Arainn (The Iron Rock Ledge) [a long submerged reef on the south-west coast of Arran] [**43**]. Known to Angus Martin as The Iron Rock Ledges.   **Cùr**: an Cinntìre eadar Càradal agus Sgibinis [in Kintyre between Carradale and Skipness]. [**43**]

l. 11 **losgadh**: see note in Poem 173 "Miannan an Tairbeartaich".   **sùil** (sgadain): rudeigin nas lugha na shoal [an "eye" (of herring): somewhat smaller than a shoal]. [**43**]

l. 12 **an duine làidir**: an capstan. [**43**]

l. 19 **drumach**: dìle-bhàithte [**43**]; see note in Poem 180 "An Druim-àrcan 's an t-Ìochdar".

A final verse was added in **11** in 1978:

> Is àrd amach a thà mo ghaol.
> Thà an Caol càrsanach.
> Is àrd amach a thà mo ghaol.
> Till, a ghaoil, slàn rium.

Far out on the sea is my love. | There's a hoarseness on the Sound. | Far out on the sea is my love. | Return to me safely, love.

274   Guidhe an Iasgair

11: 7v, 1976.
43: folder 19; published in Gairm 101, Winter 1977–8.
Date: 1976.

l. 2 **coltas**: see gloss in Poem 173 "Miannan an Tairbeartaich".

l. 3 **reòtach**: see gloss in Poem 173 "Miannan an Tairbeartaich".

275   The Fisherman's Prayer

11: 7v, 14; 1976.
20: 129, 1977?
P25: 17: 54, Summer 1977.
Date: 1976.

l. 2 **appearance**: see gloss of *coltas* in Poem 173 "Miannan an Tairbeartaich".

276   Aubade [1]

11: 12r, 18r; 1976.
P25: 17: 54, Summer 1977.
Date: 30 November 1976 (**11**).

See Poem 345 for an English version.

277   Bloigh

20: 130, 1976–7.
P25: 17: 52, Summer 1977.
Date: 1976–7.

Hay adds a note in **P25**: "Theagamh gun cuir leughadair air choireigin òran ris an rann seo" ("Perhaps some reader will add a whole song to this verse"). He himself drafted an expansion of the fragment in 1983 (see Poem 382 "Air Leathad Slèibhe").

278 Lunnainn agus Alba

11: 20, 1977.
P26: 72: 9, March 1977.
Date: 1977.

279 Irische Strophe

11a: 12r, 1976–7.
11b: 22r, 1977.
20: 139, 1977.
P11: 7: 35, Winter 1977–8.
Date: 27 February 1977 (**11**b).

The quote is from an Irish love song: "I have been sitting since the moon rose last night ...".

l. 4 (transl.) **The**: editor's emendation of Hay's "my".

280 Briseadh na Fàire 'n Albainn

11: 21, 1977.
P26: 74 8, May 1977.
Date: 27 February 1977 (**11**).

281 *Bloigh* Lebensraum

11: 26, 1977.
Date: 16 March 1977 (**11**).

282 Leum gu Taobh Life

11: 24–6, 1977.
20: 128, 1977.
P5: 18: 2, Summer 1977.
Date: 16 March 1977 (**11**).

POEMS 1978–1979

283   Do Dh'Ùistean MacDhiarmaid

20: 146, 1978.
P26: 83: 3, Feb. 1978.

Date: though sent for publication along with the January 1978 poems (see "Na Ràtaichean ..." below), the poem does not feature among the notebook drafts, and may be of earlier date (perhaps written to mark MacDiarmid's 85th birthday in August 1977?).

284   [Bigein is Aiteamh]

11: 29, 30–1; 1978.
P5: 21: 23, Spring 1978.

Date: 5 January 1978 (**11**).

Title: the verses were sent to *Carn* simply as "Dà rann in Amhrán" ("two verses in song metre").

285   Na Ràtaichean 's a' Bhàrdachd

11: 31v, 32v, 42; 1978.
20: 152–3, 1978; four verses only.
43: folder 20; published in Gairm 105, Winter 1978-9.

Date: January 1978. The translation (**20**) is dated 11 January 1978. In a letter of 14 January (Source 45), Hay writes:

> The *Wessergott* [Weather God] wasn't very *gnädig* [gracious], but being stuck in the house I wrote about ten Gaelic poems in three days, and they're now sent away to *Gairm* and the S I.

The poem is in *amhrán iomlan*, full Irish song metre, with rhyme pattern *i-à-à-e-u* running throughout the poem's original verses, and *i-o-o-a-u* in the added verses 4–6.

l. 19 **tiugh**: also "fat" or "thick"; the interpretation chosen is that given by Ronald Black in his 1999 anthology.

286   Cùinneadh Samhraidh

11: 32–31v, 1978.
20: 152–3, 1978.
43: folder 20; published in Gairm 105, Winter 1978-9.

Date: 11 January 1978 (**11**).

287 Na Gàidheil sna Bailtean

11: 35r, 1978.
20: 81, 1978; carbon of 44.
43: folder 20; published in **Gairm** *105,* **Winter** *1978–9.*

Date: 11 January 1978 (**20**).

As Hay points out in **20**, this poem and the next are in *amhrán iomlan* ("full *amhrán* metre"). This demands that in addition to internal rhyme, the same rhyme pattern should run in every line of the verse.

288 Dreuchd an Fhilidh

11: 35, 1978.
20: 81, 1978.
43: folder 20; published in **Gairm** *105,* **Winter** *1978–9.*

Date: 11 January 1978 (**20**).

A poem in *amhrán* metre.

289 Guth Thairis

11: 35, 1978.
20: 147, 1978.
P26: 84: 3, **March** *1978.*

Date: see Poem 285 "Na Ràtaichean 's a' Bhàrdachd".

A verse in *amhrán* metre.

290 Mòr à Meud

11: 36, 1978.
20: 147, 1978.
P26: 84: 3, **March** *1978.*

Date: see Poem 285 "Na Ràtaichean 's a' Bhàrdachd".

A verse in *amhrán* metre (but one variant line).

291 Bàr an Dùn Èideann

11: 34r–33v, 1978.
20: 145–6, 1978.

Date: see Poem 285 "Na Ràtaichean 's a' Bhàrdachd".

A poem in full *amhrán* metre. Rhyme pattern *o-e-e-ì-u* runs throughout the poem.

292 Stad a' Bhus

11: 34v–35r, 1978.
20: 146, 1978.

P26: 87 (June 1978), 3.

Date: see Poem 285 "Na Ràtaichean 's a' Bhàrdachd".

A poem in full *amhrán* metre. Rhyme pattern *i-u-u-a-i* runs throughout the poem.

293 An Cruinneachadh no an Tional

11: 33, 1978.
20: 145, 1978.

Date: see Poem 285 "Na Ràtaichean 's a' Bhàrdachd".

294 Tìr-mòr

20: 146, 1978.
P26: 83: 3, Feb. 1978.

Date: see Poem 285 "Na Ràtaichean 's a' Bhàrdachd".

A verse in *amhrán* metre.

295 Canzone Goliardica

11: 37r–38r–39r, 1978; fourth verse lacking.
20: 143–4, 1978.
45: letter of 21 Jan. 1978.

Date: 15 January 1978 (**11**).

Title: the Goliards were wandering renegade scholars of medieval Western Europe, notorious for their hedonism; their songs, mostly composed in Latin (and exemplified in the Bavarian collection "Carmina Burana"), celebrate the joys of riotous drinking and sexual licence, and lampoon the Church authorities. The Goliardic song became a distinct literary genre.

ll. 13–16: added for Hamish Henderson (**45**).

296 Ritornello

20: 144, 1978.
45: letter of 21 Jan. 1978.

Date: January 1978.

Title: an Italian song-form of circular repetitive structure.

297 [Rann do Shomhairle]

11: 35v, 1978.
20: 82, 1978.
P15: 102: 157, Spring 1978.

Date: January–February 1978 (note to *Gairm*, and **20**).

298 *Là Allaban Monaidh*

11: 37v, 1978.
20: 82, 1978.
P15: 102: 157–8, Spring 1978.

Date: January–February 1978 (note to *Gairm*, and **20**).

299 *Taigh nan Cumantan*

20: 82, 1978.
P15: 102: 157, Spring 1978.

Date: January–February 1978 (note to *Gairm*, and **20**).

ll. 1–2 **mañana**, **domani**: tomorrow (Spanish and Italian).

300 *Gum Chur an Aithne*

11: 36, 1978.
20: 82, 1978.
P15: 102: 157, Spring 1978.

Date: January–February 1978 (note to *Gairm*, and **20**).

ll. 1–2: Hay's patronymic may have been used by the Tarbert fishermen. A list of Tarbert nicknames noted down by him c. 1961 includes Mac Iain Dheòrsa and "The Ceathrach" (the fishermen's name for Catherine Hay) among other colourful examples such as the Big Duck (one of Calum Johnson's crew), Hail-Smiling-Morn, Ceann A' Phump and James Did-Ye-Get-Yer-Tea-Yet Bain (featured in Hay 1940a).

301 *M'Oilein is M'Altram*

11: 36v–37, 1978.
20: 83, 1978.
P15: 102: 158–9, Spring 1978.

Date: January–February 1978 (note to *Gairm*, and **20**).

302 *Summer Coinage*

20: 153, 1978; prose translation of Poem 286 "Cùinneadh Samhraidh".
47: folder 7, 1978; published in Chapman 21, Spring 1978.

Date: January–February 1978. Text **47** was sent with a letter of 12 February 1978 (Source **47**, folder 1).

303 *The Auld Border Wumman*

20: 149, 1978.
47: folder 7, 1978; published in Chapman 21, Spring 1978.

Date: 5 February 1978 (**20**).

Title: the heading quote is from Catullus' 5th Ode (c. 50 BC):

> soles occidere et redire possunt;
> nobis, cum semel occidit brevis lux,
> nox est perpetua una dormienda.

(see Simpson 1952: 3–4)

Suns may go down and rise again; | but for us, when our brief light goes down, | the night to be slept is an eternal one.

l. 12 **Tinto**: Tinto Hill, by Lanark.

304 *Larochs*

11: 42v–44, 1978.
20a: 150–1, 1978.
20b: 86–7; 1978.
P1: 14/40: 40–1, April 1979.

Date: February 1978 (**20b**).

305 *The Muirland Man, Hieland or Lawland*

20a: 150, 1978.
20b: 86, 1978.
P1: 14/40: 40, April 1979.

Date: February 1978 (**20b**).

l. 1 **fail**: turf ("Yon fail dyke" in "The Twa Corbies" and the Gaelic *balla fàil*: "a turf wall"). [**20b**]

306 *A' Cheòlraidh – Beatha Bun-os-Cionn*

11: 2v, 44; 1978.
20: 149, 1978.

Date: 5 February 1978 (**11**).

The poem was published shortly after Hay's death (see Meek 1984: 8).

307 *Airson na Cloinne – Fàilt' air a' Mhadainn*

11a: 2v, 1978.
11b: 44, 1978.
20: 149, 1978.
47: letter of 28 April 1982; published in Gairm 119, Summer 1982.

Date: 5 February 1978 (**11**).

l. 1 **mañana di domani**: tomorrow (Spanish) of tomorrow (Italian).

308 A' Chearc Gheal

10: 26v–27r, 1979.

Date: 4 January 1979.

In this draft, Hay may have been imitating an ancient Greek poetic form mentioned in his war-time essay "Poetry in the world or out of it?":

> it can be a bizarre toy like the Alexandrian πέλεκυς poems, where lines of different lengths are so arranged that the outline of the finished poem, when written, is that of a double-headed axe. (Hay 1946–7 I: 52)

l. 16 **bilean**: "lips", but "bills" may be intended, or a play on both words.

309 An Nàiseantach ga Chomhairleachadh

10: 26v–27r, 1979.

Date: 1979.

l. 1: among expressions transcribed by Hay c. 1961 is "Och, cuist. Bi glic!" (Source 13: 4).

310 [Falamh]

10: 27v, 1979.

Date: 1979.

l. 2: among phrases and expressions noted down by Hay in the early 1960s is "empty" for "destitute, skint", a usage he attributed to Gaelic (Source 12: 4).

311 Na Feansaichean

10: 28–27, 1978–9; initial draft.

Date: 1979.

The poem survives only as an unedited draft of rhyming line-clusters. The draft must have been rearranged and finalised, as Hay mentions a (finished) Gaelic poem "about fences round the hills" in a letter of 29 January 1979 (see notes to Poem 312 "The Fences"). My editorial reconstruction of the Gaelic poem is based on "The Fences".

ll. 1–8: note the following traditional verse (see Stewart 1884: 14–15; also Kennedy-Fraser 1909: 18–21):

> Thug mi gaol is gean is gràdh dhuit
> nach tug piuthar riamh gu bràthair
> nach tug bó gu laogh air àiridh
> na bean òg gu naoidhean ràidhe.

> *I gave you love and affection and fondness | such as sister never gave to brother | that cow on hill pasture never gave to calf | or a young wife to her three-month-old baby.*

ll. 34–7: the only instance of divergence between **10** and "The Fences"; markings by Hay indicate uncertainty about line order.

312 The Fences

P9: 23–4: 85, Spring 1979.

Date: January–February 1979. In a letter of 29 January (Source 47, folder 1), Hay tells the editor of *Chapman*:

> I'll spend a day or two hammering out some contributions and send them on to you ... As far as I can see at the moment, what I'll be able to offer are a four-line epigram restating "Summer Coinage" in Scots, an English translation of a Gaelic poem about fences round the hills, in the same Gaelic metre as "Summer Coinage" but rather longer ... and a prose article on my position as regards Scotland's assembly of languages .... All that you can expect long before the end of February.

313 Simmer Cunzie

48: Dalex spring-back file, 1979.
P9: 23–4: 86, Spring 1979.

Date: January–February 1979 (see note to Poem 312).

See Poem 302 "Summer Coinage".

314 To the Younger Generation

P9: 23–4: 86, Spring 1979.

Date: 1979?

315 Extempore in Bennett's Bar

P9: 23–4: 86, Spring 1979.

Date: 1979?

316 The Bard, the Drink an' the Hill

P9: 23–4: 86, Spring 1979.
12: 12r, 1980?
43: folder 20; published in Gairm 111–12, Summer–Autumn 1980.
Date: 1979?

l. 1 **The Cannie Man's**: Edinburgh public bar, one of Hay's local haunts.

POEMS 1980–1982

317 *Na h-Òrain a Bh'ann 's a Th'ann*

11: 48v–49, 1980?
43: folder 22; published in Gairm *111–12, Summer–Autumn 1980.*

Date: 1980? (Sent to *Gairm* as a new song).

Title: much of Hay's poetic activity in this period involved expanding or rewriting old songs.

318 *Muir is Tìr, no Deireadh Oidhche ri Cladach*

11: 49r–47v, 1980?; verses lacking.
43: folder 22; published in Gairm *111–12, Summer–Autumn 1980.*

Date: 1980? (Sent to *Gairm* as a new song).

Text **11** lacks three verses but has the following extra verse:

> Eadar lighe 's lunn
> eadar slighe 's stiùir
> is siud a' ghrian os cionn.

Between spate and surf | between path and helm | there goes the sun overhead.

l. 17 **maois**, **peic**: also measures of quantity, the *maois* holding 500 herrings, and the peck being a two-gallon measure (Dwelly).

l. 25 **ceannair**: the bridle-rope of a ring-net. Hay included the word in a 1938 list of Gaelic usage in Tarbert English (NLS MS 26747: 2). Around the time of composition of this poem, however, he was less specific (SSS 1979): "I heard *ceannair* often enough. I never asked, so I don't know what *ceannair* is … I thought it was a head-rope but maybe not."

ll. 34–5: as *mogall* can mean "husk" or "mesh of a net", *tobhta* "ruin" or "thwart", and *cliath* "harrow" or "shoal", the wealth of maritime and terrene allusions is impossible to evoke in translation.

l. 46 **cur**: also "weathering, getting to windward".

l. 55 **putag**: also "haft" and "strip of land" (Dwelly).

l. 56 **ulag**: also "oatmeal in cold water" (Dwelly).

319 *Hòro, Mhàiri Dhubh*

11: 38v, 1980.
47: letter of 20 Nov. 1982; published in Gairm *124, Autumn 1983.*

Date: February 1980 (List 11).

The song is based on a traditional model. Hay explains in **47**:

Thàinig mi trast air na rainn seo an seann leabhar ciùil:–

> Cha dean mi car feuma ma thrèigeas mo leannan mi,
> *Hòro, Mhàiri Dhubh, tionndaidh rium,*
> bean a' chùil duinn 's nan cuachagan camagach,
> *hòro, Mhàiri Dhubh, tionndaidh rium.*
> *A Mhàiri, nan tigeadh tu ...* [etc.]

Tha an t-òran is am fonn air aithne sa Bheurla mar "Hòro, Mhàiri Dhu, turn ye to me". Seo mar a dh'ath-rinn mi e: ...

I came across these verses in an old song-book:- "Cha dean mi ..." etc. The song and the melody are known in English as "Hòro, Mhàiri Dhu, turn ye to me". This is my new version: ...

320 Eich Mhic Nèill

11: 40, 1980; "unfinished untyped".
43: folder 24; published in Gairm 122, Spring 1983.
Date: 1980 (–1982?). The song is dated February 1980 in List 11, but the version sent to *Gairm* is of 20 November 1982 (**43**).

The model for this song is a traditional (seventeenth-century?) flyting between a Uist poet and her rival from Barra (see Campbell and Collinson 1977: 124–8, 232–7). Hay's gloss in **11** suggests that he may have intended a more ambitious "conflation" than the one finally sent for publication (which differs very little from the "unfinished" draft).

ll. 1–11: from tradition; draft **11**, however, suggests that Hay may have thought that only ll. 1–6 were traditional, or may have been uncertain which lines he was remembering and which composing.

l. 2 **dubh chapall**: the forfeit in a bardic contest (Campbell and Collinson 1977).

ll. 4–6: the heroes mentioned are sixteenth- and seventeenth-century MacNeills of Barra.

321 Chailein Òig, an Stiùir Thu Mi?

11: 38v–41, 1980; initial draft "unfinished, untyped".
43: folder 23; published in Gairm 114, Spring 1981.
Date: 1980.

In **43**, Hay cites the traditional model for his reworking:

Cha robh agam riamh den t-seann òran seo ach na sreathan a leanas:

> Chrom i 'ceann is rinn i gàire,
> *chailein òig, an stiùir thu mi?*
> nighean rìgh Èireann 's i san àirigh.
> *Chailein òig, nighean rìgh Eireann, chailein òig, an stiùir thu mi?*

Latha dhomh 's mi 'siubhal sràide,
cò a thachair ach mo nàimhdean?
– 'Ille sin shìos, ciamar a thà thu?
– Olc lem chàirdean, math lem nàimhdean.
Rug mi air caman 's chuir mi bàire.
Chuir mi a h-aon is a dhà dhiubh.
Gheall an cailein nì nach b'fheudar,
caisteal air gach cnoc an Èirinn,
muileann air gach sruthan slèibhe.
Chrom i 'ceann is rinn i gàire,
nighean rìgh Èireann 's i san àirigh.

All I've ever known of this old song are the following verses:

> *She turned her head and gave a laugh, | young girl will you guide me? | the King of Ireland's daughter at the shieling. | Young girl, daughter of the King of Ireland, young girl, will you guide me?*
>
> *One day as I walked the street, | who should I meet but my enemies? | "You there, laddie, how are you faring?" | "Badly by my friends, well by my foes". | I reached for a shinty stick and scored a goal. | I scored one and then a second. | The lass promised me something impossible, | a castle on every hill in Ireland, | a mill on every mountain stream. | She turned her head and gave a laugh, | the king of Ireland's daughter at the shieling.*

The lines recalled by Hay are a version of an old Irish-Scottish song which survived in Scottish oral tradition until the latter part of the twentieth century. Hay had already noted down two other versions of the song in the 1930s (see Source 23: 24r). More coherent versions can be found in Sinclair (1879: 21–3) and in Campbell and Collinson (1977: 44–53).

Draft **11** consists of 116 lines noted individually or in clusters, over seven pages. A third of these were abandoned for the final version.

l. 39 **mànla**: "well-mannered, gracious" (RIA 1983).

322 *Cnoc an Àtha Dhuibh*

20: 166, 160; 1980.
12: 11, 1980.
10: 41–2, 1981.
P28: *3 July 1982: 4.*

Date: 9 May 1980 (**12**).

The poem was memorably introduced by *The Scotsman*'s Gaelic editor Ronald Black as

> the nearest thing *The Scotsman* has ever published to what a resident of Morningside would have contributed to the paper exactly 1,000 years ago, when the language of the "better sort" in Edinburgh was Gaelic.

Title: Blackford Hill is in the south of Edinburgh. Hay notes in **P28** that the metrical structure of the poem (*trì rainn is amhran*) is "the Gaelic equivalent of the sonnet".

323 *Gile is Deirge nan Caorann*

7: 29v, 1980.
12: 12–13, 1980.
20: 161, 1980.
P6: 3: 28, Summer 1980.

Date: 9 May 1980 (all).

The germ of this poem was again developed in "White Rowan, Red Rowan" (Poem 334). John Burns remembers Hay experimenting with the idea in several languages before settling on Gaelic while in hospital.

324 *[Am Bàrd, an Deoch 's am Monadh]*

12: 12r, 1980.
20: 165, 1980.
43: folder 20; published in Gairm 111–12, Summer–Autumn 1980.

Date: 9 May 1980 (**12**).

This is a version of the Scots epigram "The Bard, the Drink an' the Hill" (Poem 316).

325 *[Verses in* deibhidhe *metre]*

7: 42, 49v; 1980.
12: 6, 1980.

Date: context 12 and 7.

In these drafts, Hay attempted to reproduce the medieval bardic *deibhidhe* metre. Its most distinctive feature is asymmetrical end-rhyme in the couplet (between a stressed and an unstressed syllable); in accordance with classical bardic practice, the couplets are embellished with further rhyme and alliteration.

326 *The Sunday Howffs of Morningside*

13: 11–13, 1980.

Date: 30 June 1980 (**13**).

Title: **Morningside**: Hay's locality in south Edinburgh.

l. 5 **the Hermitage**: public bar in Morningside.

ll. 23–4: The Canny Man's pub in Morningside was originally The Volunteers' Rest inn, and more recently The Volunteer Arms (see C. J. Smith 1992: 91).

l. 24 **the wa**: the Flodden Wall, remnants of which still stand.

l. 25 **Holy Corner**: crossroads in south Edinburgh marked by four churches.

ll. 27–8: three public bars in Morningside.

327 *The Lether*

13: 10, 1980.

Date: 30 June 1980 (**13**).

328 *The Twa Capitals*

13: 7–9, 1980.

Date: 30 June 1980 (**13**).

l. 25 **The Thatcher wifie**: Margaret Thatcher, elected British Prime Minister in 1979.

l. 36: "Let there be one leader only!" – Ulysses' advice to the Greek army in the *Iliad* (Book II, l. 204).

329 *The Haary Toon*

13: 9–10, 1980.

Date: 30 June 1980 (**13**).

l. 9 **Canmore**: Malcolm III, reigned 1058–93; killed in battle. **Donald Bane**: Donald III, Canmore's brother, reigned 1094–7; died in prison.

l. 13 **Rizzio**: David Rizzio, secretary to Mary Queen of Scots, murdered in Holyrood Palace in 1566.

330 *Wundward Bate*

13: 13, 1980.

Date: 1 July 1980 (**13**).

331 *The Hert's Aye the Pairt Aye …*

13: 10, 1980.

Date: 1 July 1980 (**13**).

Title: from Burns' "Epistle to Davie, a Brother Poet": "The heart's aye the part aye that makes us right or wrang" (Kinsley 1969: 51).

332 *Òran Tàlaidh*

10: 35, 1980.

Date: 1 July 1980 (**13**).

333 *The Green Gairs o England*

47: Dalex spring-back file, 1980?
10: 30, 1981.

Date: 9 January 1981 (**10**).

ll. 12, 16, 24 **growes**: editorial emendation of "grows".

334 *White Rowan, Red Rowan*

7: 29v, 1981?; one verse.
10a: 29, 1981?; thirteen lines.
10b: 31–2; 1981.

Date: 9 January 1981 (**10**).

See the related Gaelic poem "Gile is Deirge nan Caorann" (Poem 323).

Text **7** is another Envoi, as follows:

> Leaf and blossom come and go; when is our zenith overhead?
> Between when the rowans are all white and the rowans are all red.
> White is the rowan, red will be the rowan, white was the gean
> White is the rowan, red will be the rowan, the cherry is green.

335 *Do Charaid Marbh*

10: 32v–33r, 1981.

Date: 1981.

Title: Malcolm Johnson (1920–55), master mariner, son of the Tarbert fisherman on whose boat Hay worked in the 1930s.

ll. 1–9: these tercets use terzina rhyme (aba, bcd, cdc).

l. 25 **sgeul ach**: editorial emendation of difficult script; Hay seems to have written "sgleoch".

336 *[Geal]*

11: 1r, 54; 1981.
10: 28v, 35; 1981.
48a: letter of 12 Oct. 1981; published in *Gairm* 117, Winter 1981–2.
48b: letter of 28 April 1982; published in* Gairm *119, Summer 1982.

Date: 9 January 1981 (**11**).

Title: the poem was published simply as "Rann" and "Rann Amhrain" ("verse in song metre").

337 *[The Caller Wind Blows]*

10: 7v–8, 1981.

Date: 1981.

l. 2 **Lothian Road**: a main Edinburgh thoroughfare.

ll. 5, 10 **West Kip**: a peak of the Pentland Hills.

338 *Innis Sgeul Dòchais*

20: 162, 1981.
10: 32, 1981.

48: letter of 12 Oct. 1981; published in Gairm *117, Winter 1981–2.*

Date: 29 August 1981 (**10**).

339 Fàire [Aig Tobar an Tighearna]

10: 7v, 34; 1981.
48: letter of 12 Oct. 1981; published in Gairm *117, Winter 1981–2.*

Date: 29 August 1981 (**10**).

Title: the poem was published under the title "Fàire". For the history of the Lord's Well, see Appendix 2.

340 Do Shomhairle MacGill-eain

10: 1v, 34; 1981.
48: letter of 12 Oct. 1981; published in Gairm *117, Winter 1981–2.*

Date: 29 August 1981 (**10**).

l. 1 **labharag**, l. 10 **cagaran**: my thanks to Dr John MacInnes for pointing out the occurrence of these terms in Sorley MacLean's long poem "Coilltean Ratharsair":

Coille Ratharsair, | m'ionam, labharag: | mo chiall cagarain ...

The wood of Raasay, | *my dear prattler,* | *my whispered reason* ...

Coille Ratharsair an labharag, | coille bhrìodail, coille chagarain ...

The wood of Raasay is the talking one, | *the prattling, whispering wood* ...

(MacGill-eain 1989: 176–7, 178–9)

341 The Hermitage o Braid

20: 162, 1981.
10: 33, 1981.

Date: 29 August 1981 (**10**).

Title: a wood at the foot of Blackford Hill, south Edinburgh.

342 An Lonan Iuchair

10: 28v, 1981?; one line.
14: 1, 5r; 1982.
43: folder 20; published in Gairm *120, Autumn 1982.*

Date: 18 May 1982 (**14**).

343 Ballade

14: 4–5, 1982.
43: folder 24; published in Gairm *120, Autumn 1982.*

Date: 20 May 1982 (**14**).

Title: the poem is based on the three ballads from François Villon's "Testament", all on the biblical "Ubi sunt?" theme ("Where are the princes of the peoples?"). The first evokes famous women of legend and history, the second more recent rulers (including James II of Scotland). Hay quotes the opening of the first ballad and its recurrent line:

> Tell me in what land | is Flora, the beautiful Roman | ... but where are the snows of last year?

Hay's roll-call includes the legendary Deirdre and the poets Hugh MacDiarmid (1892–1978), Edwin Muir (1887–1959), William Soutar (1898–1943) and Sydney Goodsir Smith (1915–75).

344 [*Gile*]

14: 3, 1982.

Date: c. May 1982.

345 [*Aubade 2*]

14: 5r, 1982.

Date: 21 May 1982 (**14**).

This is a translation of a Gaelic verse; see "Aubade [1]" (Poem 276).

346 *Ròsan an Lethbhaile*

10: 14v, 1982; ll. 17–32 only.
48: letter of 20 Nov. 1982; published in **Gairm 124, Autumn 1983.**

Date: 19 November 1982 (**10**).

Title: **An Lethbhaile**: Halftown, Taigh-na-bruaich. [**48**]

ll. 1–16: omitted in **10**. In **48**, Hay indicates that these lines are by Evan MacColl. They are a version of the song found in the first and second editions of his collection *Clàrsach nam Beann* (1836 and 1838), and possibly learnt by Hay from Lochfyneside oral tradition; MacColl revamped the song, however, and subsequent editions (and anthologies such as Sinclair 1879) give a very different version.

347 *Mo Robairneach Gaolach*

10: 16v, 1982.
43: folder 24; published in **Gairm 124, Autumn 1983.**

Date: 19 November 1982 (**10**).

Much of verses 1, 2 and 4 can be found in a version of the traditional song transcribed by Hay in the 1930s ("Oran Slèibhteach", Source 23: 28).

l. **5 mun iomas seo**: the meaning is unclear (Hay's traditional version has *fo h-uidheam*). The word *iomas* occurs in Rob Donn's "Òran nan Greusaichean Beaga" (Gunn and McFarlane 1899: 86) meaning "confusion, trouble" (reference in the Appendix to Dwelly).

Professor William Gillies has suggested a derivation from the Irish *immas* (*imbas*) "occult knowledge", from which a meaning of "the known, the familiar" and hence "familiar territory" might be derived. A second meaning, "excessive narrowness?", suggested in the RIA Dictionary, might allow a further interpretation as "straits, narrows". There could be a connection with *iombath*, "adjoining sea, sea encompassing an island", noted as obsolete in Dwelly. I have interpreted the word as a variant of *imisg*, "proximity" (Dwelly).

348 *Is Trom Mi 'Siubhal Slèibhe*

14: 7r, 1982.

Date: 22 November 1982 (**14**).

ll. 1–3: The traditional song "Cuchulann 's a Mhac", collected in Eigg by Kenneth MacLeod (see Kennedy-Fraser 1917: 24–6), has for chorus:

> Och nan och is och èire,
> Trom mi ri siubhal beinne,
> Arm mo mhic san dara làimh,
> 'S a sgiath san làimh eile.

The song is related to the ballad "Bàs Chonlaoich", which recounts the death of the young warrior Conlaoich at the hands of his unwitting father Cù Chulainn (see J. F. Campbell 1872: 13, verse 111).

349 *A Mhnathan a' Bhaile Seo*

14: 6v–7, 1982.
48: undated typescript; published in Gairm 123, Summer 1983.

Date: 22 November 1982 (**14**).

Hay introduces the song as follows (**48**):

> Chuala mi aig piuthar mo sheanamhar, Anna NicMhaoilein, gum b' àbhaist don phìobaire an Glac a' Mhuilinn (Whitehouse, baile beag mar bheagan mhìltean do Thairbeart Loch Fìne) dìreadh suas gu mullach cnocain os cionn a' bhaile mochthrath madainn na Bliadhn' Ùire is am port seo a chluich:
>> A mhnathan a' bhaile seo, 's mithich dhuibh èirigh.
>
> Seo agaibh an t-òran a rinn mise dheth.
>
> *I heard from my grandmother's sister, Ann MacMillan, that the piper in Mill Hollow (Whitehouse, a wee township a few miles from Tarbert Loch Fyne) used to climb up to the top of the hill overlooking the town first thing on New Year's morning and play this tune: "A mhnathan ..." etc. Here's the song I've made from it.*

Hay mentioned the Whitehouse piper in a letter of 9 December 1960 (Source 46), and commented that Tarbert "is well and truly connected with Glen Coe (or Breadalbane in the North)". The traditional song, about a murderous raid, is associated with Glencoe (see Sinclair 1879: 484; and also Source 1: 31v for a version transcribed by Hay in the 1930s).

350 *Marbhrann dom Mhàthair*

10a: 11v, 1975; eight lines.
10b: 25, 1982.
P15: 123: 214, Summer 1983.

Date: 2 December 1982 (**10b**); but eight lines of the poem were drafted shortly after Catherine Hay's death on 10 June 1975.

ll. 5–8: these lines were added when Hay revised his 1975 draft.

ll. 6–8: Catherine Hay *née* Campbell was connected to Islay through her father, and to Tarbert through her mother's family the MacMillans, but she was born and brought up in the Kerry Cowal. Hay recalled c. 1982 that she was known to the Tarbert fishermen as "the Kerrach" (NLS MS 26752: 3).

351 *Somebody – The Beginnin o an Auld Sang*

14a: 8v, 10–11r (fragmentary drafts); 1982.
14b: 11v–13; 1982.

Date: 6/7 December 1982 (**14**).

A traditional model for Hay's song can be found in MacQueen and Scott (1966: 421), with chorus:

> Och hon for somebody,
> och hey for somebody.
> I wad do – what wad I not?
> for the sake o somebody.

Title: when signing the Act Ratifying and Approving the Treaty of Union in 1707, the Chancellor of Scotland, James Ogilvie, is reported to have said: "Now there's ane end of ane auld sang" (see Scott 1994: 207).

ll. 17–20, 45–8: these two verses may have originated in Gaelic, but the evidence suggests that Scots and Gaelic versions of the song were composed concurrently, with each version feeding off the other.

352 *Cuideigin*

14: 9, 8v, 11v (eleven verses); 1982.
***48: undated typescript; published in* **Gairm 128, Autumn 1984.**

Date: 6 December 1982 (**14**).

Text **14**, interspersed with drafts of "Somebody", includes the following five verses not sent for publication:

> Ach an tig e is an ruig,
> bidh Alba leis gu lèir 's a cuid,
> bidh cathair 's crùn is cùirt 's gach rud
>   is rudeigin aig cuideigin.
>
> Bidh Alba eadar bhean is fhear
> aige, is a là san ear,

ma thig e oirnn gu còrs' air lear
　　is feareigin mo chuideigin.

Cuirear chuige 'Chuigse bhàth
a spàrr rìgh fuadain suas na àit.
Bidh Lunnainn ìosal shìos fo 'làimh
　　là-eigin aig cuideigin.

Bidh an Duitseach crocht' air gad.
Dìobrar uainn a shliochd air fad.
Nì mi ruith is nì mi stad
　　am badeigin aig cuideigin.

Seinnidh mi mar eun an lios,
bidh grian òir ag òradh shlios,
cuirear claidheamhan an crios
　　is fios againn o chuideigin.

Should he but come and but arrive, | Scotland and her all will be his, | throne and crown and court and all, | and something will be had by somebody.

Scotland will be his, both women and men, | when his day rises in the east, | if over the foam he reaches our coast, | some man is my somebody.

The foolish Whig will be brought to justice, | who imposed a foreign king in his place; | London will lie prostrate under his hand, | on a day that will be somebody's.

The Dutchman will be strung up on a withe, | and his entire dynasty expelled. | I will run and I will stop | in some spot for somebody.

Like a bird in a garden I will sing, | a golden sun will gild the slopes, | swords will be slipped into belts, | when news is heard of somebody.

353　*Dh'Fhalbh Mo Leannan Fhèin*

10: 15v, 1982; two verses, one line and couplet.
43: folder 24; published in Gairm 122, Spring 1983.
Date: 1982?

ll. 1–5: traditional; see Sinclair (1879: 340–2).

354　*Nìonag a' Chùil Duinn, Nach Fhan Thu?*

43: folder 24; published in Gairm 122, Spring 1983.
Date: 1982?

ll. 1–5: o Chinntàile [from Kintail] [**43**]; see Sinclair (1879: 337–8).

355　*Cruinneag na Buaile*

48: letter of 20 Nov. 1982; published in Gairm 124, Autumn 1983.
Date: 1982.

Hay explains:

> Tha an t-òran seo san Duanaire. Seo mar a dh'ath-rinn mi e, agus fonn ga chur agam air.
>
> *This song is in [MacPherson's] Duanaire. Here's how I rewrote it, set to a tune of my own.*

Hay's tune from the 1940s is in Source 19: 5v.

ll. 1–18: traditional (see MacPherson 1868: 83–5).

356 *Musa Caledoniae*

10: front cover, 1982?; sixteen lines only.
11: 59v–60, 1982–3.

Date: 1982–3. Hay intended inserting the poem in a second edition of *Wind on Loch Fyne* (see Source 11: 63–4).

357 [*Dùrachdan Nollaige, 1982?*]

49: folder 116, Christmas card.

Date: December 1982 (calligraphical inference).

POEMS 1983

358 *Dùrd a' Ghlinne*

16: 5, 1983.

48: *letter of 3 Oct. 1983; published in* **Gairm 126, Spring 1984.**

Date: February 1983?

359 *[Am Bàta Dubh]*

16a: 4–5, 1983; shorter draft.

16b: 9–11, 1983.

48: *letter of 4 Oct. 1983; published in* **Gairm 128, Autumn 1984.**

Date: February 1983, Tarbert (**16b**).

ll. 1–8: na fhuair mi o bheul-aithris [what I got from oral tradition]. [**48**]

See Source 23: 21r for a version collected by Hay in the 1930s.

360 *Mìos a' Ghearrain*

16: 5–6, 8r–9; 1983.

48: *letter of 4 Oct. 1983; published in* **Gairm 125, Winter 1983–4.**

Date: February 1983, Tarbert (**16**).

In a letter of 1 October 1983 telling of his seven-month stay in Tarbert, Hay writes: "I had a day of trawling for prawns at the beginning of February, a wild month of Force 10 storms" (Source 48: 104).

Title: in **16b** this is followed by the proverb "Cha tig fuachd gu'n tig earrach" ("There's no cold without a Spring").

l. 1 **railleach**: stoirmeil – Albais: rallyoch. [**48**]

361 *[Killiecrankie]*

16: 7, 1983.

Date: c. February 1983. In a letter of 2 March 1983, Hay writes:
   The Muse hasn't forsaken me here [in Tarbert], neither in Scots nor in Gaelic. I have made a version of "The Braes o Killiecrankie, oh". (Source 48: 103)

362 *Dùthaich nan Craobh*

48: *letter of 4 Oct. 1983; published in* **Gairm 128, Autumn 1984.**

Date: 1983.

In **48**, Hay writes of the original song:

> 'S e 'n cunntas a bhios aca san Tairbeart gun d'rinneadh e le Tairbeartach
> (Mac 'Ille Mhìcheil) o Bhruthach na(n) Sùgh (Subh) agus, gu nàdarra, tha mi
> mòr às a sin.

> *What they'll tell you in Tarbert is that it was composed by a Tarbert man*
> *(Carmichael) ... and naturally I'm proud of that.*

ll. 1–6: na fhuair mi o bheul-aithris [what I got from oral tradition]. [**48**]

ll. 21–4: bha seo sa bheul-aithris san Tairbeart roimhn chogadh [this verse could be
heard in Tarbert before the war]. [**48**]

363 [Is Mear a Bhreabas i Sàil]
16: 6v–8r, 23r; 1983.

Date: 4 October 1983 (**16**).

364 I 'Ruith Leis
16: 23r, 1983.

Date: October 1983?

365 [Dùghall a' Seòladh]
15: 8r (ll. 1–13), 1983.
16a: 12v, 1983; short version of **15**.
16b: 6v (ll. 14–25), 7r (ll. 26–42), 8v (ll. 43–63); 1983.

Date: 1983.

Although Hay wrote in 1981 (Source 48, 8 January) that he had added a handful of
lines to "Mochtàr is Dùghall" "nach eil dona idir" ("that aren't bad at all"), there is no
evidence of any additional material until these drafts from 1983. The critical acclaim
which followed publication may have encouraged him to attempt completion of the
poem. The drafts are rough and the order not always clear; I have excluded overlap-
ping drafts (for example, a version of **15** in text **16**) and odd lines.

Title: from text **15**.

ll. 1–25: these drafts are an expansion of four lines retained from c. 1946 (all re-
corded in Source 48, Source 7: 39r and Source 20: 48):

> gus an robh gach uain' is donn is liath dheth,
> gorm am bun an speur is cian uait ...
> trast an domhain an oidhch' a' ciaradh
> a thug na dathan is an sgiamh dheth.

366 [Och-òin mar a dh'Fhalbh Sinn]
16: 13r–12v, 1983.

Date: 1983.

For a traditional sailor song with similar chorus but longer verses, see Shaw (1955: 86).

367   Homer [revised]

15a: 3v, 1983; verse 3.
15b: 6, 1983.
Date: 1983.

Hay turned to expanding this poem of fifty years earlier while attempting to organise a collected edition of his work.

ll. 5–8 **Helen**: wife of the king of Sparta; her elopement with a Trojan prince led to the siege of Troy.   **Skaean Gate**: the main entrance to Troy.   **Hector**: Trojan prince.   **Achilles**: central (Greek) hero of the Iliad.   **Priam**: king of Troy. **Odysseus**: king of Ithaca, wandering hero of the *Odyssey*.

ll. 9–12 **Demodocus**: blind bard in the *Odyssey*.   **Telemachus**: son of Odysseus; sailed in search of his father.   **Deienera**: wife of Heracles; not in Homer.   **Ilium**: Troy.   **Ajax**: Greek hero.

368   The Smoky Smirr o Rain [revised]

10: front cover, 1982; vv. 2–3.
5: 37v, 1982; vv. 2–3.
20a: 163r, 1982; vv. 1–5.
20b: 163v, 1982–3; vv. 6–7.
15: 3r–4, 1983; vv. 1–7 and v. 8.
Date: December 1982 (**20a**) to October 1983 (**15**). On 10 December 1982, Hay wrote to Angus Martin that he had rewritten the poem and added two verses (Source 24: 58). This was the five-verse version (text **20a**) which Hay envisaged for publication in Martin (1984) and which he planned to include in a reissue of *Wind on Loch Fyne* (Source 30: 9). By 15 October 1983 two further verses had been added, and an eighth drafted but not clearly incorporated into the poem.

369   We're Nae Awa tae Bide Awa

16: 18, 1983.
Date: 20 October 1983 (**16**).

ll. 9–12: this quatrain is appended below the date.

370   Fragment

15: 2v, 1983.
16: 21v, 1983.
Date: 1983.

This is a version of the Gaelic verse published as "Bloigh" (Poem 277).

371   [*Thèid na Fèilltean Seachad*]
15: 2v, 1983.
Date: 1983.
There are two further couplets drafted between the verses.

372   *The Sain*
16: 14, 1983.
Date: 22 October 1983, Edinburgh (**16**).

373   *The Toper's Night*
16: 16, 1983.
Date: 23 October 1983, Edinburgh (**16**).

374   [*The Rosyns and the Waste*]
20: 163v (ll. 17–20), 1983.
16: 15, 22v; 1983.
Date: 1983.
ll. 17–18: perhaps intended as the first verse (**16**).

375   [*The Airts Eternal*]
20: 163v, 1983.
16: 22v, 1983.
Date: 1983.

376   *A Nor'-Sea Day*
16: 20r–21, 1983.
Date: 28 October 1983, Edinburgh (**16**).

377   [*The Airts*]
16: 18, 1983.
Date: 29 October 1983, Edinburgh (**16**).

378   *Cha Tig Mòr, mo Bhean, Dhachaigh*
16: 19r–20r, 1983.
Date: 30 October 1983, Edinburgh (**16**).

This is Hay's reworking of a traditional song already translated by him into English in the 1930s (see *The Voice of Scotland* 1/4: 13–14).

ll. 1–6, 9–12, 34–6: these lines appear in a traditional version of the song (MacPherson 1868: 34–5, "A' Bhean Chomainn").

379 *Is Fada Thà Mi 'm Ònar*
16: 17, 1983.

Date: 6 November 1983, Edinburgh (**16**).

380 *[Natur's Child]*
16: 20v, 1983.

Date: 1983.

381 *[Thàin' Trath-nòin]*
16: 20v (ll. 1–16), 13v (ll. 9–20); 1983.

Date: 1983.

ll. 1–8, 9–16: the two verses are separated by the "Natur's Child" quatrain, but linked by metre and theme.

ll. 15–16: from Tarbert tradition; the verse was noted by Hay in the 1930s (Source 3: 24r), and quoted again in a letter of 9 December 1960:

> When I was small the elder of my grand-aunts gave me a verse, which she said was composed by an old shepherd near West Loch Tarbert when he was too old and feeble to go to the hill any more. It is addressed to Sliabh Gaoil ...
>
> > A Shlia' mo ghaoil,
> > 's mòr mo thlachd dhiot;
> > thusa cha tig a-nuas,
> > 's cha téid mi suas am-feast.
>
> Dòmhnall Mac Fhionnlaigh [composer of the sixteenth-century "Òran Na Comhachaig"] seems to lurk somewhere at the back of that. (Source 46)

382 *Air Leathad Slèibhe*
16: 22r–23r; 1983.

Date: 7 November 1983 (**16**).

ll. 1–4: this verse was published in 1977 as "Bloigh" (Poem 277), with the suggestion that some reader should expand the verse into a song.

Below text **16** is a verse in the same metre:

> Is fear feudar. Is fheudar dhomh
> bhith fàgail shlèibhtean nam dhèidh is chnoc;
> bhith falbh an cèin bhuapa gu Dùn Èideann,
> gu foghlam 's Beurla. Nam bheul tha "och!"

*Must commands [?]. I must | leave the hill-lands and knowes behind me; | go
far from them to Edinburgh, | to instruction and English. On my lips is "Alas!"*

383 Whan Ye Gang Awa, Jamie

16: 19v, 21v, 22v; 1983.

Date: November 1983, The Canny Man's, Edinburgh.

The song's prototype is the traditional ballad "Huntingtower" (see Greig 1892: 136–7).

384 I'm Wearan Awa, Jean

16: 25, 1983.

Date: December 1983, The Canny Man's, Edinburgh.

Subtitle: **Allermuir**: Allermuir Hill, in the Pentlands.

The song's prototype is Lady Nairne's "The Land o the Leal" (see MacQueen and
Scott 1966: 417–18).

385 Beam Sea in Biscay

16: 25v–26, 1983.

Date: December 1983, The Canny Man's, Edinburgh.

386 Over the Isles to America
Null Thar nan Eileanan dh'Ameireaga

16: 26v–28, 1983.

Date: 1983.

This is a reworking of a traditional Gaelic song, glossed "O Thàileach" ("from a Kintail
man").

387 Soraidh an Sgoileir

17: 5v, 1930s, Melody and lines 1–5.
16: 28v, 1983.

Date: 1930s and 1983 (The Canny Man's, Edinburgh). The metrical model for the
song is Rob Donn Mackay's "Cead Fhir Bhìogais don Fhrìth" which Hay had set to
the same melody (Source 19: 5).

l. 16 **soraidh ò**: see note in Poem 229 "Òran Maraiche".

Appendices

APPENDIX 1

SOURCES

1 Manuscript

AUL: Aberdeen University Libraries
EUL: Edinburgh University Library
NLS: National Library of Scotland

1   NLS MS 26721, folio notebook, c. 1933–c. 1948.
2   NLS MS 26722, quarto notebook, late 1930s, 1972.
3   NLS MS 26723, quarto notebook, late 1930s.
4   NLS MS 26727, quarto notebook, c. 1940.
5   NLS MS 26728, quarto notebook, 1938–41 (diary), 1982.
6   NLS MS 26729, quarto notebook, 1943–5.
7   NLS MS 26730, quarto notebook, 1944–5, 1972, 1980.
8   NLS MS 26731, quarto notebook, 1946.
9   NLS MS 26732, jotter of continuous drafts, c. 1950?
10 NLS MS 26734, quarto notebook, 1975–6, 1979–82.
11 NLS MS 26735, quarto notebook, 1976–82.
12 NLS MS 26736, quarto notebook, early 1960s; poetry content 1980.
13 NLS MS 26737, quarto notebook, early 1960s; poetry content 1980s.
14 NLS MS 26738, quarto notebook, late 1930s; poetry content 1982.
15 NLS MS 26739, quarto notebook, 1983.
16 NLS MS 26740, quarto notebook, 1983.
17 NLS MS 26741, musical notebook, late 1930s.
18 NLS MS 26742, musical notebook, 1930s and c. 1947.
19 NLS MS 26743, quarto musical notebook; collected melodies 1947.
20 NLS MS 26744, folder of miscellaneous poems, 1920s–1980s.
21 NLS MS 26745, quarto typescript of collected Gaelic poems, 1974?
22 NLS MS 26746, folder of prose material with poetry typescripts on some versos, 1946–7?
23 NLS MS 26748, folder of correspondence, 1941–83.
24 NLS MS 26753, folder of correspondence with Angus Martin, 1979–83.
25 NLS MS 26758, copy of U. MacDhunlèibhe, *Duain agus Òrain.*

26 NLS MS 26767, copy of Homer, *Odyssey* I–XII.

27 NLS MS 26769, copy of R. Ní Ógáin, *Duanaire Gaedhilge* III.

28 NLS MS 26773, copy of Byrne and Dillon (eds), *Táin Bó Fraích*.

29 NLS MS 26777, copy of *Fuaran Slèibh*, annotated c. 1983.

30 NLS MS 26778, copy of *Wind on Loch Fyne*, annotated 1961 and c. 1983.

31 NLS MS 26781, copy of R. MacThòmais, *An Dealbh Briste* (1951).

32 NLS MS 26783, copy of *O na Ceithir Àirdean*, annotated 1960s?

33 NLS MS 26784, copy of *O na Ceithir Àirdean*, annotated 1983.

34 NLS MS 14967, wartime poetry notebook ("Rainn is Dàin le Deòrsa Caimbeul MacGàraidh"); typescripts pasted over handscript, 1943–5 (North Africa, Italy). Deposited by Hay.

35 NLS MS 14968, wartime poetry notebook, 1945–6 (Italy, Greece, Scotland). Deposited by Hay.

36 NLS Acc. 6419/38 (a). Douglas Young papers. Letters from Hay to Young, mainly 1939–46.

37 NLS Acc. 6419/101. Douglas Young papers: (1) texts for *Scottish Verse 1851–1951*; (2) miscellaneous poems including typescripts by Hay.

38 NLS Acc. 6839/1, *Scotia Review* papers (NLS Exhibition documents).

39 NLS Acc. 7085/15. Douglas Young papers. Typescripts of Hay poems and translations, 1930s. Double-spaced typescripts by Young, single-spaced by Hay.

40 NLS Acc. 7125, *Akros* papers.

41 NLS Acc. 7980/43, Wendy Wood papers.

42 NLS Acc. 8636, Fanny MacTaggart papers.

43 NLS Acc. 9367, *Gairm* papers.

44 NLS Acc. 9927/6, letters and poems from Hay to Rev. Kenneth MacLeod, mainly 1938–40.

45 NLS Acc. 9967 (i), Hamish Henderson papers.

46 NLS Acc. 10105, letters from Hay to Prof. Robert A. Rankin, mainly 1934–9.

47 NLS Acc. 10477, *Chapman* papers.

48 NLS Acc. 11047, *Gairm* papers, including "Mochtàr is Dùghall" typescript.

48a NLS Acc. 11572/6, letters by Hay to Sorley MacLean, mainly 1940–6.

49 EUL Gen. 1733, letters to Hamish Henderson.

50 EUL Gen. 2030, letters to Maurice Lindsay.

51 Bruce-Watt MS: typescript poem given to Jeremy Bruce-Watt in February 1969.

52 Burns MS: photostat of "Mochtàr is Dùghall" typescript (1946–7), given to Dr John Burns, 1982.

53 Kirk MSS: typescript poems given to Ms Elisabeth Kirk.

54 McIntosh MSS: letters to Prof. Angus McIntosh.

55 McLean MS: poem sent to Dr Alister F. MacLean; kindly supplied by Mrs Flora MacLean.

56 Neill MSS: letters and typescripts sent to Dodo Neill.

57 Rankin *Fuaran Slèibh*: annotated copy given to Prof. Robert A. Rankin, 4 June 1976 (annotations 1960s?).

58 Scott MSS: musical MS of Hay's collected melodies, plus three typescript poems, sent to F. G. Scott in December 1947, now belonging to Ronald Stevenson.

59 AUL MS 2864/2, 32 pages of a 48-page typescript by Hay deposited by Douglas Young on 11 June 1941, almost certainly compiled before Hay's departure to Argyll in October 1940.

2   Printed Collections and Anthologies

A G. C. Hay, *Fuaran Slèibh* (Glasgow, 1948)

B G. C. Hay, *Wind on Loch Fyne* (Edinburgh, 1948)

C G. C. Hay, *O na Ceithir Àirdean* (Edinburgh, 1952).

D1 F. G. Scott, *Scottish Lyrics* (Book V) (London and Glasgow, 1939).

D2 F. G. Scott, *Seven Songs for Baritone Voice* (London and Glasgow, 1946).

D3 F. G. Scott, *Thirty-five Scottish Lyrics* (Glasgow, 1949).

E M. Lindsay (ed.), *Modern Scottish Poetry: An Anthology of the Scottish Renaissance 1925–1945* (London, 1946).

F D. Young (ed.), *Scottish Verse 1851–1951* (London, 1952).

G J. MacQueen and T. Scott (eds), *The Oxford Book of Scottish Verse* (Oxford, 1966).

H S. MacLean, G. C. Hay, W. Neill and S. MacGregor, *Four Points of a Saltire* (Edinburgh, 1970).

J D. MacAulay (ed.), *Nua-Bhàrdachd Ghàidhlig: Modern Scottish Gaelic Poems* (Edinburgh, 1976).

3   Periodicals

P1 *Akros*: Scots poetry monthly, ed. Duncan Glen (Glasgow, 1965–83).

P2 *Alba*: "A Scottish Miscellany in Gaelic and English", publ. An Comunn Gàidhealach (1948, one issue).

P3 *A' Bhratach*: "leabhar meudachaidh do Chummanacht na h-Alba", ed. Rev. John Mackechnie (1941–2, three issues).

P4 *The Bulletin and Scots Pictorial*: weekly paper (Glasgow, 1926–60).

P5 *Carn*: quarterly journal of the Celtic League (Dublin, 1973–).

P6 *Catalyst*: "For the Scottish Viewpoint", quarterly magazine of the 1320 Club (Aberdeen, 1967–74).

P7 *Cencrastus*: "Scottish and International Arts and Affairs" quarterly (Edinburgh, 1979–).

P8 *Chapbook*: "The Magazine of Scottish Achievement", bi-monthly (Glasgow, 1946–7).

P9 *Chapman*: literary quarterly (Edinburgh, 1970–).

P10 *Comhar* (Dublin, pre-1944–).

P11 *Cyphers*: poetry quarterly (Dublin, 1975–).

P12 *Evening Dispatch*: daily paper (Edinburgh, 1921–63), ed. in late 1940s by A. D. Mackie.

P13 *The Fettesian*: magazine of Fettes College, Edinburgh (Edinburgh, 1878–).

P14 *An Gàidheal*: monthly bilingual magazine of An Comunn Gàidhealach (Glasgow, 1923–67).

P15 *Gairm*: An Ràitheachan Gàidhlig, quarterly periodical (Glasgow, 1952–).

P16 *Lallans*: quarterly of the Scots Language Society (Edinburgh, 1973–).

P17 *Life and Letters Today*: literary monthly (London, 1928–50).

P18 *The Morningside Mirror*: community magazine of the Royal Edinburgh Hospital (Edinburgh, 1846–1972).

P19 *New Alliance*, later *(New Alliance and) Scots Review*: monthly journal of Scottish and Irish arts and letters (Edinburgh, 1939; 1940–51).

P20 *The New Scot*: journal of the Scottish Reconstruction Committee (Glasgow, 1945–9).

P21 *Ossian*: magazine of the Glasgow University Ossianic Society (Glasgow, 1933–).

P22 *Poetry Scotland*: collections of new Scottish poetry, ed. Maurice Lindsay (Glasgow, 1944–9; four issues).

P23 *The Saltire Review*: journal "of Arts, Letters and Life", publ. Saltire Society (Edinburgh, 1954).

P24 *The Scot*: magazine of the Glasgow University Scottish Nationalist Association (Glasgow, 1940–5; three issues).

P25 *Scotia* (then *Scotia Review*): "For the Scottish Muse and Nation", monthly then quarterly, ed. David Morrison (Thurso, 1970–2; Wick, 1972–80).

P26 *Scots Independent*: mainly monthly organ of the Scottish Self-government movement (Glasgow, new series 1936–).

P27 *The Scots Magazine*: "monthly miscellany of Scottish life and letters" (Dundee, 1924–).

P28 *The Scotsman*: daily newspaper (Edinburgh).

P29 *Scottish Art and Letters*: ed. R. Crombie Saunders (Edinburgh, 1945–9).

P30 *Scottish Field*: monthly issue (Glasgow, 1911?–).

P31 *Scottish International*: quarterly review, ed. Robert Tait et al. (Edinburgh, 1968–74).

P32 *SMT Magazine* (and *Scottish Country Life*): monthly (Edinburgh, 1935–46).

P33 *The Voice of Scotland*: Scottish Republican literary periodical, ed. Hugh MacDiarmid (Dunfermline, 1938–61).

4   Dating Lists

The following poem-listings by Hay
are referred to as dating sources in the Commentary:

List 3   Source 3: 92v, 94v–95r, c. summer 1939.

List 34   Source 34: 41v–42r, late 1944–early 1945.

List 8   Source 8: 2r, c. summer 1945; 51v–53r, c. August 1946.

List 20   Source 20: 52v, c. winter 1947.

List 10   Source 10: 23r, spring 1976.

List 11   Source 11: 58r, January 1981?

Numbers below correspond to those in parentheses in Appendix 2 opposite

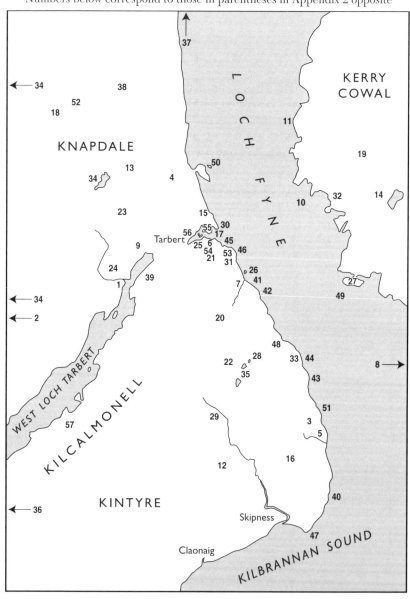

APPENDIX 2

A GLOSSARY OF LOCHFYNESIDE PLACE-NAMES

Information obtained from Ordnance Survey, 1st edn (1867–8), from Hay's own glosses and his interviews with Angus Martin, and from Angus Martin.

Abhainn nan Gillean (1): Avinagillan, "the young lads' river", at the head of West Loch Tarbert (OS: Abhainn Ghillean).

Àird MhicLaomainn: see **Ardlamont.**

Àirigh Chreagach (2): "rocky shieling", west of Loch Racadal, South Knapdale.

Àirigh Fhuar (3): "cold shieling", deserted township on the West Shore, north of Skipness.

Aisinn, an (4): Ashens, north of Tarbert.

Allt a' Ghalbhais (5): Altagalvash, a burn that runs into Loch Fyne north of Skipness.

Allt an Lìn (6): "the flax burn", just south of Tarbert (G. C. Hay).

Allt Beithe (7): "birch burn", a burn on the West Shore, and site of a deserted settlement, just south of Eilean a' Chòmhraig.

Ardlamont (8): the southern tip of Cowal.

Bàgh a' Chòmhraig: "battle bay", by Eilean a' Chòmhraig?

Bail' Ìomhair (9): Baliver, "Ivor's township", a deserted settlement at the head of West Loch Tarbert.

Bròg, the: the "shoe", on the Kerry Shore; between Caisteal Aoidh and the Buck?

Buck, the (10): Eilean a' Bhuic, small island off Glenan Bay on the Kerry Shore.

Caisteal Aoil: "lime castle", presumably Caisteal Aoidh, on Eilean Aoidh, Kerry Shore.

Caolas Bhreannain, Caol Bhranndain: "Brendan's straits", the Kilbrannan Sound between Kintyre and Arran.

Carraig nam Ban (11): "the cliff of the women", headland on the Kerry Shore, north of Ardmarnock Bay.

Ceathramh, an: Kerry, the peninsula of Kerry Cowal, from Kilfinan to Ardlamont.

Chaolbheinn, a' (12): "the narrow ben", north-west of Skipness.

Chruach Chaorainn, a' (13): "the rowan summit", Knapdale.

Cill Ainndreis or **Cill Ainndreann**: "Andrew's churchyard", the Tarbert burial-ground, off School Road.

Cnoc a' Chaisteil (14): Castle Knowe (460 ft), west of Asgog Loch (Loch a' Chaisteil) in Kerry Cowal.

Cnocan a' Chait Fhiadhaich (15): "wild cat knowe", according to Hay a rocky hillock at the head of Toll a' Bhòdaich (OS: Cnoc nan Cat Fiadhaich, situated as on map).

Cnoc na Mèine (16): "the knowe of the mine" (816 ft), north of Skipness (OS: Cnoc nam Mèin).

Cnoc nan Sgarbh (17): "cormorant hill", by Toll a' Choilich, north side of East Loch Tarbert (OS: Cnocan Sgairbh).

Coire Odhar (18): "dun corrie", on the west slopes (OS), or the "north side" (G. C. Hay) of Sliabh Gaoil.

Creag an Fhasgaidh (19): "the shelter rock", ridge running north-east of Glenan, in Kerry Cowal.

Cruach an t-Sorchain (20): "the summit of the footstool" (1,125 ft), south of Tarbert; *sorchan* is also the term for a small sand pyramid used as a shinty tee, an interpretation Hay favoured because of the shape of this summit (SSS 1979), but in his own writings always translated as "footstool".

Cruach Bhuidhe (21): "yellow summit" (446 ft), west of Rubha Meall Daraich.

Cruach Doire Lèithe (22): "grey grove summit" (1,236 ft), between Tarbert and Skipness.

Cruach Tharsainn (23): "sidelong summit" (994 ft), north-west of Tarbert, South Knapdale (there is also a Cruach Tarsainn between Tarbert and Skipness).

Cùil nan Seamrag (24): "shamrock nook", by the head of West Loch Tarbert, South Knapdale (OS: Cùil na Seamraig).

Earrann Ghoineach, an (25): "the sandy section", at the bend on Pier Road, Tarbert.

Ebbing Stone Point: see **Rubha Clach an Tràghaidh**.

Eilean a' Chòmhraig (26): "the battle isle", south of Mealdarroch Point.

Eilean Aoidh (27): "Hugh's isle", small peninsula by Asgog Bay on the Kerry Shore.

Feurlochan, am (28): "the grassy lochan", between Tarbert and Skipness.

Garbhallt, an (29): Garvalt, "the wild burn", running into Skipness River from above Cruach Tarsuinn.

Gharbhail, a' (30): Garvel, northern promontory at the mouth of East Loch Tarbert (OS: Garbh Mhaol, "rough mull").

Gharbhaird, a': "the rough height": see **a' Gharbhail**.

Glac Calltainn (31): "hazel hollow", on the West Shore, just south of Rubha Meall Daraich.

Gleannan, an (32): Glennan, site of a deserted township on the Kerry Shore, Cowal.

Kerry Shore, the: the Cowal shore of Loch Fyne, from the Otter to Ardlamont.

Kilbrennan: the Kilbrannan Sound: see **Caolas Bhreannain**.

Lagan Ròaig (33): "Ròag hollow", site of a deserted farm, on the West Shore halfway between Tarbert and Skipness.

Lagan, an/Laggan: "the hollow", see **Lagan Ròaig** and **Sean Lagan**.

Laggan Heid: see **Rubha Lagan Ròaig**.

Loch a' Chaorainn (34): "the rowan loch", by Cruach Chaorainn (OS: Loch Chaorainn)? Others lie west of West Tarbert and by Loch Caolisport.

Loch na Machrach (Mòire/Bige) (35): "the loch of the great/little machairland", two lochs between Tarbert and Skipness.

Lùb, an (36): "the bight", Loup, at the mouth of West Loch Tarbert.

Maol Dubh (37): "black mull", opposite Kilfinan Bay.

Meall Mòr (38): "muckle mound" (1,580 ft), east of Sliabh Gaoil.

Òrdag, an (39): "the thumb", "Glac na h-Òrdaig", south-west of Tarbert?

Paiste Beag, am: "the wee patch", a field on the long-deserted farm of Lagan Ròaig, and a landmark for fishermen.
[I was] at the fishing, and they said "We're in the run of the Paiste Beag", and I looked in and I could see it. (SSS October 1980)

Port a' Chruidh (40): "cattle bay", north of Skipness Point.

Rubha Bhaltair (41): "Walter's point", on the West Shore, south of Allt Beithe (G. C. Hay).

Rubha Clach an Tràghaidh (42): "ebbing stone point", on the West Shore.

Rubha Grianain (43): "sunny point", Grianan Point, on the West Shore.

Rubha Lagan Ròaig (44): a headland on the West Shore.

Rubha Loisgte (45): "scorched point", at the mouth of East Loch Tarbert.

Rubha Meall Daraich (46): Mealdarroch Point, "oaken knowe point", at the mouth of East Loch Tarbert; in later sources, Hay corrects this to **Rubha Maol Daraigh** "oaken mull point".

Rubha Sgibinis (47): Skipness Point.

Sean Lagan, an (48): Seanlagan, "the old hollow", site of a long-abandoned township on the West Shore above Fionn Phort.

Sgat Mòr, an (49): the Great Skate, off the Kerry Shore (OS: Sgat Mhòr).

Sgeir Leathann (50) : "broad skerry", north of Tarbert, off Barmore Island.

Sgìre Chalmain Eala: "the parish of St Calman Ela", Kilcalmonell, the west strip of North Kintyre.

Sgolaig (51): south of Grianan Point, on the West Shore.

Sliabh Gaoil (52) (Slia', Sleea): "love hill" (1,840 ft), in South Knapdale. The hill range was associated in tradition with the story of Diarmid and Gràinne.

Sloc Domhain, an (53): "the deep dell" (OS: Glac Dhomhain, by Mealdarroch Point?).

Stob Odhar (52): "dun peak", the highest peak on Sliabh Gaoil.

Tobar an Tighearna (54): "the lord's well", on the north slope of Cruach Bhuidhe.

A natural spring on the edge of a smooth flat, sandy and frosted with quartz around the rim, it has been kept clean and tended lovingly for many a generation. By this well it was that the emigrants from the hill-villages of Kilcalmonell came to pray before setting out on their bitter journey away from all that was familiar, and many a one landed on the shores of Canada with a bottle of its water in his possession. By it, some say, the folk who had left the Church of Patronage worshipped at the time of the Disruption, until they had built their own church. (Hay 1947a: 258)

Toll a' Bhòdaich: "the Buteman's creek", inside East Loch Tarbert?

Toll a' Cheiligh (55): "the cockerel creek", on the north side of East Loch Tarbert.

Uaraidh (56): the mound on the north side of Tarbert harbour (G. C. Hay).

West Shore, the: the west coast of lower Loch Fyne, between Tarbert and Skipness.

Whitehouse (57): Glac a' Mhuilinn, "the mill hollow", by West Loch Tarbert.

APPENDIX 3

SONG SETTINGS

Please note that lyrics are as given in Sources 19 and 58, and vary in several instances from the versions in Volume 1.

Siubhal a' Choire

(see Poem 7)

Chun - naic mi'n "Coire".___ haoi ò. Deas 's i fo h-uidh - eam. ho - rò.

Ghabh sinn a - mach air a' mhach - air uaine.___ Dh'fhu - ar sinn Garbh - ail

ghail - bheach ghru - a - mach, Leum on iardh - eas sìon - tan cruaidh oirnn. Haoi

ò. 's i'n "Coi - re" a bh'ann.__ Thog i a ceann ri ceann nam fuar - thonn

Tè___ dhubh chaol, nì gaoir___ 'na glu - a - sad, Thog i 'seinn is

rall.

rinn i rua - thar___ 'S i'n "Coi - re" i fhèin___ a bh'ann.

685

B'e Cruas na Gaoithe

(see Poem 15 "Luinneag")

Soraidh Slàn le Cinntìre

(see Poem 19)

(Tarbert, Spring 1936)

Gràdh nan Gruagach

(see Poem 28 "Òran")

Gràdh nan grua - gach, o dh'fhàs i fuar rium, Chan eil dol suas domh, no suain 'na dèidh, Mar chuir i suar - ach ar bruidh - inn chluain - eis, 'S gach coin - neimh uaign - each, dh'fhàg luath___ mo cheum. Èir - idh lath - a, 's a' ghrian le gathan - naibh, Èir - idh 'n ceathach rith' on ach - adh rèidh. Èir - idh 'n driùch - da bhàrr fhlùr is gheu - gan — Och cùin - e dh'èir - eas mo chri - dhe fhèin?

Alba Ghaoil Ò

(see Poem 75)

Ged___ tha thu nis bochd ìo - sal___ Al - ba ghaoil ò, Bidh sùil is seirc gach tìr' ort, A mhùir - neach chaomh ò. Ged tha t'ao - dach dì - blidh, Càir - ear gùn den t-sìod' ort. Thèid thu mach fo uidh - eam rìo - ghail, A Al - ba ghaoil ò.

687

Am Faillean Ùr

English version: *The Fresh Sapling*

(see Poems 152 and 153)

Faill - ean   fo   bhlàth   an   gàr - adh driùch - dach   leis   fhèin.
Sap - ling   that   grew,   with   dew   and   sun - shine   and   days.

Mai - se   is   fàs,   is   fail - eadh   ùr - ar   nan   geug.   Siud
Leaf - y   and   slen - der,   fresh   the   scent   of   its   sprays,

coim - eas   mo   gràidh,   's is feàrr   a   giù - lan   'sa   gnè.   Tha
Bloom - ing   un - known   with   none   to   speak   in   its   praise.

ait - eas   is   bàigh   am   fàil - te   mhùirn - each   a   bèil.
Where   I   steal   in   a - lone   in   sec - ret   to   gaze.

Though I Should Go Ten Hunner Mile

(see Poem 156 "Then Farewell, Tarbert")

[Dorian mode]

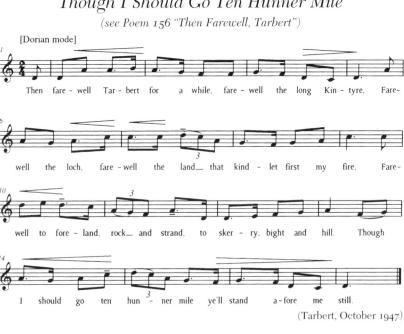

Then   fare - well   Tar - bert   for   a   while,   fare - well   the   long   Kin - tyre,   Fare-

well   the   loch,   fare - well   the   land   that   kind - let first   my   fire,   Fare-

well   to   fore - land,   rock   and   strand,   to   sker - ry,   bight   and   hill.   Though

I   should   go   ten   hun - ner   mile   ye'll   stand   a - fore   me   still.

(Tarbert, October 1947)

688

APPENDIX 4

BIBLIOGRAPHY

Accounts and Papers, vol. 76, *Census of Scotland 1881*, Report, vol. 1 (Edinburgh, 1882).

Accounts and Papers, vol. 107, *Census of Scotland 1891*, Supplement to vol. 1 (Edinburgh, 1893).

Black, M. and H. H. Rowley (eds), *Peake's Commentary on the Bible* (London, 1962).

Black, R. (ed.), *An Tuil: Anthology of 20th Century Scottish Gaelic Verse* (Edinburgh, 1999).

Bold, A. (ed.), *The Letters of Hugh MacDiarmid* (London, 1984).

Byrne, M., *Bàrdachd Mhic Iain Dheòrsa: The Original Poems of George Campbell Hay* (University of Edinburgh Ph.D. thesis, 1992).

Calvocoressi, P. and G. Wint, *Total War*, 2nd edn (London, 1989).

Campbell, J. F. (ed.), *Leabhar na Féinne* (1872; reprinted Dublin, 1972).

Campbell, J. G., *Superstitions of the Scottish Highlands* (Glasgow, 1900).

Campbell, J. L. and F. Collinson (eds), *Hebridean Folksongs*, 3 vols (Oxford, 1969, 1977, 1981).

Census records (General Register House, Edinburgh) 1841, 1881, 1891, Registration District 535.

Comunn na Pìobaireachd (The Piobaireachd Society), *Pìobaireachd*, Books 6 and 10 (Glasgow, 1936, 1961).

Croce, B., *"My Philosophy" and Other Essays on the Moral and Political Problems of Our Time*, selected by R. Klibansky, trans. E. F. Carritt (London, 1949).

— *Saggi Filosofici 12 (Discorsi di varia filosofia, vol. 2)* (2nd edn Bari, 1959).

— *The Aesthetics as the Science of Expression and of the Linguistic in General*, trans. C. Lyas (Cambridge, 1992).

Dillon, M., *Early Irish Literature* (Dublin, 1994).

Dwelly, E., *The Illustrated Gaelic–English Dictionary* (Edinburgh, 1901–11).

Dwelly, E. and D. Clyne, *The Appendix to Dwelly's Gaelic–English Dictionary* (Glasgow, 1991).

Ferguson, W. J., *Scotland: 1689 to the Present* (Edinburgh, 1968), pp. 359–82.

Finlay, R. J., *Independent and Free: Scottish Politics and the Origins of the Scottish National Party 1918–1945* (Edinburgh, 1994).

France, P. and D. Glen, *European Poetry in Scotland* (Edinburgh, 1989).

Gaskill, H. (ed.), *The Poems of Ossian and Related Works* (Edinburgh, 1996).

Gillies, W., "Deòrsa Caimbeul Hay", serialised in *Gairm*, Earrann 1: 135 (Samhradh 1986), 262–9; Earrann 2: 136 (Foghar 1986), 331–9.

Gleasure, J., "Synthetic and analytic: some comments on the Irish/Gaelic present/future", *Scottish Gaelic Studies* 14:2 (Winter 1986), 94–101.

Greene, D. and F. O'Connor (eds), *A Golden Treasury of Irish Poetry AD 600–1200* (London, 1967).

Greig, J. (ed.), *Scots Minstrelsie*, vol. 2 (Edinburgh, 1892?).

Gunn, A. and M. McFarlane, *Rob Donn: Òrain agus Dàin* (Glasgow, 1899).

Hackney, N. C. L., *Cutty Sark* (London, 1974).

Hanham, H. J., *Scottish Nationalism* (London, 1969).

Harvie, C., *Scotland and Nationalism* (London, 1977).

— *No Gods and Precious Few Heroes* (London, 1981).

Hay, G. Campbell

>1939: "Gaelic and literary form", *The Voice of Scotland* 2:1 (June–August), 14–18.

>1940a: "A night with the Beadle", *Scottish Field* (March), 35–40.

>1940b: "The lamp itsel' will tell ye", *The Scots Magazine* 34:1 (October), 62–4.

>1940–1: "Scots Gaelic poetry", serialised in *The New Alliance*, Part 1: 1:5 (Aug.–Sep. 1940), 7–9; Part 2: 1:6 (Oct.–Nov. 1940), 7–8; Part 3: 2:1 (Dec. 1940–Jan. 1941), 9–11; Part 4: 2:2 (Feb.–March 1941), 10.

>1942: "The freedom of Europe: Is that England's war aim?", *Scots Independent* (December), 4.

>1944: "Cor litreachas na Gàidhlige", *An Gàidheal* (June), 104–5.

>1945: "The dancers at Ras El-Hamra", *The Scots Magazine* 43:5 (August), 337–42.

>1946a (unpublished): "An untapped source of Scottish history", in NLS MS 26746, fos 128–63.

>1946b: "The Scotland I'd like to see", *New Scot* 2:10 (November), 16–18.

>1946c: "Seventy baskets of mackerel", *The Scots Magazine* 46:3 (December), 218–22.

>1946–7: "Poetry in the world or out of it?", serialised in *Scottish Art and Letters*, Part 1: 2 (Spring 1946), 49–58; Part 2: 3 (Spring 1947), 52–7. Written December 1944.

>1947a: "A turn on the hill", *The Scots Magazine* 46:4 (January), 257–60.

>1947b: "Caifidh Mòr na h-Òigridh, 1942", *An Gàidheal* (May), 98–9.

>1947c: "Gael warning", *Scots Review* 8:7 (November), 104–5.

>1948: "Grand stravaig – a turn after dookers on Loch Fyne", *The Scots Magazine* 48:5 (February), 337–42.

>1956: "Affinities elsewhere", *The Voice of Scotland* 7:1 (April), 26–30.

>1977: "Men on Gamila", *Lallans* 9, 21–4. Written c. February 1946.

Hay, J. MacDougall, *Gillespie* (London, 1914; 3rd edn Edinburgh, 1979).

Henderson, A., *Scottish Proverbs* (London, 1876).

Henderson, H., *Elegies for the Dead in Cyrenaica* (1948; 3rd edn Edinburgh, 1990).

HMSO, *Census of Scotland 1921*, Report, vol. 1 part 6 (Edinburgh, 1922).

Holmer, N. M., *The Gaelic of Kintyre* (Dublin, 1962).

Johnston, T., *Memories* (London, 1952).

Keating, M. and D. Bleiman, *Labour and Scottish Nationalism* (London, 1979).

Kennedy-Fraser, M. (with K. MacLeod), *Songs of the Hebrides*, 3 vols (London, 1909, 1917, 1921).

Kinsley, J., *Burns: Poems and Songs* (Oxford, 1969).

Lhôte, H., *Les Touaregs du Hoggar* (Paris, 1944).

Lindsay, M. (ed.), *Modern Scottish Poetry: An Anthology of the Scottish Renaissance 1925–1945* (London, 1946).

— "The poetry of modern Scotland", *The Lion Rampant* 1:2 (1947).

— *The Scottish Renaissance* (Glasgow, 1948).

— *Francis George Scott and the Scottish Renaissance* (Edinburgh, 1980).

MacColla, E., *Clàrsach nam Beann* (Glasgow, rev. edn 1937).

MacCormick, J. M., *Convention: An Experiment in Democracy* (Glasgow, 1943).
— *The Flag in the Wind* (London, 1955).
MacDiarmid, H. (ed.), *A Golden Treasury of Scottish Poetry* (London, 1940).
— *Collected Poems 1920–1976* (London, 1978).
MacDonald, K. N., *The Gesto Collection of Highland Music* (Leipzig, 1895).
MacFadyen, J., *Sgeulaiche nan Caol* (Glasgow, 1902).
MacGill-eain, S., *Ris a' Bhruthaich: The Criticism and Prose Writings of Sorley MacLean*, ed. W. Gillies (Stornoway, 1985).
— *O Choille gu Bearradh* (Manchester, 1989).
Mackenzie, A. M., *Òrain Iain Luim* (Edinburgh, 1964).
MacLeod, A. (ed.), *Sàr Òrain* (Glasgow, 1933).
McLeod, W., *Computer-Assisted Learning for Gaelic: Towards a Common Teaching Core* (Board of Celtic Studies (Scotland), 1998).
MacMillan, S. (ed.), *Sporan Dhòmhnaill: Gaelic Poems and Songs by the Late Donald MacIntyre* (Edinburgh, 1968).
MacNeill, S., "MacCrimmons", in D. S. Thomson (ed.), *The Companion to Gaelic Scotland* (Oxford, 1983), pp. 162–3.
MacPherson, D., *An Duanaire* (Edinburgh, 1868).
MacQueen, J. and T. Scott (eds), *The Oxford Book of Scottish Verse* (Oxford, 1966).
MacThòmais, R. (deas.), *Bàrdachd na Roinn-Eòrpa an Gàidhlig* (Glasgow, 1990).
Martin, A., *The Ring-net Fishermen* (Edinburgh, 1981).
— *Kintyre: The Hidden Past* (Edinburgh, 1984).
— Introduction to Saltire Society limited edition of "Seeker, Reaper" (Edinburgh, 1988).
— "In Fyne Fettle", *Scottish Book Collector* 6: 11 (2001), 16–18.
Meek, D. E. (ed.), *The Campbell Collection of Gaelic Proverbs and Proverbial Sayings* (Inverness, 1978).
— "Land and loyalty: the Gaelic verse of George Campbell Hay", *Chapman* 39 (Autumn 1984), 2–8.
— (ed.), *Tuath is Tighearna/Tenants and Landlords* (Edinburgh, 1995).
Murphy, G., *Early Irish Lyrics* (Oxford, 1961).
New Statistical Account of Scotland 8 (Edinburgh, 1845).
Nicolson, A., *Gaelic Proverbs* (Edinburgh, 1996; 1st edn 1881).
Ó Baoill, C. (ed.), *Bàrdachd Shìlis na Ceapaich* (Edinburgh, 1972).
Ó Rathile, T., *Búrdúin Bheaga* (Dublin, 1925).
Ó Tuama, S. and T. Kinsella, *An Duanaire 1600–1900: Poems of the Dispossessed* (Portlaoise, 1981).
Parker, H., *Flawed Texts and Verbal Icons: Literary Authority in American Fiction* (Evanston, IL, 1984).
Piccoli, V. (ed.), *Savonarola: Poesie* (Turin, 1927).
Pottinger, G., *The Secretaries of State for Scotland 1926–1976* (Edinburgh, 1979).
Race, W. H. (ed.), *Pindar*, vol. 1 (Cambridge, MA, 1996).
Rankin, R. A., "Òran na Comhachaig", *Transactions of the Gaelic Society of Glasgow* 5 (Glasgow, 1958), 122–71.
— "George Campbell Hay as I knew him", *Chapman* 40 (Winter 1984), 1–12.
Reid, H., "*Gillespie*: our forgotten masterpiece", *The Scotsman*, 21 October 1972.
RIA (Royal Irish Academy), *Dictionary of the Irish Language*, Compact Edition (Dublin, 1983).

Ross, N., *Heroic Poetry in the Book of the Dean of Lismore* (Edinburgh, 1939).

Salvini, L. (ed.), *Poeti Croati Moderni* (Milan, 1942).

Scott, P. H., *Andrew Fletcher and the Treaty of Union* (Edinburgh, 1994).

SEB (Scottish Examination Board, now Scottish Qualifications Authority), *Gaelic Orthographic Conventions* (Dalkeith, 1981).

Shaw, M. F., *Folksongs and Folklore of South Uist* (London, 1955).

Simpson, F. P. (ed.), *Selected Poems of Catullus* (London, 1952).

Sinclair, A., *An t-Òranaiche* (Glasgow, 1879).

Sinclair, A. MacL., *Gaelic Bards*, 2 vols (Charlottetown, 1890–2).

— *Na Bàird Leathanaich/The MacLean Bards*, 2 vols (Charlottetown, 1898, 1900).

Skene, W. F., *Chronicles of the Picts and Scots* (Edinburgh, 1867).

Smith, C. J., *Morningside* (Edinburgh, 1992).

Smith, E. D., *Victory of a Sort: The British in Greece 1941–46* (London, 1988).

Smith, I. Crichton, "Modern Scottish Gaelic poetry", *Scottish Gaelic Studies* 7 (1953), 199–206.

— "The heart of a nationalist poet", *The Scotsman*, 11 August 1984, p. 6.

— *Towards the Human* (Edinburgh, 1986).

Soutar, W., *Diaries of a Dying Man* (Edinburgh, 1988; 1st edn 1954).

SSS (School of Scottish Studies, Edinburgh), recordings of George Campbell Hay and Angus Martin in conversation, 14 May 1979, 3 October 1980 and 15 November 1980.

Stewart, C., *The Killin Collection of Gaelic Songs* (Edinburgh, 1884).

Tanselle, G. T., *Textual Criticism Since Greg: A Chronicle 1950–1985* (Charlottesville, 1987).

Thomson, R. L. (ed.), *Foirm na n-Urrnuidheadh: John Carswell's Gaelic Translation of the Book of Common Order* (Edinburgh, 1970).

Thorpe, J. D., *Principles of Textual Criticism* (San Marino, CA, 1972).

Warrack, G. H., *Dal Cor Gentil d'Italia: Folk Songs, Venetia to Sardinia* (Oxford, 1925).

Watson, W. J., *Bàrdachd Ghàidhlig* (Edinburgh, 1918).

— *Scottish Verse from the Book of the Dean of Lismore* (Edinburgh, 1937).

Webb, K., *The Growth of Nationalism in Scotland* (Glasgow, 1977).

Whyte, C., "George Campbell Hay: nationalism with a difference", in D. S. Thomson (ed.), *Gaelic and Scots in Harmony* (Glasgow, 1990), pp. 116–35.

Wood, W., *I Like Life* (Edinburgh, 1938).

— *Mac's Croft* (London, 1946).

— *Yours Sincerely for Scotland* (London, 1970).

Young, D. C. C., *The Free-minded Scot: The Trial and Defence of Douglas C. C. Young at the High Court, Glasgow* (Glasgow, 1942).

— *Auntran Blads* (Glasgow, 1943).

— *A Braird o Thistles* (Glasgow, 1947).

— *Chasing after an Ancient Greek* (Edinburgh, 1950).

— *A Clear Voice: Douglas Young, Poet and Polymath* (Edinburgh, 1970).

INDEX OF TITLES

Numbers given are **poem numbers**.

INDEX OF FIRST LINES

Numbers given are **poem numbers**.

INDEX OF PLACE-NAMES

Numbers given are **poem numbers**.
For brevity, names are given in their anglicised form only unless no such form exists,
and initial articles have been omitted. Rivers are indicated by (r).

INDEX OF PERSONAL NAMES

Numbers given are **page numbers**.